Unity 2020 Virtual Reality Projects
Third Edition

Learn VR development by building immersive applications and games with Unity 2019.4 and later versions

Jonathan Linowes

BIRMINGHAM - MUMBAI

Unity 2020 Virtual Reality Projects
Third Edition

Commissioning Editor: Ashwin Nair
Acquisition Editor: Larissa Pinto
Content Development Editor: Aamir Ahmed
Senior Editor: Hayden Edwards
Technical Editor: Deepesh Patel
Copy Editor: Safis Editing
Project Coordinator: Kinjal Bari
Proofreader: Safis Editing
Indexer: Tejal Daruwale Soni
Production Designer: Aparna Bhagat

First published: September 2015
Second edition: May 2018
Third edition: July 2020

Production reference: 1290720

Published by Packt Publishing Ltd.
Livery Place
35 Livery Street
Birmingham
B3 2PB, UK.

ISBN 978-1-83921-733-3

www.packt.com

This book is dedicated to Lisa—my wife, best friend, and soul mate—and the amazing family we created together: Rayna, Jarrett, Steven, and Shira, who know in their hearts that the future is theirs to embrace.

- Jonathan Linowes

Contributors

About the author

Jonathan Linowes is a long-time Unity developer and software engineer with a focus on VR and AR games and applications. He founded Parkerhill XR Studio and Reality Labs, an immersive indie studio and developer of products including the BridgeXR toolkit, the Power Solitaire VR game, and the Epoch Resources mobile game. He is a VR/AR evangelist, Unity developer, entrepreneur, and Certified Unity Instructor. Jonathan has a Bachelor of Fine Arts degree from Syracuse University, a Master of Science degree from the MIT Media Lab, and has held technical leadership positions at Autodesk and other companies. He has authored several books on VR and AR from Packt Publishing.

About the reviewer

Yash Gugale completed his Master's degree from the Department of Computer Graphics Technology at Purdue University where he specialized in VR, AR (Unity 3D), graphics programming (OpenGL and shaders), and data visualization (D3.js). He has a strong background in machine learning (Sklearn), deep learning (PyTorch), mobile (Android) and web development, photogrammetry (Meshroom), animation (Maya), UI/UX, and 360-degree videos. His work also involves volumetric videos and applying shader effects in Unity to create amazing volumetric experiences. He is currently working as a software engineer at Samsung to build TV applications and in their XR Volumetric Studios. In his free time, he enjoys salsa dancing, hiking, traveling, yoga, and scuba diving.

Packt is searching for authors like you

If you're interested in becoming an author for Packt, please visit `authors.packtpub.com` and apply today. We have worked with thousands of developers and tech professionals, just like you, to help them share their insight with the global tech community. You can make a general application, apply for a specific hot topic that we are recruiting an author for, or submit your own idea.

Table of Contents

Preface

Today, we are witnessing the burgeoning of **virtual reality** (**VR**), which is exciting new technology and a creative medium that promises to transform how we interact with our information, friends, and the world at large in a fundamental way.

Through wearing a VR **head-mounted display** (**HMD**), you can view stereoscopic three-dimensional scenes. You can look around by moving your head, walk around the space with room-scale tracking, and interact with virtual objects with positional hand controllers. With VR, you can engage in fully immersive experiences. It's like you're really in some other virtual world.

This book takes a practical, project-based approach to teach you the specifics of VR development using the Unity 3D game engine. We will walk through a series of hands-on projects, step-by-step tutorials, and in-depth discussions using Unity 2019.4 LTS or Unity 2020.x, and other free or open source software. While VR technology is rapidly advancing, we'll try to capture the basic principles and techniques that you can use to make your own VR games and applications immersive and comfortable.

You will learn how to use Unity to develop VR applications that can be experienced on devices such as Oculus Rift, Quest, HTC VIVE, and others. We'll also cover the technical considerations that are especially important and possibly unique to VR. By the end of this book, you will be equipped to develop rich and interactive VR experiences.

About the author and this third edition

Years ago, I studied 3D computer graphics in college and user interface design in graduate school, before starting a small software company developing a 3D graphics engine for managing AutoCAD engineering drawings. We sold the business to Autodesk. In the ensuing years, I focused on 2D web app development, blogged about my technical adventures, and pursued several new start-ups. Then, in March 2014, I read about Facebook purchasing Oculus for $2 billion; that certainly piqued my interest. I immediately ordered my first VR headset, the Oculus DK2 developer kit, and began developing small VR projects in Unity.

In February 2015, I had the idea to write a book on Unity VR development. Packt accepted my proposal right away, and suddenly I realized "Oh no! I have to do this!" Within 6 months, in August 2015, the first edition of this book was published. That's a short time to go from proposal to outline, to chapter drafts to review, to a final draft and publication. I was obsessed. At the time, I told my wife that I felt the book had a life of its own: "It's inside of me and struggling to get out, I just have to get out of its way." She replied, "It sounds like you're pregnant."

At the time of writing, Google Cardboard was a thing, but there were no consumer VR devices. The Oculus DK2 had no hand controllers, just an Xbox game controller. Months after the book was released, in November 2015, the HTC Vive came to market with room-scale and positionally tracked hand controllers. In March 2016, the consumer version of Oculus Rift was released. Not until December 2016, almost a year and a half after the book came out, did Oculus release its positionally tracked Touch hand controllers.

Since the first edition of this book, many new VR devices have entered the market, hardware and software features have improved, and the Unity game engine continues to add native VR SDK integrations and new features to support them. Oculus, Google, Steam, Samsung, PlayStation, Microsoft, and many others have joined the fray as the industry continues to accelerate and blossom.

Meanwhile, in 2016, I coauthored another book with Packt, *Cardboard VR Projects for Android*, a non-Unity VR book using Java and Android Studio to build Google Daydream and Cardboard applications. (In that book, you build and use your own home-grown three-dimensional graphics engine for mobile devices.) Then, in 2017, I coauthored a third book with Packt, *Augmented Reality for Developers*, an exciting and timely Unity-based project book for AR applications on iOS, Android, and HoloLens devices.

In May 2018, I published the second edition of this book, *Unity Virtual Reality Projects*. When the time came to begin the second edition, I expected it to be a relatively simple task of updating to the current version of Unity, adding support for positionally tracked hand controllers, plus a few tweaks here and there. But it wasn't so simple! While much of the fundamentals and advice in the first edition did not change, as an industry, we have learned a lot in these few short years. For example, it's really not a great idea to implement a trampoline in VR (one of our projects that got scrapped from the first edition) as that can really cause motion sickness! Every chapter and project was updated. New chapters and projects were added, including an audio fireball game, a storytelling and animation experience, and a discussion of optimization best practices.

In this third edition, the book has again been significantly revised and expanded. With the introduction of the Unity XR platform architecture, plugins, and XR Interaction Toolkit, I decided to focus on this new standard API and components throughout the book. All of the chapters and projects have been adapted to use Unity's own XR SDK instead of provider-specific toolkits because I see this to be a hugely significant development and contribution by Unity to the progress of our industry. I sincerely hope you find this book fun, educational, and helpful as we create great new VR content and explore this amazing new medium.

Who this book is for

If you are interested in VR, want to learn how it works, or want to create your own VR experiences, this book is for you. Whether you're a non-programmer and are unfamiliar with three-dimensional computer graphics or you are experienced in both but new to VR, you will benefit from this book. Any experience in Unity is an advantage. If you are new to Unity, you can also pick up this book, although you might first want to work through some of Unity's own getting-started tutorials, which are available on their website (`https://unity.com/learn`).

Game developers may already be familiar with the concepts in this book that have been reapplied to VR projects, but might still learn many other ideas that are specific to VR. Mobile and 2D game designers who already know how to use Unity will discover another dimension! Engineers and 3D designers may understand many of the 3D concepts, but will learn to use the Unity engine for VR. Application developers may appreciate the potential non-gaming uses of VR and may want to learn how to use the tools to make that happen.

What this book covers

`Chapter 1`, *Virtually Everything for Everyone*, is an introduction to the new technologies and opportunities in consumer VR in gaming and non-gaming applications, including an explanation of stereoscopic viewing and head tracking.

`Chapter 2`, *Understanding Unity, Content, and Scale*, introduces the Unity game engine as we build a simple diorama scene using primitive GameObjects, prefabs, and imported three-dimensional content.

`Chapter 3`, *Setting Up Your Project for VR*, helps you set up your system and a Unity project to build and run on your target device(s), including SteamVR, Oculus Rift, Windows Immersive MR, Oculus Quest, and Google Cardboard.

`Chapter 4`, *Using Gaze-Based Control*, explores the relationship between the VR camera and objects in a scene, including 3D cursors and gaze-based ray guns. This chapter also introduces Unity scripting in C#.

`Chapter 5`, *Interacting with Your Hands*, looks at user input events, such as controller buttons and tracked hand controllers using components from the XR Interaction Toolkit. We also build a balloon gun for inflating and popping balloons!

`Chapter 6`, *Canvasing World Space UI*, implements many examples of the **user interface** (**UI**) for VR using a Unity world space canvas, including a **heads-up display** (**HUD**), info bubbles, in-game objects, a three-dimensional dashboard, and a wrist-based menu palette.

`Chapter 7`, *Teleporting, Locomotion, and Comfort*, dives into techniques for moving yourself around a VR scene, such as glide locomotion, climbing a wall, and teleporting to other locations.

`Chapter 8`, *Lighting, Rendering, Realism*, takes a closer look at the Unity render pipelines and choosing a lighting strategy for your projects. We build interactive controls for environmental lighting, PBR materials, light objects, reflection probes, postprocessing, and more.

`Chapter 9`, *Playing with Physics and Fire*, explores the Unity physics engine, physic materials, particle systems, and more C# scripting as we build a paddle ball game to whack fireballs in time to your favorite music.

`Chapter 10`, *Exploring Interactive Spaces*, teaches you how to build an interactive art gallery, including level design with ProBuilder, artwork lighting, data management using scriptable objects, and teleporting through space.

`Chapter 11`, *Using All 360 Degrees*, explains 360-degree media and uses photos and videos in a variety of examples, including globes, orbs, photospheres, and skyboxes.

`Chapter 12`, *Animation and VR Storytelling*, builds a complete VR storytelling experience using imported three-dimensional assets and a soundtrack, as well as Unity timelines and animation.

`Chapter 13`, *Optimizing for Performance and Comfort*, demonstrates how to use the Unity Profiler and Stats window to reduce latency in your VR app, including optimizing your three-dimensional art, static lighting, efficient coding, and GPU rendering.

To get the most out of this book

Before we get started, there are a few things that you'll need. Grab a snack, a bottle of water, or a cup of coffee. Besides that, you'll need a PC (Windows or Mac) with the current version of Unity installed (Unity 2019.4 LTS or later). Access to a VR HMD is strongly recommended in order to try out your builds and get first-hand experience of the projects developed in this book.

You don't need a super-powerful computer rig. While Unity can be a beast that can render complex scenes, the requirements for the projects in this book are not that demanding. If you are targeting an Android-based VR device (such as Oculus Go or Quest), you need just enough power to run Unity and build your project as if for any Android mobile device. If you are targeting desktop VR (such as HTC Vive, Valve Index, Oculus Rift, or Oculus Quest with a Quest Link cable), you simply need to meet the VR-ready requirements of the target device.

`Chapter 3`, *Setting Up Your Project for VR*, goes into detail of what you need for each device and platform, including SteamVR, Oculus Rift, Windows MR, Oculus Go and Quest, and Google Cardboard.

That should just about do it—a PC, the Unity software, a VR device, and the other tools described in `Chapter 3`, *Setting Up Your Project for VR*, and we're good to go! Oh, some projects will also be more complete if you download the associated assets from the Packt website, as follows.

Download the example code files

You can download the example code files for this book from your account at `www.packt.com`. If you purchased this book elsewhere, you can visit `www.packtpub.com/support` and register to have the files emailed directly to you.

You can download the code files by following these steps:

1. Log in or register at `www.packt.com`.
2. Select the **Support** tab.
3. Click on **Code Downloads**.
4. Enter the name of the book in the **Search** box and follow the onscreen instructions.

Once the file is downloaded, please make sure that you unzip or extract the folder using the latest version of:

- WinRAR/7-Zip for Windows
- Zipeg/iZip/UnRarX for Mac
- 7-Zip/PeaZip for Linux

The code bundle for the book is also hosted on GitHub at `https://github.com/PacktPublishing/Unity-2020-Virtual-Reality-Projects-3rd-Edition-`. In case there's an update to the code, it will be updated on the existing GitHub repository.

We also have other code bundles from our rich catalog of books and videos available at `https://github.com/PacktPublishing/`. Check them out!

Conventions used

There are a number of text conventions used throughout this book.

`CodeInText`: Indicates code words in text, database table names, folder names, filenames, file extensions, pathnames, dummy URLs, user input, and Twitter handles. Here is an example: "Open the `Assets/Scenes/` folder."

A block of code is set as follows:

```
public class BallsFromHeaven : MonoBehaviour
{
    public GameObject ballPrefab;
    public float startHeight = 10f;
    public float interval = 0.5f;

    private float nextBallTime = 0f;

    private void Start()
    {
        nextBallTime = Time.time + interval;
    }
```

When we wish to draw your attention to a particular part of a code block, the relevant lines or items are set in bold:

```
public float startHeight = 10f;
  public float interval = 0.5f;

  private float nextBallTime = 0f;
  private ObjectPooler objectPooler;
```

```
private void Start()
{
    nextBallTime = Time.time + interval;
    objectPooler = GetComponent<ObjectPooler>();
}
```

Bold: Indicates a new term, an important word, or words that you see onscreen. For example, words in menus or dialog boxes appear in the text like this. Here is an example: "Add an **XR Rig** object by going to **GameObject** | **XR** | **Stationary XR Rig**."

Warnings or important notes appear like this.

Tips and tricks appear like this.

Get in touch

Feedback from our readers is always welcome.

General feedback: If you have questions about any aspect of this book, mention the book title in the subject of your message and email us at `customercare@packtpub.com`.

Errata: Although we have taken every care to ensure the accuracy of our content, mistakes do happen. If you have found a mistake in this book, we would be grateful if you would report this to us. Please visit `www.packtpub.com/support/errata`, selecting your book, clicking on the Errata Submission Form link, and entering the details.

Piracy: If you come across any illegal copies of our works in any form on the Internet, we would be grateful if you would provide us with the location address or website name. Please contact us at `copyright@packt.com` with a link to the material.

If you are interested in becoming an author: If there is a topic that you have expertise in and you are interested in either writing or contributing to a book, please visit `authors.packtpub.com`.

Reviews

Please leave a review. Once you have read and used this book, why not leave a review on the site that you purchased it from? Potential readers can then see and use your unbiased opinion to make purchase decisions, we at Packt can understand what you think about our products, and our authors can see your feedback on their book. Thank you!

For more information about Packt, please visit `packt.com`.

1 Virtually Everything for Everyone

This virtual reality thing calls into question, what does it mean to "be somewhere"?

Before cell phones, you would call someone and it would make no sense to say, "Hey, where are you?" You know where they are, you called their house, that's where they are.

So then cell phones come around and you start to hear people say, "Hello. Oh, I'm at Starbucks," because the person on the other end wouldn't necessarily know where you are because you became un-tethered from your house for voice communications.

So when I saw a VR demo, I had this vision of coming home and my wife has got the kids settled down, she has a couple minutes to herself, and she's on the couch wearing goggles on her face. I come over and tap her on the shoulder, and I'm like, "Hey, where are you?"

It's super weird. The person's sitting right in front of you, but you don't know where they are.

- Jonathan Stark, mobile expert, and podcaster

Welcome to **virtual reality** (**VR**)! In this book, we will explore what it takes to create VR experiences on our own. We will take a walk through a series of hands-on projects, step-by-step tutorials, and in-depth discussions using the Unity 3D game engine and other free or open source resources. Though VR technology is rapidly advancing, we'll try to capture the basic principles and techniques that you can use to make your VR games and applications feel immersive and comfortable.

In this first chapter, we will define VR and illustrate how it can be applied not only to games, but also to many other areas of interest and work productivity. We'll see that VR is all about immersion and presence, seemingly transporting you to a different place and experience. VR is not just for gaming—it can be applied to a wide spectrum of personal, professional, and educational applications. This chapter discusses the following topics:

- What is virtual reality?
- Differences between virtual reality and augmented reality
- How VR applications may differ from VR games
- Types of VR experience
- Types of VR device
- Some psychological, physiological, and technical explanations of how VR works
- Technical skills that are necessary for the development of VR

What is virtual reality?

Today, we are witnesses to burgeoning consumer-accessible VR, an exciting technology that promises to transform in a fundamental way how we interact with information, our friends, and the world at large.

What is virtual reality? In general, VR is the computer-generated simulation of a 3D environment, which seems very real to the person experiencing it, using special electronic equipment. The objective is to achieve a strong sense of being present (presence) in the virtual environment.

Today's consumer tech VR involves wearing HMD (head-mounted display) goggles to view stereoscopic 3D scenes. You can look around by moving your head, and walk around by using hand controls or motion sensors. You are engaged in a fully immersive experience. It's as if you're really there in some other virtual world. The following photo shows me, the author, experiencing an **Oculus Rift Development Kit 2** (**DK2**) in 2015:

VR is not new. It's been here for decades, albeit hidden away in academic research labs and high-end industrial and military facilities. It was big, clunky, and expensive. Ivan Sutherland invented the first HMD in 1965 (see `https://amturing.acm.org/photo/sutherland_3467412.cfm`). It was tethered to the ceiling with metal pipes! In the past, several failed attempts have been made to bring consumer-level VR products to the market:

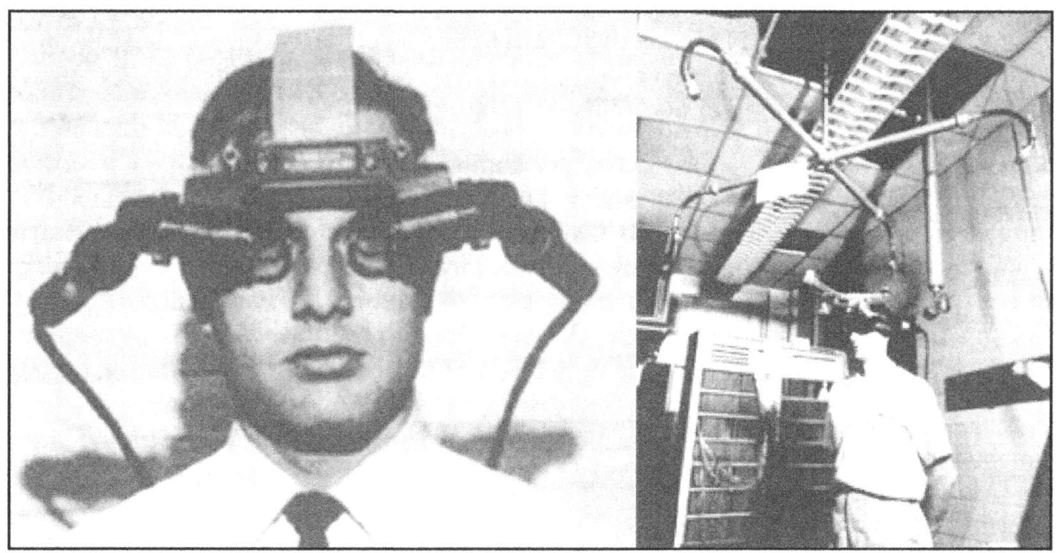

Source: `https://mashable.com/2012/09/24/augmented-reality/`

In 2012, Palmer Luckey, the founder of Oculus VR LLC, gave a demonstration of a makeshift head-mounted VR display to John Carmack, the famed developer of the Doom, Wolfenstein 3D, and Quake classic video games. Together, they ran a successful Kickstarter campaign and released a developer kit called **Oculus Rift Development Kit 1** (**DK1**) to an enthusiastic community. This caught the attention of investors, as well as Mark Zuckerberg (Facebook CEO), and in March 2014, Facebook bought the company for $2 billion. With no product, no customers, and infinite promise, the money and attention that it attracted helped fuel a new category of consumer products.

At the same time, others were also working on their own products, which were soon introduced to the market, including Steam's HTC VIVE, Google Daydream, Sony PlayStation VR, Samsung Gear VR, Microsoft's immersive Mixed Reality, and more. New innovations and devices that enhance the VR experience continue to be introduced.

Most of the basic research has already been done, and the technology is now affordable, thanks in large part to the mass adoption of devices that work on mobile technology. There is a huge community of developers with experience in building 3D games and mobile apps. Creative content producers are joining in and the media is talking it up. At last, virtual reality is real!

Say what? *Virtual reality is real?* Ha! If it's virtual, how can it be... Oh, never mind.

Eventually, we will get past the focus on the emerging hardware devices and recognize that *content is king*. The current generation of 3D development software (commercial, free, or open source) that has spawned a plethora of indie (independent) game developers can also be used to build nongame VR applications.

Though VR finds most of its enthusiasts in the gaming community, the potential applications reach well beyond that. Any business that presently uses 3D modeling and computer graphics will be more effective if it uses VR technology. The sense of immersive presence that is afforded by VR can enhance all common online experiences today, which includes engineering, social networking, shopping, marketing, entertainment, and business development. In the near future, viewing 3D websites with a VR headset may be as common as visiting ordinary flat websites today.

It's probably worthwhile to clarify what virtual reality is not by comparing VR with augmented reality.

Differences between virtual reality and augmented reality

A sister technology to VR is **augmented reality** (**AR**), which combines **computer-generated imagery** (**CGI**) with views of the real world. AR on smartphones has recently garnered widespread interest with the introduction of Apple's ARKit for iOS and Google ARCore for Android. Furthermore, the Vuforia AR toolkit is now integrated directly with the Unity game engine, helping to drive even more adoption of the technology. AR on a mobile device overlays the CGI on top of live video from a camera.

The latest innovations in AR are wearable AR headsets, such as Microsoft's **HoloLens** and **Magic Leap**. The computer graphics are shown directly in your field of view, not mixed into a video image. If VR headsets are like closed goggles, AR headsets are like translucent sunglasses that combine the real-world light rays with CGI.

A challenge for AR is ensuring that the CGI is consistently aligned with and mapped onto the objects in the real-world space and to eliminate latency while moving about so that they (the CGI and objects in the real-world space) stay aligned.

AR holds as much promise as VR for future applications, but it's different. Though AR intends to engage the user within their current surroundings, VR is fully immersive. In AR, you may open your hand and see a log cabin resting in your palm, but in VR, you're transported directly inside the log cabin and you can walk around inside it.

We are also beginning to see hybrid devices that combine features of VR and AR and let you switch between modes. For example, we're already seeing VR devices with pass-through video features, primarily used for setting up your play area bounds and floor level, and as a safety feature when the player goes out of bounds. The camera mounted on the HMD, generally used for spatial positioning, can be fed to the display. Be aware that the field of view of the video may be distorted, so it shouldn't be used for walking around.

If you are interested in developing applications for AR, please also refer to the author's book *Augmented Reality for Developers* from Packt Publishing (`https://www.packtpub.com/web-development/augmented-reality-developers`).

Next, we'll explore the ways in which VR can be used to improve our lives and entertainment.

Applications versus games

Consumer-level VR started with gaming. Video gamers are already accustomed to being engaged in highly interactive hyper-realistic 3D environments. VR just ups the ante.

Gamers are early adopters of high-end graphics technology. Mass production of gaming consoles and PC-based components in the tens of millions and competition between vendors leads to lower prices and higher performance. Game developers follow suit, often pushing the state of the art, squeezing every ounce of performance out of hardware and software. Gamers are a very demanding bunch, and the market has consistently stepped up to keep them satisfied. It's no surprise that many, if not most, of the current wave of VR hardware and software companies are first targeting the video gaming industry. A majority of the VR apps on the Oculus Store, such as Rift (`https://www.oculus.com/experiences/rift/`), GearVR (`https://www.oculus.com/experiences/gear-vr/`), and Google Play for Daydream (`https://play.google.com/store/search?q=daydreamc=appshl=en`), are for games. And of course, the Steam VR platform (`http://store.steampowered.com/steamvr`) is almost entirely about gaming. Gamers are the most enthusiastic VR advocates and seriously appreciate its potential.

Game developers know that the core of a game is the **game mechanics**, or the rules, which are largely independent of the *skin*, or the thematic topic, of the game. Game mechanics can include puzzles, chance, strategy, timing, or muscle memory. VR games can have the same mechanical elements but might need to be adjusted for the virtual environment. For example, a first-person character walking in a console video game is probably going about 1.5 times faster than their actual pace in real life. If this wasn't the case, the player would feel that the game was too slow and boring. Put the same character in a VR scene and they will feel that it is too fast; it could likely make the player feel nauseous. In VR, you want your characters to walk at a normal, earthly pace. Not all video games will map well to VR; it may not be fun to be in the middle of a hyperrealistic war zone when you're actually virtually there.

That said, VR is also being applied in areas other than gaming. Though games will remain important, nongaming applications will eventually overshadow them. These applications may differ from games in a number of ways, with the most significant having much less emphasis on game mechanics and more emphasis on either the experience itself or application-specific goals. Of course, this doesn't preclude some game mechanics. For example, the application may be specifically designed to train the user in a specific skill. Sometimes, the **gamification** of a business or personal application makes it more fun and effective in driving the desired behavior through competition.

In general, nongaming VR applications are less about winning and more about the experience itself.

Here are a few examples of the nongaming application areas that are proving successful in VR:

- **Travel and tourism**: Visit faraway places without leaving your home. Visit art museums in Paris, New York, and Tokyo in one afternoon. Take a walk on Mars. You can even enjoy Holi, the spring festival of colors, in India while sitting in your wintery cabin in Vermont.
- **Mechanical engineering and industrial design**: Computer-aided design software, such as AutoCAD and SOLIDWORKS, pioneered three-dimensional modeling, simulation, and visualization. With VR, engineers and designers can directly experience the end product before it's actually built and play with what-if scenarios at a very low cost. Consider iterating a new automobile design. How does it look? How does it perform? How does it appear when sitting in the driver's seat?
- **Architecture and civil engineering**: Architects and engineers have always constructed scale models of their designs, if only to pitch the ideas to clients and investors or, more importantly, to validate the many assumptions about the design. Currently, modeling and rendering software is commonly used to build virtual models from architectural plans. With VR, the conversations with stakeholders can be so much more confident. Other personnel, such as interior designers, HVAC, and electrical engineers, can be brought into the process sooner.
- **Real estate**: Real-estate agents have been quick adopters of the internet and visualization technology to attract buyers and close sales. Real-estate search websites were some of the first successful uses of the web. Online panoramic video walkthroughs of for-sale properties have been commonplace for years. With VR, I can be in New York and gauge the feel of a place to live in Los Angeles.
- **Medicine**: The potential of VR for health and medicine may literally be a matter of life and death. Every day, hospitals use MRI and other scanning devices to produce models of our bones and organs that are used for medical diagnosis and possibly preoperative planning. Using VR to enhance visualization and measurement will provide a more intuitive analysis, for example. VR is especially being used for medical training, such as the simulation of surgery for medical students.

- **Mental health**: VR experiences have been shown to be effective in a therapeutic context for the treatment of **post-traumatic stress disorder** (**PTSD**) in what's called **exposure therapy**, where the patient, guided by a trained therapist, confronts their traumatic memories through the retelling of the experience. Similarly, VR is being used to treat arachnophobia (fear of spiders) and the fear of flying.
- **Education**: The educational opportunities for VR are almost too obvious to mention. One of the first successful VR experiences is **Titans of Space**, which lets you explore the solar system first hand. In science, history, the arts, and mathematics, VR will help students of all ages because, as they say, field trips are much more effective than textbooks.
- **Training**: Toyota has demonstrated a VR simulation of drivers' education to teach teenagers about the risks of distracted driving. In another project, vocational students got to experience the operating of cranes and other heavy construction equipment. Training for first responders, the police, and fire and rescue workers can be enhanced with VR by presenting highly risky situations and alternative virtual scenarios. The **National Football League** (**NFL**) and college teams are looking to VR for athletic training.
- **Entertainment and journalism**: Virtually attend rock concerts and sporting events or watch music videos. Re-experience news events as if you were personally present. Enjoy 360-degree cinematic experiences. The art of storytelling will be transformed by virtual reality.

Wow, that's quite a list! This is just the low-hanging fruit. Unity Technologies, the company behind the Unity 3D engine, appreciates this and is making an all-out push beyond gaming for its engine (you can learn more about Unity Solutions at `https://unity.com/solutions`).

The purpose of this book is not to dive too deeply into any of these applications. Rather, I hope that this brief look at the possibilities helps stimulate your thinking and provides an idea of how VR has the potential to be virtually anything for everyone. Next, we'll attempt to define the spectrum of the types of VR experience.

Types of VR experience

There is not just one kind of VR experience. In fact, there are many. Consider the following types of VR experiences:

- **Diorama**: In the simplest case, we build a 3D scene. You're observing from a third-person perspective. Your eye is the camera. Actually, each eye is a separate camera that gives you a stereoscopic view. You can look around.
- **First-person experience**: This time, you're immersed in the scene as a freely moving agent. Using an input controller (a hand controller or some other technique), you can "walk" around and explore the virtual scene.
- **Room scale:** The first-person experience with physical space. Given positional tracking, you can physically walk around a predefined area. A guardian system will show when you've reached unsafe boundaries.
- **Interactive virtual environment**: This is like the first-person experience, but you're more than an observer. While you are in the scene, you can interact with the objects in it. Physics is at play. Objects may respond to you. You may be given specific goals to achieve and challenges to face using the game mechanics. You might even earn points and keep score.
- **3D content creation**: In VR, you can create content that can be experienced in VR. **Google Tilt Brush** is one of the first blockbuster experiences, as is **Oculus Medium** and **Google Blocks**, among others. Unity is working on **EditorXR** for Unity developers to work on their projects directly in the VR scene.
- **Riding on rails**: In this kind of experience, you're seated and being transported through the environment (or the environment changes around you). For example, you can ride a rollercoaster using this VR experience. However, it may not necessarily be an extreme thrill ride; it could be a simple real estate walk-through or even a slow, easy, and meditative experience.
- **360-degree media**: Think panoramic images that are projected on the inside of a sphere. You're positioned at the center of the sphere and can look all around. Some purists don't consider this *real* VR, because you're seeing a projection and not a model rendering. However, it can provide an effective sense of presence.
- **Social VR**: When multiple players enter the same VR space and can see and speak with each other's avatars, it becomes a remarkable social experience.

In this book, we will implement a number of projects that demonstrate how to build each of these types of VR experience. For brevity, we'll need to keep it pure and simple, with suggestions for areas for further investigation. Our focus will be on consumer-grade devices, described in the next section.

Types of HMD

Presently, there are two basic categories of HMDs for VR: **desktop VR** and **mobile VR**, although the distinctions are increasingly becoming blurred. Eventually, we might just talk about platforms as we do traditional computing, in terms of the operating system—for example, Windows, Android, and console VR. Let's look at each of these HMDs in more detail.

Desktop VR

With desktop VR (and console VR), your headset is peripheral to a more powerful computer that processes the heavy graphics. The computer may be a Windows PC, Mac, Linux, or a game console, although Windows is by far the most prominent PC, and PlayStation is a bestseller in terms of console VR.

The headset is connected to the computer with physical wires (tethered connection) or a near-zero latency wireless connection. The game runs on the remote machine and the HMD is a peripheral display device with a motion-sensing input. The term *desktop* is an unfortunate misnomer since it's just as likely to be stationed in your living room or den.

The **Oculus Rift** (`https://www.oculus.com/`) is an example of a device where the goggles have an integrated display and sensors. The games run on a separate PC. Other desktop headsets include the **HTC VIVE**, Sony's **PlayStation VR**, and **Microsoft Mixed Reality**.

Desktop VR devices rely on a desktop computer for CPU (general processor) and GPU (graphics processing unit) power, where more is better. Please refer to the recommended specification requirements for your specific device.

However, for the purpose of this book, we won't have any heavy rendering in our projects, and you can get by with the minimum system specifications.

Mobile VR

Mobile VR originated with **Google Cardboard** (`https://vr.google.com/cardboard/`), a simple housing device for two lenses and a slot for your mobile phone. The phone's display shows twin stereoscopic views. It has rotational head tracking, but it has no positional tracking. Cardboard also provides the user with the ability to click or *tap* its side to make selections in a game. The complexity of the imagery is limited because it uses your phone's processor for rendering the views on the phone display screen.

Google Daydream can be said to have progressed to the Samsung GearVR, requiring more performant minimum specifications in the Android phone, including greater processing power. GearVR's headsets include motion sensors to assist the phone device rather than relying on the phone's own sensors. These devices also introduced a three-**degrees-of-freedom (DOF)** hand controller that can be used as a laser pointer within VR experiences:

> *The term degrees of freedom (DoF) refers to the number of basic ways a rigid object can move through 3D space. There are six total degrees of freedom. Three correspond to rotational movement around the x, y, and z axes, commonly termed pitch, yaw, and roll. The other three correspond to translational movement along those axes, which can be thought of as moving forward or backward, moving left or right, and moving up or down.*
>
> *– Google VR Concepts*
> (`https://developers.google.com/vr/discover/degrees-of-freedom`)

Since the previous edition of this book, Google has discontinued the Daydream headset and has mad the Cardboard software open-source. Likewise, Samsung and Oculus have discontinued support for GearVR, supplanted by the Oculus Go and Quest devices.

The next generation of mobile VR devices includes all-in-one headsets, such as Oculus Go, with embedded screens and processors, eliminating the need for a separate mobile phone. The Oculus Quest further adds depth sensors and spatial mapping processors to track the user's location in 3D space, 6DOF hand controllers, and in some cases even hand tracking without hand controllers.

As of December 2020, Oculus is sunsetting the Oculus Go and will stop accepting new applications in its store.

The bottom line is that the projects in this book will explore features from the high end to the low end of the consumer VR device spectrum. But generally, our projects will not demand a lot of processing power, nor will they require high-end VR capability, so you can begin developing for VR on any of these types of devices, including Google Cardboard and an ordinary mobile phone.

Next, let's dive a little deeper into how this technology works.

How virtual reality works

So, what is it about VR that's got everyone so excited? With your headset on, you experience synthetic scenes. It appears 3D, it feels 3D, and maybe you will even have a sense of actually being there inside the virtual world. The strikingly obvious thing is that VR looks and feels *really cool!* But why?

Immersion and *presence* are the two words that are used to describe the quality of a VR experience. The Holy Grail is to increase both to the point where it seems so real that you forget you're in a virtual world. *Immersion* is the result of emulating the sensory input that your body receives (visual, auditory, motor, and so on). This can be explained technically. *Presence* is the visceral feeling that you get of being transported there—a deep emotional or intuitive feeling. You could say that immersion is the science of VR and presence is the art. And that, my friend, is cool.

A number of different technologies and techniques come together to make the VR experience work, which can be separated into two basic areas:

- 3D viewing
- Head, hand, and body tracking

In other words, displays and sensors, such as those built into today's mobile devices, are a big reason why VR is possible and affordable today.

Suppose that the VR system knows exactly where your head and hands are positioned at any given moment in time. Suppose that it can immediately render and display the 3D scene for this precise viewpoint stereoscopically. Then, wherever and whenever you move, you'll see the virtual scene exactly as you should. You will have a nearly perfect visual VR experience. That's basically it. *Ta-dah!*

Well, not so fast. Literally. Let's dig deeper into some of the psychological, physiological, and technical aspects that make VR work.

Stereoscopic 3D viewing

Split-screen stereography was discovered not long after the invention of photography. Take a look at the popular stereograph viewer from 1876 shown in the following photo (B.W. Kilborn & Co, Littleton, New Hampshire; see `http://en.wikipedia.org/wiki/Benjamin_W._Kilburn`):

A stereo photograph has separate views for the left and right eyes, which are slightly offset to create a parallax effect. This fools the brain into thinking that it's a truly three-dimensional view. The device contains separate lenses for each eye, which lets you easily focus on the photo close up.

Similarly, rendering these side-by-side stereo views is the first job of the VR-enabled camera object in Unity.

Let's say that you're wearing a VR headset and you're holding your head very still so that the image looks frozen. It still appears better than a simple stereograph. Why?

The old-fashioned stereograph has relatively small twin images rectangularly bound. When your eye is focused on the center of the view, the 3D effect is convincing, but you will see the boundaries of the view. Move your eyes around (even with your head still), and any remaining sense of immersion is totally lost. You're just an observer on the outside peering into a diorama.

Now, consider what a VR screen looks like without the headset by using the following screenshot:

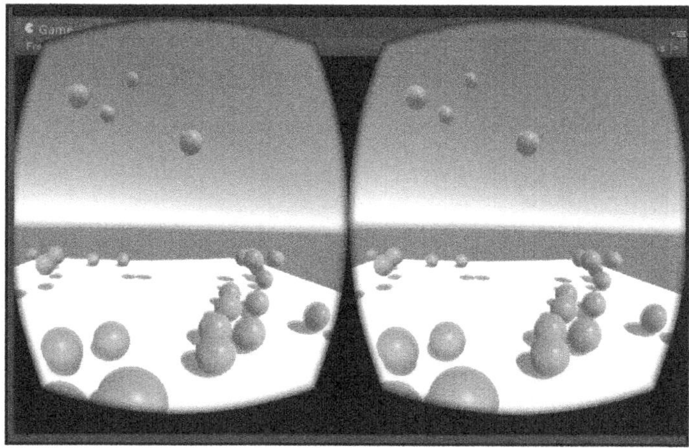

The first thing that you will notice is that each eye has a barrel-shaped view. Why is that? The headset lens is a very wide-angle lens, so when you look through it, you have a nice wide field of view. In fact, it is so wide (and tall) that it distorts the image (**pincushion effect**). The graphics software inverts that distortion by creating a **barrel distortion** so that it looks correct to us through the lenses. This is referred to as an **ocular distortion correction**. The result is an apparent **field of view** (**FOV**) that is wide enough to include a lot more of your peripheral vision. For example, the Oculus Rift has an FOV of about 100 degrees (we talk more about FOV in `Chapter 11`, *Using All 360 Degrees*).

Also, of course, the view angle from each eye is slightly offset, comparable to the distance between your eyes or the **inter pupillary distance** (**IPD**). The IPD is used to calculate the parallax and can vary from one person to the next.

To measure your IPD, hold a ruler (with millimeter markings) on your forehead in front of a mirror, as close to your eyes as possible. Open one eye and line up the 0 mark on the center of your pupil. Now, close that eye and open the other, and the distance to the center of your other pupil should be your IPD.

It might be less obvious, but if you look closer at the VR screen, you will see color separations, like you'd get from a color printer whose print head is not aligned properly. This is intentional. Light passing through a lens is refracted at different angles based on the wavelength of the light. Again, the rendering software inverts the color separation so that it looks correct to us. This is referred to as a **chromatic aberration correction**. It helps make the image look really crisp.

The resolution of the screen is also important to get a convincing view. If it's too low res, you'll see the pixels, or what some refer to as a **screen-door effect**. The pixel width and height of the display is an oft-quoted specification when comparing the HMDs, but the **pixels per inch** (**PPI**) value may be more important. Other innovations in display technology, such as **pixel smearing** and **foveated rendering** (showing higher-resolution details exactly where the eyeball is looking) help improve the apparent resolution and reduce the screen-door effect.

When experiencing a 3D scene in VR, you must also consider the **frames per second (FPS)**. If the FPS is too slow, the animation will look choppy. Things that affect FPS include the GPU performance and the complexity of the Unity scene (the number of polygons and lighting calculations), among other factors. *This is compounded in VR because you need to draw the scene twice, once for each eye*. Technology innovations, such as GPUs that are optimized for VR, frame interpolation, and other techniques, will improve the frame rates. For us developers, performance-tuning techniques in Unity that are often used by mobile game developers can be applied in VR (we will talk more about performance optimization in `Chapter 13`, *Optimizing for Performance and Comfort*). These techniques and optics help make the 3D scene appear realistic.

Sound is also very important—more important than many people realize. VR should be experienced while wearing stereo headphones. In fact, you can still have a great experience when the audio is done well but the graphics are pretty crappy. We see this a lot in TV and cinema. The same holds true in VR. Binaural audio gives each ear its own stereo *view* of a sound source in such a way that your brain imagines its location in 3D space. True 3D audio provides an even more realistic spatial audio rendering, where sounds bounce off nearby walls and can be occluded by obstacles in the scene to enhance the first-person experience and realism.

For a fun example of binaural audio, put on your headphones and visit the classic *Virtual Barber Shop* at `https://www.youtube.com/watch?v=IUDTlvagjJA`. No special listening devices are needed. Regular headphones will work (speakers will not).

Lastly, the VR headset should fit your head and face comfortably so that it's easy to forget that you're wearing it, and it should block out light from the real environment around you.

Head, hand, and body tracking

So, we have a nice 3D picture that is viewable in a comfortable VR headset with a wide field of view. If we had this setup and you moved your head, it'd feel like you had a diorama box stuck to your face. Move your head and the box moves along with it, and this is much like holding the antique stereograph device or the **View-Master**. Fortunately, VR is so much better.

The VR headset has a motion sensor (IMU) inside that detects spatial acceleration and rotation rates on all three axes, providing what's called the **six degrees of freedom (6DOF)**. This is the same technology that is commonly found in mobile phones and some console game controllers, but perhaps with higher sensitivity and accuracy. With the IMU integrated into your headset, when you move your head, the current viewpoint is calculated and used when the next frame's image is drawn. This is referred to as **motion detection**.

The previous generation of mobile motion sensors was good enough for us to play mobile games on a phone, but for VR, it's not accurate enough. These inaccuracies (rounding errors) accumulate over time, as the sensor is sampled thousands of times per second, and you may eventually lose track of where they were in the real world. This *drift* was a major shortfall of the older, phone-based Google Cardboard VR. It could sense your head's motion, but it lost track of your head's orientation. The current generation of phones, such as Google Pixel and Samsung Galaxy, which conform to the Daydream specifications, have upgraded sensors.

High-end HMDs account for drift with a separate *positional tracking* mechanism:

- **Inside out**: The original Oculus Rift CV1 did this with inside-out positional tracking, where an array of (invisible) infrared LEDs on the HMD were read by an external optical sensor (infrared camera) to determine your position. You need to remain within the *view* of the camera for the head tracking to work.
- **Outside in**: Alternatively, the Steam VR VIVE Lighthouse technology uses *outside-in positional tracking*, where two or more dumb laser emitters are placed in the room (much like the lasers in a barcode reader at the grocery checkout), and an optical sensor on the headset reads the rays to determine your position.
- **Spatial mapping**: The Oculus Rift-S, Vive Cosmos, and Windows MR headsets use no external sensors or projectors. Rather, the headset itself contains all the integrated cameras and sensors needed to perform spatial mapping of the local environment around you in order to locate and track your position in real-world 3D space.

Either way, the primary purpose is to accurately find the position of your head and other similarly equipped devices, such as handheld controllers.

Together, the position, tilt, and forward direction of your head—or the *head pose*—are used by the graphics software to redraw the 3D scene from this vantage point. Graphics engines such as Unity are really good at this.

Now, let's say that the screen is getting updated at 90 FPS, and you're moving your head. The software determines the head pose, renders the 3D view, and draws it on the HMD screen. However, you're still moving your head, so by the time it's displayed, the image is a little out of date with respect to your current position. This is called **latency**, and it can make you feel nauseous.

Motion sickness caused by latency in VR occurs when you're moving your head and your brain expects the world around you to change exactly in sync. Any perceptible delay can make you uncomfortable, to say the least.

Latency can be measured as the time from reading a motion sensor to rendering the corresponding image, or the *sensor-to-pixel* delay. Oculus's John Carmack said the following:

> *A total latency of 50 milliseconds will feel responsive, but still noticeable laggy. 20 milliseconds or less will provide the minimum level of latency deemed acceptable.*

There are a number of very clever strategies that can be used to implement latency compensation. The details are outside the scope of this book and inevitably will change as device manufacturers improve on the technology. One of these strategies is what Oculus calls the **timewarp**, which tries to guess where your head will be by the time the rendering is done and uses that future head pose instead of the actual detected one. All of this is handled in the SDK, so as a Unity developer, you do not have to deal with it directly.

Meanwhile, as VR developers, we need to be aware of latency as well as the other causes of motion sickness. Latency can be reduced via the faster rendering of each frame (keeping the recommended FPS). This can be achieved by discouraging your head from moving too quickly and using other techniques to make yourself feel grounded and comfortable. We talk more about comfort strategies in `Chapter 7`, *Teleporting, Locomotion, and Comfort.*

Another thing VR software does to improve head tracking and realism is use a skeletal representation of the neck so that all the rotations that it receives are mapped more accurately to the head rotation. For example, looking down at your lap creates a small forward translation since it knows it's impossible to rotate one's head downward on the spot.

Other than head tracking, stereography, and 3D audio, VR experiences can be enhanced with body tracking, hand tracking (and gesture recognition), locomotion tracking (for example, VR treadmills), and controllers with haptic feedback. The goal of all of this is to increase your sense of immersion and presence in the virtual world.

Technical skills that are important to VR

Being a VR developer requires the integration of multiple skills. Yes, you may likely specialize in one or a few areas. But sooner or later you're going to need at least some hands-on experience in a range of areas, as depicted in the following diagram:

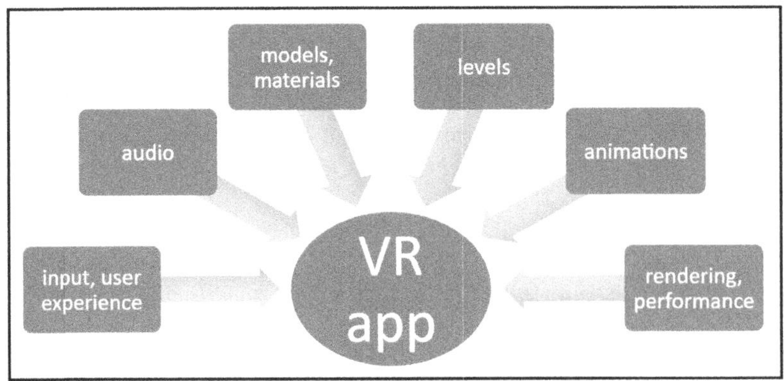

Years ago, software development was revolutionized by the web. Web development draws upon a range of engineering and artistic disciplines to make a successful website, including artists, designers, typographers, photographers, and others. With VR, the reach is an order of magnitude greater. VR is multimedia, requiring audio, animation, and 3D design. VR is software engineering, requiring programming, debugging, and platform operations. VR is architecture and modeling, requiring 3D models, level design, and space construction. VR is theater and storytelling, requiring lighting, blocking, and character development. And the list goes on. But do not be discouraged. Consider this a challenge. Dip your toes into each aspect of the whole, and, as needed, deep dive into one area or another and engage friends and colleagues who have these skills and knowledge.

Each chapter of this book introduces new technical skills and concepts that are important if you wish to build your own VR applications. You will learn about the following in this book:

- **World scale**: When building for a VR experience, attention to the 3D space and scale is important. One unit in Unity is usually equal to one meter in the virtual world.
- **First-person controls**: There are various techniques that can be used to control the movement of your agent (first-person camera), gaze-based selection, tracked hand-input controllers, and head movements.

- **User interface controls**: Unlike conventional video (and mobile) games, all user interface components are in world coordinates in VR, not screen coordinates. We'll explore ways to present notices, buttons, selectors, and other **user interface** (**UI**) controls to the users so that they can interact with the environment and make selections.
- **Lighting and rendering**: Managing the look of each scene is important to accomplishing the feel you want. This is a complex set of topics (light sources, global illumination, render pipelines, quality settings, lightmapping, and other effects!). We'll introduce enough basics to get you going.
- **Physics and gravity**: Critical to the sense of presence and immersion in VR is the physics and gravity of the world. We'll use the Unity physics engine to our advantage.
- **Animations**: Moving objects within the scene is called *animation*—duh! It can either be along predefined paths or it may use **artificial intelligence** (**AI**) scripting that follows a logical algorithm in response to events in the environment.
- **Multiuser services**: Real-time networking and multiuser games are not easy to implement, but online services make it easy without you having to be a computer engineer.
- **Build, run, and optimize**: Different HMDs use different developer kits and assets to build applications that target a specific device. We'll consider techniques that let you use a single interface for multiple devices. Understanding the rendering pipeline and how to optimize performance is a critical skill for VR development.
- **C# programming**: We will write scripts in the C# language and use features of Unity as and when they are needed to get things done.

However, there are technical areas that we will not cover. We will not go into modeling techniques, terrains, or humanoid animations. We also won't discuss game mechanics, dynamics, and strategies. All of these are very important topics that may be necessary for you (or for someone in your team) to learn, in addition to this book, to build complete, successful, and immersive VR applications.

So, let's see what this book actually covers and who it caters to.

What this book covers

This book takes a practical, project-based approach to teach the specifics of VR development using the Unity 3D game development engine. You'll learn how to use Unity 2020 to develop VR applications, which can be experienced with devices such as Oculus, Rift, Quest, HTC Vive, Cosmos, Valve Index, and even Google Cardboard.

However, we have a slight problem here—the technology is advancing very rapidly. Of course, this is a good problem to have. Actually, it's an awesome problem to have, unless you're a developer in the middle of a project or an author of a book on this technology! How does one write a book that doesn't have obsolete content the day it's published?

Throughout the book, I have tried to distill some universal principles that should outlive any short-term advances in VR technology, which include the following:

- Categorization of different types of VR experiences with example projects
- Important technical ideas and skills, especially those that are relevant to the building of VR applications
- General explanations of how VR devices and software works
- Strategies to ensure user comfort and and the avoidance of VR motion sickness
- Instructions on using the Unity game engine to build VR experiences

Once VR becomes mainstream, many of these lessons will perhaps be obvious rather than obsolete, just like the explanations from the 1980s of *how to use a mouse* would just be silly today.

Who this book is for

If you are interested in VR, want to learn how it works, or want to create VR experiences yourself, then this book is for you. We will walk you through a series of hands-on projects, step-by-step tutorials, and in-depth discussions using the Unity 3D game engine.

Whether you're a nonprogrammer who is unfamiliar with 3D computer graphics or a person with experience in both, but who is new to VR, you will benefit from this book. It could be your first foray into Unity or you may have some experience, but you do not need to be an expert either. Still, if you're new to Unity, you can pick up this book as long as you realize that you'll need to adapt to the pace of the book.

Game developers may already be familiar with the concepts in the book, which are reapplied to the VR projects along with many other ideas that are specific to VR. Engineers and 3D designers may understand many of the 3D concepts, but they may wish to learn to use the Unity game engine for VR. Application developers may appreciate the potential nongaming uses of VR and want to learn the tools that can make this happen.

Whoever you are, we're going to turn you into a *3D software VR ninja*. Well, OK, this may be a stretch for this little book, but we'll try to set you on the way.

Summary

In this chapter, we looked at virtual reality and realized that it can mean a lot of things to different people and can have different applications. There's no single definition, and it's a moving target. We are not alone, as everyone's still trying to figure it out. The fact is that VR is a new medium that will take years, if not decades, to reach its potential.

VR is not just for games; it can be a game-changer for many different applications. We identified over a dozen. There are different kinds of VR experiences, which we'll explore in the projects in this book.

VR headsets can be divided into those that require a separate processing unit (such as a desktop PC or a console) that runs with a powerful GPU and those that use mobile technologies for processing.

So, let's get to it! In the next chapter, we'll jump right into Unity and create our first 3D scene and learn about world coordinates, scaling, and importing 3D assets.

2
Understanding Unity, Content, and Scale

You may remember building a diorama project from a shoebox for school as a child. We're going to make one today, using Unity. Let's assemble our first scene, which is composed of simple geometric objects. Along the way, we'll talk about using Unity, world scale, and rendering. We'll also explore various sources for 3D content, where you can find them, and how to use them in your Unity VR scenes. In this chapter, we will get you started in creating VR projects with Unity and work through some core concepts, including the following:

- Installing Unity
- Getting started with Unity
- Creating a simple diorama
- Using prefabs
- Creating and importing content

Technical requirements

To implement the projects and exercises in this chapter, you will need the following:

- A PC or Mac with Unity 2019.4 LTS or later, the XR Plugin for your device, and the XR Interaction Toolkit installed

You can access or clone the GitHub repository for this book (`https://github.com/PacktPublishing/Unity-2020-Virtual-Reality-Projects-3rd-Edition-`) to optionally use the assets and completed projects for this chapter as follows:

- The asset files for you to use in this chapter are located in `UVRP3Files/Chapter-02-Files.zip`.
- All completed projects in this book are in a single Unity project at `UVRP3Projects`.
- The completed assets and scenes for this chapter are in the `UVRP3Projects/Assets/_UVRP3Assets/Chapter02/` folder.

Installing Unity

To get started, you first need to install Unity on your development machine. All the projects in this book will be built using the Unity 3D game engine. Unity is a powerful, cross-platform 3D development environment with a user-friendly editor.

If you don't have Unity installed on your computer yet, we'll do that now! The full-featured Personal Edition is free and runs on both Windows and Mac (for details, see `https://store.unity.com/#plans-individual`). This book is written with **Unity 2019.4** LTS and **Unity 2020.x** in mind.

Development system requirements

There are a few prerequisites that we need before we get started. You should have a Mac or Windows PC to develop on with enough resources to install and run Unity (a Linux version of Unity is also in the works). Details of the current system requirements for Unity can be found on its website (`https://unity3d.com/unity/system-requirements`), including the supported operating system versions, the graphics card, or built-in GPU, sufficient disk space, and necessary RAM.

For VR development, we recommend that you have a physical device that you are targeting for the build applications, compatible with the **Software Development Kit** (**SDK**) that you are using with Unity. That may be an Android mobile VR, such as Oculus Quest, or a Windows-based HMD, such as Oculus Rift, HTC Vive, Windows IMR (from Acer, HP, and so on), or the other VR device supported by Unity.

Installing Unity Hub

Unity Hub is a convenient desktop application for managing all your Unity projects and installed versions, and is a portal to Unity's own plethora of learning content. It is not uncommon to create a project using one version of Unity, and then at a later date start another project with a newer version of Unity. I recommend using Unity Hub for managing your Unity installs and projects (`https://docs.unity3d.com/Manual/GettingStartedUnityHub.html`).

For existing projects, hold back on updating Unity to a newer version until you've scheduled time to address possible compatibility issues that might be introduced with the upgrade. This is especially recommended with projects that are nearing release. Unity Hub is a convenient tool for managing your Unity projects and associated installed versions.

If you don't have Unity Hub installed on your development machine, do it now by going through the following steps:

1. Browse to the Unity Store **Unity Personal** download page at `https://store.unity.com/download`.
2. Download and install **Unity Hub**.
3. Sign in to your Unity account or **Create** one if you do not have an account.

Now we can install Unity itself.

Installing the Unity Editor

The next step is installing the **Unity Editor** itself, and at the same time, the modules that are needed for you to build your target platforms. To install Unity, go through the following steps:

1. Within **Unity Hub**, choose **Installs** in the left-hand menu tabs.
2. Select the **ADD** button to open the **Add Unity Version** dialog box, and choose the current version of Unity, 2019 or later.
3. Select **Next** to select the optional modules that you also want to install.
4. If you're targeting Android devices, check the **Android Build Support** module, as well as the corresponding tools (you may need to unfold the list with the arrow icon), as shown in the following screenshot.
5. Then select **NEXT**.

6. If prompted, accept any additional license terms and the download will begin:

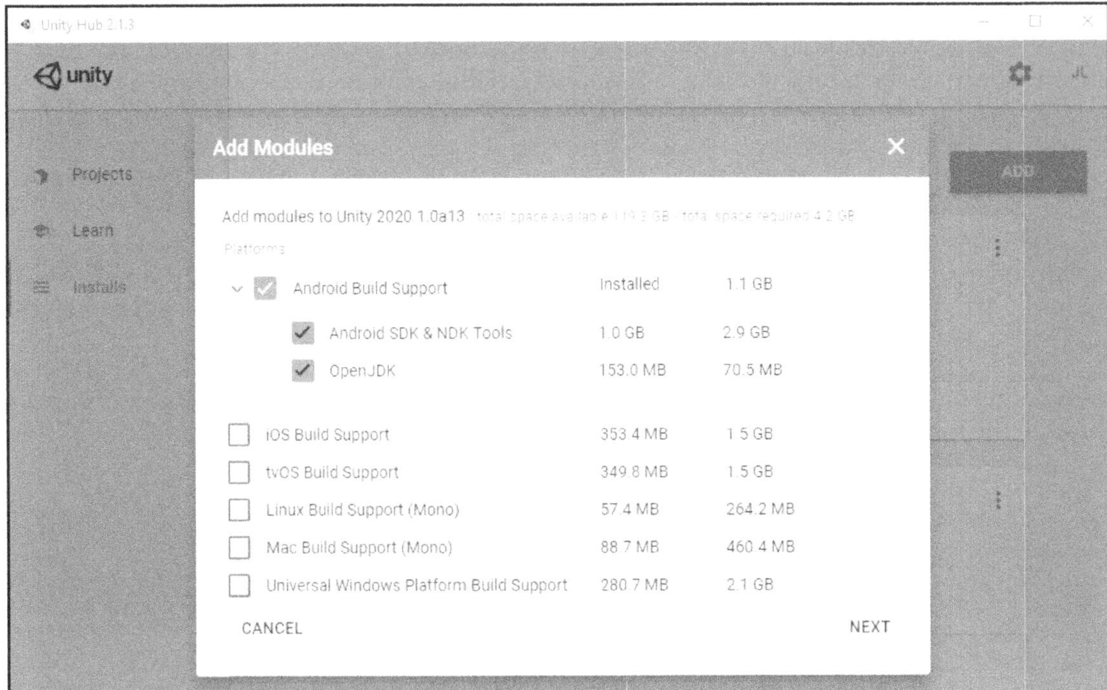

Now we're ready to create our first project.

Creating a new Unity project

Let's create a new Unity project named `VR_is_Awesome`, or whatever you'd like:

1. In **Unity Hub**, choose **Projects** in the left-hand menu tabs.
2. Select the **NEW** button (in the top-right) to start a new project (note that the **NEW** button includes a dropdown list for selecting an installed Unity version other than your default).
3. In the **Create New Project** dialog box, you will be prompted to choose a **Template**. For the projects in this book, we will use the **Universal Render Pipeline**. Select **Universal Render Pipeline**.

4. Enter a project name, such as `VR_is_awesome`. You can also select its location in your filesystem.
5. Select **CREATE** to create a new empty project and open the Unity Editor on your desktop.

When creating a new Unity project, the Unity Hub offers a choice of templates to use as your starting point. The projects in this book will focus on the **Universal Render Pipeline** template. We will discuss render pipelines and related topics in `Chapter 8`, *Lighting, Rendering, Realism.*

A **Create New Project** dialog box is shown in the following screenshot:

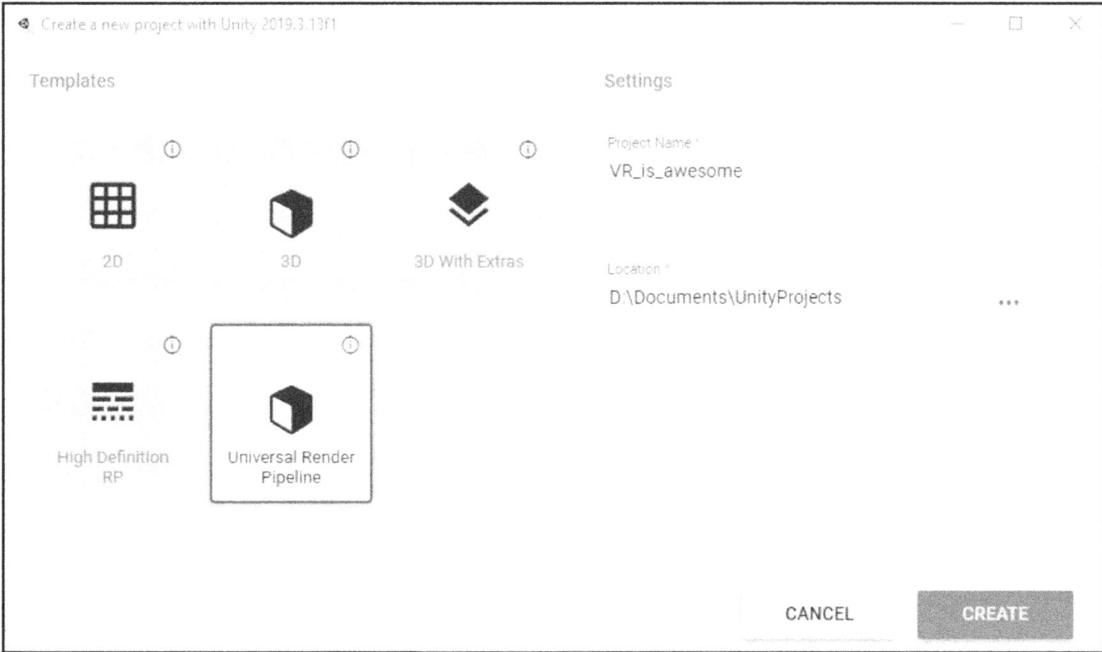

Unity Hub gives you the option to choose a template when creating a new Unity project. The projects in this book will use the Universal Render Pipeline (formerly called the Lightweight Render Pipeline). If you are aiming for high-end graphics quality, you may decide to use the **High-Definition Render Pipeline** (**HDRP**) in your own projects instead.

In addition to the tools mentioned here, I highly recommend that you use a version control manager with each of your projects. Unity has built-in support for **Perforce** and **Plastic SCM**, as well as its own **Collaborate** service (`https://unity.com/unity/features/collaborate`). These team-oriented solutions are best suited to larger projects with multiple developers and other contributors. Personally, I'm a big fan of **Git** (and **GitHub** or **BitBucket**) for personal and small team projects. Even on solo projects, version control is a sane way to backup your work, with the ability to revert changes, recover from mistakes, and explore experimental branches of your project. Setup requires some familiarity with the version control platform that you choose, and is outside the scope of this book.

Installing additional packages and assets

Once you create and open a specific Unity project, there may be more packages and assets that you want or need to install. Unity provides several avenues for extending its features, platform support, editor tools, and runtime assets:

- **Package Manager**: Use the Unity Package Manager (in Unity's top menu., go to **Window | Package Manager**) to view which packages are available for installation or are already installed in your Project (`https://docs.unity3d.com/Manual/upm-ui.html`).
- **Import Unity Package**: You can import asset package files (filename extension `.unitypackage`) from the menu **Assets | Import Package**—for example, packages can be exported from another project and shared via **Assets | Export Package**.
- **Import Asset**: You can import individual assets that are created with another app or downloaded from the web with **Assets | Import New Asset**, or simply drag and drop a file into the **Project** window in Unity.

We'll use all of these mechanisms at one time or another later in this chapter and throughout this book.

The Unity Asset Store, available through your web browser, is home to a growing library of free and commercial assets created both by Unity Technologies and members of the community. Learn more at `https://unity3d.com/quick-guide-to-unity-asset-store`. Assets you may have purchased (or got for free) on the store can be installed using the **Open In Unity** button on the web page, and also as a package listed in the **Package Manager**.

With a new project, it's always a good idea to open the **Package Manager** and review what's already installed in your project, so let's do that now:

1. Select **Window | Package Manager**.
2. By default, the filter is set to **In Project**.
3. You may notice that from time to time, newer updates to your packages will become available. With appropriate caution, you should update. Especially with point releases, these updates should only be bug fixes rather than potentially breaking features.
4. To add a package, you need to find uninstalled packages. Change the filter dropdown to **All Packages** to see all packages, including those not yet installed in your project.

The following image shows a **Package Manager** window where several packages have updates available:

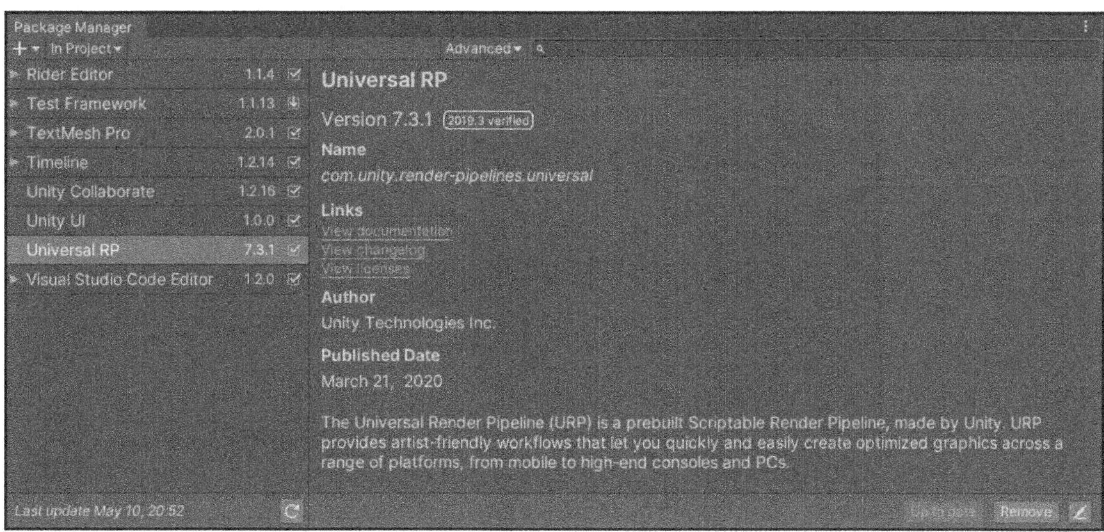

Now that you have Unity installed on your development machine, let's explore how to use the Unity Editor.

Getting started with Unity

For you beginners out there, we're going to take this chapter nice and slow, with more hand-holding than you'll get later in this book. Even if you already know Unity and have developed your own games, it may be worthwhile to revisit the fundamental concepts, since the rules are sometimes different when designing for virtual reality.

Exploring the Unity Editor

The **Unity Editor** consists of multiple nonoverlapping windows, or panels, that may be subdivided into panes. The following is a screenshot of a project with the default window layout, annotated to identify some of the panels: (1) **Hierarchy**, (2) **Scene**, (3) **Inspector**, and (4) **Project**:

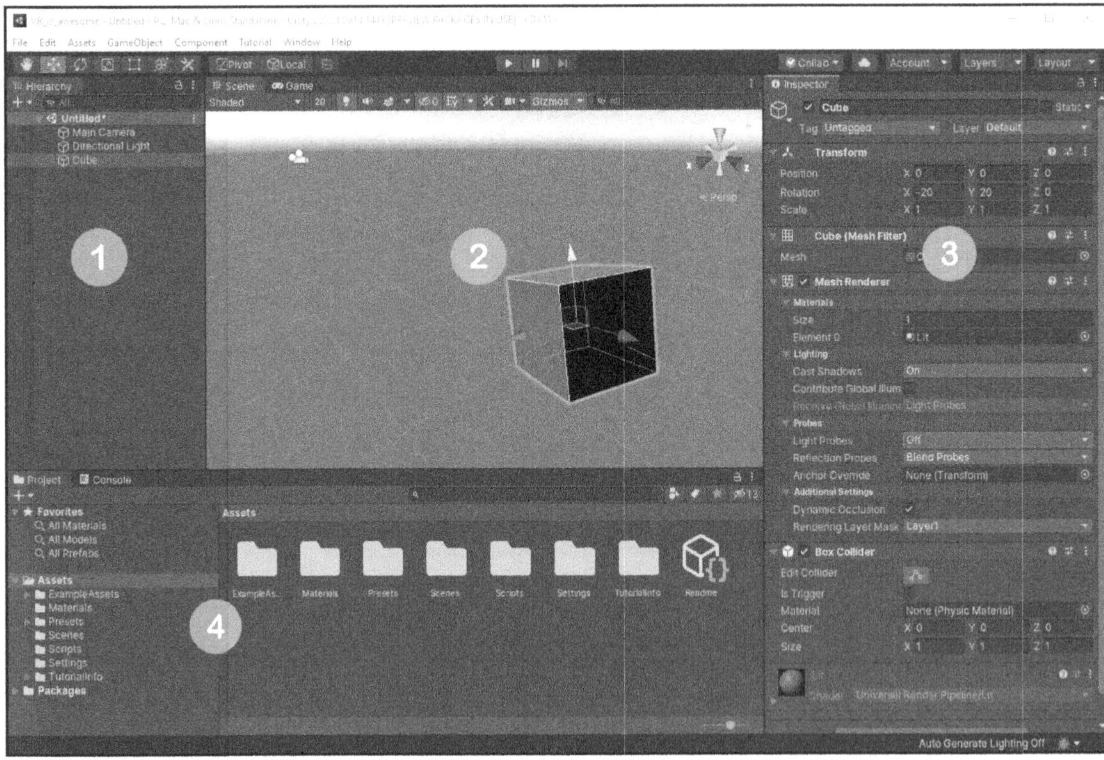

A Unity project consists of one or more scenes, containing a hierarchy of game objects. In the preceding screenshot, I have just created a new default empty scene (**File** | **New Scene**) and added a 3D cube (**GameObject** | **3D Object** | **Cube**). The **Hierarchy** window (1) shows the contents of the current scene in a hierarchical tree view. The current scene in the screenshot contains a **Main Camera** and a **Directional Light**, and we've added a **Cube**. As we'll see, objects can be nested with children objects to form nested parent–child object structures.

The **Scene** window (2) is a graphic rendering of this scene, where you can visually compose the 3D space of the current scene, including the placement of objects. There are interactive gizmos in this window for manipulating objects' positions, rotations, and scales.

In the preceding screenshot, there are additional windows of interest, although we can only see their tabs. Behind the **Scene** window (2) is a Game view, which displays what the in-game camera sees. When you press **Play** (the play triangle in the top-center toolbar), the running app is played in the Game view window.

Presently in this scene, the Cube is selected, permitting its properties to be examined in the **Inspector** window (3). Game objects can be given **Components** (such as **Transform**, **Mesh Renderer**, and **Box Collider**, shown in the preceding screenshot) that define the behavior of the object. And each component has specific properties that can be edited in the **Inspector**. For example, our Cube is positioned at the origin (`0`, `0`, `0`) and rotated along the XYZ axes by (`-20`, `20`, `0`) degrees. These Transform properties are shown in the following screenshot:

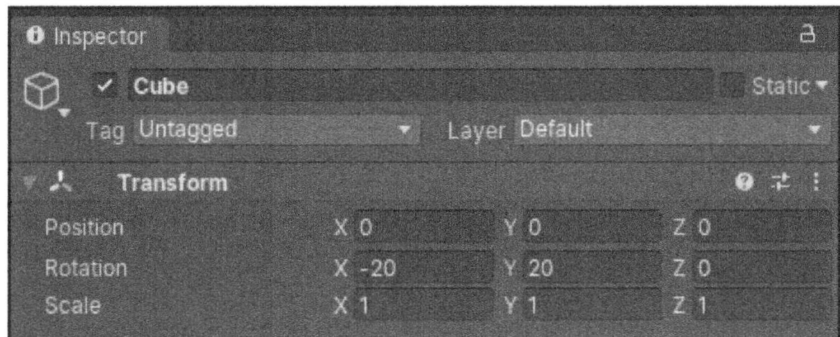

The **Project** window (4) shows the asset files on your hard drive, in the project's `Assets/` folder, which can be used in any of the project scenes. These include various reusable graphics, audio, scripts, and so on that, you've imported into the project, as well as those you'll create along the way.

Behind the **Project** window (4) is a **Console** window, which shows messages from Unity, including warnings and errors from code scripts. The **Console** window is very important during development, so you should try to arrange it so that it is always visible during development.

The **Console** window is very important during development. I usually drag it out into its own window in my editor layout so I can always see any messages.

Note that each window (and each component in the **Inspector** window) has a three-dot-icon context menu with additional item-specific options—for example, in the Inspector's context menu you can choose between **Normal** and **Debug** views. In the **Transform** component's context menu, you can **Reset** the transform values, and in the **Console** window's context menu, you can access detailed player and editor log files, as shown in the following screenshot:

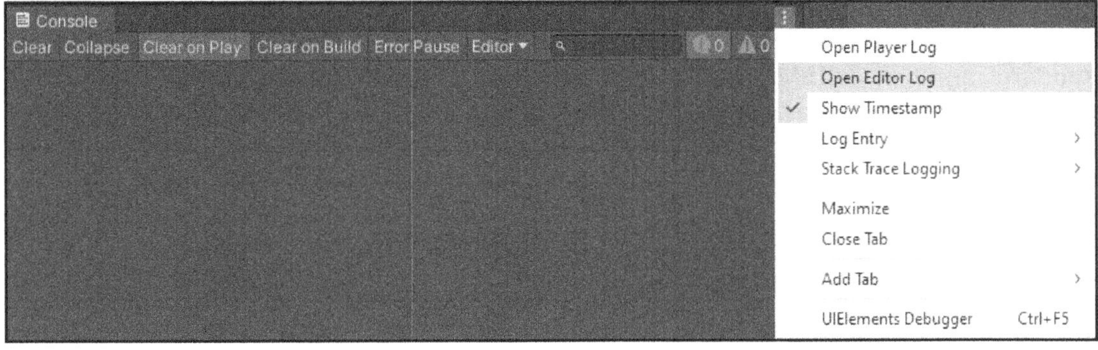

At the top is the main menu bar (on a Mac, this will be at the top of your screen, not at the top of the Unity window), and a toolbar area with various controls that we'll use later on, including the **Play** (triangle icon) button that starts **Play** mode.

In the main menu, the **Assets** menu lets you create, import, and manage assets in your **Project Assets** (the same as the + create button atop the **Project** window). The **GameObject** menu lets you add new objects to the current scene (like the + create button atop the **Hierarchy** window). The **Component** menu lets you add component behaviors to the currently selected object (the same as the **Add Component** button in the **Inspector** window). From the menu bar's **Window** menu, you can open additional windows as needed. Go ahead—click and explore these now.

The editor's user interface is configurable—each window can be rearranged, resized, and tabbed by grabbing one of the panel tabs and dragging it or even completely undocking it from the editor itself. On the upper right-hand side is a **Layout** selector that lets you either choose between various default layouts or save your own preferences.

Most of the Unity screenshots in this book show the Professional color theme (**Edit** | **Preferences** | **General** | **Editor Theme**). If you are using the Personal edition, your editor will be a light gray. Also, you will see in later screen captures, I often arrange the windows in a custom layout that I prefer, to maximize productivity and keep relevant information together for screen captures.

Like most professional design and development applications, the Unity editor has a lot to it. The key to not getting overwhelmed is to focus on just the functions you are using at the moment and basically ignore the rest until you need them. That is how I'll present Unity throughout this book. Let's start by creating and reviewing a new, empty scene.

Understanding the default new scene

Start a new scene in Unity as follows:

1. Using the main menu at the top of the editor, select **File**.
2. Then, from the menu, select **New Scene**.

A default empty Unity scene consists of a **Main Camera** object and a single **Directional Light** object. These are listed in the **Hierarchy** window and depicted in the **Scene** window. The **Scene** window also shows a perspective of an infinite reference ground plane grid, like a piece of graph paper with nothing on it. The grid spans across the x (red) and z (blue) axes. The y axis (green) is the vertical axis.

An easy way to remember the Gizmo axes colors is by keeping in mind that R-G-B corresponds to X-Y-Z.

The **Inspector** window shows the details of the currently selected item. Select the **Directional Light** with your mouse, either from the **Hierarchy** list or within the scene itself, and look at the **Inspector** window for each of the properties and components associated with the object, including its transform. An object's transform specifies its position, rotation, and scale in the 3D world space. For example, a **Position** of (`0, 3, 0`) is three units above (in the *Y* direction) the center of the ground plane (*X* = `0`, *Z* = `0`). A **Rotation** of (`50, 330, 0`) means that it's rotated 50 degrees around the *x-axis* and 330 degrees around the *y*-axis (the same as -30, since 360 is a full circle). As you'll see, you can change an object's **Transform** values numerically here or directly with the mouse in the **Scene** window.

Similarly, if you click on the **Main Camera**, it may be located at the (`0, 1, -10`) position with no rotation—that is, pointed straight ahead, towards the positive *Z* direction. If the **Game** window is visible, you'll see the camera view rendered there.

Unity provides a rich set of scene-editing tools, including built-in grid and snapping features, which we'll look at next.

Using grid and snap

Unity provides a grid system to visualize and snap. You have control over the grid displayed in the **Scene** view. It is for editing only, and so is not part of the **Game** view. It's accessed using the **Grid Visibility** button at the top of the **Scene** view. You can control which plane to grid (*X*, *Y*, or *Z*) and the opacity of the grid lines, as shown in the following screenshot:

The three-dot-icon menu opens the **Grid and Snap** settings window to show more controls:

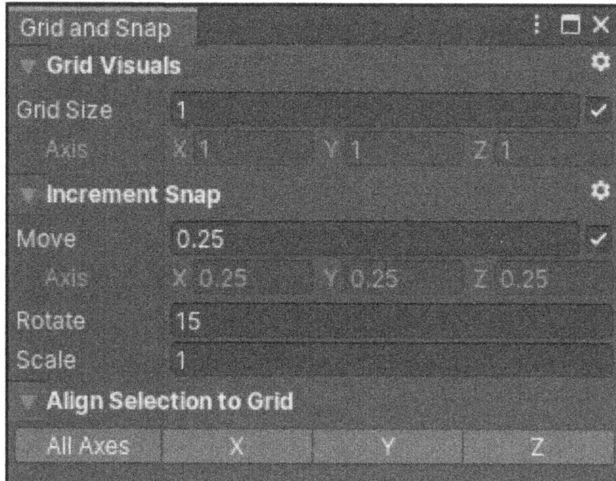

You can see the default **Grid and Snap** settings in the preceding screenshot. The visual grid size is set to 1 unit (normally meters). When snap is enabled, moving an object will snap to 0.25 units on any axis, rotations will be snapped to 15 degrees, and scaling will be snapped in increments of 1.

To enable snapping, toggle the **Grid Snapping** button (the icon with a grid and magnet) so that it's enabled. Note that you'll also need to have **Global handles** enabled (the **Global** icon to the left of the **Grid Snapping** one), as shown in the following screenshot:

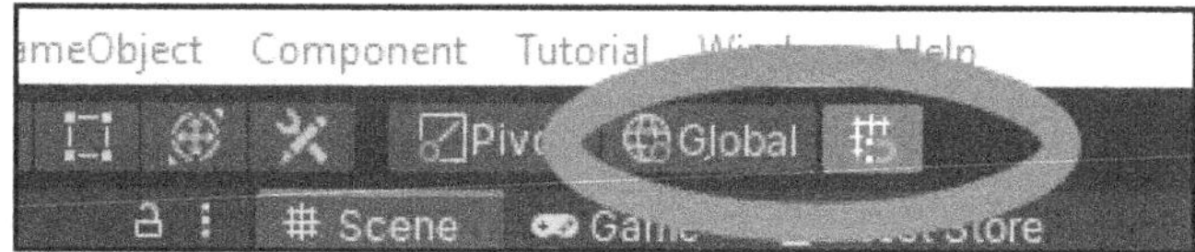

As you grow more familiar with Unity, you'll continue to configure and refine its settings to your liking.

A couple more options

Next, we'll add a couple of settings that I like for any new project. Consider these tips and suggestions. Among the settings I like for any new project are the following two:

- Personalized windows layout
- Play mode editor color

Personally, I prefer my editor layout to have the scene **Hierarchy** window adjacent to the **Inspector** window, and I like the **Console** window to be visible all the time. In the layout shown in the following screenshot, for example, there's a column on the left with the **Scene**, **Game**, and **Console** windows (top to bottom). The center column contains the **Hierarchy** and **Project** windows. On the right is the **Inspector**, with tabs for **Lighting**, **Project Settings**, and other less frequently used windows:

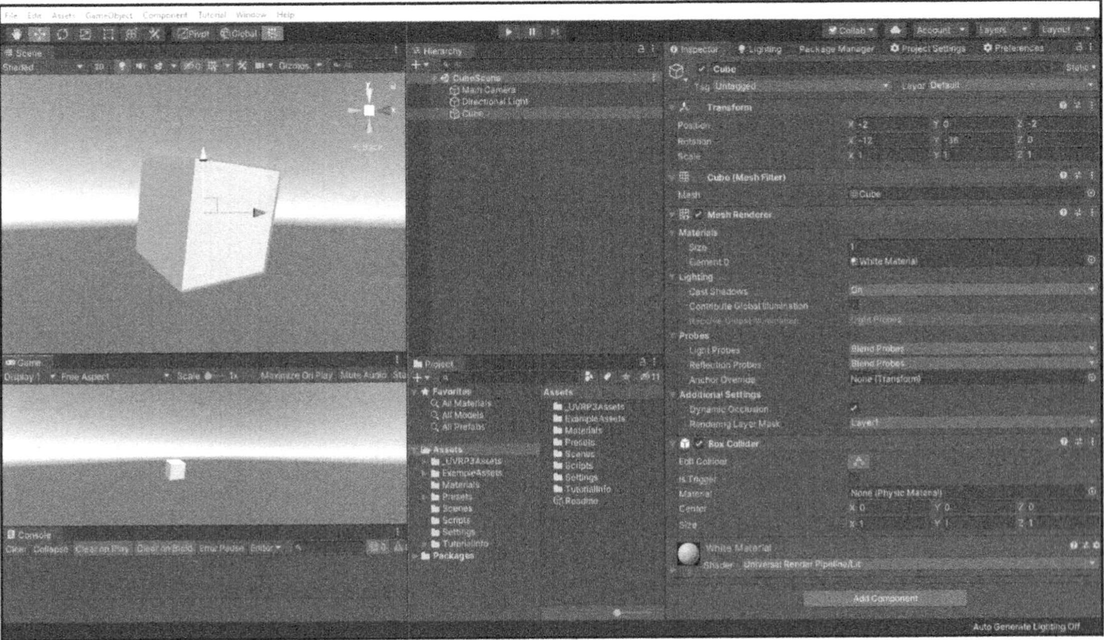

You can save the layout configuration using the **Layout** dropdown menu in the upper-right of the editor, as shown in the following screenshot. With this, you can readily switch between layouts:

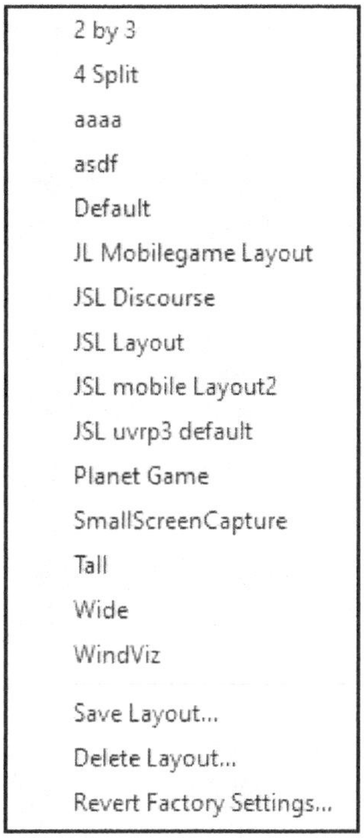

2 by 3
4 Split
aaaa
asdf
Default
JL Mobilegame Layout
JSL Discourse
JSL Layout
JSL mobile Layout2
JSL uvrp3 default
Planet Game
SmallScreenCapture
Tall
Wide
WindViz
Save Layout...
Delete Layout...
Revert Factory Settings...

In Unity, when you press **Play** and the scene is running, it's convenient to have visual feedback to show that you are in **Play Mode**. This is important because the changes you make to a GameObject in the **Inspector** are not preserved after you exit **Play** mode, so it's good to be reminded of the mode. Although the triangular **Play** button is highlighted, I like to use a more prominent reminder by changing the background color. You can set the editor play mode color as follows:

1. Open the **Preferences** window (**Edit | Preferences...**).
2. Select the **Colors** tab on the left.

3. Modify the **Playmode tint** color—for example, I like a reddish tint, which is listed as `#EAC4B2`, as shown in the following screenshot:

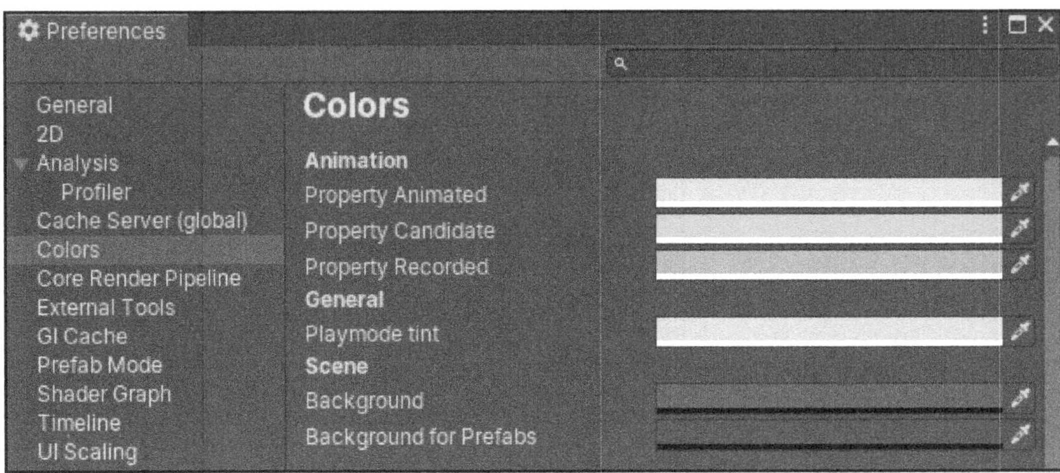

Now that you have Unity installed and have walked through an introduction on how to use it to create and edit 3D scenes, let's build a simple diorama scene.

Creating a simple diorama

We will add a few objects to the scene, including a unit cube, a flat plane, a red ball, and a photographic backdrop. Here is a photograph of a physical mock-up of the diorama we will build in VR:

To begin, let's create a new scene and name it `Diorama`:

1. If you haven't already, start a new scene in your opened project by selecting **File | New Scene**.
2. Then select **File | Save As....**
3. Open the `Assets/Scenes/` folder.
4. Set the file name to `Diorama`.
5. Press **Save**.

Ok, now we'll add stuff.

Adding a cube and a plane

Let's add the first object to the scene, a unit-sized cube:

1. Within the **Hierarchy** window, click on the **+** (create) menu in the upper-left corner.
2. Click on **3D Object | Cube**. The same selection can also be found in the main menu bar's **GameObject** menu.

A default cube will be added to the scene, centered on the ground plane at the (`0, 0, 0`) position, with no rotation and a scale of 1, as you can see in the **Inspector** window. The **Transform** component should have **Position** (`0, 0, 0`), **Rotation** (`0, 0, 0`), and **Scale** (`1, 1, 1`). These are the reset settings. If for some reason your cube has other **Transform** values, set them in the **Inspector** panel, or go through the following steps:

1. Click the three-dot menu icon in the upper right-hand side of the **Inspector** window's **Transform** component.
2. Select **Reset** to reset the **Transform** values.

This cube has the dimensions of one unit on each side. As we'll see later, one unit in Unity corresponds to one meter in world coordinates. Its local center is the center of the cube.

To reset the **Transform** values of an object, in **Inspector**, use the Transform's three-dot menu or right-click and click **Reset**.

Now, let's add a ground plane object to the scene:

1. In the **Hierarchy** window, click on the + (create) menu in the upper-left (or main **GameObject** menu).
2. Select **3D Object** | **Plane**.
3. If necessary, reset its **Transform** values.
4. A default plane is added to the scene, centered on the ground plane at **Position** (`0, 0, 0`). Rename it as `GroundPlane` in the name field at the top of its **Inspector**.

Note that at a scale of (`1, 1, 1`), Unity's plane object actually measures 10 by 10 units in *X* and *Z*. In other words, the size of `GroundPlane` is 10 by 10 units and its transform's **Scale** is 1.

The cube is centered at **Position** (`0, 0, 0`), just like the ground plane; however, maybe it doesn't look like it to you. The **Scene** window may show a **Perspective** projection that renders 3D scenes onto your 2D computer monitor. The **Perspective** distortion makes the cube not seem centered on the ground plane, but it is. Count the grid lines on either side of the cube. As you'll see, when it is viewed in VR and you're actually standing in the scene, it won't look distorted at all. This is shown in the following screenshot (the default colors may look different on your screen than in this image; we'll adjust that soon):

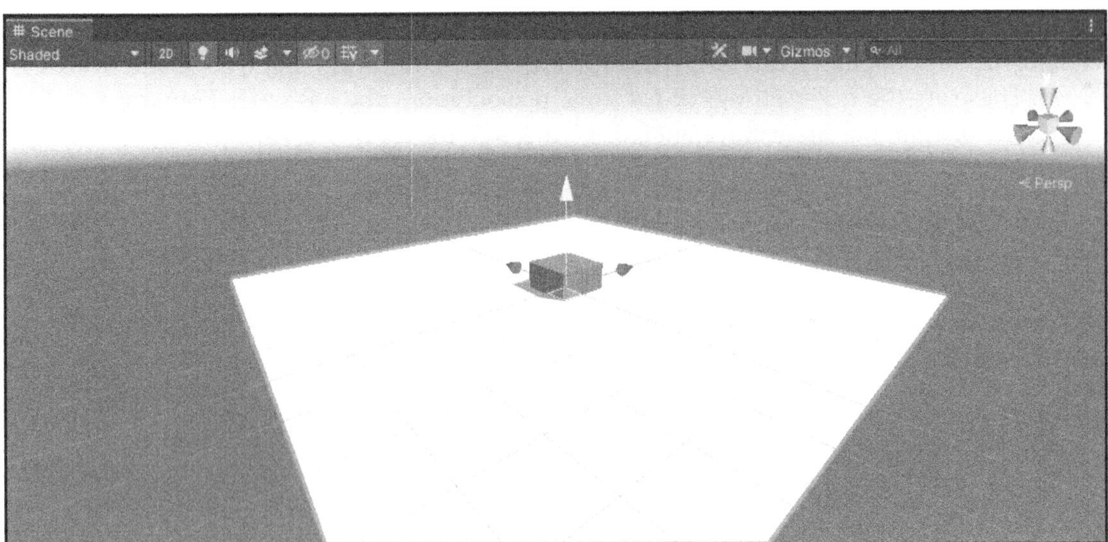

The **Cube** is submerged in the **GroundPlane** because its local origin is at its geometric center—it measures 1 by 1 by 1 and its middle point is (`0.5, 0.5, 0.5`). This might sound obvious, but it is possible for the origin of a model to not be its geometric center (such as one of its corners). The **Transform** component's position is the world space location of the object's local origin. Let's move the cube as follows:

1. Move the **Cube** onto the surface of the **GroundPlane**—in the **Inspector** panel, set its **Y** position to `0.5`: **Position** (`0, 0.5, 0`).
2. Let's rotate the cube a bit around the *y-axis*. Enter `20` into its **Y** rotation: **Rotation** (`0, 20, 0`).

Note the direction in which it rotates—that's 20 degrees clockwise. Using your left hand, give a thumbs-up gesture. See the direction your fingers are pointing? Unity uses a *left-handed coordinate system*. (There is no standard for the coordinate system handedness; some software uses left-handedness, others use right-handedness).

Unity uses a left-handed coordinate system, and the *y*-axis is up.

In the previous screen capture, our **GroundPlane** is white. Yours probably still has the default gray color. Let's fix that by creating a new **Material** for the plane, as follows:

1. In the **Project** window, open the `Materials` folder. (If there isn't one, select **Create** | **Folder**, and name it `Materials`).
2. With the **Materials** folder selected, click on **+** | **Material** (or right-click in the **Project** folder) to create a new material and name it `White Material`.
3. In the **Inspector** window, click the white rectangle to the right of **Base Map**, which opens the **Color** window. Select white (hexadecimal `#FFFFFF`).
4. Drag the **White Material** from the **Project** window onto the **Ground Plane** in the **Scene** window.
5. Also, for this demonstration, let's **Auto Generate** the environment lighting by selecting **Window** | **Rendering** | **Lighting** (or **Lighting Settings** in Unity 2019). Ensure that the **Scene** tab is selected at the top of the window and check the **Auto Generate** checkbox at the bottom of the window (the **Lighting settings** window is discussed in more detail in later chapters).

Before we go much further, let's save our work by clicking **File** | **Save** and continue building our scene.

Adding a red ball

Next, let's add a sphere to the scene:

1. From the main menu, select **GameObject** | **3D Object** | **Sphere**.
2. If necessary, select **Reset** from the **Inspector** panel's **Transform** component as we did earlier (using its three-dot-menu or by right-clicking).

Like the **Cube**, the **Sphere** has a radius of 1.0, with its origin at the center. It's hard to see the **Sphere** as it is embedded in the **Cube**. We need to move the **Sphere** position.

This time, let's use the **Scene** window's **Gizmos** tool to move the object. In the **Scene** view, you can select graphical controls, or **Gizmos**, to manipulate the object's transforms, as shown in the following illustration from the Unity documentation (`http://docs.unity3d.com/Manual/PositioningGameObjects.html`):

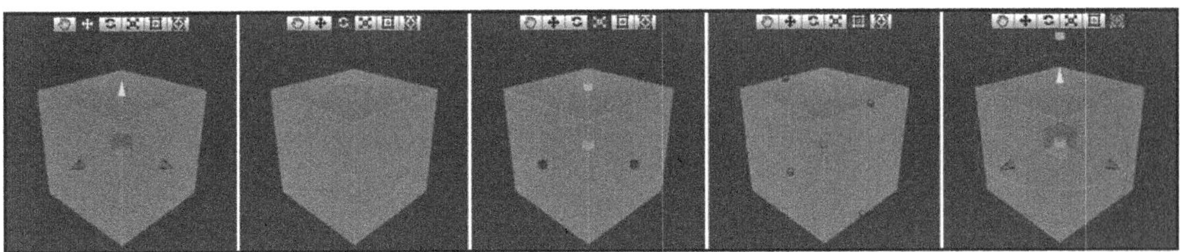

In the **Scene** window, with the **Sphere** selected, make sure that the **Move** tool is active (the second icon in the top-left icon toolbar) and use the arrows of the *x*-, *y*-, and *z*-axes to position it. I left mine at **Position** (`3, 0.75, -1.75`).

A gizmo is a graphical control that lets you manipulate the parameters of an object or a view. Gizmos have grab points or handles that you can click and drag with the mouse.

Let's make this **Sphere** into a red ball, with a new **Material**:

1. In the **Project** window, with the `Materials/` folder selected, Click **Create** | **Material** and name it `Red Material`.
2. In the **Inspector** window, click the white rectangle to the right of **Base Map**, which opens the **Color** window. Choose a nice juicy red.

3. Drag the **Red Material** from the **Project** window onto the **Sphere** (note that you can drag it onto the **Sphere** in the **Scene** window, in the **Hierarchy**, or, provided the Sphere is currently selected, directly onto its **Inspector** window).

In Unity materials and shaders, the main color is sometimes named **Albedo** or **Base Map**, or perhaps something else. They usually refer to the same thing, the main color and texture of the material. The word *albedo* is a scientific term for the color reflected off of an object's surface.

The **Sphere** should now look red. Save your scene.

One more thing. The view in the **Scene** window is never necessarily aligned with the camera that renders the scene in the **Game** window. It's easy to align the two:

1. In the **Hierarchy**, select the **Main Camera**.
2. From the main menu, click **GameObject** | **Align View to Selected** (don't click **Align With View**, as this would change the **Main Camera** rather than the **Scene** view camera; if you make that mistake, press *Ctrl* + *Z* to undo, or click **Edit** | **Undo**).

Here's what my scene looks like now:

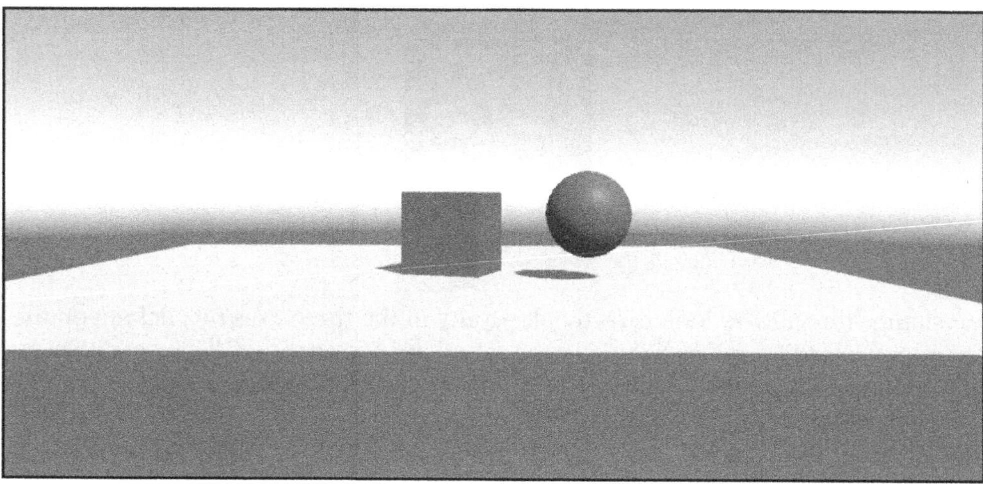

Let's look at other ways of changing the scene view next.

Changing the scene view

You can change the scene view any time in a number of ways, and this varies depending on whether you have a mouse with three-buttons, two-buttons, or a Mac mouse with only one button. Read up on it in the Unity Manual (which can be found at `https://docs.unity3d.com/Manual/SceneViewNavigation.html`) to find out what works for you.

In general, combinations of left and right mouse clicks with the *Shift* + *Ctrl* + *Alt* keys will let you perform the following actions:

- Drag the camera around.
- Orbit the camera around the current pivot point.
- Zoom in and out.
- Press *Alt* and right-click to swing the current eye orbit up, down, left, and right.
- When the hand tool is selected (in the upper-left icon bar), the right mouse button moves the eye.

In the upper-right-hand side of the **Scene** window, you have the **Scene View Gizmo**, which depicts the current scene view orientation, as shown in the following screenshot. It may indicate, for example, a **Perspective** view, with *X* extending back to the left and *Z* extending back to the right:

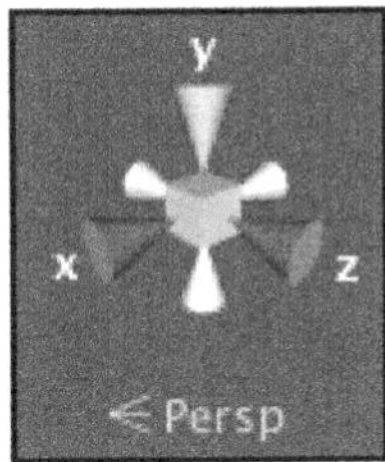

You can change the view to look directly along any of the three axes by clicking on the corresponding colored cone, as shown in the following screenshot. Clicking on the small cube in the center changes the **Perspective** (3D) view to the **Orthographic** (2D nondistorted) view:

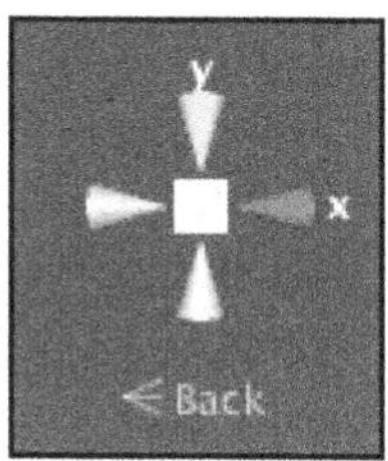

For a full list of Unity shortcut hotkeys and the **Shortcuts Manager**, see `https://docs.unity3d.com/Manual/ShortcutsManager.html`.

Next, let's improve our diorama with some image textures.

Making a Crate Material

We've already used Materials to apply an albedo color to the simple geometry in the scene, including the white plane and the red sphere. But Materials can do more, much more. Materials define how a surface should be rendered, including the textures for the object's surface and how it reacts to lights. This information is used by the **shader** code associated with the Material.

A **texture** is an image file that gets "painted" onto the object's surface, not unlike wallpaper or package labeling. It is used for simulating details and making objects appear more realistic. Let's make our **Cube** look like a wooden crate. We've included a `crate.jpg` texture file with this book, or you can Google search `wooden crate texture` to find one on your own:

1. In the **Project** window, created another **Asset** subfolder named `Textures` (by clicking on **+** | **Folder**).
2. Drag the crate image file from your filesystem into the Unity project's `Textures` folder. Ours is named `crate.jpg`.
3. In the **Project** window, in the `Assets/Materials/` folder, create another material (right-click, then go to **Create** | **Material**) named `Crate Material`.
4. In **Inspector**, select the little doughnut icon next to the **Base Map** to open a **Select Texture** dialog box, then choose the crate one (note that the search bar at the top of the dialog has the keyboard focus, so you can readily start typing the first few letters of the name to search).

5. Select the texture with a double-click (or single-click, then close the box with the red **X** in the upper right).
6. Set the **Base Map** to full color (white) by clicking its color chip and selecting white (`#FFFFFF`) so that the full fidelity of the texture pixels is not tinted.
7. Now, drag the **Crate Material** from the **Project** window onto the **Cube** in the **Scene** (or in the **Hierarchy** list).
8. Let's be more specific about our crate box. Rename it as `Crate` by selecting it in the **Scene** or **Hierarchy** and editing its name at the top of the **Inspector**.
9. Save your work (**File | Save**).

The following screenshot shows the **Crate Material** in the **Inspector**, already applied to the cube. I've also opened the **Base Map** texture for preview by *Ctrl*-clicking the texture tile with the mouse:

In computer graphics, an image that is mapped onto an object is called a *texture*. While objects are represented in the *x*, *y*, and *z* world coordinates, textures are said to be in *U* and *V* texture coordinates.

Next, we'll add another texture to the scene, this time as a backdrop image.

Adding a photo

Let's add a photo of the big-screen backdrop of our diorama. We've included with this book a photo I took at the Grand Canyon, but you can use one of your own (the idea is to use a vista image with no nearby objects in the foreground). The steps are similar to the ones we used for the crate:

1. Drag the photo image from your filesystem into the Unity project's `Textures/` folder. Ours is named `GrandCanyon.jpg`.
2. Create a quadrilateral (a simple four-sided square) 3D primitive object by navigating to **GameObject** | **3D Object** | **Quad** and naming it `Photo`.
3. In **Inspector**, reset its transform if necessary (**Transform** | **3-dot-icon** | **Reset**).
4. Scale it to the size of the `GroundPlane`. Set its transform **Scale** to (`10, 10, 10`) (you may recall that the planes in Unity are 10 by 10 units, whereas other primitives, such as **Cube** and **Sphere**, are 1-unit sized).
5. Move it to the edge of the **GroundPlane** at a **Position** value of **Z** = `5`, and above, at **Position** value of **Y** = `5`.
6. In the **Project** window, in the `Materials/` folder, create another material (right-click and go to **Create** | **Material**) named `GrandCanyon Material`.
7. Drag the **GrandCanyon Material** from the **Project** window onto the **Photo** quad in the **Scene** (or in the **Hierarchy** list).
8. In the **Inspector**, select the little doughnut icon next to the **Base Map** to open a **Select Texture** dialog box, then double-click to choose the **GrandCanyon** one.
9. Set the **Base Map** to full color (white) by clicking its color chip and selecting white (`#FFFFFF`).

You may notice that **Quads** and **Planes** are only visible from their front. If you flip the **Scene** view around, they might seem to disappear. All surfaces in computer graphics have a front-facing direction (normal vector). The view camera must be towards the front face; otherwise, the object will probably not be rendered. This is a performance optimization. If you require a plane that is visible from all sides, try using a **Cube** instead, scaled thinly, or maybe two separate **Planes** back-to-back, facing away from each other. You can also modify the **Material Render Face** property to **Both**, if that property is available in its shader. Alternatively, you can create a custom shader that does not cull back faces.

In my scene, the image looks a little squished compared to the original. My original photo is 2576 x 1932 pixels or a 0.75 aspect ratio. But our quad is square. Let's fix that up:

1. Select the **Photo** quad in the scene.
2. Set its transform **Scale Y** to `7.5`.
3. Set its transform **Position Y** to `3.75` (this is its new center offset, 7.5 / 2; in fact, you can type `7.5/2` into the *Y* value slot and Unity will evaluate the calculation).

Why 3.75? The height started at 10, so we scaled it to 7.5. The scaling of objects is relative to their origin. So now, half of the height is 3.75. We want to position the center of the backdrop 3.5 unit above the ground plane.

You can type arithmetic equations into the Inspector's numerical property fields and Unity will perform the calculation.

We have the size and position set up, but the photo looks washed out. That's because the ambient lighting in the scene is affecting it. You might want to keep it that way, especially as you build more sophisticated lighting models and materials in your scenes. But for now, we'll disallow lighting effects on the photo using the **Unlit** shader. With **Photo** selected, change it to **Unlit** by going through the following steps:

1. Select the **Photo** object.
2. In **Inspector**, note that the photo's **GrandCanyon Material** component in the **Inspector** window has its default **Shader** set as **Universal Render Pipeline/Lit**.
3. Change the Material's **Shader** to **Universal Render Pipeline/Unlit** using the dropdown selection list.

One more thing: let's adjust the GroundPlane color to better match the photo ground:

1. Create a new material in the `Materials` folder and name it `Ground Material`.
2. Drag it onto the **GroundPlane** object.
3. Then, change its **Base Map** color. I suggest using the dropper (icon) to pick a sandy tone from the image in your photo plane.

Here's what mine looks like; yours should be similar:

There! That looks pretty good. Save your scene.

In Unity, some properties seemingly attached to a specific **GameObject** are actually assets themselves, and changing a value in one place will change any other object that references the same asset. Materials are one example of this. When you select a **GameObject** and edit its **Material** in the **Inspector**, that will modify the **Material** asset (in the **Project** `Assets/` folder). Any other objects that use the same **Material** will also see those changes.

We have created a 3D diorama scene consisting of a few geometry primitives, including a **Plane**, **Cube**, **Sphere**, and **Quad**, and applied some simple **Materials**. Obviously, Unity is capable of using more complex and interesting graphics. Next, we'll look at using Unity **prefabs** for managing reusable GameObjects.

Using prefabs

Unity **prefabs** (short for *prefabricated object*) allow you to create, store, and modify GameObjects as reusable assets together with all its components, property values, and child GameObjects. Prefabs are easily created by dragging an object from the scene **Hierarchy** window into the **Project** window, or they may be imported as part of a Unity asset package. You can read more about prefabs in the Unity Manual at `https://docs.unity3d.com/Manual/Prefabs.html`.

Let's see how this works by creating a simple reusable model built from simple geometric elements.

Creating and instantiating a prefab

We're going to create a reusable character prefab named `BobHead`. First, let's build the little guy from a few primitive 3D objects, as follows:

1. In the **Hierarchy**, create an empty GameObject named `BobHead` (by clicking on **+** | **Create Empty**; name it `BobHead`).
2. Set its position to something like **Position** (`3, 0.75, 1.25`).
3. Create a child **Sphere** for its head (right-click the **BobHead** and click **3D Object** | **Sphere**). Name it `Head`.
4. In the **Project** `Materials/` folder, create a new **Material**, named `BobHead Material`, and make it a dark blue (for example, `#191963`).
5. Drag the **BobHead Material** onto the **Head**.

To help you focus on specific objects in your scene you can temporarily disable other objects from view. One way to do this is to fully disable the object in the **Inspector** (uncheck the **Enable** checkbox in the upper-left corner), or better, in the **Hierarchy** window, you can click the View eye icon in the far-left of the **Crate** GameObject, for example, to temporarily hide it while working on the scene.

Now, add the eyes:

1. Create a child white-colored eye (right-click the **BobHead**, then click **3D Object** | **Sphere**) and name it `Eye`.
2. Set its **Transform Position** (`0.15, 0.2, -0.35`) and **Scale** (`0.15, 0.25, 0.25`).

3. Drag the **White Material** that we created earlier from the **Project** `Materials/` folder onto the **Eye**.
4. Duplicate the eye (select the **Eye** and press *Ctrl* + *D*).
5. Change its **Transform Position X** to `-0.15`.

The resulting model, including the scene **Hierarchy,** is shown in the following screenshot:

Now to create a prefab of the object. We'll save it in a project folder named `Assets/Prefabs/` by going through the following steps:

1. In the **Project** window, create a new folder named `Prefabs` (at the root `Assets/`, right-click, then click **Create** | **Folder** and name it `Prefabs`).
2. In the **Hierarchy** window, click and drag the **BobHead** GameObject into the **Project** window's `Prefabs/` folder we just created.

Note that a few things have changed in the editor, as shown in the following screenshot:

- The **Project** `Assets/Prefabs/` folder contains the `BobHead.prefab` file, with a preview image.
- Because the asset is presently selected, the **Inspector** shows its component values and a button to **Open Prefab** for editing. We'll get to that in a moment.

- The **BobHead** object name in the **Hierarchy** is now blue, indicating that it's now a prefab instance.
- There's also a > icon on the **BobHead** that you can click to edit the prefab asset (the same as the **Open Prefab** button).

The **BobHead** prefab is now available as a template for other **BobHead** GameObjects; you may want to add one or more to your scenes. All instances of the prefab will inherit the properties of the prefab. To add a new instance, just drag it from the **Project** window into the scene. Let's do that now:

1. In the **Project** window, click the **BobHead** prefab and drag it into the scene (either the **Scene** view window or the **Hierarchy**).
2. Once positioned as you like, drop it into the scene.
3. Add a few more too.

The following screenshot shows the scene with multiple **BobHead** instances. In the **Hierarchy**, the **BobHead** objects are blue because they reference prefab assets:

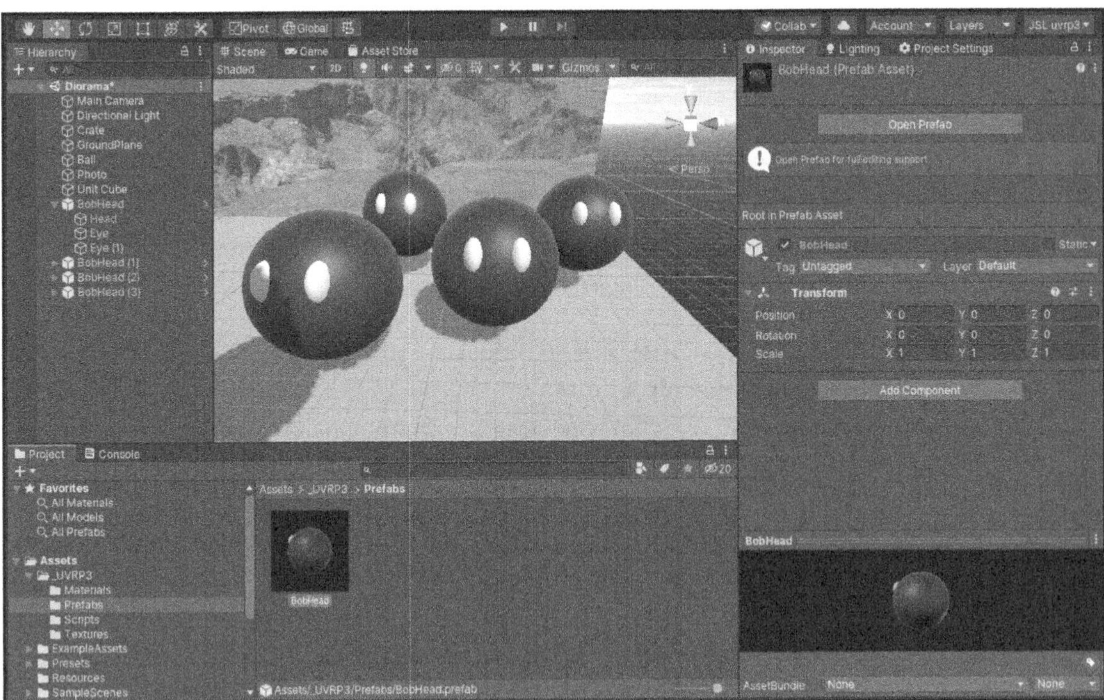

You can now modify the instance as you like, such as adjusting its position and scale.

Keep in mind that a prefab is an asset file that resides in a folder like any other file on your computer. It can reference other assets, such as **Textures** and **Materials**, and Unity will remember those links. But a prefab asset cannot have any direct references to objects in the **Scene Hierarchy**—for example, if you drag a GameObject from the **Hierarchy** onto a slot of a component of another object, and then save that object as a prefab, the reference to the GameObject will be lost, and it will have a `null` value when instantiated at a later time.

In summary, we have learned the following definitions:

- **GameObject**: Generally refers to game objects in the Scene and Hierarchy, containing a geometric mesh, material, and other components that define its behavior.
- **Asset**: Refers to files in the **Project** `Assets/` folder that can be added to a scene, including prefab GameObjects, materials, audio clips, and more.
- **Prefab asset**: A GameObject saved as an asset.
- **Prefab instance**: A prefab that's been added to a scene is said to be instantiated.

Now that we have a prefab, let's see how to edit it.

Editing and overriding a prefab

Suppose that you now decide that the **BobHead** needs adjustment; perhaps you want to add a hat. You can modify the prefab and all of the instances will be updated. You could select the **BobHead** prefab in the **Project** `Prefabs/` folder and select **Open Prefab** to edit it (or just double-click it). Right now, we'll edit it first in the scene **Hierarchy**, then apply the overrides:

1. To add a hat, select one of the **BobHead** objects in the hierarchy, right-click, and select **Create Empty**, then rename it `Hat`.
2. Set its **Position** to (`0`, `0.5`, `0`).
3. Right-click the **Hat** and select **3D Object** | **Cylinder** to add a cylinder as a child of `Hat`— name it `HatTop`.

4. Set its **Transform Scale** to (`0.5, 0.1, 0.5`).
5. Drag the **Red Material** from the Project's `Materials/` folder (created earlier in this chapter) onto the **HatTop**.
6. Right-click the **Hat** again and select **3D Object** | **Cylinder** to add a cylinder as a child—name it `Brim`.
7. Set its **Transform Scale** to (`0.75, 0.01, 0.75`) and **Position** to (`0, -0.075, 0`).
8. Drag the **Red Material** from the **Project**'s `Materials/` folder onto the **Brim**.
9. Adjust the **Hat** transform to **Rotation** (`0, -15, 25`) and **Position** (`-0.2, 0.5, 0`).

That looks cool! Presently, only one of the **BobHead** instances has a hat. Suppose we want each of them to have one too. Select the **BobHead** object in **Hierarchy**; note the **Overrides** dropdown in the **Inspector**. Click it to show the modifications that you have made relative to the original prefab, as shown in the following screenshot: that'd be the Hat:

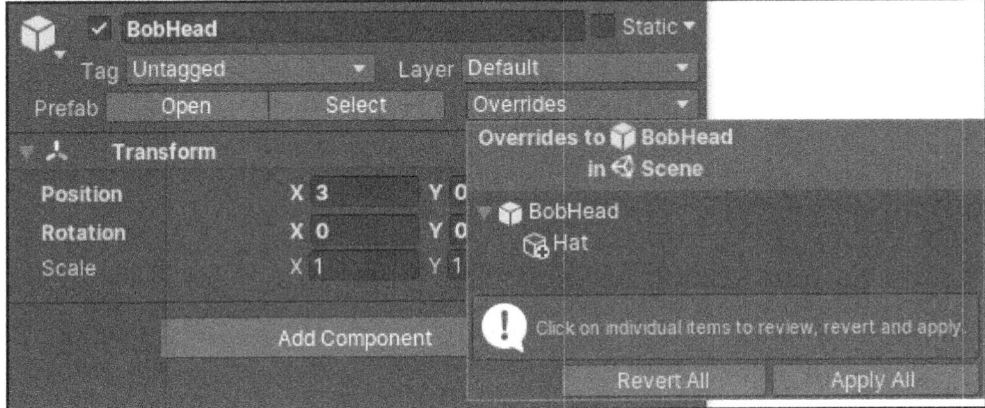

Do the following steps to actually apply the overrides:

1. Click the **Overrides** in **Inspector**.
2. Press **Apply All**.

Voila! Now all the BobHeads in the scene have been updated, as shown in the following screenshot:

Because prefabs may include child objects, it is possible for a child to be another prefab. That's perfectly fine. This is called a **nested prefab**, and will behave as you expect—for example, we could have made the **Hat** object its own separate prefab and then inserted it into the **BobHead** prefab. If you change the original child prefab, then that change will be reflected in the parent prefab.

In addition, modified instances of a prefab can be saved as a separate **prefab variant**. In that case, the new prefab still references the original prefab so that if the original prefab is changed and said properties have not been overridden by the variant, then the variant (and all its instances) will inherit those changes.

One more thing to point out. When you edit a prefab instance in Unity, you have the option to view it in the **Scene** window in the context of its position within the scene (**Normal**), to gray out the surrounding scene (**Gray**), or hide the context altogether (**Hidden**). The following image shows a **BobHead** being editing with a **Gray** context:

There you have it! Prefabs are a very powerful feature of Unity that we will use throughout this book. Next, we'll look at how to import content from outside of Unity.

Importing content

So far, we have shown you how to use Unity and be productive in creating a scene, but with pretty simple content. Normally, Unity is not a 3D-modeling or asset-creation tool. Rather (as the name *Unity* suggests), it's a unified platform for pulling together content from a variety of sources to assemble and program a game or experience involving animation, physics, rendering effects, and so on. If you are a 3D artist, then you may know how to create content in other programs, or you can find a plethora of models on the web.

Creating 3D content for VR

Unity offers some basic geometric shapes, but when it comes to more complex models, you'll need to go beyond Unity. The **Unity Asset Store** and many other sites have tons of amazing models. Where do they come from? Will you run into problems while importing them into Unity?

For example, **Blender** is a free and open source 3D animation suite (`http://www.blender.org/`) that you can use to make a model and then import it into Unity. Other popular software, for both hobbyists and professionals, includes **ZBrush**, **3DS Max**, **Maya**, and **Cinema4D**. A detailed list of 3D modeling software can be found at `https://en.wikipedia.org/wiki/List_of_3D_modeling_software`.

Actually, there are content creation tools that run right inside the Unity editor. **Polybrush** and **ProBuilder** are two examples, bought by Unity Technologies in 2019 and provided free with Unity itself (we will be using both these packages in later chapters in this book). Many other in-editor tools can be found on the **Unity Asset Store**, for example, by searching `modeling or painting tools` (`https://assetstore.unity.com/tools?category=tools%2Fmodeling%5Ctools%2FpaintingorderBy=1`).

In addition to traditional 3D-modeling software, there is a new generation of 3D design apps that let you directly create inside VR. Let's be honest: it's pretty awkward trying to use an inherently 2D desktop screen with a 2D mouse to form, sculpt, and manipulate 3D models. If only it could be more like real-life pottery, sculpture, and construction. Well, why not just do it directly in VR? Some of the growing number of VR 3D content creation tools include the following:

- **Google Tiltbrush** (`https://www.tiltbrush.com/`): 3D painting and sculpture; import directly into Unity with Unity SDK (`https://github.com/googlevr/tilt-brush-toolkit`).
- **Google Blocks** (`https://arvr.google.com/blocks/`): 3D modeling and painting.
- Tiltbrush and Blocks models can also be uploaded to **Google Poly** (`https://poly.google.com/`) and imported into Unity with the **Poly Toolkit** on the Asset Store (`https://assetstore.unity.com/packages/templates/systems/poly-toolkit-104464`).

- **Microsoft Marquette** (`https://www.maquette.ms/`): Import with the Unity Addon (`https://www.maquette.ms/unity-addon`).
- **Adobe Medium** (originally by Oculus) (`https://www.oculus.com/medium`): Digital clay tool.
- **Adobe Substance Painter** (originally by Allegorithmic) (`https://www.substance3d.com/products/substance-painter/`): Design **PBR (physically based rendering**) textures and materials.
- **Oculus Quill** (`https://www.oculus.com/experiences/rift/1118609381580656/`): Illustration and animation tool.
- **VR Gravity Sketch** (`https://www.gravitysketch.com/`): Sculpting tool for 3D models.
- **Unity Editor XR** (`https://github.com/Unity-Technologies/EditorXR`): An experimental extension of the Unity editor that operates in VR, with 3D gizmos for scene editing and access to all the Unity windows, including **Inspector** and **Project** assets.

Let's see how to import assets from the store in the next section.

Importing from the Unity Asset Store

One terrific source is the **Unity Asset Store** (`https://www.assetstore.unity3d.com/en/`). Many asset packs are free, especially starter ones, with possible paid upgrades if you want more. These can be very useful, for instance, if you are looking for a few things to get your learning and experimental projects going.

As of Unity 2020.1, you are expected to browse and purchase assets from the Unity Asset Store website using your web browser. You can then find and import packages that you already own using the Package Manager (by going to **Window | Package Manager**). The Package Manager window with the **My Assets** filter selected is shown in the following screenshot:

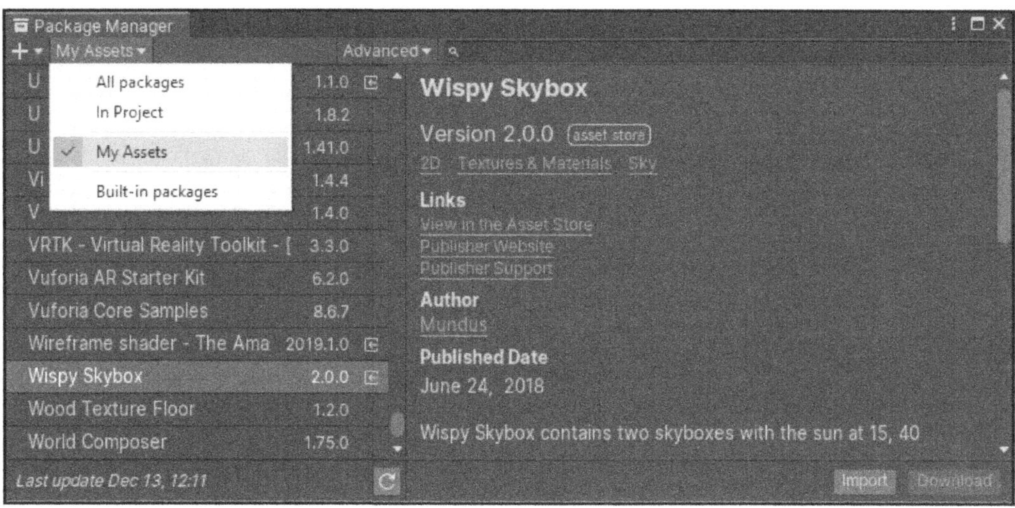

Unfortunately (or fortunately), Unity keeps evolving, and some asset packages can get left behind. The Asset Store is filled with popular packages that were built for older versions of Unity and may have problems importing into the current version, possibly including the following:

- Unsupported shaders
- Obsolete C# script APIs

In this book, we created our Unity project using the **Universal Render Pipeline**, derived from the new **Scriptable Render Pipeline** (**SRP**) system that replaces the built-in render pipeline (`https://docs.unity3d.com/Manual/ScriptableRenderPipeline.html`). As we'll see, Unity provides tools to help upgrade materials for your **Render Pipeline** (**RP**). Sometimes that works, but sometimes it needs manual adjustment, as we'll show you next.

The **Unity Scripting API** (programmer interface) also evolves. When importing old scripts, Unity will try to automatically update them to work with the current version. Sometimes it cannot. Usually, if an API function has changed, Unity will give a warning that it is *deprecated*, and then eventually it will become *unsupported* after a number of Unity updates. You may find assets on the Asset Store that have not been updated and will throw errors when you try to import. Sometimes, this incompatibility makes the package unusable and obsolete. But sometimes a minor script edit can take care of the problem without having to chase down the developer and request a fix.

Let's run through a couple of these scenarios now, while at the same time learning more about Unity.

A **skybox** is a panoramic texture drawn behind all objects in the scene to represent the sky or another vista at a far distance. You can find many skyboxes to use in your projects; one of my favorites is the free **Wispy Skybox** from MUNDUS. Let's add it to our project now:

1. In your browser, go to the **Asset Store** (`https://assetstore.unity.com/`) and search for `Wispy Skybox`, or go directly to `https://assetstore.unity.com/packages/2d/textures-materials/sky/wispy-skybox-21737`.
2. Click **Open in Unity**.
3. In Unity, the **Import Unity Package** dialog box will pop up, with all the contents selected. Click **Download** (if present), and then click **Import**.
4. Check your console window for errors (by going to **Window** | **General** | **Console**). I see none, so that's good.
5. Open the scene's **Lighting** window (by going to **Window** | **Rendering** | **Lighting**).
6. Select the **Environment** tab at the top of the window.
7. At the top is a slot for **Skybox Material**. Click the doughnut icon, which opens the **Select Material** dialog.
8. Search using the string `wispy`.
9. Select one of the skyboxes to use in the scene.

Voila! That's good.

Next, let's import a model with a relatively high-quality PBR material. For fun, let's add the *FREE Snowman* from Angry Mesh:

1. In your browser, go to the Asset Store (`https://assetstore.unity.com/`) and search for `free snowman`, or go directly to `https://assetstore.unity.com/packages/3d/props/free-snowman-105123`.
2. Click **Open in Unity**.
3. In Unity, **Import** the package.
4. In the **Project** window, go to the `Assets/ANGRY MESH/Snowman/Prefabs/` folder.
5. Drag the **Snowman_01** prefab into the scene.

Oh no! It looks all magenta. That's Unity telling you that the object's materials are missing or not compatible with the current render pipeline:

To fix it, we'll try converting the imported materials to our RP:

1. Select **Edit** | **Render Pipeline** | **Universal Render Pipeline** | **Upgrade Project Materials to UniversalRP Materials**, then click **Proceed**:

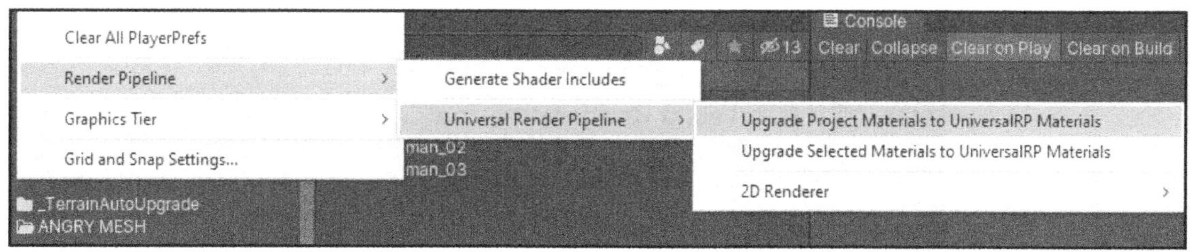

There we go. Now he looks happier:

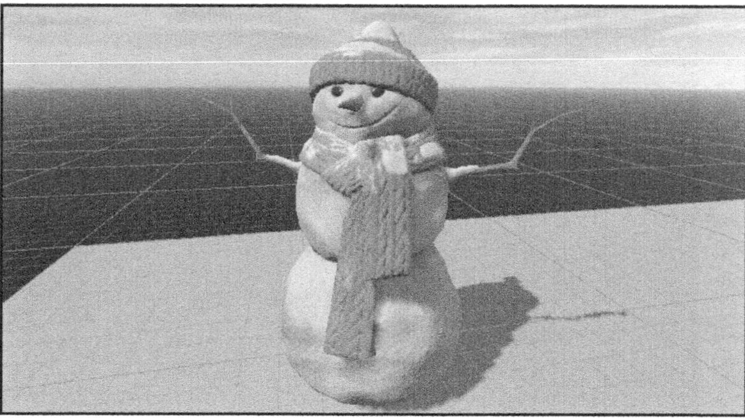

If you were to open the `Demo_Snowman` demo scene that comes with the package, you will see three snowmen in a terrain of *pink* snow! The upgrade tool didn't work on the terrain. Let's see why:

1. Save your current work by going to **File | Save**.
2. Go to **File | Open Scene** and select the scene `Assets/ANGRY MESH/Snowman/Scene/Demo_Snowman`.
3. Select the **Terrain** GameObject.
4. In **Inspector**, click the gear icon to open its **Terrain Settings** (you may need to first click **Active** to enable this object if the gear icon is disabled). Note that its **Material** property is called **Default-Terrain-Standard**.

As we've seen, Unity has a number of built-in default materials—for example, when you create a new object, its default material is **Lit** with the **URP/Lit** shader, because that's compatible with our current render pipeline. The default material with the imported terrain is not compatible with our render pipeline. We can create new material instead by going through the following steps:

1. In the Terrain's **Inspector**, next to the **Material** slot, click the **Create...** button.
2. Name it `Snow Terrain Material`.
3. Set its **Shader** to **Lit (Universal Render Pipeline/Terrain/Lit)**.

There, that works! Although we're not using this terrain in our scene, it was worthwhile seeing how to drill down into the game object properties to fix the unsupported shader that it was using.

We will not be doing much with terrains in the projects in this book. To learn more about the Unity Terrain Engine, see `https://docs.unity3d.com/Manual/terrain-UsingTerrains.html`.

Next, let's look at some assets that we will definitely be using in the projects in this book.

Using Unity Legacy Standard Assets

Several of the chapters in this book use a variety of assets that Unity has provided as a Standard Assets package for a long time; however, while still useful and fun, the package as a whole has grown stale and unsupported. Since Unity 2018, it was removed from the standard Unity install and became available on the Asset Store instead. We're still going to use this package, but we'll need to make some adjustments for compatibility with Unity 2019.3 or later and the Universal RP.

A copy of a subset of the Standard Assets that we will be using, already converted to be compatible with Unity 2019 or later, and the Universal RP, is also provided as a download with the files for this book. You can import that package in lieu of following the steps in this section.

You can import the entire package or a subset as described in the following steps:

1. In your browser, go to the **Asset Store** (`https://assetstore.unity.com/`) and search for `Unity Standard Assets`, or go directly to `https://assetstore.unity.com/packages/essentials/asset-packs/standard-assets-for-unity-2017-3-32351`.
2. Click **Open in Unity,** click **Download,** and then click **Import**.
3. In Unity, the **Import Unity Package** dialog box pops up, with all the contents selected.
4. Uncheck the `SampleScenes` folder.
5. Uncheck the `Standard Assets/2D` folder.
6. Uncheck the `Standard Assets/Cameras` folder.
7. Uncheck the `Standard Assets/Characters/FirstPersonCharacter` folder.
8. Uncheck the `Standard Assets/Characters/RollerBall` folder.
9. Uncheck the `Standard Assets/Vehicles` folder.

The import box with items that we don't need for this book is shown in the following image:

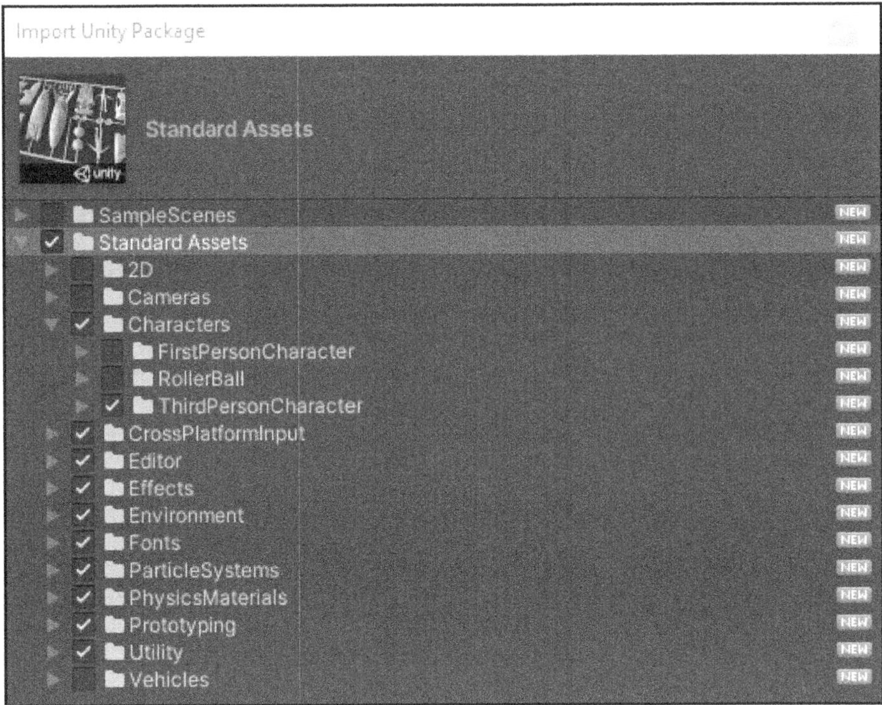

Import the assets, then correct any import errors as follows:

1. Click **Import**.
2. Check your **Console** window for errors by going to **Window** | **General** | **Console**.
3. There may be numerous import errors, but most of them will have been corrected by Unity. Click the **Clear** button (in the top-left of the **Console** window).
4. The remaining errors need to be resolved manually. I see two script files with obsolete references. We could update the scripts rather easily, but since we will not need time at all, they can just be deleted.

5. Clicking an error message will take you to the offending file in the **Project** window. Locate the file, right-click it, and select **Delete**. At the time of writing, the broken files will be as follows:
    - `Assets\Standard Assets\Utility\ForcedReset.cs`
    - `Assets\Standard Assets\Utility\SimpleActivatorMenu.cs`
6. The import can now continue. More errors may be found and fixed by Unity. Click **Clear** again.

Generally, you should be cautious in deleting assets from the `Assets` folder, as there is no way to undo it. This is another good reason to use a version control system, such as Git, to let you recover from errors by going to a previously committed save point. In the case of imported asset packages, if you inadvertently delete or modify a file, you can reimport the original package.

That should complete the import. Next, let's attempt to convert materials to the current render pipeline:

1. Select **Edit** | **Render Pipeline** | **Universal Render Pipeline** | **Upgrade Project Materials to UniversalRP Materials** and then click **Proceed**.

You can browse the warning messages, but don't worry about them; we'll find incompatible materials soon enough.

One of the models that we plan to use soon is the Ethan humanoid model. Let's add him to the scene:

1. In the **Project** window, drill down to the `Assets/Standard Assets/Characters/ThirdPersonCharacter/Prefabs/` folder.
2. Drag the **ThirdPersonController** into the **Scene**.
3. You may want to turn him around so that he's facing the camera by going to **Transform** | **Rotation** | **Y**: `180`.

Say hi to Ethan!

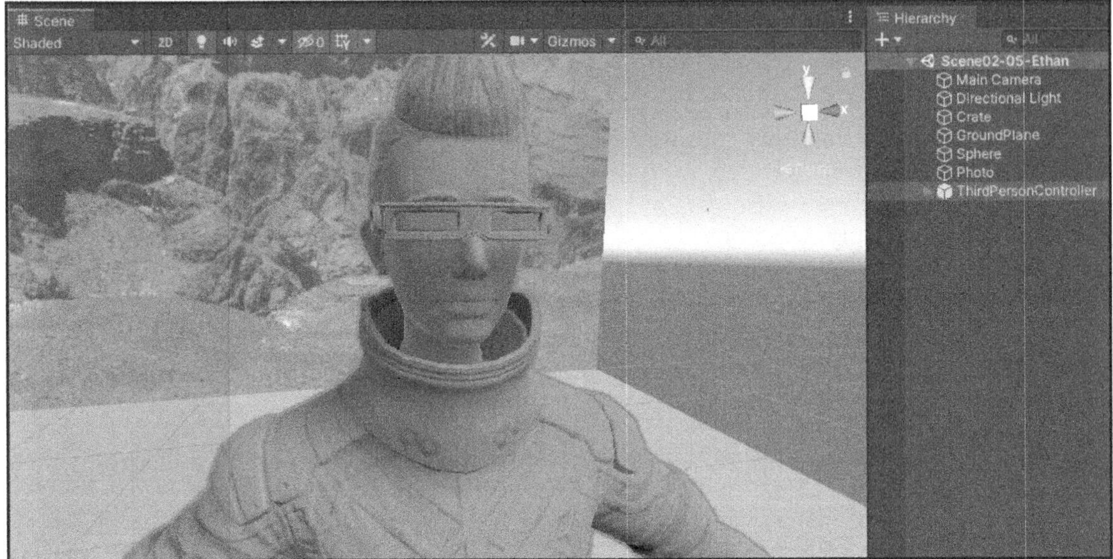

Ethan has a third-person control script that lets you control his animation with user input. We will work on VR input devices in later chapters, so for now, let's try it out with just the keyboard:

1. Click on the **Play** icon at the top of the Unity window in the center to start your game.
2. Use the *W*, *A*, *S*, and *D* keys to move him around. *Run, Ethan! Run!*
3. Be careful not to let him fall over the edge of our playground, or he'll fall down forever.
4. Click on the **Play** icon again to stop the game and return to edit mode.

Other than creating geometry inside Unity and getting asset packages from the Asset Store, content is otherwise imported from other graphics software.

Importing models in supported formats

Unity has built-in support for reading and importing models in a few generic file formats, including `.fbx` and `.obj`. Most 3D-modelling software can export these files. No extra software or licenses are required to use these files. In general, you should try to obtain 3D models in `.fbx` or `.obj` file format.

Unity also supports importing models in a number of proprietary formats, provided that you have the corresponding applications that edit these files on your development machine. These include Autodesk 3ds Max (`.max`) and Blender (`.blend`). This can be an advantage if you or your team is actively working on 3D models with one of these applications, and you have the software licenses to install it on your system (if needed). *But you must have a copy of the application on your own system for Unity to know how to import the files.* Not having to export files to `.fbx`, for example, before using them in Unity saves a step, especially if the models are still being developed and modified. Unity can import proprietary files from the following 3D-modelling software (from the Unity Manual, `https://docs.unity3d.com/Manual/3D-formats.html`):

- Autodesk® 3ds Max®
- Autodesk® Maya®
- Blender (a free and open source 3D application)
- Cinema4D
- Modo
- LightWave
- Cheetah3D

For models that have been imported in Unity, you can modify their **Import Settings** and reimport as needed. The following is a screenshot of the import settings for the snowman FBX file we used earlier—for example, you can change the **Scale Factor** and **Units** if the source file was built at a scale other than Unity's 1-unit equals 1-meter scale. There are settings to select what to import from the file's scene, the mesh, and geometry.

Depending on the capabilities of the model, the **Rig**, **Animation**, and **Materials** tabs provide additional import parameters. If you change settings, click **Apply** to reimport the object with the new settings:

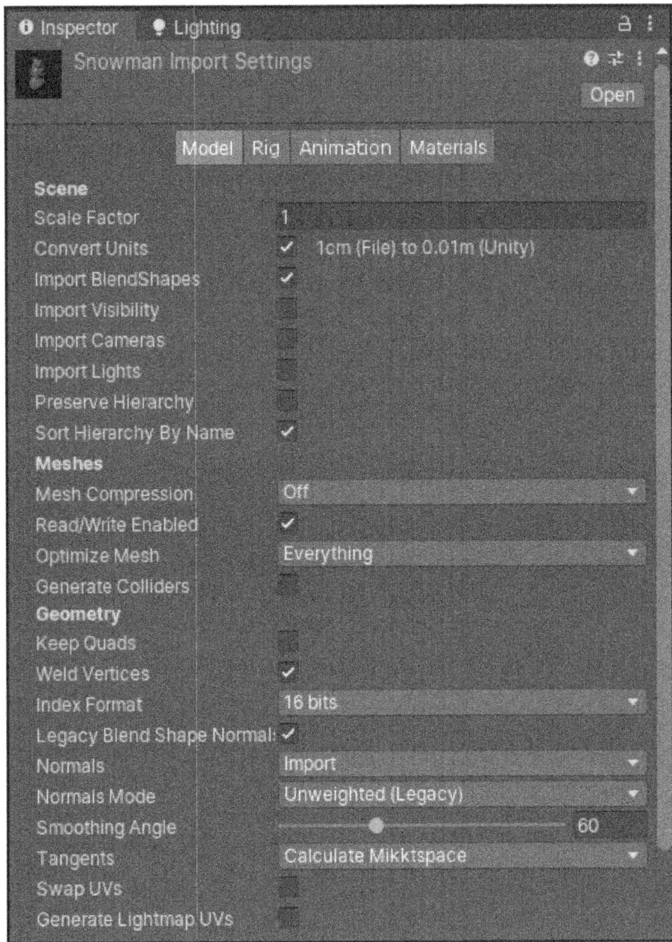

When the source model has materials, you can instruct Unity to use those Materials automatically, or you have the option to extract the Materials into separate Unity Material files that can be modified and adjusted like any other Material in Unity.

Additional details and tips for import models into Unity can be found at `https://docs.unity3d.com/Manual/ImportingModelFiles.html`.

While Unity provides a lot of import parameters, if you have access to the original modeling software, you can also gain control of the file that is using that software's export settings—for example, in Blender, its default coordinate system has the *z-axis* up, while Unity's is y. This can be compensated by rotating it once inside Unity, or you can adjust Blender's FBX export settings as shown in the following screenshot:

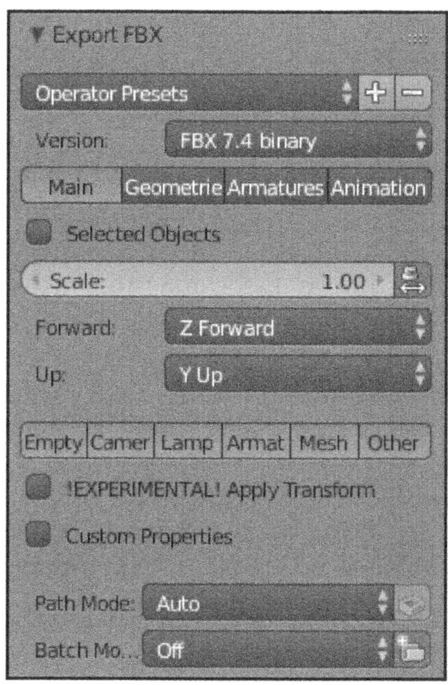

Next, we'll consider the workflows related to creating and importing 3D assets.

Round-trip geometry workflows

All this said, Unity is increasingly more capable of creating and modifying geometry within the Unity Editor itself—for example, the **ProBuilder** package that is integrated into Unity (which we'll use in `Chapter 10`, *Exploring Interactive Spaces*) is useful for white-boxing (prototyping) level designs and creating simple buildings with walls, passageways, and windows. There are many other third-party tools to be found on the Asset Store.

Unity is supporting advanced workflows with the **FBX Exporter** package, available in **Package Manager**, which provides round-trip workflows between Unity and other 3D software. With this package, GameObject hierarchies, animations, lights, and cameras can now be exported from Unity and shared with other applications.

The tool also allows you to preconfigure an integration with a specific 3D-modeling software. Presently, only Autodesk Maya and 3ds Max are supported, but more may be available by the time you read this. For details and instructions on using the FBX Exporter, see `https://docs.unity3d.com/Manual/HOWTO-exportFBX.html`. The package is presently still in preview, but is very promising.

As you can see, building a VR project requires you to not just understand how to use the many features of Unity itself, but how to import artwork and other assets from other sources into your project.

Summary

In this chapter, you built a simple diorama, became more acquainted with the Unity editor, and learned about importing content into your project. We started by installing Unity via Unity Hub, creating a new VR project with the Universal Render Pipeline, and installing additional packages using **Package Manager**.

Then you learned some basics of the Unity editor, such as how to navigate between its many windows and how to use the **Scene** editing gizmos, including grid and snap. We built a simple diorama scene with a ground plane, a crate (cube), a red ball, and a photo backdrop. You then created a BobHead prefab and learned about prefab editing, overrides, variants, and nesting, which we'll be seeing more of in upcoming chapters.

You also looked at the value of, and potential problems with, importing assets and Unity asset packages, including ones from the **Asset Store**. We learned about the issues with importing legacy assets that are not necessarily compatible with the version of Unity and render pipeline that you are using and how to fix it. Lastly, you learned how Unity is growing support for round-trip geometry workflows with the **FBX Exporter** package.

When developing for VR, you need to set up Unity for the specific platform and device that you plan to target, as well as the SDK external to Unity that is used to build the executable project. In the next chapter, we'll set up your development system and Unity settings to build and run the project to play on your VR headset.

3
Setting Up Your Project for VR

Yeah well, this is cool and everything, but where's my VR? I WANT MY VR! Hold on, kid, we're getting there.

In this chapter, we are going to set up our system and configure our project so that it can be run with a virtual reality **head-mounted display** (**HMD**). This chapter is very nuts and bolts. Although Unity aims to provide a unified platform for *create once, build many*, you are still going to need to do some system setup, project configuration, and maybe even include object components specifically for your target devices. After the first couple of topics in this chapter, you can jump to the section(s) that address your specific target devices.

In this chapter, we will cover the following topics:

- Using the Unity XR platform
- Managing virtual reality plugins for your platform
- Installing the XR Interaction Toolkit package
- Creating a VR-enabled camera rig
- Setting up your development machine to build and run VR projects from Unity
- Targeting desktop VR, including SteamVR, Oculus Rift, and Immersive Windows Mixed Reality
- Targeting mobile VR, including Oculus Quest, and Google Cardboard

Let's get started!

Technical requirements

To implement the projects and exercises in this chapter, you will need the following:

- A PC or Mac capable of running Unity 2019.4 LTS or later, along with an internet connection to download files.
- A VR headset supported by the Unity XR platform.

Introducing the Unity XR platform

Unity's **XR platform** aims to provide the tools necessary to achieve the core principle of the Unity engine – "Build once, deploy anywhere" – for VR and AR projects so that you can target any number of different platforms and devices with a single version of your content. In the past, VR developers have been plagued by incompatible device-specific, vendor-specific, platform-specific SDKs and toolkits. Various other "solutions," both open source and proprietary, have had serious shortcomings and limited support. The XR platform architecture has a technology stack that enables direct integrations of multi-platform deep integration, new features, and optimization. The XR tech stack is shown in the following diagram, which has been taken from the Unity Manual's *XR Plug-in Framework* page (`https://docs.unity3d.com/Manual/XRPluginArchitecture.html`):

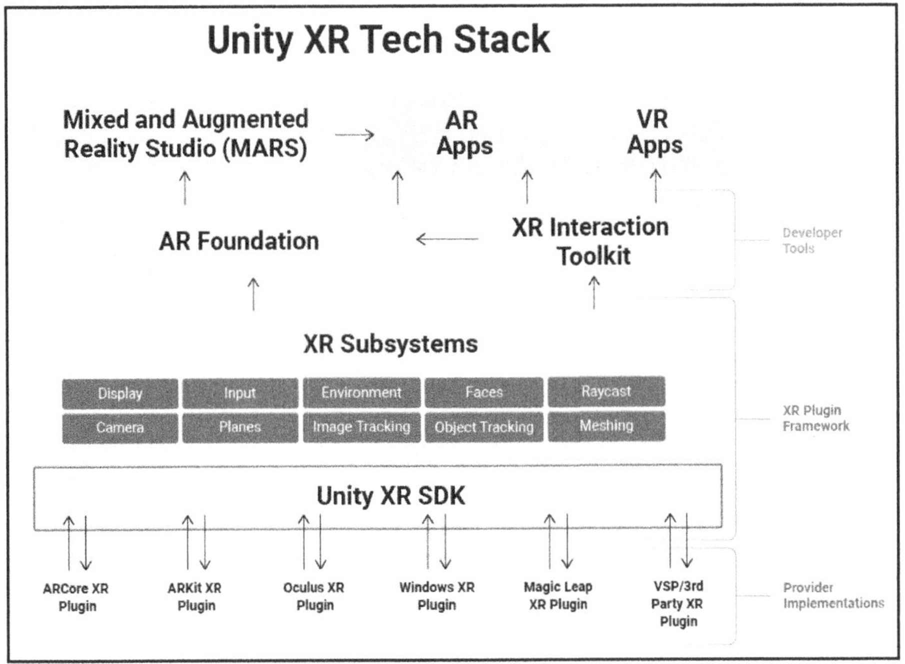

At the bottom of the stack are device-specific **XR plugins**. Some are provided and directly supported by Unity. Others are provided and supported by third-party developers for their own devices. This XR plugin architecture itself is a very important design as it decouples device-specific updates from the core Unity release cycle, as well as allows device providers to independently add and update their own device support in Unity (using the **Unity XR SDK**).

Using these provider plugins, the **XR subsystems** deliver core capabilities in a modular design, organized and separated by feature category. This allows developers to choose which XR features they want to build into a project and allows Unity to update individual subsystem modules independently. As a developer, you can use these subsystem components and C# classes directly in your projects, keeping the project content relatively device-independent. This way, you can focus on your own project's features instead of fighting differences between specific device APIs.

On top of the XR plugin framework, Unity offers two toolkits. **AR Foundation** is for augmented reality projects and won't be considered in this book. The **XR Interaction** (**XRI**) **Toolkit** is for both VR and AR, and we are going to use it extensively in the projects in this book. As we'll see, XRI provides components for tracking camera rigs and hand controllers, as well as for interaction with objects in the scene such as grabbing and throwing, teleportation, and other interactions common in virtual reality.

To get started with your Unity project ready for VR, you should identify the VR platform(s) and device(s) you initially plan to target.

Choosing your target VR platforms and toolkits

While much of your development will focus on the artwork, behaviors of game objects, and interactive game mechanics of your application, from the very beginning of your project, you should also identify which platforms and devices you are targeting. In ordinary Unity projects, it's often sufficient to simply choose the **Build Settings** target platform (for example, Android or Windows) and then configure **Player Settings** for build runtime options. But for VR, there's more. You need to manage the VR plugins you will need and use additional toolkit(s) for developing the project. Generally, your Unity VR project will need to include the following:

- Select a **Target Platform** for your builds (for example, Android versus Standalone/Windows).
- Install an **XR Plugin** that drives the VR devices.
- Within your scene, you will include a VR-enabled camera rig for tracking head and hand locations in 3D space.

- Using other components provided with Unity's **XR Interaction Toolkit** for handling interaction with game objects and locomotion in your scenes.
- Alternatively, you may choose to include device-specific toolkits, often provided by device manufacturers that have been tuned to their specific devices and often include a suite of prefabs, components, and shaders. These higher-level add-ons help you create interactive, responsive, and comfortable VR experiences tailored to a specific platform.

Unity has a growing library of built-in classes and installable packages to support VR (or rather, *XR* including augmented reality devices), including stereo rendering, input tracking, user interactions, and audio spatializers. Some features are limited by specific platform capabilities, but generally, they're designed to be device-independent.

I will walk you through the details of installing and configuring your project in this chapter. If you are not sure which platform, XR plugin, and device toolkit to include in your project, consult the following table, which shows many of the major consumer VR devices available today and the options for the development platform, target device platform, VR runtime, XR plugin, and optional device toolkit. The first table identifies the plugins provided and supported directly by Unity:

Device	Dev Platform	Target Platform	VR Runtime	Official XR Plugin	Optional Device Toolkit
Oculus Rift	Windows	Standalone/Windows	Oculus Desktop	Oculus	**Oculus Integration (OVR)**
Windows MR	Windows	**Universal Windows Platform** (**UWP**) or Standalone/Windows	Mixed Reality Portal	Windows MR	Mixed Reality Toolkit (MRTK)
Oculus Quest	Windows, macOS X	Android	Oculus Quest	Oculus	OVR
Oculus Go	Windows, macOS X	Android	Oculus Go	Oculus	OVR

The following table includes plugins provided by third parties:

Device	Dev Platform	Target Platform	VR Runtime	XR Plugin	Optional Device Toolkit
HTC Vive	Windows, macOS X	Standalone/Windows, Mac	SteamVR	OpenVR	SteamVR Input System and Interaction Toolkit
Valve Index	Windows, macOS X	Standalone/Windows, Mac	SteamVR	OpenVR	SteamVR Input System and Interaction Toolkit
Oculus Rift (OpenVR)	Windows	Standalone/Windows	SteamVR (via Oculus Desktop)	OpenVR	SteamVR Input System and Interaction Toolkit
Windows MR (OpenVR)	Windows	Standalone/Windows	SteamVR (via Mixed Reality Portal)	OpenVR	SteamVR Input System and Interaction Toolkit

The following table shows plugins that have been announced but are not currently available (at the time this was written):

Cardboard	Windows	Android	Android	Cardboard	Cardboard Unity
Cardboard	macOS X	iOS	Android	Cardboard	Cardboard Unity

Note that Valve's OpenVR supports multiple VR devices, although OpenVR with Oculus or immersive Windows MR devices also require their corresponding runtime app be running in the background (Oculus Desktop or Mixed Reality Portal, respectively). Also note that, as of October 2019, Google discontinued Daydream and open-sourced the Cardboard SDK. As of December 2020, Oculus is sunsetting the Oculus Go and will stop accepting new applications in its store.

If you try to install multiple device toolkit packages in a Unity project, you may get irreconcilable errors caused by code conflicts. You can temporarily remove folders from `Assets/` by renaming the offending folder with a trailing tilde (~) outside of Unity (for example, in Windows Explorer or macOS X Finder). For example, rename `SteamVR` to `SteamVR~` and Unity will then ignore the folder and think it's been removed. However, note that your revision control tool (for example, Git) will still have the files.

So, let's get started by enabling VR in the project's scene.

Enabling virtual reality for your platform

The Diorama scene we created in the previous chapter was a 3D scene using the Unity default `Main Camera`. As we saw, when you pressed **Play** in the Unity Editor, you had the scene running in the **Game** window on your 2D computer monitor. We will now enable the project and scene so that it runs in virtual reality. These first couple of tasks are similar, regardless of which device you are targeting:

- Setting the **target platform** for your project builds
- Installing the **XR plugin** for our device
- Installing the **XRI package**
- Creating a VR enabled **XR Rig** camera rig

We'll take care of these details now. After doing this, you'll need to set up your Unity project and development system software, depending on your specific target. This will include completing the following tasks, which we'll cover on a case-by-case basis in the rest of this chapter:

- Ensuring your VR device is connected and you're able to normally discover and use its home environment.
- Ensuring your device's development mode is enabled.
- Installing any system software on your development machine that's required for you to build your target platform.
- Optionally, importing the device toolkit for your target device into your Unity project and using the provided camera rig instead of the XR Rig.

Now, let's configure the project for your specific VR headset.

As you know, installation and setup details are subject to change. We recommend that you double-check with the current Unity Manual pages and your device's *Getting started* documentation for the latest instructions.

Setting your target platform

New Unity projects normally default to targeting standalone desktop platforms. If this works for you, you do not need to change anything. Let's take a look at this now:

1. Open the **Build Settings** window (**File | Build Settings...**) and review the **Platform** list.

2. Choose your target platform; such as one of the following, for example:
    - If you're building for Oculus Rift or HTC Vive, for example, choose **PC, Mac & Linux Standalone**.
    - If you're building for Windows MR, choose **Universal Windows Platform.**
    - If you are building for Oculus Quest, or Google Cardboard on Android, choose **Android**.
    - If you are building for Google Cardboard on iOS, choose **iOS**.
3. Then, click **Switch Platform**.

Unity may need to reimport your assets for a different platform. This will happen automatically and may take a while, depending on the size of your project. The editor will be locked out until the process is completed.

If the platform you require is not present in the list, you may need to install the corresponding module. To do this, you need to go back into **Unity Hub**, as follows. These steps are similar to the ones described in the previous section, *Installing the Unity Editor*:

1. Quit the current Unity session (**File | Exit**).
2. Open **Unity Hub** on your computer desktop.
3. From the left-hand side menu, choose **Installs**.
4. Find the version of Unity that you're using in this project.
5. Use the three-dot menu to choose **Add Modules**.
6. Review the list and check the checkbox for each of the modules you require. The module may have additional tools. Be sure to unfold the module name and check any sub-options. In particular, the **Android Build Support** module has child **Android SDK & NDK Tools** and **OpenJDK** sub-modules, which should also be checked.
7. Press **DONE** to install the additional modules.
8. Reopen your Unity project. The added platform should now be included in the **Build Settings' Platform** list.

Next, we'll enable VR for the project.

Installing XR Plugin Management

When VR is enabled in your Unity project, it renders stereoscopic camera views and runs on a VR headset. Unity 20193 and later sports a new **XR Plugin Management** tool, which you'll use to install and manage VR device SDKs. You can do this using **XR Plugin Management**, as follows:

1. Open the **Project Settings** window (**Edit** | **Project Settings**).
2. Select **XR Plugin Management** from the left tab menu.
3. If necessary, click **Install XR Plugin Management**, as shown in the following screenshot:

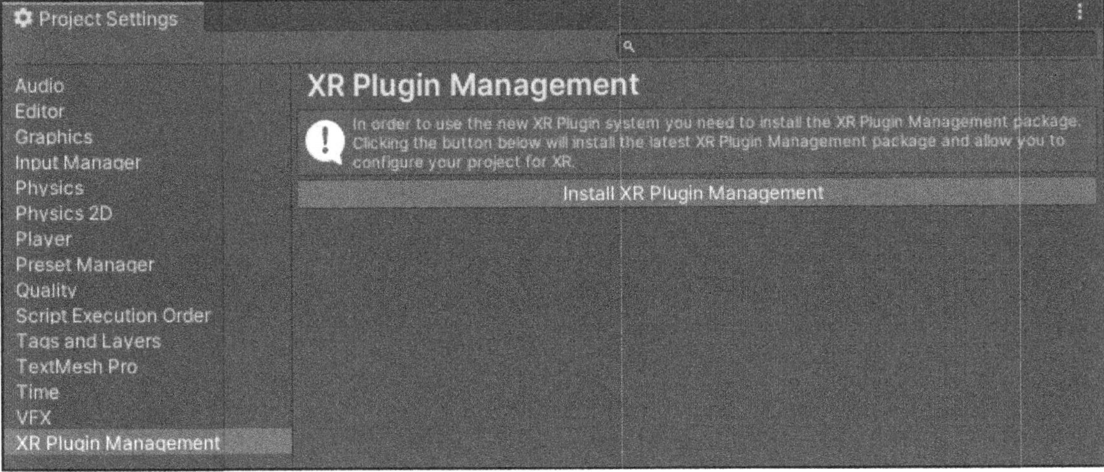

Next, you'll need to install the loaders for the specific device(s) you plan to target with this project. We'll go through the details in the device-specific topics later in this chapter. Meanwhile, you may see the following warning:

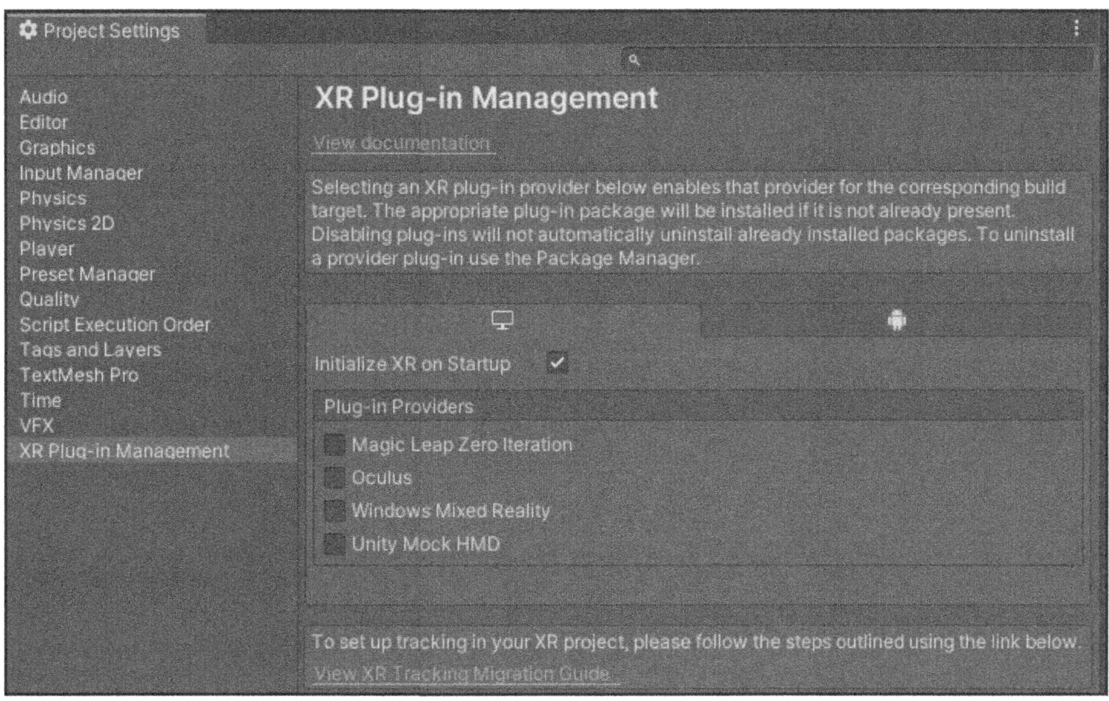

Then, once one or more of the desired plugins have been installed, the plugin will be added to the list in the left-hand menu, under **XR Plug-in Management**. In the following screenshot, for example, I've installed the Oculus plugin and you can see that the Oculus settings are now available:

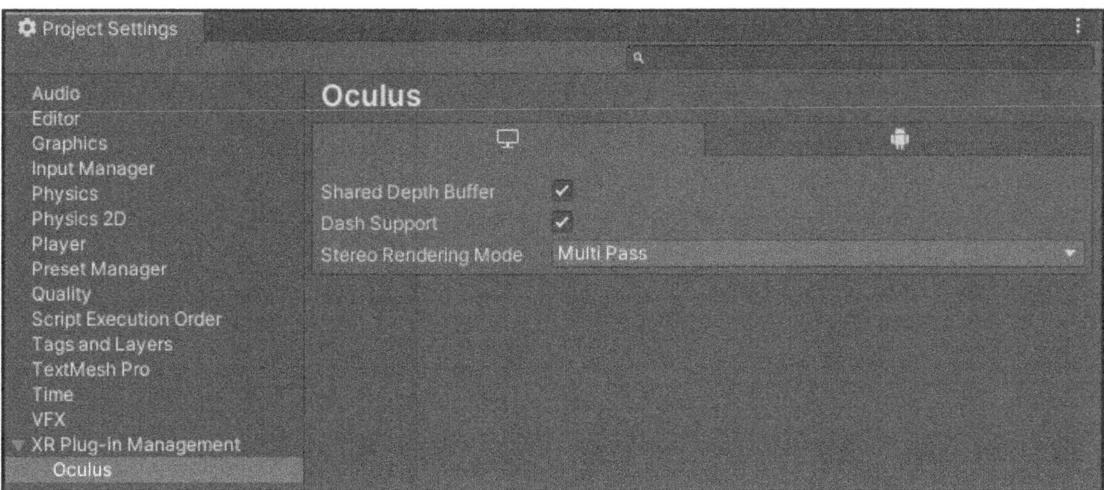

When you install **XR Plug-in Management**, other dependency packages may also be installed. In fact, using the **Install Plug-in Management** button we used previously is a shortcut for doing the same through **Package Manager** (**Window | Package Manager**). In the following screenshot, you can see the package in **Package Manager** where I've selected **Show Dependencies** from the **Advanced** drop-down menu, so you can see that two additional (hidden) required packages are also installed: **XR Legacy Input Helpers** and **Subsystem Registration**:

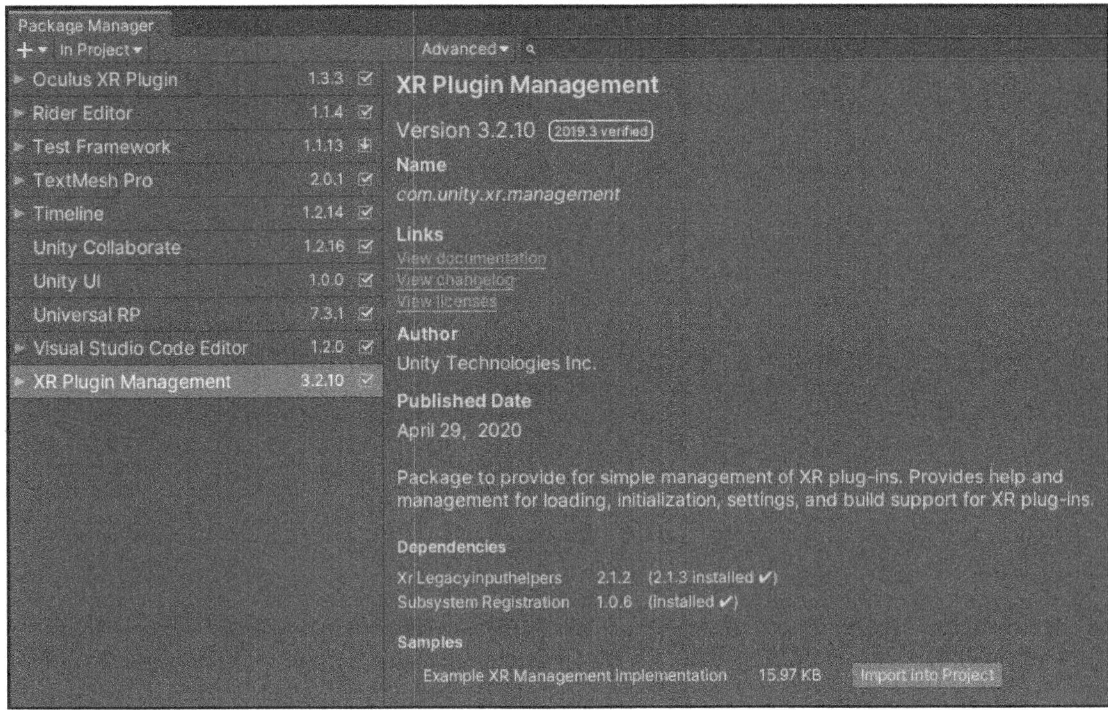

Good. At this point, the project is VR-ready, since we've set the target platform and installed the XR plugins for the target device. If you want to develop a project directly using the native XR SDK, you could stop here. However, if you want to develop a project for one specific platform, you can use an optional device toolkit, such as **Oculus Integration** (**OVR**), SteamVR Interaction Toolkit, or **Windows Mixed Reality Toolkit** (**MRTK**). In this book, we will focus on the Unity XR Interaction Toolkit. We'll install this next.

Installing the XR Interaction Toolkit

We are going to be using Unity's new **XRI Toolkit** in the projects throughout this book. XRI provides higher-level components for interaction in VR and AR projects, including cross-platform hand controller input for grabbing objects. It also provides components for setting up a VR camera rig that handles stationary and room-scale VR experiences.

The XR Interaction Toolkit can be installed using **Package Manager**. Follow these steps to install it in your project:

1. Open **Package Manager** (**Window** | **Package Manager**).
2. Filter the list to **All Packages** (Use the drop-down list at the top-left of the window).
3. At the time of writing, XRI is still in preview, so you may also need to select **Show Preview Packages** from the **Advanced** dropdown menu.
4. Type `xr interaction` in the search area and, with the package selected, press **Install**.

The XR Interaction Toolkit package is shown in the following screenshot:

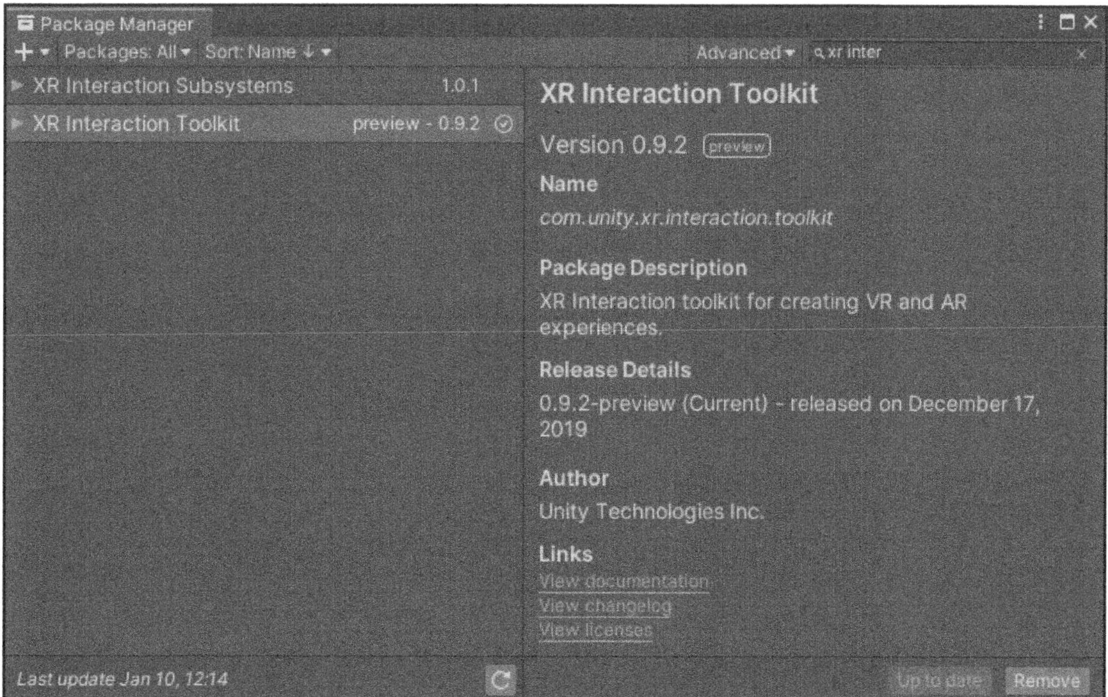

With XRI installed, you now have access to its components through the main menu bar, that is, **Component** | **XR**. As shown in the following screenshot of the menu, these include **XR Rig**, **XR Controller**, **XR Interaction Manager**, and **XR Simple Interactable**:

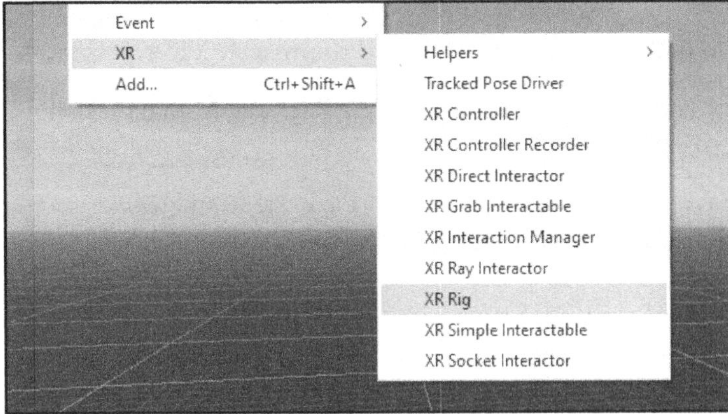

There are some pre-made game objects you can readily add to your scenes through the main **GameObject** | **XR** menu, as shown in the following screenshot:

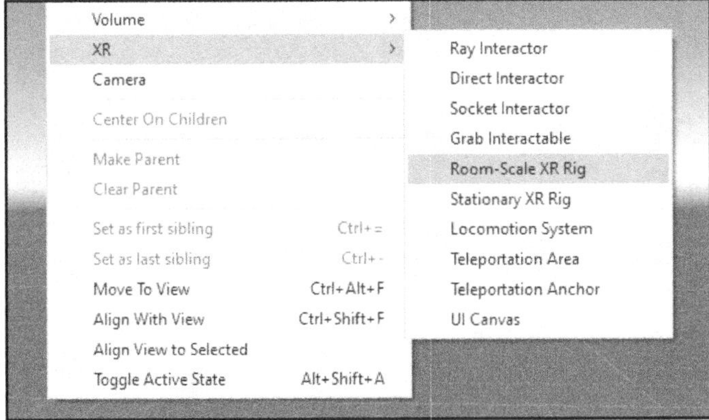

For example, here, you can find the **Room-Scale XR Rig** and **Stationary XR Rig** game objects, both of which use the **XR Rig** component. We're going to add one of these to our scene next. At this point, you should have set up the target platform and installed an XR Plugin and the XRI Toolkit. Now, we'll replace the default main camera with the XR camera rig in the scene.

Adding the XR camera rig

The XR camera rig places a camera object in the scene that tracks the position and pose of the physical VR HMD. It also includes game objects that track the player's hands. There are two versions you can readily add to your project – one for room-scale VR and one for stationary VR. Room-scale mode enables the player to walk around within a configured play area (for example, Guardian on Oculus or Chaperone on SteamVR). In stationary mode, the player is assumed to be seated or standing in place; they can still move their head to look around the scene, but the player rig is stationary.

Please decide which mode you would like to use in your project. Don't worry if you change your mind; they both use the same XRI components, but with different default settings that you can change as needed later on.

To replace the default Main Camera with a pre-configured XR camera rig of your choice, use the following steps. We'll also adjust its initial position so that it's a few meters back from the center of our ground plane:

1. From the main menu, select **GameObject** | **XR** | **Stationary XR Rig** or **Room-Scale XR Rig**.
2. Position **XR Rig** at **Z**=`-3` (select **XR Rig** in **Hierarchy**, then in **Inspector** set **Transform Position Z** = `-3`).

This adds two new objects to the root of your scene hierarchy: **XR Interaction Manager** and **XR Rig**. It also removes the default Main Camera from the Hierarchy, as XR Rig has its own Main Camera child object. At this point, if you have a VR device that's supported in Editor Play mode, when you press **Play**, you can enjoy your scene in VR!

Let's take a moment to explore what this **XR Rig** is made of.

Exploring the XR Rig objects and components

Using the **GameObject** | **XR** menu to add an XR Rig to the scene adds the **XR Rig** and **XR Interaction Manager** objects to the scene. Let's take a closer look.

Select the **XR Interaction Manager** object. In the **Inspector** window, you can see that it has a corresponding **XR Interaction Manager** component. XRI requires you have one **XR Interaction Manager** component in the scene so that you can manage communications between the *interactors* and *interactables* in the scene (we'll go into more depth about these and start using them in `Chapter 5`, *Interacting with Your Hands*).

The scene now also includes an **XR Rig** object, which has a child hierarchy of GameObjects. As shown in the following screenshot, it has an **XR Rig** component, which includes the option to set **Tracking Origin Mode**; for example, for room-scale (**Floor**) or stationary (**Device**). It also has a **Camera Y Offset**. This defines the camera's (player's head) default height above the floor and is needed when we're not using **Floor** as the tracking origin:

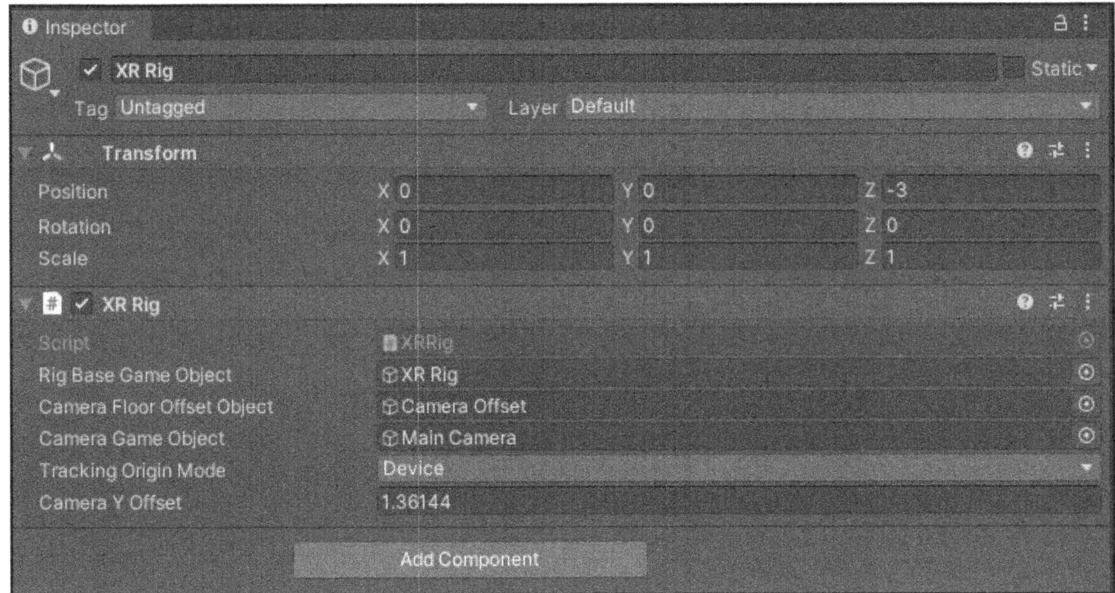

Camera Y Offset is pertinent for *stationary tracking* and will be applied to the rig's child **Camera Offset** transform. In stationary mode, the Y offset sets the child **Camera Offset** object to this fixed Y position. Conversely, in *room-scale* mode, the camera Y offset will be automatically set to zero and use the device's runtime tracking of the HMD to determine the eye level. The **Camera Offset** object is shown in the following screenshot:

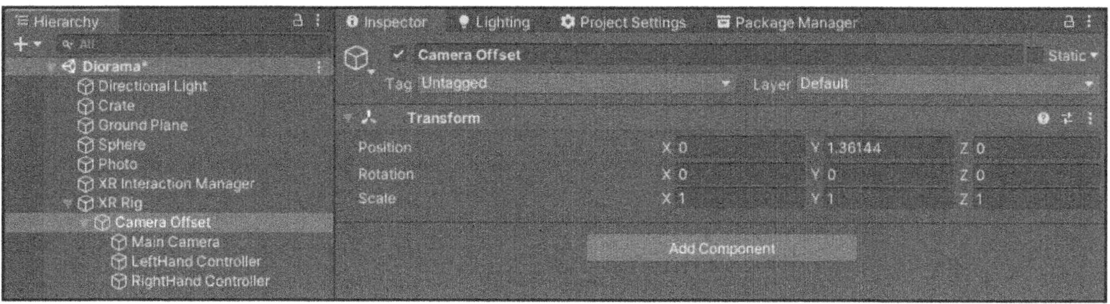

The height for the average seated person is about 1.3 meters. The height of an average human female is 1.6 meters and 1.75m for males. The actual averages vary by ethnicity/locale (`https://en.wikipedia.org/wiki/Average_human_height_by_country`).

The children of **Camera Offset** are the **Main Camera**, **LeftHand Controller**, and **RightHand Controller** objects. Like any camera in a Unity scene, the XR Rig's **Main Camera** has a **Camera** component, with default settings. But it also has a **Tracked Pose Driver** component configured as a **Center Eye - HMD Reference** pose source. **Tracked Pose Driver**, as its name suggests, tracks physical devices in 3D space, and in this case, it'll be tracking the head-mounted display device. The Main Camera's **Tracked Pose Driver** is shown in the following screenshot:

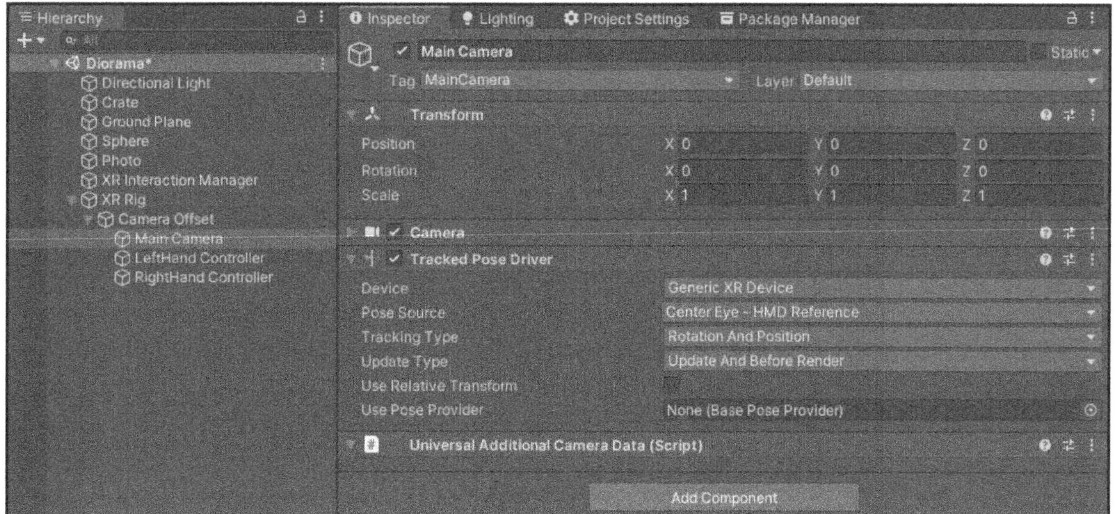

While we're here, you may want to set the near clipping plane of the camera to `0.01` (the smallest value Unity allows). This option can be found in **Camera** | **Projection** | **Clipping Planes** | **Near**, in the **Inspector** window. The camera's clipping planes define the distances from the camera where rendering starts and stops. Any objects in front or behind the near and far clipping planes, respectively, are not drawn in the view, and any objects partially crossing this plane will be clipped. The default value may be fine for conventional apps, but in VR, you really put your face into the scene and likewise, may bring your rendered hands close to your face, so we should set the near clipping plane so that it's as small as possible.

In the **Hierarchy** window, you can see siblings of **Main Camera**, which are the left- and right-hand controller objects. Each of these is a more complex combination of XR components, including the following:

- **XR Controller**: Interprets **Input System** events as XRI interactor position, rotation, and interaction states.
- **XR Ray Interactor**: Used for interacting with objects at a distance using raycasts.
- **XR Interactor Line Visual**: A helper component that gets line point and hit point information for rendering.
- **Line Renderer**: Renders the visual line that's cast from the controller when the user is in VR.

An *interactor* is an object in the scene that can select or move another object in the scene. This XR Rig uses a **Ray Interactor** by default that selects objects from a distance using a raycast in the direction the user is pointing. Another type is **Direct Interactor**, which selects objects when they're directly touching the target interactable object. An interactor requires an XR Controller component.

The **XR Controller** component converts physical device controller input, such as button presses, into interaction events, including Hover, Select, Activate, and UI button presses. You can also specify the model prefab for the hand to show in VR. Details of the **XR Controller** component are shown in the following screenshot, with the **Model** option highlighted:

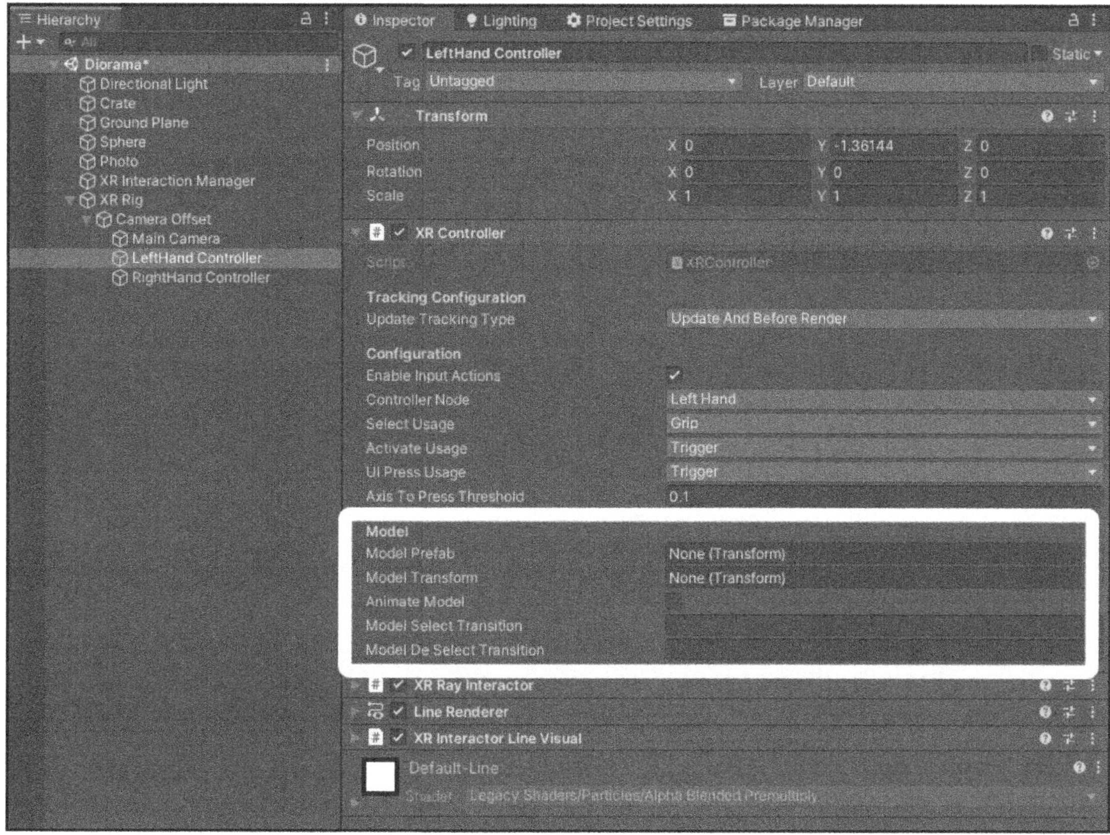

You also can see that, currently, the controller **Grip** button is used for selection, while the **Trigger** button will be used to activate an object or interact with UI elements.

The **XR Interactor Line Visual** and **Line Renderer** components are used in conjunction with **Ray Interactor** to display laser beam-like lines within VR so that the user knows where they're pointing. You may want to explore the many parameters that control the look of the rays.

Your scene is now set up with a camera rig that enables viewing in virtual reality. Depending on the VR headset you're using (for example, ones tethered to your PC), you may be able to press **Play** now and review the scene in VR. However, you should make sure you can build and run the project on your physical device too. Let's do that now.

Building and running your project

It's always a good idea to actually build and run your project as early as possible in your VR development projects. A good first time to try is once things are set up. Then, you can continue to iterate the develop, build, run, and test cycle frequently throughout development. I'll remind you of this as we develop our projects.

So far, you have set the target platform for your build, for example, as standalone Windows or Android. You've installed the XR packages and SDK required for your device. Finally, you've set up an XR camera rig in the scene using the XR Interaction Toolkit. Before you can build, you may also need to configure additional player settings.

Configuring the player settings

There are a wide variety of **Player Settings** you may need to configure, depending on your target platform. These control the runtime player that is deployed on the target platform and runs your Unity project. These settings include GPU rendering settings, scripting compiler configuration, and optimizations.

In Unity, the word "player" is used in several contexts. There's the end user "player" of your game, the camera rig as a "first-person player," and the hand controller, which is sometimes referred to as the "player controller," But in **Project Settings**, "Player" refers to the program deployed on the target host platform that plays your Unity project, such as a media *player* that plays videos or a music *player* that plays MP3 files. **Player Settings** configures the deployed Unity player for the specific target hardware and system software.

It is a good idea to get familiar with these settings as soon as possible. With each new project, for example, you should set **Company Name** (defaults to `DefaultCompany`) and **Project Name** (defaults to the name provided when you created the project in Unity Hub). Android projects require a **Package Name** (for example, `com.[companyname].[projectname]`).

I will provide the details of the settings required per platform/device in the corresponding topics later in this chapter. We will adjust them occasionally in the projects throughout this book. Some settings are required for any build to be run. Others are only needed to be configured when you're preparing to publish to a store. These settings are organized into panels, including **Icons**, **Resolution And Presentation**, and perhaps the most important catch-all (modestly named), **Other Settings**. Explanations can be found in the Unity Manual at `https://docs.unity3d.com/Manual/class-PlayerSettings.html`.

Building, running, and testing your VR project

Depending on your target device, you may have a few more things to set up before you can build and run. These will be addressed in the device-specific topics that follow in this chapter. Then, when you're ready, simply choose **File** | **Build And Run** (or use the **Build And Run** button in the **Build Settings** box).

You may need to complete the setup of your project, according to the appropriate section later in this chapter, before completing the **Build And Run** steps in this topic.

I strongly recommend that you frequently test your VR scenes in a VR headset during development with **Build And Run**. Quick development and iteration using the Editor's **Play** mode is great for rapid development. But just because something seems to work in the Editor does not guarantee it will work in a build. Continue to build, run, and test frequently throughout development and especially after you've implemented any new feature in your project before you say it's "done."

The scene or scenes you can build are specified in the **Build Setting** dialog box's **Scenes in Build** list, as shown in the following screenshot. To add the current open scene, press **Add Open Scenes**. Alternatively, you can drag and drop a scene from the **Project** `Assets` folder into the list. In multi-scene projects, the first one in the list will be the initial default scene that's loaded when your application starts; other scenes can be loaded via C# scripts by calling `SceneManager.LoadScene` (for scripting examples, see `https://docs.unity3d.com/ScriptReference/SceneManagement.SceneManager.LoadScene.html`):

When it's time to **Build And Run**, you'll be prompted to specify a folder for the build files. I recommend a folder named `Builds/` in the root of your project.

If you're using Git for revision control, you can list the build folder in your `.gitignore` file (`/Builds/`) so that its content is not committed to your repository.

The following screenshot shows the built app running in VR with the default laser raycast hands:

The rest of this chapter will continue to set up Unity and your development system software for the specific platform and device you plan to target. Please skip to the specific section that is relevant to you.

Building for SteamVR

This section describes how to set up and build your VR project so that it runs on a SteamVR supported VR device. VR applications that run on SteamVR are built using the OpenVR plugin. It can drive a variety of models of VR, including HTC Vive, Valve Index, Oculus Rift, and Windows MR devices; that is, basically all the major PC-based **six degrees of freedom (6-DOF)** VR rigs with trackable hand controllers.

Before you get started, ensure you have your VR device connected to the PC and that you're running the SteamVR runtime. This may include installing the Lighthouse base stations for the HTC and Valve devices that require it. If you're running SteamVR for an Oculus Rift, you also need to be running the Oculus desktop app. Likewise, if you're running SteamVR for immersive **Windows Mixed Reality** (**WMR**), you need to be running the Mixed Reality Portal. Test that you can see and interact with the SteamVR Home in the headset.

Setting up for OpenVR

The **OpenVR XR** plugin is provided and maintained by Valve (not by Unity). At the time of writing, you must install the plugin using **Package Manager** using a GitHub URL. Please review the README instructions on the GitHub page at `https://github.com/ValveSoftware/steamvr_unity_plugin` before completing this section, as it may be more up to date than this book.

To target SteamVR, use the following **Build Settings**:

1. Configure your Unity **Build Settings** so that they target the **Standalone** platform, if they aren't already (**File** | **Build Settings...** | **PC, Mac & Linux Standalone** | **Switch Platform**).
2. Set **Target Platform** to **Windows** and **Architecture** to **x86_64**.

Use the following steps to install the **OpenVR** XR plugin:

1. Open the **Package Manager** window using **Window** | **Package Manager.**
2. Press the **+** button in the upper left of the window.
3. Select **Add Package from GIT URL**.
4. Paste in the following URL: `https://github.com/ValveSoftware/steamvr_unity_plugin.git#UnityXRPlugin`.
5. Open **XR Management Settings** using **Edit** | **Project Settings** | **XR Plug-in Management**.
6. If you see **OpenVR** in the **Plug-in Providers** list, check its checkbox.
7. You will see that the **OpenVR** plugin is now listed under **XR Plug-in Management**. Click it to review its settings.

The **OpenVR** plugin has several options. Generally, you'll keep the default values, as shown in the following screenshot:

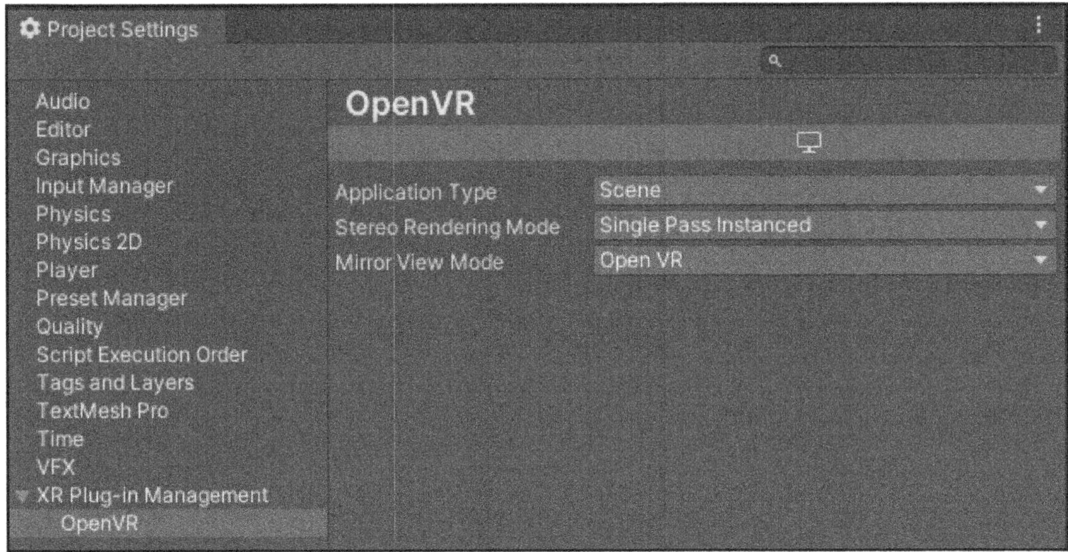

If you press **Play** now, you should see the scene playing in your VR headset. At this point, it's also advised that you **Build And Run** the project to verify it will build correctly and run as expected in your VR device.

The SDK we've installed is sufficient for the projects in this book. We are going to use the XR Interaction Toolkit, including the Tracked Pose Driver, for the left- and right-hand controllers. However, Steam provides an alternative input system that uses the SteamVR input bindings and 3D controller models.

Installing the SteamVR Unity Plugin toolkit

As a SteamVR app, you have the option of using the SteamVR plugin for the Unity toolkit from Valve Software, which provides user rebindable inputs, skeletal inputs, 3D controller models, and more, including an example interaction system with useful scripts and assets and some pretty good example scenes that are fun and instructional. Details can be found at `https://valvesoftware.github.io/steamvr_unity_plugin/articles/intro.html`.

Note that the use of the word "plugin" for this SteamVR Unity Plugin toolkit is a high-level toolkit unrelated to the low-level Unity XR plugins. You've already installed the separate low-level OpenVR plugin device driver for the XR Management system.

For the projects in this book, we do not depend on having this toolkit installed, and it is best to not try to mix the SteamVR Unity Plugin toolkit assets with the Unity XR ones in your project scenes, especially while you're learning the basics of VR development and following along with our project tutorials. I recommend that you do **not install** it here. For your own projects, however, you can decide to use the SteamVR Input System instead of the Unity one, especially if you plan to only target the Steam Store and target only the desktop VR devices supported by SteamVR.

At the time of writing, there are two versions of the **SteamVR Unity Plugin**. The older one is compatible with the Unity built-in XR, which supports Unity versions earlier than Unity 2019.3. It can be installed from the Asset Store (`https://assetstore.unity.com/packages/tools/integration/steamvr-plugin-32647`). The newer version is presently in prerelease and can be downloaded as a `.unitypackage` file from GitHub (`https://github.com/ValveSoftware/steamvr_unity_plugin/releases`).

To install the **SteamVR Plugin** version that is compatible with **XR Plugin Management** from GitHub, use the following steps (subject to change in the future):

1. In your web browser, go to `https://github.com/ValveSoftware/steamvr_unity_plugin/releases` and choose the current **Assets file** link to begin the download.
2. Import the package into Unity using **Assets** | **Import Package** | **Custom Package** or simply drag and drop the package file into the **Project** window.
3. At the bottom of the **Import Unity Package** window, select **Import**.
4. Since we're using the **Universal Render Pipeline**, you should convert the imported materials by selecting **Edit** | **Render Pipeline** | **Universal Render Pipeline** | **Upgrade Project Materials**.

The package installs several new folders in your **Project** `Assets/`, including `SteamVR/`, `SteamVR_Resources/`, and `StreamingAssets/SteamVR/`. If you drill down into the `Assets/SteamVR_Resources/Resources/` folder and select the **SteamVR_Settings**, you will be able to see the current settings in the **Inspector** window, as shown in the following screenshot:

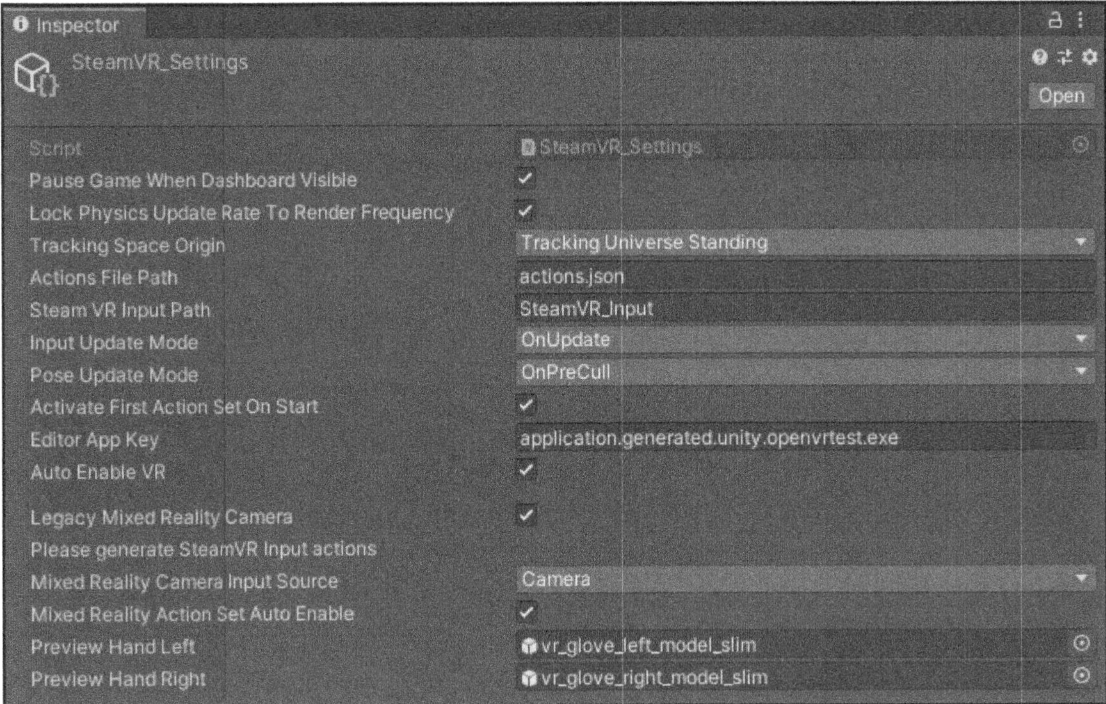

For more information, review the `SteamVR Unity Plugin.pdf` and `SteamVR Unity Plugin - Input System.pdf` documents, which can be found in the `Assets/SteamVR/` folder. Be sure to explore the various example scenes, such as **Simple Sample** in `SteamVR/`, `Interactions_Example` in `SteamVR/InteractionSystem/Samples/`, and multiple example scenes in `SteamVR/Extras/`.

Please refer to the plugin documentation for details on the features and usage of the assets. For example, in your own projects, you can choose to replace our **XR Rig** camera rig with the `[CameraRig]` prefab provided with the SteamVR Plugin, which can be found in the `Assets/SteamVR/Prefabs/` folder and is used in their various example scenes. The plugin includes the following:

- **Render Models**: The virtual 3D models of the hand controllers adapt to the actual physical VR device the player is using.
- **SteamVR Input**: Manage user input actions. Handles user rebindable input mappings that are controlled from a `.JSON` file and are accessible via the **Window** | **SteamVR Input** window.
- **Skeleton Input**: Hand animation with a full finger and joint estimates and range of motion.
- **Interaction System**: A set of scripts, prefabs, and other assets that serve as examples. These can be used in your own projects.
- **Skeleton Poser**: Tools you can use to design your own hand poses and finger constraints, used together with Skeleton Input.

If you don't need to set up an additional VR device, you can move onto the next chapter. We will consider the setup for Oculus Rift next.

Building for Oculus Rift

This section describes how to set up and build your VR project on an Oculus Rift desktop VR device. Using a Rift requires the Oculus Windows app to be running, and in Unity, you'll build with the Oculus SDK. (Alternatively, you can build for OpenVR and run your Oculus in SteamVR, in which case, follow the instructions in the previous section instead).

Using the Oculus SDK is required if you plan to publish on the Oculus Store or use any of the many advanced **Oculus Integration** platform features, including avatars, **in-app-purchases** (**IAP**), achievements, and more. See `https://developer.oculus.com/platform/` for a list of features that are part of the Oculus platform solutions.

Before getting started, be sure you have your Rift connected to a PC (or a Quest connected with an Oculus Link cable) and that you're able to see and interact within the Oculus Home environment.

Setting up for Oculus desktop

To target the Oculus desktop, use the following **Build Settings**:

1. Configure your Unity **Build Settings** so that they target the **Standalone** platform, if they're not already (**File** | **Build Settings...** | **PC, Mac & Linux Standalone** | **Switch Platform**).
2. Set **Target Platform** to **Windows** and **Architecture** to **x86_64**.

Now, if you haven't already, add the Oculus XR plugin using the following steps:

1. Open**XR Plugin Management** in **Project Settings** using **Edit** | **Project Settings** | **XR Plug-in Management**.
2. In the **Plug-in Providers** list, check the **Oculus** checkbox.
3. You'll now see the **Oculus** option in the left tab menu. Select it.
4. Optionally, set **Stereo Rendering Mode** to **Single Pass Instanced** for better performance.

Notice that the Oculus SDK has several options. By default, **Shared Depth Buffer** and **Dash Support** are enabled. These allow the Oculus system software to render into the same view while your app is running, for example, for popup Dash menus. The Oculus plugin options are shown in the following screenshot:

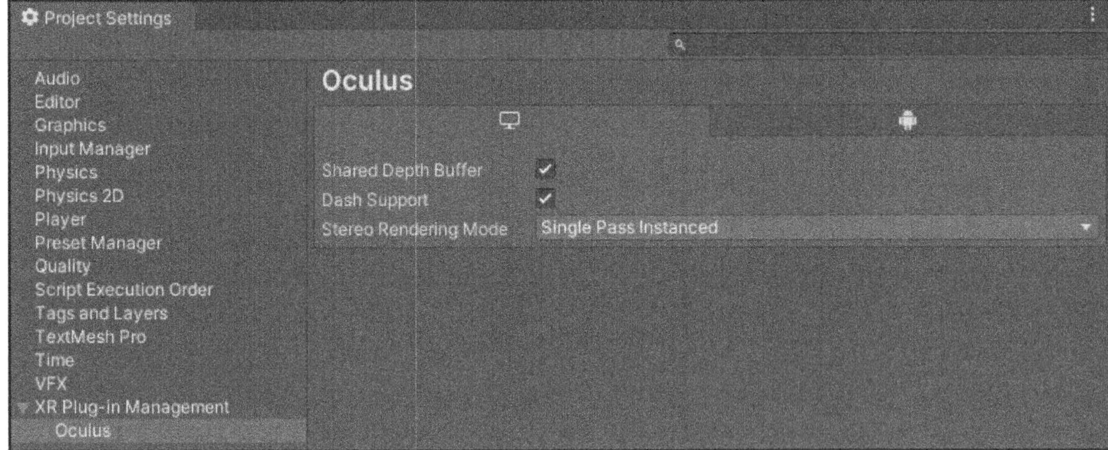

If you press **Play** now, you should see the scene playing in your VR headset. At this point, it's also advised that you **Build And Run** the project to verify it will build correctly and run as expected on your VR device.

The SDK we've installed is sufficient for the projects in this book. However, Oculus provides a rich collection of optional tools in the Oculus Integration toolkit.

Installing the Oculus Integration toolkit

As an Oculus app, you have the option of using the Oculus Integration toolkit for Unity, which is built on top of the native XR SDK. Oculus maintains this plugin, which provides advanced rending, social platform, audio, avatars, lipsync, and more. For the projects in this book, we do not depend on having this toolkit installed, but from time to time, we may give additional tips on using it to enhance a project. To install the Oculus Integration toolkit from the Asset Store, follow these steps:

1. In your web browser, go to `https://assetstore.unity.com/packages/tools/integration/oculus-integration-82022`.
2. Click **Open In Unity** and **Install** it into your project.
3. If prompted, also allow updates to the **OVRPlugin for the Unity Editor** and/or other assets.
4. Since we're using the Universal Render Pipeline, you should convert the imported materials (**Edit** | **Render Pipeline** | **Universal Render Pipeline** | **Upgrade Project Materials**).

The package installs a lot of stuff under the **Project** `Assets/Oculus/` folder. I encourage you to explore the various subfolders, open example scenes, and even read through the scripts. A good place to start is **StartScene** in the `Oculus/SampleFramework/Usage/` folder, as shown in the following screenshot:

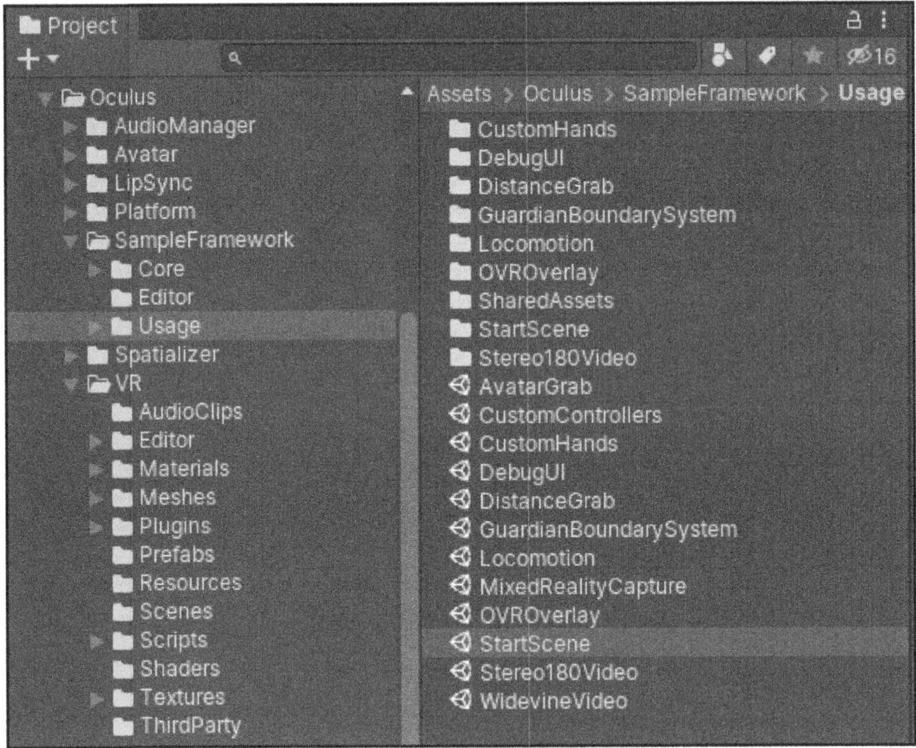

The Oculus package also installs helpful menu items on the Unity Editor menu bar's **Oculus** menu. We won't go into details here, and they are subject to change. We encourage you to explore the options and shortcuts they provide. For more information on the Oculus Integration toolkit for Unity, see `https://developer.oculus.com/unity/`:

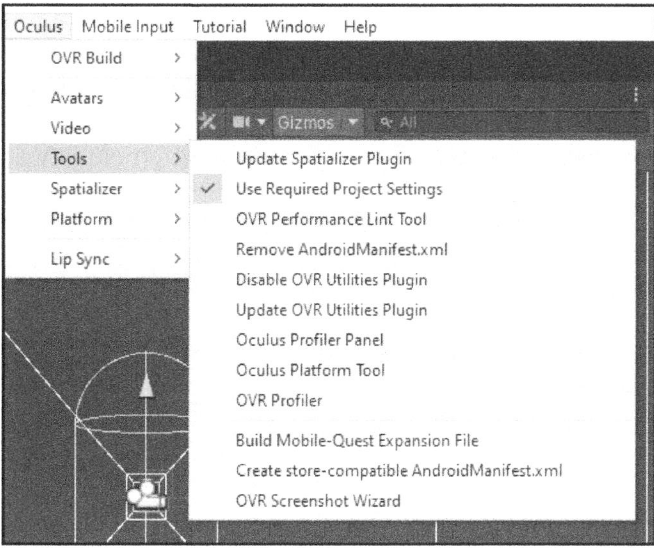

In your own projects, you can choose to replace our **XR Rig** camera rig with the **OVRCameraRig** prefab provided in the Oculus Integration, which can be found in the `Assets/Oculus/VR/Prefabs/` folder. It is used in their various example scenes.

If you do not need to set up an additional VR device, you can move on to the next chapter. Next, we will consider the Windows Immersive Mixed Reality setup.

Building for Immersive Windows MR

This section describes how to set up and build your VR project so that it runs on a **Windows Mixed Reality** (**WMR**) immersive VR headset. This allows it to be run on Windows 10. You can choose to target **Standalone / Windows** in **Build Settings** or **Universal Windows Platform** for development. (Alternatively, you can build for **OpenVR** and run your WMR device in SteamVR, in which case, follow the instructions in that section instead). However, to publish to the Windows Store, you must build to target **Universal Windows Platform**.

Microsoft's 3D media **Mixed Reality** strategy is used to support a spectrum of devices and applications, from virtual reality to augmented reality. This book and our projects are about VR. At the other end of this spectrum is the Microsoft HoloLens wearable AR device. Developing for MR requires that you're using a Windows 10 PC and have Visual Studio installed. At the time of writing, the minimum requirement is Visual Studio 2019 (16.2 or higher). See `https://docs.microsoft.com/en-us/windows/mixed-reality/install-the-tools` for more details. Targeting the Universal Windows Platform and using the Windows Mixed Reality SDK are required if you plan to publish on the Windows Store. We'll set that up now.

Before getting started, be sure you have your WMR headset connected to the Windows 10 PC, that **Mixed Reality Portal** is running, and that you're able to see and interact with the home environment.

Setting up for Immersive WMR

To target Windows Mixed Reality VR devices, you can target the **Standalone / Windows** platform, as follows:

1. Configure your Unity **Build Settings** so that they target the **Standalone** platform via **File | Build Settings... | PC, Mac & Linux Standalone | Switch Platform.**
2. Set **Target Platform** to **Windows** and **Architecture** to **x86_64**.

If you plan to publish on the Windows Store, you need to target the Universal Windows Platform. In that case, I recommend that you develop and build for that target early in your development process by setting it up as follows:

1. Configure your Unity **Build Settings** so that they target **Universal Windows Platform** via **File | Build Settings... | Universal Windows Platform | Switch Platform**.
2. If you do not see **Universal Windows Platform** in the platforms list, or when you pick it if you see a message stating that the module is not loaded, you may need to go back to **Unity Hub** and install the module, as described earlier in this chapter.
3. Set **Target Device** to **Any Device**.
4. Set the **Architecture** to **x64**.
5. Set **Build Type** to **D3D**.

If you see a warning about missing components in Visual Studio, don't worry – we'll address that soon. Next, add the **Windows Mixed Reality** plugin to your project using these steps:

1. Open **XR Plug-in Management** in **Project Settings** using **Edit | Project Settings | XR Plugin Management**.
2. In the **Plug-in Providers** list, check the **Windows Mixed Reality** checkbox. This will install the SDK files.
3. You'll now see the **Windows Mixed Reality** option in the left tab menu. Select it.

Examine the **Windows Mixed Reality** settings, as follows:

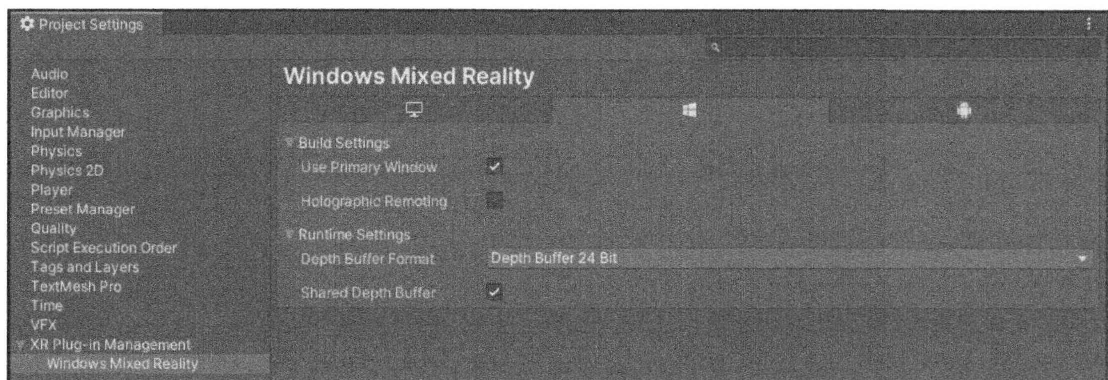

If you press **Play** now, you should see the scene playing in your VR headset. Before you can build and run your project, though, you need to ensure you have the necessary Visual Studio components installed.

Installing Visual Studio workloads

Visual Studio is a powerful **integrated development environment** (**IDE**) for all kinds of projects. When we build for UWP from Unity, we will actually build a Visual Studio-ready project (a `.csproj` file) that you can then open in Visual Studio to complete the compile, build, and deploy process, which will allow you to run the app on your device.

To build for UWP, ensure you have the required Visual Studio workloads, as follows:

1. From Unity, open your C# project in Visual Studio (**Assets** | **Open C# Project**).
2. In Visual Studio, select **Tools** | **Get Tools and Features** from the main menu.
3. Select the **Workloads** tab and choose the **.NET Desktop Development** and **Desktop Development with C++** workloads, and then press **Modify** to install it (if it's not already installed).
4. Choose the **Universal Windows Platform Development** workload and then press **Modify** to install it (if it's not already installed).
5. You may find that you'll need to download and install additional .NET targeting packs. If you see a message to that effect when you build, follow the instructions provided.

My **Workloads** section looks as follows. The ones with the checkboxes ticked have been installed:

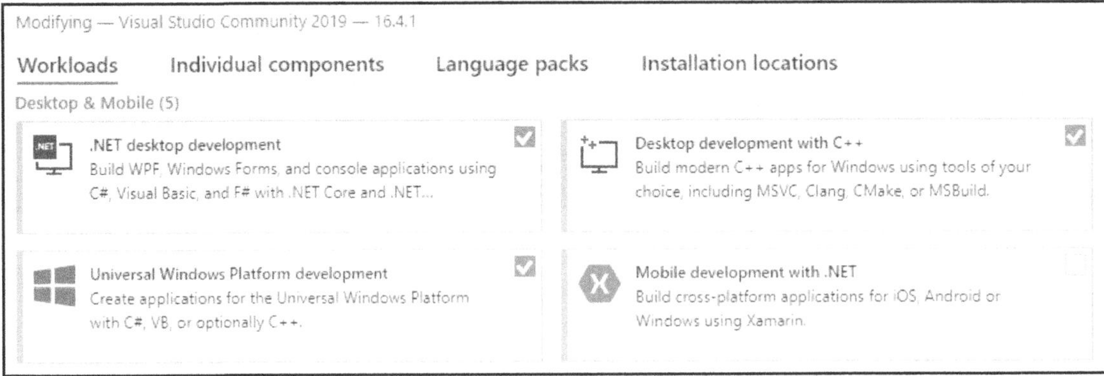

In order to sideload unsigned UWP apps and debug them, including development projects built with Unity and Visual Studio, you need to enable **Developer Mode** in Windows on your PC. In your Windows 10 desktop, open the **For Developer** settings (in Windows, go to **Start** | **Settings** | **Update & Security** | **For Developers**) and select **Developer Mode**.

At this point, it's also advised that you **Build And Run** the project to verify it will build correctly and run as expected on your VR device. The SDK we've installed is sufficient for the projects in this book. However, Microsoft provides a rich collection of optional tools in the Mixed Reality Toolkit.

Installing the Mixed Reality Toolkit (MRTK)

As a Windows MR app, you have the option of using the **Microsoft Mixed Reality Toolkit** (**MRTK**) for Unity, which is built on top of the native XR SDK. Microsoft maintains this project, which provides high-level support for both immersive MR headsets, OpenVR headsets, and HoloLens. MRTK is a richly featured, well-designed, device-independent software toolkit. You can read more about its architecture at `https://microsoft.github.io/MixedRealityToolkit-Unity/Documentation/Architecture/Overview.html`. It is an open-source project and can be found on GitHub at `https://github.com/microsoft/MixedRealityToolkit-Unity`.

The projects in this book do not depend on you having this toolkit installed. If you would like to use it in your own projects, follow the latest getting started instructions at `https://microsoft.github.io/MixedRealityToolkit-Unity/Documentation/GettingStartedWithTheMRTK.html`. Note that some of the prerequisites and instructions that are given pertain to HoloLens development and are not necessary for VR devices. To install MRTK, follow these steps:

1. Browse to the **MRTK Releases** downloads page at `https://github.com/Microsoft/MixedRealityToolkit-Unity/releases`.
2. Click the specific packages to download; such as the following, for example:
    - Required: `Microsoft.MixedReality.Toolkit.Unity.Foundation.2.1.0.unitypackage`
    - Optional: `Microsoft.MixedReality.Toolkit.Unity.`**`Tools`**`.2.1.0.unitypackage`
    - Optional: `Microsoft.MixedReality.Toolkit.Unity.Extensions.2.1.0.unitypackage`
    - Other example packages may be fun and useful
3. Once downloaded, drag each `.unitypackage` file into your **Project** window to install them (or use **Assets** | **Import Package** | **Custom Package**) and click **Import**.
4. Note that the package adds a new **Mixed Reality Toolkit** menu to the main menu, as shown in the following screenshot. Convert the imported materials into Universal RP using **Mixed Reality Toolkit** | **Utilities** | **Upgrade MRTK Standard Shader to Render Pipeline**.

5. Then, convert any example materials into URP using **Edit** | **Render Pipeline** | **Universal Render Pipeline** | **Upgrade Project Materials**:

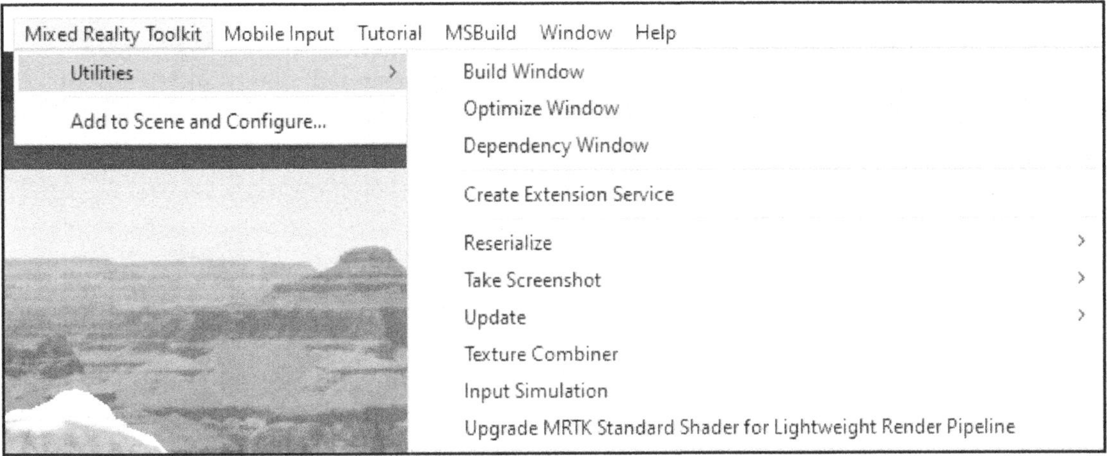

The packages install several folders in your Project Assets, including ones named `MixedRealityToolkit/`, `MixedRealityToolkit.Extensions/`, `MixedRealityToolkit.SDK/`, `MixedRealityToolkit.Tools/`, and so on. I encourage you to explore the various subfolders, open example scenes, and even read through the scripts.

The toolkit includes a handy build tool that provides a shortcut to the build and player settings. For example, to build the project, follow these steps:

1. Open the MRTK Build window, which can be opened using **Mixed Reality Toolkit** | **Utilities** | **Build Window**.
2. Select **Any Device** in **Quick Options**.
3. Click **Build Unity Project**.

In your own projects, you can choose to replace our **XR Rig** camera rig with the camera and input prefabs provided in the MRTK.

If you do not need to set up for an additional VR device, you can move onto the next chapter. Now, we will consider setting up Android-based mobile VR devices.

Building for Oculus Quest

This section describes how to set up and build your VR project on an Oculus mobile VR device, including Quest. Internally, these devices run Android, so developing from Unity has a lot in common with developing for any Android device. For VR, you set **XR Plugin** to **Oculus** and configure your project so that it builds and runs on the mobile VR device.

Before we begin, ensure your device is in **Developer Mode**, as follows:

1. Open the **Oculus** companion app on the phone connected to the device.
2. Go to the **Settings** menu (lower-right corner).
3. Select the device (for example, Oculus Quest).
4. Select **More Settings** | **Developer Mode** and switch it on, as shown in the following screenshot:

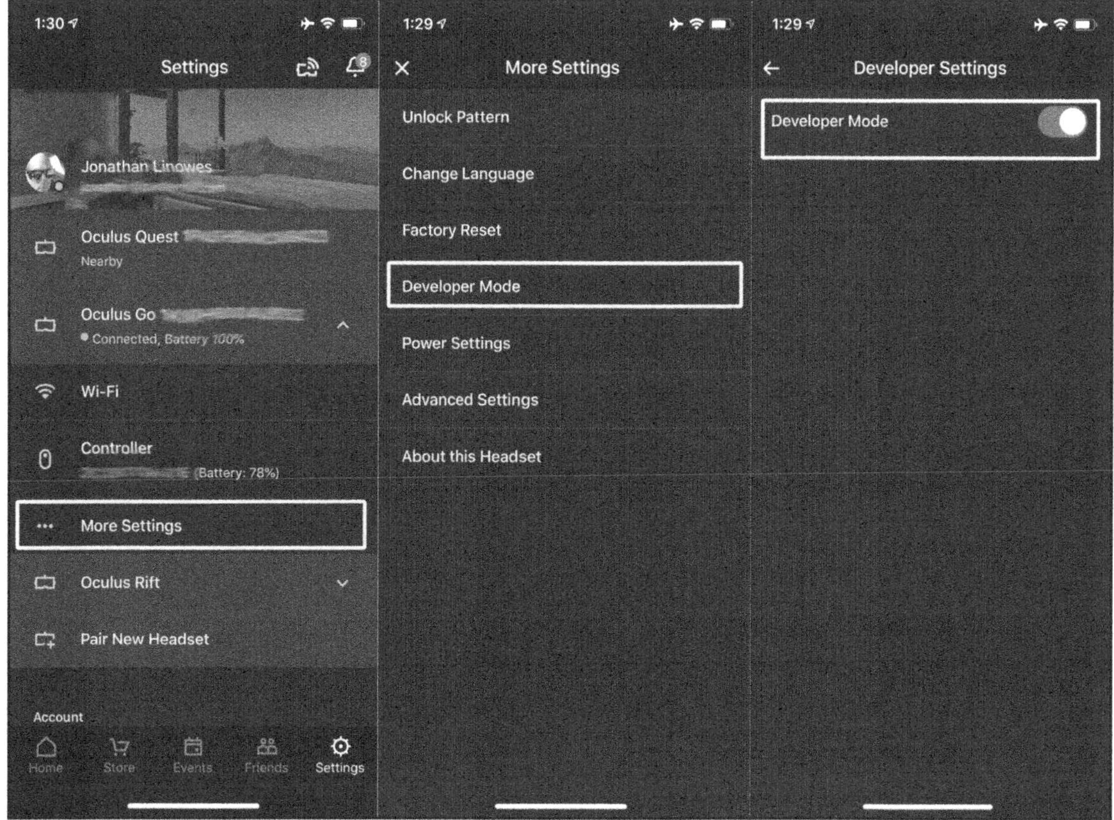

Next, we'll make sure you can build from Unity for a target Android platform.

Installing the Android tools

To develop VR apps that will run on Oculus Go and Oculus Quest (and other Android mobile VR devices such as Google Cardboard), you will need to set up your development machine for Android development. The requirements are not specific to virtual reality; they're the same for any Android app from Unity. The process is also well-documented elsewhere, including the Unity documentation at `https://docs.unity3d.com/Manual/android-sdksetup.html`.

OK; let's get going. Developing for Android devices requires that you prepare your development system with the Android SDK, NDK, and JDK external tools (short for *software development kit*, *native development kit*, and *Java development kit*, respectively). Your current version of Unity may have been already installed with the **Android Build Support** module, including **Android SDK & NDK Tools** and **OpenJDK**. You can double-check this in **Unity Hub** by going to the **Installs** tab, clicking the three-dot button for your current release, and choosing **Add Modules**, as follows:

If necessary, install the missing tools. Your Unity configuration should then be automatically set up. You can check this by opening Unity and doing the following:

1. Select **Edit** | **Preferences...** to view the configured external tools.
2. Verify that **JDK Installed with Unity** is checked.
3. Verify that **Android SDK Tools Installed** with Unity is checked.
4. Verify that **Android NDK Installed with Unity** is checked.

This **Preferences** window can be seen in the following screenshot:

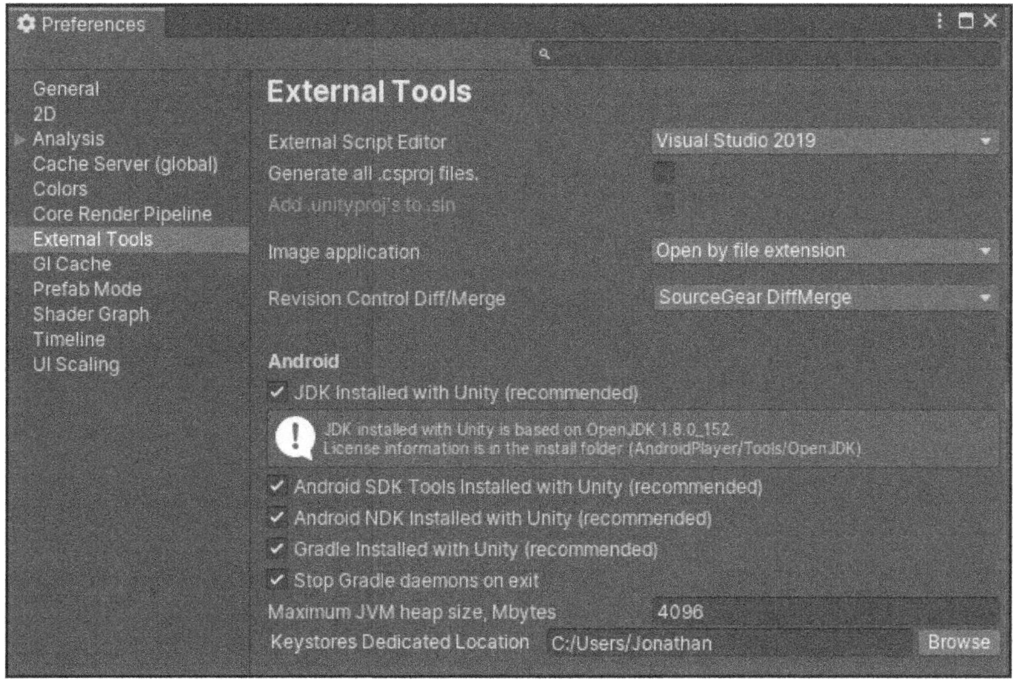

If Unity complains it cannot find a required tool version, you may need to install it manually. For Android SDK, you can install just the command-line tools from the Android Studio downloads page at `https://developer.android.com/studio/`. (Scroll to the bottom of the page for the **Command-Line Tools Only** section). Then, NDK can be downloaded from `https://developer.android.com/ndk/downloads`.

Now you can set up your project for Oculus mobile VR devices.

Setting up for Oculus mobile VR

To target Android-based Oculus mobile VR, configure your Unity **Build Settings** so that they target the **Android** platform via **File | Build Settings... | Android | Switch Platform**. Next, if it's not already installed, add the **Oculus XR Plugin**, as follows:

1. Open **XR Plug-in Management** in **Project Settings** using **Edit | Project Settings | XR Plugin Management**.

2. Click the **Android** tab.
3. In the **Plug-in Providers** list, check the **Oculus** checkbox. The Oculus SDK will be installed.
4. You'll now see an **Oculus** option in the left tab menu. Select it.
5. Press **Create** to create a serialized instance of the settings data in order to modify the default Oculus settings.
6. Check the **V2 Signing** checkbox, especially if you're targeting Quest.

The Oculus settings for Android are shown in the following screenshot:

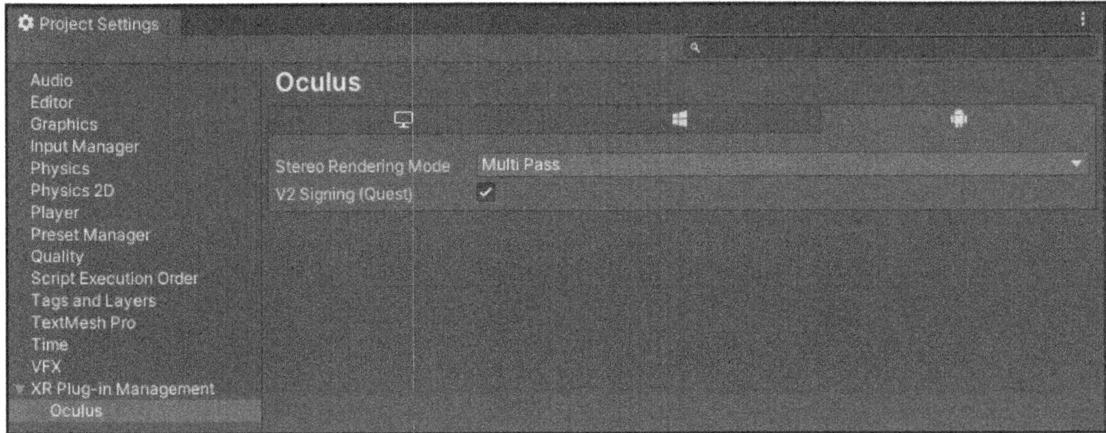

To preview the scene in your device, you could use **OVR Scene Quick Preview**, which is included with the Oculus Integration Toolkit. This will be described later in this chapter. If you have an Oculus Quest connected to your PC with an Oculus Link Cable and the Oculus Link settings are enabled, you can view your scenes in VR (for details, see `https://support.oculus.com/525406631321134`). Otherwise, if you press **Play** now, you can run the scene in the editor's Game window but not remotely on the VR device. To see it in VR, you need to do a build.

Oculus Link connects Quest to a PC. It's marketed as an expansion of the Quest so that you can play PC-based VR games for Rift and SteamVR. But it can also be used in Unity for viewing VR scenes in **Play** mode.

Other Android and optimization settings

To build for an Android device, you also need to configure other **Player Settings**. Some settings are required for it to run, while others are recommended for it to run better:

1. At the top, set **Company Name** and **Product Name**. The product defaults to the project name that was used when it was created via Unity Hub.
2. In **Other Settings** | **Package Name**, set a unique app ID using a Java package name format. It defaults as a composite of the company and product names; for example, mine is `com.UVRP3.VR_is_awesome`.
3. The minimum API level will vary, depending on your target device. Oculus Quest requires **Minimum API Level: Android 6.0 Marshmellow (API Level 23)**. Oculus Go requires a minimum of **Android 5.0 Lollipop (API Level 21)**.

There are many other options in **Player Settings**. Refer to the Oculus documentation for the current recommendations, including the following:

- `https://developer.oculus.com/documentation/unity/unity-conf-settings/`
- `https://developer.oculus.com/blog/tech-note-unity-settings-for-mobile-vr/`
- `https://developer.oculus.com/documentation/unity/latest/concepts/unity-mobile-performance-intro/`

Some of these current recommended settings include the following:

- **Build Settings** | **Texture Compress: ASTC**.
- **Player** | **Other Settings** | **Color Space: Linear**.
- **Auto Graphics:** Unchecked. **OpenGLES3** should be the first in the list. **Vulcan** should be the second, if at all, but not on Go.
- **Multithreaded Rendering**: Checked.
- Also, review the recommended **Graphics pipeline** and **Quality** settings.

Give this a shot by clicking **Build And Run**.

The SDK we've installed is sufficient for the projects in this book. However, Oculus provides a rich collection of optional tools in the **Oculus Integration toolkit**.

Installing the Oculus Integration toolkit

As you're building an Oculus app, you have the option of using the Oculus Integration toolkit for Unity, which is built on top of the XR plugins. It provides support for advanced rendering, social platform interaction, audio, avatars, lipsync, and more. This is the same as what we had for Oculus Rift, which we mentioned earlier in the *Building for Oculus Rift* section. Look there for a discussion of this. In summary, to install the Oculus Integration toolkit from the Asset Store, follow these steps:

1. In your web browser, go to `https://assetstore.unity.com/packages/tools/integration/oculus-integration-82022`.
2. Click **Open In Unity** and **Install** it in your project.
3. If prompted, also allow updates to the **OVRPlugin for the Unity Editor** or other packages.
4. Since we're using the Universal Render Pipeline, you should convert the imported materials using **Edit** | **Render Pipeline** | **Universal Render Pipeline** | **Upgrade Project Materials**.

In addition to the collection of example scenes, frameworks, and Oculus platform support, it installs an Oculus menu in the main menu bar, which includes some shortcuts, especially for mobile VR development, as shown in the following screenshot:

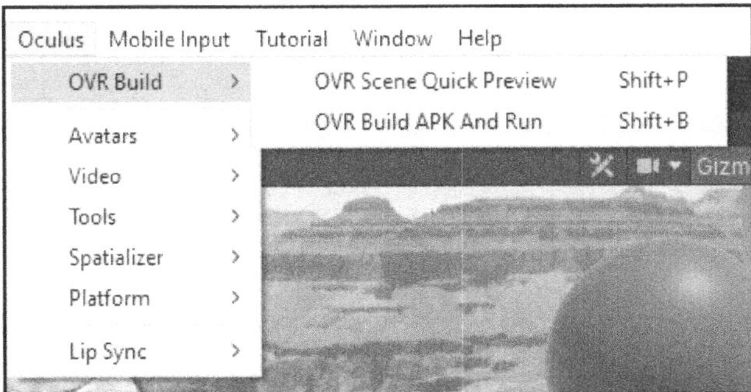

Press the **OVR Scene Quick Preview** button to play the scene in your device. You may be prompted to install the OVR Transition APK. The Transition APK helps Unity launch your working scene in the device. After doing this, press **Build And Deploy Scene** to quick-build the scene for preview in the HMD. The dialog box is shown in the following screenshot:

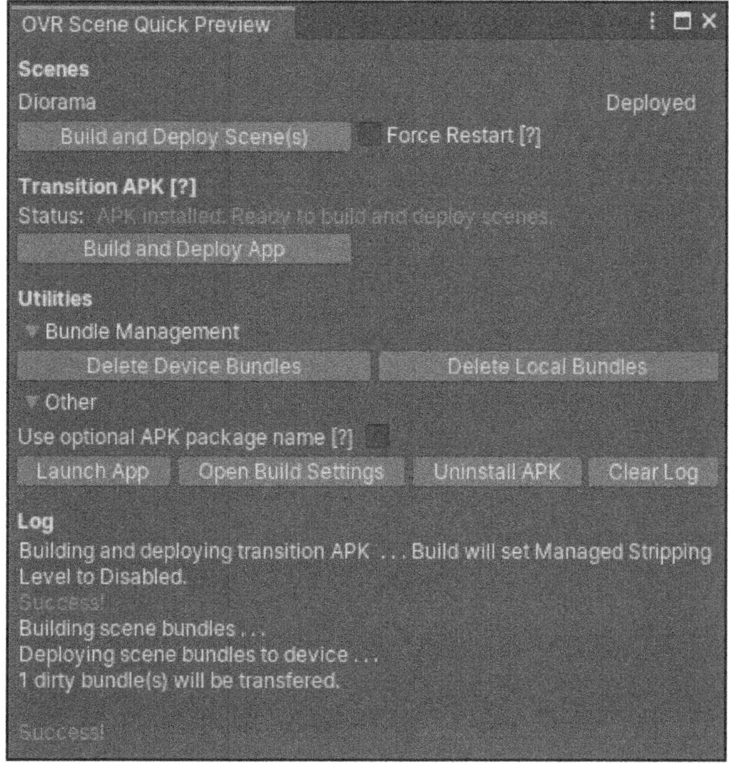

To build and run this, press the **OVR Build APK And Run** option.

In your own projects, you may choose to replace our **XR Rig** camera rig with the OVRCameraRig prefab provided in the Oculus Integration package, which can found in the `Assets/Oculus/VR/Prefabs/` folder and is used in their various example scenes.

One more thing worth mentioning is that the **Android Debug Bridge** (**adb**) tool is something you should get to know sooner rather than later for installing Android APK builds and examining runtime logs. We'll take a look at this next.

Using adb

When you build a project from Unity, it creates an `.apk` file and installs it on the mobile device connected to your development machine. If you already have an `.apk` file, you can install it manually using the Android `adb` command-line tool.

The **Android Debug Bridge (adb)** is an important command-line tool that you should get to know so that you can communicate with an Android device for side-loading apps and debugging. It's included with the Android SDK. The full documentation can be found at `https://developer.android.com/studio/command-line/adb`. If you do not have the `adb` command on your system, you can install it as follows:

1. Download **Android Platform Tools** from `https://developer.android.com/studio/releases/platform-tools`.
2. Unzip the folder.
3. Navigate to the folder containing `adb.exe`.
4. Open the Terminal/Command Prompt at this folder. For example, in Windows Explorer, you can type `cmd` into the address bar.

I like to move the unzipped `platform-tools/` folder into my `/Program Files/` folder and add it to the Windows environment `PATH`.

Now, when you type `adb devices` at the Command Prompt, you should see the connected Android device. To install the APK file built from Unity, use the `adb install [path to apk file]` command. Other useful `adb` commands include the following:

- `adb help`: Lists the available `adb` commands
- `adb devices`: Lists the currently connected devices
- `adb install [path to apk file]`: Sideload installs an APK package on your device
- `adb install -r [path to apk file]`: Installs and replaces a package
- `adb shell pm list packages -3`: Lists the packages already installed on the device
- `adb uninstall [packagename]`: Removes a package from the device; for example, `com.UVRP3.VR_is_Awesome`

If you have trouble running `adb install`, you may need to add the **Oculus ADB Drivers**. Follow these steps to do so:

1. Download the zip file containing the driver from `https://developer.oculus.com/downloads/package/oculus-adb-drivers/`.
2. Unzip the file.
3. Right-click on the `.inf` file and select **Install**.

`Adb` can also be used to access the Android device logs, which are very useful when you're debugging:

- `adb logcat -v time -s Unity >logs.txt`: Streams the logs, filtered for Unity messages, and pipes them to the local `logs.txt` file. Run this command and then start your app.
- `adb logcat -d  -v time -s Unity >logs.txt`: Dumps the most recent Unity log messages into `logs.txt` and exits.
- `adb logcat -c`: Clears the logs on the device.

Unity includes an **Android Logcat** package that adds support for displaying log messages coming from Android devices in the Unity Editor. Install the **Android Logcat** package via Package Manager (**Window** | **Package Manager** | **All Packages** | **Android Logcat** | **Install**). Then, open the window using **Window** | **Analysis** | **Android Logcat**. You can filter the message list; for example, using the `Unity` string.

If you do not need to set up an additional VR device, you can move onto the next chapter. Next, we'll consider setting up Google Cardboard for either Android or iOS.

Building for Google Cardboard

This section describes how to set up and build your VR project for Google Cardboard on a mobile phone, including Android smartphones and Apple iPhones (iOS). With this, you set up **XR Plugin** for Google Cardboard and configure your project so that it builds and runs on the mobile VR device.

Smartphone-based virtual reality is not as popular as it was when the previous editions of this book were written. Google no longer supports Daydream and has now open sourced the Cardboard SDK (`https://github.com/googlevr/cardboard`) as a baseline starter VR platform. Similarly, Oculus has dropped support for GearVR in its ecosystem. Nonetheless, Cardboard lives on, in both Android and iOS, as a fun and educational low-end VR display. The scene is displayed on the phone screen with separate left and right eye views that provide 3D stereographic viewing using a low-cost cardboard or plastic goggles with Fresnel lenses. Tracking is limited to **three degrees of freedom** (**3DOF**), which tracks your head's orientation in space but not its position.

Most of the projects in this book can run on smartphones with Cardboard, but maybe with some limitations. The only input device supported by Google Cardboard is a single button click. Unlike its next-level cousins (Daydream and GearVR), a Google Cardboard solution does not directly support Bluetooth hand controllers. However, a 3DOF handheld pointer controller can be bought for around $10 and used in your projects for pointing with a little extra work.

The following topics will review what it takes to set up your project for Google Cardboard with the Unity XR Platform on Android and iOS.

Setting up for Google Cardboard

The Google Cardboard XR plugin is an open source project supported by Google (not directly by Unity). At the time of writing, you must install the plugin using **Package Manager** using a GitHub URL. Please review the current Quickstart instructions on the Google page at `https://developers.google.com/cardboard/develop/unity/quickstart` before completing this section, as it may be more up to date than this book.

Use the following steps to install the Google Cardboard XR plugin:

1. Open the **Package Manager** window using **Window** | **Package Manager**.
2. Press the + button in the upper left of the window.
3. Select **Add Package from GIT URL**.
4. Paste the following URL: `https://github.com/ValveSoftware/steamvr_unity_plugin.git#UnityXRPlugin`.
5. Open **XR Management Settings** using **Edit** | **Project Settings** | **XR Plug-in Management**.
6. Check the **Cardboard XR Plugin** checkbox in the **Plug-in Providers** list, as shown in the following screenshot:

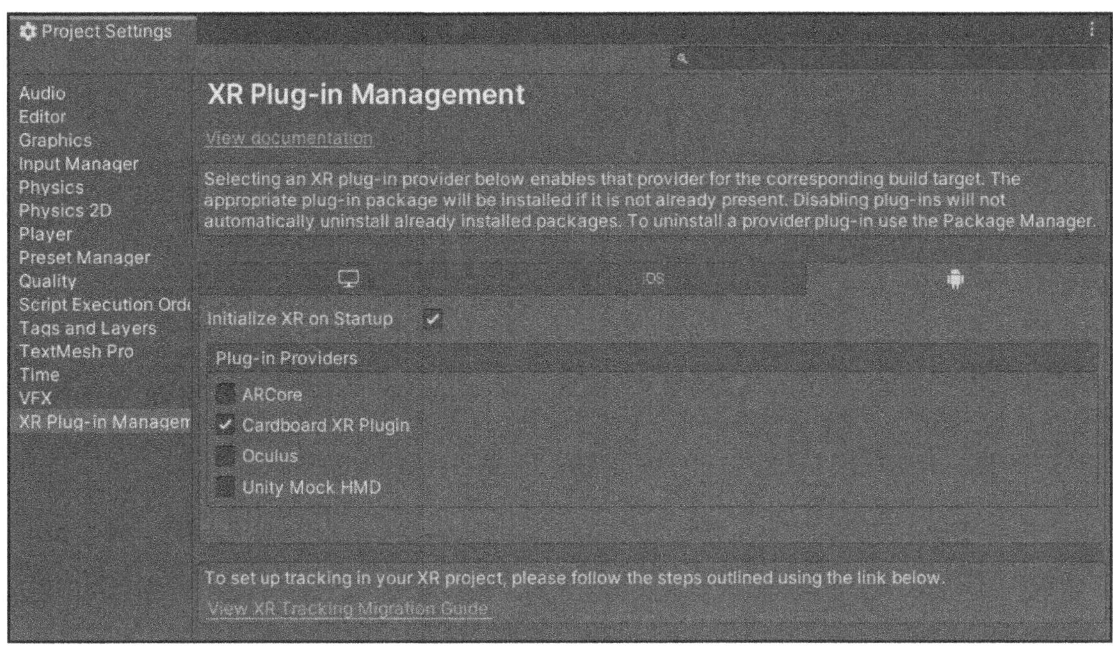

At the time of writing, the Cardboard plugin does not work in the Editor's **Play** mode. (Hopefully, this has been fixed in the current version, `https://github.com/googlevr/cardboard/issues/51`.) Meanwhile, you can install the legacy Google VR package from `https://github.com/googlevr/gvr-unity-sdk/releases` and then add the `GvrEditorEmulator` prefab to your scene. This will allow you to use the *Alt* and *Ctrl* keys on the keyboard to change the camera's orientation with your mouse movements.

Once the plugin has been installed, I recommend that you also install and review the "Hello Cardboard" sample package. In **Package Manager** | **Google Cardboard Plugin for Unity**, select the **Samples** | **Hello Cardboard** | **Import** button. In the installed assets is a sample scene called `HelloCardboard` you should open and try to **Build And Run** to verify your installation is complete and working, after finishing the following settings according to your platform.

The following **Player Settings** pertain to both Android and iOS projects. Open the **Edit | Project Settings | Player** window and do the following:

- In **Player Settings | Resolution and Presentation**, use the following setting:
    - **Default Orientation: Landscape Left**
- In **Player Settings | Splash Image**, use the following setting:
    - **Show Splash Screen**: Uncheck (Unity Plus and Pro only)
- In **Player Settings | Other Settings**, do the following:
    - Specify the company domain under **Package Name**. Note that this defaults to the **Company Name** and **Product Name** fields at the top of the window.

Now, use these settings according to your target platform – Android or iOS.

Targeting Android for Cardboard

To target Android, configure your Unity **Build Settings** to target the Android platform, if it's not already (**File | Build Settings... | Android | Switch Platform**). Ensure your Unity install includes **Android Build Support**, along with the Android SDK and NDK tools and OpenJDK. See the *Installing the Android tools* section earlier in this chapter for more details.

Then, follow the instructions at `https://developers.google.com/cardboard/develop/unity/quickstart` for the specifics. I am not duplicating these instructions here because they are likely subject to change. Note that, currently, these instructions require you to create a **Custom Main Gradle Template** and edit the `mainTemplate.gradle` file in your project.

In the installed assets is a sample scene called `HelloCardboard` that you should open and try to **Build And Run** to verify your installation is complete and working.

Targeting iOS for Cardboard

This section will help you set up your Mac for iOS development from Unity for iPhones. The requirements are not specific to virtual reality; these are the same steps required for anyone building any iOS app from Unity. The process is also well-explained elsewhere, including the Unity documentation at `https://docs.unity3d.com/Manual/iphone-GettingStarted.html`. To participate in Apple's closed ecosystem, you must use a Mac as your development machine to develop for iOS. You will need to do/have the following:

- Have an Apple ID.
- Install Xcode.
- Set up a Provisioning Profile and Signing ID in Xcode.
- Configure the Unity Build Setting Target Platform.
- Configure the Unity Player Settings.

To target iOS, configure your Unity **Build Settings** so that they target the iOS platform, if it's not already (**File** | **Build Settings...** | **iOS** | **Switch Platform**). Ensure you have installed the iOS build modules using Unity Hub. Ensure your Unity install includes **iOS Build Support**. And, of course, you need to be developing on a Mac (OS X) and have Xcode installed (see `https://docs.unity3d.com/Manual/iphone-GettingStarted.html`).

Then, follow the instructions given at `https://developers.google.com/cardboard/develop/unity/quickstart` for the specifics. I am not duplicating the instructions here because they are likely subject to change.

In the installed assets is a sample scene called `HelloCardboard` that you should open and try to **Build And Run** to verify your installation is complete and working. Note that the iOS Cardboard companion app also needs to be installed on your phone so that you can run your Cardboard-based Unity project.

Summary

In this chapter, you set up your system for VR development and built your project for your target platform and devices using the Unity XR Platform features. We discussed the different levels of device integration software and then installed the plugins and packages that are appropriate for your target VR device. While we have summarized the steps, all of these details are well documented in the Unity Manual and on the device providers' sites, so I encourage you to look at the relevant up-to-date documentation as you get started. Be aware that things have changed as of Unity 2019.3+, so be sure you are looking at the documentation pertinent to the version of Unity you are using.

At this point, you should be able to preview your VR scene in Unity Editor's **Play** mode. You should also be able to **Build And Run** your project and install and run it as a binary directly on your device.

In the next chapter, we'll do more work on the Diorama scene and explore the techniques we can use to control objects in virtual reality. From a third-person perspective, we'll interact with objects in the scene (Ethan, the zombie) and implement gaze-based control.

4
Using Gaze-Based Control

Right now, our diorama is a third-person virtual reality experience. When you go into it, you're like an observer or a third-person camera. Sure, you can look around and add controls that let you move the camera's viewpoint. However, any action in the scene is seen from a third-person perspective.

In this chapter, we'll pretty much stay in third-person mode, but we'll get a little more personally involved. We will explore techniques that can be used to control objects in your virtual world by looking and staring. Our character, Ethan, will be under your control, responding to where you look. Furthermore, we'll start programming the Unity scripts. Along the way, we will discuss the following topics:

- Adding AI (artificial intelligence) and a navmesh to our third-person character, Ethan
- Unity programming in C#
- Using your gaze to move a 3D cursor
- Shooting and killing Ethan, the zombie, to good effect

Most introductions to Unity development tip-toe you through the easy stuff and maybe never even get to the more interesting, although more complex, things. We're going to mix things up in this chapter, throwing you into a few different 3D graphics topics, some of which will be a little advanced. If it's new to you, think of this as a survey tutorial. Nonetheless, we'll go through it step by step, so you should be able to follow along and have a lot of fun too!

Technical requirements

To implement the projects and exercises in this chapter, you will need the following:

- A PC or Mac with Unity 2019.4 LTS or later, the XR plugin for your device, and the XR Interaction Toolkit installed
- A VR headset supported by the Unity XR platform

You can access or clone the GitHub repository for this book (`https://github.com/PacktPublishing/Unity-2020-Virtual-Reality-Projects-3rd-Edition-`) to optionally use the following assets and completed projects for this chapter:

- The asset files for you to use in this chapter are located in `UVRP3Files/Chapter-04-Files.zip`.
- All the completed projects for this book are in a single Unity project at `UVRP3Projects`.
- The completed assets and scenes for this chapter are in the `UVRP3Projects/Assets/_UVRP3Assets/Chapter04/` folder.

Adding Ethan, the walker

Gaming is a common application of virtual reality. So, we might as well start out from there, too! We are going to give our character, Ethan, a life of his own. Well, sort of (or not), because he's going to become a zombie!

We left off the Diorama scene at the end of `Chapter 2`, *Understanding Unity, Content, and Scale*, with Ethan hanging out. If, by chance, you skipped that part and don't have Ethan in your Project assets, import the Unity **Standard Assets** package (`https://assetstore.unity. com/packages/essentials/asset-packs/standard-assets-for-unity-2017-3-32351`) by following the instructions in the *Using Unity Legacy Standard Assets* section in `Chapter 2`, *Understanding Unity, Content, and Scale*, in this book. You may need to delete any error scripts (that we won't be using) and convert imported materials into the current render pipeline. We then need to drag a copy of the **ThirdPersonController** version of Ethan from the **Project** `Assets/Standard Assets/Characters/ThirdPerson Character/Prefabs/` folder. When you press **Play**, the Ethan character animates idly; press the *W*, *A*, *S*, and *D* keys on the keyboard to move him around.

Naturally, keyboard input is not appropriate for VR. In the next chapter, `Chapter 5`, *Interacting with Your Hands*, we will go into handheld input controllers. For now, we will consider another way to make him move around; that is, using the direction of your gaze while wearing your VR headset. Before we attempt this, we'll first transform Ethan into a zombie and have him walk around aimlessly without any user control. We'll do this by giving him some AI and writing a script that sends him to random target locations.

AI controllers and *navmesh* are somewhat advanced topics in Unity, but we're going to throw you into it just for fun. Besides, it's not as scary as zombies! Unity uses the term *artificial intelligence* in reference to intelligent pathfinding algorithms. A *navmesh* defines the area that an AI agent is allowed to walk in.

Before we begin, let's make sure we have a scene with an XR camera rig by following these steps:

1. Open the `Diorama` screen we created earlier using **File** | **Open Scene** (or double-click the scene file in the **Project** window's `Scenes/` folder).
2. Add an **XR Rig** using **GameObject** | **XR** | **Stationary XR Rig**.
3. Save the scene with a new name using **File** | **Save As**.

In the following sections, we are going to replace the Ethan third-person controller with an AI version of the controller, then define a position target where he should move to. Then, we'll generate a navigation mesh (navmesh) that defines the allowable walking area.

Artificially intelligent Ethan

To start, we want to replace the `ThirdPersonController` prefab that we used initially with Unity's AI character, `AIThirdPersonController`. We'll do this by inserting the AI version into the scene, copying the transform from the old character, and pasting those values into the new one. Follow these steps to do so:

1. Start by opening the Unity project and Diorama scene we created in `Chapter 2`, *Understanding Unity, Content, and Scale*.
2. In the **Project** window, open the `Standard Assets/Characters/ThirdPersonCharacter/Prefabs` folder and drag `AIThirdPersonController` into the scene. Name it `Ethan`.
3. In the **Hierarchy** window, select the previous `ThirdPersonController` (the old Ethan), if present. Then, in **Inspector**, choose the three-dot icon to the upper right of the **Transform** panel and select **Copy Component**.

4. Select the new `Ethan` object from the **Hierarchy** and on its **Inspector Transform**, choose the three-dot icon and select **Paste Component Values**.
5. Now, you can delete the old `ThirdPersonController` object from the scene (in Hierarchy, **right-click** | **Delete**).

The **Transform** context menu where you can copy/paste the values that were used in these steps can be seen in the following screenshot:

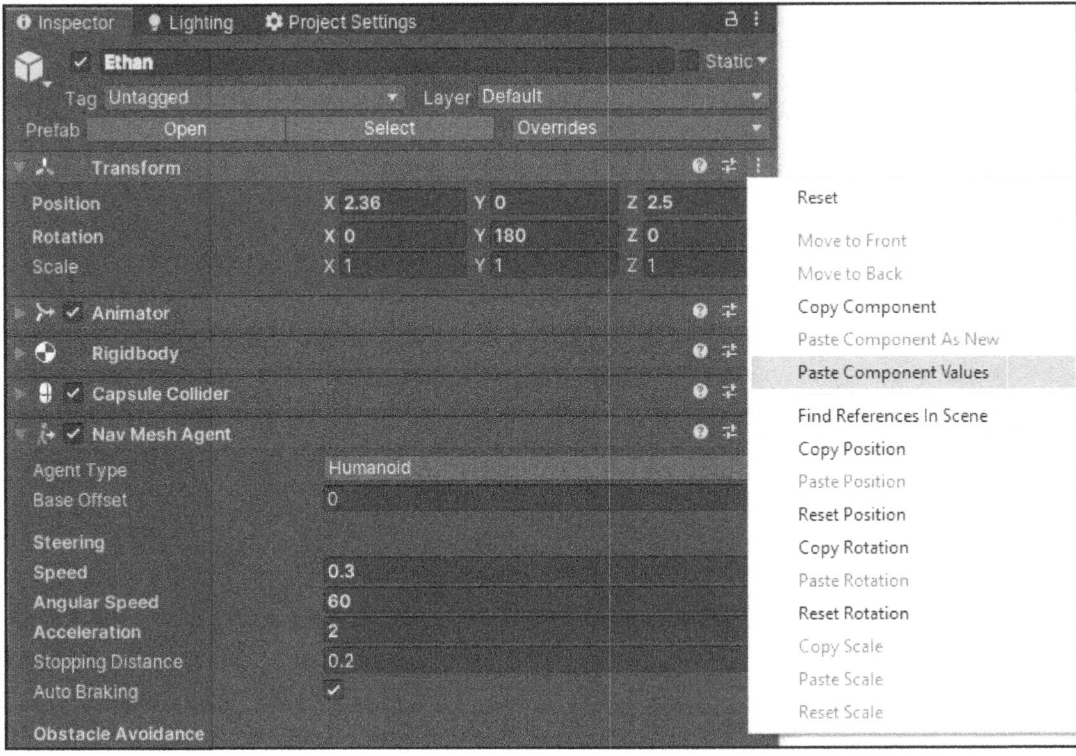

The Ethan object has `Nav Mesh Agent` and `AI Character Control` components. `Nav Mesh Agent` has parameters for how Ethan will move around the scene. On the other hand, `AI Character Control` takes a target object where Ethan will walk to. Let's populate this, as follows:

1. Add an empty game object to the Hierarchy (**GameObject** | **Create Empty**) and rename it `WalkTarget`.
2. Reset its **Transform** values to position (`0,0,0`) (**Transform** | **right-click** | **Reset**).

3. Select Ethan and drag `WalkTarget` into the **Target** property in the **Inspector** panel's **AI Character Control** component, as shown here:

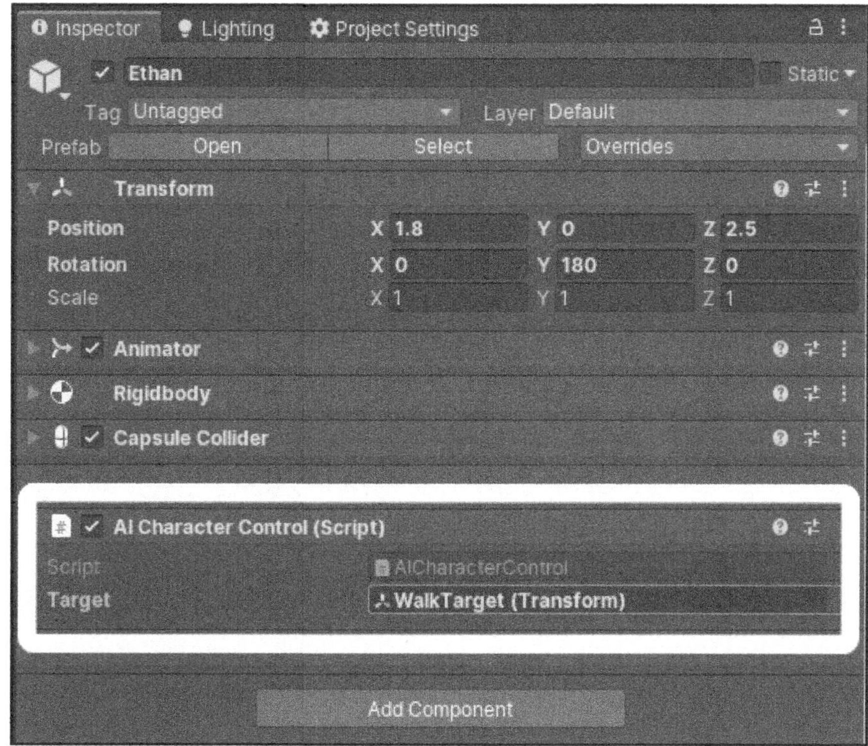

We now have an AI character in the scene (`Ethan`), an empty game object that will be initially used as a navigation target (`WalkTarget`) in the center of our scene, and we told `AI Character Controller` to use this target object. When we run the game, wherever `WalkTarget` is, Ethan will go there. But not yet.

It is common in Unity to use an empty game object just for its Transform component in order to specify a location in your scene. In this case, the WalkTarget's position will be used by the `AI Character Control` component.

Next, we'll add a NavMesh that defines the walkable areas in the scene.

The NavMesh bakery

Ethan cannot just go walking around without being told where he's allowed to roam! We need to define a *navmesh*, a simplified geometrical plane that enables a character to plot its path around obstacles.

In our scene, Ethan is a navmesh agent (he has a `Nav Mesh Agent` component attached). The *navmesh* says where he's allowed to walk. We'll create a navmesh by marking the static objects in the scene that should block navigation and then baking the navmesh. To do this, follow these steps:

1. Open the **Navigation** window (**Window** | **AI** | **Navigation**). The **Navigation** window is shown in the following screenshot.
2. Select its **Object** tab.
3. Select **Ground Plane** in **Hierarchy**. Then, in the **Navigation** window, check the **Navigation Static** checkbox, as shown in the following screenshot. (Alternatively, you can use the object's **Inspector** window **Static** dropdown list.)
4. Repeat *step 3* for each of the objects that should get in his way; for example, in my scene, these are **Crate**, **Ball**, and **UnitCube**.
5. In the **Navigation** window, select the **Bake** tab.
6. Unfold the **Advanced** options and check the **Height Mesh** checkbox (this will prevent Ethan from hovering above the ground).
7. Then, click on the **Bake** button at the bottom of the panel:

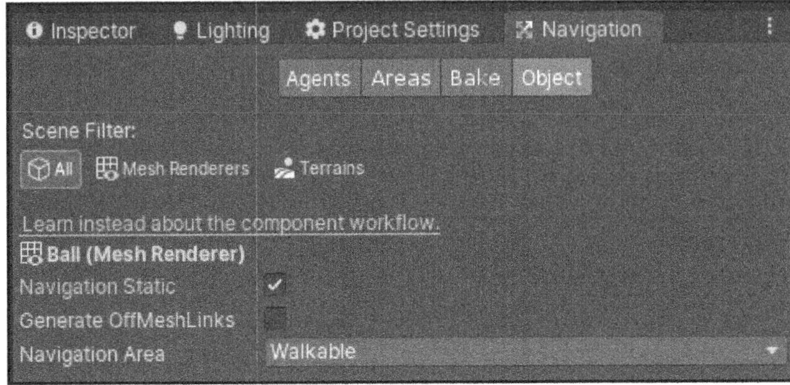

The **Scene** view should now show a blue overlay where the navmesh is defined, as shown in the following screenshot (if you don't see the blue navmesh areas, ensure the **Navigation** window is active, the **Gizmos** button is enabled at the top of your **Scene** window, and the **Show NavMesh** checkbox is checked in the lower-right of the **Scene** window):

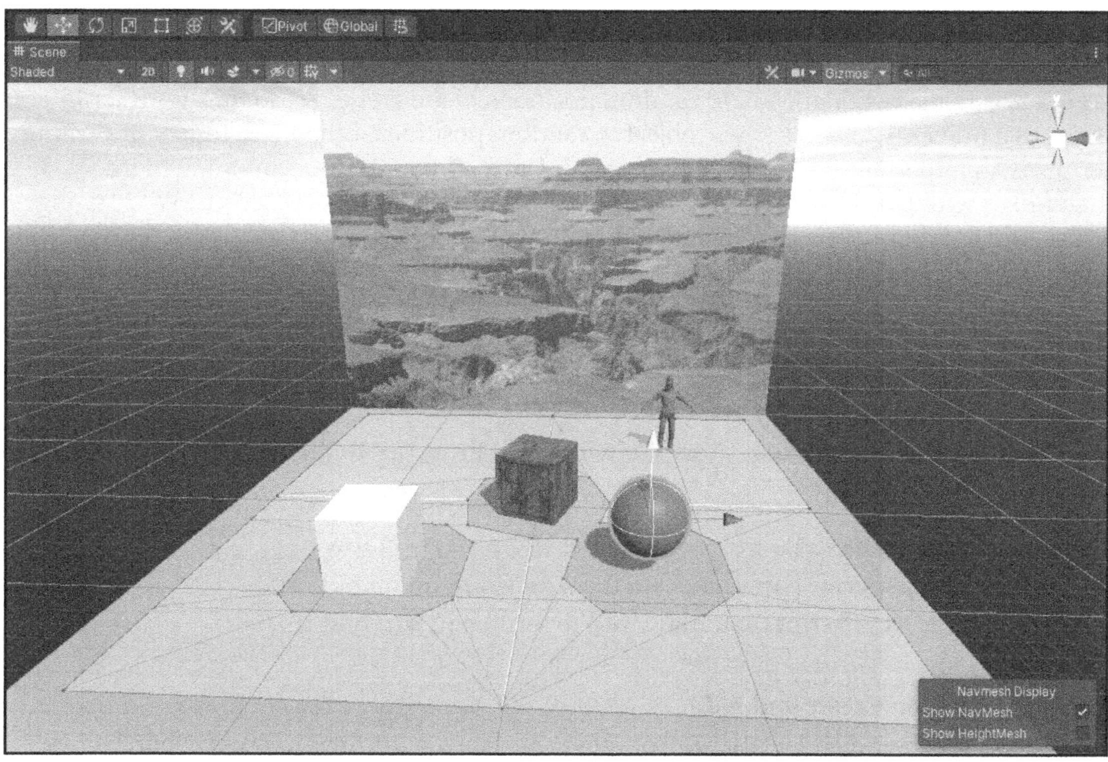

To test this out, follow these steps:

1. Ensure that the **Game** window's **Maximize on Play** setting is not selected.
2. Click on the **Play** button (the triangle at the top of the editor).
3. In the **Hierarchy** window, select the `WalkTarget` object and ensure that the **Translate** gizmo is active in the **Scene** panel (you can use the *W* key shortcut on the keyboard).
4. Now, drag the red (**X-axis**) and/or the blue (**Z-axis**) arrow handles onto the `WalkTarget` object to move it around the floor plane. As you do, Ethan should follow!
5. Click on **Play** again to stop Play mode.

Now, we have Ethan, the nav agent, a navmesh defined in the scene, and a target that Ethan automatically walks toward. Next, we'll write a script that moves the `WalkTarget` object to random places.

Scripting a random walk target

Our goal is to make Ethan walk to random positions in the scene. To do this, we'll write a script that moves the `WalkTarget` object to random positions. Ethan will follow it. Writing scripts is an important part of developing with Unity. If you've done anything more than tinker with Unity, you've probably already written at least some scripts. We're going to use the C# programming language to do this.

If you are new to programming, don't panic! We'll provide a general introduction to Unity scripting at the end of this chapter. You can jump to that now and come back if you wish, or just follow along.

For this first script, we'll take it slow. We will attach the script to the `WalkTarget` object. To do that, follow these steps:

1. Select the `WalkTarget` object in the **Hierarchy** window.
2. In its **Inspector** panel, click on the **Add Component** button.
3. Select **New Script** (you may need to scroll down to find it).
4. Name it `RandomPosition`.
5. Click on **Create and Add**.
6. This should create a script component on the `WalkTarget` object. Double-click on the `RandomPosition` script slot, as shown here, and open it in your code editor (for example, Visual Studio):

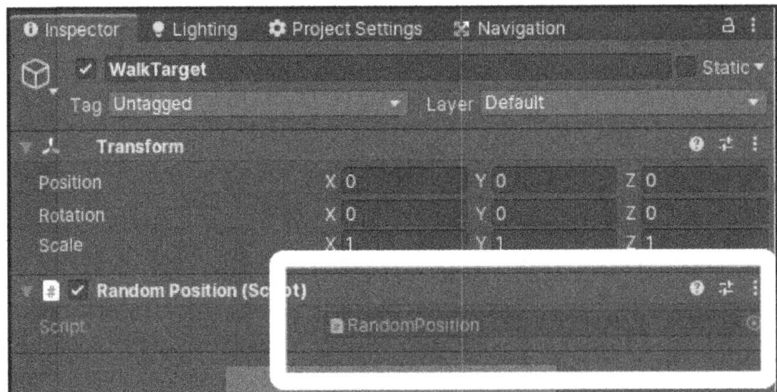

We want to move the `WalkTarget` object to a random location so that Ethan will head in that direction, wait a few seconds, and move the `WalkTarget` object again. That way, he'll appear to be wandering around aimlessly. We can do this with a script. Rather than developing the script incrementally, I'm presenting the finished version first, and we'll go through it line by line. The `RandomPosition.cs` script looks like this. Type or paste the following code into Visual Studio for the `RandomPosition.cs` file:

```
using System.Collections;
using UnityEngine;

public class RandomPosition : MonoBehaviour {
    void Start()     {
        StartCoroutine(RePositionWithDelay());
    }

    IEnumerator RePositionWithDelay() {
        while (true) {
            SetRandomPosition();
            yield return new WaitForSeconds(5f);
        }
    }

    void SetRandomPosition() {
        float x = Random.Range(-5.0f, 5.0f);
        float z = Random.Range(-5.0f, 5.0f);
        Debug.Log("X,Z: " + x.ToString("F2") + ", " +
           z.ToString("F2"));
        transform.position = new Vector3(x, 0.0f, z);
    }
}
```

This script defines a `MonoBehaviour` subclass named `RandomPosition`. The first thing we do when defining a class is declare any variables that we'll be using. A variable is a placeholder for a value. This value can be initialized here or assigned elsewhere, as long as it has a value before the script uses it.

The meat of the script is further down, in the function named `SetRandomPosition()`. Let's see what that does.

As you may recall, the `GroundPlane` plane is 10 units square, with the origin in the middle. So, any (*x*, *z*) location on the plane will be within a range from `-5` to `5` along each axis. The line `float x = Random.Range (-5.0f, 5.0f)` picks a random value within the given range and assigns it to a new `float x` variable. We do the same thing to get a random **z** value.

The line `Debug.Log ("X,Z: " + x.ToString("F2") + ", " + z.ToString("F2"))` prints the `x` and `z` values in the **Console** panel when the game is running. It'll output something like `X, Z: 2.33, -4.02` because `ToString("F2")` says round up to two decimal places. Note that we're using plus (+) signs to combine the parts of the output string.

We actually move the target to the given location with the line `transform.position = new Vector3 (x, 0.0f, z);`. We're setting the transform position of the object that this script is attached to. In Unity, values that have X, Y, and Z coordinates are represented by the `Vector3` objects. So, we create a new one with the `x` and `z` values that we generated. We set `y=0` so that it sits on `GroundPlane`.

The last mysterious bit is how we handle time delays in Unity, which is by using coroutines. A **coroutine** is a piece of code that runs separately from the function in which it was called. This is a somewhat advanced coding technique, but very handy. In our case, the transform position should get changed once every 5 seconds. It's solved in the following ways:

- In the `Start()` function, there's the line `StartCoroutine (RePositionWithDelay());`. This line starts the `RePositionWithDelay()` function in a coroutine.
- Inside the coroutine function, there's a `while (true)` loop, which, as you might have guessed, runs forever (as long as the game object is enabled).
- It calls the `SetRandomPosition()` function, which actually changes the object's position.
- Then, at the bottom of this loop, we do a `yield return new WaitForSeconds (5f);` statement, which basically says to Unity, *hey, go do what you want for 5 seconds and then come back here so that I can go through my loop again.*
- For all of this to work, the `RePositionWithDelay` coroutine must be declared as the `IEnumerator` type (because the documentation says so).

This coroutine/yield mechanism, although an advanced programming topic, is a common pattern in time-sliced programs such as Unity. For more details about coroutines and yield statements, visit the Unity Manual (`https://docs.unity3d.com/Manual/Coroutines.html`) and tutorial (`https://learn.unity.com/tutorial/coroutines`).

Save the script in Visual Studio (**File** | **Save**). We are now good to go. Return to the Unity editor and click on **Play**. Ethan is running from one place to another like a madman! OK, that's pretty random.

As you may have noticed, Ethan seems to be hovering above the ground – or sinking below – the capsule collider. To edit the collider, use the **Edit Collider** button on Ethan's **Capsule Collider** component and adjust the bottom node. Alternatively, you may need to add a **Height Mesh** to the NavMesh. In the **Navigation** window's **Bake** tab, under the **Advanced** options, check the **Height Mesh** checkbox and then **Bake** it again.

In summary, we have added a third-person AI controller to the scene and made him walk around to random positions. The `RandomPosition` script we just wrote moves the target position to random new locations. However, he looks more like a spaceman athlete rather than a zombie. Let's fix that.

"Zombie-izing" Ethan!

The first thing we can do to make Ethan more like a zombie walker is to slow him down to a nice zombie-like pace. Let's adjust the navmesh's steering parameters, as shown in the following steps:

1. Select `Ethan` in **Hierarchy**.
2. In the **Inspector** window, in the **Nav Mesh Agent** component's **Steering** parameters, set the following values:
    - **Speed**: `0.3`
    - **Angular Speed**: `60`

- **Acceleration**: 2:

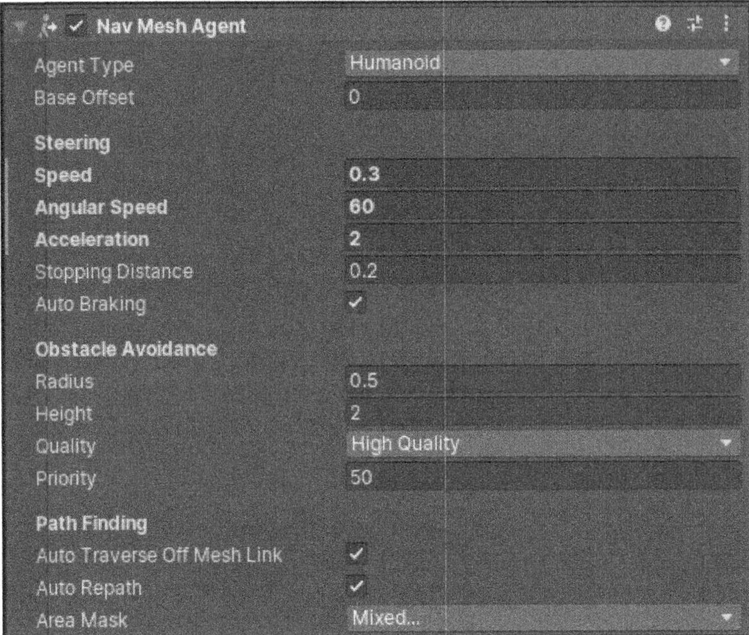

Press the **Play** button again. He has slowed down. That's better. Ethan now walks like a zombie, but he doesn't really look like one yet:

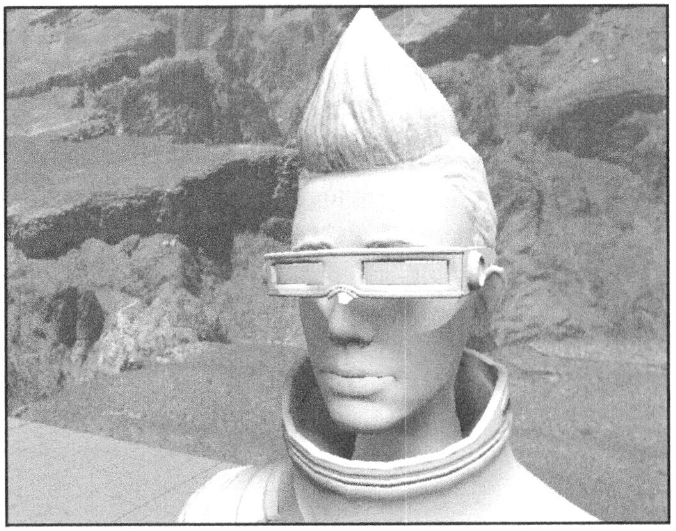

First, he really needs to lose those glasses. To do that, follow these steps:

1. In the **Hierarchy** window, unfold the **Ethan** game object and select **EthanGlasses.**
2. In the **Inspector** window, uncheck the enable checkbox to disable and hide the glasses.

The following screenshot shows Ethan with his glasses hidden:

Next, we'll give him some zombie skin.

Adding a zombie material

To give our Ethan zombie some decaying skin, let's make a copy of his body's material to work with. To do that, follow these steps:

1. In the **Hierarchy** window, select the **EthanBody** object.
2. In the **Inspector** window, click the material (for example, **EthanGray**), which can be found under **Skinned Mesh Renderer** | **Materials** | **Element 0**. That'll highlight the material file in the **Project** window.
3. In **Project**, duplicate the material (with the material file selected, press *Ctrl* + *D* on Windows, or *Cmd* + *D* on Mac).
4. Rename the copy `EthanZombie`.
5. Again, ensure **EthanBody** is selected in **Hierarchy**.

6. Next, drag the **EthanZombie** material from the **Project** window onto the **Materials** | **Element 0** slot, as shown in the following screenshot:

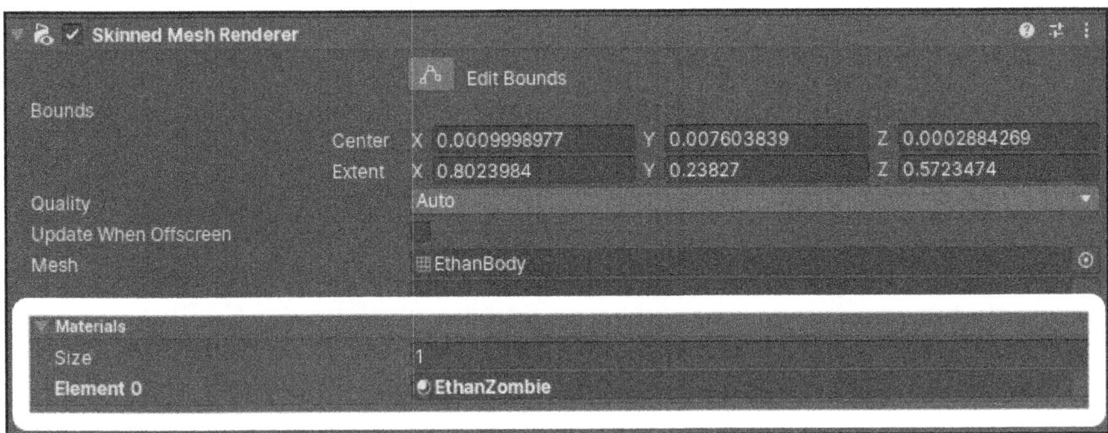

Let's adjust his body's base color from gray to white by following these steps:

1. In the **EthanBody** inspector, unfold the **EthanZombie** material.
2. Click the **Base Map** color swatch (right of the **Base Map** label).
3. Select white (`FFFFFF`).

Now, let's add a zombie face texture to Ethan's face. I have created a zombie face texture for Ethan you can use. It's a texture image named `EthanZombie.png` that's included with this book. Now that you have the file, follow these steps:

1. From the main menu, select **Assets** | **Import New Asset....**
2. Navigate to the files folder with the assets that came with this book.
3. Select the `EthanZombie.png` file and click **Import**. For tidiness, ensure that it resides in the `Assets/Textures` folder. (Alternatively, you can just drag and drop the file from Windows Explorer into the **Project** window.)
4. With **EthanBody** selected in **Hierarchy**, drag the **EthanZombie** texture from **Project** onto the **Base Map** texture chip (left of the **Base Map** label).

His portrait is featured in the following screenshot. *What'd you say? That's not a scary enough zombie??* Well, maybe he's just recently turned. Go ahead and make a better one yourself. Use Blender, Gimp, or Photoshop and paint your own (or even import a whole different zombie humanoid model to replace `EthanBody` itself):

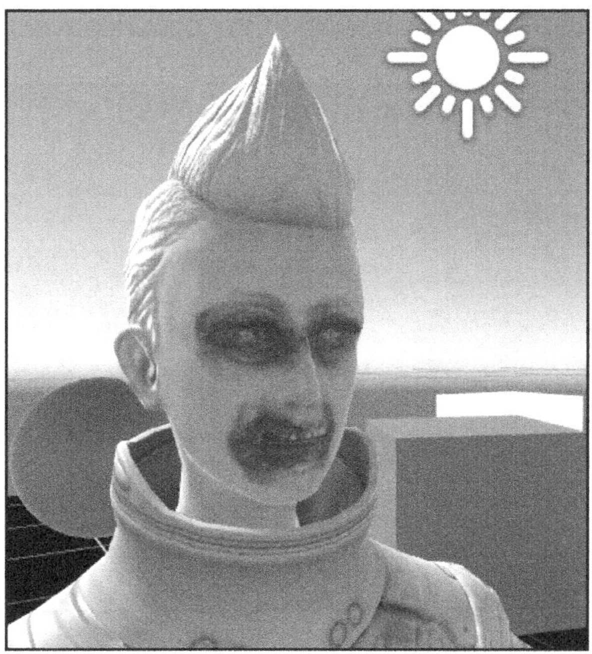

Photoshop, for example, offers 3D tools you can use to edit 3D textures that have been viewed applied to a 3D model mesh (see `https://helpx.adobe.com/photoshop/using/3d-texture-editing.html`). Unity has a built-in tool, PolyBrush, with limited 3D texture painting support. We'll provide a quick introduction to the Unity Polybrush tool next.

Painting models with Polybrush

In this section, we'll go on a tangent (entirely optional) as I'll be giving you a quick introduction to the **Polybrush** package included with Unity. **Polybrush** is a lightweight mesh painting and sculpting tool you can use directly within the Unity editor. It may be sufficient for some zombie skin painting. More about Polybrush can be found at `https://docs.unity3d.com/Packages/com.unity.polybrush@1.0/manual/index.html`.

First, we'll install Polybrush into our project and import its shaders for the Render Pipeline we're using. To install this, follow these steps:

1. Open Package Manager (**Window** | **Package Manager**).
2. Filter the list to **All Packages** (the drop-down list in the top left of the window).
3. Type `polybrush` into the search area and with the package selected, press **Install**.

4. Also, press the **Shader Examples (LWRP)'s Import into Project** button:

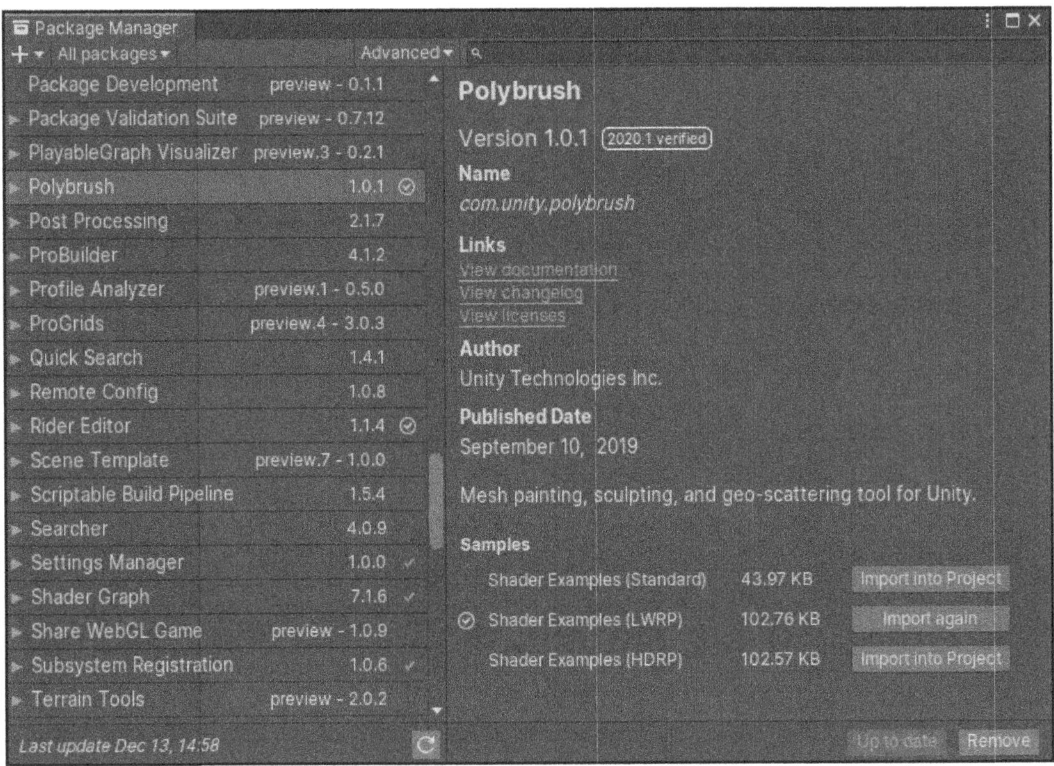

Polybrush requires its own shaders (or ones you've customized for compatibility) for you to edit the texture. Let's change the material's shader to one we imported with Polybrush. If you skipped the previous section, make a copy now of the material you plan to edit. In our case, we're editing the `EthanBody` game object's material. If you have the `EthanZombie.png` texture image, we'll use it as the base map texture. Otherwise, its fair to repurpose the occlusion map one, `EthanOcclusion.png`, which can be found in the `Assets/Standard Assets/Characters/ThirdPersonCharacter/Textures/` folder. To begin, we need to switch shaders in the material and assign the texture image to it, as follows:

1. With **EthanBody** selected, set the material's **Shader** to **Polybrush | Lightweight Render Pipeline | Lit Vertex Color LWRP**.
2. Drag the **EthanZombie** texture onto the material's **Albedo Texture** chip:

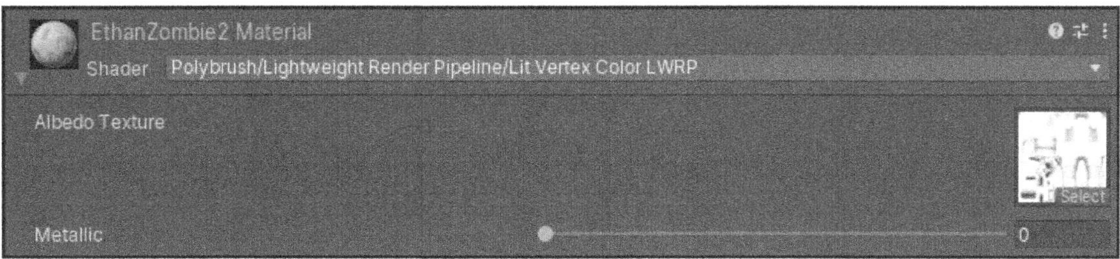

Now, we can begin editing the texture, as follows:

1. Open the **Polybrush** window (**Tools** | **Polybrush** | **Polybrush Window**).
2. Ensure **EthanBody** is the currently selected object in **Hierarchy**.
3. In the **Polybrush** window, adjust the brush radius to **Outer Radius**: `0.01` and **Inner Radius**: `0`.
4. Select the middle tab icon for **Paint Vertex Colors on Meshes**.
5. Select a paint color.
6. Begin painting on the model.

OK, that's an improvement... my new masterpiece-in-progress (haha!) is shown in the following screenshot:

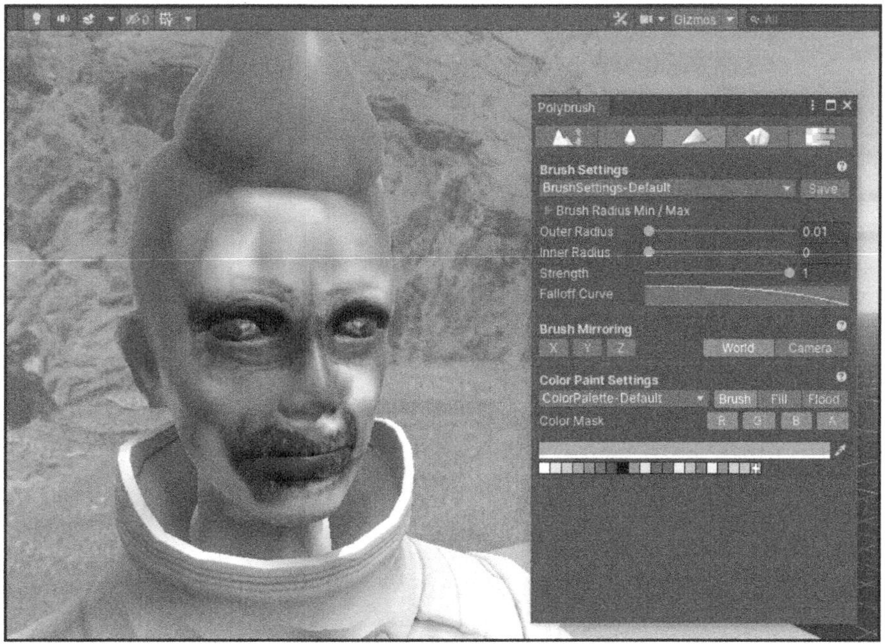

You can now go and build the project and try it in VR. We're participating from a third-person perspective. You can look around and watch what's going on. It's kind of fun, and it's pretty interesting – and it's passive. Now, let's get more active.

In the next part of this project, we'll replace the random walk target with a gaze tracking mechanic so that Ethan will walk to any location we look at with the headset in VR.

Going where I'm looking

For our next objective, instead of being random, we'll send Ethan to wherever you look. As you know, the VR camera object in your scene moves with your head. This means you can tell where on the ground you're looking by drawing a line (a ray) from the camera, in the direction you're looking, until it penetrates the ground plane. The X, Y, Z points at which it hits the ground plane is where we will move **WalkTarget** to.

In Unity, this is accomplished by using ray casting. It's like shooting a ray from the camera and seeing what it hits. Ray casts are detected on objects that have a collider attached to them. In our scene, most of the objects we're using presently are built-in primitive 3D game objects (cube, sphere, and so on), and by default, Unity's 3D primitive game objects have a collider already attached. If you inspect **GroundPlane** in the scene, for example, you will see the following:

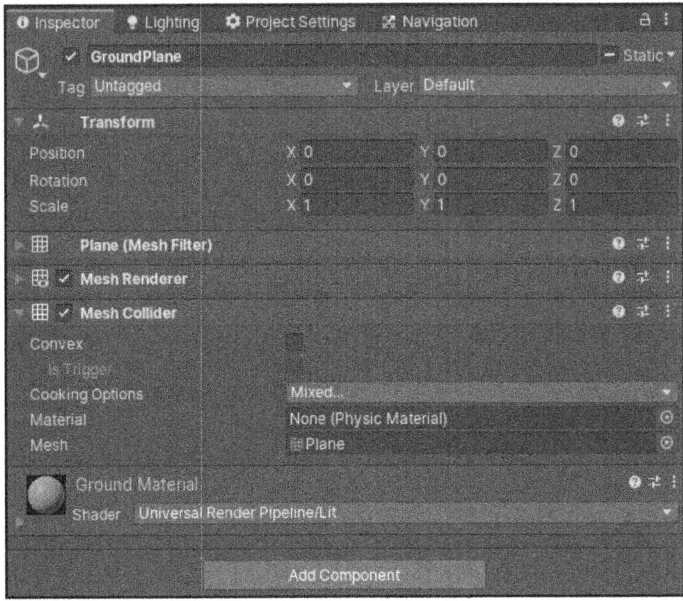

As we'll see in a moment, you can call the Unity `Physics.Raycast` function from a C# script to find a hit point. (For more information, visit `http://docs.unity3d.com/Manual/CameraRays.html`.) Let's write this script now.

The LookMoveTo script

Earlier, we attached the `RandomPosition` script to **WalkTarget** to move it randomly. Now, we'll make a new script that moves the target where you're looking by creating a script named `LookMoveTo` (like we did previously for the `RandomPosition.cs` script), as follows:

1. Select the `WalkTarget` object in **Hierarchy**.
2. In its **Inspector**, click on the **Add Component** button.
3. Select **New Script**.
4. Name it `LookMoveTo`.
5. Click on **Create And Add**.
6. Disable or remove the **RandomPosition** component by unchecking its checkbox, or **right-click** | **Remove Component**.

This should create a script component on the `WalkTarget` object. Double-click on it to open it in your code editor.

This `LookMoveTo` script replaces the `RandomPosition` script we created previously. Disable or remove the `RandomPosition` component of `WalkTarget` before proceeding.

In our script, each time `Update()` is called, we'll read where the camera is pointing to (by using its transform position and rotation), cast a ray in that direction, and ask Unity to tell us where it hits the ground plane. Then, we'll use this location to set the `WalkTarget` object's position. Here's the full `LookMoveTo.cs` script:

```
using UnityEngine;
using System.Collections;

public class LookMoveTo : MonoBehaviour {
    public GameObject ground;

    void Update() {
        Transform camera = Camera.main.transform;
        Ray ray;
        RaycastHit hit;
```

```
        GameObject hitObject;

        Debug.DrawRay(camera.position, camera.rotation *
             Vector3.forward * 100.0f);

        ray = new Ray(camera.position, camera.rotation *
             Vector3.forward);
        if (Physics.Raycast(ray, out hit)) {
            hitObject = hit.collider.gameObject;
            if (hitObject == ground) {
                Debug.Log("Hit (x,y,z): " + hit.point.ToString("F2"));
                transform.position = hit.point;
            }
        }
    }
}
```

Let's go through the script a bit at a time:

```
public GameObject ground;
```

The first thing the script does is declare a variable for the `GroundPlane` object. Since it's `public`, we can use the Unity editor to assign the actual object:

```
void Update () {
  Transform camera = Camera.main.transform;
  Ray ray;
  RaycastHit hit;
  GameObject hitObject;
```

Inside `Update()`, we define a few local variables – `camera`, `ray`, `hit`, and `hitObject` – all of which have data types that are required by the Unity functions that we're going to use. `Camera.main` is the currently active camera object (that is, tagged as `MainCamera`). We get its current transform, which will be assigned to the camera variable:

```
ray = new Ray (camera.position, camera.rotation * Vector3.forward);
```

Ignoring the handy `Debug` statements for a moment, we first determine the ray from the camera using `new Ray()`. A **ray** is a direction vector, defined by a 3D starting point and the direction it's pointing in. Its starting point is a `Vector3` consisting of X, Y, Z coordinates. Its direction is another `Vector3` consisting of the X, Y, Z offset relative to the starting point. To determine the ray of the camera's forward direction, we start with `camera.position` and calculate the forward direction as `camera.rotation * (0, 0, 1)` (in Unity, the `Vector3.forward` constant has a value of `(0,0,1)`):

```
if (Physics.Raycast (ray, out hit)) {
```

Then, we cast the ray and see if it hits anything. If so, the `hit` variable will now contain more details about what was hit, including the specific object in `hit.collider.gameObject` (the `out` keyword means that the `hit` variable value is filled in by the `Physics.Raycast()` function):

```
if (hitObject == ground) {
  transform.position = hit.point;
}
```

We check whether the ray hit the `GroundPlane` object and if so, we'll assign that as the position to move the `WalkTarget` object to the `hit` location.

The compare operator, ==, should not be confused with =, which is the assignment operator.

This script contains two `Debug` statements, which are a useful way to monitor what's going on while a script is running in **Play** mode. `Debug.DrawRay()` will draw the given ray in the **Scene** view so that you can actually see it, while `Debug.Log()` will print the current hit position to the console if there's a hit.

Save the script, switch to the Unity editor, and perform the following steps:

1. With `WalkTarget` selected, in **Inspector**, the `LookMoveTo` script component now has a field for the `GroundPlane` object.
2. From the **Hierarchy** window, select and drag the `GroundPlane` game object onto the **Ground** field.

Save the scene. The script pane looks like this:

Then, click the **Play** button. Ethan should follow our gaze (at his own pace).

In projects with more than a few objects with colliders, in order to optimize the performance of your ray cast, it is advised to place the objects on a specific layer (for example, named `Raycast`) and then add that layer mask to the `Raycast` call. For example, if `Raycast` is layer 5, `int layerMask = 1 << 5`, then `Physics.Raycast(ray, out hit, maxDistance, layerMask);`. See `https://docs.unity3d.com/ScriptReference/Physics.Raycast.html` and `https://docs.unity3d.com/Manual/Layers.html` for details and examples.

For a bit of housecleaning, it's inefficient to ask Unity for the main camera on every update. Rather, it's recommended you do this once at the start of the app and then reference it. Modify your script first by adding the following code:

```
private Transform camera;

void Start() {
    camera = Camera.main.transform;
}
```

Then, remove the line of code that declares `camera` as a local variable in `Update` (remove the line `Transform camera = Camera.main.transform;` from `Update`).

Next, we'll make the interaction a little more user-friendly by adding a visual feedback cursor to the location the user is looking in.

Adding a feedback cursor object

You may have noticed it's not always obvious where your gaze is hitting the ground plane. Due to this, we'll add a cursor to the scene. It's really easy because what we've been doing is moving an invisible, empty `WalkTarget` object along the ground. Let's add an object to make it visible. Follow these steps:

1. In **Hierarchy**, right-click the **WalkTarget** object and select **3D Object** | **Cylinder**. This will create a cylindrical object parented by `WalkTarget`. Rename it `CursorDisk`.
2. Reset its transform (in **Inspector**, **right-click Transform** | **Reset**).
3. Change its **Scale** to (`0.4`, `0.05`, `0.4`). This will create a flat disk with a diameter of `0.4`.

4. Disable its **Capsule Collider** by unchecking that checkbox. We don't need to use its physics.
5. As a performance optimization, in **Mesh Renderer**, you can also disable **Cast Shadows**, **Light Probes**, and **Reflection Probes** (set them to **Off**).

Now, click **Play** again. You will see that the cursor disk follows your gaze.

If you want, decorate the disk with a material (in the **Project** window, **right-click** | **Create** | **Material**, name it `WalkTarget Material`, and drag it onto the **CursorDisk** object). Then, find an appropriate texture. For example, there is a texture named `Grid` in Standard Assets (in the **WalkTarget** material's **Base Map**, click **doughnut-icon**, and search for `grid` to select that texture). The **WalkTarget** cylindrical cursor disk with a cross-hair texture is shown in the following screenshot:

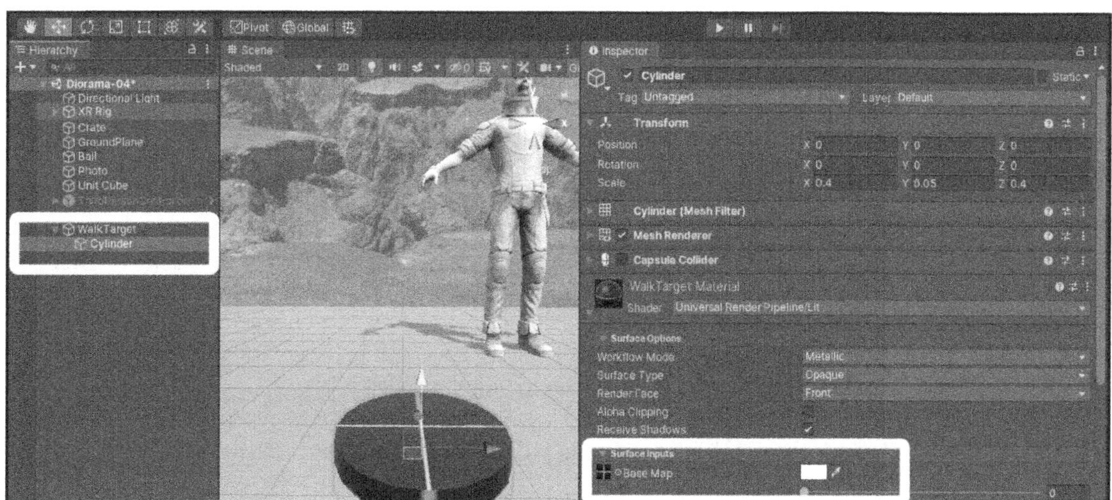

For adding a gaze-based reticle cursor, such as a gun sight that follows where you're looking, using the XR Interaction Toolkit, see the corresponding topic in `Chapter 6`, *Canvasing the World Space UI*.

So far, we've got Ethan to follow where we're looking by moving the **WalkTarget** object to a position on **GroundPlane** that's determined by raycasting from the camera and seeing where it intersected that plane.

Observing through obstacles

You may have noticed that the cursor seems to get *stuck* when we slide our gaze over other solid objects, such as the crate and ball. That's because the **physics engine** has determined which object is hit first, never getting to the ground plane.

In our script, we have the `if (hitObject == ground)` conditional statement before `WalkTarget`. Without it, the cursor would float over any object in a 3D space where the ray cast hits something. Sometimes, that's interesting, but in our case, it isn't. We want to keep the cursor on the ground. However, now, if the ray hits something other than the ground, it doesn't get repositioned and seems *stuck*. Can you think of a way around this? Here's a hint: look up `Physics.RaycastAll`. Alright; I'll show you. Replace the body of `Update()` with the following code:

```
void Update()
{
    Transform camera = Camera.main.transform;
    Ray ray;
    RaycastHit[] hits;
    GameObject hitObject;

    Debug.DrawRay(camera.position, camera.rotation *
       Vector3.forward * 100.0f);

    ray = new Ray(camera.position, camera.rotation *
       Vector3.forward);
    hits = Physics.RaycastAll(ray);
    for (int i = 0; i < hits.Length; i++)
    {
        RaycastHit hit = hits[i];
        hitObject = hit.collider.gameObject;
        if (hitObject == ground)
        {
            Debug.Log("Hit (x,y,z): " + hit.point.ToString("F2"));
            transform.position = hit.point;
        }
    }
}
```

On calling `RaycastAll`, we get back a list (a C# array) of hits. Then, we loop through each one looking for a ground hit anywhere along the path of the ray vector. When you press **Play**, our cursor will trace along the ground, regardless of whether there's another object in between.

Extra challenge: Another more efficient solution is to use the *layer system*. Create a new layer, assign it to the plane, and pass it as an argument to `Physics.raycast()`. Can you see why that's much more efficient?

Making a look-to-kill system

We've got this far, so we might as well try to kill the zombie, right? (haha!). Here are the specifications for this new feature:

- Looking at Ethan hits him with our line-of-sight raygun.
- Sparks are emitted when the gun hits its target.
- After 3 seconds of being hit, Ethan is killed.
- When he's killed, Ethan explodes (we get a point) and then he respawns at a new location.

Again, if you're new to programming, it's OK to just follow along and copy/paste the code. Alternatively, you can use a completed copy of these scripts, which can found in the download files for this book from the publisher. I will try to include a little explanation for each line of code as we go through it. The first thing we'll do is write a script, named `KillTarget`, which will kill Ethan when the user stares at him. Then, we'll add some visual effects, using the Unity particle system, to show when Ethan is being hit and killed.

The KillTarget script

This time, we'll attach the script to a new empty **GameManager** object by performing the following steps:

1. Create an empty game object and name it `GameManager`.
2. Using **Add Component**, attach a new C# script to it named `KillTarget`.
3. Open the script for editing.

Here's the completed `KillTarget.cs` script:

```
using System.Collections;
using System.Collections.Generic;
using UnityEngine;

public class KillTarget : MonoBehaviour {
    public GameObject target;
```

```
public ParticleSystem hitEffect;
public GameObject killEffect;
public float timeToSelect = 3.0f;
public int score;

Transform camera;
private float countDown;

void Start() {
    camera = Camera.main.transform;
    score = 0;
    countDown = timeToSelect;
}
```

The script continues, as follows:

```
void Update()
{
    bool isHitting = false;
    Ray ray = new Ray(camera.position, camera.rotation *
        Vector3.forward);
    RaycastHit hit;

    if (Physics.Raycast(ray, out hit))
    {
        if (hit.collider.gameObject == target)
        {
            isHitting = true;
        }
    }

    if (isHitting)
    {
        if (countDown > 0.0f)
        {
            // on target
            countDown -= Time.deltaTime;
            // print (countDown);
            hitEffect.transform.position = hit.point;
            if (hitEffect.isStopped)
            {
                hitEffect.Play();
            }
        }
        else
        {
            // killed
            Instantiate(killEffect, target.transform.position,
```

```
                target.transform.rotation);
            score += 1;
            countDown = timeToSelect;
            SetRandomPosition();
        }
    }
    else
    {
        // reset
        countDown = timeToSelect;
        hitEffect.Stop();
    }
}
```

Finally, add the last function for the script, `SetRandomPosition`, as follows:

```
void SetRandomPosition() {
        float x = Random.Range(-5.0f, 5.0f);
        float z = Random.Range(-5.0f, 5.0f);
        target.transform.position = new Vector3(x, 0.0f, z);
    }
}
```

Let's go through this. First, we declare a number of public variables, as follows:

```
public GameObject target;
public ParticleSystem hitEffect;
public GameObject killEffect;
public float timeToSelect = 3.0f;
public int score;
```

Like we did in the previous `LookMoveTo` script, we are going to look at a target. However, in this case, the target is Ethan, and rather than move something, we're going to activate a particle effect (`hitEffect`) to show that he's being shot. We're also adding a `killEffect` explosion and a countdown timer, `timeToSelect`. Lastly, we'll keep `score` of our kill count.

The `Start()` method, which is called at the start of the gameplay, initializes the score to zero and sets the `countDown` timer to its starting value.

Then, in the `Update()` method, like in the `LookMoveTo` script, we cast a ray from the camera and check whether it hits our target, Ethan. In this code, we use a local `isHitting` variable to know if it's a hit.

When it hits, we check the `countDown` timer. If the timer is still counting, we decrement its value by the amount of time that's gone by since the last time `Update()` was called, using `Time.deltaTime`, and make sure that `hitEffect` is emitting at the hit point. If the ray is still on its target and the timer is done counting down, Ethan will be killed. He explodes, we bump up the score by one, we reset the timer to its starting value, and move (respawn) Ethan to a random new location.

For an explosion, we'll use one of Unity's standard assets, which can be found in the `ParticleSystems` package. To activate it, `killEffect` should be set to the prefab named `Explosion`. Then, the script *instantiates* it. In other words, it makes it an object in the scene (at a specified transform), which kicks off its awesome scripts and effects.

Lastly, if the ray did not hit Ethan, we reset the counter and turn off the particles.

Save the script and open the Unity Editor.

Extra challenge: Refactor the script so that it uses coroutines to manage the delay timing, as we did in the `RandomPosition` script at the start of this chapter.

Next, we'll add some visual effects to the scene by providing an introduction to Unity's particle system.

Adding particle effects

Unity's particle system allows us to generate lots of particles with small lifespans that are used to create many varied visual effects, including fire, explosions, sparkles, smoke, water, and more. For a single effect, hundreds of tiny particles can be generated, moving in prescribed directions and velocity, changing size and color over time, and quickly "burning out." Unity's legacy Particle System is a component that you add to an object in the scene with dozens of parameters for defining the behavior of the effect. We'll look into that now for our shoot and kill effects.

Unity has recently introduced its next-generation visual effects editor, **VFX Graph**. It includes a graph node visual editor for creating, editing, and testing particle systems and even more complex behaviors. It can provide much better performance than the legacy particle systems as the computation has been moved from the CPU to the GPU. We will use VFX Graph in a later project in this book.

Now, to populate the `public` variables, we will perform the following steps:

1. Select **GameManager** from **Hierarchy** and go to the **Kill Target (Script)** pane in **Inspector**.
2. Drag the **Ethan** object from **Hierarchy** onto the **Target** field.
3. From the main menu bar, navigate to **GameObject** | **Effects** | **Particle System** and name it `SparkEmitter`.
4. Reselect **GameManager** and drag **SparkEmitter** onto the **Hit Effect** field.

We created a default particle system that will be used as the spark emitter. Now, we need to set that up to our liking. I'll get you started. You can play with it as you desire, as follows:

1. Select **SparkEmitter** from the **Hierarchy** panel. You'll see it playing in the **Scene** window.
2. In its **Inspector**, under **Particle System**, set the following values:
    - **Start Size**: `0.15`
    - **Start Color**: Pick a red/orange color
    - **Start Lifetime**: `0.3`
    - **Start Speed**: `0.3`
    - **Max Particles**: `50`
3. Under **Emission**, set **Rate over Time**: `100`
4. Under **Shape**, set **Shape**: **Sphere** and **Radius**: `0.01`

This will spray a bunch of fire-colored particles at the hit location when Ethan is hit.

For the **Kill Effect**, we're going to use a premade explosion effect from Standard Assets. If you don't have them, please import the Unity **Standard Assets** package (`https://assetstore.unity. com/packages/essentials/asset-packs/standard-assets-for-unity-2017-3-32351`) by following the instructions in the *Using Unity Legacy Standard Assets* section in `Chapter 2`, *Understanding Unity, Content, and Scale* of this book. Now, let's add an explosion. Follow these steps:

1. In the **Project** window, find the `Explosion` prefab in `Standard Assets/ParticleSystems/Prefabs`.
2. Drag the `Explosion` prefab onto the **GameManager** | **Kill Target** | **Kill Effect** field.

The script pane looks as follows:

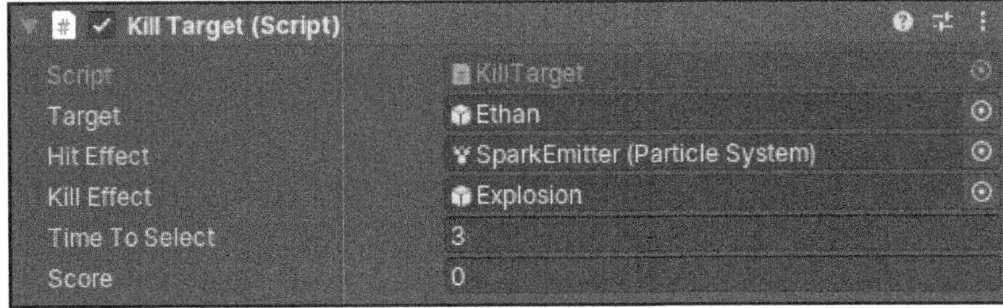

If you'd like to experiment with the standard particle prefab's settings, duplicate the prefab in the Project Assets first and modify your own working copy. Just be sure to remember to reference your version in the **Kill Target** effects slots instead.

Here's what my **Scene** view looks like as I run **Play** mode and zap Ethan in the chest:

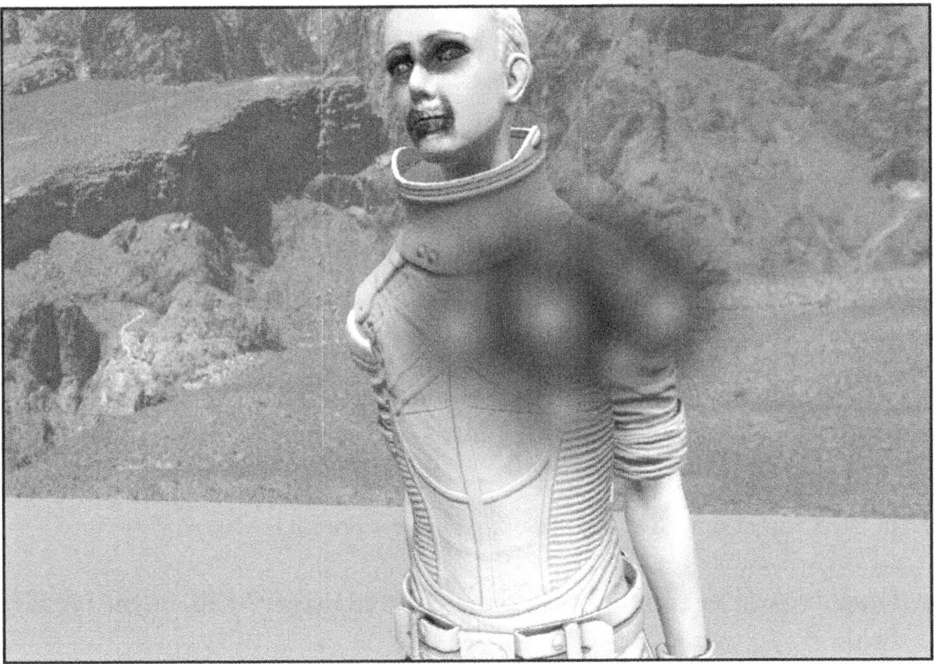

When Ethan is shot, the `hitEffect` particle system is activated. After 3 seconds (or whatever value you set in the `TimeToSelect` variable), his *health* is depleted, the explosion effect is instantiated, the score is incremented, and he respawns at a new location. In `Chapter 6`, *Canvasing World Space UI*, we'll see how we can show the current score to the player. That chapter also implements a gaze-based reticle cursor.

(If you find it annoying for your gaze to be doing double-duty with both **Kill Target** and **Look Move To**, you can disable the **Look Move To** component and enable the **Random Position** one we wrote earlier instead).

One last thing before we're done: let's clean up the `Assets` folder a bit and move all the scripts into an `Assets/Scripts/` subfolder. Follow these steps to do so:

1. Select the `Assets/` folder in the **Project** window.
2. Create a new folder (**right-click** | **Create** | **Folder**) and name it `Scripts`.
3. Finally, drag each of the scripts we created in this chapter into it.

There it is – we've accomplished a lot in this chapter using some really fun and interesting features of Unity, including AI and navmeshes, particle effects, and, of course, C# programming. In the next section, I'll provide a more structured but brief introduction to C# programming for Unity.

Introducing Unity C# programming

As we just saw, Unity does a lot of things: it manages objects, renders them, animates them, calculates the physics of those objects, and so on. Unity itself is a program. It's made of code; probably a lot of good code written by some very smart people. This internal Unity code can be accessed by you, the game developer, through the Unity Editor point-and-click interface that we've already been using. Within the Unity Editor, scripts are manifested as configurable components. However, it's also made more directly accessible to you through the Unity scripting API.

Application Programming Interface (**API**) refers to public software functions that you can access from your own scripts. Unity's API is very rich and nicely designed. That's one reason why people have written amazing applications and plugin add-ons for Unity.

There are many programming languages in the world. Unity has chosen to support the C# language from Microsoft. Programming languages have a specific syntax that must be obeyed. Otherwise, the computer will not understand your script. In Unity, script errors (and warnings) appear in the **Console** window of the editor, as well as in the bottom footer of the editor window.

The default script editor for Unity is Microsoft's Visual Studio. It has some powerful features such as coding suggestions that pop up as you type, automatic formatting rules, and easy-to-use cross-referencing for symbols in your project. The editor understands the C# language, the Unity API and docs, and details about your own Unity project (see IntelliSense at `https://docs.microsoft.com/en-us/visualstudio/ide/using-intellisense` for more information).

C# scripts are text files that are named with a `.cs` extension. In a Unity C# script, some of the words and symbols are a part of the C# language itself, some come from the Microsoft .NET Framework, and others are provided by the Unity API. And then there's the code that you write.

Be aware that the script's filename must match the class name declared in the script. When you create a new script, Unity automatically sets the class name the same as the initial filename. If you rename one, you must rename the other so that they match. Likewise, the script file name must only use valid C# symbol characters, for example, no spaces, dashes, or other special characters (except underscores), and must begin with an alphabetic character.

An empty default Unity C# script looks like this:

```
using System.Collections;
using System.Collections.Generic;
using UnityEngine;

public class DoSomething : MonoBehaviour {
    // Start is called before the first frame update
    void Start() {
    }

    // Update is called once per frame
    void Update() {
    }
}
```

Let's dissect it. The first two lines indicate that this script needs some other stuff to run. The `using` keyword belongs to the C# language. The line using `UnityEngine` says that we'll be using the `UnityEngine` API. The line using `System.Collections` says that we might need to use a library of functions named `Collections` to access lists of objects.

In C#, each line of code ends with a semicolon. Double slashes (`//`) indicate comments in the code, and anything from there to the end of that line will be ignored.

This Unity script defines a class named `DoSomething`. **Classes** are like code templates with their own variable properties and behavior functions. Classes derived from the `MonoBehaviour` base class are recognized by Unity and used when your game runs. The line `public class DoSomething: MonoBehaviour` basically says *we are defining a new public class named* `DoSomething`*, which inherits all the abilities of the* `MonoBehaviour` *Unity base class*, including the capabilities of the `Start()` and `Update()` functions. The body of the class is enclosed in a pair of curly braces (`{ }`).

When an object, function, or variable is `public`, it can be seen by other code outside this specific script file. When it's `private`, it can only be referenced within this file. We want Unity to see the `DoSomething` class.

Classes define variables and functions. A **variable** holds data values of a specific type, such as `float`, `int`, `Boolean`, `GameObject`, `Vector3`, and so on. **Functions** implement logic (step-by-step instructions). Functions can receive *arguments* – variables enclosed in a parenthesis used by its code – and can return new values when they're done. Numeric `float` constants, such as `5.0f`, require an `f` at the end in C# to ensure that the data type is a *simple* floating-point value and not a *double-precision* floating-point value.

Unity will automatically call some special functions if you've defined them. `Start()` and `Update()` are two examples. Empty versions of these are provided in the default C# script. The data type in front of a function indicates the type of value that's returned. `Start()` and `Update()` do not return values, so they're `void`.

Each `Start()` function from all the `MonoBehaviour` scripts in your game is called before the gameplay begins when the attached game object is created. It's a good place for data initialization. All the `Update()` functions are called during each time slice, or frame, while the game is running. This is where most of the action lies.

Once you've written or modified a script in the Visual Studio editor, remember to save it. Then, switch to the Unity Editor window. Unity will automatically recognize that the script has changed and will reimport it. If errors are found, they will report them right away in the **Console** window.

This is just a cursory introduction to Unity programming. As we work through the projects in this book, I will explain additional bits as they're introduced.

Summary

In this chapter, we explored the relationship between the VR camera and objects in the scene. First, we made Ethan (the zombie) walk randomly around the scene and enabled him to move by using a **NavMesh**, but then we directed his wanderings using a 3D cursor on the **X**, **Z** ground plane. This cursor follows our gaze as we look at new locations on **GroundPlane** in virtual reality. Lastly, we also used our gaze to shoot a ray at Ethan, causing him to lose health and eventually explode. These look-based techniques can be used in non-VR games, but in VR, it's very common and almost essential. We'll be using them more in the later chapters of this book too.

In this chapter, you learned and used more features of Unity, all of which are very important for VR development. We used several different built-in components that control the behavior of game objects, including **NavMesh** and **Particle Systems**. We modified **Materials** and **Textures**, including painting with **PolyBrush**. Finally, we created our own components from C# scripts, including the `RandomPosition`, `LookMoveTo`, and `KillTarget` scripts.

In the next chapter, we will use our hands to interact with the virtual scene. We'll learn how to use the Unity XR input system for tracking the hand controller and detecting button presses, as well as using the XR Interaction Toolkit.

5
Interacting with Your Hands

When we're in a virtual world with all this cool stuff, it is in our nature to try to reach out and touch something. While the gaze-based selection that we used in the previous chapter is a good first step for interacting with virtual scenes, most people intuitively want to use their hands. Most VR devices provide a hand controller to select, grab, and interact with virtual objects in the scene.

In this chapter, we introduce practices for capturing user input in Unity, illustrating how to use them in a simple VR scene. Everyone loves balloons, so in this project, we will make balloons. We may even pop a few. We will continue with our work in the previous chapter, using C# programming for basic scripting, and exploring several software design patterns for user input. We will discuss the following topics:

- Polling for input device button presses
- Invoking and subscribing to Unity events
- Using the XR Interaction Toolkit and interactable components

For this project, we'll build a fun little balloon gun for creating and inflating balloons and releasing them to float up into the sky. And at the end, we will add a projectile ball that you can throw at a balloon to pop it! Let's begin by setting up a simple scene.

Technical requirements

To implement the projects and exercises in this chapter, you will need the following:

- PC or Mac with Unity 2019.4 LTS or later, XR Plugin for your device, and the XR Interaction Toolkit installed
- A VR headset supported by Unity XR platform

You can access or clone the GitHub repository for this book (`https://github.com/PacktPublishing/Unity-2020-Virtual-Reality-Projects-3rd-Edition-`) to optionally use assets and completed projects for this chapter as follows:

- Asset files for you to use in this chapter are located in `UVRP3Files/Chapter-05-Files.zip`.
- All completed projects in this book are in a single Unity project at `UVRP3Projects`.
- The completed assets and scenes for this chapter are in the `UVRP3Projects/Assets/_UVRP3Assets/Chapter05/` folder.

Setting up the scene

To begin our exploration of input mechanisms, let's set up our scene. The plan is to let players create balloons. Everyone loves balloons!

For this scene, you could start with a new scene (**File** | **New Scene**) and then add an **XR Rig** from the **GameObject** | **XR** menu. Instead, I've decided to start with the **Diorama** scene used in the previous chapter and remove all but the **GroundPlane** and **PhotoPlane**, as follows:

1. Open the **Diorama** scene.
2. Remove all the objects, except for **XR Rig, XR Interaction Manager, Directional Light, GroundPlane** and **PhotoPlane**.
3. Position the **XR Rig** a few feet from the scene origin, **Position** (`0, 0, -1`).
4. Select **File** | **Save Scene As** and give it a name, such as `Balloons`.

Now that the scene stage is set, we are first going to define a balloon game object, make it a prefab, and add an empty controller object in the hierarchy and script that will instantiate the balloon prefab.

Defining a balloon game object

For the balloon, you can simply use a standard Unity sphere 3D primitive if you want, or you can find an object in the Unity Asset Store or elsewhere. We are using a low poly balloon object that I found on Google Poly (`https://poly.google.com/view/a01Rp51l-L3`) (created by Louis DeScioli), a copy of which is provided with the download files for this chapter under the name `BalloonModel.fbx`. Generally, I recommend using the FBX format version of a model when it's available, as Unity provides native support and it includes materials.

Google Poly (`https://poly.google.com/`) is a website created by Google for you to browse, distribute, and download 3D objects. Poly Toolkit is a Unity package that lets you browse and import Poly objects directly within Unity, available for free on the Asset Store (`https://assetstore.unity.com/packages/templates/systems/poly-toolkit-104464`).

Import the model into your project. If you're using the one provided with this book, then please go through the following steps:

1. Create an asset folder named `Models` (in the **Project** window, right-click **Create** | **Folder** and name it).
2. By dragging and dropping, locate the `BalloonModel.fbx` file in Windows Explorer (or Finder on OSX), and drag it into the **Models** folder you just created. Alternatively, with the **Models** folder selected, navigate to **Assets** | **Import New Asset** from the main menu.

Now, when we add the model to the scene, we're going to *parent the object* (make it a child of another object) and adjust its position so that the bottom of the balloon model becomes its origin (pivot point), as follows:

1. In **Hierarchy**, create an empty object (**+** | **Create Empty**, as shown in the following screenshot) and name it `Balloon`.
2. Reset its transform (**Transform** | **3-dot-icon** | **Reset**).
3. Drag the balloon model into the **Hierarchy** as a child object of **Balloon** (for example, from the `Assets/Models/` folder).

4. In the **Scene** window, use the **Move Tool** to adjust the position of the model so that it sits with its bottom aligned with the origin of its parent, such as (`0, 0.5, 0`). See the following screenshot to see what we're trying to accomplish. If you are using the original model downloaded from Google Poly, I found the **Position** (`0.66, -0.54, 0.1`) works well. If you have the version of `BalloonModel` included with this book, then it is already recentered (I used Blender, which you can get from `https://www.blender.org/`), so adjustment may not be necessary.
5. If you do not have a balloon model, then use a sphere (**Create | 3D Object | Sphere**) and add a material, like the **Red Material** we created in the previous chapter.

Note that to create the game object you can use the **GameObject** menu in the main menu bar or use the **+** create menu in the **Hierarchy** window:

Why are we parenting the model under an empty GameObject? To adjust the relative origin (pivot point) of an object, you can make it a child of an empty game object; however, it may not be clear in the **Scene** window where the origin of that empty object is. A trick I use is to add a small, temporary child object as a reference marker—for example, add a cube scaled to `0.05` and positioned at `(0,0,0)` as a sibling of the balloon model. Then move the balloon to that marker.

The current scene and hierarchy are shown in the following image, with the Balloon game object at the origin. Note that the balloon's local origin (pivot point) is at the bottom of the balloon:

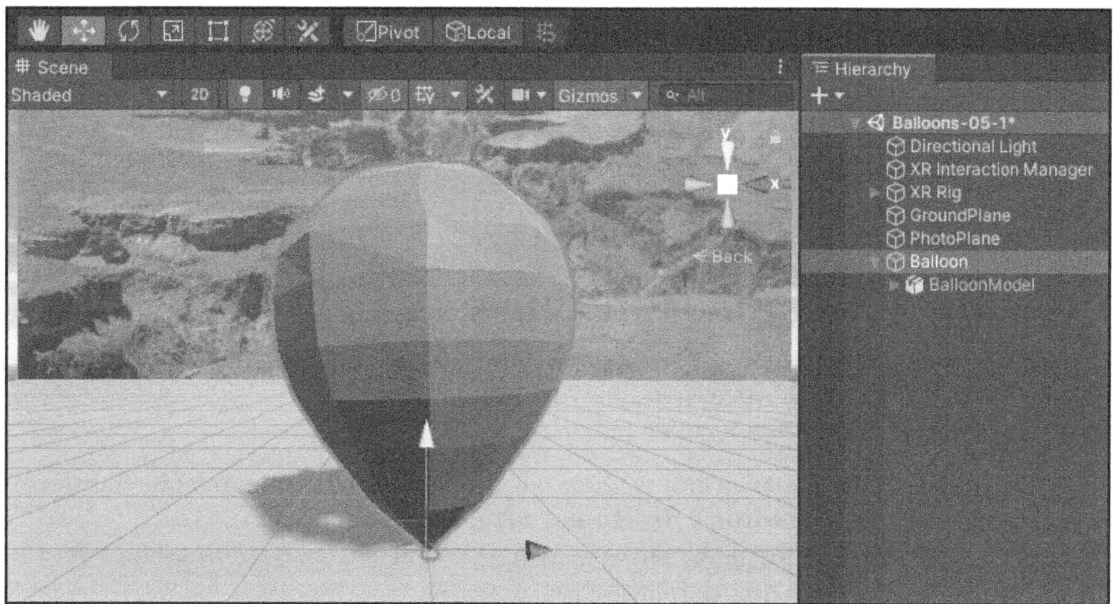

Let's continue to work on our balloon so we can instantiate multiple balloons in the scene by making it into a prefab.

Making the balloon prefab

Our intent is to instantiate new balloons from a prefab when our user presses a button on their controller. When the button is released, the balloon is released and floats away.

Let's scale and position the balloon in the scene at a starting size and workable distance. We're going to expect the balloon to float into the sky when you release it, so we'll also give it some physics properties by adding a `RigidBody` component. But unlike heavy objects, we do not want it to fall to the ground because of gravity, so we are going to disable gravity. Instead, we'll make it float by applying an upward force with our own script later in this project.

Add a Rigidbody and make the object a prefab, as follows:

1. Select your **Balloon** object in **Hierarchy**.
2. From the main menu, **Component** | **Physics** | **Rigidbody**.
3. Uncheck the Rigidbody's **Use Gravity** checkbox.

4. Drag the **Balloon** object from the **Hierarchy** to the **Project** window into your `Prefabs/` folder to make it a prefab object.
5. Delete the original **Balloon** object from the **Hierarchy**.

Next, we'll create a Balloon Controller for handling the user interaction with balloons in the scene.

Creating a Balloon Controller

The last step in our initial scene setup is to create an empty game object named balloon controller and attach a script correspondingly named `BalloonController.cs`. We'll work on this script over the next few sections:

1. In **Hierarchy**, create an empty game object (**+** | **Create Empty**), reset its transform (**Transform** | **3dot-icon** | **Reset**), and name it `Balloon Controller`.
2. Create a new script on the object named `BalloonController` (from the inspector, go to **Add Component** | **New Script** | `BalloonController`).
3. Open it for editing (double-click the script file).

You can create a new C# script using the **Add Component** button on a specific object's inspector. That will create the `.cs` file in the currently selected folder in the **Project** assets folder. If that is not your `Scripts/` folder, then you may need to then move the file there to keep your assets orderly. Alternatively, you can create a new C# script first, directly in the **Project** assets folder (**+** | **C# Script**), and then add it to the object. In that case, you must remember to drag the file from the **Project** window onto the game object to add it as a component.

Okay, so far we've set up a scene environment, created a Balloon prefab with a model and rigid body, and created a Balloon Controller with a script that handles user input. Now let's play around with input buttons using the legacy Input Manager.

Using an Input Manager button

Unity's legacy input manager includes a standard **Input Manager** for accessing traditional game controllers, keyboard, mouse, and mobile touchscreen input. This includes specific button presses and joystick axes. It also supports input from VR and AR input controllers mapped to logical input axes.

The Input Manager provides an abstraction layer over the physical input devices. You can define logical inputs, such as the `Fire1` button to fire a gun, which may be mapped to a physical finger trigger button. Unity has a collection of preset inputs that are available when you create a new project. You can review and edit these settings in your project in the Input Manager settings window (**Edit** | **Project Settings** | **Input Manager**). For a general overview and details of the Unity Input Manager, see `https://docs.unity3d.com/Manual/ConventionalGameInput.html`.

The hand controllers for VR often have a lot of different buttons and axes, and it can get pretty complex. For example, you may think of the (index finger) trigger as a binary button that's either pressed or not, but on some controllers, you may also be able to detect just a finger touch and the amount of pressure you're putting on the trigger (read as an axis value between 0.0 and 1.0). The following screen capture shows a portion of the table provided in the Unity documentation for **XR Input Mappings**. You can see that the trigger is defined as an **Axis** type input using input indexes 9 and 10, for left- and right-hand controllers respectively. For a complete reference, see `https://docs.unity3d.com/Manual/xr_input.html`:

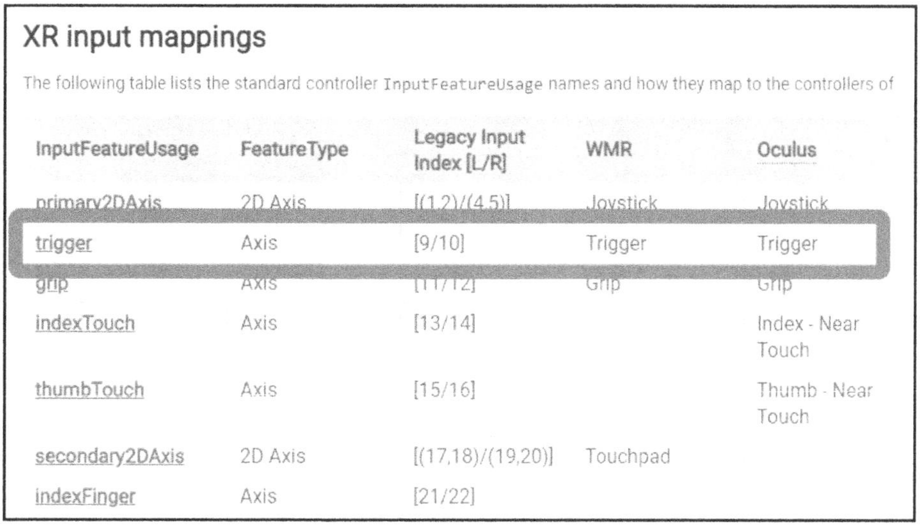

XR input mappings

The following table lists the standard controller `InputFeatureUsage` names and how they map to the controllers of

InputFeatureUsage	FeatureType	Legacy Input Index [L/R]	WMR	Oculus
primary2DAxis	2D Axis	[(1,2)/(4,5)]	Joystick	Joystick
trigger	Axis	[9/10]	Trigger	Trigger
grip	Axis	[11/12]	Grip	Grip
indexTouch	Axis	[13/14]		Index - Near Touch
thumbTouch	Axis	[15/16]		Thumb - Near Touch
secondary2DAxis	2D Axis	[(17,18)/(19,20)]	Touchpad	
indexFinger	Axis	[21/22]		

Fortunately, the Unity XR Platform has simplified this by providing a rich set of input bindings. Let's add these bindings now to our project as follows:

1. Open the Input Manager settings (**Project Settings** | **Input Manager**).
2. From the main menu, select **Assets** | **Seed XR Input Bindings**.
3. In **Input Manager**, if necessary, click to unfold the **Axes** settings.

You can see that a long list of new bindings has been added, a portion of them shown in the following screenshot. In this screenshot, I have unfolded the binding definition for **XRI_Right_Trigger**; you can see that it maps to the **10th axis (Joysticks)**, which is the right-hand index finger trigger button on your hand controller, regardless of which device the user is using, whether Oculus, WMR, OpenVR, or any other:

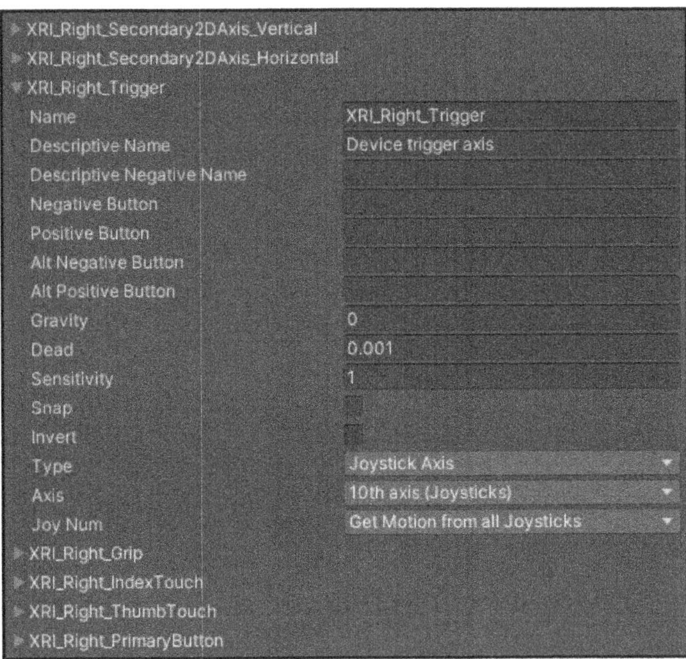

Unity is in the process of transitioning from its legacy Input Manager to a new **Input System Package**, which will replace the original Input Manager described here. You can switch your project between the systems in **Player Settings** (**Project Settings** | **Player** | **Other Settings** | **Configuration** | **Active Input Handling**). For more information on the Input System Package, see the introductory blog post (`https://blogs.unity3d.com/2019/10/14/introducing-the-new-input-system/`) and the documentation (`https://docs.unity3d.com/Packages/com.unity.inputsystem@1.0/manual/Installation.html`). The one that you choose here will not affect the projects in this book beyond the current section topic, as we will be using the VR-specific **XR Interaction Toolkit** instead of either of those (set up later this chapter) throughout the book to handle VR controller input.

Let's take a look at how this works. To start, we will get a specific button state and see how the Unity Input class works.

Polling the XRI_Right_Trigger button

The simplest way to obtain user input is to just *get* the current state from the Input Manager. This process of polling the input state is shown in the following diagram:

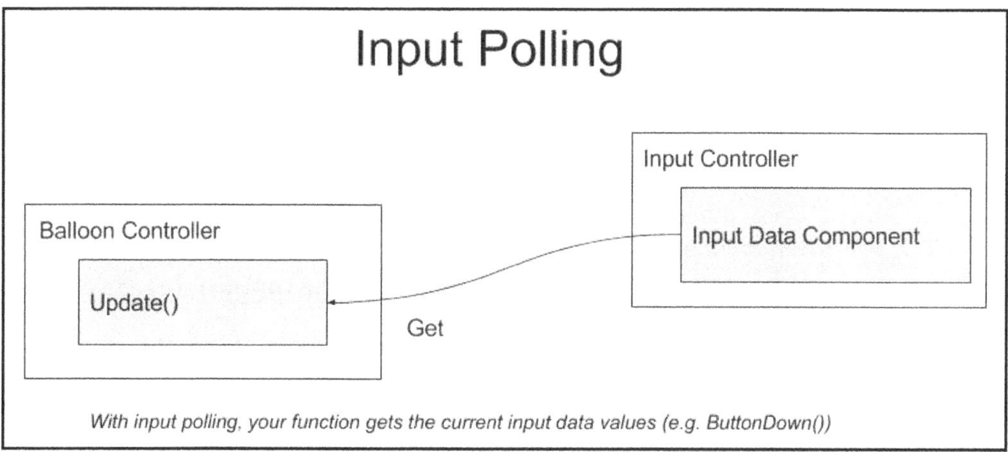

You may recall that Unity calls the `Update()` function once every frame update. We can poll for button presses in each frame by checking the button state for each update. Open the `BalloonController.cs` file in your editor and edit the script as follows:

```
public class BalloonController : MonoBehaviour
{
  void Update()
  {
    if (Input.GetButtonDown("XRI_Right_TriggerButton"))
    {
      Debug.Log("Trigger down");
    }
    else if (Input.GetButtonUp("XRI_Right_TriggerButton"))
    {
      Debug.Log("Trigger up");
    }
  }
}
```

In this script, for each update, we first call `Input.GetButtonDown ("XRI_Right_TriggerButton")`, which returns a Boolean (true or false) value indicating whether the trigger button has just been *pressed*. If so, we print a message on the **Console** window; otherwise, we call `Input.GetButtonUp ("XRI_Right_TriggerButton")`, which says whether the trigger has just been *released*. If it has, then we print that message.

This example uses the legacy Input Manager. For this example to work, ensure that you have **Active Input Handling** set to **Input Manager (Old)** in **Player Settings**.

Let's try it out by going through the following steps:

1. Press **Play** in the Unity editor to run the scene.
2. When you press the trigger on your input controller, you will see the **Input: Trigger down** message as output.
3. When you release the trigger button, you will see the **Input: Trigger up** message.

Feel free to experiment with using other logical input names (**Edit** | **Project Settings** | **Input Manager**). For more on scripting the `Input` class, see `https://docs.unity3d.com/ScriptReference/Input.html`. Now we can use these input functions to control the creation and release of balloons in the game.

Controlling balloons with the input trigger

Now we're ready to implement the meat of our game. When the trigger is pressed, the controller script creates a new balloon by instantiating the Balloon prefab in the scene. When the trigger is released, the balloon object is permitted to float up into the sky. And while the button is held, we'll grow (inflate) the balloon's scale. Let's begin.

Creating balloons

The `BalloonController.cs` script should now create a new balloon when the trigger button gets pressed. In your code editor, change the `Update` function to the following:

```
void Update()
  {
    if (Input.GetButtonDown("XRI_Right_TriggerButton"))
      {
```

```
            CreateBalloon();
        }
    }
```

We need to write this `CreateBalloon()` function. It will reference the Balloon prefab that we created earlier in this chapter and create a new instance of it in the scene. So first, declare a `public GameObject` variable named `balloonPrefab` at the top of the `BalloonController` class and add a private variable to hold the current instance of the `balloon`, as follows:

```
public class BalloonController : MonoBehaviour
{
    public GameObject balloonPrefab;
    private GameObject balloon;
    ...
```

Now, add the `CreateBalloon` function that calls the Unity `Instantiate` function to create a new instance of the `balloonPrefab` and assign it to the `balloon` variable:

```
public void CreateBalloon()
{
    balloon = Instantiate(balloonPrefab);
}
```

This `CreateBalloon` function will be called from `Update` when `GetButtonDown` is true. Next, we'll handle the trigger release case. (Note that we are declaring our functions as `public` for use later in the chapter).

Releasing balloons

The `ReleaseBalloon` function should be called when the player releases the trigger button. Let's add that to `Update` now, as follows:

```
void Update()
  {
    if (Input.GetButtonDown("XRI_Right_TriggerButton"))
     {
       CreateBalloon();
     }
       else if (Input.GetButtonUp("XRI_Right_TriggerButton"))
        {
          ReleaseBalloon();
        }
      }
```

To release the balloon into the sky, we apply a gentle upward force on the balloon so that it floats skyward. For this, we'll define a `floatStrength` variable and apply it to the object's Rigidbody. (When a Rigidbody is on an object, Unity will include that object in its physics calculations). It's initially set to `20.0`; you can later change this value in the **Inspector**. Add this variable with the others declared at the top of the `BalloonController` script:

```
public GameObject balloonPrefab;
public float floatStrength = 20f;
private GameObject balloon;
```

Now, we can write the `ReleaseBalloon` function as follows:

```
public void ReleaseBalloon()
{
    Rigidbody rb = balloon.GetComponent<Rigidbody>();
    Vector3 force = Vector3.up * floatStrength;
    rb.AddForce(force);

    GameObject.Destroy(balloon, 10f);
    balloon = null;
}
```

The first few lines of the new function contain a chain of actions. First, we query the balloon object for its Rigidbody component (`GetComponent<Rigidbody>()`) and assign it to a local variable, `rb`. Then, we calculate the force that we want to add to the object as the `floatStrength` value in the up direction (`Vector3.up * floatStrength`). Then that force is applied to the balloon's Rigidbody (`AddForce()`) to give it some velocity (see `https://docs.unity3d.com/ScriptReference/Rigidbody.AddForce.html`).

In the latter part of the function, we tell Unity to remove the balloon from the scene, after letting it float for 10 seconds. We also set the currently held `balloon` to `null`, clearing the variable for the next balloon.

It's generally a good idea to remove from the scene any game objects that are no longer visible and can be discarded. Repeatedly creating and destroying objects over time can cause memory issues at runtime. We discuss this issue and solutions such as *object pooling* in `Chapter 9`, *Playing with Physics and Fire*.

Save the file. Go back into Unity and assign the Balloon prefab to the variable in our script as follows:

1. In the **Hierarchy** window, make sure that the **Balloon Controller** is currently selected.
2. In the **Project** window, locate the **Balloon Prefab** that we created earlier.
3. Drag the **Balloon** prefab from the **Project** window to the **Inspector** window and onto the BalloonController's **Balloon Prefab** slot.

The **BalloonController** now looks like this in the Inspector:

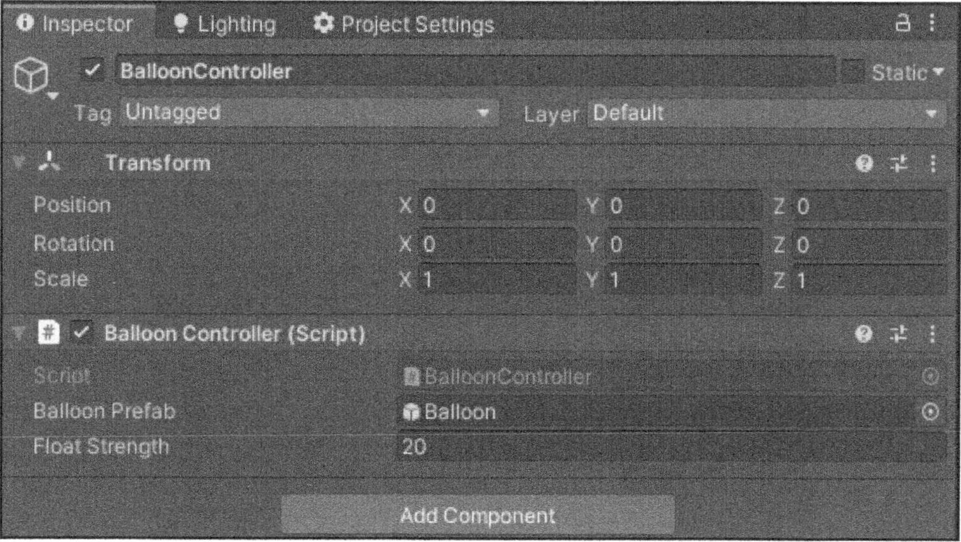

When you're ready, press **Play**. Then, inside the VR world, when you press the trigger button, a new balloon will be instantiated. When you release it, the balloon will float upward. In the following game window, I have pressed the button multiple times in succession, creating a series of balloons, *haha!* Not exactly what you'd expect, but it's what we have implemented so far. (The overlap will get fixed when we add Colliders to the balloon later in the project):

And here is the scene hierarchy of this, showing the cloned balloons in the **Hierarchy** window. There will be a new instance (clone) of the balloon prefab each time the button is pressed:

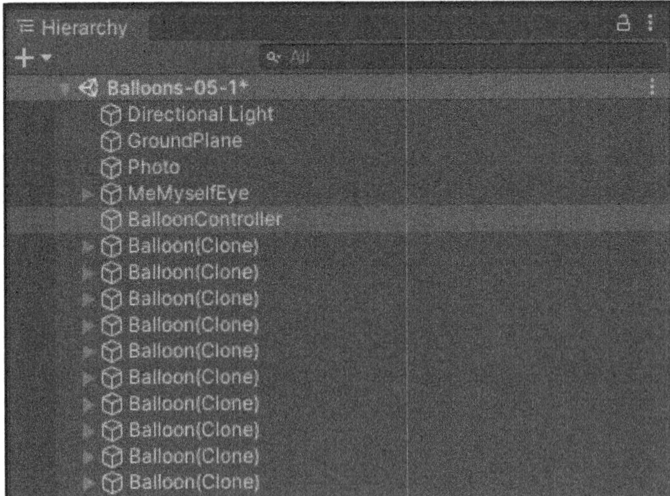

The next thing we want to do is inflate the balloon while the trigger is still pressed so that the user will press the trigger to create the balloon, hold to enlarge it, and release it to release it into the sky.

Inflating a balloon while pressing the trigger

The next thing we want to do is inflate the balloon while we hold down the button. The balloon should start out small and then grow. We can do this by checking whether there's a current balloon instance from a button press, and modify its scale each update by a specified grow rate—say, 1.5 times bigger per second.

First, let's create a small balloon at one-tenth of its original size. Modify the `CreateBalloon` function as follows. When a new balloon is instantiated, we set its local scale to `0.1f` on all three axes:

```
public void CreateBalloon()
{
    balloon = Instantiate(balloonPrefab);
    balloon.transform.localScale = new Vector3(0.1f, 0.1f, 0.1f);
}
```

Next, we'll declare a `growRate` variable that will be used to change the balloon scale. We'll initialize it to `1.5`, but you can adjust that value in the Inspector later. Add the following declaration at the top of the class, among the other variables:

```
public float growRate = 1.5f;
```

Now, modify the `Update` function with a third `if` condition as follows:

```
else if (balloon != null)
{
    GrowBalloon();
}
```

Then add the `GrowBalloon` function like this:

```
public void GrowBalloon()
{
  float growThisFrame = growRate * Time.deltaTime;
  Vector3 changeScale = balloon.transform.localScale * growThisFrame;
  balloon.transform.localScale += changeScale;
}
```

The `GrowBalloon` function modifies the balloon's size by a percentage based on the `growRate` and the time since the last update. First, we define a local variable, `growThisFrame`, which is the growth factor for this specific frame, calculated from our `growRate` per second by multiplying this figure by the number of seconds (or fractions of second) since the last frame update (`Time.deltaTime`). Next, we calculate by how much we should change the balloon's size in this frame by applying the `growThisFrame` factor to its current scale. Lastly, we actually change the balloon's scale by incrementing the current balloon size by this `changeScale` amount, using the `+=` to modify the current local scale values.

Note that this `GrowBalloon` function could be refactored into a single line of code, as shown in the following code:

```
public void GrowBalloon()
{
    balloon.transform.localScale += balloon.transform.localScale
        * growRate * Time.deltaTime;
}
```

Press **Play** in Unity. When you press the controller button, you'll create a balloon, which continues to inflate until you release the button. Then the balloon floats up. Wow, that's actually pretty fun!

Try improving the `GrowBalloon` function by, for example, setting a maximum scale for the balloon so that it doesn't grow beyond that size. For advanced balloon ideas with deformation animations, check out the cool post on water balloons by August Yadon at `https://www.auggodoggogames.com/source/balloon/`!

In summary, we now have three functions in the BalloonController. The `CreateBalloon` function instantiates a new balloon from the Balloon prefab as a new game object in the scene. It starts out small, as if deflated. The `GrowBalloon` function modifies the scale of the balloon, making it appear to inflate over time at a given growth rate. The `ReleaseBalloon` function deploys the balloon, causing it to float up into the sky. The software pattern we used here is *polling* the input device for changes. During each frame update, we call the `Input.GetButtonDown` and `GetButtonUp` functions to see whether a specific button has changed. Next, let's look at a different software pattern for handling user input—*events*.

Using Unity events for input

Events allow the decoupling of the source of the event from the consumer of the event. Basically, events are a messaging system where one object triggers an event. Any other objects in the project can listen for the event. It can subscribe to a specific function to be called when the event occurs.

Events are a very rich topic, and we can only introduce them here. We will be using the event pattern in various contexts throughout this book, including UI, collisions, and XR interactions. For more information on using Unity events, there are a lot of good references online, including the Unity tutorials at `https://learn.unity.com/tutorial/events-uh` and `https://learn.unity.com/tutorial/create-a-simple-messaging-system-with-events`.

For this example, we'll create a separate input controller that reads the input button's state and invokes an event and then modify the `BalloonController` to subscribe to the events. The following diagram illustrates the relationship between our input controller, which invokes events, and the balloon controller, which subscribes to the events, as shown in the following illustration. As you'll see, you can set this up by dragging and dropping via the Unity Inspector, or you can subscribe listener functions to scripts:

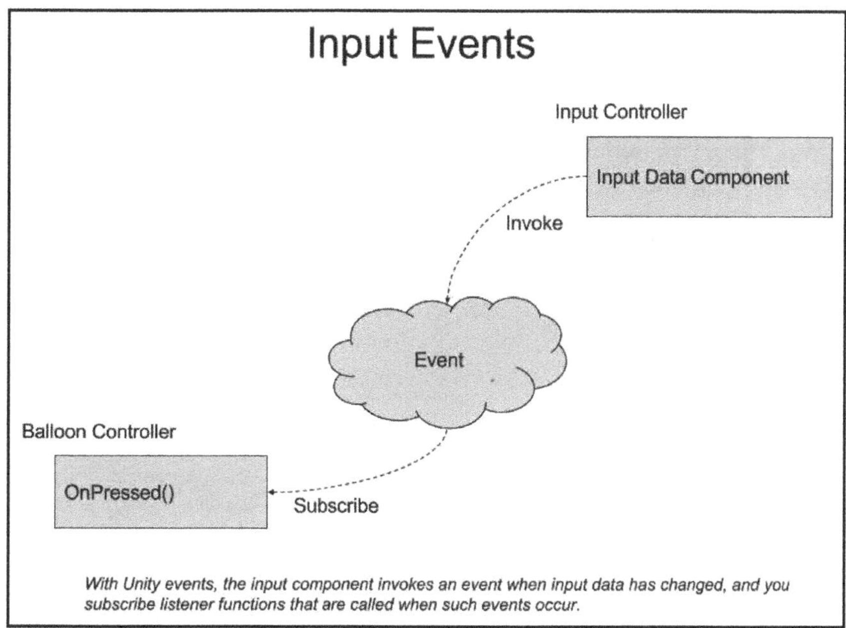

With Unity events, the input component invokes an event when input data has changed, and you subscribe listener functions that are called when such events occur.

To begin, create an empty **Input Controller** game object and add a corresponding new C# script:

1. In **Hierarchy**, create an empty game object (**+** | **Create Empty**), reset its transform (**Transform** | **3dot-icon** | **Reset**), and name it `Button Input Controller`.
2. Create a new script on the object named `ButtonInputController` (**Add Component** | **New Script**).
3. Open it for editing (double-click the script file).

If you are a developer and are familiar with C#, it may help to know that Unity events are delegates. As explained in the Unity manual, "*UnityEvents can be added to any MonoBehaviour and are executed from code like a standard .Net delegate. When a UnityEvent is added to a MonoBehaviour it appears in the Inspector and persistent callbacks can be added.*" It's important to note that, unlike normal C# events, Unity events do not need to be unsubscribed.

Now, we can start editing the script.

Invoking our input action events

To implement our example using events, we'll first have the `ButtonInputController` trigger events when the trigger button is pressed and another event when the button is released.

First, at the top of the script, we need to declare that we are using the Unity event API. Then we declare the two `UnityEvents` that we will invoke. The `Update()` function only needs to invoke one event or the other as they happen.

The entire `ButtonInputController.cs` is as follows:

```
using UnityEngine;
using UnityEngine.Events;

public class ButtonInputController : MonoBehaviour
{
    public UnityEvent ButtonDownEvent = new UnityEvent();
    public UnityEvent ButtonUpEvent = new UnityEvent();

    void Update()
    {
        if (Input.GetButtonDown("XRI_Right_TriggerButton"))
        {
```

```
            ButtonDownEvent.Invoke();
        }
        else if (Input.GetButtonUp("XRI_Right_TriggerButton"))
        {
            ButtonUpEvent.Invoke();
        }
    }
}
```

As you can see, we simply declare a couple of Unity events—`ButtonDownEvent` and `ButtonUpEvent`—and initialize them to a new Unity event object. Then, when the user presses the trigger button on their controller, we invoke the `down` event, and when they release the button, we invoke the `up` event.

That's it for this side of the equation. Now the `BalloonController` can subscribe to these events.

Subscribing to input events

When using events, `BalloonController` does not need to check for input actions each update—all of that conditional logic can be bypassed. Instead, we'll drag and drop the components to subscribe them to events. The `Update` function now only needs to grow the balloon if it's already instantiated (that is, when the `balloon` variable is not `null`). Modify its `Update` function so it reads as follows:

```
void Update()
{
    if (balloon != null)
    {
        GrowBalloon();
    }
}
```

Also, verify that you have declared its `CreateBalloon` and `ReleaseBalloon` functions as `public`, as I instructed earlier, so that we can reference them outside of this file. To wire up the input events to the Balloon Controller, go through the following steps:

1. In **Hierarchy**, select **Button Input Controller** and look at its **Inspector** window.
2. You will see that the script component now has two event lists, as we declared them in its script.
3. On the **Button Down Event** list, click the + in the lower-right corner to create a new item.
4. Drag the **BalloonController** from **Hierarchy** into the empty object slot.

5. In the function select list, choose **BalloonController** | **CreateBalloon**.

Repeat the process for the Button Up Event as follows:

1. On the **Button Up Event** list, press the **+** in the lower-right corner to create a new item.
2. Drag the **BalloonController** from **Hierarchy** into the empty object slot.
3. In the function select list, choose **BalloonController** | **ReleaseBalloon**.

The component should now look like this:

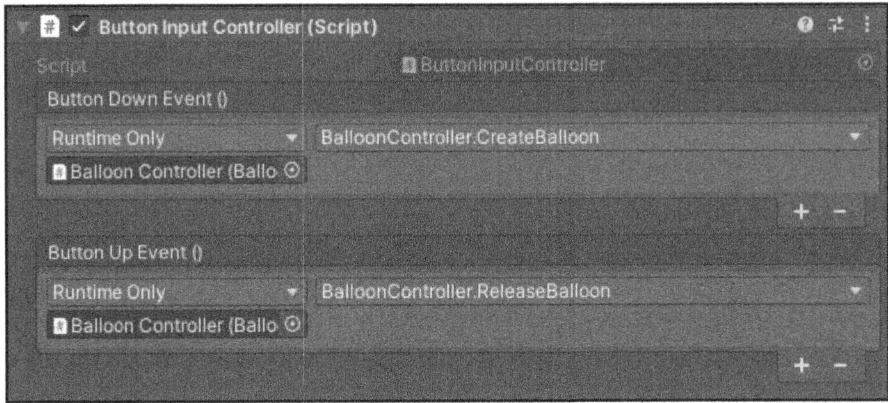

Now, when you press **Play** and press the trigger, the input controller invokes the **Button Down Event**, and the `CreateBalloon` function that is listening for these events gets called (likewise for the **Button Up Event**). When the trigger is released, the input controller invokes the other event, and `ReleaseBalloon` gets called.

This mechanic can also be done entirely using scripting. *The following is for explanation purposes only; don't add it to your code now.* But if you wanted to subscribe to the button events in a script, you could write a `Start()` function that adds `CreateBalloon` and `ReleaseBalloon` as listeners on the corresponding `ButtonController` events as follows. In this way, instead of the `ButtonController` having to know what other objects should listen to its events, the `BalloonController` references the `ButtonController` directly to subscribe to its events:

```
void Start()
{
    buttonController.ButtonDownEvent.AddListener(CreateBalloon);
    buttonController.ButtonUpEvent.AddListener(ReleaseBalloon);
}
```

So now we have a scene that lets you blow up balloons by pressing a button on the controller. We implemented two ways to handle button input: polling or events. When you press the trigger/button, a new balloon is instantiated and grows until you release the button. Then the balloon floats up into the sky. But the balloon starts out positioned at the center of the ground plane (origin `0,0,0`), at ground level, so it appears to grow more like a flower than a balloon! The next step is to attach it to your hands.

Tracking your hands

To start taking advantage of the positional tracking of your hands, we simply need to parent the balloon prefab to the hand model. Our scene includes an **XR Rig** that contains not only the **Main Camera** that is positionally tracked with the player's head-mounted display, but it also contains a **LeftHand Controller** and **RightHand Controller** that are tracked with the player's hand controllers. Any game object that is a child of the hand controller object will be tracked along with it. To implement this, we will first modify the `CreateBalloon` function so that new balloons are attached to your hand controller and move with it as you move your hands. As we'll see, this introduces a new problem where the balloons are not necessarily positioned upright, so we'll fix that as well.

Parenting the balloon to your hand

The Balloon Controller will need to know which hand pressed the button and parent the balloon to that controller object. Specifically, we'll pass the hand `GameObject` to the `CreateBalloon` function and then pass its transform to the `Instantiate` function, as follows:

```
public void CreateBalloon(GameObject parentHand)
{
    balloon = Instantiate(balloonPrefab, parentHand.transform);
    balloon.transform.localScale = new Vector3(0.1f, 0.1f, 0.1f);
}
```

Unity's `Instantiate` function has several variants. Originally, we passed just one parameter—the prefab to be used. This time, we're passing a second parameter, the `parentHand` transform. When a parent transform is given, the instantiated object will be made a child of it (see `https://docs.unity3d.com/ScriptReference/Object.Instantiate.html`).

Likewise, `ReleaseBalloon` must detach the balloon from the hand before sending it on its way, as follows:

```
public void ReleaseBalloon()
{
    balloon.transform.parent = null;
    balloon.GetComponent<Rigidbody>().AddForce(Vector3.up
      * floatStrength);
    GameObject.Destroy(balloon, 10f);
    balloon = null;
}
```

How do we pass the hand `GameObject` to `CreateBalloon`? Assuming that your project is presently using the Unity events that we set up in the previous topic, it's very easy. In **Inspector,** we need to update the **Button Down Event** function, since it now requires the game object argument:

1. In the Unity editor, select the **Button Input Controller** object.
2. In the **Button Down Event** list, the function may now say something like `<Missing BalloonController.CreateBalloon>`.
3. Select the **Function** dropdown and choose **BalloonController | CreateBalloon(GameObject)**.
4. Unfold the **XR Rig** object in **Hierarchy** and look for the **RightHand Controller** object, then drag it onto the empty **Game Object** slot.

The **Button Input Controller** component now looks like this:

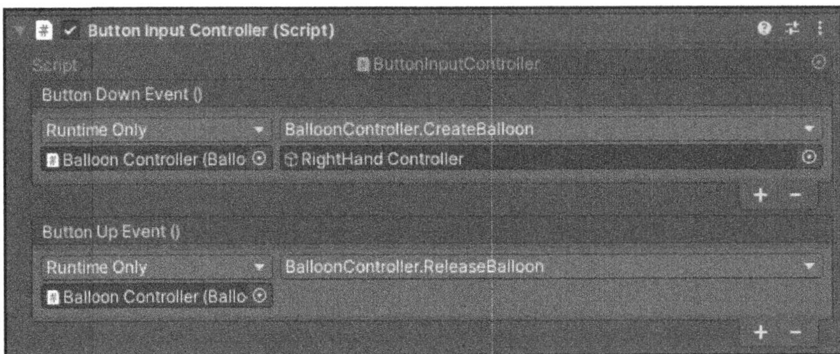

Press **Play**. Now, when you press the trigger button, the balloon is created attached to your hand, and when released, it is released into the scene from that hand location at the time.

But now we have a new problem. Not only is the balloon tracking the position of your hand, but it is also tracking its orientation, making it look and feel unnaturally sideways!

Forcing balloons to float upright

When we first instantiated the balloons at the ground plane, it was also oriented at its default vertical rotation. But now the balloons are instantiated as a child of the hand controller and oriented relative to its rotation (as well as position). We didn't notice this 'bug' earlier, but we need to fix it now:

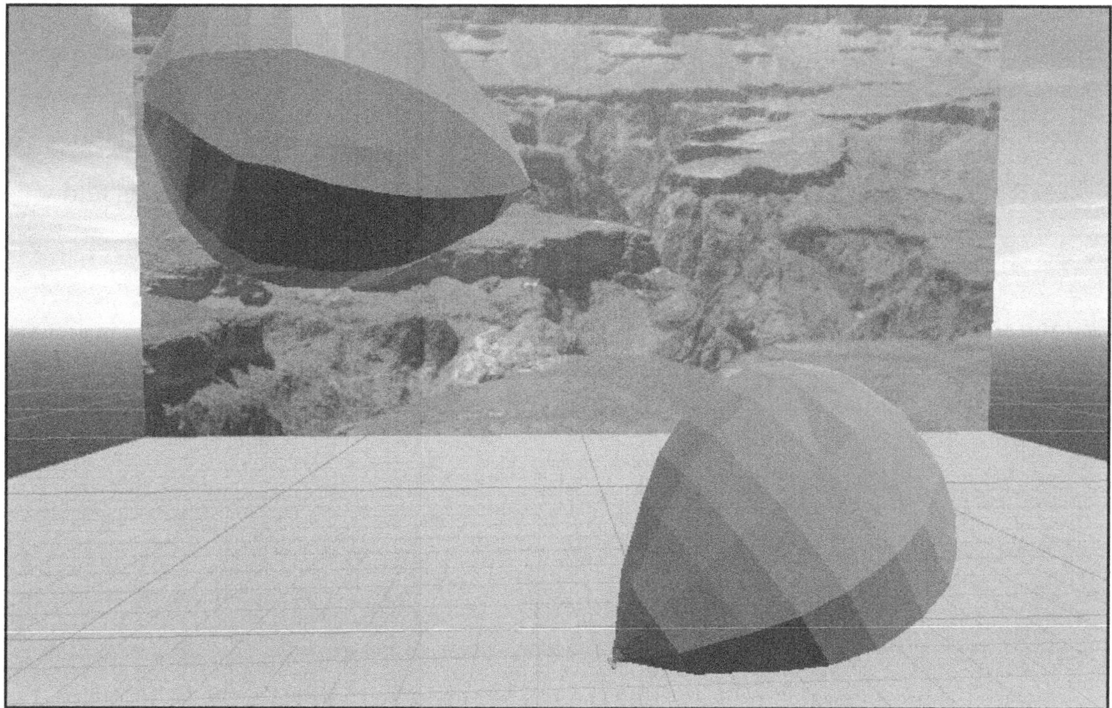

Let's write a component script, `KeepUpright`, that orients the balloon to remain upright. This will also animate it into position gradually, more like a real balloon. To do this, we'll use a linear interpolation of the rotation of the balloon so that it incrementally changes to an upright position over time. Rotations in transforms are internally represented as a *quaternion*, and we can use Unity's `Quaternion.Slerp()` function to calculate a *spherical linear interpolation* between two angles—the balloon's current rotation and the preferred upright one.

Rotations in transforms are internally represented as a *quaternion*—a mathematically efficient representation of a 3D rotation matrix. They are easier to interpolate (that is, find a linear path between two 3D orientations) than Euler angles (independent *x*, *y*, *z* rotations), and they avoid *gimbal lock*, a problem with Euler angles where one dimension is overridden by the other two angles. Euler angles are more intuitive for humans, so Unity uses them in the editor's **Inspector Transform Rotation** user interface, but internally, rotations are represented as quaternions (see `https://docs.unity3d.com/ScriptReference/Quaternion.html`).

Let's write this script now and add it to the **Balloon** prefab object:

1. Select your **Balloon** prefab in the **Project** window (in the `Assets/Prefabs/` folder).
2. Create and add a new script named `KeepUpright` (by navigating to **Add Component** | **New Script** | `KeepUpright` | **Create And Add**).
3. For tidiness, in the **Project** window, drag the new script into your scripts folder (`Assets/Scripts/`).
4. Double-click the script to open it for editing.

Edit the script as follows:

```
public class KeepUpright : MonoBehaviour
{
 public float speed = 5f;

 void Update()
 {
 transform.rotation = Quaternion.Slerp(transform.rotation,
    Quaternion.identity, Time.deltaTime * speed);
 }
}
```

We declare a `speed` variable representing the rate it may take to upright the balloon. In each frame `Update`, we modify the balloon's world space rotation between the balloon's current rotation and an upright position.

Press **Play**. Here is a screenshot of me generating a bunch of balloons that appear to be flying over the Grand Canyon. Fun!

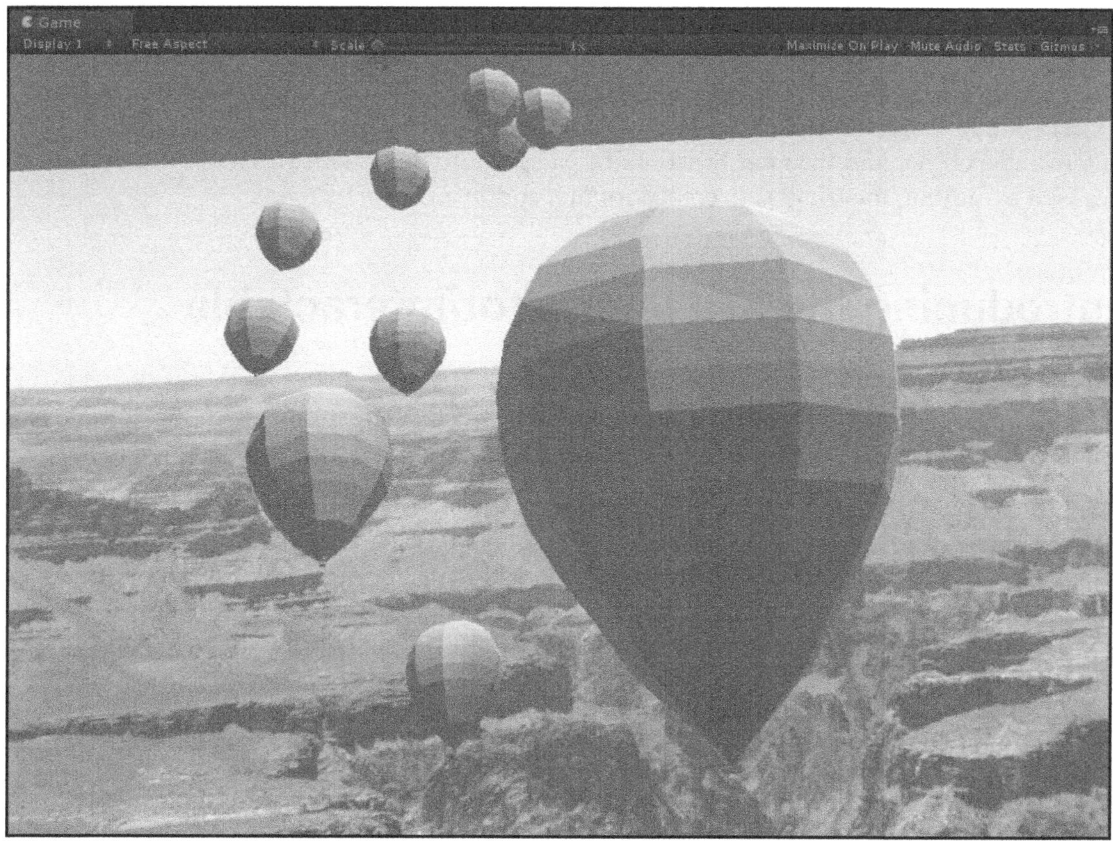

So far we have created a balloon prefab that can be inflated and float into the sky when released, uprighting itself. The balloon is created and tracked with your hand position. But presently, we are still using the default hand controller settings from XR Interaction Toolkit's XR Rig, including the laser interactors. To make this a more familiar VR experience, we should be holding something in our hands, like maybe a *balloon gun* that makes the balloons. We'll build that next.

Interacting with a balloon gun

For this part of the project, I'm going to show you how to grab and use interactable objects. Let's make a balloon gun. You'll pick up the gun, and when you pull the trigger, a balloon comes out! *Haha!*

The implementation uses a different approach to building interactions. Rather than a main central controller script that reads the user input and directs the actions, we are going to use a more object-oriented *interactor/interactable* paradigm provided by the **XR Interaction** (**XRI**) Toolkit. With our toolkit, we'll create a grabbable balloon gun by making it an interactable object, and then use the toolkit to respond to the interactor's `Activate` events (caused by pulling the trigger) to create, inflate, and release the balloons.

Introducing the XRI Interactor/Interactable architecture

The XR Interaction Toolkit implements an object-oriented interaction system that couples interactor objects, such as your hands, with interactable objects, such as a gun or a ball.

An **Interactor** is a component that handles the actions of hovering and selecting other objects. Typically, that'd be your left- and right-hand controllers. These are the Interactors in a VR scene. XRI provides several types of Interactors, including a **Ray Interactor** that casts a laser-beam-like ray for selecting objects (as we've seen in the default XR Rig). There's a **Direct Interactor** that expects you to directly touch the target object with your hand model to interact with it and a **Socket Interactor** that locks the object at a position in the world. Other features of Interactors include interaction events that you can hook into, haptics, and sounds. Interactors only interact with *Interactable* objects.

An **Interactable** is a component that is added to a game object to make it interactable. Interactables are objects that can respond to hover, select, and activate interactions from an Interactor. The Interactable object controls its own response to these interaction events, so each Interactable object can respond in its own way appropriate for that object.

In XRI, there are three interaction states: *hover*, *select*, and *activate*. These are described as follows:

- **Hover**: Hovering on an object indicates your intention to interact with it. Hovering usually doesn't change the behavior of an Interactable object, but it might change color or display another visual indicator for this state. To enter and exit the hover state triggers events, you can use `OnFirstHoverEnter`, `OnHoverEnter`, `OnHoverExit`, and `OnLastHoverExit`.
- **Select**: Selecting an Interactable object requires a user action such as a grip button or trigger press. A common response is to grab the object, and it becomes attached to your hand controller. Entering and exiting the select state triggers the `OnSelectEnter` and `OnSelectExit` events.

- **Activate**: Activating an Interactable object requires a user action, such as a trigger or button press, that typically affects the currently selected object. This lets you further interact with the object you've selected. Entering and exiting the activate state triggers the `OnActivateEnter` and `OnActivateExit` events.

Tying these together, the **Interaction Manager** associates sets of Interactors and Interactables. There can be multiple Interaction Managers, but every scene requires at least one. On Awake, both Interactors and Interactables register with the first Interaction Manager found in the Scene, unless you have already assigned them a specific Interaction Manager in the Inspector. Note that the interaction system also supports UI events, which we will be using in the next chapter.

When you add an **XR Rig** to your scene, as we've done earlier (using the **GameObject** | **XR** menu), it will automatically also create an **XR Interaction Manager** object containing an **XR Interaction Manager** component. Likewise, the XR Rig's child controllers (**LeftHand Controller** and **RightHand Controller**) contain an **XR Ray Interactor**, as well as line rendering helper components for drawing the ray. We'll use these defaults, but note that you can replace it with an **XR Direct Interactor** or another type of interactor.

In the XRI Toolkit, the **Ray Interactor** casts a laser-beam-like ray from your hand into the scene to interact with objects. Alternatively, the **Direct Interactor** interacts with objects using a Collider on your hand to detect touching an object. You can use either (or both) on a hand controller. With the **Direct Interactor**, you would reach out and actually touch the object you want to select, grab, and/or activate.

We can now use the interaction system. In this project, we are going to create a gun in the scene, sitting atop a pedestal, that you can grab and trigger to make balloons! Let's get started.

Creating a grabbable balloon gun

First, we'll create a grabbable gun. If you have a gun model, you can use that. I don't, so I'm just going to make a white-box one from a few 3D primitives, using the following steps. The important things are to make this model into a prefab and make sure that it includes a Transform that we can use to define the tip of the gun where new balloons will be instantiated:

1. In **Hierarchy**, create an empty game object named `BalloonGun` (**+** | **Create Empty**), and reset its **Transform** (**3-dot-icon** | **Reset**).
2. For its `Body`, create a child 3D **Cube** and **Scale** it to (`0.04, 0.1, 0.2`).

3. For its `Barrel`, create a child 3D **Cylinder**, with **Scale** (`0.02, 0.04, 0.02`), **Rotation** (`90, 0,0`), and **Position** (`0, 0.04, 0.14`).
4. Define the tip of the barrel where balloons will be instantiated and create an **Empty GameObject** named `Tip` at **Position** (`0, 0.04, 0.18`).

My gun looks as in the following screenshot (I also made it into a prefab). Your mileage may vary. You could also add some materials other than the default, for example. The **Tip** object is presently selected in the following screenshot:

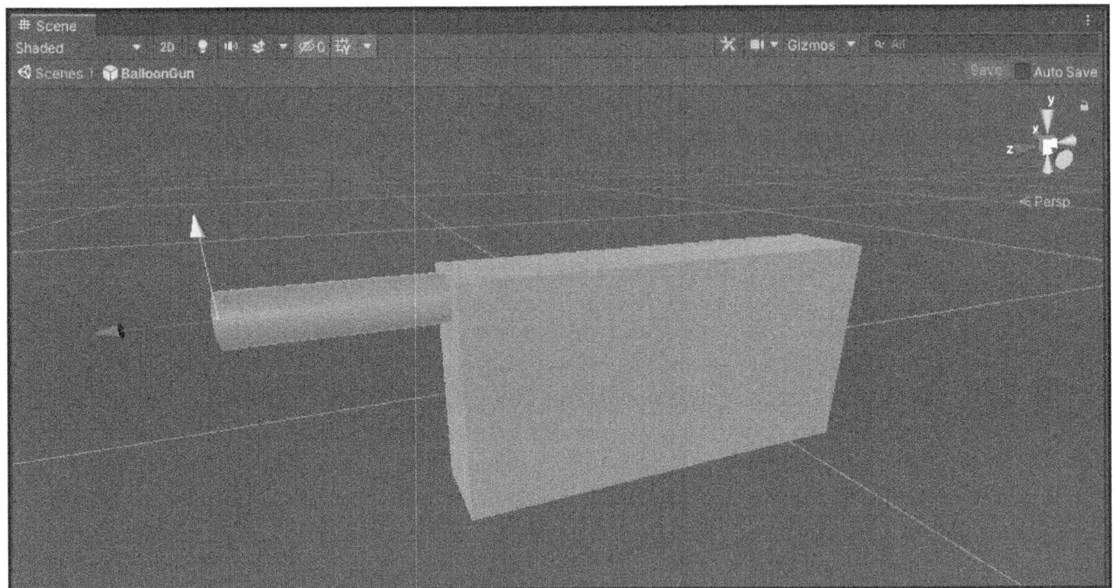

White-boxing is the use of temporary simplistic models as a placeholder to develop a project until actual artwork can be used. It's an important technique for prototyping. White-boxing also helps the team focus on other issues like game mechanics and interactions apart from the graphics details.

Now that we have a gun model, let's make it an Interactable object as follows:

1. Ensure that the root **BalloonGun** object is selected in **Hierarchy**.
2. Add a **XR Grab Interactable** component (from the main menu, select **Components** | **XR** | **XR Grab Interactable**).
3. Change the Interactable **Movement Type** to **Instantaneous**.

Note that adding the Interactable also adds a **Rigidbody** to the object, if one is not already there. The **BalloonGun**'s **Inspector** now looks as follows:

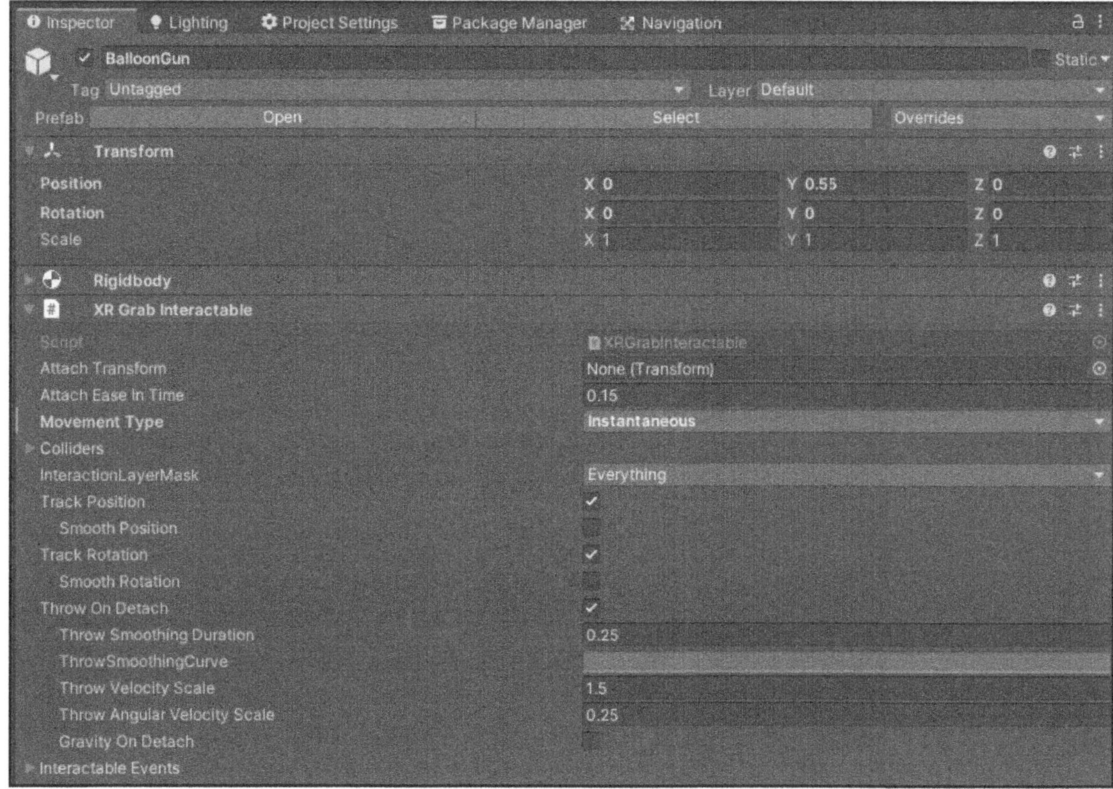

As you can see, the **XR Grab Interactable** component includes a lot of interesting parameters. The **Movement Type** refers to how the selected object is tracked with your hand; we're keeping it simple and using the **Instantaneous** option rather than physics. The component also provides the ability to throw the object when you let go, which also uses physics. We'll try that later on.

We're ready to add the gun to the scene. Let's build a pedestal to place our objects on:

1. Create a cylinder at the root of your **Hierarchy** (**+** | **3D Object** | **Cylinder**) and rename it `Pedestal`.
2. Set its **Scale** (`0.5, 0.25, 0.5`) and **Position** at the origin (`0, 0.25, 0`).

3. Make it white by creating a new material or using an existing one (by dragging **White Material** from **Project** `Assets/Materials/` onto the **Pedestal**).
4. Place the gun on the pedestal by setting its **Position** to (`0, 0.55, 0`).

If you look at the **Pedestal** cylinder object, you'll find it has a **Capsule Collider** with a rounded top (as the name implies, it is shaped like a pill capsule). We need to make sure that it has a flat top so we can put things on it without them rolling or sliding off. We can do this by replacing the capsule with a mesh that matches the cylinder's actual shape, as follows:

1. Disable or remove the Pedestal's **Capsule Collider** component (**3-dot-icon** | **Remove Component**).
2. Add the **Mesh Collider** (**Component** | **Physics** | **Mesh Collider**).

Press **Play** to try it out in VR now. Using the ray interactor with either hand, you can point the laser at the gun, then squeeze the **grip button** (middle finger) (as **Select Usage** designates) and it will fly into your hand. Release the grip button and it drops to the ground, or you can throw it. The following is a screen capture of the Scene view using the laser ray just before grabbing the gun:

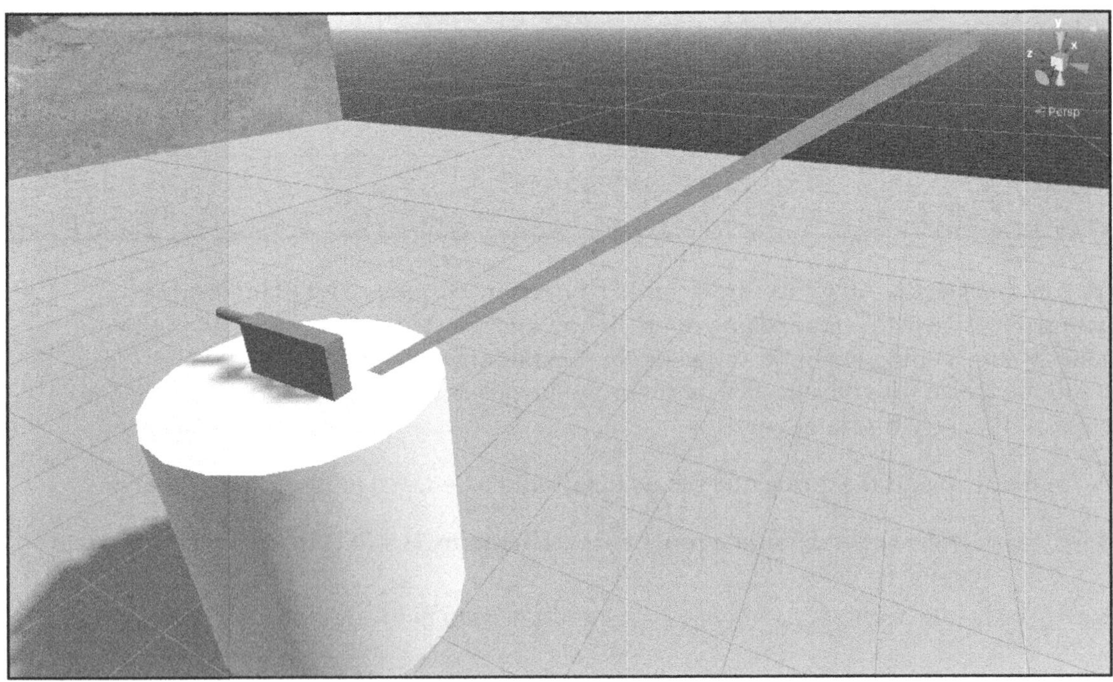

Now let's activate the trigger button.

Handling Activate events

We now need to wire up the **On Activate** events to the `BalloonController`. The main thing that changes from our previous implementation is that we can remove the global **Balloon Controller** object and attach the `BalloonController` script directly to the gun. One way to do this is to copy the existing **Balloon Controller (Script)** component onto the **BalloonGun** GameObject by going through the following steps:

1. In **Hierarchy**, select the **Balloon Controller**.
2. In **Inspector**, select the **3-dot-icon** for the **Balloon Controller** component and select **Copy Component**.
3. In **Hierarchy**, select the **BalloonGun**.
4. In **Inspector**, select the **3-dot-icon** of the **Transform** (or any other) component, and select **Paste Component As New**.
5. In **Hierarchy**, select the **Balloon Controller** and delete or disable it (**right-click | Delete**).

Now to wire up the interactable events. First, we'll define the **On Activate** event (which is invoked when the user pulls the trigger) to call the `CreateBalloon` function in `BalloonController`. If you recall, this function takes one parameter—the game object that will parent the new balloon. In this case, we want the balloon to be at the **Tip** of the gun. To do this, go through the following steps:

1. Select the **BalloonGun** in **Hierarchy**.
2. In **Inspector**, unfold the **Interactable Events** list on its **XR Grab Interactable** component.
3. For the **On Activate** event, click the **+** button to add one.
4. Drag this **BalloonGun** object from **Hierarchy** onto the **Object** slot.
5. In its **Function** dropdown, select **BalloonController | CreateBalloon**.
6. From **Inspector**, drag the **Tip** child object onto the **Game Object** parameter slot.

When the user releases the trigger, the **On Deactivate** event is invoked, and we want to release the balloon. Let's set this up by going through the following steps:

1. For the **On Deactivate** event, click the **+** button.
2. Drag this **BalloonGun** object from **Hierarchy** onto the **Object** slot.
3. In its **Function** dropdown, select **BalloonController | ReleaseBalloon**.

The following screenshot of a portion of the BalloonGun's **Inspector** shows these two events defined along with the **Balloon Controller** component that we added:

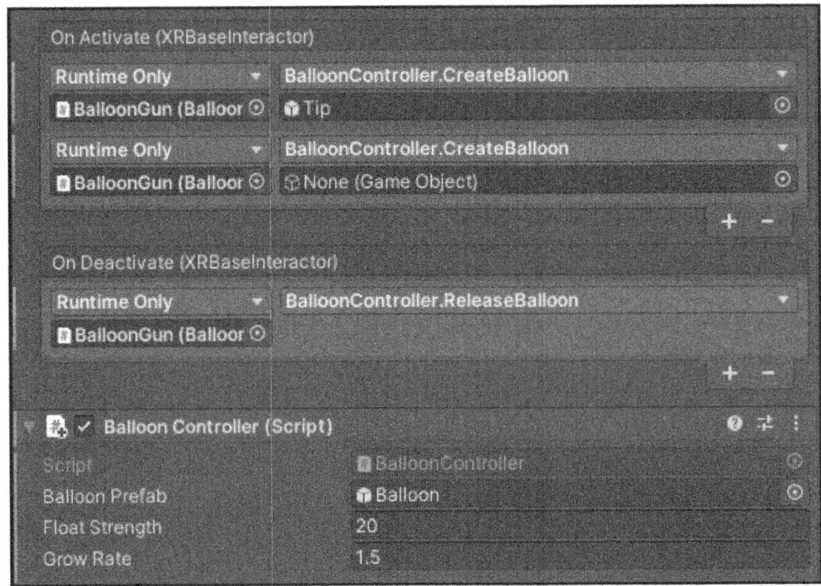

When you **Play** the scene, you should now be able to grab the gun with either hand and use the trigger button to create, inflate, and release balloons. Now our interactable gun is not just a gun, but a *balloon gun*!

Using the XR Interaction Debugger

When you're developing for VR, it's sometimes difficult to understand what the device tracking, Interactors, and Interactables are doing. Unity provides an XR Interaction Debugger window to give you more insight. To open the debugger, select **Window** | **Analysis** | **XR Interaction Debugger**. This feature (presently) is only available when running in the Editor **Play** mode. In the following screenshot, I am running the scene. I have selected just the Interactables tab. It shows all the Interaction Managers (just one in this scene) and associated Interactables (just the **BalloonGun** in this scene). You can see that its state shows that it is presently selected:

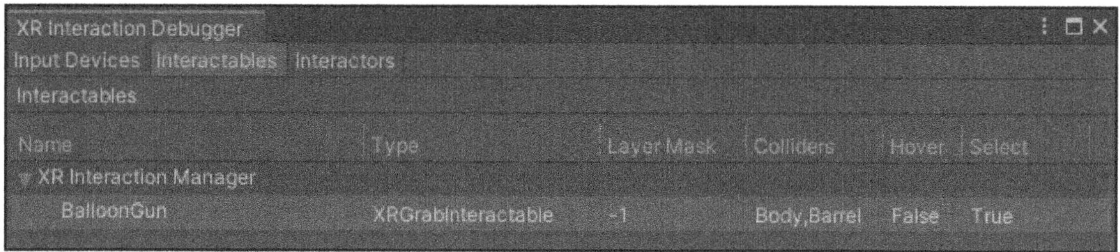

Well, that's awesome, isn't it! We have a VR project that lets you grab and shoot a gun that makes floating balloons. But to be honest, it's really hard to think about creating balloons without also wanting to pop them!

Popping balloons

Do you want to pop some balloons? "*No*", said no one ever! Let's add that feature and make a little game out of this. First, we'll make the balloons poppable with collision detection and an explosion. Then we'll add a ball to the scene that you can throw at a balloon to pop it. And after the ball is thrown, we'll fetch it back by resetting it to its original position after a short delay.

Making the balloons poppable

The Unity physics engine can detect when two objects collide. To do this, each object must have a Collider component attached. You can then have the collision trigger an event. We can also subscribe to that event to make something else happen, like play an explosion effect. This is set up on the balloon prefab. Let's do that now:

1. In the **Project** `Prefabs/` folder, open your Balloon prefab for editing by double-clicking it.
2. Select **Component** | **Physics** | **Sphere Collider**.
3. To scale and center the Collider into position, click the **Edit Collider** icon in its component.
4. In the **Scene** window, the green Collider outline has small anchor points that you can click to edit. Note that the *Alt* key pins the center position and *Shift* locks the scale ratio.
5. Or you can edit the **Center** and **Radius** values directly. I like **Radius** `0.22` and **Center** (`0, 0.36, 0`) on my balloon.

Now, we will add a script to handle the collision events:

1. Create a new C# script on the **Balloon**, named `Poppable`.
2. Open it for editing.

The `Poppable` script will provide a callback function for `OnCollisionEnter` events. When another object with a Collider enters this object's Collider, our function will get called. At that point, we'll call `PopBalloon`, which instantiates the explosion and destroys the balloon:

```
public class Poppable : MonoBehaviour
{
    public GameObject popEffectPrefab;

    void OnCollisionEnter(Collision collision)
    {
        if (transform.parent == null &&
          collision.gameObject.GetComponent<Poppable>() == null)
        {
            PopBalloon();
        }
    }

    private void PopBalloon()
    {
        if (popEffectPrefab != null)
        {
            GameObject effect = Instantiate(popEffectPrefab,
               transform.position, transform.rotation);
            Destroy(effect, 1f);
        }
        Destroy(gameObject);
    }
}
```

There are a lot of different ways that you can decide when it's appropriate to pop the balloon on collision. In this case, I've decided that the balloon must already have been released (`transform.parent == null`) and the object it collided with is not another balloon (assuming that only balloons have a poppable component, `collision.gameObject.GetComponent<Poppable>() == null`). You can see that the `OnCollisionEnter` gets a `Collision` argument with information including what game object collided with it (see more at `https://docs.unity3d.com/ScriptReference/Collision.html`).

The `PopBalloon` function instantiates the pop effect object if one has been assigned (in the **Inspector**) and lets it play for one second before it is destroyed. It also destroys the balloon itself.

Save the script. Try it in Unity. Press **Play**. When you create a balloon and release it, whack it with your hand. It disappears. Now, let's make a little popping explosion effect.

Adding a popping explosion

If you recall, in `Chapter 4`, *Using Gaze-Based Control*, we used an explosion particle-effect prefab from Standard Assets. Let's reuse that here, with some modifications to make it smaller (and less like a hand grenade!):

1. In the **Project** window, navigate to the `StandardAssets/ParticleSystems/Prefabs/` folder.
2. Select and duplicate the **Explosion** prefab (**Edit** | **Duplicate**).
3. Rename the copy as `BalloonPopEffect` and move it into your own `Prefabs/` folder.

Edit the **BalloonPopEffect** prefab by double-clicking it and going through the following steps:

1. In the root **BalloonPopEffect**, set its **Transform Scale** to (`0.01, 0.01, 0.01`).
2. Remove or disable the **Explosion Physics Force** component (**right-click** | **Remove Component**).
3. Remove or disable the **Light** component.
4. Change the **Particle System Multiplier's Multiplier** value to `0.01`.
5. In **Hierarchy**, delete or disable the child **Fireball** game object.
6. Delete or disable the child **Shockwave** game object.
7. Save the prefab and exit back to the scene hierarchy.

Now assign the effect to the Balloon:

1. Open the **Balloon** prefab again by double-clicking on it.
2. Drag the **BalloonPopEffect** prefab onto the **Poppable**'s **Pop Effect Prefab** slot.
3. Save and exit to the scene.

Press **Play**, create and release a balloon, and hit it with your hand. Pow! Okay, maybe it's too pyrotechnical for a balloon pop effect, but I like it. Next, we'll do some best practice housekeeping regarding the rigid physics of the balloon.

Disabling rigid physics while in hand

Now that we've added both a **Rigidbody** and a **Collider** to the balloon, it interacts with other physics objects in the scene. Oftentimes, you will want to disable this behavior while the object is being grabbed and enable it once the player releases the object. This is controlled using the Rigidbody's `IsKinematic` flag. When an object is kinematic, the Unity physics engine will not control its velocity and other behavior. To implement this, we just need to add a few things. First, at the top of the class, add a variable to hold the current balloon's Rigidbody, as follows:

```
private Rigidbody rb;
```

In the `CreateBalloon` function, add the following lines to get the balloon's Rigidbody and make it kinematic:

```
public void CreateBalloon(GameObject parentHand)
{
    balloon = Instantiate(balloonPrefab, parentHand.transform);
    balloon.transform.localScale = new Vector3(0.1f, 0.1f, 0.1f);
    rb = balloon.GetComponent<Rigidbody>();
    rb.isKinematic = true;
}
```

Then, restore the physics in `ReleaseBalloon`, as follows:

```
public void ReleaseBalloon()
{
    rb.isKinematic = false;
    balloon.transform.parent = null;
    rb.AddForce(Vector3.up * floatStrength);
    GameObject.Destroy(balloon, 10f);
    balloon = null;
}
```

Now, if the explosions created a physical force, for example, it would affect any free-floating balloons in the sky, but will not affect a balloon that is held in your hand with the balloon gun.

Lastly, we'll add a ball that you can grab with your other hand and try to throw at a balloon in the sky.

Throwing a ball projectile

Our final step is to add a ball to the scene that also has a Collider so that you can throw it at a balloon to pop it. We've done just about all of the steps before, so I'll just list them out as follows:

1. In the scene **Hierarchy** root, create a new sphere (by going to **+** | **3D Object** | **Sphere**) and name it `Ball`.
2. **Scale** the ball to (`0.1, 0.1, 0.1`) and place it on the **Pedestal** at **Position** (`-0.125, 0.55, 0`).
3. Make it red by adding new material or using the **Red Material** in your `Materials/` folder (drag the material onto the **Ball**).
4. Add a **Grab Interactable** component (**Component** | **XR** | **XR Grab Interactable**).
5. On its **Rigidbody** component, change the **Collision Detection** to **Continuous**.
6. On its **XR Grab Interactable** component, change the **Throw Velocity Scale** to `2`.

Setting its **Collision Detection** to **Continuous** (versus **Discrete**) helps prevent the ball from accidentally falling through the **Ground Plane** by instructing Unity to more continuously check for collisions. Changing the **Throw Velocity Scale** helps accentuate the ball's velocity when you throw it; you can try other values to make it go faster.

The pedestal with the gun and ball are shown in the following scene view screenshot:

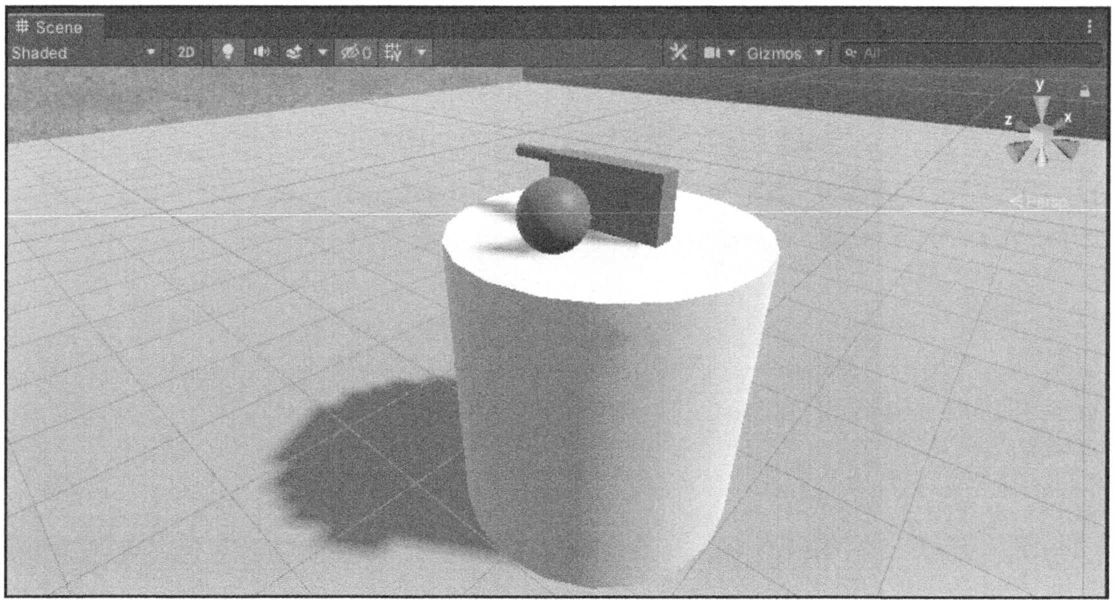

Press **Play**. Grab the gun with one hand and inflate a balloon. Grab the ball with the other hand and throw it at the balloon. *Kaboom!* This could actually be fun! After throwing the ball, I can grab it again using the hand controller ray cast. But wait: what if you throw it off the edge of our playground? Let's add a script to retrieve the ball and reset it to the start position after a delay.

Resetting the ball position

To reset the ball position back onto the pedestal after you've thrown it, we'll create one more script. Create a new C# script named `ResetAfterDelay`, attach it to the **Ball**, and edit it as follows:

```
public class ResetAfterDelay : MonoBehaviour
{
 public float delaySeconds = 5f;
 private Vector3 startPosition;

 private void Start()
 {
 startPosition = transform.position;
 }

 public void Reset()
 {
 StartCoroutine(AfterDelay());
 }

 IEnumerator AfterDelay()
 {
 yield return new WaitForSeconds(delaySeconds);
 transform.position = startPosition;

 Rigidbody rb = GetComponent<Rigidbody>();
 rb.velocity = Vector3.zero;
 rb.angularVelocity = Vector3.zero;
 }
}
```

On `Start`, the script will get the ball's starting position and save it into a `startPosition` variable.

The public function Reset will reset the object's Position after a delay. We implement the delay using a *coroutine*. This is not the first time we've used coroutines in this book, but to remind you, a coroutine is a function that runs separately from the function in which it was called. It must be declared as IEnumerator, it is started using the StartCoroutine function, and it must contain at least one yield return statement. In this case, we yield for five seconds (delaySeconds), and then it does its work.

The reset operation restores the ball's position to its starting position and stabilizes its physics by zeroing out its velocity and angular velocity. If we didn't reset the Rigidbody values, the ball would keep moving even after it's placed on the pedestal.

Save your script, and back in Unity, we can wire up the Reset function by calling the function when the player throws (or otherwise lets go of) the Ball. This is when the **XR Grab Interactable**'s **On Select Exit** event is invoked:

1. With the **Ball** selected in **Inspector**, unfold the **Interactable Events** list on its **XR Grab Interactable** component.
2. At the **On Select Exit** event, add a new response by pressing its **+** button (in the lower-right corner).
3. Drag the **Ball** from **Hierarchy** onto the event's **Object** slot.
4. In the **Function** drop down, select **ResetAfterDelay | Reset**.

The Inspector is shown in the following screenshot:

When you press **Play**, grab the ball and throw it. Five seconds later, the ball will return to its original position.

You could continue improving this game, but I'm going to stop here. It certainly could use some sound effects when the balloon pops. The hand controllers could use some haptic feedback when an object is selected. Another thing you could do is not allow balloons to intersect one another (as you'd expect), even at their tip, by adding a small second Collider component near its base. Oh, and you could display a scoreboard, which requires a UI Canvas. We are actually going to learn about that in the next chapter.

Summary

In this chapter, we explored a variety of software patterns for handling user input for your VR projects. The player uses a controller button, the trigger, to create, inflate, and release balloons into the scene. First, we tried the standard `Input` class for detecting logical button clicks, like the `XRI_Right_TriggerButton` button, and implemented it using a polling design pattern. Then we replaced that with Unity events instead of polling, decoupling our `BalloonController` script from the input itself. Later, this was even more important when we used the XR Interaction Toolkit's Interactor events to implement the same mechanic.

We learned about the XR Interaction Toolkit and its Interactor/Interactable design pattern. We saw how the XR Rig's hand controllers are the Interactors in the scene. We also created Interactables, including the balloon gun and the ball projectile, that you can grab, activate, and throw. We learned how to wire into the Interaction events, including **OnActivate**, **OnDeactivate**, and **OnSelect** events, to call public functions that we wrote to make things work together.

Along the way, we gained more experience with game objects, prefabs, particles, Rigidbodies, and Colliders. We wrote several C# scripts, including `BalloonController`, `KeepUpright`, `Poppable`, and `ResetAfterDelay`, that instantiate, modify, and destroy game objects in the scene. We learned a little more about directly modifying components such as **Transform** and **Rigidbody** through API functions.

In the next chapter, we will further explore user interactions using the Unity UI (user interface) system for implementing information canvases, buttons, and other UI controls.

6
Canvasing the World Space UI

In the previous chapter, we discovered how to interact with game objects in the world space scene. Not only can these objects be balls and toys or tools and weapons, but they can also be buttons you interact with and other **graphical user interface** (**GUI**)—or just **UI**—widgets. Furthermore, Unity includes UI canvas components and an event system for building menus and other UIs.

UI usually refers to onscreen, two-dimensional graphics, which overlay the main gameplay and present information to the user with status messages, gauges, and input controls, such as menus, buttons, sliders, and so on. In Unity, UI elements always reside on a **canvas**. The Unity manual describes the `Canvas` component as follows:

> *The* `Canvas` *component represents the abstract space in which the UI is laid out and rendered. All UI elements must be children of a* `GameObject` *that has a* `Canvas` *component attached.*

In conventional video games, UI objects are usually rendered in a **screen space** canvas as an overlay. The screen space UI is analogous to a piece of cardboard pasted onto your TV or monitor, overlaying the game action behind it. Normally, in games and apps (as with traditional art and photography), the edges of the screen are very important for the composition of the view and the layout of the UI elements. On a phone, the top edge has the status icons and pull-downs for system widgets and the side edges access menu drawers and allow you to swipe between pages, to give a couple of examples.

However, that doesn't work in VR. If you attempt to use screen space for UI in VR, you'll run into issues. Since there are two stereoscopic cameras, you need separate views for each eye. While conventional games may co-opt the edges of the screen for the UI, *VR has no screen edges*!

Instead, in VR, we use various approaches that place the UI elements in **world space**, rather than screen space. In this chapter, we will characterize a number of these types. We'll define these types in detail and show you examples of them throughout this chapter:

- **Heads-up display** (**HUD**): The canvas appears in front of the user. We will explore two types—a **visor HUD**, where the canvas appears at the same spot in front of your eyes, regardless of your head movement, and a **windshield HUD**, where the panel is floating in three-dimensional space, such as a windshield in a cockpit.
- **In-game element UI**: The canvas is part of the **Scene** gameplay, such as a scoreboard in a stadium.
- **Info bubble**: This is a UI message that is attached to objects in the scene, such as a thought-bubble hovering over a character's head.
- **Reticle cursors**: Similar to visor HUDs, a cross-hair or a pointer cursor is used to select things in the scene.
- **Interactive dashboard**: This is a control panel that is a part of the gameplay, usually at waist or desk height.
- **Wrist-based menu palette**: With two-handed input controllers, one hand can hold a menu palette while the other makes selections and uses the selected tool.

The differences between these UI techniques basically comes down to where and when you display the canvas and how the user interacts with it. In this chapter, we're going to try each of these in turn. Along the way, we'll become familiar with the graphic layout of canvas UIs and the use of interactive toggle buttons. By the end of this chapter, you will be able to build your own fully functioning menus and control panel in VR projects.

Technical requirements

To implement the projects and exercises in this chapter, you will need the following:

- A PC or Macintosh with Unity 2019.4 LTS or later, XR Plugin for your device, and the XR Interaction Toolkit package installed
- A VR headset supported by the Unity XR platform

You can access or clone the GitHub repository for this book (`https://github.com/PacktPublishing/Unity-2020-Virtual-Reality-Projects-3rd-Edition-`), to optionally use assets and completed projects for this chapter, as follows:

- Asset files for you to use in this chapter are located in `UVRP3Files/Chapter-06-Files.zip`.
- All completed projects in this book are in a single Unity project at `UVRP3Projects`.
- The completed assets and scenes for this chapter are in the `UVRP3Projects/Assets/_UVRP3Assets/Chapter06/` folder.

Let's talk about VR design principles in the next section.

Studying VR design principles

Before we get into the implementation details, I want to introduce the topic of designing three-dimensional UIs and VR experiences. A lot of work has been carried out in these areas over the past few decades, even more so in the past few years.

With consumer VR devices being so readily available and the existence of powerful development tools, such as Unity, it's not surprising that a lot of people are inventing and trying new things, continuously innovating and producing really excellent VR experiences. You are probably one of them. However, the context of today's VR progress cannot be viewed in a vacuum. There is a long history of research and development that feeds into present-day work. The following are some examples:

- The *3D User Interfaces: Theory and Practice* (Bowman et al) book, for example, is a classic academic survey of three-dimensional user interaction for consumer, industrial, and scientific applications and research.
- An easy-to-read but practical introduction to VR user experience design is the medium.com *Get Started with VR User Experience Design* (`https://medium.com/vrinflux-dot-com/get-started-with-vr-user-experience-design-974486cf9d18`) article by Adrienne Hunter, the co-creator of the popular VR physics package NewtonVR. It identifies important core principles, including attention, lighting, audio, and space.

- Another great article is *Practical VR: A Design Cheat Sheet* (`https://virtualrealitypop.com/practical-vr-ce80427e8e9d`), intended to be an up-to-date primer with VR design guidelines, processes, tools, and other resources that the author intends to maintain and update.
- You can also check out Oculus's series of articles on VR design best practices, including one on user input (`https://developer.oculus.com/design/latest/concepts/bp-userinput/`).
- Look for presentations from the Unity Unite annual conferences, the Oculus Connect conferences, the **Game Developer Conference** (**GDC**), and the VRDC conference. Have fun reading and watching videos.

One of my favorite studies of design for VR is *VR Interface Design Pre-Visualization Methods* produced by Mike Algers as a grad student in 2015. His inspiring video (which can be found at `https://vimeo.com/141330081`) presents an easily digestible thesis of design principles, especially for seated VR experiences, based on established ergonomics of workspaces and visual perception. We'll use some of these ideas in this chapter. Algers also explores button design for VR, mock-up workflows, and concepts for VR operating system design. (Algers presently works in the Google VR development group). In his thesis, Algers establishes a set of comfort zones radially around the user's first-person location, as shown:

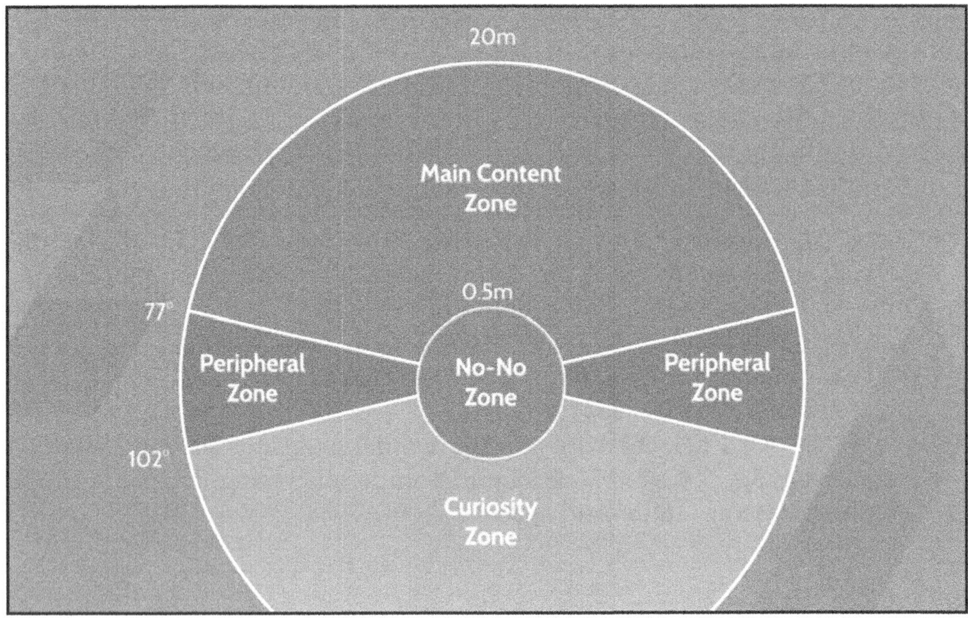

Anything closer than `0.5` meters is too close for comfort; you might have to cross your eyes just to focus and follow objects at that range. Anything beyond `20` meters is too far away to have meaningful interactions and is also too far for depth perception with parallax. Your peripheral zones (between `77` to `102` degrees) should not contain primary content and interactions but can have secondary ones. Behind you is what Algers calls the curiosity zone; you'd need to stretch (or swivel your chair or turn around) to see what's going on there, so it had better be important yet not imperative. The main content zone is your normal workspace. Then, accounting for the directions your arm can reach (forward, up, and down) and other normal human movements in a workspace, Algers defines the optimal virtual work zone for a seated VR experience, as shown:

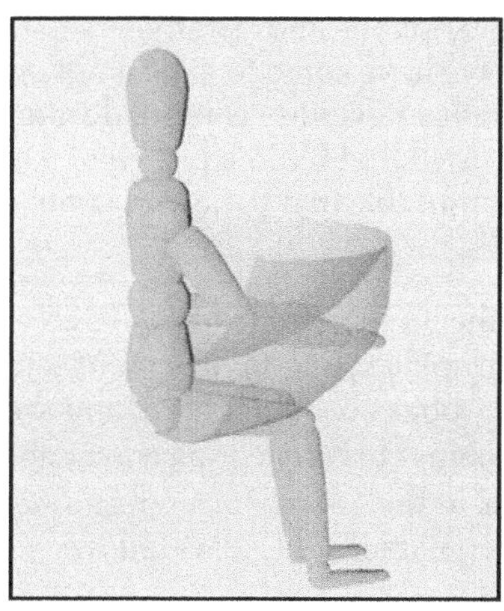

For standing and room-scale VR, the workspace is different. When standing, it may be much easier (and expected) to be able to turn around to access things all around you. With room-scale, you can walk around (and jump, duck, and crawl, for that matter). Alex Schwartz and Devin Reimer of Owlchemy Labs (which has since been acquired by Google), in their talk at Oculus Connect 2 (`https://www.youtube.com/watch?v=hjc7AJwZ4DI`), discuss the challenges of designing standing VR experiences for their popular *Job Simulator* game, including accommodation for real-world ergonomics and varied height experiences.

Of course, this just scratches the surface, and more is being published about VR every day. Meanwhile, let's get back to work. It's time to implement a VR UI ourselves. The first thing we'll do is create a default **Canvas** prefab that we can reuse in the various examples in this chapter.

Making a reusable default canvas

A Unity **canvas** is a two-dimensional planar surface that is a container for UI graphics, such as menus, toolbars, and information panels. In conventional applications, canvases are commonly rendered in screen space that overlays the scene's gameplay graphics and has the ability to stretch and conform to a huge variety of screen sizes, aspect ratios, and orientations (landscape versus portrait). In contrast, in VR, we never use screen space because the VR "screen" has no edges and differs for the left and right eyes. Instead, in VR, we use a world space canvas that floats (albeit still on a two-dimensional surface) in the same three-dimensional space as all your other **Scene** objects.

Unity's UI canvas provides many options and parameters to accommodate the kinds of graphical layout flexibility that we have come to expect not only in games but also from websites and mobile apps. With this flexibility comes additional complexity. To make our examples in this chapter easier, we'll first build a prefab of a canvas that has our preferred VR default settings and make it reusable in a variety of contexts that we'll explore in the various topics of this chapter.

We will start this chapter with the `04-Navmesh` scene we created in `Chapter 4`, *Using Gaze-Based Control*, which includes our play space environment with a baked NavMesh, an `AIThirdPersonController` object named `Ethan`, and scripts that control where the `Ethan` character is allowed to roam. This scene is also available in the assets that you may have downloaded from GitHub, in the `Chapter06-Files.zip` folder. Save a working copy of the scene for this chapter, named `06-UI`, as follows.

1. Open the `04-Navmesh` scene.
2. Go to **File** | **Save As** and name it `06-UI`.
3. You may need to rebake the NavMesh by selecting **Window** | **Navigation** | **Bake**.

We now have a working scene named `06-UI` for this chapter.

Creating a default canvas prefab

We want to create a default VR canvas prefab that we can use in the examples throughout this chapter and other projects in this book. To start, create a new world space XR UI canvas, as follows:

1. Add a new canvas to the scene (**GameObject** | **XR** | **UI Canvas**).
2. Rename the canvas `Default Canvas`.
3. Notice that **Render Mode** is set to **World Space** (if not, change it now).
4. Also, note the canvas **Event Camera** setting will be preset to **Main Camera** in **XR Rig**.

The **Rect Transform** component defines the grid system on the canvas itself, like the lines on a piece of graph paper. It is used for the placement of UI elements on the canvas. The pixel grid is defined by width and height and then scaled down to a world space size. We'll set it to a convenient value of `1000 x 750`, giving it a `0.75` aspect ratio, as follows:

1. In **Rect Transform**, set **Width** to `1000` and **Height** to `750`.
2. In **Scale**, set **X**, **Y**, and **Z** to `0.001`, `0.001`, and `0.001`, respectively. This is the size for one of our canvas units in world space units.
3. Now, position the canvas centered above the ground plane. In **Rect Transform**, set **Pos X**, **Pos Y**, and **Pos Z** to `0`, `1.5`, and `0`, respectively.

The canvas has a **Rect Transform** component, whose **Width** and **Height** values define the grid system on the canvas itself, like the lines on a piece of graph paper. These dimensions help in the placement of UI elements on the canvas. However, unless you want one pixel to be 1 meter wide in world space(!), we must compensate by downscaling the entire canvas by 1/width (or height).

The **Default Canvas** scope's **Inspector** window is shown in the following screenshot. Note the **Width**, **Height**, and **Scale** values, as well as the additional default components—**Canvas**, **Canvas Scaler**, **Graphic Raycaster**, and **Tracked Device Graphic Raycaster**:

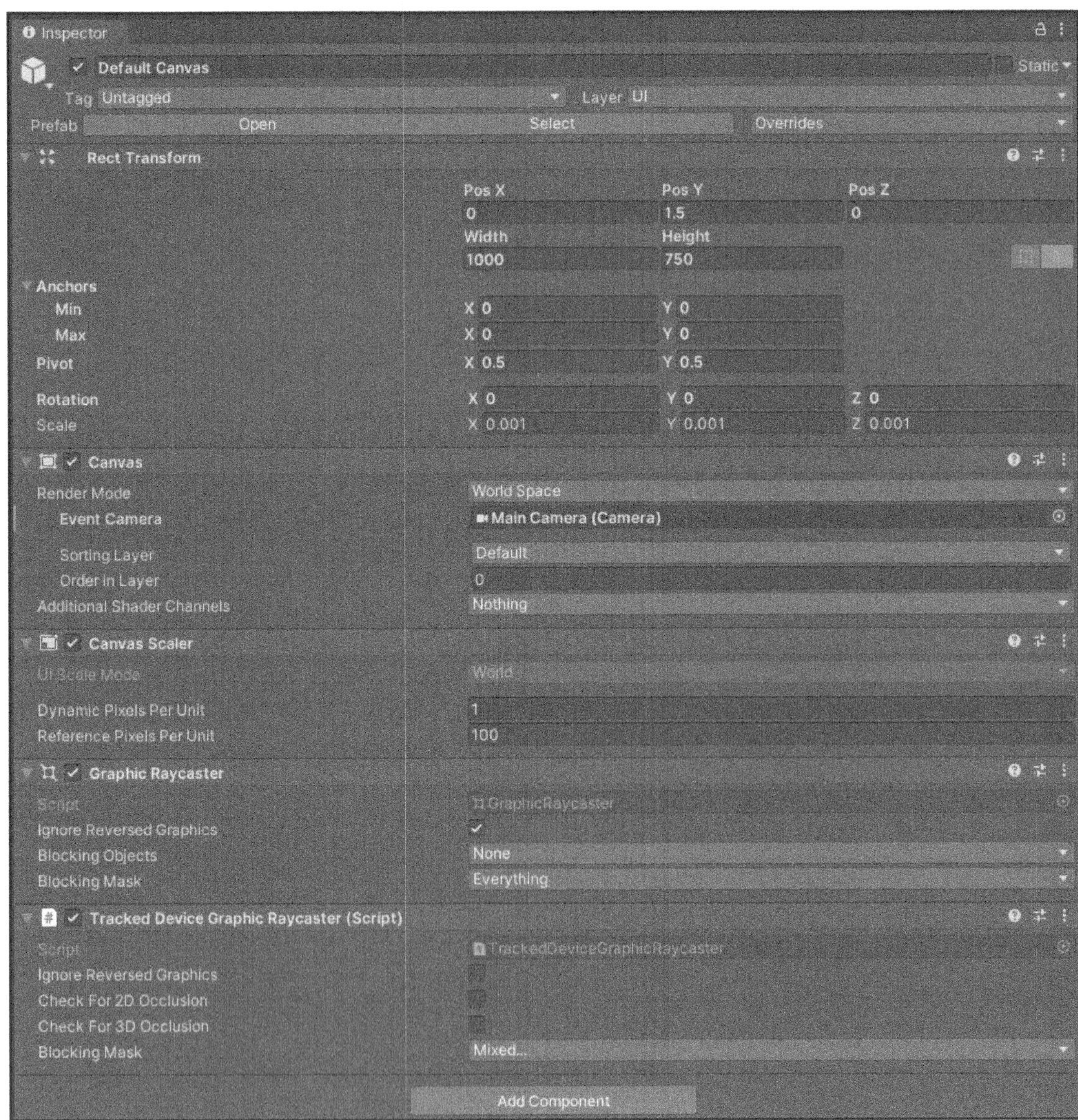

An empty canvas is rendered in the **Scene** view as just a thinly outlined rectangle. We will add a child **Panel** element (with a translucent white background) to help us see the canvas:

1. With **Default Canvas** selected, right-click and choose **UI** | **Panel** (ensure that it's created as a child of **Default Canvas**; if not, move it under **Default Canvas**).
2. With **Panel** selected, note that at the upper left of its **Rect Transform** pane, there is an **Anchor Presets** button (shown in the following screenshot) that is set by default to **stretch-stretch** so that it fills the canvas. Selecting this opens the **Anchor Presets** dialog box.
3. Now, you can press and hold the *Alt* key to see and set the **Anchors** position and/or the *Shift* key for the **Pivot** setting:

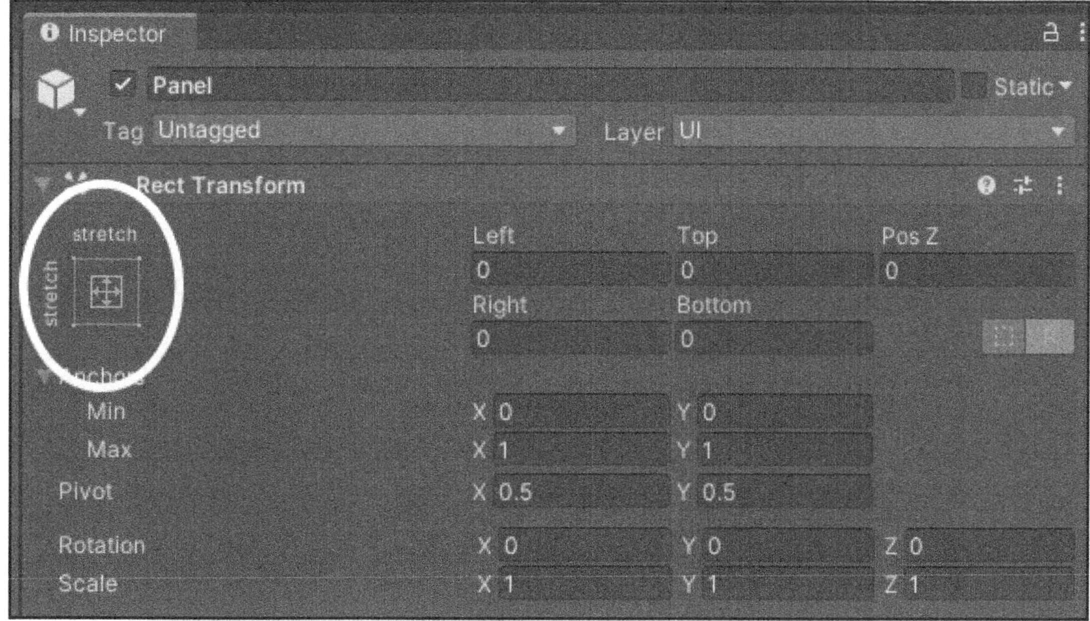

Add a **Text** element under the panel with useful new settings, as follows:

1. With **Panel** selected, right-click and choose **UI** | **Text** (ensure that it's created as a child of **Panel**; if not, move it under **Panel**). `New Text` should appear on the canvas, although the text may be too small to easily notice.
2. Set its **Anchors** setting to **stretch-stretch** using the **Anchor Presets** widget at the upper left of its **Rect Transform** pane.

3. Also, set its **Position** setting to **stretch-stretch** using the *Alt* key while the **Anchor Presets** box is still open.
4. Choose a larger font. With **Text** selected, set **Font Size** to `72`.
5. Center the text on the panel. With **Text** selected, set **Alignment** to **Center Align** and **Middle Align**.

The modified **Text** settings are shown in the following screenshot:

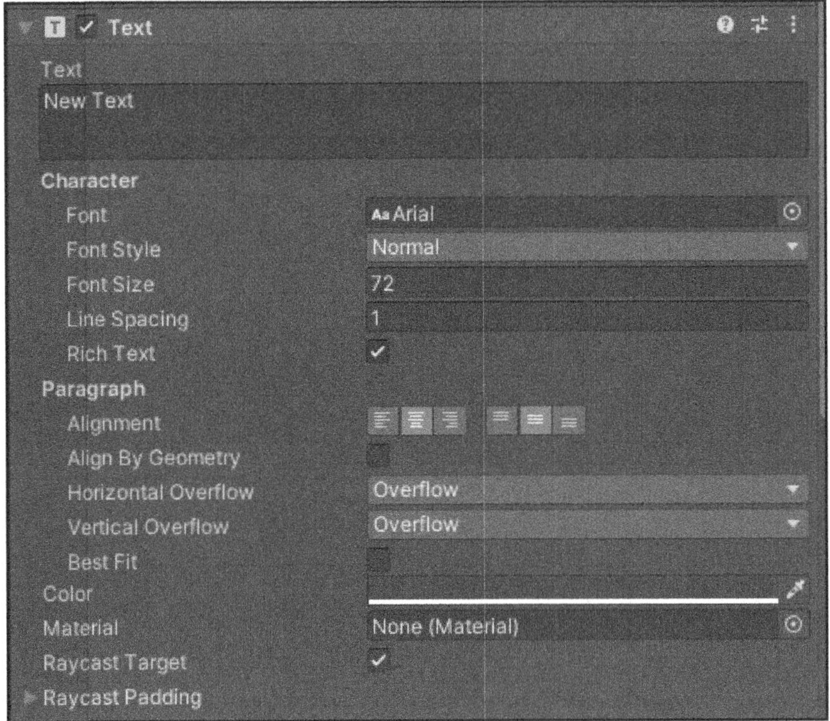

Note that if you increase the font size without first increasing the text's **Rect Transform** setting, the text may disappear. This can be remedied by modifying its **Horizontal Overflow** and **Vertical Overflow** settings to **Overflow**.

If the text's font appears fuzzy, you can increase the pixel resolution of your canvas by selecting the canvas object and setting **Canvas Scaler** | **Dynamic Pixels Per Unit** to `10`, for example. However, you'll then need to increase the **Scale** value of your text elements to compensate.

Please note that any UI elements in a scene (such as **Button**) must be a child of a canvas. If you try to add a UI element to the **Hierarchy** window that is not nested under a canvas, Unity will automatically parent the new element to the first canvas it can find in the **Hierarchy** window, or if it cannot find one, it creates a new one. In the latter case, the new canvas may not be in world space and may not contain the **Tracked Device Graphic Raycaster** component needed for XR interactions. Likewise, the same is true if you create a canvas using the standard **GameObject | UI | Canvas** setting. This is why I recommend using the **GameObject | XR | UI Canvas** menu instead, which will generate a world space canvas with the required **Tracked Device Graphic Raycaster** component.

When you add an XR canvas (**GameObject | XR | UI Canvas**), Unity generates an **EventSystem** component with an **XRUI Input Module** component in your scene, along with a canvas with a **Tracked Device Graphic Raycaster** component. Normally, in order for users to interact with UI elements on a canvas, the canvas needs at least one **Graphic Raycaster** component. This is used to determine whether a user input event, such as mouse clicks or screen touches, has hit any UI elements on the canvas. The **raycaster** looks at all the graphics on the canvas and determines whether any of them have been selected by the user. In an XR project, you should use a **Tracked Device Graphic Raycaster** component instead of the default **Graphic Raycaster** one, which handles XR UI input events. Likewise, the scene must contain an **Event System** component with an **XRUI Input Module** component.

Finally, save your work as a prefab asset that you can reuse throughout the chapter in the following manner:

1. If necessary, in **Project Assets**, create a new folder named `Prefabs`.
2. Drag the **Default Canvas** object into the `Assets/Prefabs` folder of the Project to create a prefab.
3. Delete the **Default Canvas** instance in the **Hierarchy** panel (right-click and select **Delete**).

OK, I'm glad we got that out of the way! Now, we can use the **Default Canvas** prefab with different VR UI examples. In our projects, we can now simply drag the **Default Canvas** prefab into the scene. However, there's a new problem—the canvas reference to **Main Camera** is not retained in the prefab version of the canvas. Let's fix that now.

Initializing the default main camera

When you save a game object as a prefab, the prefab cannot have any direct references to objects in the **Scene** view's **Hierarchy** window. This may be confusing at first, but if you think about it, it becomes obvious. Files in the `Assets/` folder of **Project** are potentially available for use in the scene, in multiple instances, and/or in multiple different scenes, or not at all. They may be exported into a Unity package and shared worldwide. Objects in the scene, on the other hand, are a specific instantiation of an object. So, prefab objects cannot reference instantiated objects in a particular scene. In the case of world space canvases, the instantiated canvas may have a reference to **Main Camera**, but our **Default Canvas** prefab has lost this reference. When we drag the **Default Canvas** prefab into a scene, we need to assign the camera again. Let's write a script to take care of that automatically at runtime, assuming it will use the current main camera:

1. Open the **Default Canvas** prefab for editing (double-click on **Default Canvas** in the **Project** window's `Prefabs/` folder.)
2. Select the root **Default Canvas** object.
3. Create a new C# script on the object, named `AssignCanvasEventCamera`.

Open the script and write it as follows to assign `Camera.main` to the `Canvas` if it isn't already assigned:

```
public class AssignCanvasEventCamera : MonoBehaviour
{
    void Start()
    {
        Canvas canvas = GetComponent<Canvas>();
        if (canvas && canvas.worldCamera == null)
        {
            canvas.worldCamera = Camera.main;
        }
    }
}
```

We can now drag the **Default Canvas** prefab into the scene whenever we want to add a canvas. With this script attached, you need not worry about forgetting to assign the world camera manually. Additionally, if necessary, Unity will also automatically create an **Event System** component in **Hierarchy**.

Including an Event System component with XRUI Input Module

If a canvas contains interactive UI elements, such as a button or slider, it must be configured to detect when your user is pointing at one of these elements, respond with some user feedback (such as showing a pressed-button highlight color or moving the slider handle), and trigger a corresponding input event. This is handled by the Unity event system. There must be one, and only one, **Event System** component in the scene.

User interactions with UI elements (such as pressing a **Button** and so on) also require an event system to be in the scene. If you add a canvas to a scene and an event system is not present, Unity will automatically create one in the hierarchy. If this default event system contains a **Standalone Input Module** component and not the **XRUI Input Module** component needed for XR interactions, you can delete the standalone one and add the XRUI one yourself. Using the **GameObject** | **XR** | **UI Canvas** menu instead will generate, if necessary, the proper event system with the **XRUI Input Module** component instead of **Standalone Input Module**.

I will explain the use of the **XRUI Input Module** and **Tracked Device Graphic Raycaster** components later in this chapter. To start, we will be using canvases for non-interactive, display-only graphics. The first thing we'll look at is a couple of variations of HUD information.

Implementing a HUD

The term HUD originates from its use in an aircraft, where a pilot is able to view information while looking forward rather down at their instrument panels. In Unity, a HUD may be implemented as a canvas-based UI floating in your field of view, overlaying the gameplay scene. Typically a HUD is more about displaying information than providing interactable buttons or controls. In this section, we'll test two different variations of HUDs—what I characterize as **visor HUD** and **windshield HUD**. We'll start with the visor HUD and then add a little script that gracefully hides the panel with a fadeout when we want it to disappear.

Creating a visor HUD

For a visor HUD, the UI canvas is attached to the camera object in the scene, so when you move your head, the canvas doesn't appear to respond to your head movement. Rather, it seems to be *stuck to your face (haha)*! For a nicer way to describe it, suppose you're wearing a helmet with a glass see-through visor in front of your eyes, and the UI appears projected onto that visor. (Tony Stark in the *Iron Man* movies was a big fan of the visor HUD in his Iron Man suit.) There may be contexts where this is OK in VR, but otherwise, it could break the sense of immersion and should generally only be used when wearing a visor is part of the gameplay.

Let's make a visor HUD with a welcome message and see for ourselves how it feels, as follows:

1. In the **Hierarchy** window, unfold the **XR Rig** object and then drill down to the **Main Camera** object.
2. From the **Project** window, drag the **Default Canvas** prefab onto the camera object so that it becomes a child of it, and rename it `Visor Canvas`.
3. In the **Inspector** window for the canvas, change the **Rect Transform** component's **Pos X**, **Pos Y**, and **Pos Z** values to `0`, `0`, and `1`, respectively.
4. Unfold **Visor Canvas** and select the child **Text** object.
5. In the **Inspector** window, change the text to `Welcome! My reality is your reality`. (You can enter line breaks in the input text area.)
6. Change its **Horizontal Overflow** setting to **Wrap**
7. Change the text **Color** setting to something bright and colorful.
8. Select the parent **Panel** object and disable its **Image** object so that only the text shows by un-checking its **enable** checkbox in **Inspector**.
9. Save the scene and try it in VR.

As you can see, in the following **Scene** view and **Hierarchy** window, the canvas is a child of the camera and stays in view, regardless of where the user is looking. In VR, when you move your head, the text follows along as if it's attached to a visor in front of your face:

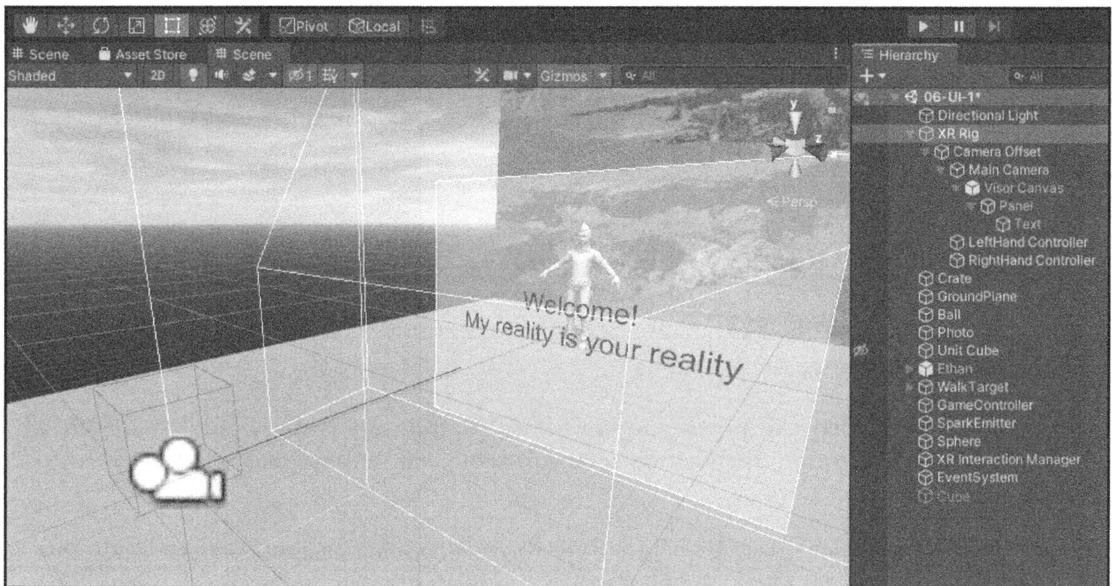

A visor HUD appears like it is attached to the helmet visor you're wearing on your head. It moves in unison with your head, regardless of where you are positioned in the environment. The canvas is set up as a child object of the camera.

Now, go ahead and disable **Visor Canvas**, or just delete it (in the **Hierarchy** panel, right-click on it and select **Delete**) because we're going to display the welcome message in a different way next—as a windshield HUD.

The windshield HUD

With a **windshield HUD**, like the visor HUD, is an information panel that overlays the gameplay, but it isn't attached to your head. Instead, you can think of it as being attached to your vehicle while you're seated in its cockpit. You can freely move your head and look around; the HUD stays stationary relative to your body's position but moves along with you if you navigate or teleport to a different location in the scene.

A windshield HUD appears as if it's attached to a glass windshield as you sit in a vehicle. It stays stationary as you move your head, but it moves along with you as the vehicle moves through the environment. The canvas is set up as a child of the camera rig.

Let's create a simple windshield HUD by performing the following steps:

1. From the **Project** window, drag the **Default Canvas** prefab onto the `XR Rig` object in the **Hierarchy** panel so that it becomes an immediate child of `XR Rig` (not under the camera this time).
2. Rename it `Windshield Canvas`.
3. With `Windshield Canvas` selected, set the **Rect Transform** component's **Pos X**, **Pos Y**, and **Pos Z** values to `0`, `1.5`, and `1`, respectively.
4. Now, we'll set the **Text** component. With **Text** under `Windshield Canvas` selected, change the text to `Welcome! My reality is your reality`.

That's pretty straightforward. When you view it in VR, the canvas starts out just in front of you, but as you look around, its position seems to remain stationary and relative to the other objects in the scene.

As we'll see in the next chapter, `Chapter 7`, *Teleporting, Locomotion, and Comfort*, when the player moves through the scene, the HUD canvas will stay in front of you, relative to the position of your body object, `XR Rig`. You can try it now in the editor:

1. Select **XR Rig** in **Hierarchy**.
2. Press **Play**.
3. Then, in the **Scene** window, using the **Move** gizmo, move the **XR Rig** object's position. In VR, you'll see that the HUD follows along like it's part of your body or a spaceship's cockpit, as in the following **Scene** view:

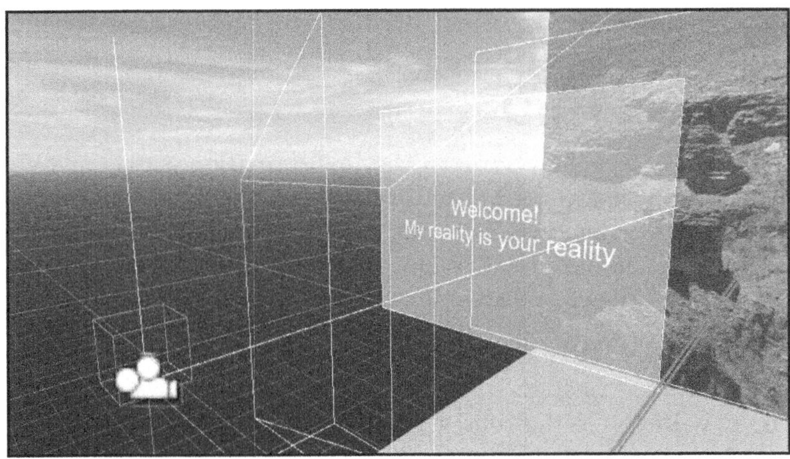

You might have realized that it's possible for objects in the scene to obfuscate the HUD panel since they're all occupying the same world space. If you want to prevent this, you have to ensure that the canvas is always rendered last so that it appears in front of any other objects, regardless of its position in three-dimensional space. In a conventional monoscopic game, you can do this by adding a second camera for the UI and changing its render priority; or, more simply, use the **Screen Space** mode with the canvas. In stereoscopic VR, you have to accomplish this differently, possibly by writing a custom shader for your UI object or doing per-layer occlusion culling. This is an advanced topic; see the *World Space canvas on top of everything?* discussion thread for details at `https://answers.unity.com/questions/878667/world-space-canvas-on-top-of-everything.html`.

A variant of this HUD is to turn the canvas so that it's always facing you, while its position in three-dimensional space is fixed. We'll write a script for that in the *Info bubble* topics of the next section. But first, let's consider one more feature—hiding the HUD panel with a nice fade-out effect.

Hiding the panel using Canvas Group

For kicks, let's write a script that removes the welcome message after 5 seconds. When the time is up, we could just call `SetActive(false)` to make it disappear. But instead, we'll give it a gentler fade-out effect, using a **Canvas Group** component. Let's add that now, as follows:

1. With **Windshield Canvas** selected, add a **Canvas Group** component (go to the main menu, then **Component | Layout | Canvas Group**).
2. Note that **Canvas Group** has an **Alpha** parameter. Try changing its value to somewhere between `1` and `0` to fade the canvas.
3. Add a new script, `HideAfterDelay`, to the canvas (go to **Add Component | New Script**, name it `HideAfterDelay`, and then click **Create And Add**).
4. Open the script for editing.

Here's the `HideAfterDelay.cs` script:

```
public class HideAfterDelay : MonoBehaviour
{
    public float delayInSeconds = 5f;
    public float fadeRate = 0.25f;
```

```
    private CanvasGroup canvasGroup;
    private float startTimer;
    private float fadeoutTimer;

    void OnEnable()
    {
        canvasGroup = GetComponent<CanvasGroup>();
        canvasGroup.alpha = 1f;

        startTimer = Time.time + delayInSeconds;
        fadeoutTimer = fadeRate;
    }

    void Update()
    {
        // time to fade out?
        if (Time.time >= startTimer)
        {
            fadeoutTimer -= Time.deltaTime;

            // fade out complete?
            if (fadeoutTimer <= 0)
            {
                gameObject.SetActive(false);
            }
            else
            {
                // reduce the alpha value
                canvasGroup.alpha = fadeoutTimer / fadeRate;
            }
        }
    }
}
```

This script maintains two timers. The first one (`startTimer`) determines when its time to start hiding the canvas. It is initialized in `OnEnable()` to the game time when the fade should start (the time plus `delayInSeconds`—for example, the current time+ 5 seconds). Then, in `Update()`, we check the current time to see whether it's time for the fade out.

The second timer, `fadoutTimer`, calculates the change in the canvas' alpha value over time. It is initialized to one-quarter of a second. Then, in `Update`, we modify the alpha value to the percentage that the timer is done (`fadeoutTimer / fadeRate`). Once the timer has run out, we hide the canvas altogether by calling `SetActive(false)`. Note that when a GameObject is not active anymore, the `Update` function will stop being called by Unity, saving a tiny bit of processor performance.

You may notice that I'm using `OnEnable` to initialize the timers. I could just as well have used `Start()`, which is called only once in the lifetime of the object. On the other hand, `OnEnable` is called any time that the object is enabled, so for example, if you were to re-activate the canvas later on, it will again wait 5 seconds and then fade out again.

This script could be simplified using the **DOTween** package from Demigiant (available for free in Asset Store at `https://assetstore.unity.com/packages/tools/animation/dotween-hotween-v2-27676`. There is also a Pro version for a small cost). The entire fade-out part of the code could be written as a single statement, as follows:

```
void Update()
{
    if (Time.time >= startTimer)
    {
        canvaGroup.
            DOFade(0f, fadeRate).
            OnComplete(() => { gameObject.SetActive(false); });
    }
}
```

In summary, we have implemented a couple of variations of a HUD. The visor HUD stays put in front of your eyes, even as you move your head, like a helmet with a glass visor in front, by parenting the canvas to **Main Camera**. The windshield HUD is more like a vehicle windshield; it follows your body's position, but is not attached to your head, by parenting the canvas to **XR Rig**. Then, I demonstrated how to make the UI panel fade out (or in) using the **Canvas Group Alpha** values, making the hide/show experience a bit more pleasant.

Next, we will look at using UI elements that are integrated into your scene as game objects.

The in-game world space UI

Game objects in your game world that use UI elements might include billboards, scoreboards, control panels, handheld menu palettes, puzzles, and so on. What all of these have in common is that they are objects in the scene that are meant to convey some information and/or indicate that the user should interact with them to perform some operations. They are better served if they are able to dynamically update with runtime information, so a pre-saved texture image or sprite will not be sufficient. In this section, we will try a couple of different scenarios—a scoreboard and an info bubble. We will also introduce the powerful **TextMesh Pro** (**TMP**) tools, which are built into Unity and give greater control over your text graphics. We'll start with the scoreboard game element example, and then implement an info bubble.

Making a scoreboard

When `Ethan` gets killed in the diorama scene from `Chapter 4`, *Using Gaze-Based Control*, the score value in the `GameController` object's `KillTarget` script is updated, but the current score isn't shown to the player (set up in that chapter). We'll do this now, adding a scoreboard into the scene at the top-left corner of the backdrop **Photo** image:

1. From the **Project** window, drag the `Default Canvas` prefab directly into the **Scene** view and rename it `Scoreboard`.
2. Position and size the canvas in the corner of the image (with `Scoreboard` selected, set the **Rect Transform** component's **Pos X**, **Pos Y**, and **Pos Z** values to(`-2.8`, `7`, and `4.9`, respectively, and the **Width** and **Height** values to `2000` and `750`, respectively).
3. Hide the **Panel** background (select the child **Panel** object and in the **Inspector** window, un-check the **Image** component **enable** checkbox).
4. Enlargen the text (select the **Text** object and in the **Inspector** window, set **Font Size** to `300`).
5. Choose a noticeable color, such as red, for the **Text** object.
6. Enter the `Score: 0` sample string for **Text**.

Note that you can use **Rect Tool** in the **Scene** editor window to interactively modify the **Rect Transform** component without affecting the pixel scale of its contents. The selection of **Rect Tool** from the toolbar is shown in the following screenshot:

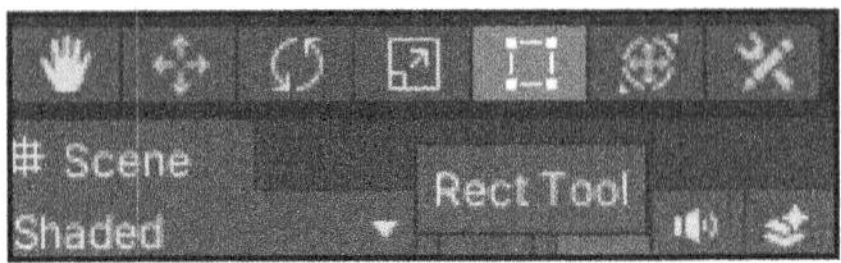

We have added another canvas to the scene, then sized and placed it where we want, and formatted the text for display. It should look something like this:

Now, we need to update the KillTarget.cs script, as follows:

1. First, we will be using the UnityEngine.UI classes, so declare using UnityEngine.UI at the top of the file:

    ```
    using UnityEngine.UI;
    ```

2. Add a public variable for scoreText at the top of the class:

    ```
      public Text scoreText;
    ```

3. Add a line to Start() to initialize the score text:

    ```
    scoreText.text = "Score: 0";
    ```

4. Then, add a line to Update() to change the score text when the score changes:

    ```
    score += 1;
    scoreText.text = "Score: " + score;
    ```

5. After saving the script file, go back into the Unity editor, select GameController from the **Hierarchy** panel, and then drag and drop the **Text** object under **Scoreboard** from **Hierarchy** onto the **Score Text** field in the **Kill Target** component.
6. Run the scene in VR. Each time you kill Ethan (by staring at him), your score will be updated on the Scoreboard component at the upper left of the Photo plane.

This was an example of using an object that's a part of the scene for information display. Our example is pretty simplistic. You might want to make a nicer modeled scoreboard, such as the one you'd actually see in a stadium. You can also use a better font; we'll learn in the next topic how to use TMP. The scoreboard is a part of the scene and unlike HUDs, to see the message, you might have to actually turn your head and look at it.

Using TextMesh Pro

To make a billboard glow like a neon sign, you can use **TextMesh Pro** (**TMP**), an advanced text-rendering toolkit that gives you a lot of flexibility and high-quality text styling and texturing functionality. Some time ago, TMP was a third-party asset that was very popular in Asset Store, then Unity acquired the product and now distributes it free with Unity. In fact, it may already be installed on your Unity project by default. Even so, you probably still need to install the TMP asset into your project if you want to use it, as follows:

1. Open **Package Manager** (**Window** | **Package Manager**).
2. In the search bar, search for `TextMeshPro`. If necessary, in the left-side filter dropdown, choose **All** instead of **Packages In Project**.
3. Click **Install** to install the package, or if necessary, select **Update** to install the current version.
4. Import the **TMP essential assets** into your project (**Window**| **TextMeshPro** | **Import TMP Essential Resources**) and then select **Import** in the import box.
5. This should open a new **TMP Importer** window. Press the **Import TMP Essentials** button to complete the import.
6. Likewise, import the **TMP examples and extras** by selecting **Import TMP Examples and Extras**, and carry out the previous step:

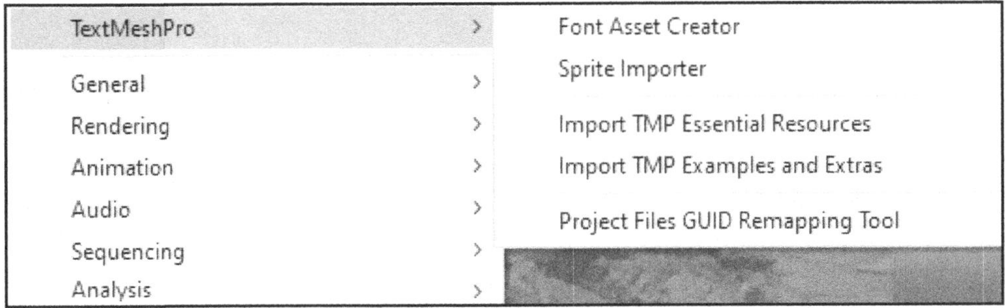

Now, we can use TMP text in the project. For example, we can do the following:

1. With **Scoreboard Panel** selected in **Hierarchy**, create a new TMP text element (right-click, then go to **UI** | **Text - TextMeshPro)**. Notice its default name is `Text (TMP)`.
2. This replaces our standard UI text element, so disable the **Text** object (un-check the **enable** checkbox at the top left of **Inspector**).
3. Let's set up the **Text (TMP)** object like we had the original text one. Go to **Rect Transform** | **Anchor Presets** | **Stretch-Stretch**, and then press *Shift* + *Alt* and click **Stretch-Stretch**.
4. For the **Text** string, set the **Score** value to `0`, **Font Size** to `300`, **Wrapping** to **Disabled**, **Overflow** to **Overflow**, and **Alignment** to **Left, Middle**.

Now, we'll experiment with some fonts. Let's try **Bangers**:

1. In the **Font Asset** area, pick the doughnut icon to open the **Select TMP Font Asset** window and choose **Bangers SDF**.
2. For its **Material Preset** setting, use **Bangers SDF Glow**.
3. Scroll to the **Glow** settings in the **Material** pane to adjust the colors and other settings as you desire.

In C# scripts, the TMP text object class is not the same as the standard Unity UI text object. In your scripts, if you are using TMP text objects, you must declare the variable as `TMP_Text` instead of `Text`.

We now need to tell the `KillTarget` script that we're using a TMP text object rather than the standard UI text object. Modify `KillTarget.cs` as follows. First, declare that we are using the Unity Engine TMP classes:

```
using TMPro;
```

Replace the data type of the `scoreText` variable with `TMP_Text`:

```
    public TMP_Text scoreText;
```

The rest of the script is unchanged since `TMP_Text` has a `text` sub-property, just as the UI text does. Save the script. Back in Unity, drag the **Text (TMP)** object from **Hierarchy** onto the **Score Text** slot in **Inspector**. The following is a screenshot of the scoreboard text using a glow effect with TMP and its material's **Inspector** settings: The orange color is achieved by setting the material's **Texture** setting using the `Gradient Diagonal (Color)` image asset:

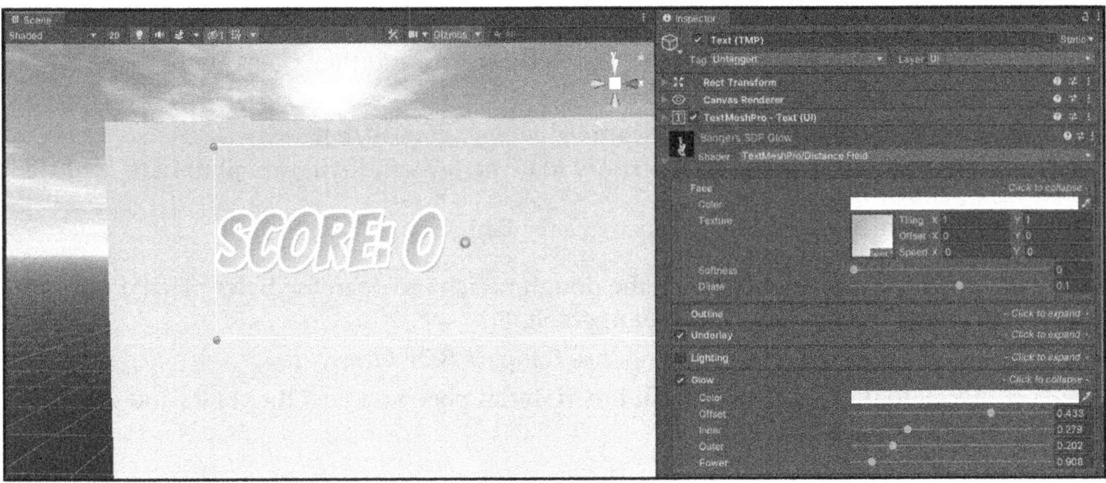

TMP can be used wherever basic `Text` objects are used in a scene, including buttons, dropdowns, and input field UI elements. Uniquely, TMP also lets you add three-dimensional text objects directly into a scene as a mesh, without the need for a canvas (from the main menu, go to **GameObject** | **3D Object** | **Text - TextMeshPro**). While this chapter continues to focus on world space canvases, you might want to keep all of this in mind. Next, we'll consider another scenario where text elements can be used as game objects in a scene—info bubbles.

Info bubbles

In a comic book, when a character says something, it's shown in a **speech bubble**. In many online social VR worlds, participants are represented by avatars, and often, hovering above someone's avatar is their name. I call this type of UI an **info bubble**. Another example is a health meter hovering over a character. Info bubbles are located in world space at a specific three-dimensional position, but the canvas should always be facing the user (camera). We can set this with a script.

In this example, we'll display the *X* and *Z* location of the `WalkTarget` object (set up in `Chapter 4`, *Using Gaze-Based Control*), controlled by the `LookMoveTo.cs` script. To add the info bubble, take the following steps:

1. From the **Project** window, drag the `Default Canvas` prefab directly into the **Hierarchy** window so that it's a child of `WalkTarget`.
2. Rename it `InfoBubble`.
3. Use **Rect Tool** in the **Scene** window to adjust the **InfoBubble** canvas size. Set **Pos X**, **Pos Y**, and **Pos Z** to `0`, `0.2`, and `0`, respectively, and **Width** and **Height** to `600` and `150`, respectively.
4. On the child **Text** element, enter the `X:00.00, Z:00.00` string for **Text**.

Verify that the canvas and text look good. My `InfoBubble` canvas with the `WalkTarget` object's **CursorDisk** component is shown in the following screenshot:

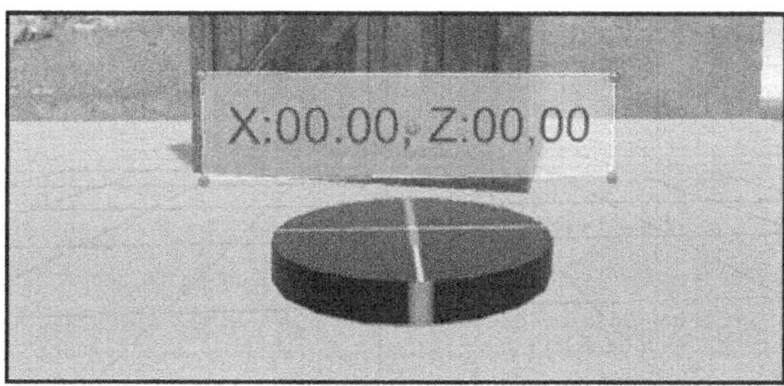

Now, we will modify the `LookMoveTo.cs` script to show the current `WalkTarget` object's *X* and *Z* position. Open the script in the editor and add the following code (highlighted in bold). First, declare the `infoBubble` and `infoText` variables, then initialize `infoText` in `Start`:

```
using UnityEngine;
using UnityEngine.UI;

public class LookMoveTo : MonoBehaviour
{
  public GameObject ground;
  private Transform camera;

  public Transform infoBubble;
  private Text infoText;

  void Start()
  {
    camera = Camera.main.transform;
```

```
        if (infoBubble != null)
        {
            infoText = GetComponentInChildren<Text>();
        }
    }
```

The `using UnityEngine.UI;` line states that this script will need access to the Unity UI API. We defined a `public Transform infoBubble` variable, which will be set to the **WalkTarget** | **InfoBubble** object. We also defined a `private Text infoText` variable, which gets set to the `InfoBubble` object's **Text** object. The script assumes that the given `InfoBubble` object has a child **Text** UI object.

Then, add `Update` to the code, which updates the `infoText` object with the current position of the target. Rotate the canvas to always face the camera, as follows:

```
    void Update()
    {
      Ray ray;
      RaycastHit[] hits;
      GameObject hitObject;

      ray = new Ray(camera.position, camera.rotation * Vector3.forward);
      hits = Physics.RaycastAll(ray);
      for (int i = 0; i < hits.Length; i++)
      {
        RaycastHit hit = hits[i];
        hitObject = hit.collider.gameObject;
        if (hitObject == ground)
        {
          if (infoBubble != null)
          {
            infoText.text = "X:" + hit.point.x.ToString("F2") +
                            ", " +
                            "Z:" + hit.point.z.ToString("F2");

            infoBubble.LookAt(camera.position);
            infoBubble.Rotate(0, 180f, 0);
          }
          transform.position = hit.point;
        }
      }
    }
```

In `Start()`, we found the `WalkTarget/InfoBubble/Text` object's **Text** component, assigned to `infoText`. Then, in `Update()`, we set a string value of `infoText.text` to show the coordinates on the bubble canvas.

Unfortunately, the overuse of the word `text` can be confusing. The `infoText` variable references the scene's **Text** game object, which has a **Text** component (the C# `Text` class), which has a `text` string property! You can see what I mean in the Unity **Inspector** window. When `InfoBubble/Text` is selected, it contains a **Text** (**Script**) component, which has a **Text** field. This **Text** field is where we write our messages. In code, the text field is referenced as `infoText.text`.

Also, in `Update()`, we transform the `infoBubble` canvas so that it's always facing the user, using `infoBubble.LookAt()` and passing the camera position. The result of `LookAt()` has the canvas facing the same forward direction as the camera (away from us), so we also need to rotate it around the y-axis by 180 degrees to face us.

Save the script and drag the `InfoBubble` object from **Hierarchy** onto the **Info Bubble** slot in the **Look Move To** component. If you don't assign the `InfoBubble` canvas, the script will still run because we test for `null` objects before we reference them. Run the scene in VR and you'll see that `WalkTarget` has a little info bubble telling us about its X and Z position.

An info bubble UI canvas is attached to other game objects, moving when they move and always facing the camera.

As we have seen, info bubbles are useful when you need to display UI messages that belong to specific objects in the scene and may move around with objects. We can use the `LookAt` function to make sure its canvas is always facing the player. Other in-game UIs may include a scoreboard, as we implemented to display the kill count in our little game. The TMP package is a powerful text toolkit for more advanced text display, textures, and effects, and can even be used to add three-dimensional text meshes to your scene.

Want to try something else? Implement a health meter bar for `Ethan` as an info bubble. Use the `countDown` variable in the `KillTarget` script to determine the percentage of health `Ethan` has remaining, and try to display a health meter (a horizontal bar) above his head when it's not at 100 percent. Progress bars can be implemented using the **Background** panel's **Image** component, setting its **Image Type** setting to **Filled** and **Horizontal**. Then, modify **Fill Amount** by the health value between `0` and `1`. My implementation is included in the `Chapter 6` scene on GitHub.

In the next topic, we'll consider ways of adding a reticle cursor to the UI.

The reticle cursor

A variant of the visor HUD is a **reticle** or crosshair cursor that, for example, is essential in first-person shooter games. The analogy here is to imagine you're looking through a gun-sight or an eyepiece (rather than a visor) and your head movement is moving in unison with the gun or turret itself. You can do this with a regular game object (for example, use **Quad** and a texture image), but this chapter is about UI, so we'll use a world space canvas. Then, we'll re-implement the reticle using XRI toolkit components instead, first as part of the interactor hand controller, and then as a HUD reticle.

Adding a canvas reticle to gaze-based interaction

The first step in creating a canvas reticle is to add a crosshair graphic to a canvas. I've included a sprite image named `GUIReticle.png` with the files for this book that you can use, or you can find another. (If you are importing your own image, be sure to first set its **Import Settings** | **Texture Type** setting to **Sprite (2D and UI)** and click **Apply**.) Add the reticle by taking the following steps:

1. Find your **Main Camera** object in the **Hierarchy** window under **XR Rig**, as we did previously.
2. From the **Project** window, drag the `Default Canvas` prefab onto the camera object so that it becomes a child of the camera. Name it `Reticle Canvas`.
3. Set the **Rect Transform** component's **Width** and **Height** values to `128` and `128` respectively, and position **Pos X**, **Pos Y**, and **Pos Z** to `0`, `0`, and `1`, respectively.
4. Disable the child **Text** object by un-checking its **enable** checkbox in **Inspector.**
5. Set the panel's **Source Image** setting to your reticle image (drag the `GUIReticle` image from the `Project` folder onto the panel's **Source Image** slot, or use its doughnut icon to browse).
6. To change its color, use the **Image** | **Color** property. I picked green. Set it to opaque (set the alpha value to `255`).
7. Save the scene and try it in VR.

We set the **Pos Z** canvas position to `1.0` so that the reticle floats in front of you at a 1-meter distance. A fixed distance cursor is fine in many UI situations, such as when you're picking something up from a flat canvas that is also about the same fixed distance from you. However, there could be a problem if another object is between you and the reticle—the reticle will be obfuscated.

Also, where there are objects in the scene at varying distances, as is the case in our scene here, it could make you go cross-eyed in VR! When you look at something that is much farther away, you refocus your eyes and will have trouble viewing the closer cursor at the same time, and vice versa. To emphasize this problem, try moving the cursor closer—for example, change the **Pos Z** position of `ReticleCursor` to `0.5`. You might have to strain your eyes to see it. To compensate for these issues, we can raycast and move the cursor to the actual distance of the object that you're looking at, resizing the cursor accordingly so that it appears to stay the same size. Let's write a script to handle this:

1. With `Reticle Canvas` selected, click on **Add Component** | **New Script** and name it `CursorPositioner`, and click on **Create And Add**.
2. Open the script by double-clicking on the name.

Here's the `CursorPositioner.cs` script:

```
public class CursorPositioner : MonoBehaviour
{
    private float defaultPosZ;
    private Transform camera;

    void Start()
    {
        camera = Camera.main.transform;
        defaultPosZ = transform.localPosition.z;
    }

    void Update()
    {
        Ray ray = new Ray(camera.position, camera.rotation *
            Vector3.forward);
        RaycastHit hit;
        if (Physics.Raycast(ray, out hit))
        {
            if (hit.distance > defaultPosZ)
            {
                transform.localPosition = new Vector3(0, 0,
                    hit.distance * 0.95f);
            }
            else
            {
                transform.localPosition = new Vector3(0, 0,
                     defaultPosZ);
            }
        }
    }
}
```

In `Start`, we record the default Z position of the reticle and assume that's the closest distance we'll allow. Then, in `Update`, we raycast to see what the player is looking at and move the reticle to that distance away. I've introduced a little hack, which is actually adjusting the position 5% closer so that it's a little in front of the hit point. An improvement to our algorithm could also be to rotate the reticle so that it conforms to the surface normal (`hit.normal`), thus appearing to hug the surface of the object you're looking at. Another improvement could be to ensure the reticle remains a constant size, regardless of its distance (objects further away appear smaller, but a reticle perhaps should not follow that rule) by up-scaling the reticle by the inverse-square of its distance.

We just implemented our own cursor reticle, but many VR SDKs now also provide reticles, including the XR interaction toolkit. Let's replace ours with that one now. First, we'll attach it to the hand controller.

Adding a reticle to the XR interactor hand controller

In the previous chapter, `Chapter 5`, *Interacting with Your Hands*, we got familiar with the XRI toolkit, interactors, and interactables. We saw how **XR Rig** includes a **RightHand Controller** object (and a left hand one), with **XR Ray Interactor**, **XR Interactor Line Visual**, and **Line Renderer** to draw the laser beam to select objects in the scene. We will now enhance this by adding a reticle to the tip of the ray to further identify the object you're pointing at.

The first thing we need to do is make a prefab of our reticle graphic, contained in an empty parent game object. You could move or copy the one we just built, but I'll just remake it, as follows:

1. In the **Hierarchy** root, select **GameObject** | **Create Empty** and name it `Reticle Prefab`, then reset its **Transform** value (click on the three-dots icon and click **Reset**).
2. Drag the **Default Canvas** prefab from its **Project** folder as a child of **Reticle Prefab** and rename it `Reticle`.
3. Set the **Reticle** position's **X**, **Y**, and **Z** values to `0`, `0.01`, and `0`, respectively, **Width** and **Height** to `64` and `64`, respectively, and **Rotation** to `90, 0, 0` so that it's upright.
4. Set its child, by going to **Panel** | **Source Image**, then to **GUIReticle**, setting **Color** to green, and setting no alpha transparency (`255`).
5. Disable its child **Text** object (un-check its **enable** checkbox).

6. Drag **Reticle Prefab** into your **Project** window's `Prefabs/` folder to save it as a prefab.
7. Delete the working copy of **Reticle Prefab** from the **Hierarchy** panel.

Now, we can add the reticle to the hand controller using the following steps:

1. In the **Hierarchy** window, unfold the **XR Rig** object and select the **RightHand Controller** object.
2. In the main menu, select **Components** | **XR** | **Helpers** | **XR Interactor Reticle Visual**.
3. Drag **Reticle Prefab** from the **Project** window onto the **Reticle Prefab** slot of the **XR Interactor Reticle Visual** component.
4. Repeat these steps for the **LeftHand Controller** object if you want.

The new component should now look like this:

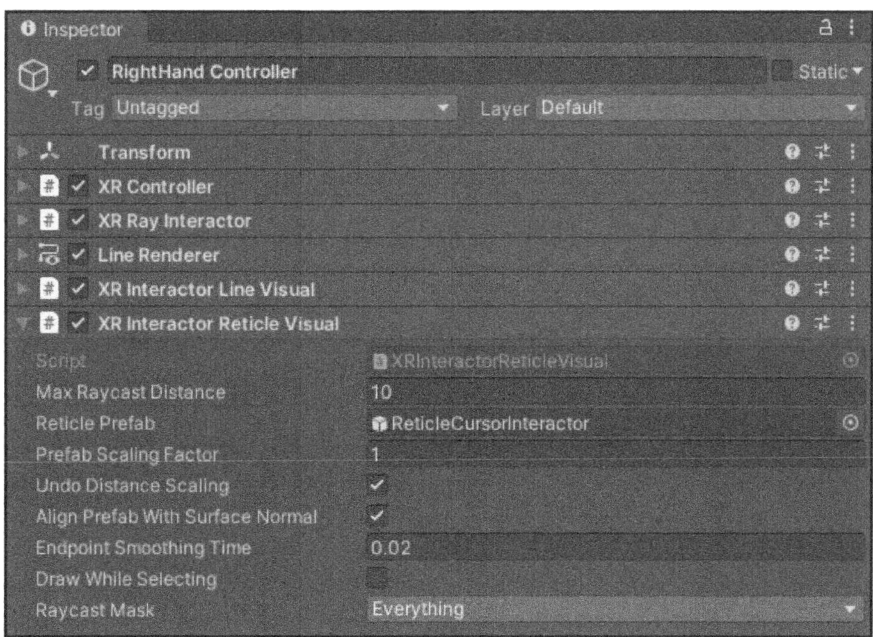

You can see it has all the options we talked about in the previous section with our home-grown one, including **Undo Distance Scaling**, **Align Prefab With Surface Normal**, and more.

When you press **Play** and use the hand controller to point at objects in the scene, there's now a reticle at the end of the laser ray. Next, we'll add the same feature to our gaze input.

Adding a gaze-based reticle using XRI

In gaze-based interactions, you can think of your head pose (**Main Camera**) as a kind of interactor. It's not a full-featured one like the hand controllers because, for example, there are no input buttons on your head. However, to use the **XR Interactor Reticle Visual** component on the camera, we need to make the camera a basic interactor.

These instructions may change if Unity adds this feature to XRI, for example for the Google Cardboard SDK.

XRI does not provide a basic interactor component, but we can make one from the abstract `XRBaseControllerInteractor` class. Create a new C# script named `BasicInteractor` and edit it as follows. The following code simply implements an `XRBaseControllerInteractor` class with no support for interactable targets:

```
using System.Collections.Generic;
using UnityEngine.XR.Interaction.Toolkit;

public class BasicInteractor : XRBaseControllerInteractor
{
    public override void GetValidTargets(List<XRBaseInteractable>
       validTargets) { }

    protected override List<XRBaseInteractable> ValidTargets { get; }
}
```

Now, in Unity, we can use this new script, as follows:

1. If you haven't already, disable or delete the **Reticle Canvas** child of **Main Camera** since we're going to use a different implementation now.
2. With **Main Camera** selected, from the main menu, select **Component** | **XR** | **XR Interactor Reticle Visual**.
3. Notice how this forces an **XR Controller** component to also be added. Let's disable its interactive features. (If not, please add the component now using **Component** | **XR** | **XR Controller**.) Un-check the **Enable Input Actions** checkbox.
4. Set its **Controller Node** setting to **Center Eye**. Ignore the other settings.
5. With **Main Camera** still selected, drag the `BasicInteractor` script onto it.
6. Drag **Reticle Prefab** from the **Project** panel's `Prefabs/` folder onto the reticle component's **Reticle Prefab** slot.

When you press **Play**, you should see a full-featured reticle cursor following your gaze, maintaining its scale, and aligning with the surface normals.

In summary, in this section, we saw how to add a reticle cursor to your interactions. Usually, a reticle is a crosshair cursor that tracks with your head, but as we've seen, it can also be usefully added to hand controllers as a pointer. We first implemented the reticle by parenting it to **Main Camera** and writing our own `CursorPositioner` script to give it depth so that the player will not go cross-eyed in VR. Then, we considered how to implement a reticle instead of using the components provided with the XRI toolkit, which offers more options and a standard implementation.

Next, we will dive further into interactive UIs for VR by building a dashboard with UI buttons.

Building an interactive dashboard

Up to now, we have been using the canvas primarily as a container of display-only information. However, the canvas can also contain interactive UI elements, including **Button**, **Toggle**, **Slider**, and the **Dropdown** lists option. In this section, we will be building an in-game interactive dashboard or control panel that is integrated into the game environment itself.

Earlier in this chapter, we discussed windshield HUDs. Dashboards are pretty much the same thing. One difference is that the dashboard may be more obviously part of the level environment and not simply an auxiliary information display or a menu. A typical in-game scenario is an automobile or a spaceship, where you are seated in a cockpit. In VR, dashboards are familiar in the home environments—for example, the Oculus **Home** menu is depicted in the following screenshot:

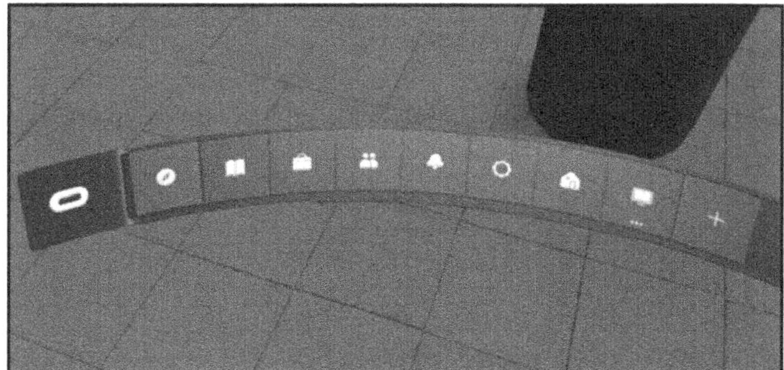

In this part of our project, we'll operate a water hose in the scene to help fend off the zombies. *Why not!* We will make a simple dashboard with one toggle button that starts and stops a spray hose. To implement this feature, we will add a water hose to the scene to fend off our zombie `Ethan` character, create a dashboard canvas with a toggle button, and wire it to the hose. So, let's get to it.

Adding a dynamic water hose

First, we'll add a powerful water hose to the scene. If we aim it strategically, it might even fend off rogue zombies. Coincidentally, the Unity `Particle Systems` folder under **Standard Assets**, which we imported earlier, has a water hose that we can use. (If you have not imported **Standard Assets**, please refer to the *Using Unity Legacy Standard Assets* section in `Chapter 2`, *Understanding Unity, Content, and Scale*). Add it to the scene, as follows:

1. In the **Project** window, find the `Assets/Standard Assets/Particle Systems/Prefabs/Hose` prefab and drag it into the **Hierarchy** window.
2. Set its **Transform** component's **X**, **Y**, and **Z** values to `-3`, `0`, and `1.5`, respectively, and **Rotation** to `-20`, `90`, and `0`.
3. Ensure that **Hose** is enabled (check its **Enable** checkbox).
4. The hose comes with two control scripts—`Hose` and `Simple Mouse Rotator`—that we will not use, so remove both components (click on the three-dots icon and select **Remove Component**).
5. Unfold the **Hose** object in **Hierarchy** so that you can see its child **WaterShower** particle system. Select it.
6. In the **Scene** window, you'll now notice a **Particle Effect** control. If necessary, press **Restart** to see the hose spray in action.
7. In the **Inspector** window, in the **Particle System** properties for **WaterShower**, ensure the **Play On Awake** checkbox is checked.

Per *step 4*, please remove the **Hose** and **Simple Mouse Rotator** components from the **Hose** GameObject as we are not using these and they'll interfere with our implementation.

Our plan is to use a UI button to turn on the water by enabling the **Hose** object and to stop the water by disabling the object. As an aside, note that if `Ethan` walks in the way of the water stream, he will get knocked away because **WaterShower** has collisions enabled and is configured via its child **Callback Particles** | **Collision** properties.

Let's make the dashboard and button now.

Creating a dashboard with a toggle button

The dashboard will be a canvas positioned as a dashboard about 1 meter off the ground and a little out in front of the player, as follows:

1. From the **Project** window, drag the `Default Canvas` prefab onto the `XR Rig` object in the **Hierarchy** window so that it becomes a child.
2. Rename it `Dashboard`.
3. With `Dashboard` selected, set the **Rect Transform** setting to a comfortable size, then position and angle it. For example, set **Width** and **Height** to `800` and `600`, respectively, **Pos X**, **Pos Y**, and **Pos Z** to `0`, `0.8`, and `0.15`, respectively, and **Rotation** to `60`, `0`, and `0`. Feel free to adjust the position for your preferred comfort zone and specific VR device camera rig.
4. Disable the **Text** child object of `Dashboard/Panel/`.

For a *work-in-progress* look, I've included an image sketch of a vehicle dashboard named `DashboardSketch.png` that you can use, as follows:

1. If necessary, import the `DashboardSketch.png` file into your **Project** panel (such as the `Assets/Textures` folder). Set it as a sprite (set **Import Settings** | **Texture Type** to **Sprint (2D and UI)** and press **Apply**).
2. Select the **Panel** child of **Dashboard** and drag **DashboardSketch** onto its **Source Image** slot (replacing the default white **Background** image).
3. Adjust its **Color** alpha value if you want to make it opaque.

Next, we will add the start-stop toggle button. You may first be inclined to use a UI **Button** element (**GameObject** | **UI** | **Button**), whose default behavior is that it stays on only while you click and hold it and turns off when you release it. Instead, in our case, we want it to act like a **switch** that you click once to turn it on, and the hose stays on until you click it again to turn it off. For this, we'll use a **Toggle** element and modify it to look like a button instead of its default checkbox graphics:

1. With the **Panel** object selected, choose **GameObject** | **UI** | **Toggle**, move it to a child of **Panel**, and rename it `WaterHose Toggle`.
2. Set its **Width** and **Height** values to `128` and `128`, respectively, and **PosX**, **PosY**, and **PosZ** to `65`, `148`, and `1`, respectively.
3. On its child **Background** object, stretch its anchor to **stretch-stretch** (click on the anchor icon, then **stretch-stretch**, and then press *Alt* + *Shift* and click **stretch-stretch**).
4. Change the **Background Source Image** setting to **Knob** (use the doughnut icon to select a new sprite) and change its **Color** property to a red (`#FF0000`) for its off state.
5. Instead of the checkmark image for the on state, we'll overlay a green circle. Select the child **Checkmark** object, set its anchor to **stretch-stretch**, then press *Alt* + *Shift* and select **stretch-stretch**.
6. Change the **Source Image** setting to **Knob** and set its **Color** property to green (`#00FF00`).
7. Change **Label** to `Hose` (select the **Label** object, set **Text** | **Text** to `Hose`, set **Text** | **Alignment** | **Middle** and **Center**, and **Color** to white, `#FFFFFF`).
8. We'll start the scene with the toggle disabled (with **WaterHose Toggle** selected, uncheck the **Is On** checkbox).
9. Likewise, disable **Hose** (select **Hose** in **Hierarchy** and uncheck its **enable** checkbox).

These settings are shown in a later screenshot. The resulting panel looks something like this:

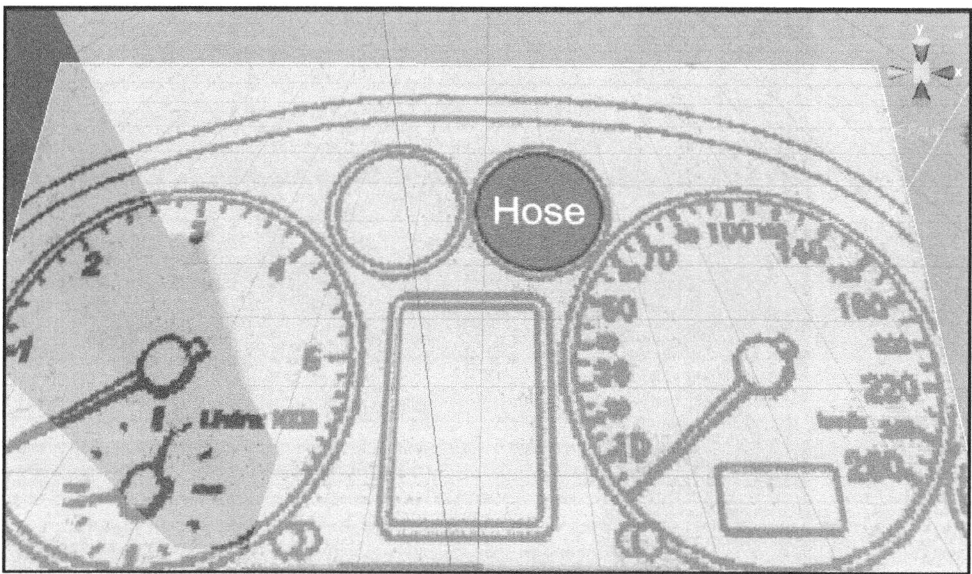

The way a **Toggle** UI element works is that when it is off, only the **Background** red circle is displayed; when it is on, the foreground **Checkmark** green circle is displayed (on top of the **Background** one). You can verify your work by selecting the **WaterHose Toggle** object and clicking its **Is On** checkbox on and off. The button should change between green and red. (When done, leave it off—that is, leave **Is On** unchecked.) Now, we can connect the button to the hose, as follows:

1. Ensure **WaterHose Toggle** is selected in **Hierarchy**.
2. In its **Toggle** component's **On Value Changed** events, click the **+** button to add an event response.
3. Drag the **Hose** object from **Hierarchy** onto the **Runtime object** slot.
4. From the **Function** dropdown, select **GameObject | SetActive**.

The resulting **WaterHose Toggle** settings look as in the following screenshot in the **Inspector** window:

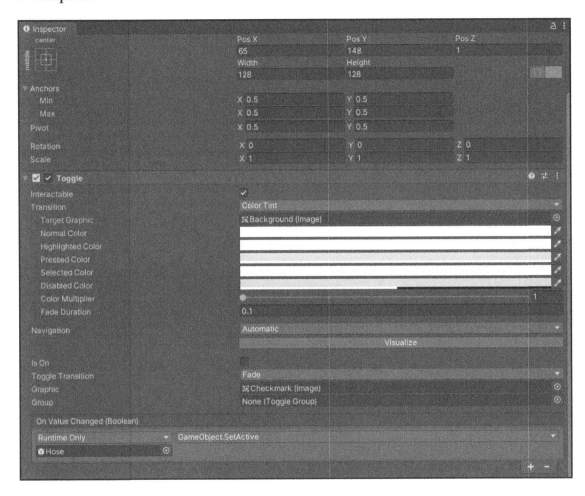

Press **Play** and try it in VR. You can point the hand controller to the toggle button and pull the trigger to interact. Press once to turn on the hose and again to turn it off.

Note that the XR ray interactor on the hand controller has the **Enable Interaction with UI Elements** option. Make sure this checkbox is checked if you expect the interactor to work with UI elements such as **Button** and **Toggle**.

You may notice that the laser pointer ray passes through the dashboard canvas into the scene behind, even when you're selecting the button. Let's fix this next so that it's more intuitive to the user that the laser ray is interacting with the dashboard.

Stopping the ray interactor at the canvas

This topic may change if XRI changes this behavior. The solution described here is as used in the XRI demo scene. There's also a code fix to the XRI script; see `https://forum.unity.com/threads/xr-interaction-toolkit-preview-release.795684/page-3#post-5386755`.

If you have a UI canvas that is interactable with a ray interactor, you probably do not want the ray beam to extend past the canvas onto other objects in the scene behind it. This can be fixed by adding a **Collider** component behind the dashboard by taking the following steps. Remember, as a child of the canvas, the units are in world *pixels*, not *meters*, so we have to make adjustments accordingly:

1. Select the **Panel** child of the **Dashboard** canvas.
2. Add a child **Cube** object (right-click and select **3D Object Cube**) and name it `Backstop`.
3. The default **Cube** object already has a **Box Collider** component, which we want to be the size of the canvas. Set the cube's **Rect Transform Scale** property to match its parent canvas (`800, 600, 1`).
4. Position it so that it is a little behind the panel and set **Position** to `0, 0, 5`.
5. Disable its **Renderer** component (un-check the **enable** checkbox of its **Mesh Renderer** component.

Now, when you press **Play** and use the hand controller with its ray interactor, the ray line extends from your hand to the dashboard, but not beyond the `Backstop` object we just added.

In summary, we created a control panel dashboard with a toggle button and we added a water hose to the scene. Pressing the button turns on the hose and pressing it again turns the hose off. Presently, the hand controllers are still using the laser pointer to select and interact with the UI elements. Next, we'll make it so that you can directly touch the button to click it.

Direct interaction with UI elements

Up to now in this chapter, we've been using the XR ray interactor on hand controllers to interact with the UI. In the previous chapter, we learned that there other kinds of interactors, including a direct interactor. To implement the ability to reach out and directly touch an object in your scene, rather than cast a ray, you could use a direct interactor instead of a ray interactor.

This implementation may change if XRI adds support for UI objects with the direct interactor. Presently, I have described a workaround.

Let's see what it will take to change our UI to support direct interactions with the toggle button. The direct interactor works by using physics colliders to detect when the hand is touching an interactable object. Let's switch to that now and see what happens. (We'll work on a copy so its easy to switch back if you want:)

1. In **Hierarchy**, select **RightHand Controller** (under **XR Rig/Camera Offset/**), duplicate it (press *Ctrl* + *D*), and rename the copy `RightHand Direct`.
2. Disable the original **RightHand Controller** object (uncheck its **enable** checkbox).
3. On **RightHand Direct**, remove all of its components other than **XR Controller** (right-click on the components and select **Remove Component**).
4. Add a **Direct Interactor** component (go to the main menu and select **Component** | **XR** | **XR Direct Interactor**).

For the interactor to detect an object, it needs a collider. We'll add one here:

1. With **RightHand Direct** selected, add a sphere collider (**Component** | **Physics** | **Sphere Collider**).
2. Set the collider's **Radius** property to `0.1`.
3. Check its **Is Trigger** checkbox.

We need a way to visualize where your hand is. In the previous chapter, we made a little gun from a cube and cylinder. Here, we'll just make a sphere "fist." (Or, instead, you could use a prefab on the **XR Controller** | **Model Prefab** slot:)

1. With **RightHand Direct** selected, add a sphere (right-click and select **3D Object** | **Sphere**).
2. Set its **Scale** value to `0.1, 0.1, 0.1`.

Next, we also need to make the UI button an interactable object by adding a corresponding interactable and collider components to the button. We'll use a **Simple Interactable** component to do this:

1. With the **WaterHose Toggle** setting in the **Dashboard** panel selected, add a **Simple Interactable** component (**Component** | **XR** | **XR Simple Interactable**).
2. This also automatically adds a **Rigidbody** component, which is required. Since we don't really want to apply any physics to the button, we should constrain it. Uncheck the **Use Gravity** checkbox.
3. Then, check all six of the **Constraints** checkboxes—the **Freeze Position** property's **X**, **Y**, and **Z** settings and the **Freeze Rotation** property's **X**, **Y**, and **Z** settings.
4. Add a collider so that the hand controller can find it. We'll use a **Box Collider** object, which can be more easily flattened than a sphere. (**Component** | **Physics** | **Box Collider**) and set its **Size** property to `100, 100, 5`.

These settings are shown in the screenshot of the **Inspector** window later on in this section. Remember, as a child of a canvas, the units are in world *pixels,* not meters, so we set the collider size in pixels. Finally, we can connect the **Interactable On Hover Enter** event, which is triggered when the hand touches the button, to equate to a toggle button selection. We need a little helper script to translate the interactable events to toggle events and ensure the toggle's `OnValueChanged` event is invoked:

1. On the **WaterHose Toggle** object, create a new C# script named `ForceToggle`.
2. Open the script for editing and write it as follows:

```
using UnityEngine;
using UnityEngine.UI;

public class ForceToggle : MonoBehaviour
{
    private Toggle toggle;

    private void Start()
    {
        toggle = GetComponent<Toggle>();
    }

    public void Toggle()
    {
        toggle.isOn = !toggle.isOn;
    }
}
```

Note that in our case, since we're using the "old" UI objects, we need to be sure our script is `using UnityEngine.UI` (rather than the new `UnityEngine.UIElements` script. In the script's `Toggle` function, the `!` operator returns the inverse of a Boolean value, so when `toggle.isOn` is `true`, it's now set to `false`, and vice versa. Modifying this `isOn` property will automatically invoke the `OnValueChanged` event. Now, we can use it in our UI:

1. Ensure this new script is added to the **WaterHose Toggle** object.
2. On the **XR Simple Interactable | On First Hover Enter** event actions, click the **+** button to add a new event response.
3. Drag the same **WaterHose Toggle** object from **Hierarchy** onto the **Runtime Only** object slot.
4. From the **Function** dropdown, select **ForceToggle | Toggle()**.

The new components we added to the **WaterHose Toggle** look like this:

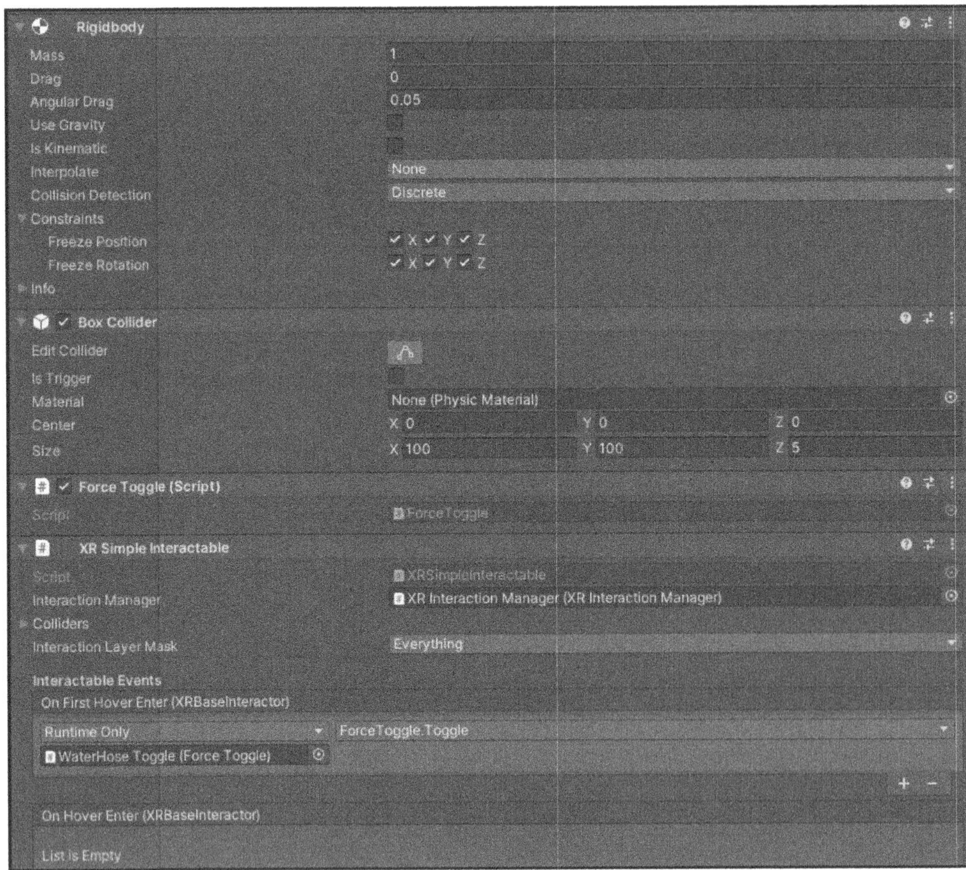

Now, when you touch the button with the controller, it'll be like you've pressed the button. Let's try it. Press **Play**. Move your hand toward the dashboard's **Hose** button. When it touches it, the button will turn green and the hose will start shooting water. Pull away and reach again to touch the button again. It toggles off to red and the water stops.

Want another challenge? Improve your UI to use a three-dimensional switch button, rather than just a sprite image, that more realistically appears pressed in when on and pops back up when released. Another improvement could be to add controls that let your user move and re-position the whole dashboard to their preference.

In VR, you will often see a curved canvas used instead of a flat one. This is because a curved canvas is more comfortable, especially when it's relatively close to you. Look on Asset Store for various packages, including the popular **Curved UI** package (which costs $25):

`https://assetstore.unity.com/packages/tools/gui/curved-ui-vr-ready-solution-to-bend-warp-your-canvas-53258`

We have built a UI dashboard with a button that you can interact with by directly pressing it. We used the **XRI Direct Interactor** and **Simple Interactable** components to implement this, along with colliders for triggering the collision events. This dashboard is positioned at a fixed location. It's also possible to make it a handheld menu palette. We'll look at that next.

Building a wrist-based menu palette

Some VR applications that are designed for two-handed setups give you a virtual menu palette attached to the player's wrist while the other hand selects buttons or items from it. Let's see how that is done. *This scenario will assume you have a two-hand controller VR system.* Converting our dashboard control panel into a wrist palette is not too difficult. We just need to scale it appropriately and attach it to the hand controller.

We'll duplicate and re-purpose the `Dashboard` object to use it on your left wrist:

1. In **Hierarchy**, right-click on **Dashboard** and choose **Duplicate**.
2. Rename the new object `Palette`.
3. Disable the old `Dashboard` object.
4. Drag the **Palette** object so that it is a child of the **LeftHand Controller** object (under **XR Rig/Camera Offset**).

Now, we'll modify the **Palette** graphics, as follows. Feel free to change the settings for what works for you:

1. On the **Palette** obejct itself, set its **PosX**, **PosY**, and **PosZ** values to `0`, `0.1`, and `-0.1`, respectively, **Rotation** to `90, -150, -115`, and **Width** and **Height** to `240` and `180`, respectively.
2. In the **Panel** child of **Palette**, replace **Source Image** with **Background** (using the doughnut icon).
3. Move the **WaterHose Toggle** button to **Pos XYZ** (`0, 0, 1`).

That's it! All of the interaction wiring we set up for the **Dashboard** object works without change. The following is a screenshot that shows what it looks like to have the palette attached to the left-hand controller (with the **Hose** toggle button on a panel) while touching the button with the right-hand controller (represented as a sphere). As you can see, thankfully, Ethan the Zombie is behind the hose barrier:

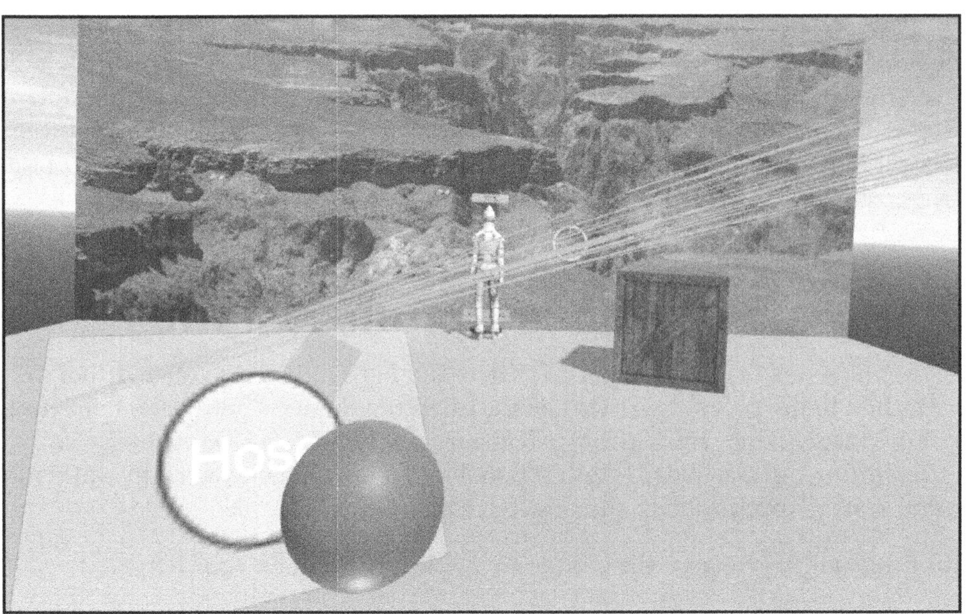

Naturally, the palette can be extended with other buttons and input controls. If you had multiple panels arranged as the sides of the cube (such as the **TiltBrush** menu), you could use the thumb pad to scroll or rotate between the various menus. That's how it's done!

Summary

In Unity, UIs that are based on a **Canvas** object and the Event System include buttons, text, images, sliders, and input fields, which can be assembled and wired to objects in the scene. At the start of the chapter, I reviewed some of the UI design principles to consider when building your own UIs for VR.

We took a close look at various world space UI techniques and how they can be used in VR projects. We considered the ways in which the UI for VR differs from the UI for conventional video games and desktop applications, never using screen space UI. We implemented over a half-dozen of them, learning how each can be constructed, coded, and used in our own projects. These range from passive HUD info panels and dynamic in-game displays to interactive control panels with buttons. We learned about using TMP to make text information a truly graphical element. Our C# scripting got a little more advanced, probing deeper into the Unity Engine API and modular coding techniques as we wrote a few simple C# scripts for custom behaviors with the UI.

You now have a broader vocabulary to approach the UI in your VR projects. Some of the examples in this chapter can be directly applicable to your own work. However, not all need to be home-grown. VR UI tools are increasingly being provided in the XRI toolkit—for example, scenes and third-party Unity Asset Store packages.

In the next chapter, we will add a first-person character controller to our scene. We'll learn about avatars and methods to control navigation in VR so that we can comfortably move around within the virtual world. Also, we'll learn about managing one of the negative aspects of VR experiences—VR motion sickness.

7
Teleporting, Locomotion, and Comfort

Up to this point in this book, the player's point-of-view camera has been stationary. In this chapter, we'll start to move around as we consider various mechanics for locomotion and teleportation. **Locomotion** in **Virtual Reality** (**VR**) generally refers to moving around a virtual scene and, specifically, moving in a *continuous* way. **Teleportation** refers to moving to a new location in a single discrete *jump*. Both of these techniques are compatible with stationary and room-scale tracking. In **stationary** tracking, locomotion and teleportation are the only means for moving within the scene.

In **room-scale** tracking, the player can physically walk around the scene within the bounds of the play space, yet can also use locomotion and teleportation to move to a new location. In that case, the play space origin itself (for example, **XR Rig**) is moved, as we'll see in the various examples in this chapter.

By the end of this chapter, you will know how to implement various techniques for locomotion and teleportation in VR, including the use of components provided with the XR Interaction Toolkit. This chapter will cover the following topics:

- Driving around a scene (glide locomotion) using the hand-controller thumbstick
- Climbing a vertical wall using hand-over-hand grab holds using **Extensible Resource Identifier** (**XRI**) interactables
- Using and integrating with the XRI Locomotion System
- Teleporting to areas and anchor points using the XRI Teleportation System
- Managing VR motion sickness

Technical requirements

To implement the projects and exercises in this chapter, you will need the following:

- A PC or Mac with Unity 2019.4 LTS or later, an XR Plugin for your device, and the XR Interaction Toolkit installed
- A VR headset supported by the Unity XR Platform

You can access or clone the GitHub repository for this book (`https://github.com/PacktPublishing/Unity-2020-Virtual-Reality-Projects-3rd-Edition-`) to optionally use assets and completed projects for this chapter, as follows:

- Asset files for you to use in this chapter are located in `UVRP3Files/Chapter-07-Files.zip`.
- All completed projects in this book are in a single Unity project at `UVRP3Projects`.
- The completed assets and scenes for this chapter are in the `UVRP3Projects/Assets/_UVRP3Assets/Chapter07/` folder.

Implementing basic glide locomotion

Locomotion refers to moving around the scene in a continuous way. In this first example, we'll implement a basic **glide locomotion** mechanic using the thumbstick on your hand controller to move you in a given direction. We'll start with moving forward (and backward) with a vertical push of the thumbstick. There are several ways you can decide what "forward" means, either based on the direction the player is looking (camera forward direction) or based on the direction the hand controller is pointing, or by using the horizontal press of the thumbstick to rotate. Our script will support all these options: camera forward, hand forward, and thumbstick rotate.

Caution is advised when using glide locomotion in VR as it can cause motion sickness in some players. For this reason, teleportation is often the preferred mechanism in VR. This can be mitigated, for example, if the player is driving "inside" a vehicle because a window frame and dashboard moving along with the player provides a frame of reference that helps provide a critical sense of orientation. There is more discussion on VR motion sickness at the end of this chapter.

You can start this chapter with any simple scene, such as the **02-Diorama** scene we created in `Chapter 2`, *Understanding Unity, Content, and Scale*, which includes a play space environment, or create a similar new scene to use in this chapter, with the following steps:

1. Create a new scene, using **File** | **New Scene**.
2. Create a ground plane using **GameObject** | **3D Object** | **Plane**, rename this as `Ground Plane`, reset its transform with **Transform** | right-click | **Reset**, and apply a colored material such as the **Ground Material** created in `Chapter 2`, *Understanding Unity, Content, and Scale* (such as selecting **Mesh Renderer** | **Materials** | **Element 0** | **doughnut-icon** | **Ground Material**.)
3. Create a photo wall using **GameObject** | **3D Object** | **Quad**, rename this as `Photo`, then set **Transform** | **Position** (`0, 3.75, 5`), **Transform** | **Scale** (`10, 7.5, 10`), and apply the **Grand Canyon** photo material using **Mesh Renderer** | **Materials** | **Element 0** | **doughnut-icon** | **GrandCanyon**.
4. Add an **XR Rig** using **GameObject** | **XR** | **Stationary XR Rig** or **Room-Scale XR Rig**, and **Reset** its **Transform** to the origin.
5. Save the scene with the name `07-Locomotion-0` (**File** | **Save As**.)

This starting scene is also available on this book's GitHub repository, with the name `07-Locomotion-0`. We now have a working scene for this chapter, and we can make a working copy using the following steps:

1. Open the `07-Locomotion-0` scene using **File** | **Open Scene**
2. Save into a new scene named `07-Locomotion-1` for this topic, with **File** | **Save As**

To help visualize these behaviors in the Unity editor, let's add a **Capsule** object to represent the player rig, as follows:

1. With **XR Rig** selected in the **Hierarchy**, add a child **Capsule** (right-click | 3D **Object** | **Capsule**)
2. Set its **Y** position to `1` (**Transform** | **Position** to (`0, 1, 0`) and **Scale** `0.5, 1, 0.5`)
3. Add another **Capsule** as its "nose" to show the forward direction (as a child of the first **Capsule**, right-click | **3D Object** | **Capsule**, set **Position** (`0, 0.75, 0.5`), **Rotation** (`90, 0, 0`), and **Scale** (`0.1, 0.2, 0.05`))

Our capsule body will look like the following screenshot:

Note that in VR, you may see this self-avatar, depending on your position. No worries: it's intended to help demonstrate our development and will not be part of the final scene (later, we'll disable its Mesh Renderer component). Now, we'll write a script to enable us to move around using the thumbstick on the hand controller. After that, we'll see how to change direction and avoid obstacles.

Moving forward with the thumbstick

The glide locomotion behavior will move the player rig—**XR Rig**—position based on the thumbstick press, and maximum velocity value. To begin, create a new script, `GlideLocomotion`, on the **XR Rig**, as follows:

1. Select the **XR Rig** in **Hierarchy**.
2. Create a new C# script by selecting **Add Component** | **New Script** (named `GlideLocomotion`)| **Create And Add**.
3. Open the script for editing, and write it as follows:

```
public class GlideLocomotion : MonoBehaviour
{
    public Transform rigRoot;
    public float velocity = 2f; // meters per second

    private void Start()
    {
```

```
        if (rigRoot == null)
            rigRoot = transform;
    }

    private void Update()
    {
        float forward = Input.GetAxis("
             XRI_Right_Primary2DAxis_Vertical");
        if (forward != 0f)
        {
            Vector3 moveDirection = Vector3.forward;
            moveDirection *= -forward * velocity
                * Time.deltaTime;
            rigRoot.Translate(moveDirection);
        }
    }
}
```

In this script, we first declare two public variables.
The `rigRoot` variable references the root object that will be moved in the locomotion, and `velocity` is the maximum rate of movement, in meters per second. In `Start()`, we initialize `rigRoot` to this game object's transform, if not already set up in the **Inspector**.

In each frame `Update`, we poll the hand controller's right-hand thumbstick (`XRI_Right_Primary2DAxis_Vertical`) using a call to `Input.GetAxis`, which returns a value between `-1.0` and `1.0`. If the stick is pushed forward any amount (the axis is not zero), we calculate the distance to move as the forward direction (`0, 0, 1`) multiplied by the velocity and the time frame (`Time.deltaTime`). Note that the `GetAxis` value returns negative values when pressed forward (that's just the way it works), so we negate the value before using it in the formula. The call to `rigRoot.Translate` increments the transform's world position by the given amount.

4. Save the script and go back to Unity.
5. With the **GlideLocomotion** script attached to **XR Rig**, drag the **XR Rig** game object onto the **Rig Root** slot.
6. Press **Play**.

In VR, using the right-hand controller, press the thumbstick forward and you'll glide forward. Pull the thumbstick back, and you'll glide backward. The next thing we'll add is the ability to also rotate your direction by pushing the thumbstick side to side (horizontal axis).

Rotating with the thumbstick

In addition to gliding forward, we can also rotate the entire player rig by pressing the thumbstick from side to side (horizontal axis). Use the following steps to add this to the `GlideLocomotion` script. First, at the top of the class, add a `rotationSpeed` variable, as shown in the following code snippet:

```
public float rotationSpeed = 100f; // degrees per second
```

Then, in the `Update()` function, add the following code:

```
float sideways = Input.GetAxis("
   XRI_Right_Primary2DAxis_Horizontal");
if (sideways != 0f)
{
  float rotation = sideways * rotationSpeed
    * Time.deltaTime;
  rigRoot.Rotate(0, rotation, 0);
}
```

Now, when the thumbstick is pressed sideways, the player rig will rotate. You can simultaneously push the stick forward and to the side to drive around the scene. The following screenshot shows a top-down view of the scene after I have moved to a new position and rotated using the right-hand thumbstick:

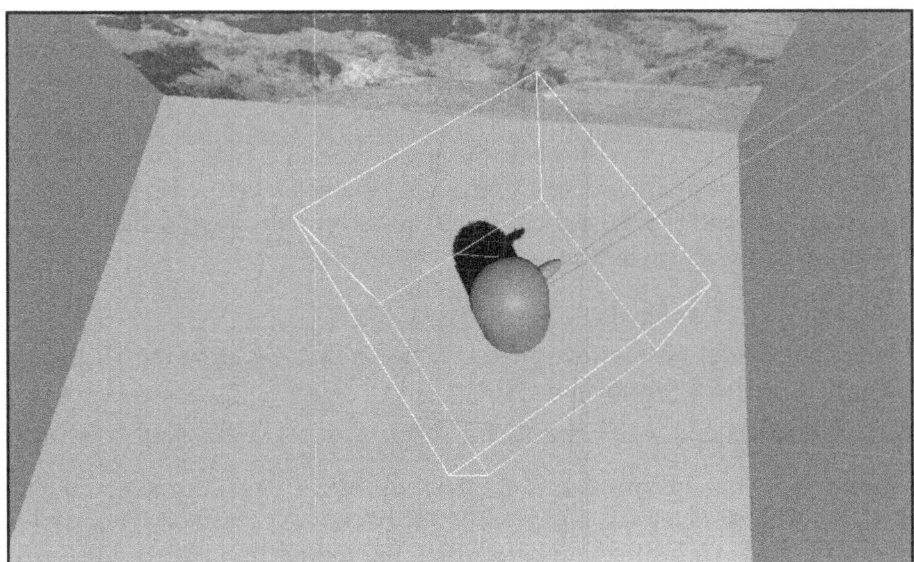

A modification of this mechanism is to limit the rotation angle to discrete "snaps" in increments such as 45 degrees at a time. We implement such snap turns later in this chapter. Alternatively, instead of rotating the forward direction of the player rig, you can have the player glide in the direction of their gaze (using the **Head-Mounted Display** (**HMD**) camera forward direction) or where they are pointing with the hand controller without actually rotating. We'll add this option next.

Moving in the direction you're looking or pointing

A variation of this mechanic is to dynamically change the forward direction using the player's gaze or by pointing in a direction with the hand controller. In order to determine a *dynamic* forward direction, we will use the transform of a tracked object. For example, this can be the **Main Camera** (which tracks the player's head pose), or it can be the **RightHand Controller** (which tracks the player's right hand). In either case, the script only needs its transform. So, to add this feature to our script, first declare a `trackedTransform` variable at the top of the `GlideLocomotion` class, as shown in the following code snippet:

```
public Transform trackedTransform; // camera or controller, null for
                                                          thumbstick
```

Then, in `Update()`, we'll use the device's forward direction rather than the fixed `Vector3.forward` one, as follows:

```
  float forward = Input.GetAxis("
     XRI_Right_Primary2DAxis_Vertical");
   if (forward != 0f)
   {
     Vector3 moveDirection = Vector3.forward;
     if (trackedTransform != null)
     {
        moveDirection = trackedTransform.forward;
        moveDirection.y = 0f;
     }
     moveDirection *= -forward * velocity
        * Time.deltaTime;
     rigRoot.Translate(moveDirection);
   }
```

In `Update()`, we've added a condition that assigns the `moveDirection` as the forward direction of the tracked device. Also, we zero out the *Y* coordinate as we only want to move along the *X-Z* plane, not up or down. The player will glide along the *X-Z* plane, while the orientation (rotation) of the player **XR Rig** does not change.

Lastly, we should disable the use of the horizontal thumbstick for rotation, as these modes are mutually exclusive. Wrap that code around another condition, as follows:

```
if (trackedTransform == null)
  {
    float sideways = Input.GetAxis("
       XRI_Right_Primary2DAxis_Horizontal");
    if (sideways != 0f)
    {
      float rotation = sideways * rotationSpeed
         * Time.deltaTime;
      rigRoot.Rotate(0, rotation, 0);
    }
  }
```

Save the script and go back to Unity and assign the **Main Camera** to the tracked transform, as follows:

1. With **XR Rig** selected in the **Hierarchy**, drag the child **Main Camera** object onto the **Tracked Transform** slot. The component looks like the following in the **Inspector**:

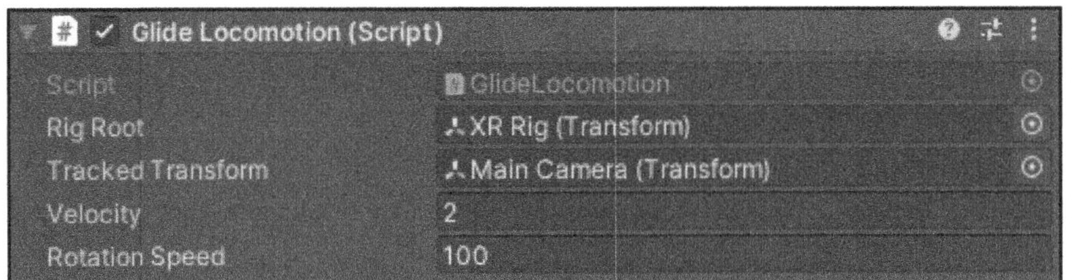

2. Press **Play**.
3. In VR, using the right-hand controller, press the thumbstick forward and you'll glide forward. As you move, turn your head to look in a different direction, and you'll move in the direction you are looking for.

   If you're using a room-scale tracking rig, you'll notice that the whole play space is moving along with you. That is, your relative location within the tracking space does not change as you travel within the scene. Although you can change the direction you are moving within the scene by turning your head, the forward direction of the tracking space within the scene is not changed.

Alternatively, instead of the gaze direction, we can use the hand controller to point in the direction to move. The change is simple. We just need to change **Tracked Transform** from **Main Camera** to the **RightHand Controller**, as follows:

1. With **XR Rig** selected in the **Hierarchy**, drag its child **RightHand Controller** game object onto the **Glide Locomotion | Tracked Transform** slot. The component now looks like this:

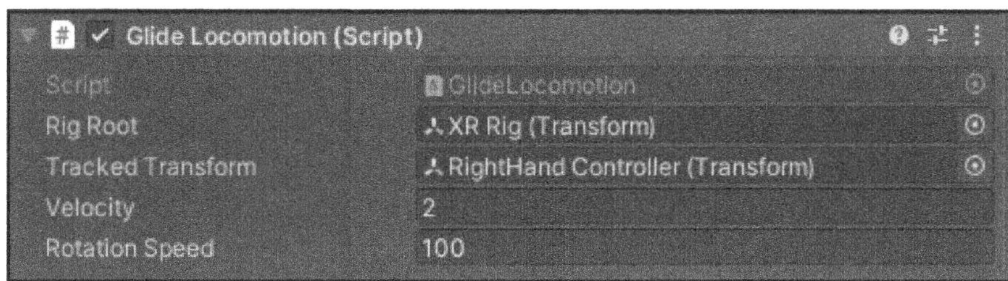

Now, when you press **Play**, you can point with your hand controller in the direction you want to glide and press the thumbstick forward. Simultaneously, you can push the thumbstick to the side to also twist the rig's orientation and default forward direction. Or, if you prefer the original method, you can use the thumbstick to rotate and remove the **Tracked Transform** assignment altogether, as follows:

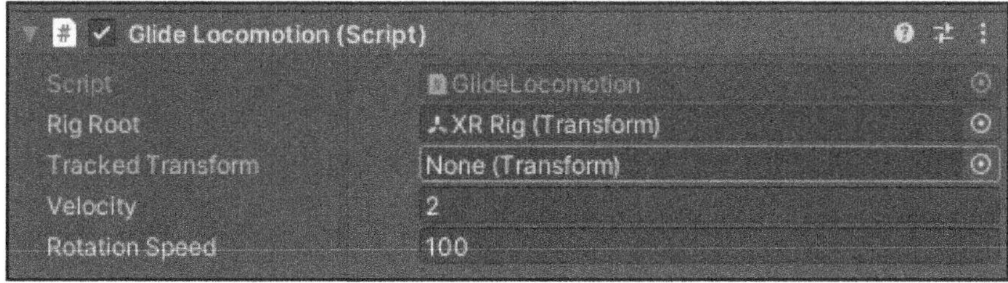

Whichever way you choose to go, we still have another issue. When the scene includes other objects, you'll find that the player can just glide right through them. We'll accommodate that next.

Avoiding obstacles

In VR, you probably want to maintain the illusion that objects are solid. But currently in our scene, as you glide along within the scene, there is nothing to prevent you from passing through walls or other objects. Let's demonstrate this by adding some solid obstacles in the scene, such as a couple of crates. Follow the steps given here:

1. Add a **Cube** object to the scene, using **GameObject | 3D Object | Cube**, positioned at (`-2.5, 0.5, 1.5`.)
2. Add another cube with right-click, then **Cube | Duplicate**, positioned at (`2.5, 0.5, -1.5`.)
3. If you'd like, apply the **Crate Material** we created in `Chapter 2`, *Understanding Unity, Content, and Scale,* to both cubes.

If you were to press **Play** now and move about, you'd find you can pass through the crates as if you're a ghost. To prevent this, we can introduce a **Rigidbody** to the **XR Rig** with appropriate constraints to keep it from falling over, as follows:

1. Add a **Rigidbody** to the **XR Rig**: with **XR Rig** selected, select **Component | Physics | Rigidbody**.
2. Uncheck the **Use Gravity** checkbox.
3. Check the **Freeze Rotation X, Y, Z** checkboxes.

Now, when you press **Play** and move around the scene, if you bump into an object, you'll either get stopped or slide around it as the curved surface of your capsule collider rubs against the surface of the object.

Note that the **Rigidbody** is using the collider of the object and the **Capsule Collider** of the player capsule that we added to the **XR Rig** earlier. If you want to maintain this behavior but hide the capsule, disable its **Mesh Renderer** component instead of the whole game object.

Challenge: Build a scene including uneven surfaces, such as ramps and steps. How would you move through such a scene? Try using the **Use Gravity** option on the **Rigidbody**. Or, for a more advanced, use a **NavMesh** (introduced in `Chapter 4`, *Using Gaze-Based Control*) to control the allowed navigation areas, ramps, and step elevations. But be aware that gliding like this can aggravate motion sickness in VR.

In summary, we have developed the mechanics for moving around the scene by locomotion—that is, driving or gliding along the ground plane, and using the thumbstick to press forward. We implemented several methods for defining what we mean by "forward," either using the player's gaze direction (camera forward), pointing with a hand controller, or using the side-to-side (horizontal) press of the thumbstick to rotate. We also learned how to avoid passing straight through solid objects using the **Rigidbody** and **Collider** components. Next, we'll look at a different mechanic for locomotion, using your hands to grab and pull. In this example, we'll climb up a climbing wall.

Climbing a wall

Many VR games include the ability to climb a wall or ladder; that is, locomotion in a vertical direction. In this section, we will implement a wall-climbing exercise using a hand-over-hand grab-and-pull mechanic. Given a climbing wall, the player can reach up and grab a hold, then pull themself up, reach with the other hand to grab another hold, and so on. But if you let go with both hands, you'll fall! For this, we're going the use the XRI Toolkit's **Interactor** and **Interactable** components. We'll build a wall with a series of **GrabHold** prefabs. Then, we'll write two scripts. A `GrabPull` script notifies the `ClimbController` when the player has grabbed or released a hold. The `ClimbController` moves the **XR Rig**, and it detects when the player has completely let go, causing them to fall.

Begin with a basic scene such as the one defined at the top of this chapter, as follows:

1. Open the scene by clicking **File** | **Open Scene**, and select `07-Locomotion-0`.
2. Save into a new scene named `07-Locomotion-2` for this topic, using **File** | **Save As**.

Now, we can start by building a climbing-wall game object.

Building a wall with grab holds

In this project, we are going to climb a climbing wall. The wall will be a simple cube slab with grab-holds that the player can use to pull themselves up. To create a wall, follow the steps given next:

1. Create an empty game object (**GameObject** | **Create Empty**), and name it `ClimbingWall`.
2. Position it a half-meter from the player, at **Position** (`0, 0, 0.5`.)

3. Create a child **Cube** for the wall (**right-click** | **ClimbingWall** | **3D Object** | **Cube**), and name it `Wall`.
4. Set its **Scale** (`3, 5, 0.1`) and **Position** (`0, 2.5, 0`.)

Next, we'll add a grab-hold object on the wall, make it a prefab, and copy it to multiple positions up the wall. To do that, follow the steps given next:

1. Create a small cube on the wall (right-click **ClimbingWall** | **3D Object** | **Cube**), and name it `GrabHold`.
2. Set its **Scale** (`0.1, 0.1, 0.1`), and position it at an easy reaching distance—for example, (`0.5, 0.8, -0.1`.)
3. Give it a distinct color—for example, using the **Red Material** created in a prior chapter (**Mesh Renderer** | **Materials** | **Element 0** | **doughnut-icon** | **Red Material**.)
4. Make it a prefab by dragging the **GrabHold** from the **Hierarchy** window into your **Project** window's `Prefabs/` folder.

Then, duplicate the **GrabHold** on the **Wall**, and move each to various locations such as the following X, Y coordinates:

- (`0.5, 0.8`)
- 1: (`-0.5, 1.2`)
- 2: (`0.3, 1.8`)
- 3: (`-0.4, 2.3`)
- 4: (`0.4, 2.6`)
- 5: (`-0.6, 3.0`)
- 6: (`0.25, 3.5`)
- 7: (`-0.5, 4.0`)
- 8: (`0.4, 4.7`)

My climbing wall looks like this:

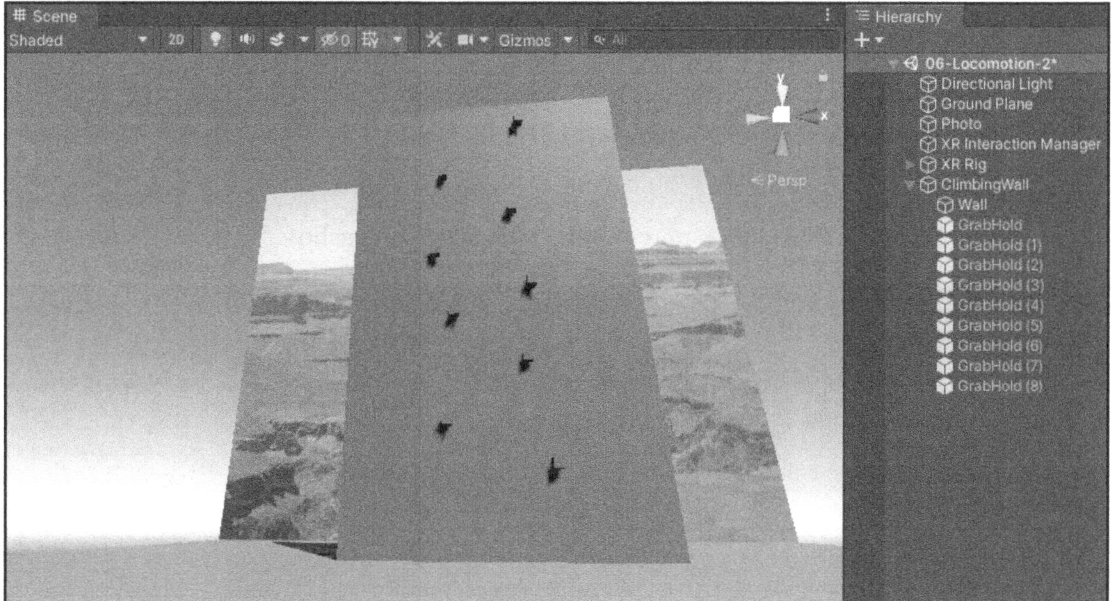

The next step is to make the grab-holds interactable.

Adding the XRI Interactor and Interactable components

To make the grab-holds grabbable, we'll use the Unity XR Interaction Toolkit components. If you recall from our previous chapters, XRI implements an interactor-interactable pattern, where the hand controllers have an **Interactor** component, which in turn can select and activate any game objects in the scene with an **Interactable** component.

The first step is to replace the default hand controllers (that have an **XR Ray Interactor**) with ones using an **XR Direct Interactor**. It's easy enough to just disable or delete the default ones and create new ones, as follows:

1. In the **Hierarchy** window, unfold the **XR Rig** so that you can see the **RightHand Controller** and **LeftHand Controller** objects.
2. Disable both **RightHand Controller** and **LeftHand Controller** objects (uncheck its **Enable** checkbox.)

3. Create a new **Direct Interactor** named `RightHand Direct Interactor` (**GameObject** | **Create** | **XR** | **Direct Interactor**) and rename it `RightHand Direct Interactor`.
4. Drag it as a child of **Camera Offset** (sibling of the original **RightHand Controller**.)
5. Change its **Controller Node** to **Right Hand**.
6. Repeat *steps 3-5* for the `LeftHand Director Interactor`.

The **XR Rig** hierarchy is shown in the following screenshot:

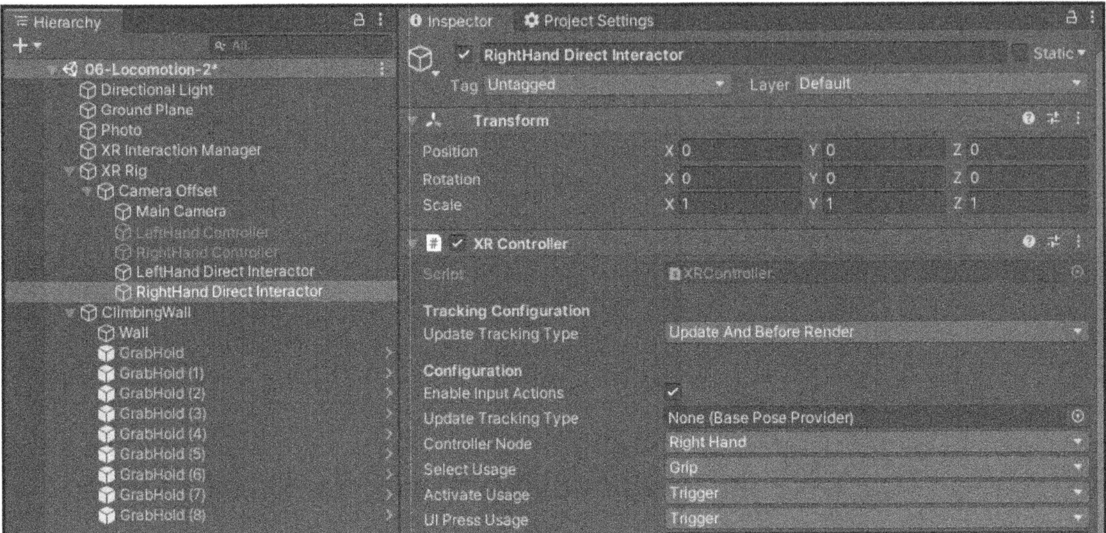

It's important to confirm that you have the **Select Usage** option set to the **Grip** button, as we want to be sure that the player will squeeze the grip handle button to grab a handhold.

We should add a hand graphic so that the player will be able to see where their hands are in VR. For simplicity, we'll just use a sphere "fist," as follows (or, instead, you could use a better graphic prefab on the **XR Controller** | **Model Prefab** slot):

1. Right-click, then go to **RightHand Direct Interactor** | **3D Object** | **Sphere**.
2. Set its **Scale** (`0.1, 0.1, 0.1`.)
3. Repeat for the **LeftHand Direct Interactor**.

To make all the **GrabHold** objects interactable, open the **GrabHold** prefab for editing and add an **XR Simple Interactable** component, as follows:

1. Double-click the **GrabHold** to open it for editing
2. With its root **GrabHold** object selected, add a **Simple Interactable** (**Component** | **XR** | **XR Simple Interactable**.)

(While we're calling these objects "grab holds" that the player will grab to climb the wall, it's not a "grab interactable" such as a gun or a knife that the player can grab and throw.) Note that this also adds a **Rigidbody** that the **Interactable** needs. But we do not want the **GrabHold** to move when it's grabbed, so let's constrain it by following the steps given next:

1. Uncheck the **Use Gravity** checkbox.
2. Check the **Constraints** | **Freeze Position** | **X, Y, Z** checkboxes.
3. Check the **Constraints** | **Freeze Rotation** | **X, Y, Z** checkboxes.
4. **Save** your changes to the prefab.

We now have interactor hand controllers and a climbing wall with interactable grab holds. We're ready to implement the grab-and-pull mechanic for climbing the wall.

Adding a ClimbController script

The first thing we're going to do to implement the climb mechanic is writing a `ClimbController` script that will handle the grab/pull/release actions coming from any of the **GrabHold** objects. Add a new script to the **ClimbingWall** named `ClimbController`, as follows:

1. With **ClimbingWall** selected, create a new C# script (**Add Component** | **New Script** | `ClimbController` | **Create And Add**.)
2. Open the script for editing.
3. Create a first iteration of the script, as follows:

```
public class ClimbController : MonoBehaviour
{
    public GameObject xrRig;

    private void Start()
    {
        if (xrRig == null)
            xrRig = GameObject.Find("XR Rig");
    }
```

```
        public void Grab()
        {
        }

        public void Pull(Vector3 distance)
        {
            xrRig.transform.Translate(distance);
        }

        public void Release()
        {
        }
    }
```

We declare a variable for the `xrRig` transform. If you forget to assign it in the **Inspector**, the `Start()` function will find the **XR Rig** in your **Hierarchy** and assign it for you. The `Grab()` and `Release()` functions are placeholders for now; we'll build them out later. The `Pull()` function is called with a pull `distance` and moves the player rig (`xrRig`) the given distance. Save the script. Then, back in Unity, drag the **XR Rig** onto the **ClimbingWall** | **Climb Controller** | **XR Rig** slot.

Avoid the use of `GameObject.Find()` as it can be a time-consuming operation. If you must, use it in `Start()` but never in `Update()`. Better still, be sure to assign any object references in the **Inspector** rather than searching at runtime.

Now, we'll write the `GrabPull` script behavior that the **GrabHold** objects will use for calculating the pull distance and notify the `ClimbController`.

Adding the GrabPull script and actions

As an **Interactor**, each **GrabHold** object on the wall will know when it's being selected by the user's hand controller. At that time, it should begin tracking how far the player has pulled at the **GrabHold** in the current frame and pass that distance on to the `ClimbController`. Create a `GrabClimb` script on the **GrabHold** prefab, as follows:

1. Double-click the **GrabHold** prefab to open it for editing.
2. With its root **GrabHold** object selected, create a new C# script by selecting **Add Component** | **New Script** | `GrabClimb` | **Create And Add**.
3. Open the script for editing.

4. Start writing the script, as follows:

```
using System.Collections.Generic;
using UnityEngine;
using UnityEngine.XR.Interaction.Toolkit;

public class GrabClimb : MonoBehaviour
{
    private XRSimpleInteractable interactable;
    private ClimbController climbController;
    private bool isGrabbing;
    private Vector3 handPosition;

    private void Start()
    {
        interactable = GetComponent<XRSimpleInteractable>();
        climbController = GetComponentInParent<ClimbController>();
        isGrabbing = false;
    }
```

At the top of the file, be sure to declare that we're using `UnityEngine.XR.Interaction.Toolkit` as we'll be using the XRI toolkit **application programming interface (API)** functions. At the top of the class, we declare a number of private variables, which get initialized in `Start`. The `interactable` variable holds the `XRSimpleInteractable` component we added to this **GrabHold**. The `climbController` contains the `ClimbController` component we added to the **ClimbingWall**. And finally, an `isGrabbing` Boolean variable identifies when this **GrabHold** is presently being grabbed so that we can continue to update the pull distances. Next, add the following code:

```
public void Grab()
{
    isGrabbing = true;
    handPosition = InteractorPosition();
    climbController.Grab();
}

private Vector3 InteractorPosition()
{
    List<XRBaseInteractor> interactors =
       interactable.hoveringInteractors;
    if (interactors.Count > 0)
        return interactors[0].transform.position;
    else
        return handPosition;
}
```

The public `Grab` function will be called when the user grabs this hold (**On Select Enter**). It sets the grabbing state to `true`, registers the current `handPosition`, and then notifies the `ClimbController` that a grab has been initiated (`climbController.Grab`).

We get the current hand controller's position with a private `InteractorPosition` function, which uses the XRI API to get the list of `hoveringInteractors` and, for simplicity, returns the position of the first one. If for some reason we thought we're still grabbing but the interactable has no interactors, we return the last known `handPosition`. Finally, add the final two functions, as follows:

```
private void Update()
{
    if (isGrabbing)
    {
        Vector3 delta = handPosition - InteractorPosition();
        climbController.Pull(delta);
        handPosition = InteractorPosition();
    }
}

public void Release()
{
    isGrabbing = false;
    climbController.Release();
}
```

As we know, `Update` gets called every frame. If we're presently grabbing a grab hold (`isGrabbing` is `true`), we calculate the `delta` distance the hand controller (`Interactor`) has moved since the previous frame and pass that distance to the `climbController.Pull` function. Then, we update the current `handPosition` in preparation for the next `Update`.

Lastly, the `Release` function is called when the player lets go of the grab-hold. We reset the `isGrabbing` state and notify the `ClimbController` that this hold has been released.

Save the script. Now, back in Unity, let's connect the `Grab` and `Release` functions to the interactor Select events, as follows:

1. Double-click the **GrabHold** prefab to open it for editing.
2. On its **XR Simple Interactable** | **Interactable Events** | **On Select Enter**, press the **+** button to add a new event action.

3. Drag the same **GrabHold** game object onto the **Runtime Only** object slot.
4. In its **Function** dropdown, select **GrabClimb | Grab**.
5. Likewise, on its **On Select Exit** event, press the **+** button to add a new action.
6. Drag the same **GrabHold** game object onto the **Runtime Only** object slot.
7. In its **Function** dropdown, select **GrabClimb | Release**.
8. Save the prefab changes.

The **XR Simple Interactable** events now look like this:

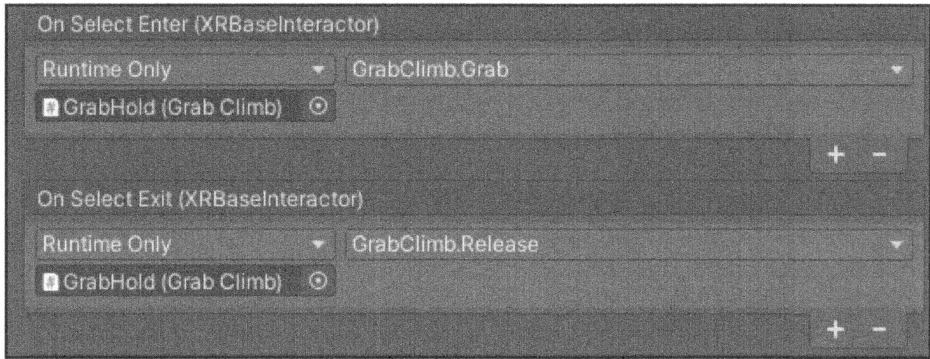

Wow! That should do it. Let's try it out. Press **Play** and go into VR. Reach out to one of the grab-holds and squeeze the grip button, then pull yourself up. Repeat with each hand as you climb the wall. The following screenshot shows my view while hanging on and looking down after having climbed to the top of the wall:

That seems to work pretty well. You can now climb the wall using the **Interactor** hand controller to grab a **Simple Interactable** grab-hold. While grabbing, the `GrabClimb` script calculates the distance you have moved the controller and passes that to the `ClimbController`, which in turn moves the player rig the same distance, resulting in the effect that you've pulled yourself up by the grab-hold. But if you release both hands, you just hover in space as if in zero-gravity. Let's add a consequence to letting go, and fall back to the ground.

Falling

To make you fall down to the ground when you've let go with both hands, we must do several things. First, we need to keep track of how many hands are presently holding onto a grab-hold. When you're not grabbing any, we can implement falling by enabling gravity on a **Rigidbody** attached to the player rig. The Unity Physics engine will take care of moving the rig in accordance with the laws of gravity, yet we should make sure you don't fall below the ground level and continue descending forever.

First, we will add a **Rigidbody** to the rig. Note that there are several ways to disable the effects of falling with a **Rigidbody**—toggling the **Use Gravity** value, or toggling the **Is Kinematic** value, or toggling the **Freeze Position Y** value. We'll use the **Is Kinematic** one, as this, when `true`, tells the Unity Physics engine to ignore this **Rigidbody** in its calculations altogether. (You might choose a different way to handle this if, for example, you also wanted the player to swing while holding with one hand, or add the ability to jump to a new grab-hold with the other hand.) Let's set up a basic vertical gravity fall now. Follow the steps given next:

1. Add a **Rigidbody** to the **XR Rig** (with **XR Rig** selected in **Hierarchy**, choose **Component | Physics | Rigidbody**.)
2. Ensure the **Use Gravity** checkbox is checked.
3. Check the **Is Kinematic** checkbox, to temporarily disable the physics.
4. Constrain the fall to downward only. Check the **Constraints | Freeze Position X, Z** and **Freeze Rotation X, Y, Z** options. Leave the **Position Y** constraint *unchecked*.

The **Rigidbody** settings are shown in the following screenshot:

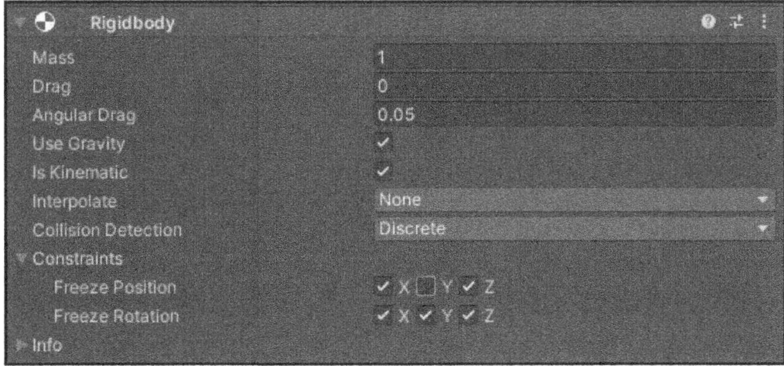

Now, we should update the `ClimbController` script in the following ways. First, add new variables for the `grabCount`, `rigidBody`, and `groundLevel` and initialize them in `Start`, as follows:

```
public class ClimbController : MonoBehaviour
{
    public GameObject xrRig;

    private int grabCount;
    private Rigidbody rigidbody;
    private float groundLevel;

    private void Start()
    {
        if (xrRig == null)
            xrRig = GameObject.Find("XR Rig");
        grabCount = 0;
        rigidbody = xrRig.GetComponent<Rigidbody>();
        groundLevel = xrRig.transform.position.y;
    }
```

The `Grab` function will increment the `grabCount`, and make the **Rigidbody** kinematic (thus, disabling any gravity effects), as illustrated in the following code snippet:

```
public void Grab()
{
    grabCount++;
    rigidbody.isKinematic = true;
}
```

The `Pull` function needs no changes. But the `Release` function now decrements the `grabCount`, and, if neither hand is grabbing, enables the **Rigidbody** gravity (by disabling `IsKinematic`), as illustrated in the following code snippet:

```
public void Release()
   {
     grabCount--;
     if (grabCount == 0)
     {
       rigidbody.isKinematic = false;
     }
   }
```

Finally, we can add an `Update` function that ensures the rig never goes below ground level, and if so, resets the Y position and **Rigidbody** kinematics, as illustrated in the following code snippet:

```
private void Update()
   {
     if (xrRig.transform.position.y <= groundLevel)
     {
        Vector3 pos = xrRig.transform.position;
        pos.y = groundLevel;
        xrRig.transform.position = pos;
        rigidbody.isKinematic = true;
     }
   }
```

Save the script. In Unity, press **Play**. Now, you can climb the wall, but don't let go, or you'll fall down and have to start over. And there it is!

In this section, we've built a little wall-climbing game. First, we built a wall game object from a 3D cube and added a sequence of grab-holds. We made the holds interactable using the **XR Simple Interactable** component and using an **XR Direct Interactor** on the left- and right-hand controllers. Each grab-hold detects when it's been selected and calls its own `GrabPull` script, which begins tracking the pull distance from frame to frame and passes this distance to the `ClimbController`, which moves the player rig that distance, resulting in a climbing mechanic. When you release the controller grip, the **On Select Exit** event calls the `GrabPull.Release` function, resetting the grabbing state, and tells the `GrabController` you've let go with one hand. If the `GrabController` sees that no hands are presently grabbing, it enables the **Rigidbody** physics to let gravity make you fall back down to the ground.

Now, we'll switch our attention from locomotion to teleportation, using the XR Interaction Toolkit's Locomotion System.

Using the XRI Locomotion System

The Unity XR Interaction Toolkit includes what they call the **Locomotion System**, a framework for managing the relocation of the player rig at runtime. They use the word *Locomotion* to encompass both *teleportation* and my narrower definition of *locomotion*. By my definition, *locomotion* refers to a smooth movement of the player in the scene, whereas *teleportation* refers to a discrete jump from one location to another. The XRI Locomotion System has an architecture that can be extended with custom **Locomotion Providers**, some of which they provide, and others you can write, such as the `GlideLocomotion` and `ClimbController` components we developed earlier in this chapter.

In this section, we will introduce the architecture of the XRI Locomotion System, Locomotion Providers, and its control-locking protocol for managing user interactions. We will then install the XRI examples assets, provided separately by Unity, into our project.

Understanding the Locomotion System

The **Locomotion System** is responsible for changing the location of the player in the scene, handling the **XR Rig** position and rotation. Also, the Locomotion System can restrict access to the **XR Rig** transform, preventing other actions from changing it while one **Locomotion Provider** has control moving it. For example, suppose the user activates a teleport to a new location in the scene; the Locomotion System will lock the **XR Rig**, ensuring that the user can't do another action, such as snap turning or teleporting again, until the current action is completed. After the teleport is done, the Teleportation Provider releases its exclusive lock, allowing another Locomotion Provider to request changes to the XR Rig in turn.

The overall flow of a Locomotion request is as follows:

1. The Locomotion Provider checks whether the Locomotion System is currently busy.
2. If not, the Provider requests exclusive access to the Locomotion System.
3. If the request is successful, the Provider moves the **XR Rig.**
4. When the Provider has finished modifying the user's transform position and/or rotation, the Provider relinquishes exclusive access.
5. If the system is busy, or the Provider is unable to get exclusive access, the Provider will not modify the **XR Rig.**

This lock allows teleport actions to be animated over multiple frames without interruption. For example, rather than an instantaneous jump to the new location, the Provider could do a fast glide, show a vignette, and/or a blink-effect that helps reduce motion sickness, as explained later in this chapter. Let's jump right in by adding a **Snap Turn Provider** to the glide locomotion scene we built earlier in this chapter, in the *Implementing basic glide locomotion* section.

Turning in a snap

The XR Interaction package provides an example implementation of a Locomotion System **Snap Turn Provider**. Snap Turn is a type of locomotion that rotates the user in place by a fixed angle. In the glide locomotion scene at the top of this chapter, we wrote our own `GlideLocomotion` script. Let's add to this the ability to turn direction in discrete "snap" angles, using the **Snap Turn Provider** component.

To do this, first, add a Locomotion System component to the **XR Rig**, as follows:

1. Open the `07-Locomotion-1` scene (**File** | **Open Scene**.)
2. Select the **XR Rig** game object in **Hierarchy**.
3. Add a **Locomotion System** component (in **Inspector**, **Add Component**, search `locomotion` | **Locomotion System**.)
4. Save it to a new working scene, `07-Locomotion-3` (**File** | **Save As**.)

Then, add the **Snap Turn** component to the **XR Rig**. Because we set up our scene using the right-hand controller's thumbstick for moving around the scene, we'll connect the snap turn action to the left-hand controller stick only by following the steps given next:

1. With **XR Rig** selected, in **Inspector**, press **Add Component**.
2. Search `snap` and select **Snap Turn Provider** to add the component.
3. To add the left-hand controller, grow the **Controller** list by setting the **Snap Turn Provider** | **Controller** | **Size** to `1`.
4. Drag the child **LeftHand Controller** game object from the **Hierarchy** window onto the **Controllers** | **Element 0** slot.

The component looks like this:

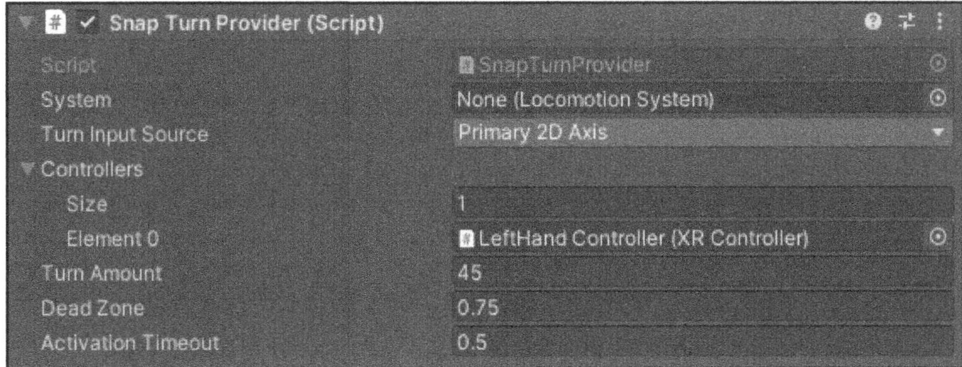

5. Also, clear the **Glide Locomotion** | **Tracked Transform** slot if you tried experimenting with that mechanic earlier.

Now, when you press **Play** and press the left-hand controller's thumbstick sideways, you'll snap turn in that direction. In accordance with the parameters we have set, when the thumbstick is pressed to the side, at least 75% off-center (**Dead Zone**), the player rig will be rotated 45 degrees (**Turn Amount**) in that direction. When you release the stick, you need to wait at least 0.5 seconds (**Activation Timeout**) before a new press will register another turn. The **System** value, which is unassigned, will get filled at runtime by the first **Locomotion System** found in the hierarchy.

It's currently possible to use both the left and right thumbsticks to move (using our `GlideLocomotion` script) and snap turn simultaneously. That's not a great idea, according to Unity XRI best practices. If we integrate the `GlideLocomotion` script with the Locomotion System, however, they'll work in coordination, one at a time.

Integrating scripts with Locomotion System

The XR Interaction package supplies two built-in **Locomotion Providers**: the **Teleportation Provider** and the **Snap Turn Provider**. Both implement the `LocomotionProvider` abstract class. The `LocomotionProvider` class has a simple interface to request and relinquish exclusive access. The `LocomotionProvider` abstract class defines the following methods and events:

- `BeginLocomotion`—Request exclusive access to the Locomotion System.
- `EndLocomotion`—Relinquish access to the Locomotion System.

- `CanBeginLocomotion`—Check if the Locomotion System is currently in exclusive mode before attempting to call `BeginLocomotion` to acquire it.
- `startLocomotion`—This event is invoked on a successful call to `BeginLocomotion`.
- `endLocomotion`—This event is invoked on a successful call to `EndLocomotion`.

We can update our `GlideLocomotion` script developed earlier in this chapter to integrate with the Locomotion System. (In the GitHub files for this book, the script is named `GlideLocomotionXRI`.) Follow the steps given next:

1. Open the `GlideLocomotion` script file for editing, and update it as follows. First, we'll make it a type of `LocomotionProvider` (which itself is a type of `MonoBehaviour`) by changing its declaration, as follows:

```
using UnityEngine.XR.Interaction.Toolkit;

public class GlideLocomotion : LocomotionProvider
{
```

2. Next, add a private flag to track when we're moving, like this:

```
private bool isMoving;
```

3. Then, change `Update` to call the `LocomotionProvider` functions, as follows:

```
private void Update()
{
    if (!isMoving && !CanBeginLocomotion())
        return;

    float forward = Input.GetAxis("
        XRI_Right_Primary2DAxis_Vertical");
    float sideways = Input.GetAxis("
        XRI_Right_Primary2DAxis_Horizontal");
    if (forward == 0f && sideways == 0f)
    {
        isMoving = false;
        EndLocomotion();
        return;
    }

    if (!isMoving)
    {
        isMoving = true;
        BeginLocomotion();
    }
```

```
        if (forward != 0f)
        {
            Vector3 moveDirection = Vector3.forward;
            if (trackedTransform != null)
            {
                moveDirection = trackedTransform.forward;
                moveDirection.y = 0f;
            }

            moveDirection *= -forward * velocity * Time.deltaTime;
            rigRoot.Translate(moveDirection);
        }

        if (trackedTransform == null && sideways != 0f)
        {
            float rotation = sideways * rotationSpeed * Time.deltaTime;
            rigRoot.Rotate(0, rotation, 0);
        }
    }
```

First, if we're not presently moving (`!isMoving`), we check whether the Locomotion System is available. If not, then we just return.

Then, we poll the thumbstick input values, and if it's not being pressed at all (zeros), we reset the `isMoving` flag to `false` and release the Locomotion System (`EndLocomotion`).

Otherwise, if we have just started moving, we set `isMoving` to `true` and lock the Locomotion System. The rest of the function is largely the same, with minor refactoring changes.

Now, when you press **Play** and use the right thumbstick to move through the scene, the left thumbstick, **Snap Turn**, is locked out and will not operate. Once you stop moving, the system is unlocked and you can use the left hand controller to snap turn.

In this section, we learned about the XRI Locomotion System and Provider components for implementing one or more locomotion mechanics in a scene. We learned about the Locomotion System architecture and API, including the abstract `LocomotionProvider` base class. We learned how to add a **Locomotion System** component to the **XR Rig** and use one type of provider, the **Snap Turn Provider**. Then, we modified our homegrown `GlideLocomotion` script to also be a type of `LocomotionProvider` and integrate cleanly with other providers in the same scene.

Next, we'll look at adding teleportation for jumping between locations in the scene.

Teleporting between locations

Teleportation is a type of locomotion that teleports the user from one position to another position, in discrete jumps rather than a continuous gliding motion. Teleportation is generally more user-friendly in VR, reduces the risk of motion sickness, and is often more convenient to use. Normally, as a developer, you designate specific locations or areas where the player is allowed to go. The player then uses the hand controller to point at and select a target location and triggers a jump from here to there. The selection is often indicated with a glowing laser arc ray and a glowing teleportation location disk, showing where the player will end up.

To implement teleportation in our scene, we will use components included with the XRI Toolkit package, but we also need graphics for the arc laser and location anchors effects. For this, it'll be easier to use some of the assets included with the `XR Interaction Toolkit Examples` project, so let's install that first. Then, we'll add the teleportation components and set up the scene with a Teleportation Area interactable and several Teleportation Anchor points.

Installing the XRI examples

The Unity XR Interaction Toolkit Examples repository on GitHub (`https://github.com/Unity-Technologies/XR-Interaction-Toolkit-Examples`) includes examples, presets, and assets for using the XR Interaction package, including teleportation. As we've already witnessed, the XRI examples assets are not required in order to use the XRI Toolkit in your own projects, but it will make our demonstration of teleportation a little easier by avoiding our having to duplicate the effort, using assets they've already provided.

Unfortunately (at the time of writing), the assets are not provided directly as a Unity package. They must be cloned from the GitHub repository, opened as a separate Unity project, and exported into a Unity package that you can then import into your own project. To accomplish this, follow these steps using the **GitHub Desktop**. (Or, if you are already familiar with Git and GitHub, you may choose a different tool.) Note that the repository contains two separate Unity projects, one with VR examples and another with **augmented reality** (**AR**) examples. Obviously, for now, we're just interested in the VR one. Follow the steps given next:

1. If you do not presently have **GitHub Desktop**, use your internet browser to go to `https://desktop.github.com/` to download and install the tool.

2. Then, in your internet browser, go to the `XR Interaction Toolkit Examples`. repository (`https://github.com/Unity-Technologies/XR-Interaction-Toolkit-Examples`)
3. Click the **Clone Or Download** button, then **Open In Desktop**.
4. This will open the GitHub Desktop package and you should see the **Clone A Repository** dialog box. You may choose a **Local Path** into which you want to place your cloned files. Then, click the **Clone** button.

Once the repository has been cloned and downloaded, open it in Unity Hub. (You can have more than one copy of Unity open at a time on your desktop, but I recommend that you first save your changes to any open projects before opening an additional Unity instance.) Follow the steps given next:

1. Open the **Unity Hub** desktop application on your PC.
2. Navigate to the **Projects** tab, and select **Add**.
3. Find the repository folder you just downloaded, and navigate to the `VR` folder (it will contain subfolders named `Assets`, `Packages`, and `ProjectSettings`). Click **Select Folder** (this will add the project to the Unity Hub **Projects** list.)
4. In the **Projects** list, if necessary, select a **Unity Version** from the drop-down list with a version you presently have installed on your machine.
5. Then, click the `VR` project name to open the XRI sample VR project in Unity. If it asks you *Do you want to upgrade your Project to a newer version of Unity?*, press **Confirm**.

This will open Unity with the specified project. Now in Unity, we'll export everything from the Unity package to a file named `XRI-Examples-VR.unitypackage`, using the following steps:

1. In the **Project** window, right-click the root `Assets/` folder (we want to export all of the **Project** folders we just cloned.)
2. Choose **Export Package...**, then **Export**.
3. Choose a filename and location, such as `XRI-Examples-VR.unitypackage`.

You now have a Unity package with the current assets of the `Examples` repository that you can use in this and other projects. I recommend you periodically check the GitHub repository for newer updates, and, if necessary, in GitHub Desktop, choose **Repository | Pull** to get the latest files, then repeat the preceding steps for exporting to a fresh `.unitypackage` file.

We can now import the examples into our own project. With the current project open (for example, `VR_Is_Awesome` is the name we used, starting in `Chapter 2`, *Understanding Unity, Content, and Scale*), do the following:

1. Select **Assets** | **Import Package** | **Custom Package...**
2. Navigate to and choose the `XRI-Examples-VR` package we just created, and choose **Open**.
3. In the **Import Unity Package** dialog box, click **Import**.
4. Because we're using the **Universal Windows Platform** (**UWP**) render pipeline, you might need to convert the imported materials (select **Edit** | **Render Pipeline** | **Universal Render Pipeline** | **Upgrade Project Materials to UWP Materials**.)

While you're here, you might want to explore some of the example scenes including **Locomotion**, **UI Canvas**, and **WorldInteractionDemo**. Now, we're ready to add teleportation to a scene.

Adding teleportation

As noted previously, the XRI Teleportation Provider supports different types of teleportation interactable objects, including a **TeleportationArea** and a **TeleportationAnchor**. *Areas* let the player choose a location on a surface they wish to teleport to. *Anchors* teleport the user to a specific predefined location they choose. Both types of destinations are implemented as a type of `BaseTeleportationInteractable` abstract class, as the starting point for shared code. These are intended to be used with an **XR Ray Interactor**, which uses the intersection point of the ray and the area's collision volume to determine the location where the user wants to teleport.

For our example, let's begin with the first locomotion scene we created earlier in this chapter—that is, `07-Locomotion-1`. First, add a **Locomotion System** and save the scene as a new working scene, as follows:

1. Open the `07-Locomotion-1` scene (**File** | **Open Scene**.)
2. Select the **XR Rig** game object in **Hierarchy**.
3. Add a **Locomotion System** component (in **Inspector**, **Add Component**, search `locomotion` | **Locomotion System**.)
4. Now, we can add a Teleportation Provider to the **XR Rig** (in **Inspector**, **Add Component**, search `teleport` | **Teleportation Provider**.)
5. Save it to a new working scene, `07-Locomotion-4` (**File** | **Save As**.)

That's the Provider side of the equation. Now, we can add some teleport interactables to the scene. Let's add one area and several anchors. First, we'll add a teleport area by dragging the `TeleportArea` prefab to the back-left corner of the play area, as follows:

1. From the **Project** window, locate the **TeleportArea** prefab (this can be found in `Assets/Prefabs/`.)
2. Drag it into the scene
3. Set its **Scale** to (`0.5, 1, 0.5`) and **Position** to (`-3, 0, 3`.)

Notice that this prefab has a number of things already set up. The **Scene** view, **Hierarchy**, and **Inspector** with a **TeleportArea** are shown in the following screenshot:

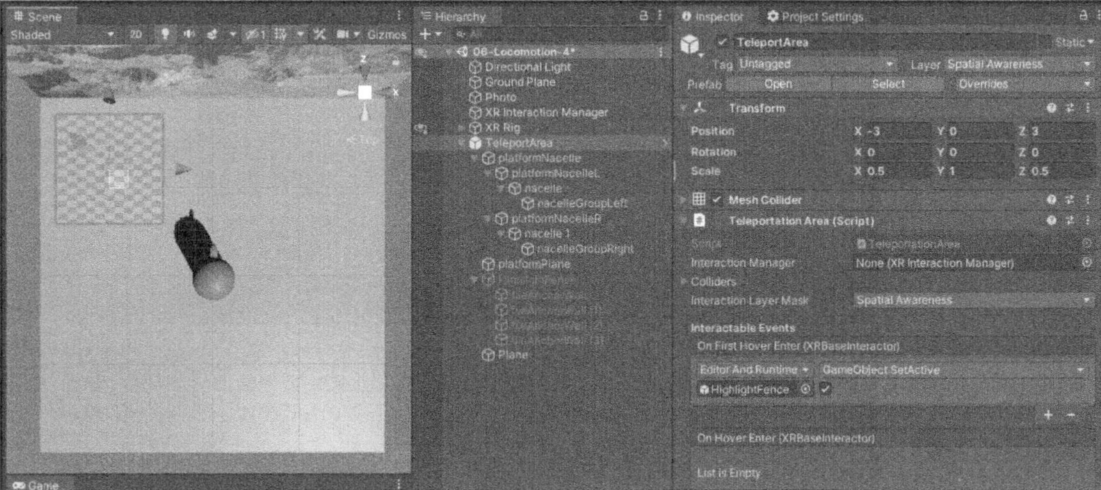

As you can see, the game object has children objects that can be used to highlight the area while it's being selected for teleportation, including one named **HighlightFence** that highlights the rectangular perimeter of the area. Its **Teleportation Area** component defines two event actions: **On Hover Enter** will enable the **HighlightFence**, and **On Hover Exit** will disable the fence. Also (not shown in the preceding screenshot), the **Teleportation Area** specifies a **Custom Reticle** that will be displayed at the actual teleportation location you are pointing at.

When you press **Play** and point with the hand controller at the **TeleportArea**, it highlights the **HighlightFence** around its perimeter, and the **TeleportReticle** is displayed at the target position. Obviously, you can change each of these graphics to suit your specific game requirements. Squeeze the grip button (or whichever button is configured to activate the teleport), and the **XR Rig** is moved to the selected location. In the following screenshot, I am pointing at the **TeleportArea**, and you can see the area perimeter and teleport location reticle are highlighted:

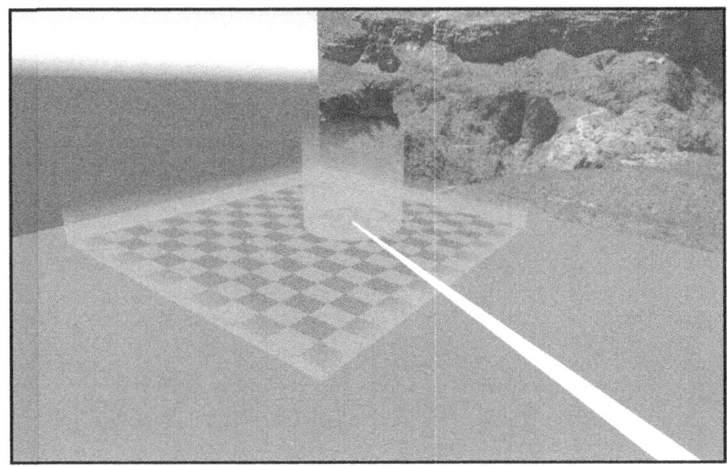

Likewise, we can add individual teleportation anchor points in the scene. Use the following steps to make three separate **TeleportAnchor** instances in three quadrants of the ground plane:

1. From the **Project** window, locate the **TeleportAnchor** prefab (this can be found in `Assets/Prefabs/`.)
2. Drag it into the scene and set its **Position** to (`3, 0, 3`) and **Rotation** (`0, -135, 0`.)
3. Add another at **Position** (`-3, 0, -3`) and **Rotation** (`0, 45, 0`.)
4. And another at **Position** (`3, 0, -3`) and **Rotation** (`0, -45, 0`.)

Notice that the anchors can be rotated to a specific orientation. When the player teleports to that anchor, they'll end up also facing the forward direction of the anchor. In our example, we have each of the three anchors facing toward the middle of the play area. The following screenshot depicts me standing at one corner and selecting a **TeleportAnchor** at the opposite corner. If you look closely, you can see that the anchor has a **DirectionArrow** showing the player which way I'll be facing, if and when I go there. This can be seen here:

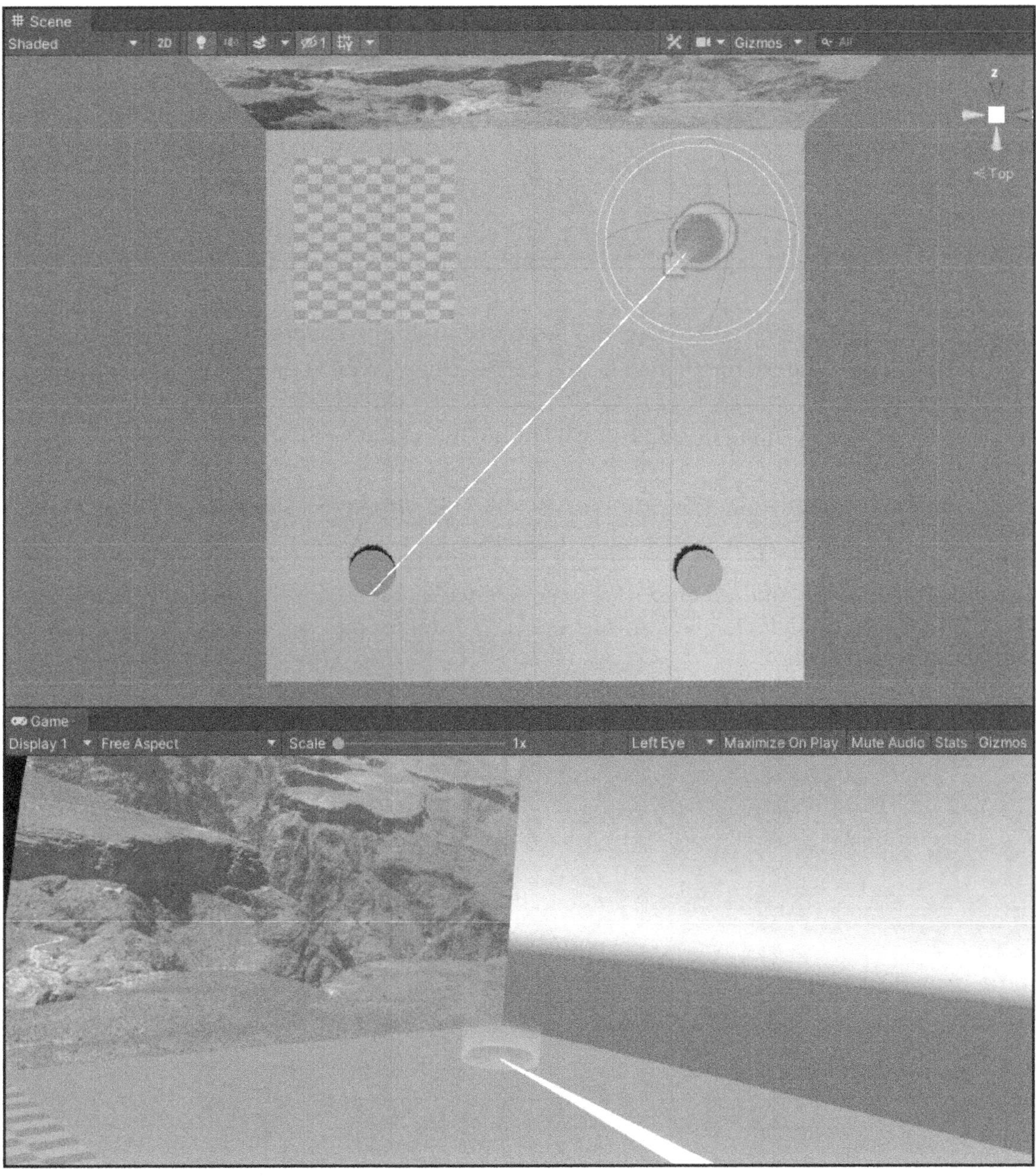

As you can see, it is very easy to add teleportation features to your game using the XRI Teleportation System and interactable teleportation platforms' areas and anchors.

Restricting interaction to a specific layer

When your scene contains many interactable objects, you will want to limit the work required to select teleportation interactables by placing them on a specific layer. The default objects we've been using may be on any layer (**Everything**) or could be already set up to use **Layer 31**, named `Spatial Awareness` or `Teleport` by XRI. If not, you can create a layer now, using the following steps:

1. In the **Layer** dropdown in the top-right of the **Inspector**, choose **Add Layer...** or **Edit Layers....**
2. This opens the **Tags & Layers** window. Unfold the **Layers** list.
3. Choose an undefined layer slot. It can be **User Layer 31** or another one. Type the name `Teleport`.
4. Select the **TeleportArea** GameObject again in **Hierarchy** to restore its **Inspector** view.
5. Set its **Layer** value to `Teleport` and its **Teleport Area** | **Interaction Layer Mask**, as shown in the screenshot that follows.

You'll notice that each of the **Teleport** areas and anchors are assigned to this layer, and their Mesh Collider component is given this layer for its **Interaction Layer Mask**, as shown in the following screenshot:

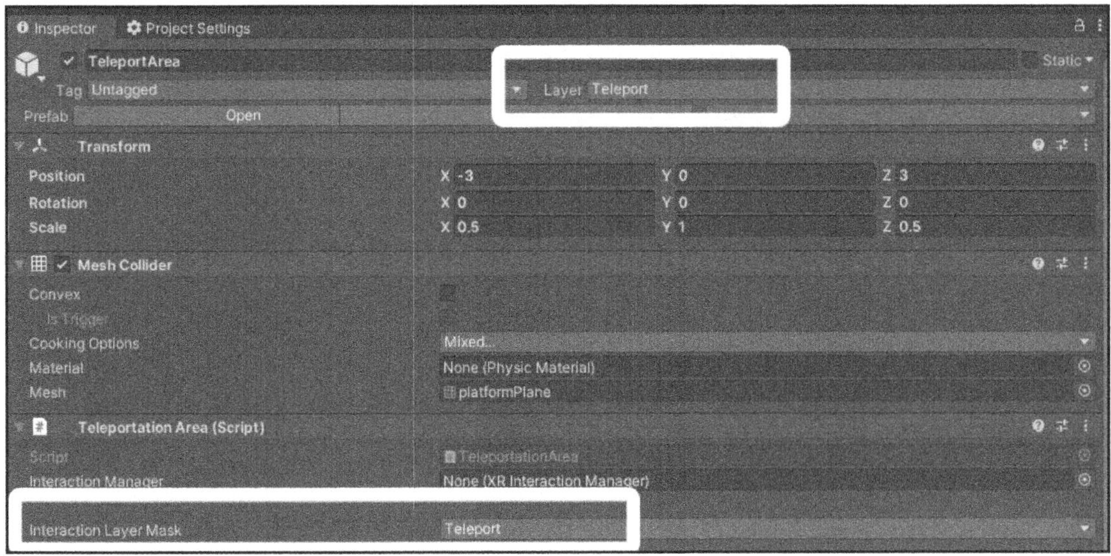

And likewise, the Interactors need to know in which layer to find items. On each of the hand controllers' XR Ray Interactor, the Interaction Layer Mask can also be set to this layer and the Raycast Mask.

Layer masks restrict the search for objects during a raycast and interaction detection. This can be very important to improve performance in large scenes with many game objects. Masks can specify multiple layers. To edit a layer mask for multiple layers, first, select **Nothing** to clear the list, then select the individual layers you want to be included.

The XR Interaction system also provides various line-rendering options that we'll explore in more detail next.

Ray interactors for teleportation

We were introduced to the **XR Ray Interactor** in `Chapter 5`, *Interacting with your Hands*, as it is part of the default **XR Rig** we've been using in our scenes. The ray is rendered as a straight laser-beam ray, using an **XR Interactor Line Visual** helper and **Line Renderer** components. Straight lines are good for selecting objects and UI items in a scene, but usually, we use an arcing curve for teleportation. This is because we're usually trying to select a location on a horizontal (or near-horizontal) surface, so you'd want the ray to end in a downward-facing vector. XRI provides two alternatives to the straight line: a Projectile Curve and a Bezier Curve. They are explained as follows:

- A **Projectile Curve** draws a curve that approximates a projectile being thrown a distance and highlights the landing point. As you lift the hand controller, the landing point goes further away, then comes closer if you keep lifting the controller.
- A **Bezier Curve** draws a curve between the start point (your controller) and a fixed-distance end selection point. You can control the height of the curve at its peak, and the distance via C#.

For teleportation, I recommend using the Projectile Curve. For example, the following steps will render a projectile curve that drops off near the end instead of a straight-line ray:

1. Select the **RightHand Controller** in **Hierarchy**.
2. In **Inspector**, set its **Line Type** to **Projectile Curve**.
3. Set its **Velocity** to `10`.

The curved ray is shown in the following screenshot, interacting with a `TeleportArea`:

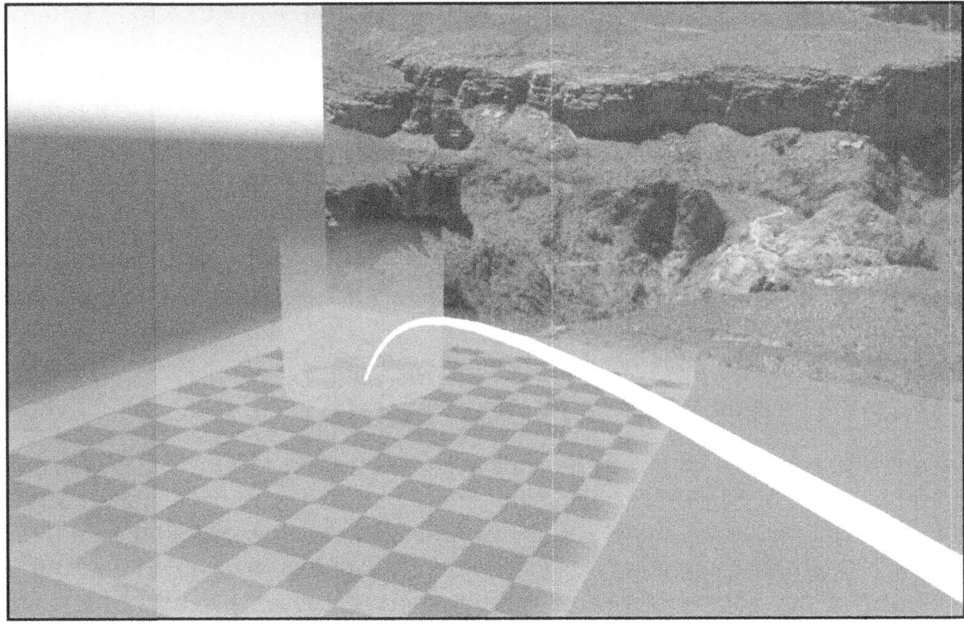

So far, we've only been considering hand controller Interactors that perform a single interaction. In a real game, you're more likely to need multiple interaction modes in a scene. Let's consider this next.

Switching between Interactors

Suppose you have a scene where the player can interact in a variety of ways: teleport with a Projectile Curve ray; grab and use an object by directly touching and picking it up; use a menu **user interface** (**UI**) by pointing with a straight-line ray. Each of these may require different controller interactors, configured in their own ways. Unity has thought about this and provides an example scene in the XR Interaction Toolkit Examples project, named `WorldInteractionDemo`. This scene uses an enhanced **XR Rig** prefab named **XRRig_Demo**, with two different hand controllers for each hand (four in total) separating the teleportation one (for example, **RightTeleportController**) from the direct interaction one (for example, **RightBaseController**).

The **XRRig_Demo** object includes a script named `ControllerManager` that allows the player to switch between hand controllers with the press of a button. Its **Inspector** is shown in the following screenshot:

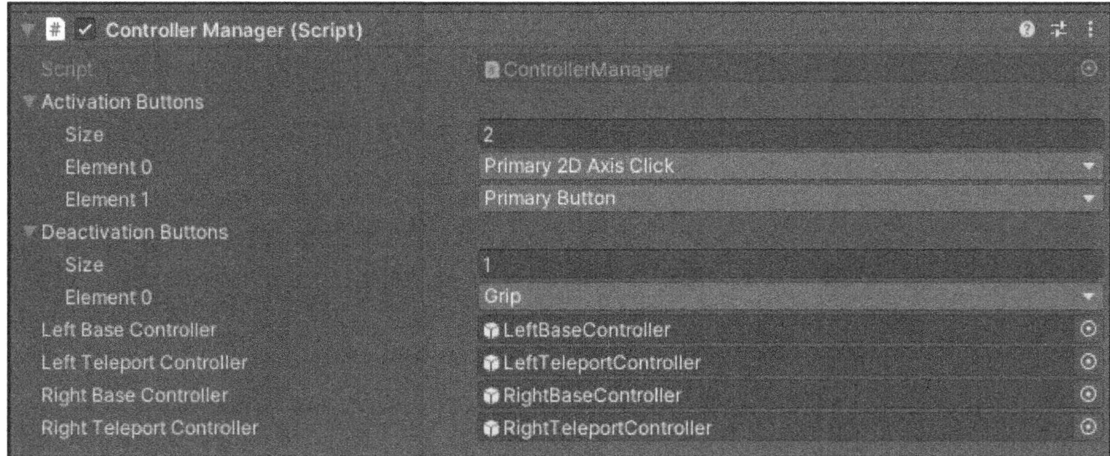

As you can see, the four controller game objects are assigned to their respective parameter slots. The **Activation Buttons** functionality on the controller will trigger a transition to the **Teleport Controller**, currently set up as either the thumbstick click or the primary button (for example, **A** or **X**). The **Deactivation Buttons** functionality, set as the **Grip** button, will force deactivation of the teleport mode. When the right or left-hand controller switches between base interaction and teleport interaction, the code will automatically manage this.

You can use this rig directly in your own projects, or modify the `ControllerManager` script for your own purposes. You could, for example, replace the default **XR_Rig** with the **XRRig_Demo** and be well on your way.

In this section, we have learned how to use the XRI Teleportation System for moving to new locations in a scene. The target location can be selected from a **Teleport Area** or a **Teleport Anchor**, where the player can choose any location in an Area, or pick a specific anchor location and direction. The teleportation provider interoperates with other locomotion providers in the XRI Locomotion System. We also looked at restricting the teleport interactables to a specific Unity layer for efficiency, how to modify the Ray Interactor to use a Projectile Curve, and ideas for handling multiple kinds of interactor controllers in a scene.

For the final topic in this chapter, we will look into the wide variety of concerns and mechanics related to locomotion, teleportation, VR comfort, and motion sickness.

Locomotion and comfort in VR

Locomotion and teleportation in VR is not a settled science. Many techniques have been tried; some have proven successful and represent best practices. We've demonstrated some of these in this chapter. Others have failed and are discouraged. New advancements in hardware, software, and player mechanics keep the options fresh and open to innovation. In this section, I present a bagful of ideas, in no particular order, for your consideration and amusement, including other locomotion mechanics and techniques for managing VR motion sickness.

Other locomotion mechanics

In the first edition of this book (2015), we implemented a game where you could ride an "elevator" to a high platform, and then jump off onto a trampoline. You'd hit the trampoline, bounce up, and down, bounce up again, and down until you settled. I assumed that would be really fun in VR, but it turned out to be a really bad idea! Unless you want to invoke nausea in your players and make people hate you, I would avoid a mechanic such as this.

If you want to offer your players a VR ride, you can define a predefined *track* to glide along, such as a guided tour of a building or art gallery. Tracks can be 3D, moving you up and down too, with gravity, such as VR roller coasters, or without gravity, such as a space tour. We do not recommend this mechanic except for the most hardcore thrill seekers as it also has a good chance of causing motion sickness.

We looked at using a hand-over-hand mechanic for climbing (vertical locomotion). You could also try using your hands not for climbing, but for horizontal locomotion—for example, reaching and pulling like a rope, or swinging your arms like a runner, or even a circular pulling motion as if you're operating a wheelchair.

With room-scale VR tracking, you can walk within a subset of your scene, within the safety boundaries that you have configured for your physical room. There also are hardware devices that implement locomotion mechanisms using your feet to walk or run, such as the following:

- VR treadmills where you walk in place with your feet and legs to walk and run in VR
- Exercise bikes where you can cycle and even hang glide in VR
- Body-tracking sensors can be used not just for player locomotion but also motion capture for representing full-body avatars in a social VR room

A technique for comfort during locomotion is to use a **vignette**. During the movement, the camera is cropped with a circular vignette and simple background, such as a grid being displayed in the player's peripheral vision, so they only see what is directly before them. Eliminating peripheral vision while moving can reduce the chance of motion sickness, as illustrated in the following screenshot (source: `https://developers.google.com/vr/elements/tunneling`, under the `Creative Commons Attribution 4.0 License` license):

You can use a similar technique for teleportation. Rather than just start at one location and suddenly appear at the new location, you could animate glide locomotion to the new location, but at a very fast speed. And also, you can use a vignette. This can help preserve the player's orientation of where they've ended up on the scene.

Likewise, **blink teleport** is a technique that does a fade-out fade-in between the change in player position. It is said to provide an additional degree of comfort. Some have even found fading with a literal blink effect is quite natural, where you rapidly fade out from top to bottom, and fade in the bottom to top, like an eyelid closing and opening.

Another teleportation technique is to provide a third-person view of the scene from above, sometimes called a **mini-map**, **god view**, or **dollhouse view**. From this perspective, the player could point to a new location to teleport. This mini version of the scene could be an object the player uses as a tool in the main scene, or you transition to this view mode during the teleportation selection process.

You can also teleport to a different scene. Combined with the fade-out/in, you would call `SceneManager.LoadScene("OtherSceneName")` rather than simply changing the transform position. You must add the other scene to the **Build Settings Scenes to Build** list (see `https://docs.unity3d.com/ScriptReference/SceneManagement.SceneManager.LoadScene.html`). It is recommended you fade to a dark color rather than white, which could be startling in a VR headset.

Clever use of teleportation and the player's direction can lead to efficient use of limited play space and give the perception of the VR space being much larger than it is actually is in real life. For example, in room-scale VR, if you have the player walk toward the edge of the play space and enter an elevator, they could be facing the back of the elevator going in and must turn around when the doors open on the new level, and can now physically walk forward. In fact, infinite corridors and connected rooms could be implemented this way while maintaining player immersion.

I've mentioned motion sickness multiple times here. In the next topic, I discuss the issue in a little more detail.

Managing VR motion sickness

VR motion sickness, or simulator sickness, is a real symptom and a concern for VR. Researchers, psychologists, and technologists with a wide array of specializations and PhDs are studying the problem to better understand the underlying causes and find solutions.

A cause of VR motion sickness is a lag in screen updates—or **latency.** When you're moving your head, your brain expects the world around you to change exactly in sync. Any perceptible delay can make you feel uncomfortable, to say the least.

Latency can be reduced by faster rendering of each frame, keeping to the recommended **frames per second** (**FPS**). Device manufacturers see this as their problem to solve, in both hardware and runtime driver software. **Graphics processing unit** (**GPU**) and chip manufacturers see it as a processor performance and throughput problem. We will undoubtedly see leaps and bounds in improvements over the coming years. Likewise, as developers, we also need to take responsibility.

VR developers need to be aware of latency and other causes of VR motion sickness. We need to look at it as though it's our problem too because ultimately, it comes down to performance and ergonomics. With an ongoing dichotomy of mobile VR versus desktop VR, there will always be upper bounds on the performance of devices that our players will be using.

But it's not just technology. I can get nauseous riding a real-world roller coaster. So, why wouldn't a VR one have a similar effect? Things to consider that help improve your players' comfort and safety include game mechanics and a user experience design such as the following:

- **Don't move fast**: When moving or animating a first-person character, don't move too fast. High-speed first-person shooter games that work on gaming consoles and desktop PCs may not work out so well in VR.
- **Look forward**: When moving through a scene, if you're looking to the side rather than straight ahead, you're more likely to feel nauseous.
- **Don't turn your head too fast**: Discourage users from turning their head quickly with the VR headset on. The latency in updating the HMD screen is aggravated by larger changes in the viewport in small time slices.
- **Offer comfort mode**: When a scene requires you to quickly turn yourself a lot of times, provide a ratcheted (snap turn) rotation mechanism, also known as comfort mode, which lets you change the direction in which you look in larger increments.
- **Use fade or blink** cuts during teleportation and scene changes. When fading, go to a dark color, as white can be startling.
- **Use tunneling** or other techniques during locomotion. Reduce what is visible in the peripheral vision by masking the camera, except what is just in front of you.
- **Use a third-person camera**: If you have high-speed action but you don't necessarily intend to give the user a thrill ride, use a third-person camera view.
- **Stay grounded**: Provide visual cues that help the user stay grounded, such as horizon lines, nearby objects in your field of view, and relative fixed-position objects, such as dashboards and body parts.
- **Provide an option to recenter the view**: Mobile VR devices, in particular, are subject to drift and the need to be recentered on occasion. With wired VR devices, this helps you avoid getting tangled in HMD wires. As a safety issue, recentering your view relative to the real world may help you avoid hitting furniture and walls in the physical space.
- **Don't use cut scenes**: In traditional games (and movies), a technique that can be used to transition between levels is to show a 2D cutscene movie. This does not work well in VR as it breaks the immersion. An alternative is to simply fade to black and then open the new scene.

- **Optimize rendering performance**: It is important for all VR developers to understand the underlying causes of latency, especially with regard to rendering performance, and what you can do to optimize it, such as lowering the poly count and choosing lighting models carefully. Learn to use performance monitoring tools in order to keep the FPS within the expected and acceptable limits.
- **Encourage users to take breaks**: Or, alternatively, you can maybe just provide a puke-bag with your game! Just kidding.

We will continue discussing many of these considerations throughout this book. In the next chapter, we examine the rendering pipeline and techniques for optimizing rendering performance while maintaining quality results. In `Chapter 11`, *Using All 360 Degrees*, we look at 360-degree media and VR comfort related to that. And in `Chapter 13`, *Optimizing for Performance and Comfort*, we dive deeper into performance optimization and Unity profiling tools for detecting and ironing out any performance bottlenecks that can affect latency and comfort.

Summary

In this chapter, we explored a variety of mechanics for moving the player within your virtual environments. We started by implementing a glide locomotion mechanic, using the thumbstick on the hand controller to drive through the scene. This included alternative ways to define what "moving forward" means, using the gaze direction, pointing with a hand controller, or rotating using the horizontal axis of the thumb controller. Then, we built a climbing wall using a hand-over-hand grab-and-pull mechanic. We even made the player fall to the ground if they let go!

We also learned about the XR Interaction Toolkit's Locomotion System that uses Locomotion Providers to implement various features. First, we added a **Snap Turn Provider** to turn the player in discrete angle increments with the thumbstick, and we learned to use the XRI API to integrate our own `GlideLocomotion` script with the Locomotion System. Next, we implemented teleportation using a Teleportation Provider along with interactable **TeleportArea** and **TeleportAnchor** objects. Using assets from the `XR Interaction Toolkit Examples` project from Unity, we quickly added effective and high-quality visuals to the teleportation mechanics in our scene.

We also gained a deeper understanding of the use of layers, ray interactor visuals, and managing multiple interactor controllers. Finally, we surveyed a wide variety of locomotion and teleportation techniques and concerns that might affect player comfort and motion sickness.

In the next chapter, we'll step away from the interactivity we've been doing the past few chapters and learn about the Unity rendering pipeline, lighting, and realism.

8
Lighting, Rendering, Realism

Up to now, we've focused on the mechanics of developing interactive 3D scenes, starting with understanding 3D coordinates and scale, to interacting with your gaze and your hands, then displaying text and **user interface** (**UI**) elements, and finally, moving through the scene with locomotion and teleportation. In this chapter, we consider a different yet equally important aspect of your **virtual reality** (**VR**) project—the visual fidelity of your scene. We will examine many of Unity's powerful tools for lighting, rendering, and realism.

Rendering and lighting are complex topics, broad and deep. It can take years of experience and artistic skills to master the quality we have come to expect in AAA video games and Hollywood movie productions. Unity is amazing because it provides many simple, easily accessible tools for getting your scenes to look very good even if you have limited experience, while also providing a plethora of controls, parameters, and components that would please even the most advanced, perfectionist, visual artist. Unity also appreciates the division of roles between artists and developers. As an artist, you can create 3D assets outside of Unity and import them into the project, and then control and refine materials, textures, and illumination. As a developer, you can build the scenes, script behaviors, design game mechanics, and refine the player experience with temporary artwork, and, at a later time, integrate the actual assets.

In this chapter, we'll learn about lighting and rendering to make the scene look realistic. The project will be the inverse of the other projects in this book—that is, instead of starting with an empty scene and building up the project step by step, we will start with an existing scene and see what happens when you remove or modify existing properties. The scene will be the default `SampleScene` that Unity includes when you create a new project using the URP template. As we examine different topics in rendering and lighting, we'll add UI controls and scripts for manipulating some settings so that you can see first-hand the effects in VR.

We will begin by reviewing the workflow and best practices that Unity recommends for planning your lighting. After setting up our in-game menu panels, you'll learn about environmental lighting. Then, you'll learn more about materials, including how to modify shader parameters from C# scripts. Next, we'll look at lighting GameObjects and light emission with Materials that contribute to lighting in the scene. After that, you'll see how adding Light Probes and Reflection Probes can really improve the realism and fidelity of your graphics. Finally, we'll look at the post-processing effects, which can be the crowning finish to making your scene look more realistic and cinematic. In this chapter, we will cover the following topics:

- Lighting and rendering strategies
- Using environmental lighting
- Using **physically based rendering** (**PBR**) materials and **Universal Render Pipeline** (**URP**) Shaders
- Using Light objects and Emission surfaces
- Using Light Probes and Reflection Probes
- Enhancing your scenes with post-processing effects

The intent of this chapter is to give you an interesting overview of the many, many ways of controlling lighting in your VR scenes. By the end of this chapter, you should have a richer understanding of lighting in VR and a launching point for your own explorations.

We will begin with a discussion of the key concepts and an overview of Unity's lighting and rendering tools.

Technical requirements

To implement the projects and exercises in this chapter, you will need the following:

- PC or Mac with Unity 2019.4 LTS or later, an XR Plugin for your device, and the XR Interaction Toolkit package installed
- A VR headset supported by the Unity XR Platform

You can access or clone the GitHub repository for this book (`https://github.com/PacktPublishing/Unity-2020-Virtual-Reality-Projects-3rd-Edition-`) to optionally use assets and completed projects for this chapter, as follows:

- All completed projects in this book are in a single Unity project at `UVRP3Projects`.
- The completed assets and scenes for this chapter are in the `UVRP3Projects/Assets/_UVRP3Assets/Chapter08/` folder.

Lighting and rendering strategies

Lighting your scenes starts with your project's requirements and your own decisions about the look and style you are aiming for. Do you want high-quality realism or simpler geometric rendering? Do you want lifelike objects or cartoon-like graphics? Are you lighting an outdoor scene or an indoor one? Just as important, you also need to ask yourself what are the primary target platforms, especially: is it mobile, desktop, or console? At some point in your projects, before creating the final assets and lighting, you need to figure out your lighting strategy, as Unity recommends:

> *Altering your lighting strategy late in development has a high impact on your workflow. Taking the time to get this right before you enter production saves time overall, and allows you to achieve better performance and higher visual fidelity.*

In this section, I'll try to break down the different types of lighting sources and settings you can use in your project. First, some definitions, as follows:

- **Direct lighting** is emitted, hits a surface once, and is then reflected into the camera.
- **Indirect lighting** is any other light that ultimately is visible, including multi-bounced light and sky.
- **Global Illumination** (**GI**) refers to the combination of direct and indirect lighting that provides realistic lighting results.
- **Real-time** lighting is calculated at runtime.
- **Baked** lighting is precomputed before your program is built and saved as lighting data (such as **Lightmap** images) and used at runtime.
- **Mixed** lighting is when your project utilizes a combination of real-time and baked lighting.

- **Render Pipeline** is the sequence of operations performed to draw a scene on the screen. Unity lets you choose between multiple render pipelines.
- **Shader** is a program running on the **graphics processing unit** (**GPU**) that calculates the value of each pixel on the screen from a set of geometry and texture data prepared by the **central processing unit** (**CPU**).

I will refer you to the *Lighting strategy* article in *Unity Best Practices Guides: Making Believable Visuals In Unity* (`https://docs.unity3d.com/Manual/BestPracticeMakingBelievableVisuals3.html`), which outlines five different common lighting setups, as follows:

- **Basic real-time lighting**: The specular highlights from the light are visible, but there is no indirect lighting.
- **Baked lighting**: Soft baked shadows are visible, and static indirect lighting is visible in high resolution, but there are no specular highlights from lights, and dynamically lit GameObjects don't cast shadows.
- **Mixed lighting**: Similar to baked lighting, but there is a specular response from lights, and dynamically lit GameObjects do cast shadows.
- **Real-time lighting and GI**: Proper indirect lighting response and specular response are visible, and lights are all moveable and updateable, but there's no angular soft shadow.
- **All options enabled**: Depending on the settings of each light, you can achieve a combination of all the preceding options.

Open the **Lighting settings** window by selecting **Window** | **Rendering** | **Lighting**, and review the options. Your settings can vary from one scene to the next in your project. The **Scene** tab settings are shown in the following screenshot, where the **Baked Global Illumination Mixed Lighting** option with **Lighting Mode** is set to **Baked Indirect**. Review the other many **Lightmapping Settings** shown here:

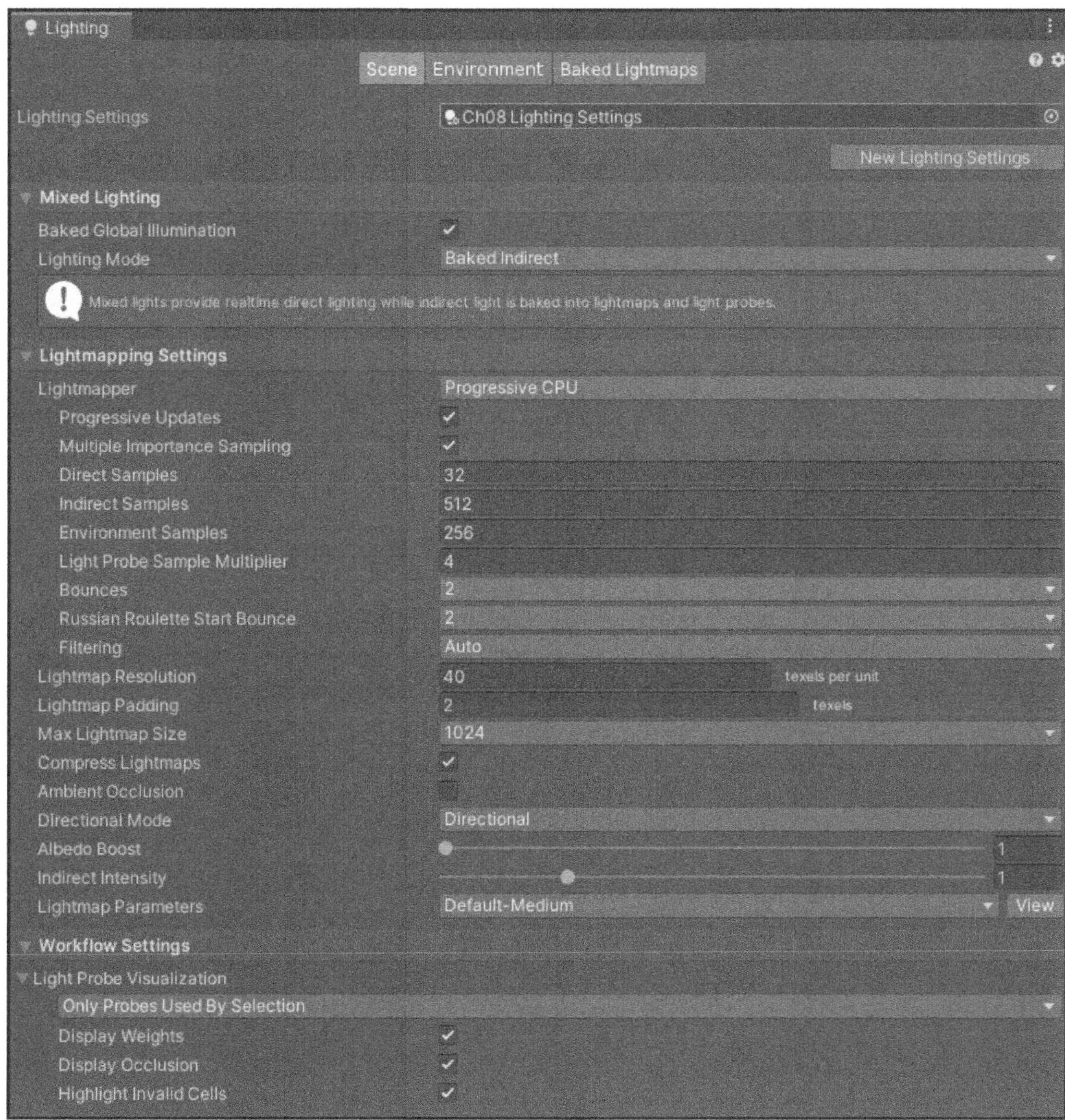

Given that you have an idea of your visual requirements and target platforms, the first step in setting up your lighting strategy is to choose a Render Pipeline for the project, and then choose lighting settings and light GameObjects in the scene.

Choosing a Render Pipeline

In setting up a new Unity project, one of the very first decisions you make is to choose a **render pipeline**. We did this at the start of this book and decided all of our projects will use the URP, picking the corresponding template from the **Unity Hub**. A render pipeline performs a sequence of operations that displays the content of a scene onto the screen, frame by frame. Different render pipelines have different capabilities and performance and are suitable for different applications and platforms. A render pipeline is responsible for three major process steps, as follows:

1. **Culling**: The first step is to list the objects to be rendered, choosing only the objects visible in the camera frustum (viewing volume) and eliminating those occluded (obscured) by other objects.
2. **Rendering**: The second stage is drawing the objects into pixel buffers, with correct lighting, shadows, reflections, and so on.
3. **Post-processing**: The final stage is performed on the pixel buffers before being copied onto the display screen, including effects such as bloom and color grading.

Prior to Unity 2019, Unity had a single **Built-in Render Pipeline**. Presently, this is still available and may be selected using one of the first three templates when creating a new project in the **Unity Hub**. The last two options, for **High Definition Render Pipeline** (**HDRP**) and URP, use the new **Scriptable Render Pipeline** (**SRP**) instead of the built-in one. I recommend you use one of these, such as **Universal Render Pipeline**, if you can, as this is the future of Unity. This option is shown in the following screenshot:

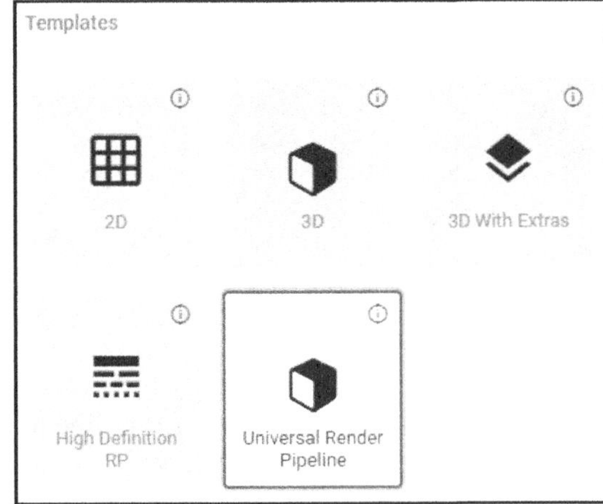

In addition to the HDRP and URP pipelines provided with Unity, you can create your own custom ones. The SRP pipeline allows you to control rendering via a C# script, giving graphics programmers very advanced control over the processing and rendering details of their projects.

In your project, you set up the **Scriptable Render Pipeline Settings** in the **Graphics** settings window, found by navigating to **Edit | Project Settings | Graphics**, as shown in the following screenshot. Details can be found in the Unity Manual (`https://docs.unity3d.com/Manual/class-GraphicsSettings.html`):

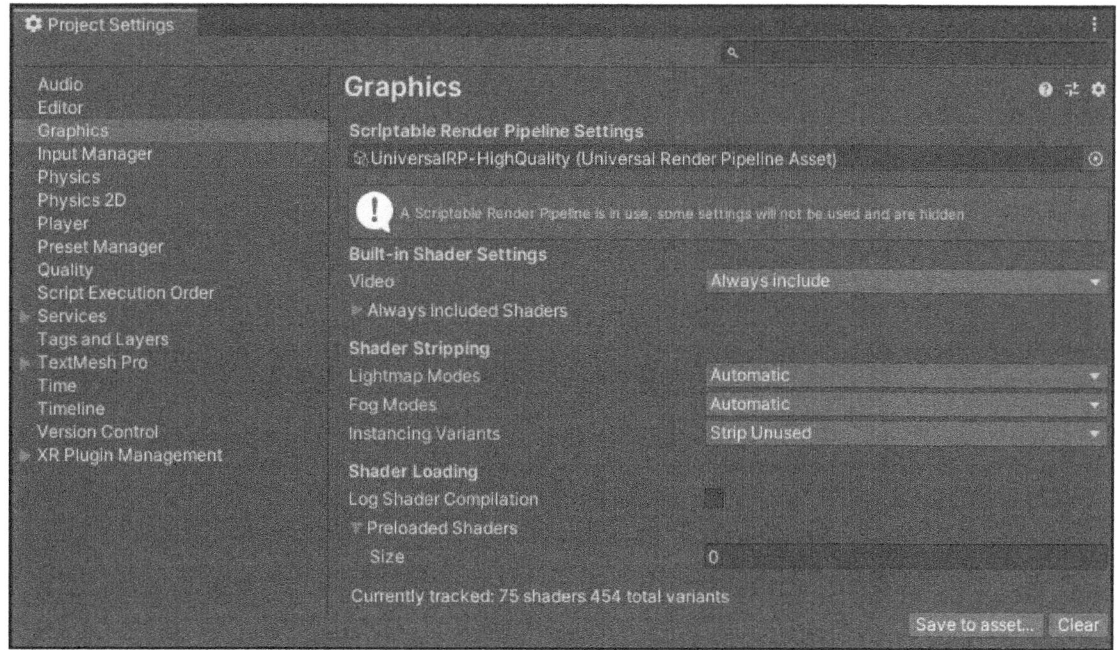

When using a **Scriptable Render Pipeline**, its settings are stored in a separate data asset file found, by default, in the `Assets/Settings/` folder. In the **Settings** window shown in the preceding screenshot, it's referencing the `UniversalRP-HighQuality` asset.

Clicking that asset, you can review and modify its settings in the **Inspector**, as shown in the following screenshot:

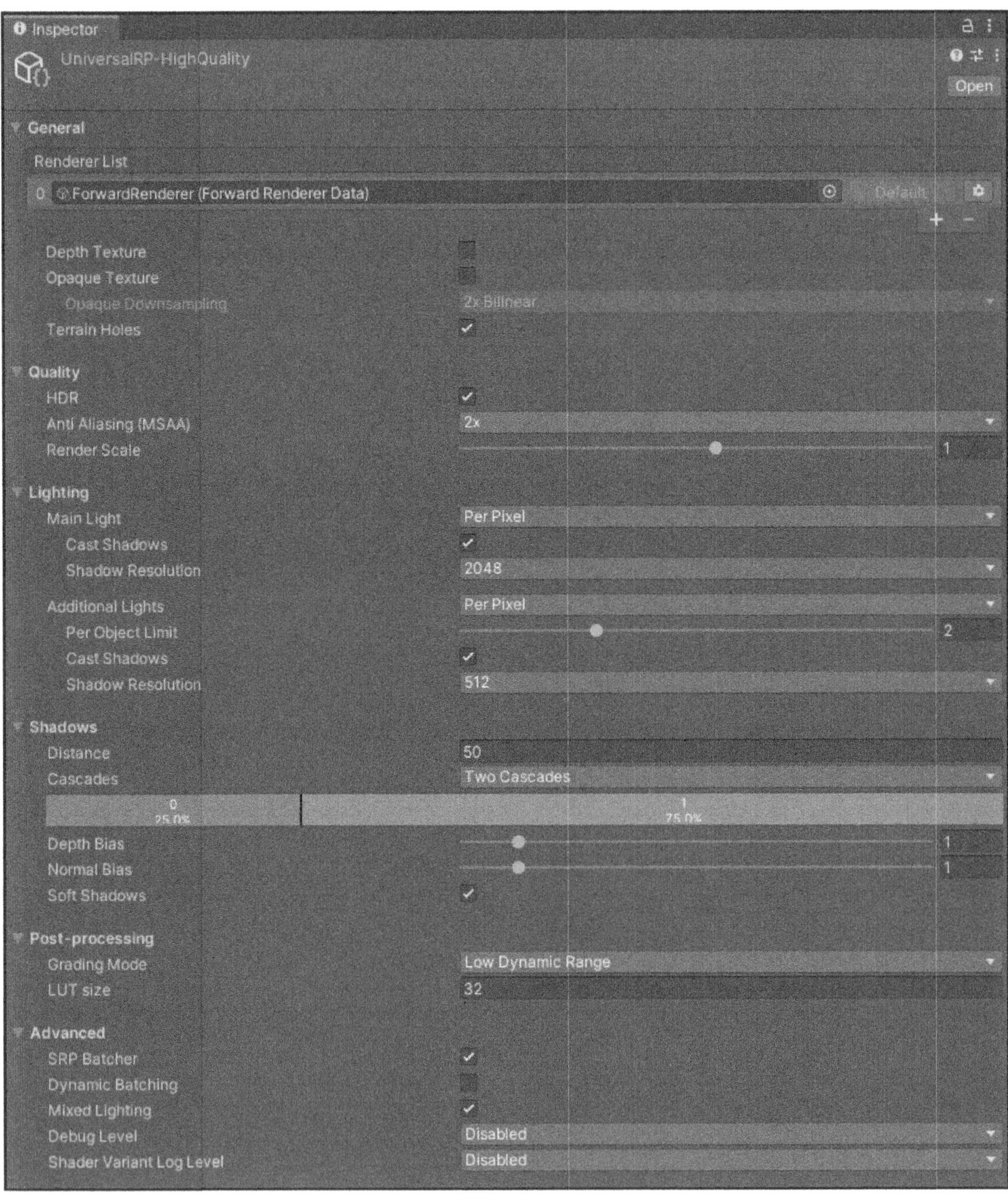

I won't go into the meaning of each individual setting here, as this can be found in the Unity Manual. As you can see, it is wise to choose your Render Pipeline before you even create and start your project. It can be changed later, but it's always best sooner rather than later. The key points to remember include the following:

- It can be difficult and disruptive to switch a project from one Render Pipeline Instance to another. For example, Shaders written specifically for HDRP may not work properly with URP.
- With a Render Pipeline Instance chosen, you can modify its graphics settings by inspecting its corresponding data asset.
- You can save and use different configurations of settings for your chosen render pipeline by creating new Render Pipeline data asset files. You can change Render Pipeline settings assets at runtime but they must reference a compatible Render Pipeline Instance.

Having decided on a Render Pipeline, the next step in your lighting strategy is to choose the **Lighting settings** and add Light GameObjects to the scene.

Choosing Lighting Settings and GameObjects

I recommend you review the flowcharts and decision trees found in the **Unity Best Practices Guide** (`https://docs.unity3d.com/Manual/BestPracticeLightingPipelines.html`) for developers deciding how to light a project. That article includes detailed decision trees and comparisons of settings and options. Along the main decision tree, as mentioned in the previous topic, your first step is to select a render pipeline for the project. In the book, we always use the **Universal Render Pipeline** option, which provides the best performance for a wide range of target devices including VR.

The next step in establishing a lighting strategy is to pick a **Global Illumination** mode. My recommendation is to choose **Mixed Lighting** by default, by checking the **Baked Global Illumination** option in the **Lighting settings** window. Then, you'll need to pick a mode from the **Lighting Mode** option. Not all modes are available for all render pipelines but they are all listed here:

- **Subtractive**—almost 100% baked, with directional light shadowing for dynamic effect
- **Baked Indirect**—100% real-time lighting and shadowing with baked indirect lighting
- **Shadowmask**—real-time light, baked shadows for static objects
- **Distance Shadowmask**—real-time shadows at show range, baked beyond

For mobile VR, I recommend **Subtractive** mode for simple outdoor scenes and mobile devices. Otherwise, use **Baked Indirect** mode, which provides real-time shadows of dynamic objects using fixed lights. These settings are shown in the following screenshot:

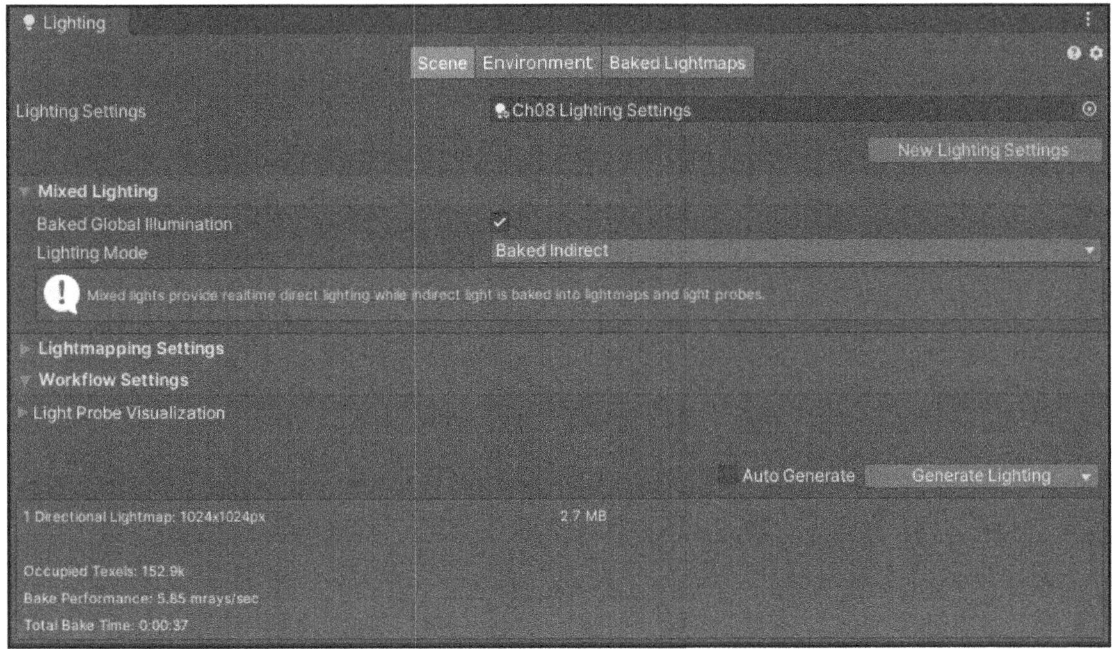

Note that when **Baked Global Illumination** is enabled, you also have the option to **Auto Generate** the lightmaps whenever you make changes to the scene or light settings that warrant it. Generally, you want to avoid **Auto Generate**, especially in larger scenes, as it can slow down your workflow and development iteration. When not using **Auto Generate**, you will need to remember to periodically press the **Generate Lighting** button to manually regenerate the lightmaps.

The next thing is the placement of lighting GameObjects in your Scene. **Light** objects include **Directional**, **Point**, **Spotlight**, and **Area**. Other GameObjects can have **Materials** with light **Emission** properties that make them glow and cast light onto other nearby objects. When object **Materials** are smooth and shiny and reflect other objects in the scene, you can precompute their reflections using **Reflection Probes**. To help you keep track of the various light sources in your scene, you can open the **Light Explorer** window, using **Window** | **Rendering** | **Light Explorer**.

It has tabs for **Lights**, **Reflection Probes**, **Light Probes**, and **Static Emissives**, as shown in the following screenshot:

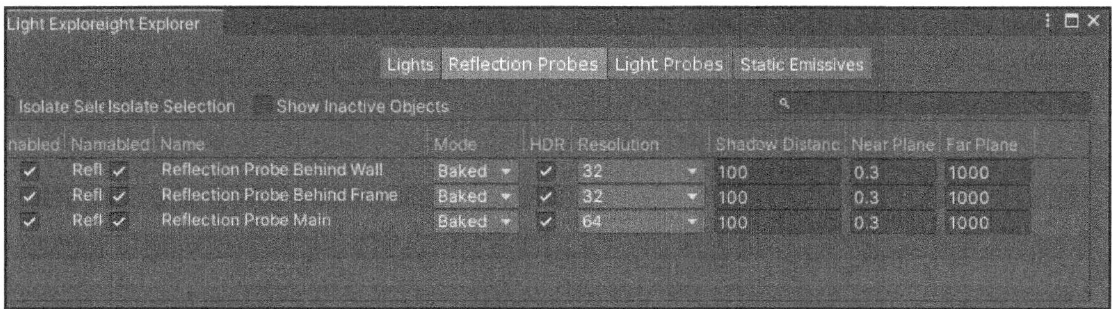

Finally, you can add a **Post-processing** stack to the scene that produces a variety of camera and cinematic visual effects that make the scene look extra fantastic. We will explore each of these in the corresponding topics later in this chapter and use some of them in other projects in the book.

In this topic, we have taken an overview of the lighting settings and objects you can include in your VR projects. In establishing a lighting strategy for your project, you should start by first choosing a render pipeline. In this book, we are using URP. Then, you have a sequence of other decisions to make, including the **Scene** and **Environment Lighting settings**, **Light** GameObjects, and the **Post-processing** stack. We'll explore each of these in this chapter. But first, let's set up a demo scene that already includes examples of many of these lighting features.

Setting up our demo scene

To demonstrate lighting and rendering in Unity, we'll start the project for this chapter with an existing scene and observe the effect of removing or modifying certain lighting settings and GameObjects. When you start a new project from the **Unity Hub** using the **Universal Render Pipeline** template, it contains a default sample scene named `SampleScene`. For this chapter, we'll decompose the `SampleScene` rather than build up a new scene. (There is a risk that the `SampleScene` is subject to change in the future, so please adapt the instructions herein as needed.)

In the Scene, we'll create a tabbed menu panel with which you can interact within VR. I'm going to attach it to the **LeftHand Controller**, but if you prefer to place it as a dashboard panel in world space, feel free to do that. First, we'll adopt this `SampleScene` and add a **VR Rig**, then we'll disable lightmap baking so we can change lighting settings at runtime, and then we'll create a UI control panel for manipulating the lighting.

Using the SampleScene

Let's begin by modifying the default `SampleScene`. (If you have removed this scene or its assets, you can start a new URP project first). Follow these steps:

1. Open the scene from the **Project** window by navigating to the `Scenes/` folder and double-click on `SampleScene`.
2. Save it as a new scene using **File** | **Save As**, and give it a name such as `LightingDemos`.
3. Add a VR rig using **GameObject** | **XR** | **Stationary XR Rig**.
4. Before I forget, minimize the near clipping plane by selecting the **Main Camera** GameObject (**XR Rig/Camera Offset/Main Camera**) and set **Clipping Planes** | **Near** to `0` (`0.01`).
5. Position the rig to match the camera in the original sample scene, **XR Rig** | **Transform** | **Position** to (`3.3, 0, 1.6`), and **Rotation** to (`0, 220, 0`).
6. Likewise, for development, set the camera height by setting **XR Rig/Camera Offset** | **Transform** | **Y** to `1.36`.
7. Lastly, align the **Scene** view by selecting **Main Camera** in the **Hierarchy** and choosing **GameObject** | **Align View To Selected**.

The scene we are working with can be seen in the screenshot that follows. I think it's a salute to the classic **Website Under Construction** pages! In the **Hierarchy** (not shown here), you will find it contains a **Workshop Set** GameObject containing the **Ground**, **Drywall Panel**, and **Stud Frame**. There's a group of **Props**, including the **Workbench** with tools. And for lighting, there's a **Construction Light**, **Directional Light**, **Light Probe Group**, **Reflection Probes**, and a **Post-process Volume**. Have a look at the following screenshot:

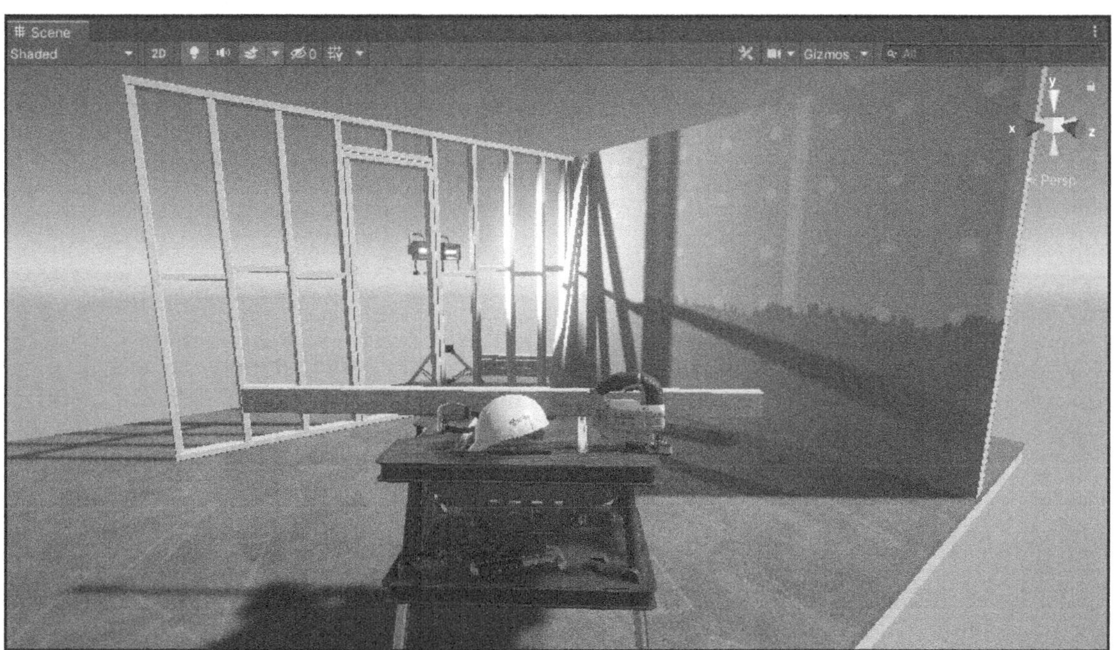

An alternative example scene you could use in this project is the **Spotlight Tunnel** sample scene included with the *Unity Best Practices Guides: Making Believable Visuals In Unity* articles (`https://docs.unity3d.com/Manual/BestPracticeMakingBelievableVisuals.html`).

Our next step is to disable baked lighting so that we can manipulate more settings at runtime within VR.

Disabling baked lighting

For this exercise, we are going to completely disable baked lighting—that is, we'll use **Realtime GI** and not **Mixed Lighting**. Ordinarily, I would not recommend this, especially in VR projects, as it imposes a lot of runtime processing overhead that could slow the frame update rate and have a negative impact on your user experience. But for this project, we want to manipulate the lighting at runtime, *frames-per-second be damned*. To disable **Baked GI**, use the following steps:

1. Open the **Lighting settings** window by going to **Window** | **Rendering** | **Lighting**.
2. Select the **Scene** tab at the top of the window.

3. Let's make a settings configuration asset unique to this scene by clicking the **New Lighting Settings** button (Unity 2020+).
4. Uncheck the **Baked Global Illumination** checkbox.

OK—with that done, let's build a UI control panel where we can add toggle buttons and value sliders for controlling the lighting settings.

Creating a menu panel

Now, we'll create a world-space **Canvas** with a tabbed menu panel where we'll add UI controls to interact with various lighting settings in the scene. Be sure to use the XR menu item, not the non-XR Canvas one, so that the **Canvas** will contain the necessary **Tracked Device Graphic Raycaster** component and create an **EventSystem** with an **XRUI Input Module** component (as explained in `Chapter 6`, *Canvasing World Space UI*). Begin with the following steps:

1. Create a new XR UI Canvas by selecting **GameObject** | **XR** | **UI Canvas**, and name it `Menu Canvas`.
2. Set its **Width** and **Height** to `1024` and `768`, respectively, and its **Scale** to `0.0005, 0.0005, 0.0005`.
3. Create a child panel for the tab by right-clicking **Menu Canvas** | **UI** | **Panel**, and name it `Tabs`.
4. Set its **Anchor Preset** to **top-stretch**, **Height**: `150`, **Pos Y**: `-75`, and pick a background **Image** | **Color** such as `#417AAD` with **Alpha**: `200`.
5. Create another child of **Menu Canvas** for the UI panels via **Menu Canvas** | **UI** | **Panel**, and name it `Panels`.
6. Set its **Anchor Preset** to **stretch-stretch, Top**: `150`.
7. Set its **Image** | **Color** to a darker gray, such as `#8C8C8C` with Alpha `200`.

To make it a hand palette menu, move the **Menu Canvas** to be a child of the **LeftHand Controller**, as follows (This step is optional. If you want, you can leave the **Menu Canvas** fixed in world space, especially if your VR device does not have two tracked hands.):

1. In the **Hierarchy**, move the **Menu Canvas** GameObject to become a child of **XR Rig / Camera Offset / LeftHand Controller**.
2. Set the Canvas **Position** to (`0, 0, 0`) and **Rotation** (`0, 0, 0`).

3. On the **LeftHand Controller** we don't need its interactor, so uncheck the **LeftHand Controller** | **XR Ray Interactor** component's enabled checkbox (while leaving the **LeftHand Controller** object itself active).
4. It may be convenient to align the **Scene** view by selecting the **Menu Canvas** in **Hierarchy** then choosing **GameObject** | **Align View With Selected**, then zoom back a little bit (using the mouse scroll wheel, or pressing *Alt* + *right-mouse* to zoom backward).

At this point, you should be able to press **Play** and see an empty menu palette attached to your left hand.

To add buttons in the tab bar, we'll make it a **Horizontal Layout** and add a **Toggle Group** of **Toggle** objects that act as buttons, using the following steps:

1. With the **Tabs** panel selected in **Hierarchy**, select **Add Component** | **Horizontal Layout Group**.
2. Set its **Padding** values to `5` (for all **Left**, **Right**, **Top**, **Bottom**, and **Spacing**), check the **Control Child Size Width** and **Height** checkboxes, and check the **Child Force Expand Width** and **Height** checkboxes (leaving the other checkboxes unchecked).
3. Also, add a **Toggle Group** by selecting **Add Component** | **Toggle Group**.
4. Create a child **Toggle** element by right-clicking the **Tabs** panel | **UI** | **Toggle**, and rename it `Tab Button`.
5. Unfold the **Toggle** in **Hierarchy**, select its **Background** object, and modify it as follows: set the **Anchor Preset** to **stretch-stretch**, set **Left/Right/Top/Bottom** all to `0`, and its **Image** | **Color** to a blue color (for example, `#08158D`).
6. Unfold the **Background** in **Hierarchy**, select its child **Checkmark** object, and modify it as follows: rename it `Selected`, set the **Anchor Preset** to **stretch-stretch**, set **Left/Right/Top/Bottom** all to `0`, delete the contents of the **Image** | **Source Image** parameter, and choose an **Image** | **Color** with a lighter blue (for example, `#4958CA`).
7. Then, select the **Label** GameObject and set its **Text** | **Color** to white, **Alignment** to **Center, Middle**, and check the **Paragraph** | **Best Fit** checkbox.
8. Now, save the **Tab Button** as a prefab by dragging the **Tab Button** object from **Hierarchy** into the **Project** window `Assets/Prefab/` folder.

Let's make a total of five buttons in the tab bar, as follows:

1. In **Hierarchy**, duplicate the **Tab Button** four times (*Ctrl* + *D*) so that there are five buttons in the **Tabs** bar.
2. Update the **Label** | **Text** for the buttons to read as `Environ`, `Materials`, `Lights`, `Probes`, and `Post Process`.
3. Lastly, we want to make the toggle buttons a group so that only one can be selected at a time. Select a **Tab Button** in **Hierarchy**, and drag the parent **Tabs** panel onto the **Toggle** | **Group** field.
4. Repeat *step 3* for each of the tabs (tip: you can multi-select all five tab objects and assign the field in one step).

The resulting menu panel with the first tab button selected now looks like this:

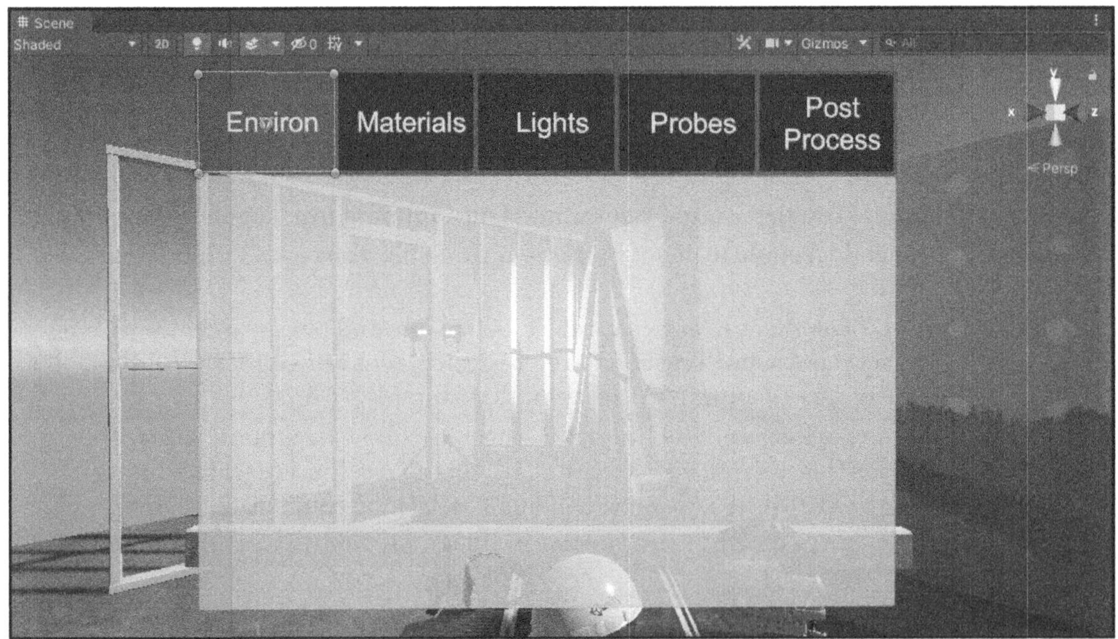

Finally, we'll create five separate panels to contain the collection of UI controls for each of the menu tabs, and wire them up to the corresponding Tab Button. Use the following steps:

1. In **Hierarchy**, select the **Panels** GameObject (child of **Menu Canvas**), right-click | **UI** | **Panel**, and name it `Control Panel`.
2. Delete its **Image** component using right-click | **Remove Component**.
3. Give it a vertical layout by selecting **Add Component** | **Vertical Layout Group**.

4. Set the **Vertical Layout Group** | **Padding Left/Right/Bottom/Spacing** to `50`, setting the **Top** value to `20`.
5. Check the **Control Child Size** | **Width** and **Child Force Expand** | **Width** checkboxes, unchecking all the others.
6. Now, under that panel, add a title by right-clicking **Control Panel** and select **UI** | **Text**, then rename it `Title`.
7. Set its **Height** to `50`, check the **Paragraph** | **Best Fit** checkbox, set **Alignment** to **Middle**, **Center**, and **Color** to blue (`#08158D`).
8. Then, set the **Text** | **Text** to say `Environmental Lighting`.
9. Duplicate this Control Panel four times (*Ctrl* + *D*), and modify their **Label** | **Text** accordingly, as follows:
    - `Materials and Shaders`
    - `Light GameObjects`
    - `Probes`
    - `Post Processing Stack`
10. Finally, for each of the tab buttons, select **Tab Button**, then select **Toggle** | **On Value Changed** | **+** to add an event action.
11. Drag the corresponding **Control Panel** GameObject from **Hierarchy** onto the **Runtime Only Object** slot, and choose **GameObject** | **SetActive** from the function select list.
12. Repeat *steps 9-10* for the other four **Tab Buttons**.
13. Note, as a toggle group, only one of the tabs, **Toggles**, can have **Is On** checked at a time. Likewise, you should set all the corresponding panels to not active except the current tab one.
14. Save your scene with **File** | **Save**.

If you play the scene now, the menu palette is attached to your left hand as you move your hand. Operate it using the right-hand controller to point, and click a tab button to open the corresponding controls panel.

As a bonus exercise, you might also want to add a frames-per-second counter display on the **Menu Canvas** so that you can monitor any impact the lighting changes may have on performance. For this, you can use the `FramesPerSecondText` script written in `Chapter 13`, *Optimizing for Performance and Comfort*.

You now have set up a copy of the `SampleScene` with an XR Rig, saved it as a new scene, disabled baked lightmaps, and created a **Menu Canvas** that will contain the control panels for operating the scene's lighting settings. The **Menu Canvas** has a tab bar with five buttons that enable the corresponding control panel UI. We're now ready to explore the lighting in the scene. We'll start by looking at environment lighting and adding UI controls for changing some of those settings.

Using environment lighting

The **Environment** lighting settings offer the ability to specify contributors to environmental illumination including a Skybox and Fog. A Skybox is a panoramic texture representing the sky that is drawn behind all objects in a scene as if at a far distance. We used the **Wispy Skyboxes**, for example, in previous chapters, and Skyboxes are discussed in more detail in `Chapter 11`, *Using All 360 Degrees*. More than rendering how the sky looks, with the **Environment Lighting settings** opened (using **Window** | **Rendering** | **Lighting** | **Environment**), you can specify if and how much the Skybox texture contributes to the **Global Illumination** and set its intensity level, as shown in the following screenshot:

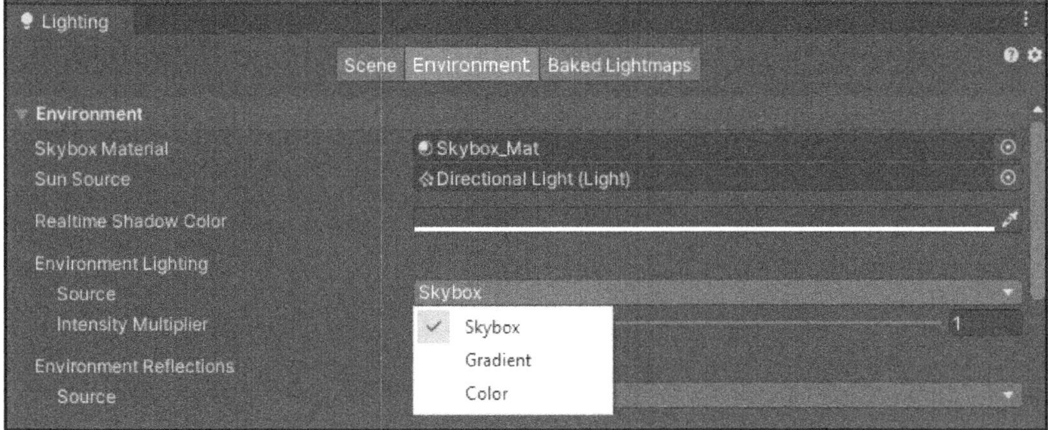

For more details on using these and other settings in this window, consider the following pages from the Unity Manual:

- *Outdoor lighting and scene setup*—`https://docs.unity3d.com/Manual/BestPracticeMakingBelievableVisuals6.html`
- *Lightmapping*—`https://docs.unity3d.com/Manual/Lightmappers.html`
- *Scripting API: RenderSettings*—`https://docs.unity3d.com/ScriptReference/RenderSettings.html`

Let's add the first two controls to the control panel—a **Skybox Toggle** checkbox and an **Intensity Multiplier Slider** that lets you interactively modify these values while in VR. As we go, we'll also save this UI as a prefab so that we can reuse this work elsewhere in this chapter.

Environment lighting source

To demonstrate the effects of some of these settings in your VR scene, we'll add controls to our menu palette that modify environmental lighting through an `Environment LightingControls` script. Let's create that script now and build it out as we go. Start with the following steps:

1. Create an empty GameObject in the **Hierarchy** root, named `Render Controller`, by selecting **GameObject** | **Create Empty**.
2. Reset its **Transform** with right-click | **Reset**.
3. Create a new script named `EnvironmentLightingControls` and add it to the `Render Controller`.

Using this script and a couple of UI prefabs that we'll create next, we will control the **Environment Light** setting including the Skybox and Fog, and see how it looks in VR. The script uses Unity's `RenderSettings` **application programming interface** (**API**) class (`https://docs.unity3d.com/ScriptReference/RenderSettings.html`). Let's start with a way to toggle the Skybox on and off. Edit the `EnvironmentLightingControls` script, as follows:

```
using UnityEngine;
using UnityEngine.Rendering;
using UnityEngine.UI;

public class EnvironmentLightingControls : MonoBehaviour
{
    public Toggle useSkyboxToggle;

    public bool UseSkybox
    {
        get => (RenderSettings.ambientMode == AmbientMode.Skybox);
        set
        {
            RenderSettings.ambientMode = (value) ?
              AmbientMode.Skybox : AmbientMode.Flat;
        }
    }
```

```
        private void Start()
        {
            useSkyboxToggle.isOn = UseSkybox;
        }
    }
```

Since we're interested in using the `RenderSettings` API, we add the `using UnityEngine.Render;` line.

Although we want the user to simply toggle the Skybox on or off, Unity actually offers three options for the **Environment** Lighting Source (as you have seen in the previous screenshot): **Skybox**, **Gradient**, and **Color**. So, our plan is that, when the Skybox is turned off, we'll switch the **Source** from **Skybox** to **Color**. In the code, I declare a Boolean property, `UseSkybox`. When `UseSkybox` is referenced, it returns either `true` or `false`, whether `RenderSettings.ambientMode` is presently `AmbientMode.Skybox` or not. Likewise, when `UseSkybox` is set, we set the `RenderSettings.ambientMode` to `AmbientMode.Skybox` or `AmbientMode.Flat` (aka **Color**). In the `Start()` function, we initialize the UI toggle switch according to the default `RenderSettings` value when the project is built.

This script introduces a few new C# concepts we have not used before. For example, the `UseSkybox` parameter is defined using separate `get` and `set` expressions that are executed when you access or assign the variable value, respectively. In this example, the `get` expression uses a *lambda expression* (`get => [expression]`) as a shortcut. The `set` expression uses a multi-statement body (surrounded by curly brackets).

Now, let's add the toggle UI element to the menu panel. Create a new toggle switch in the menu panel by following these steps:

1. In the **Hierarchy**, on the **Menu Canvas / Panels** select the (first) **Control Panel**, which is designated for **Environmental Lighting**.
2. Right-click, then select **Control Panel** | **UI** | **Toggle** and name it `Skybox Toggle`.
3. Set its **Rect Transform** | **Height** to `50`.
4. Unfold the **Skybox Toggle** in **Hierarchy** and, on its **Label**, set **Anchor Preset: top-left**, **Pos** (`0, 0, 0`), **Width, Height**: (`450, 50`), **Font Size**: `38`, **Color:** White, **Alignment: Right**.
5. For its **Text**, write `Use Skybox`.

6. Select the **Background** child of Skybox Toggle, set **Anchor Preset: top-right**, **Pos (-200, 0, 0)**, **Width, Height**: (`50, 50`).
7. And, for the **Background** own child **Checkmark**, set **Width, Height**: (`50, 50`).

Now, we can connect the toggle to the `UseSkybox` property in the script we wrote, as follows:

1. Select the **Skybox Toggle**, and in **Inspector**, select **Toggle** | **On Value Changed** | **+** to add an event action.
2. Drag the **Render Controller** object from **Hierarchy** onto the **Object** slot.
3. Then, from the **Function** dropdown, select **EnvironmentLightingControls** | **UseSkybox**.
4. Lastly, select the **Render Controller** object in **Hierarchy**, and drag the **Skybox Toggle** object from **Hierarchy** onto the **Environmental Lighting Controls** | **Use Skybox Toggle** slot.
5. Save with **File** | **Save**.

If you press **Play**, then in VR you can point and click on the checkbox to disable or enable the Skybox environment lighting.

Let's save this Toggle object as a prefab so we can reuse it for other properties, as follows:

1. Select the **Skybox Toggle** from **Hierarchy**.
2. Drag it into the `Assets/Prefabs/` folder in the **Project** window.
3. In the `Assets` folder, rename the prefab `ToggleUI`.

Next, we will add a UI slider to change the environment light intensity.

Adding Environment Light Intensity

To control the **Environment Light Intensity Multiplier**, we'll add a slider to the menu panel. The **Intensity** only applies when the light source is a **Skybox**, so this slider will only be enabled while the **Use Skybox** toggle is checked. Let's add it to the control script by editing `EnvironmentLightingControls`. The new lines of code are highlighted in bold in the following code block:

```
public class EnvironmentLightingControls : MonoBehaviour
{
    public Toggle useSkyboxToggle;
    public Slider skyboxIntensitySlider;
    public Text skyboxIntensityText;
```

```
        public bool UseSkybox
        {
            get => (RenderSettings.ambientMode == AmbientMode.Skybox);
            set
            {
                RenderSettings.ambientMode = (value) ?
                    AmbientMode.Skybox : AmbientMode.Flat;
                skyboxIntensitySlider.interactable = value;
                skyboxIntensityText.gameObject.SetActive(value);
            }
        }

        public float SkyboxIntensity
        {
            get => RenderSettings.ambientIntensity;
            set
            {
                RenderSettings.ambientIntensity = value;
                skyboxIntensityText.text = value.ToString("F1");
            }
        }

        private void Start()
        {
            useSkyboxToggle.isOn = UseSkybox;
            skyboxIntensitySlider.value = SkyboxIntensity;
        }
    }
```

The script adds a new `float SkyboxIntensity` property that can `get` and `set` the current `RenderSettings.ambientIntensity` value. In addition to the slider UI element, it also references a `Text` object that displays the current intensity multiplier value on the menu panel. We'll let the intensity value range from `0` to `3`. Let's create these UI elements with the following steps:

1. In the **Hierarchy**, on the same **Environmental Lighting Control Panel**, right-click | **Create Empty** and rename it `Intensity Slider`.
2. Add a child Slider UI element using right-click | **UI** | **Slider**.
3. On the Slider, set **Anchor Preset: middle-right, Pos** (`-200, 0, 0`), **Width, Height**: (`350, 50`).
4. Under the parent **Intensity Slider**, add a child Text element using **right-click** | **UI** | **Text**, rename it `Label`.

5. On the Label, set its **Text** to read `Skybox Intensity Multiplier`, and set **Anchor Preset: middle-left, Pos** (`240, 0, 0`), **Width, Height**: (`450, 50`), **Font Size**: `38`, **Color**: white, **Align: Right**.
6. Under the **Slider / Handle Slide Area**, find the **Handle** object, then right-click | **UI** | **Text**. Set its **Pos** (`35, 42, 0`), **Font Size**: `38`, **Color**: white, **Align: Center, Horizontal/Vertical Overflow: Overflow**.
7. On the Slider, set the **Min Value** to `0` and **Max Value** to `3`.
8. Connect the slider to the script. On the Slider, select **Slider** | **On Value Changed** | **+**, drag the **Render Controller** object from **Hierarchy** onto the **Object** slot, and set the function to **EnvironmentLightingControls** | **SkyboxIntensity**.
9. Lastly, select the **Render Controller** object in **Hierarchy**, and drag the **Slider** element from **Hierarchy** onto the **Environmental Lighting Controls** | **Skybox Intensity Slider** slot.
10. Then, drag the Handle's **Text** object onto the **Skybox Intensity Text** slot.
11. Let's also save this slider as a prefab so that we can use it for other properties. Drag the parent **Intensity Slider** from **Hierarchy** into the **Project** `Assets/Prefabs/` folder and rename the prefab `SliderUI`.
12. Save with **File** | **Save**.

The following screenshot shows the **Menu Canvas** hierarchy we just created:

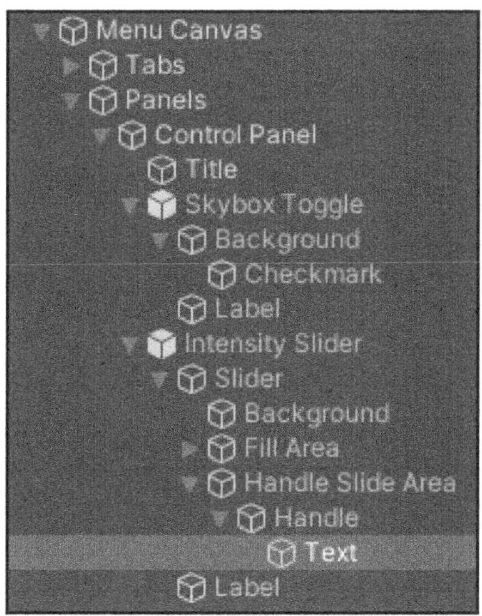

If you press **Play**, then in VR you can modify the Skybox intensity with the slider (when the **Use Skybox** functionality is enabled). The following screenshot shows a capture of the scene in VR with the **Canvas Menu** on the **Environ** tab and the **Skybox Intensity Multiplier** pushed up to **1.9**:

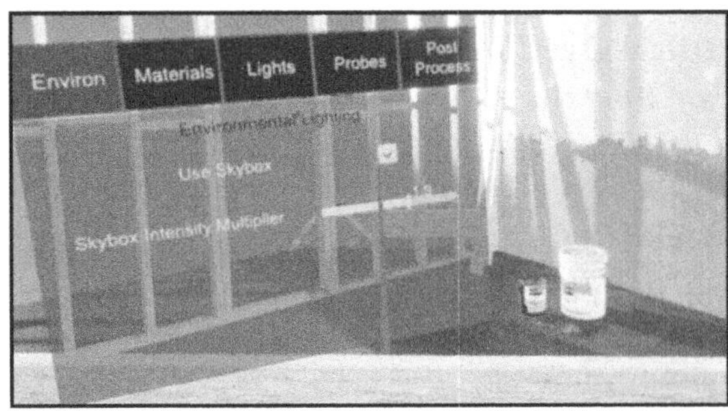

Next, we'll add a toggle for disabling or enabling environmental Fog.

Adding a Fog effect

Let's add one more toggle for the environment lighting. The Fog added to the scene will make objects in the distance appear washed out, improving the sense of depth and realism, especially in outdoor scenes. You have a number of **Fog** properties available, including **Color**, **Mode**, and **Density**. We'll simply toggle the **Fog** off and on to see its effects in VR. Edit the `EnvironmentLightingControls` script by adding the following code:

```
public Toggle enableFog;

public bool EnableFog {
    get => RenderSettings.fog;
    set => RenderSettings.fog = value;
}
```

And in `Start()`, initialize the `Toggle` state, as follows:

```
enableFog.isOn = EnableFog;
```

To add this toggle to our panel, we can use the **ToggleUI** prefab we just created, as follows:

1. From the **Project** window `Assets/Prefabs/` folder, drag the **ToggleUI** prefab into **Hierarchy** as the bottom child of the **Control Panel** we are working on (sibling of the **Intensity Slider**).
2. Rename it `Fog Toggle`.

3. Unfold **Fog Toggle**, and modify the **Label** | **Text** to read `Enable Fog`.
4. On the **Fog Toggle** | **Toggle** component, drag the **Render Controller** onto the **On Value Changed** | **Object** field, and select **EnvironmentLightingControls** | **EnableFog**.
5. Lastly, select the **Render Controller** and drag the **Fog Toggle** game object from **Hierarchy** onto the **Environment Lighting Controls** | **Enable Fog** slot.

The following screenshot shows the **Environment Lighting Controls** component with its current properties:

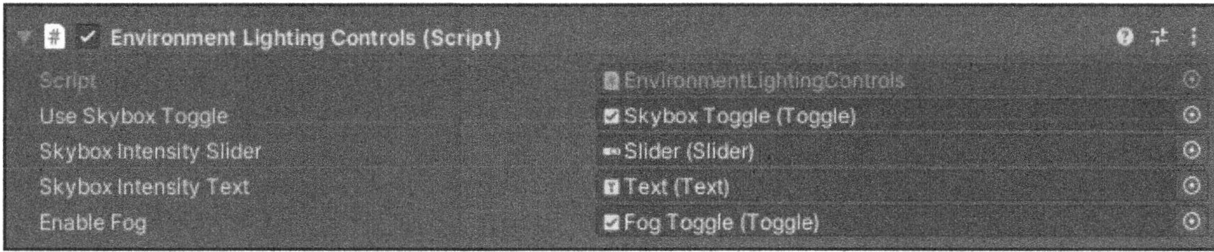

Press **Play**. You can now see the effect of disabling and enabling Fog in your scene. The UI menu panel we just created now looks like this (I improved the panel titles' color in my version):

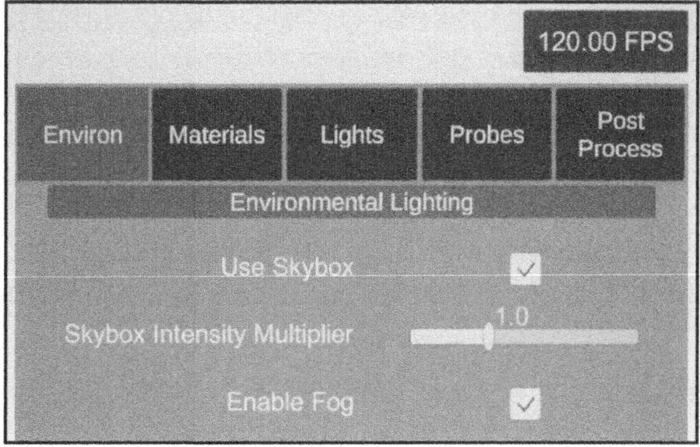

Environmental lighting is usually baked into lightmaps but for this scene, it's not, so we can control it at runtime. In this section, we created the first Control Panel in the Menu Canvas, with a checkbox to **Use Skybox** and a value slider for the **Skybox Intensity Multiplier**. We also added a checkbox for the Fog. With these controls (and feel free to add others on your own), you can experience the effect of modifying these Environment Light settings inside VR.

Next, we'll take a look at the effect of PBR materials and shader parameters on the realism of objects in the scene.

Using PBR materials and URP Shaders

3D objects can be rendered simplistic, such as a cube with flat-shaded faces, or very realistically, such as the same cube as a realistic wooden crate. This magic is performed with PBR materials and advanced Shaders.

A 3D object in Unity consists of a geometry mesh that defines the points, edges, and faces of the object, forming a surface that can then be rendered to appear as a solid object. Each object has a **Renderer** component that specifies the properties and behavior of this particular object rendered in the scene. It includes references to any **Materials** that will be applied to the object. A **Material** is an asset that specifies a specific **Shader** script that drives the actual work of drawing the object on the screen. You can learn more about all of this in the Unity Manual and Unity Learn sites, among many other resources. The following web pages provide more information:

- *Best Practices Guide: Making Believable Visuals: Modeling*—`https://docs.unity3d.com/Manual/BestPracticeMakingBelievableVisuals4.html`
- *Best Practices Guide: Making Believable Visuals: Shading*—`https://docs.unity3d.com/Manual/BestPracticeMakingBelievableVisuals5.html`
- *Unity Manual: Shadows*—`https://docs.unity3d.com/Manual/Shadows.html`

In this book, we focus on the URP and thus are limited to the Shaders compatible with that RP. Ordinarily, we use the default **Lit** shader in the Materials we are using because it offers a lot of variety, options, and settings while being quite efficient at runtime. Shaders are small programs that are compiled to run in the GPU. They process your 3D vectors and polygons (triangles), prepared by the game engine on the CPU, along with lighting information, texture maps, and other parameters, to generate pixels on the display.

Unity comes with a rich set of Shaders. The **Universal Render Pipeline/Lit** Shader we've been using throughout this book is a powerful and optimized one that supports textures, normal maps, occlusion maps, emission maps, specular highlights, reflections, and more. And, depending on which features of the particular shader you actually use in a material, Unity will compile a highly optimized shader variant file to run the processing in the GPU.

Writing Shaders is an interesting and complex topic outside the scope of this book, but I encourage you to take at least an introductory look. Unity's new **Shader Graph** tool allows you to build custom Shaders visually. See `https://unity.com/shader-graph`.

For example, consider the `HardHat_Mat` material used in our scene for the hardhat prop, as shown in the following screenshot:

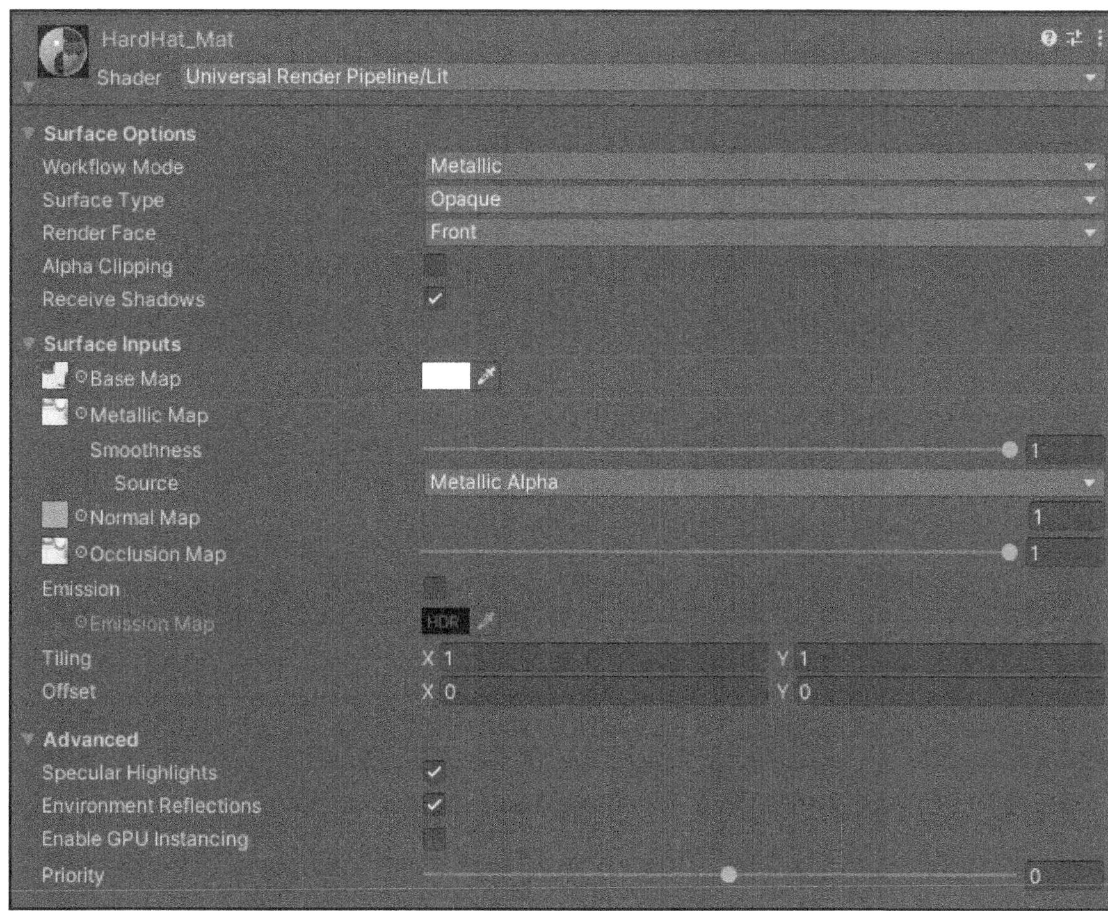

You can see this Material uses the **Universal Render Pipeline/Lit** shader. It selects the **Metallic Workflow Mode** with an **Opaque** surface. The surface properties include a **Base Map** texture, which is the basic color texture (Albedo) of the model. It also has a **Metallic Map** texture that controls shininess, a **Normal Map** that provides the appearance of bumps and grooves on the surface, and an **Occlusion Map** that further enhances the realism by accenting surface shadows associated with occlusion. You can examine the individual texture images by clicking one of the texture map chips and viewing the asset in the **Inspector**.

For this project, we will create slider controls that let you adjust the properties of materials, including the following:

- Smoothness factor (0 to 1)
- Normal scaling factor (-3 to 3)
- Occlusion factor (0 to 1)

To begin, create a new script named `MaterialsControls` on the **Render Controller** game object. Then, edit it as follows. I'll begin with the first part of the script, where we declare a set of `public` variables that reference the UI `Slider` (and the handle `Text`) for each smoothness, normal scaling, and occlusion factor. We also have a `Renderer` list that you'll populate in the **Inspector**, and which will be manipulated by the script. When you modify a factor value at runtime with the menu panel, the script will set this factor on all the Materials in the given list, like this:

```
using System.Collections;
using System.Collections.Generic;
using System.Linq;
using UnityEngine;
using UnityEngine.UI;

public class MaterialsControls : MonoBehaviour
{
    public Slider smoothnessSlider;
    public Text smoothnessText;
    public Slider normalSlider;
    public Text normalText;
    public Slider occlusionSlider;
    public Text occlusionText;

    public List<Renderer> renderers = new List<Renderer>();
```

And in `Start()`, I'll initialize the sliders to a normal value of `1`, like this:

```
    private void Start()
    {
        smoothnessSlider.value = 1f;
        normalSlider.value = 1f;
        occlusionSlider.value = 1f;
    }
```

Next, I have separate `float` type properties for `Smoothness`, `Normal`, and `Occlusion`, with their corresponding `get` and `set` methods. Internally, we keep a cache of the current values (using the underscore prefix-naming convention to denote it's a private variable). As we did in the previous section, when you `set` one of the values, we also update its `Text` display on the slider, as illustrated in the following code block:

```
        private float _smoothness;
        private float _normal;
        private float _occlusion;

    public float Smoothness {
    get => _smoothness;
    set {
        SetFloatProperty("_Smoothness", value);
        smoothnessText.text = value.ToString("F2");
        }
    }

    public float Normal {
    get => _normal;
    set {
        SetFloatProperty("_BumpScale", value);
        normalText.text = value.ToString("F2");
        }
    }

    public float Occlusion {
    get => _occlusion;
    set {
        SetFloatProperty("_OcclusionStrength", value);
        occlusionText.text = value.ToString("F1");
        }
    }

    private void SetFloatProperty(string name, float value)
    {
    for (int i = 0; i < renderers.Count; i++)
     {
       renderers.ElementAt(i).material.SetFloat(name, value);
     }
    }
   }
```

The sliders will send a value to the corresponding property. The `set` method calls our private `SetFloatProperty` function that loops through all the `renderers` we want to modify and then sets the value using the `material.SetFloat` call.

When getting and setting property values within a shader, you can only reference it indirectly with its name string. To discover what the name is of a specific property, you can open the `Shader` script to find it. For example, on the `HardHat_Mat` material, use the three-dot context menu to select **Edit Shader**, which opens the file in your text editor. The lines of code that I referenced to find the `_Smoothness`, `BumpScale`, and `_OcclusionStrength` properties look like the following in the shader file (this is just for your information):

```
_Smoothness("Smoothness", Range(0.0, 1.0)) = 0.5
_BumpScale("Scale", Float) = 1.0
_OcclusionStrength("Strength", Range(0.0, 1.0)) = 1.0
```

Save the script. Now, back in Unity, we want to provide a set of object renderers to the component, as follows:

1. With **Render Controller** selected in **Hierarchy**, add the **MaterialsControls** script (if it's not already a component).
2. In **Inspector**, set the **Materials Controls** | **Renderers** | **Size** to `5`.
3. Drag the **Safety Hat** game object from **Hierarchy** (**Example Assets / Props / Workbench**) onto the **Element 0** slot.
4. Drag the **Jigsaw** game object onto **Element 1**.
5. Drag the **Stud** game object onto **Element 2**.
6. Drag the **Hammer** game object onto **Element 3**.
7. Drag the **Bench Top** game object onto **Element 4**.

We can now add the sliders to the **Control Panel** in our menu, using the following steps:

1. In **Hierarchy**, find the second **Control Panel** under your **Menu Canvas** corresponding to the **Materials** tab button.
2. From the **Project** `Assets/Prefabs` folder, drag the **SliderUI** prefab into **Hierarchy** as a child of the **Control Panel**.
3. Rename it `Smoothness Slider`.
4. Change its **Label** | **Text** to say `Smoothness`.
5. Select its **Slider** object and select **Slider** | **On Value Changed** | **+** to add an event action, drag the **Render Controller** onto the **Object** slot, and select the **MaterialsControls** | **Smoothness** function.
6. Then, with the **Render Controller** selected in **Hierarchy**, drag this **Slider** object onto the **Materials Controls** | **Smoothness Slider** slot.

7. Then, drag the handle **Text** object (found under **Slider / Handle Slide Area / Handle /**) onto the **Smoothness Text** slot.
8. Repeat *Steps 2-7* for the `Normal` and `Occlusion` properties.

Note that the **Slider** range (**Min Value, Max Value**) for **Smoothness** and **Occlusion** are (`0`, `1`), but for **Normal**, make the range (`-3`, `3`).

In this exercise, we are only modifying existing values in the shader, not adding or removing them. Ordinarily, you have to be very careful about using shader properties in code for it to work in a build. Unity cleverly examines how each shader is used and compiles separate *shader variants* for each permutation. If you introduce a new property usage without Unity knowing, it may not have a corresponding variant in the build.

With this menu panel implemented, you can now **Play** the scene and see the effect of modifying these three properties at runtime in VR. The following screenshot shows the **Normal** scale being greatly exaggerated at `3` (while **Use Skybox** lighting is disabled) on the wooden **Stud**, **Bench Top**, and **Jigsaw** objects:

The UI menu panel we just created now looks like this:

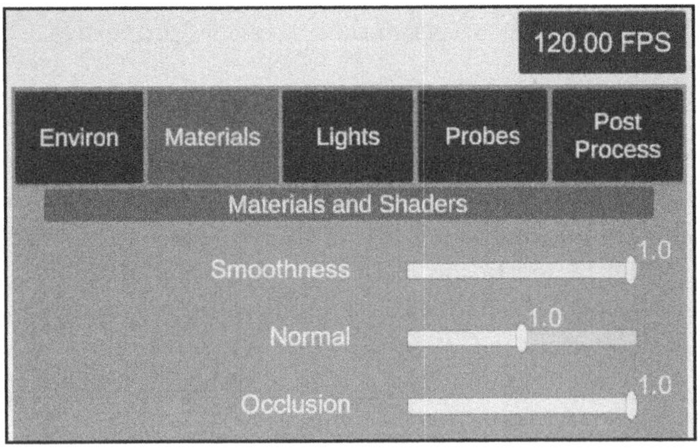

In this section, we considered how PBR materials contribute to the realism of objects in a scene. With our interactive control panel, you created sliders for modifying the **Smoothness**, **Normal** factor, and **Occlusion** contributions of the corresponding texture map for a set of materials. In the process, you also learned how to access Shader properties via C# script.

Next, we'll look at adding **Light** GameObjects for local illumination of your scene and using light emission materials.

Using Light objects and Emission surfaces

For indoor and local lighting, you will want to add Light objects to your scene. These are GameObjects that are not rendered themselves as meshes but rather emit light in a specific pattern, such as a cone (for example, a **Spot** light), sphere (for example, a **Point** light), or unidirectionally (for example, a **Directional** light). Also, you can specify individual objects to illuminate from their inside by assigning Materials with **Emission** properties. For more information on designing and using light objects, see the following links:

- *Best Practices Guide: Making Believable Visuals: Indoor and local lighting*—`https://docs.unity3d.com/Manual/BestPracticeMakingBelievableVisuals7.html`
- *Unity Manual: Types of light*—`https://docs.unity3d.com/Manual/Lighting.html`
- *Emission*—`https://docs.unity3d.com/Manual/StandardShaderMaterialParameterEmission.html`

Lights can be added to your scene using the **GameObject | Light** menu, as shown in the following screenshot:

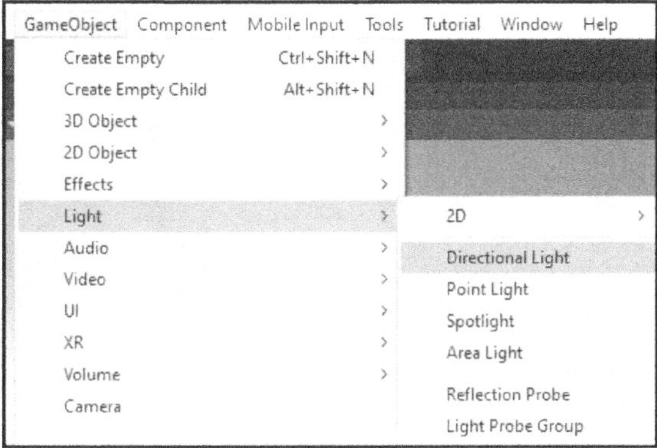

In our scene in this project, we have two lights and one Emission surface. First, there is a **Directional Light**, which you'd get when you create a **New Scene**. Directional lights cast in the same direction everywhere in the scene, like the sun illuminates the Earth because it's very far away. As you can see from its properties shown in the following screenshot, the **Directional Light** in our scene is set at an angle in the sky, with an **Intensity** value of 2, and casts **Soft Shadows**:

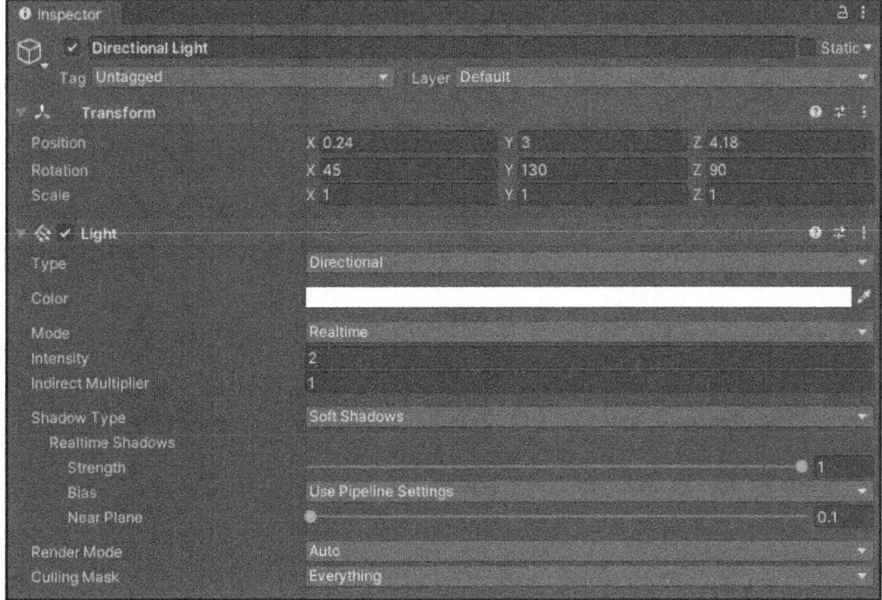

Also in the scene is a **Construction Lamp** prop (found in **Example Assets / Props**) that includes a **Spot Light** (standing behind the studded wall). In the following screenshot, the **Spot Light** is selected in **Hierarchy**, and you can see the **Scene** top-down view depicting the **Range** and **Inner/Outer Spot Angles** of the light. It's a bright light with an **Intensity** value of `12`:

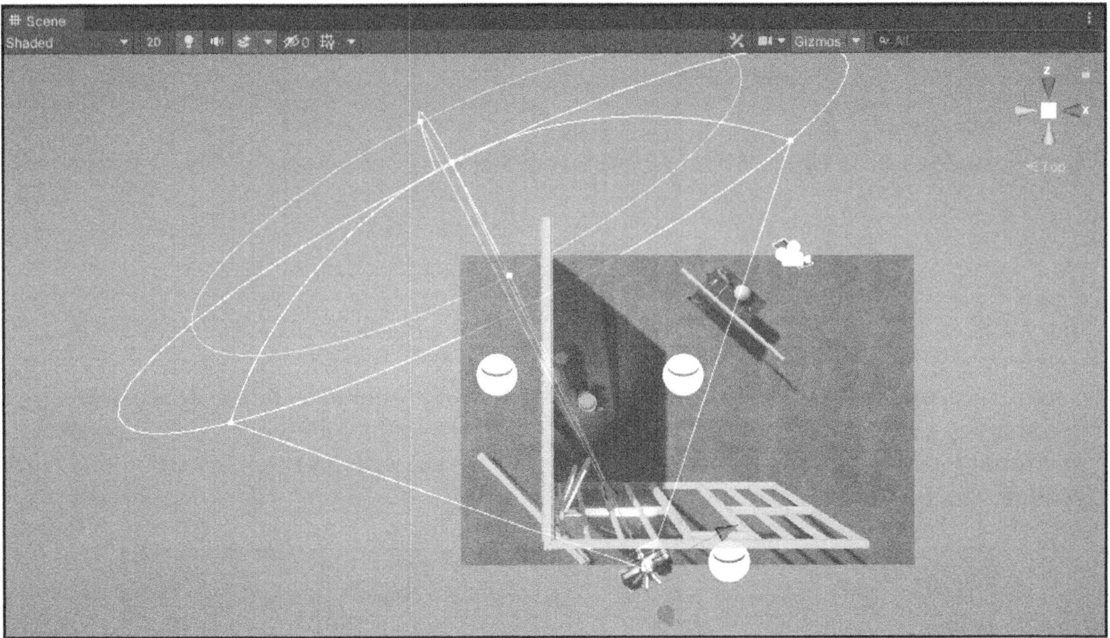

Within the **Construction Light** model is a lightbulb (**Light_Bulbs_Low**) that has a **LightBulb_Mat** material with a white emission that makes the lightbulb appear to be glowing.

For this project, we will create slider controls that let you adjust the following light object properties:

- Directional angle (*x* axis) (0 - 180)
- Directional intensity (0 - 2)
- Spot intensity (0 - 24)
- Spot Bulb emission toggle

To begin, create a new script, named `LightsControls`, on the **Render Controller** game object. Then, edit it as follows. We can begin with the first part of the script, where we declare a set of `public` variables that reference a UI `Slider` for the directional angle, directional intensity, and spot intensity, and a UI `Toggle` for the Spot Bulb object's emission property. We also declare variable references to the GameObjects themselves. Have a look at the following code block:

```
using UnityEngine;
using UnityEngine.UI;

public class LightsControls : MonoBehaviour
{
    public Slider directionalAngleSlider;
    public Slider directionalIntensitySlider;
    public Slider spotIntensitySlider;
    public Toggle bulbEmissionToggle;

    public Light directionalLight;
    public Light spotLight;
    public Renderer spotBulb;

    private Text directionalAngleText;
    private Text directionalIntensityText;
    private Text spotIntensityText;

    private bool _bulbEmission;
    private Color _emissionColor;
```

This time around, I've declared the `Text` object references for the slider handles as `private`, and find them at runtime in `Start()`. Lastly, I declare a `_bulbEmission` Boolean that says when we've disabled or enabled the bulb emission property. To turn off the emission, I will set its **Emission Color** to black, and restore its original color (`_emissionColor`) when enabled. The `Start()` function is written as follows, initializing these variables:

```
    private void Start()
    {
        directionalAngleText = directionalAngleSlider.
              GetComponentInChildren<Text>();
        directionalIntensityText = directionalIntensitySlider.
              GetComponentInChildren<Text>();
        spotIntensityText = spotIntensitySlider.
              GetComponentInChildren<Text>();

        directionalAngleSlider.value = DirectionalAngle;
        directionalIntensitySlider.value = DirectionalIntensity;
```

```
        spotIntensitySlider.value = SpotIntensity;

        _emissionColor = spotBulb.material.
              GetColor("_EmissionColor");
        _bulbEmission = (_emissionColor != Color.black);
        bulbEmissionToggle.isOn = BulbEmission;
    }
```

Now, we can add the four properties we are controlling, implemented with their `get` and `set` methods. The `DirectionalAngle` property simply modifies the object's **Transform**. The `DirectionalIntensity` property modifies the **Light** component property. Likewise for `SpotIntensity`, as illustrated in the following code block:

```
    public float DirectionalAngle
    {
        get => directionalLight.transform.localEulerAngles.x;
        set
        {
            Vector3 angles = directionalLight.transform.
                                                localEulerAngles;
            angles.x = value;
            directionalLight.transform.localEulerAngles = angles;
            directionalAngleText.text = value.ToString("F0");
        }
    }

    public float DirectionalIntensity
    {
        get => directionalLight.intensity;
        set
        {
            directionalLight.intensity = value;
            directionalIntensityText.text = value.ToString("F1");
        }
    }

    public float SpotIntensity {
        get => spotLight.intensity;
        set
        {
            spotLight.intensity = value;
            spotIntensityText.text = value.ToString("F1");
        }
    }

    public bool BulbEmission
    {
```

```
        get => _bulbEmission;
        set
        {
            spotBulb.material.SetColor("_EmissionColor",
                value ? _emissionColor : Color.black);
            _bulbEmission = value;
        }
    }
```

We can now add the sliders to the **Control Panel** in our menu, using the following steps:

1. In **Hierarchy**, find the third **Control Panel** under your **Menu Canvas** corresponding to the **Lights** tab button.
2. From the **Project** `Assets/Prefabs` folder, drag the **SliderUI** prefab into **Hierarchy** as a child of the **Control Panel**.
3. Rename it `DirectionalAngle Slider`.
4. Change its **Label** | **Text** to say `Directional Light Angle`.
5. Set the **Slider** | **Min Value** and **Max Value** to (`0, 180`).
6. Select its **Slider** object and select **Slider** | **On Value Changed** | **+** to add an event action.
7. Drag the **Render Controller** onto the **Object** slot.
8. Select the **LightsControls** | **DirectionalAngle** function.
9. Then, with the **Render Controller** selected in **Hierarchy**, drag this **Slider** object onto the **Materials Controls** | **Directional Angle Slider** slot.
10. Repeat *steps 2-7* for the `DirectionalIntensity` and `SpotIntensity` properties.

Note that the **Slider** range (**Min Value, Max Value**) for intensity is (`0, 1`) but for the light angle, make the range (`0, 180`).

Also, add the toggle for the lightbulb emission, as follows:

1. From the **Project** window `Assets/Prefabs/` folder, drag the **ToggleUI** prefab into **Hierarchy** as the bottom child of the **Control Panel** we are working on (sibling of **SpotIntensity Slider**).
2. Rename it `Emission Toggle`.
3. Unfold **Emission Toggle**, and modify the **Label** | **Text** to read `Enable Bulb Emission`.

4. On the **Emission Toggle** | **Toggle** component, drag the **Render Controller** onto the **On Value Changed** | **Object** field, and select **LightsControls** | **BulbEmission**.
5. Lastly, select the **Render Controller** and drag the **Emission Toggle** GameObject from **Hierarchy** onto the **Light Controls** | **Bulb Emission** slot.

With this menu panel implemented, populate the lights GameObjects as follows:

1. Select **Render Controller** in **Hierarchy**.
2. Drag the **Directional Light** onto the **Lights Controls** | **Directional Light** slot.
3. Drag the **Spot Light** (found under **Props / Construction Light Low**) onto the **Spot Light** slot.
4. Drag the **Light_Bulbs_Low** object (which has an Emission material) onto the **Spot Bulb** slot.

You can now **Play** the scene and see the effect of modifying these properties at runtime in VR. Notice when you change the directional light angle, in addition to the shadows moving, you can actually see the "sun" moving in the sky. This is because in the **Lighting settings** window, **Sun Source** is set to the **Directional Light** game object, and Unity renders a sun-like blob in the sky at its location. Also, notice that when you disable the **Bulb Emission**, the lightbulbs are still rendered but their glow is turned off. The UI menu panel we just created now looks like this:

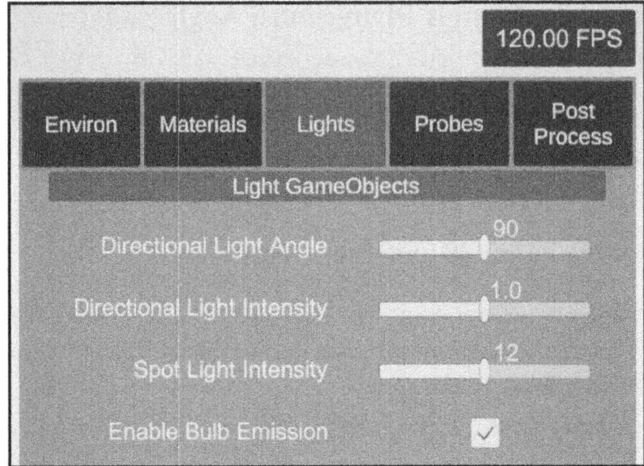

In this section, we saw how the **Light** GameObject can be used to contribute to the lighting of a scene. We created interactive controls for the **Directional Light** angle and intensity, and one for the **Spot Light** intensity. We also learned about the Emission property of Materials—in this case, the lightbulbs glow.

Next, we'll look at some more advanced objects you can add to the scene that are especially important when you are baking lightmaps: using Light Probes and Reflection Probes.

Using Light Probes and Reflection Probes

For non-static GameObjects to receive global illumination, you need to have **Light Probes** distributed in the Scene. These provide high-quality lighting for moving (dynamic) objects. **Light Probes** are positions in the scene where information is captured about the light that is passing through the empty space in your Scene. This information is baked similar to lightmaps and then used when the scene is rendered at runtime to approximate the indirect light hitting dynamic objects, based on proximity to the **Light Probes** nearest to that object. For more information on **Light Probes**, see `https://docs.unity3d.com/Manual/LightProbes.html` and the corresponding subpages.

> *The difference between* ***light probes*** *and* ***lightmaps*** *is that while lightmaps store lighting information about light hitting the surfaces in your scene, light probes store information about light passing through empty space in your scene. - Unity Manual*

A group of **Light Probes** is defined with a single **Light Probe Group** GameObject. In our scene, the **Light Probe Group** contains dozens of probes. As shown in the following screenshot, the **Light Probe Group** is selected in **Hierarchy**, the **Edit Light Probes** button is pressed in the **Inspector**, and one of the probes is selected in the **Scene** window (shaded blue), with its **Selected Probe Position** (**X**, **Y**, **Z**) location shown in the **Inspector**:

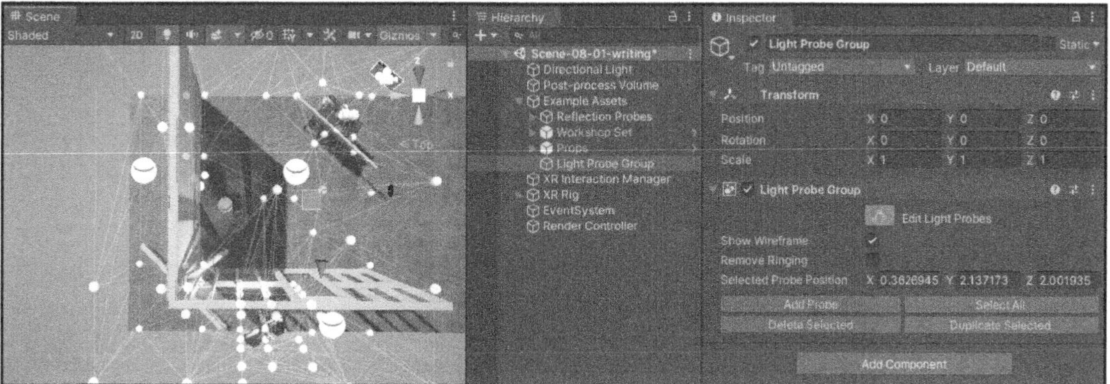

Another kind of probe, a **Reflection Probe**, provides an efficient means of calculating realistic reflections on object surfaces, giving a sense of connection and cohesion to objects in the scene. It turns out that for the human eye to obtain this perceptual effect, this does not require 100% visual accuracy and detail in the reflections. A low-resolution reflection map can be baked beforehand and used in rendering. To achieve this, you can insert **Reflection Probe** GameObjects into the scene that will capture a panoramic view (cubemap) of the surroundings from that viewpoint. When a reflective object passes near to a probe, the sampled visual data is used for the reflection map. For more information on **Reflection Probes**, see `https://docs.unity3d.com/Manual/ReflectionProbes.html` and the corresponding subpages.

You'll find in the **Hierarchy** that our scene contains three **Reflection Probes**. The one named **Reflection Probe Main** is positioned in the middle of the construction space. Shown in the following screenshot, it looks like a perfectly reflective ball hovering in space. Of course, it's not itself rendered in the scene but is used to provide approximate reflections in nearby shiny objects:

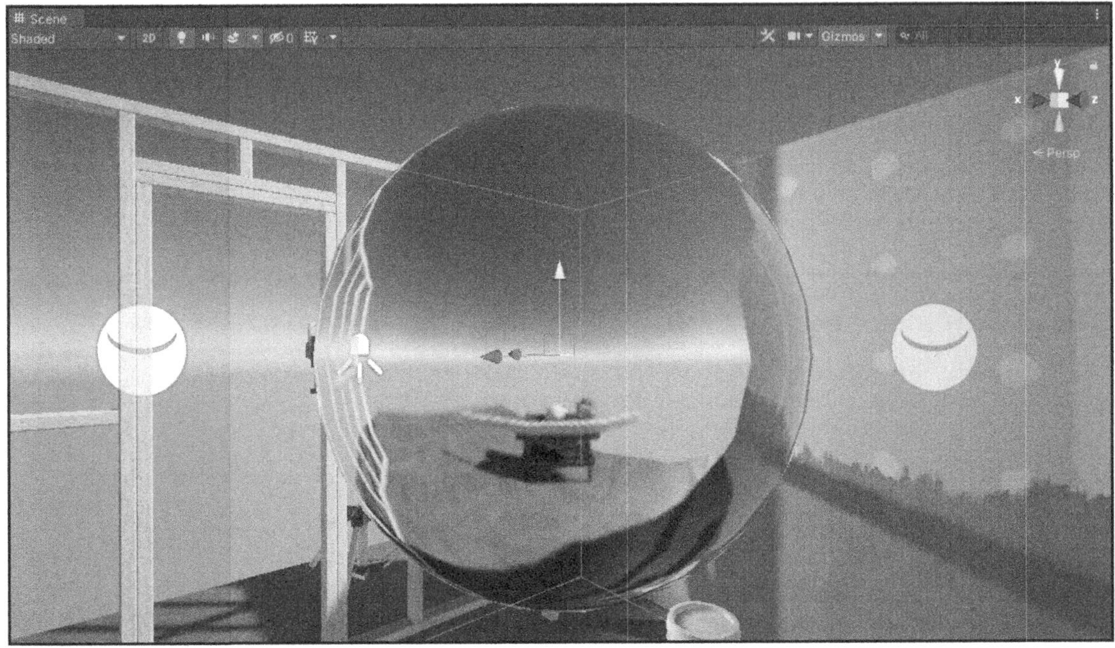

This **Reflection Probe** is defined with a 64-pixel **Resolution**, set in the **Light Explorer** window (**Window | Rendering | Light Explorer | Reflection Probes**). The baked cubemap image gets saved (by default) in a subfolder in your `Scenes/` folder as an **Extended Dynamic Range** (**EXR**) file format. In this case, its size is 64 x 384 (for the six faces of the cubemap). Panoramic and cubemap images are discussed more in `Chapter 11`, *Using All 360 Degrees*.

For this project, we will add two **Toggle** controls to enable or disable the **Light Probes** and **Reflection Probes**. To begin, create a new script, named `ProbesControls` on the **Render Controller** GameObject. Then, edit it as follows (the entire script is shown because it's relatively short):

```
using UnityEngine;
using UnityEngine.UI;

public class ProbesControls : MonoBehaviour
{
    public Toggle lightProbesToggle;
    public Toggle reflectionProbesToggle;

    public GameObject lightProbes;
    public GameObject reflectionProbes;

    public bool LightProbes
    {
        get => lightProbes.activeInHierarchy;
        set => lightProbes.SetActive(value);
    }

    public bool ReflectionProbes
    {
        get => reflectionProbes.activeInHierarchy;
        set => reflectionProbes.SetActive(value);
    }

    private void Start()
    {
        lightProbesToggle.isOn = LightProbes;
        reflectionProbesToggle.isOn = ReflectionProbes;
    }
}
```

I provide `public` variables for the `Toggle` UIs and the probes' `GameObject`. The `LightProbes` and `ReflectionProbes` Boolean properties with the `get` and `set` methods simply `SetActive` the given GameObjects in the scene. Drag the **Light Probes** and **Reflection Probes** objects onto the corresponding component slots.

We can now add the toggles to the **Control Panel** in our menu, using the following steps:

1. In **Hierarchy**, find the fourth **Control Panel** under your **Menu Canvas** corresponding to the **Probes** tab button.
2. From the **Project** window `Assets/Prefabs/` folder, drag the **ToggleUI** prefab into **Hierarchy** as the bottom child of the **Control Panel**.
3. Rename it `Light Probes Toggle`.
4. Unfold **Light Probes Toggle**, and modify the **Label** | **Text** to read `Enable Light Probes`.
5. On the **Light Probes Toggle** | **Toggle** component, drag the **Render Controller** onto the **On Value Changed** | **Object** field, and select **ProbesControls** | **LightProbes**.
6. Then, select the **Render Controller** and drag the **Light Probes Toggle** GameObject from **Hierarchy** onto the **Probes Controls** | **Light Probes** slot.
7. Repeat *steps 2-6* for the `ReflectionProbes` property.

The UI menu panel we just created now looks like this:

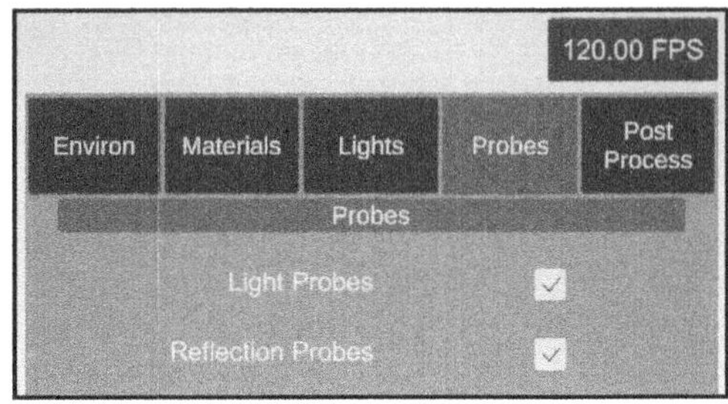

With this menu panel implemented, populate the **Lights** GameObjects as follows:

1. Select **Render Controller** in **Hierarchy**.
2. Drag the **Light Probes Group** GameObject from **Hierarchy** onto the **Probes Controls** | **Light Probes** slot.
3. Drag the **Reflection Probes** GameObject from **Hierarchy** onto the **Reflection Probes** slot.

You can now **Play** the scene and see the effect of modifying these properties at runtime in VR. The following screenshot shows the scene side by side, with the probes enabled (on the left), and all the **Light Probes** and **Reflection Probes** disabled (on the right):

In this section, you learned about using Light Probes to add environment lighting to dynamic objects, and Reflection Probes to add environment reflections to shiny surfaces. We added checkbox controls that let you turn these on and off in the scene at runtime to see their effect.

Next, we'll look at how post-processing effects can be used to enhance the realism and cinematic effects of your scenes.

Enhancing your scenes with post-processing effects

So, we've seen how the **Render Pipeline** can use environment lighting, PBR Materials, Light GameObjects, and Probes to render realistic views of your scene. *But wait! There's more!* You can add post-processing effects to the fullscreen camera buffer image before it appears on the screen. Post-processing effects are often used to simulate the visual properties of a physical camera and film. Examples include **Bloom** (fringe lighting extending the border of extremely bright light), **Color Grading** (adjusts the color and luminance of the final images, like an Instagram filter), and **Anti-aliasing** (removing jaggy edges). You can stack a series of available effects that are processed in sequence.

For example, the **Vignette** effect darkens the edges of the image and leaves the center brighter. In VR, during a fast-paced scene (such as a racing game or roller coaster), or when teleporting, using a **Vignette** can help reduce motion sickness. On the other hand, some other effects, including **Lens Distortion**, **Chromatic Aberration**, and **Motion Blur** are best avoided in VR.

For more information on creating and using post-processing effects, see the following links:

- *Best Practices Guide: Making Believable Visuals: Understanding post-processing*—`https://docs.unity3d.com/Manual/BestPracticeMakingBelievableVisuals8.html`
- *Unity Manual: Post-processing* (and its subpages)—`https://docs.unity3d.com/Manual/PostProcessingOverview.html`
- *Post-processing in the Universal Render Pipeline*—`https://docs.unity3d.com/Packages/com.unity.render-pipelines.universal@8.1/manual/integration-with-post-processing.html`

In our scene, the post-processing effects are defined on a GameObject in the **Hierarchy** named **Post-process Volume**, which contains a **Volume** component that has several effects—namely, **Tonemapping**, **Bloom**, and **Vignette**. Its **Inspector** is shown in the following screenshot:

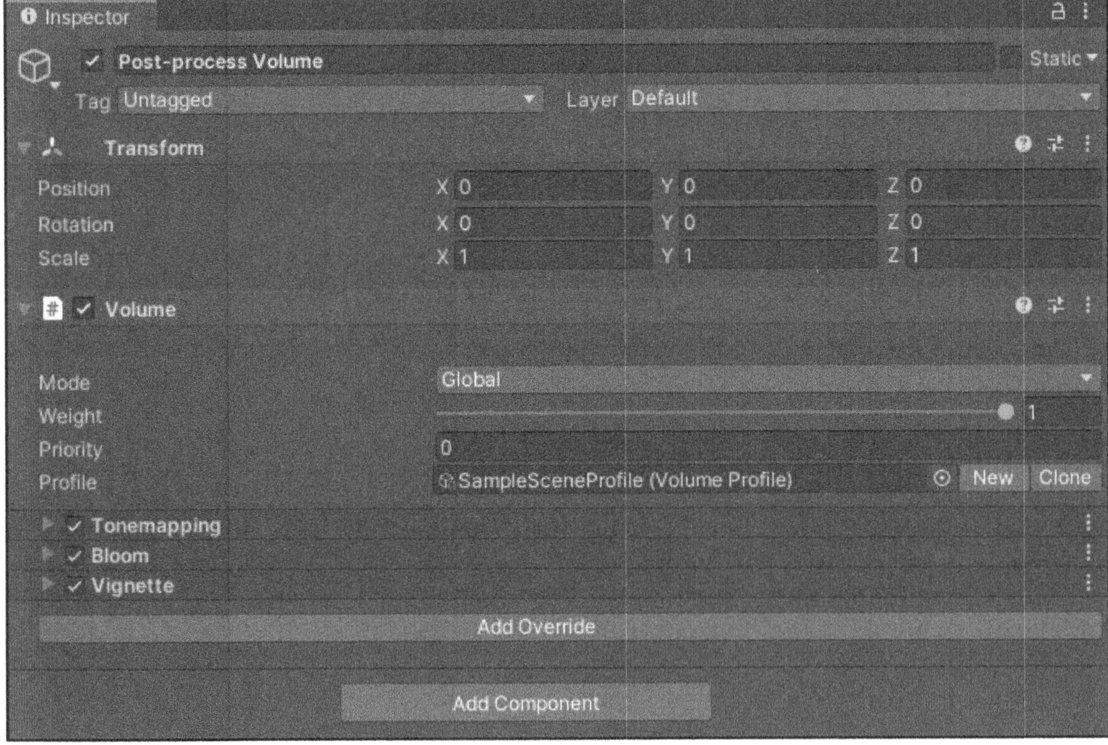

For this project, we will dynamically instantiate **ToggleUI** checkboxes for each post-processing effect we find on the **Volume**. To begin, create a new script named `PostProcessControls` on the **Render Controller** GameObject. Then, edit it as follows (the entire script is shown because it's relatively short):

```
using System.Collections.Generic;
using System.Linq;
using UnityEngine;
using UnityEngine.Rendering;
using UnityEngine.UI;

public class PostProcessControls : MonoBehaviour
{
    public Transform uiPanel;
    public GameObject togglePrefab;
    public Volume postProcessVolume;

    private VolumeProfile profile;
    private List<VolumeComponent> components;
    private List<Toggle> toggles = new List<Toggle>();

    private void Start()
    {
        profile = postProcessVolume.profile;
        components = profile.components;

        for (int i = 0; i < components.Count; i++)
        {
            GameObject go = Instantiate(togglePrefab, uiPanel);
            Toggle toggle = go.GetComponent<Toggle>();
            int index = i;
            toggle.onValueChanged.AddListener((value) =>
                { components.ElementAt(index).active = value; });
            Text text = go.GetComponentInChildren<Text>();
            text.text = components.ElementAt(i).name;
            toggles.Add(toggle);
        }
    }
}
```

In the script, we declare a `public` variable for the `uiPanel` control panel, within which we'll create the UI toggles. There's a reference to the `togglePrefab` object to instantiate and a reference to the post-processing `Volume` component in the Scene. The only function is `Start()`, where we grab the list of `VolumeComponent` instances from the `Volume`. Then, for each effect component, we create a **ToggleUI** instance.

For each toggle, we display the post-processing `VolumeComponent` name in the `Text` label. We then define an event action for `onValueChanged`—when the user checks or unchecks the toggle, it will set the `active` component to `true` or `false`.

The `AddListener` call I've written uses a C# syntax you may not have seen yet. Instead of declaring a separate function for the listener to call when the toggle value changes, we create a **lambda expression**—an unnamed anonymous function. This is especially useful and can be more readable when the body of the function is only a single line, as in this case.

Now, in Unity, we don't need to manually add any UI elements to the Control Panel because the script will do this. Populate the variable values as follows:

1. In **Hierarchy**, select the **Render Controller**.
2. From **Hierarchy**, drag the last (fifth) **Control Panel** GameObject under the **Menu Canvas / Panels /** onto the **Post Process Controls** | **UI Panel** slot.
3. From the **Project** `Assets/Prefabs` folder, drag the **ToggleUI** prefab onto the **Post Process Controls** | **Toggle Prefab** slot.
4. From **Hierarchy**, drag the **Post-process Volume** GameObject onto the **Post Process Controls** | **Post Process Volume** slot.

With this menu panel implemented, you can now play the scene and see the effect of toggling these effects at runtime in VR. The following screenshot shows the **Control Panel** populated at runtime with the post-processing effects stack (**Volume** components) in this scene, where **Bloom** is disabled. You'll notice in this screenshot that in the background, the wall studs are illuminated by the construction lamp, but are not **Bloom**, as they were in screenshots earlier in this chapter:

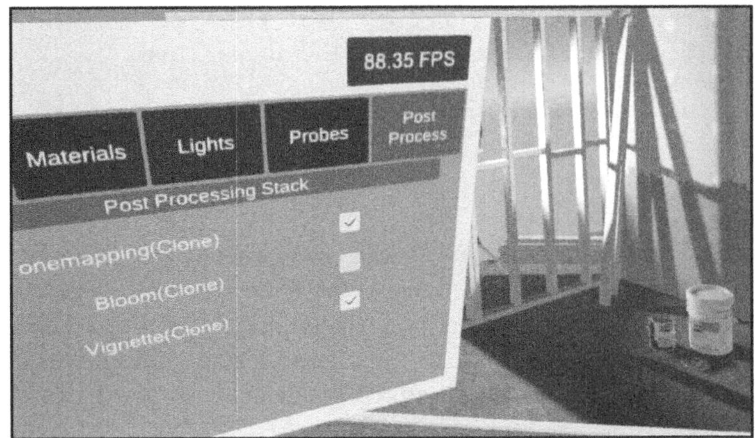

In this section, you learned how this scene is using post-processing **Volume** effects, including **Tonemapping**, **Bloom**, and **Vignette**. You also learned how to access the components for each of these effects from C#. We added checkbox controls that let you turn each post-processing component on and off to see their effect at runtime in VR.

Summary

In this chapter, we explored how to create visual realism in your VR scenes using environmental lighting, **Light** GameObjects, emissive materials, post-processing, and other tools included with Unity. We started by walking through a lighting strategy for configuring and enhancing your scenes, using decision trees and best practices suggested in the *Unity Best Practices Guides*. Then, using a sample scene, you created a menu palette with control panels for manipulating various lighting settings in the scene at runtime, while in VR.

You learned about the **Lighting settings** window, **Global Illumination** baking, and the **Environment** light settings, adding UI controls to modify the **Skybox** and **Fog** contribution to lighting. Then, you learned about PBR materials for creating realistic 3D objects in the scene, adding UI controls to modify the **Material** properties of various texture maps. Next, you learned how to use **Light** GameObjects and **Emission Material** properties to add local lighting in the scene, and explored this with UI controls to modify the **Directional Light** and the construction **Spot Light** in the scene, plus the **Emission** property for the lightbulb. You saw how lighting can be further enhanced with **Light Probes**, for pre-calculating lighting at specific locations in the scene for dynamic objects, and **Reflection Probes**, for pre-calculating reflections on shiny surfaces. Lastly, you learned about **Post-processing Volumes** that add cinematic effects and enhancements to the camera image before it is drawn on your device screen, dynamically adding UI checkbox controls to your menu panel to turn on and off individual effect components at runtime in VR.

Along the way, you learned some more advanced C# coding techniques, including class properties (with getter and setter methods), using the specific Unity namespace API including `UnityEngine.Rendering`, accessing material and shader properties, using `List` collections, and using **lambda expressions**.

In the next chapter, we'll build a real VR application, a paddle-ball game that shoots fireballs in sync with music beats that you try to hit back into a target. You'll learn more about the Unity physics engine, particle effects, and C# GameObject pooling, as well as other techniques important for VR development.

9 Playing with Physics and Fire

We've used Unity Physics and Rigidbodies already in some of the prior chapters. Here, we'll dive a little deeper. In this chapter, we will use physics and other Unity features to build variations of an interactive ball game, including headshots, paddleball, and a rhythm beat game. Along the way, we will explore managing object lifetimes, Rigidbody physics, particle effects, and adding sound effects and music to your projects. We'll also continue to gain experience with C# scripting, Unity's **application programming interface** (**API**), and events. In this chapter, you will learn about the following topics:

- The Unity Physics engine, **Rigidbody** components, and Physic Materials
- Using velocity and gravity to make bouncy balls
- Managing object lifetimes and object pooling to avoid **Garbage Collection** (**GC**)
- Hitting balls with your head and your hands
- Building a fireball using particle effects
- Synchronizing with music

By the end of this chapter, you will have learned to build several different ball games using Unity Physics, while managing the life cycle of game objects. You'll also learn about adding juice to your games, including visual effects, sound effects, and scene environments.

Technical requirements

To implement the projects and exercises in this chapter, you will need the following:

- A PC or Mac with Unity 2019.4 LTS or later, XR Plugin for your device, and the XR Interaction Toolkit installed
- A **virtual reality** (**VR**) headset supported by the Unity XR Platform

You can access or clone the GitHub repository for this book (`https://github.com/PacktPublishing/Unity-2020-Virtual-Reality-Projects-3rd-Edition-`) to optionally use assets and completed projects for this chapter, as follows:

- Asset files for you to use in this chapter are located in `UVRP3Files/Chapter-09-Files.zip`.
- All completed projects in this book are in a single Unity project at `UVRP3Projects`.
- The completed assets and scenes for this chapter are in the `UVRP3Projects/Assets/_UVRP3Assets/Chapter09/` folder.

Understanding Unity physics

In Unity, the physical behavior of an object is defined separately from its mesh (shape), rendering options, and materials (textures and shader). Unity's built-in physics is based on the NVIDIA **Physx** real-time physics engine that implements classical Newtonian mechanics for games and 3D applications. The items that play into physics include the following:

- **Rigidbody**: A component that enables the object to act under the control of the physics engine, receiving forces and torque to move in a realistic way.
- **Joints**: Allows the connection one Rigidbody to another or a fixed point in space, thereby restricting its movement in space.
- **Collider**: A component that defines a simplified, approximated shape of the object used for calculating collisions with other objects.
- **Physic Material**: Defines the friction and bounce effects of colliding objects.
- **Physics Manager**: Applies global settings for 3D physics to your project.

Basically, physics (in this context) is defined by the positional and rotational forces that affect the transform of an object, such as gravity, friction, momentum, and collisions with other objects. It is not necessarily a perfect simulation of physics in the real world because it's optimized for performance and separation of concerns to facilitate animation.

For more advanced physics simulations, Unity also offers the **Havok Physics** engine, built on the **data-oriented technology stack** (**DOTS**). Havok is a high-performance physics engine that is scalable for large, complex (for example, open-world) games, supports interpenetrating objects, an advanced friction model, and more. We do not cover Havok Physics or DOTS in this book.

A key to physics is the **Rigidbody** component that you add to objects. Rigidbodies have parameters for gravity, mass, and drag, among others. Rigidbodies can automatically react to gravity and collisions with other objects. No extra scripting is needed for this. During gameplay, the engine calculates each rigid object's momentum and updates its transform position and rotation.

Unity projects have a global Gravity setting, found in the project's Physics Manager by navigating to **Edit | Project Settings | Physics**. As you might expect, the default gravity setting is a **Vector3** setting with values (`0`, `-9.81`, `0`) that apply a downward force to all Rigidbodies, measured in meters-per-second-squared. The Physics settings window is shown in the following screenshot and explained in the Unity Manual (`https://docs.unity3d.com/Manual/class-PhysicsManager.html`):

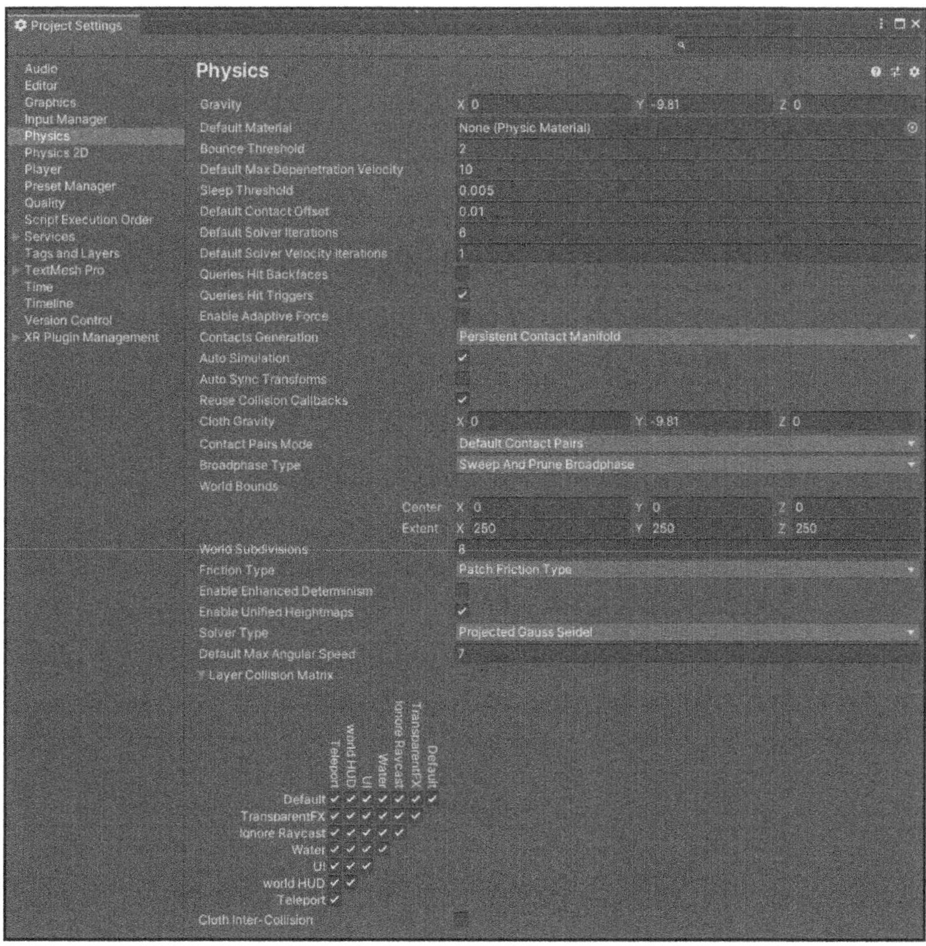

In order to detect a collision, both of the colliding objects must have a `Collider` component. There are built-in colliders with basic geometric shapes such as a box, sphere, cylinder, and mesh. In order to react to a collision with physics, the object must have a `Rigidbody` component. When game objects that contain both `Collider` and `Rigidbody` collide, the forces of one are applied to the other. The values of the resulting forces are calculated based on the objects' current velocity and body mass. Gravity and drag (that is, resistance) factors are also taken into consideration. You also have options to add constraints to freeze the position or rotation of a given object in any of its *x*, *y*, and *z* axes. Since this calculation can be expensive, especially with many objects, you can constrain the engine—for example, to only consider collisions between objects on specific layers (as shown in the **Layer Collision Matrix** at the bottom of the previous screenshot).

A mesh collider uses an arbitrarily shaped mesh. If you can, it's best to use one or multiple basic collider shapes that approximately fit the actual object rather than a mesh, so as to reduce the work calculating collisions during gameplay. Unity requires that mesh colliders be marked as **Convex** to collide with other meshes' colliders and cannot be used with higher-accuracy **Continuous** collision detection.

The calculations can be further affected when a **Physic Material** is assigned to the object's collider, which adjusts the friction and the bounciness effects of the colliding objects. These properties will be applied only to the object that owns the Physic Material. (Note that it is spelled *Physic Material* rather than *Physics Material*, for historical reasons.)

So, let's say that Object A (ball) hits Object B (brick). If Object A has bounciness and Object B does not then, Object A will have an impulse applied in the collision, but Object B will not. However, you have options to determine how their friction and bounciness combine, as we'll see next. It's not necessarily an accurate simulation of real-world physics. It's a game engine, not a computer-aided engineering modeler.

From a scripting point of view, Unity will invoke events—for example, when objects collide (`OnCollisionEnter`) and when they've stopped colliding (`OnCollisionExit`).

If this sounds daunting, read on. The rest of this chapter breaks it down into understandable examples. We'll begin by demonstrating the use of Rigidbody and gravity by dropping bouncy balls.

Creating bouncy balls

For our first demonstration, we will implement a simple bouncing ball. When a ball drops from mid-air and hits the ground, we want it to bounce up, then fall down again, bounce up again and fall, with diminishing velocity and height over time. We are going to start simply with a new scene that consists of a ground plane and a sphere. Then, we'll add physics to it, a bit at a time, as follows:

1. Create a new scene named `09-BallsFromHeaven` by clicking **File** | **New Scene** and **File** | **Save As**
2. Add an **XR Rig** by selecting **GameObject** | **XR** | **Stationary XR Rig** or **Room-Scale XR Rig**.
3. Position it toward the back of the ground plane (set **Position** `0, 0, -4`).
4. Set the **Main Camera** | **Camera** | **Clipping Planes** | **Near** to `0.01`

And set up the GameObjects, as follows:

1. Create a plane named `Ground Plane` using **GameObject** | **3D Object** | **Plane**, and reset its transform (**Transform** | right-click | **Reset**)
2. Create a sphere named `BouncyBall` by clicking **GameObject** | **3D Object** | **Sphere**
3. Set its **Scale** to (`0.25`, `0.25`, `0.25`) and **Position** to (`0`, `5`,`0`) so that it's above the center of the ground plane
4. Add a **Red Material** (drag the **Red Material** from **Project** `Assets` created in `Chapter 2`, *Understanding Unity, Content, and Scale* onto the ball, or create a new material to use via **Assets** | **Create** | **Material**, and color it red)

Our sphere now looks like a ball, hanging in space. Click on the **Play** button. Nothing happens. The ball just sits in mid-air and doesn't move. Now, let's give it a **Rigidbody**, as follows:

1. With `BouncyBall` selected, note that it has a **Sphere Collider** by default
2. Add a **Rigidbody** (**Component** | **Physics** | **Rigidbody**)
3. Set its **Collision Detection** to **Continuous**
4. Click on the **Play** button—it drops like a lead brick

Note that the default **Discrete Collision Detection** could let the ball fall through the ground plane when the ball is falling faster than the physics has a chance to detect a collision, so we changed it to **Continuous**. Alternatively, you could have used a flattened cube for the ground "platform" (for example, **Scale** `10, 0.1, 10`) instead of a zero-thickness plane. Another option, as we'll see later, is to increase the rate of the physics engine updates (**Time** | **Fixed Timestep**).

Let's make it bounce, as follows:

1. Create a `Physics` folder for our new physic materials (in the **Project** window, select **+** | **Folder**)
2. Create a **Physic Material** named `Bouncy Physic Material` (**Assets** | **Create** | **Physic Material**)
3. Set its **Bounciness** value to `1`
4. With the `BouncyBall` sphere selected in **Hierarchy**, drag the `Bouncy Physic Material` asset from **Project** onto the ball's **Sphere Collider** | **Material** field in **Inspector**

Click on the **Play** button. OK, it bounces, but it doesn't go very high. We used the maximum value for **Bounciness** as `1.0`. What's slowing it down? It's not the **Friction** settings either. Rather, the **Bounce Combine** is set to **Average**, which determines how much of the bounciness of the ball (`1`) is mixed with that of the plane (`0`). So, it diminishes by half each bounce. If we want the ball to retain *all* its bounciness, have the material use the Maximum of the two colliders by following the steps given next:

1. Change the `Bouncy Physic Material` object's **Bounce Combine** to **Maximum**.
2. Click on the **Play** button. Much better. Actually, too much better. The ball keeps bouncing back up to its original height, never slowing down.
3. Now, change the **Bounciness** to `0.8`. The bounces diminish, and the ball will eventually come to a stop.

OK—let's have some more fun. Make it rain bouncy balls! To do this, we'll make the ball a prefab and write a script that instantiates new balls, dropping them from random positions above the ground, as follows:

1. Drag the `BouncyBall` object from **Hierarchy** into the **Project** `Prefabs` folder, making it a prefab.
2. Delete the `BouncyBall` object from the **Hierarchy**, since we'll be instantiating it with a script.

3. Create an empty game object named `Ball Controller` to attach the script to **(GameObject | Create Empty).**
4. Create a new C# script named `BallsFromHeaven` (**Add Component** | **New Script**) and open the script for editing, as follows:

```
public class BallsFromHeaven : MonoBehaviour
{
    public GameObject ballPrefab;
    public float startHeight = 10f;
    public float interval = 0.5f;

    private float nextBallTime = 0f;

    private void Start()
    {
        nextBallTime = Time.time + interval;
    }

    void Update()
    {
        if (Time.time > nextBallTime)
        {
            Vector3 position = new Vector3(
                Random.Range(-4f, 4f),
                startHeight,
                Random.Range(-4f, 4f));
            NewBall(position);

            nextBallTime = Time.time + interval;
        }
    }

    private void NewBall(Vector3 position)
    {
        Instantiate(ballPrefab, position, Quaternion.identity);
    }
}
```

In `Update`, when it's time, the script drops a new ball from a random position (**X, Z** between `-4` and `4`) and a given `startHeight` at the rate of every half-second (`interval`). The `NewBall` function calls `Instantiate` to add a new ball to the scene **Hierarchy**.

Save the script. We now need to populate the **Ball** field with the **BouncyBall** prefab, as follows:

1. With **Ball Controller** selected in **Hierarchy**, drag the **BouncyBall** prefab from the **Project** `Prefabs` folder onto the **Ball Prefab** slot in the **Balls From Heaven** component in **Inspector**.
2. **Save** the scene. **Play** it in VR.

I love how even the simplest things can be fun to watch in VR! This is what I get:

In summary, we created a sphere with a Rigidbody and added a **Physic Material** with a **Bounciness** property of `0.8` and **Bounce Combine** set to **Maximum**. Then, we saved the `BouncyBall` as a prefab and wrote a script to instantiate new balls that drop from random positions above the ground plane. This scene also exposes a new issue we should address: the life cycle of game objects. As the scene plays, we keep making more and more balls, forever. Let's do something about that.

Managing the GameObject life cycle

Whenever you have a script that instantiates `GameObjects`, you must be aware of the life cycle of the object and possibly arrange to destroy it when it is no longer needed. In **object-oriented programming (OOP)**, the life cycle of an object begins when a block of memory is allocated that is large enough to hold the object. When the object is destroyed, its memory is released and reclaimed by the system. In this section, we will examine different strategies on how to decide when to destroy GameObjects you have created, including destroying after they're no longer visible in the scene, or after a specific life duration. Then, we'll use a technique called *object pooling* to avoid problems caused by repeatedly instantiating and destroying objects at runtime.

Removing fallen objects

In our scene, we have a limited-size ground plane and as balls hit one another, some will fall off the plane into oblivion. At that point, we can discard the ball and remove it from the scene. In Play mode, watch the **Hierarchy** panel as new balls are instantiated. Note that some balls end up bouncing off the plane platform but remain in the **Hierarchy** panel. We need to clean this up by adding a script that removes the balls that are out of play. Use the following steps to create a new script named `RemoveSelf` to the **BouncyBall** prefab:

1. Open the `BouncyBall` prefab for editing by double-clicking the prefab in your **Project** `Prefabs` folder
2. Add a new script named `RemoveSelf` by clicking on **Add Component** | **New Script**, open it for editing, and add the following lines of code:

```
public class RemoveSelf : MonoBehaviour
{
    public bool checkOutOfBounds = true;
    public Vector3 minBounds = Vector3.negativeInfinity;
    public Vector3 maxBounds = Vector3.positiveInfinity;

    private void Update()
    {
        if (checkOutOfBounds)
        {
            Vector3 pos = transform.position;
            if (pos.x < minBounds.x || pos.x > maxBounds.x ||
                pos.y < minBounds.y || pos.y > maxBounds.y ||
                pos.z < minBounds.z || pos.z > maxBounds.z)
            {
                Remove();
            }
```

```
        }
    }

    private void Remove()
    {
        Destroy(gameObject);
    }
}
```

This script is reusable for any object you want to remove from the scene when it goes out of bounds. You'll see in a moment why I've decided to make the `checkOutOfBounds` test optional. The min and max boundaries define a cuboid space, initialized to infinity, so everything will be in bounds until we set an actual boundary value. In the **Inspector**, you can set the actual boundaries as you need.

In programming, conditional statements such as `if` and `while` use a binary condition to test whether to run the body of the statement. Conditional expressions can simply test the value of a Boolean variable (for example, `whenOutOfBounds`), use a comparison operator (for example, < for less-than, and > for greater-than) and combine these with Boolean operators such as `&&` for "and" where both must be true, and `||` for "or" where either may be true.

Save the script and back in Unity, modify the **Min Bounds Y** value to `-5`, as shown in the following screenshot, so that when the ball falls more than 5 meters below ground level, it is destroyed:

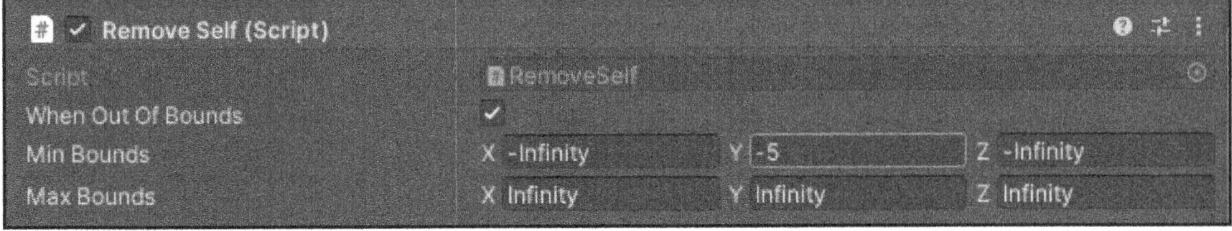

Save the prefab changes and press **Play.** You can see that when balls fall off the edge of the ground plane, they'll be destroyed and removed from the scene. Another strategy is to set a time limit on an object.

Setting a limited lifetime

Another strategy for managing an object's life cycle is to limit its duration of existence. This is especially effective for things such as projectiles (bullets, arrows, bouncy balls) or other objects that the player cares about most when it's instantiated and then isn't paying attention as gameplay moves on. We first used this technique in `Chapter 5`, *Interacting with Your Hands*, when we set balloons to disappear after a time limit. Here, we'll extend our `RemoveSelf` script with the option for the object to remove itself when time runs out. Follow the steps given next:

1. Update the `RemoveSelf` script, and at the top of the class, add the following:

```
public bool checkTimeout = true;
public float timeOut = 15f;
private float timer;

private void OnEnable()
{
   if (checkTimeout)
  {
   timer = Time.time + timeOut;
  }
}
```

   The script now offers a second option, `checkTimeout`, and a `timeOut` duration (in seconds). In `OnEnable`, we initialize the `timer`, and then in `Update`, we check if the `timer` has run out and remove the object.

2. Add to `Update` the following code:

```
if (checkTimeout && Time.time > timer)
{
    Remove();
}
```

3. **Save** the script, and in Unity, **Save** the prefab. The **RemoveSelf** component now offers the two options, as shown in the following screenshot:

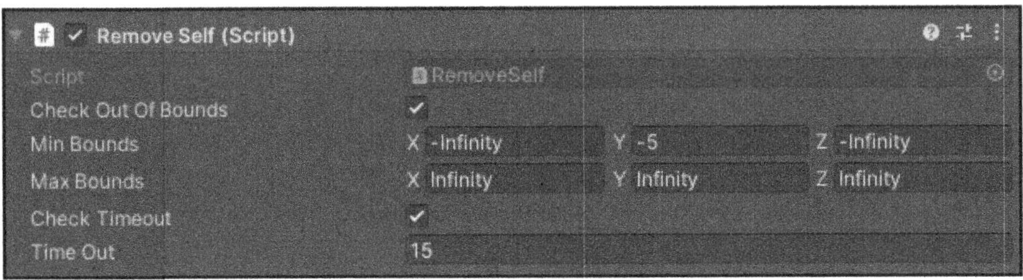

   When **Check Timeout** is checked, every ball will destroy itself after 15 seconds. When you press **Play**, after some time, notice that the ground plane remains substantially less crowded than before. With both options checked, each **Bouncy Ball** will be destroyed after 15 seconds or when it has fallen off the ground plane, whichever comes first.

Nonetheless, it's not a good idea to continuously create and destroy game objects at runtime, as this can cause memory fragmentation that requires GC (recovering unused memory fragments). We can manage this issue using an *object pool*.

Implementing an object pool

When you instantiate a game object, Unity allocates runtime memory for the object. When you destroy a game object, Unity frees its memory, but that memory is not immediately available for reuse. A separate GC process is periodically run in the background by the internal Unity system to recover it. GC is a time-consuming procedure that can affect frame rate and latency in VR applications and is best avoided whenever possible. Using *object pooling* can help avoid this issue.

Object pooling is when you create a list of reusable objects to be used in your game. Rather than continuously instantiating new ones, you activate and deactivate a pooled object instead. To implement this, we will write a generic reusable object pooler and add it to the `Ball Controller` in the scene.

For this, we are also introducing the concept of lists in C#. As the name indicates, a list is an ordered collection of objects, like an array, but lists can be easily searched, sorted, and otherwise manipulated (see `https://docs.microsoft.com/en-us/dotnet/api/system.collections.generic.list-1?view=netframework-4.8`). We'll use a list to hold our pre-instantiated objects. Let's name the script `ObjectPooler`. Proceed as follows:

1. Select the `Ball Controller` in **Hierarchy**
2. Navigate to **Add Component** | **New Script** and name it `ObjectPooler`
3. Open the `ObjectPooler.cs` for editing. Let's start by declaring several variables at the top of the `ObjectPooler.cs` file, as follows:

```
using System.Collections.Generic;
using UnityEngine;

public class ObjectPooler : MonoBehaviour
{
    public GameObject prefab;
    public int poolSize = 20;

    private List<GameObject> pooledObjects =
        new List<GameObject>();
}
```

The `prefab` public variable will get the prefab GameObject we want to instantiate—namely, `BouncyBall`—and `poolSize` says how many objects to initially instantiate. The actual list is held in `pooledObjects`. Now, when the scene starts, we initialize the list with the number of objects specified in `poolSize`, as follows:

```
void Start()
{
   for (int i = 0; i < poolSize; i++)
  {
    GameObject obj = (GameObject)Instantiate(prefab);
    obj.SetActive(false);
    pooledObjects.Add(obj);
  }
 }
```

The `for` loop repeats `poolSize` a number of times, instantiating a new GameObject from the prefab, setting it as inactive, and adding it to the list. Now, when we want a new object, we'll call `GetPooledObject`, which searches the list for one that is presently not active, sets it as active, and returns it to the caller. If none is available for reuse (all of them are active), we return `null`, as follows:

```
public GameObject GetPooledObject()
 {
   for (int i = 0; i < pooledObjects.Count; i++)
 {
     if (!pooledObjects[i].activeInHierarchy)
     {
         pooledObjects[i].SetActive(true);
         return pooledObjects[i];
     }
 }

   return null;
 }
```

4. We can also enhance the script to optionally grow the list so that it never returns `null`. Add the following option at the top:

```
public bool willGrow = true;
```

5. Add the following statements to `GetPooledObject` after the `for` loop; if we haven't found one in the list, instantiate a new one anyway and add it to the list, like this:

```
public GameObject GetPooledObject()
{
   for (int i = 0; i < pooledObjects.Count; i++)
{
    if (!pooledObjects[i].activeInHierarchy)
    {
        pooledObjects[i].SetActive(true);
        return pooledObjects[i];
    }
 }

 if (willGrow)
 {
    GameObject obj = (GameObject)Instantiate(prefab);
    pooledObjects.Add(obj);
    return obj;
}
```

```
        return null;
    }
```

Save the script. In Unity, assign the **BouncyBall** prefab to the **Object Pooler** using the following steps:

1. Select the `Ball Controller` in **Hierarchy**
2. Drag the **BouncyBall** prefab to the **Object Pooler** | **Prefab** slot

   Now, we need to modify our `BallsFromHeaven` script to call `GetPooledObject` from `ObjectPooler` instead of `Instantiate`, as follows. (Note that, in the GitHub project accompanying this book, the script is renamed `BallsFromHeavenPooled`.) At the top of the class, add a reference to the `ObjectPooler` and initialize it in `Start`. Editing the `BallsFromHeaven.cs` file, make the following changes:

```
    public float startHeight = 10f;
    public float interval = 0.5f;

    private float nextBallTime = 0f;
    private ObjectPooler objectPooler;

    private void Start()
    {
    nextBallTime = Time.time + interval;
    objectPooler = GetComponent<ObjectPooler>();
    }
```

3. Then, change `NewBall` to use `objectPooler.GetPooledObject` instead of `Instantiate`.

   Since we're not instantiating new objects but reusing them, we may need to reset any object properties to their starting values. In this case, we reset not just the **Transform**, but set the Rigidbody's velocity to zero, as illustrated in the following code snippet:

```
private void NewBall(Vector3 position)
 {
    GameObject ball = objectPooler.GetPooledObject();
    if (ball != null)
   {
     ball.transform.position = position;
     ball.transform.rotation = Quaternion.identity;
     ball.GetComponent<Rigidbody>().velocity = Vector3.zero;
   }
 }
```

4. The last part is to modify `RemoveSelf` to just disable the object rather than literally destroy it, as follows. Edit the `RemoveSelf.cs` file. (Note that, in the GitHub project for this book, the script is renamed `RemoveSelfPooled`.) Have a look at the following code snippet:

```
private void Remove()
    {
        gameObject.SetActive(false);
    }
```

Instead of calling `Destroy`, we changed it to `gameObject.SetActive(false)`. The `ObjectPooler` will later see this object is not active and thus is available for reuse when searching for a `GetPooledObject`.

Now, when you press **Play**, you can see in **Inspector** that new **BouncyBalls** are instantiated at the start of the game to initialize the list. As time goes on, the objects are disabled as they are returned to the pool, and reactivated when reused, as shown in the following screenshot (deactivated **BouncyBall(Clone)** objects are dimmer than the activated ones):

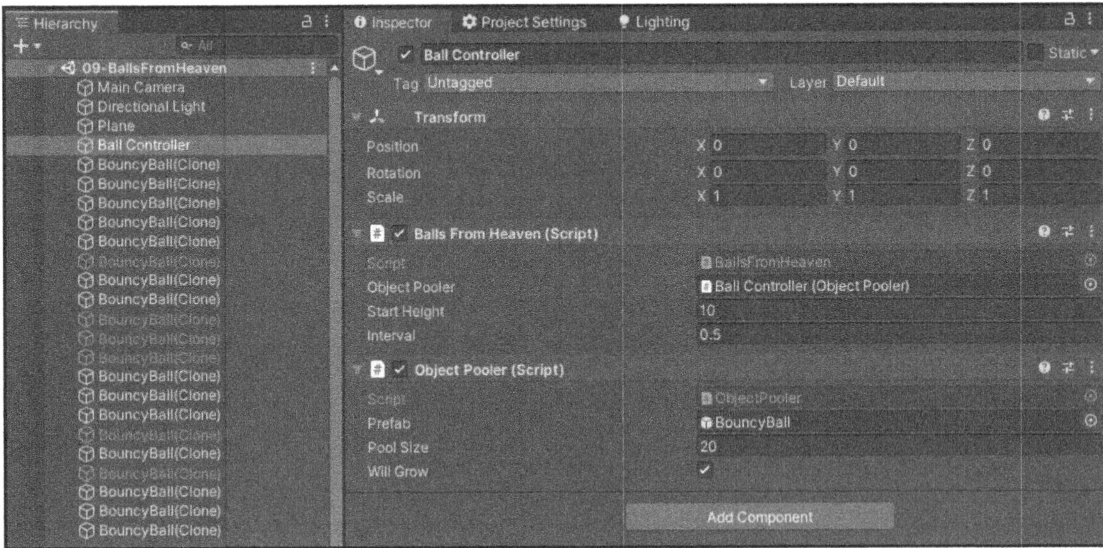

In this section, we learned some best practices in managing game objects at runtime. We used a couple of different strategies for removing objects from the scene—when it goes out of bounds, and when it times out. However, continually instantiating and destroying objects will fragment memory and require the GC to run at the expense of your user experience. So, we replaced the use of `Instantiate` and `Destroy` with an `ObjectPooler` that instantiates a list of objects at the start of the game, and then recycles them as needed for the duration of the game, using the `SetActive` and `isActiveInHierarchy` properties to identify busy versus available objects in the pool.

Next, we'll add some more interactivity with our falling bouncy balls—let's build a *headshot game*!

Building a headshot game

Wouldn't it be fun to actually play with these bouncy balls? Let's make a game where you aim the ball at a target using your head as a paddle. For this game, balls drop one at a time from above and bounce off your forehead (face), while you try aiming for a target. To implement this, we will create a cube as a child of the camera object that provides a collider that tracks the player's head movement. I decided a cube-shaped collider would be better for this game than a sphere or capsule because it provides a flat surface that will make the bounce direction more predictable. For a target, we'll use a flattened cylinder. We'll also add sound-effect cues to indicate when a new ball has been released and when a ball has hit the target.

To begin, we can build on the previous scene, adding an **XR Rig**. To do that, follow the steps given next:

1. Save the current scene named `09-2-BallGame` by clicking **File** | **Save As**
2. Position the **XR Rig** object toward the back of the ground plane (set **Position** `0, 0, -4`)
3. Delete the **Ball Controller** object by right-clicking | **Delete**

To add a **Box Collider** that tracks with the head, which the player can use to deflect balls, we'll create a Cube and disable its Renderer, as follows:

1. In **Hierarchy**, unfold **XR Rig**, drilling down, and select the **Main Camera** object
2. Create a child **Cube** by right-clicking **Main Camera** | **3D Object** | **Cube**
3. Disable the cube's **Mesh Renderer** (uncheck its enable checkbox)

Next, we'll write a `Ball Game Controller` that serves balls to the player and manages other game functions.

Serving a ball

We will add a controller script to the scene that serves a new ball, dropping it from above the player onto their head. The player will look up and try to deflect the ball toward a target. Create an empty GameObject with the object pooler and a new `BallGame` script, as follows:

1. Create a new empty `Ball Game Controller` by clicking **GameObject | Create Empty**
2. Drag the **ObjectPooler** script from the **Project** window `Scripts` folder onto the **Ball Game Controller**, as we'll use pooling
3. Drag the **BouncyBall** prefab from the **Project** window `Prefabs` folder onto the **Object Pooler | Prefab** slot
4. Create a script on it named `BallGame` (**Add Component | New Script**) and open it for editing, as follows:

   The script is very similar to the `BallsFromHeaven` script we wrote earlier, with just a few changes. First, we'll add a public `dropPoint` position where we release new balls from, as follows:

   ```
   public class BallGame : MonoBehaviour
   {
       public Transform dropPoint;
       public float interval = 3f;

       private float nextBallTime = 0f;
       private ObjectPooler objectPooler;

       void Start()
       {
           objectPooler = GetComponent<ObjectPooler>();
       }
   ```

   The `Update` function is also nearly identical to the `BallsFromHeaven` function, except we drop the ball from that `dropPoint` instead of a random one. We instantiate a new ball every 3 seconds (`interval`) from the `dropPoint` position, as illustrated in the following code snippet:

   ```
   void Update()
   ```

```
{
    if (Time.time > nextBallTime)
  {
      NewBall(dropPoint.position);
      nextBallTime = Time.time + interval;
  }
}
```

And the `NewBall` function is identical to the earlier one, as illustrated in the following code snippet:

```
private void NewBall(Vector3 position)
 {
    GameObject ball = objectPooler.GetPooledObject();
    if (ball != null)
 {
    ball.transform.position = position;
    ball.transform.rotation = Quaternion.identity;

    Rigidbody rb = ball.GetComponent<Rigidbody>();
    rb.velocity = Vector3.zero;
    rb.angularVelocity = Vector3.zero;

    ball.SetActive(true);
 }
}
```

Save the script. Back in Unity, we need to specify the drop point. For now, let's place it at a height of 10 meters, above the center of the play space just slightly in front (0.2 meters). We'll mark this location with an empty GameObject and then assign it to the script's `dropPoint`, as follows:

1. Create an empty child object of **XR Rig** named `Drop Point` by right-clicking **XR Rig** | **Create Empty**
2. Reset its transform by clicking **Transform** | right-click | **Reset**)
3. Set its **Position** to `0, 10, 0.2`
4. Drag this **Drop Point** onto the **Ball Game Controller** | **Ball Game** | **Drop Point** slot

Try it in VR. Press **Play** and look up. When a ball drops, let it hit your face and bounce off. *Haha!* It's a little hard to know when a new ball has been released, so let's add sound effects to indicate when a ball is dropped.

Adding sound effects

There are a lot of very good sound effect assets on the Unity Asset Store (`https://assetstore.unity.com/?category=audioorderBy=1`) and elsewhere on the web, many of them free. I pretty much picked one randomly for this project: **Free SFX Pack** by Olivier Girardot. Feel free to find and use your own favorites. If you want to use them, follow the steps given next:

1. Click the link to open the asset in your browser (`https://assetstore.unity.com/packages/audio/sound-fx/free-sound-effects-pack-155776`)
2. Click **Add To My Assets**, then **Open In Unity**; then, in Unity Package Manager, click **Download**, and then **Import**
3. And then, in the **Import Unity Package** window, press **Import** to add them to your project

To add an audio clip to the ball game controller, follow the steps given next:

1. Add an **Audio Source** to the `Ball Game Controller` by selecting **Component | Audio | Audio Source**
2. Uncheck its **Play On Awake** checkbox as we'll be playing it via a script
3. Add the **Audio Clip** of a shooting sound named `Cannon impact 9` (drag it onto the **Audio Clip** field, or use the **doughnut-icon** to find it)

When there's an **Audio Source**, you also must have an **Audio Listener** in the scene for it to play through the VR headset speakers. Ordinarily, this component is on the **Main Camera**. Use the following steps to add an **Audio Listener** to the camera and use it in the `BallGame` script, as follows:

1. Select the **Main Camera** in **Hierarchy** (child of **XR Rig**)
2. If there is no **Audio Listener**, add one by selecting **Component | Audio | Audio Listener**
3. Now, in the `BallGame` script, tell it to play the sound when the ball drops. Add a variable for the `AudioSource` and initialize it in `Start`, as follows:

```
private AudioSource soundEffect;

void Start()
{
    objectPooler = GetComponent<ObjectPooler>();
    soundEffect = GetComponent<AudioSource>();
}
```

4. Then, in `NewBall`, also play the sound when a new ball is served, as follows:

```
private void NewBall(Vector3 position)
 {
    GameObject ball = objectPooler.GetPooledObject();
    if (ball != null)
   {
      ball.transform.position = position;
      ball.transform.rotation = Quaternion.identity;
      ball.GetComponent<Rigidbody>().velocity = Vector3.zero;
      ball.SetActive(true);
      soundEffect.Play();
   }
 }
```

5. Ready? Press **Play**.

When you hear the ball, look up and aim the angle of your face to direct the bounce of the ball. *COOOL!* Next, we'll set up a target so that you can try your aim where the ball goes.

Hitting the target

For our target, we'll create a flattened cylinder out in front of the player on the ground. Perform the following steps:

1. Create a **Cylinder** named `Target` by clicking **Game Object** | **3D Object** | **Cylinder**
2. Set its **Scale** to (`3`, `0.1`, `3`) and **Position** at (`0`, `0.2`, `2.5`)
3. Make it blue, using an existing material (for example, **Blue Material** from `Chapter 2`, *Understanding Unity, Content, and Scale*) or create a new one by clicking **Assets** | **Create** | **Material**; set its **Base Map** | **Color** to a blue color, and then drag the material onto the **Target**

Note that, by default, a **Cylinder** has a capsule-shaped collider (hemispheres on the top and bottom) that would put a domed collider on the **Target**. Instead, we should use a mesh that conforms to the cylinder shape. Follow the steps given next:

1. Remove the **Capsule Collider**; then, on the **Capsule Collider**, select its three-dot icon **Remove Component**
2. Then, add a **Mesh Collider** instead by clicking **Component Physics** | **Mesh Collider**

While we're at it, we'll also add an audio clip for when the target is successfully hit, as follows:

1. Add an **Audio Source** component to **Target** by clicking **Component** | **Audio** | **Audio Source**
2. Assign an **Audio Clip** to the **Audio Source** (for example, use the doughnut-icon of the **Audio Clip** slot to open the **Select AudioClip** dialog box, and choose a clip—for example, the clip named `Indiana Jones Punch`
3. Uncheck the **Play On Awake** checkbox
4. Add a new script named `CollisionSound` (**Add Component** | **New Script**) and open it for editing

In the script, add the following code. As you can see, we include the `OnColliderEnter` function that will get called when another collider hits this **Target** object. The following function will play the `hitSoundEffect` audio clip:

```
public class CollisionSound : MonoBehaviour
 {
    private AudioSource hitSoundEffect;

    private void Start()
   {
     hitSoundEffect = GetComponent<AudioSource>();
    }

   private void OnCollisionEnter(Collision collision)
  {
     hitSoundEffect.Play();
  }
}
```

Try it in VR. It's a VR game! The following screenshot shows the scene with the first person's colliders and a ball bouncing off the cube-head toward the target:

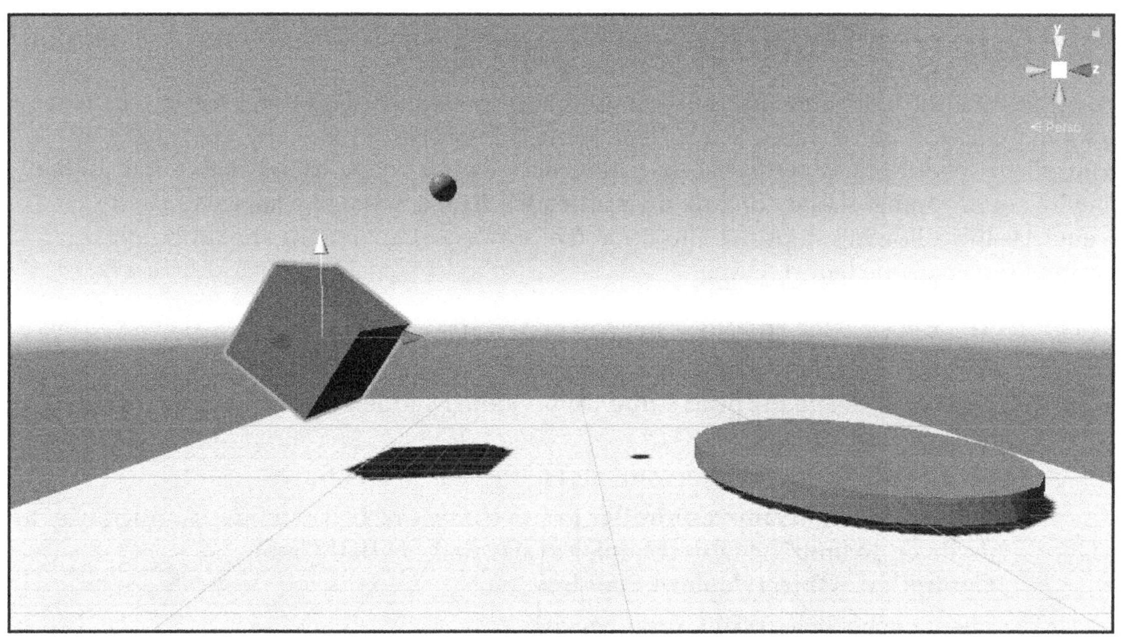

That's our headshot game. To build this game, we added a box collider (**Cube**) as a child of the **Main Camera** so that it tracks with the player's head. We created a `BallGame` script that serves balls from a fixed position above the player and plays a sound effect when a new ball is dropped. The player tries to deflect the ball at the target. If the ball hits the target (`OnColliderEnter`), a different sound clip is played.

Extra challenges: Here are some other ideas to continue building out this game. Keep score. Provide an aiming reticle. Add a backboard. Add other features to make the game more challenging, such as varying the fire interval or increasing the initial ball velocity.

For the next iteration of the game, let's get our hands involved, hitting balls with a paddle instead of your head.

Building a Paddleball game

To build a paddle ball game that lets you use hand-controlled paddles for hitting the ball, we'll make simple game paddles from geometric primitives, parented by the hand controllers in your player rig. Let's serve the balls a little further out in front of you so that they're not dropping directly on top of your head, which is more reachable. To set up the scene, use the following steps to build upon the previous one, moving the drop point and limiting serves to one ball at a time:

1. You can save the current scene with a new name, `Scene-09-Paddleball`, by clicking **File** | **Save As**
2. Disable or delete the head **Cube** we previously added as a child of the **Main Camera**, if present
3. Modify the **Drop Point** forward and to the side at **Position** (`0.6, 10, 0.6`)
4. Modify the **Ball Game Controller** to serve only one ball at a time. A quick way to do this is to limit the **Object Pooler** to size one. Set **Ball Game Controller** | **Object Pooler** | **Pool Size** | `1`
5. Then, uncheck the **Will Grow** checkbox

Next, we will create a paddle prefab that attaches to the hand controller.

Creating a hand paddle

To create a paddle, we'll construct a very simple model using cylinders. First, let's create the handle by following the steps given next:

1. Create an empty **GameObject** named `Paddle` (**GameObject** | **Create Empty**) and reset its **Transform**
2. Create a child cylinder object (right-click | **3D Object** | **Cylinder**) and name it `Handle`
3. Set the **Scale** of the `Handle` object to (`0.02`, `0.1`, `0.02`)

Next, create the paddle pad from another cylinder. Follow the steps given next:

1. Create another **Cylinder** as a sibling of **Handle**, and name it `Pad`
2. Set the **Scale** of the `Pad` cylinder to (`0.2`, `0.005`, `0.2`), **Rotation** (`90`, `0`, `0`), and **Position** (`0`, `0.2`, `0`)

3. In your **Project** `Materials` folder, create a new material named `Paddle Material` from **Assets** | **Create** | **Material**
4. Give the material **Base Map** a wooden color, such as (`110`, `85`, `40`)
5. Then, drag the material onto the **Handle** and **Pad** objects

Now, modify the colliders to a flat collider on the pad only by following the steps given next:

1. Select the **Handle**, and delete its **Capsule Collider**
2. Select the **Pad**, and delete its **Capsule Collider**
3. With **Pad** selected, add a **Box Collider** from **Component** | **Physics** | **Box Collider**

Save the paddle as a prefab, as follows:

1. Drag the **Paddle** into your **Project** `Prefabs` folder
2. Delete the **Paddle** from your **Hierarchy**

We want to parent the **Paddle** to your hands. Let's assume you want to use the right hand. In `Chapter 5`, *Interacting with Your Hands*, we learned how to grab an interactable object (in that case, it was a Balloon Gun). To simplify things here, we'll instead use the **XR Controller** | **Model Prefab** (and remove the default **XR Ray Interactor**). To do that, follow the steps given next:

1. Select the **RightHand Controller** (child of **XR Rig**)
2. Remove the following components: **XR Ray Interactor**, **XR Interactor Line Visual**, and **Line Renderer** via the three-dot-icon | **Remove Component**
3. Drag the **Paddle** prefab from the **Project** window onto the **RightHand Controller** | **XR Controller** | **Model Prefab** slot

If you press **Play** now, you should have a paddle in your right hand. The position and orientation of the paddle may feel awkward in your hand. We can refine this by providing an attach point. An **attach point** is defined with an empty child GameObject whose Transform provides a relative position where the paddle is attached to the hand. Follow the steps given next:

1. Add an empty `GameObject` child of **RightHand Controller** named `Paddle Attach` by right-clicking | **Create Empty**
2. Set its **Rotation** to (`20, 90, 90`)

3. Select the **RightHand Controller** in **Hierarchy**, and drag the **Paddle Attach** object onto the **XR Controller | Model Transform** slot

   Now, when you press **Play**, if you examine the **Hierarchy**, you can see that the **Paddle** has been instantiated as a child of the **Paddle Attach**, as shown in the following screenshot:

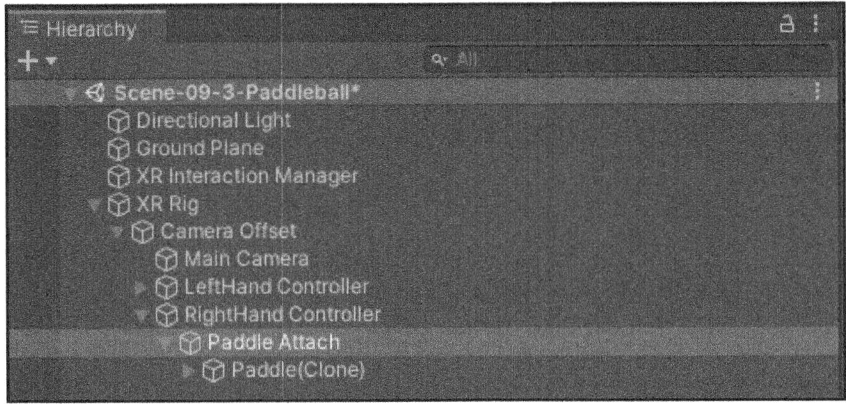

With the current settings, I suggest trying to just deflect the ball like with a shield rather than quickly swatting at it. When the ball and/or paddle are moving "too" fast, no collisions may be detected. There are various things you can do to improve collision detection. One is to use **Continuous** detection (**Rigidbody | Collision Detection**) that we've set on the ball's **Rigidbody** earlier. Likewise, we're using a primitive (non-mesh) box collider on the paddle. Another is to modify the **Fixed Timestep** (**Edit | Project Settings | Time | Fixed Timestep**) to make the physics check for collisions more frequently. The default is 0.02 or 50 **frames per second** (**FPS**). Try changing to 0.01 or even 0.001 (1,000 FPS). Of course, this is a computationally expensive global project setting and should be used prudently.

One important lesson in this project is the use of attach points for defining relative positions for specific behaviors. These are empty GameObjects where all we're interested in is its **Transform** to mark a relative. The object itself is not rendered in the scene. We used a **Drop Point** to mark the X, Z position where balls are dropped from. We used an **Attach Point** to mark the relative position and rotation of the paddle in your hand. We could have added a **Grip Point** to the paddle itself to specify its relative origin. Attach points can also be used to attach guns and swords to the hand correctly after being picked up, for example.

In summary, in this paddle ball game, we have a paddle with a collider as our XR hand-controller model. We drop a ball from above the player and they try to hit it with the paddle, into the target. The following screenshot is of me playing the game:

For the next version of this project, we'll take the game to a new level and shoot balls toward the player instead of dropping them from above.

Building a shooter ball game

For the next iteration of the game, we'll shoot balls toward the player, and you have to hit them at a target on a wall. Not a lot of changes are required to make this version work. It shows how you can take an existing mechanic and turn it on its side (both literally and figuratively). Follow the steps given next:

1. Save the current scene with a new name, `Scene-09-Shooterball`, by selecting **File** | **Save As**
2. We're going to replace the control script, so remove the **Ball Game** component from the **Ball Game Controller** by right-clicking | **Delete**)
3. Also, **Delete** the **Drop Point** object child of **XR Rig**

Next, we'll make a shooter wall with the target on it. Then, we'll change the controller script to shoot balls at the player rather than dropping them from above.

Making a shooter wall

To begin, let's make a wall and put the target on it, as follows:

1. In the **Hierarchy** root, create an **Empty** game object named `TargetWall` from **GameObject** | **Create Empty**
2. **Position** it at (`0`, `0`, `5`)
3. Create a child **Cube** and name it `Wall` by right-clicking | **3D Object** | **Cube**
4. Set the **Scale** of the **Wall** object to (`10`, `5`, `0.1`) and **Position** to (`0`, `2.5`, `0`)
5. Create a new **Material** named `Wall Material` from **Assets** | **Create** | **Material** and drag it onto the **Wall** object
6. Set its **Surface Type** to **Transparent**, and its **Base Map** color to (`85`, `60`, `20`, `75`) so that it's a translucent glossy color

Put the target "onto" the wall, as follows:

1. Move the **Target** to a child of `TargetWall`
2. Modify the Target **Transform Scale** to (`1.5`, `0.1`, `1.5`), **Rotation** (`90`, `0`, `0`), and **Position** (`0`, `2.5`, `-0.15`) so that it's smaller and just in front of the wall itself

Next, instead of serving balls by dropping them out of the sky and relying on gravity, we'll shoot balls at you from a source on the wall, as follows:

1. Create a **Sphere** object as a child of **TargetWall**, named `Shooter`, by right-clicking **3D Object** | **Sphere**
2. Set its **Scale** to (`0.5`, `0.5`, `0.5`) and **Position** to (`4`, `2.5`, `-0.25`)
3. Set its **Rotation** to (`0, 180, 0`)
4. Remove its **Sphere Collider** component (three-dot-icon | **Remove Component**)
5. Create a new **Material** named `Shooter Material`, with **Base Map** color (`45`, `22`, `12`, `255`), and drag it onto the **Shooter** object

I had you rotate the shooter 180 degrees so that it is "facing" the player. You can't necessarily see that now, so let's add a gun barrel to the shooter that sticks out its front, like this:

1. Create a **Cylinder** object as a child of **Shooter**, named `Barrel`
2. Set its **Scale** (`0.1`, `0.1`, `0.1`), **Rotation** (`90`, `0`, `0`), and **Position** (`0`, `0`, `0.55`)
3. Remove its **Capsule Collider** component (three-dot-icon | **Remove Component**)
4. Assign it a color material, such as `Red Material`

5. Duplicate the **Shooter** and set the second one's **Position X** to `-4` so that there's one on both sides of the **Target**

Here is a screenshot of the **Scene** view of the **TargetWall** with its shooters:

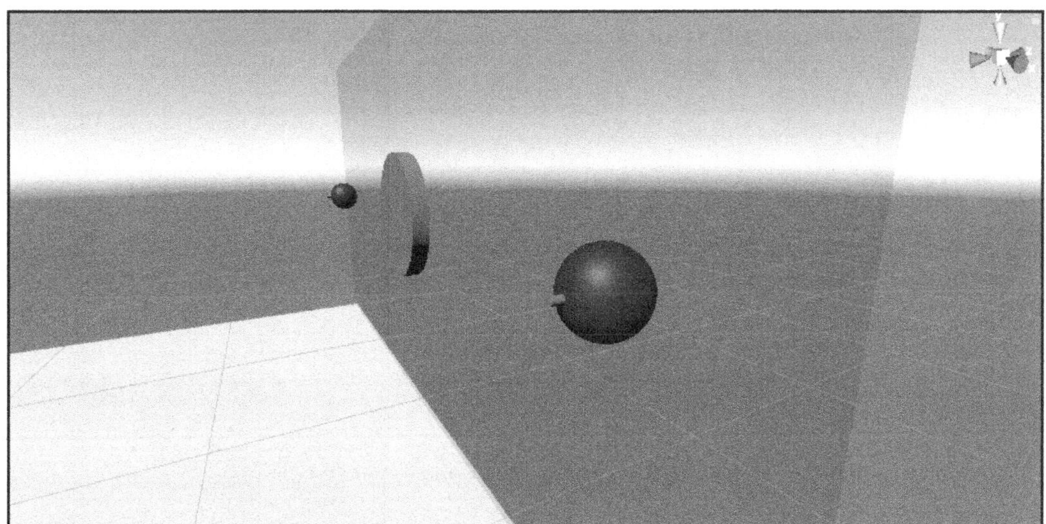

Now, we can fire the balls at the player.

Shooting balls toward the player

The game controller script is similar to the `BallGame` one we have, but sufficiently different that we should create a new script. It'll have **Object Pooler** and new **Shooter Ball Game** components, as follows:

1. On the **Ball Game Controller**, remove the **Ball Game** component (three-dot-icon | **Remove Component**) if it's still present
2. Create a new C# script named `ShooterBallGame` from **Add Component** | **New Script** on the **Ball Game Controller**, and open it for editing
3. Write the `ShooterBallGame` script as follows. We give it two shooters, and the script alternates between them to shoot balls in the direction of a `shootAt` location. It plays a sound each time a ball is shot. First, let's define the public and private variables we will need, as follows:

```
public class ShooterBallGame : MonoBehaviour
{
```

```
        public Transform shootAt;
        public Transform shooter0;
        public Transform shooter1;
        public float speed = 5.0f;
        public float interval = 3.0f;

        private float nextBallTime = 0f;
        private ObjectPooler pool;
        private AudioSource soundEffect;
        private int shooterId;
    }
```

The `Start` function initializes the variable we get at runtime. I've added some additional error checking this time around, as can be seen in the following code block:

```
void Start()
  {
    if (shootAt == null)
      shootAt = Camera.main.transform;

  soundEffect = GetComponent<AudioSource>();
  if (soundEffect == null)
     Debug.LogError("Requires AudioSource component");

   pool = GetComponent<ObjectPooler>();
   if (pool == null)
      Debug.LogError("Requires ObjectPooler component");

   if (shooter0 == null || shooter1 == null)
   Debug.LogError("Requires shooter transforms");

   Time.fixedDeltaTime = 0.001f;
  }
```

Note that because this is a faster action game, I've modified the **Project Time Fixed Timestep** by setting `Time.fixedDeltaTime = 0.001f`. I've done this in a script so that it will not affect other scenes in the project, only when the `ShooterBallGame` is present. (If you've already modified the project setting, **Edit** | **Project Settings** | **Time** | **Fixed Timestep**, you can reset it back to the default `0.02` value now and let the script handle it.)

Now, write the `Update` function that shoots the balls at specified intervals, alternating between the two shooter locations. The `shooterId` variable has the value of either `0` or `1`, indicating which shooter to use next, as illustrated in the following code block:

```
void Update()
 {
    if (Time.time > nextBallTime)
    {
       if (shooterId == 0)
       {
          ShootBall(shooter0);
          shooterId = 1;
       }
       else
       {
          ShootBall(shooter1);
          shooterId = 0;
       }

       nextBallTime = Time.time + interval;
    }
  }
```

Finally, here's the `ShootBall` function, similar to the `NewBall` one we wrote earlier. We get a ball from the `pool` and set its starting `position` as the current shooter. We point the shooter to be aiming directly at the player (`shooter.transform.LookAt(shootAt)`, where `shootAt` is the `Main Camera` transform). Then, we initialize the ball's Rigidbody `velocity` to the shooter's forward direction and ball speed (`shooter.forward * speed`), as illustrated in the following code block:

```
private void ShootBall(Transform shooter)
{
    GameObject ball = pool.GetPooledObject();
    if (ball != null)
    {
        ball.transform.position = shooter.position;
        ball.transform.rotation = Quaternion.identity;

        Rigidbody rb = ball.GetComponent<Rigidbody>();
        rb.angularVelocity = Vector3.zero;
        shooter.transform.LookAt(shootAt);
        rb.velocity = shooter.forward * speed;

        ball.SetActive(true);
```

```
            soundEffect.Play();
        }
    }
```

Back in Unity, we need to populate the public variable slots. To do that, follow the steps given next:

1. With the **Ball Game Controller** game object selected in **Hierarchy**, drag the **Shooter** object (child of **TargetWall**) onto the **Shooter Ball Game | Shooter 0** slot
2. Drag the other **Shooter (1)** object onto the **Shooter Ball Game | Shooter 1** slot
3. In the previous game, we limited the **Object Pooler** to one ball; let's bump that back up to 20 by selecting **Object Pooler | Pool Size | `20`**

   Leave the **Shoot At** slot empty for now so that it will default to the player's live head position. The game controller now looks like this in **Inspector**, including **Object Pooler**, **Shooter Ball Game**, and **Audio Source** components:

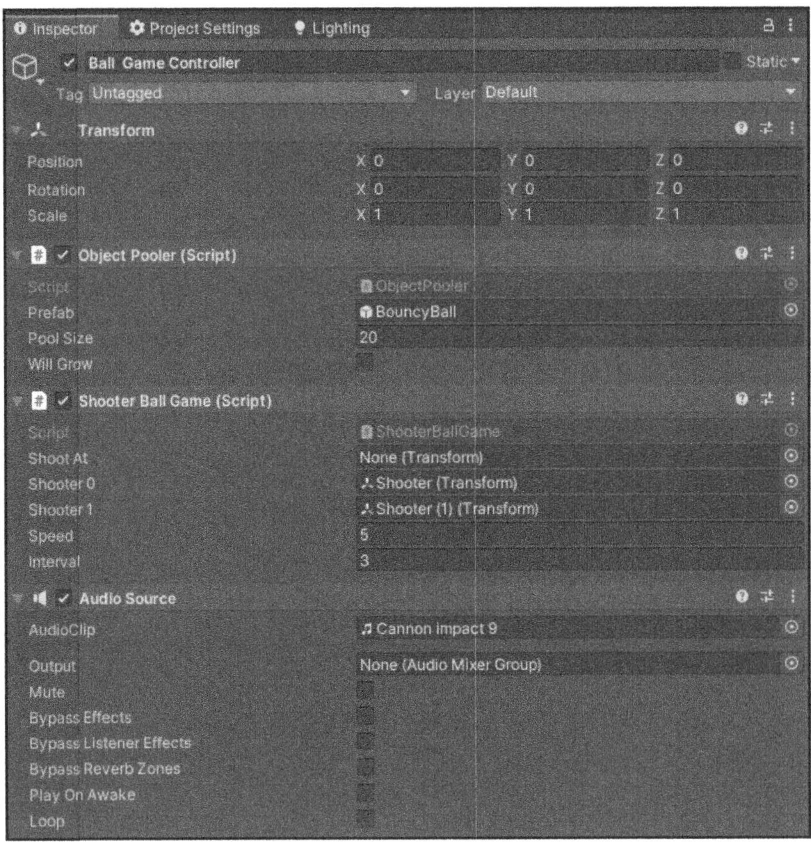

Press **Play**. *Not bad*. But the balls are too big and heavy. Let's create a new ball prefab with different properties.

Improving the ball

The falling bouncy ball feels kind of clunky now, being spat out of the shooter toward the player but dropping quickly to the ground. I think it's the gravity that's pulling it down. Let's fix this by making a new ball prefab with different properties. Follow the steps given next:

1. Open the `BouncyBall` prefab for editing from your **Project** `Prefabs` folder, then double-click the prefab
2. Save it with the name `ShooterBall` from **File** | **Save As** (note that this menu command is repurposed to save the currently open prefab rather than the scene **Hierarchy**)
3. Set its **Scale** to (`0.1`, `0.1`, `0.1`)
4. Uncheck the **Use Gravity** checkbox in its **Rigidbody** component
5. Save your changes by using the **<** icon in the top-left of **Hierarchy**, and select **Save**, to exit **Prefab** edit mode
6. Select `Ball Game Controller` in **Hierarchy**, and drag the **ShooterBall** onto its **Object Pooler** | **Prefab** slot

Now, the object pool will use the new **ShooterBall** game object. Press **Play**. *Oh yeah!* The game is now much more interesting.

We could have tried other things instead of just disabling gravity. Try adjusting the ball's RigidBody **Mass** property. Or, perhaps change the project's **Gravity** so that all falling objects are pulled down less as though you're on the Moon (**Project Settings** | **Physics** | **Gravity** value).

Of course, there's a lot of other things you can do to improve gameplay. For example, try modifying the **Interval** and **Speed** settings of the ball shooter. Some other gameplay ideas may come to mind. You could make a moving target, perhaps in a predictable oscillating motion, or completely random. You could keep score, using `OnCollisionEnter` on the **Target**. You could disqualify bank shots that bounce first on the floor (using `OnCollisionEnter` on the ground plane), and so on. You could also juice up the scene with a more enticing environment. Let's try that next.

Juicing the scene

Having the basic mechanics implemented, we can now *juice it*! First, we'll replace our red bouncy balls with hot fireballs. Then, we'll replace our ground plane and wall with a more graphic 3D artwork skull platform, and we can turn this into a rhythm beat game by synchronizing the balls to music!

The term *juice it* for game design was popularized by Jonasson and Purho in their presentation talk from 2012, *Juice it or lose it—a talk by Martin Jonasson & Petri Purho* (`https://www.youtube.com/watch?v=Fy0aCDmgnxg`). A juicy game feels alive and responds to everything you do, with tons of cascading action and response for minimal user input.

Great balls of fire

Let's change the balls from being red bouncy balls to balls of fire! Instead of mesh geometry, we will use a **Particle System** to render it. There are a lot of ways to get particle effects into your Unity project. If you recall, in `Chapter 4`, *Using Gaze-Based Control* we added a water hose, spark emitter, and explosion effects from the `Unity Standard Assets` package. Here, we'll build our own, but use one of the materials provided with the `ParticleFireCloud` Standard Assets package. In the Unity Asset Store, you can find many offerings of particle effects and system enhancements too.

First, make a new prefab derived from **ShooterBall**, named `FireBall`, as follows:

1. Duplicate the **ShooterBall** prefab and rename the copy to `FireBall` (in the **Project** `Prefabs` folder, select **ShooterBall**, and then **Edit** | **Duplicate**
2. Open **FireBall** for editing (double-click)
3. Disable its **Mesh Renderer** component (uncheck its **Enable** checkbox)—don't remove the component (yet), as we're going to use it for reference
4. Create a child **Particle System** named `Fire Particles` (right-click | **Effects** | **Particle System**)

There are a lot of details in working with particles, many options, and configuration parameters. As we step through this quick implementation of fireballs, observe the effects of each change as we make them one at a time. Note that you can preview the particle effects in the **Scene** window. Feel free to experiment on your own.

Unity now has an alternative to the Particle System called **Visual Effects (VFX) Graph**. Whereas Particle Systems are simulated on the **central processing unit** (**CPU**), the new VFX Graph moves many of the calculations to compute shaders on the **graphics processing unit** (**GPU**). It targets higher-end rendering in particular, using the **High Definition Render Pipeline** (**HDRP**). At the time of writing this, VFX Graph is not available for **Universal Render Pipeline** (**URP**) (but support is planned) and is not covered in this book. Eventually, Particle System will be deprecated and replaced by VFX Graph on all platforms.

As we saw earlier in the book, including in `Chapter 2`, *Understanding Unity, Content, and Scale*, where we first imported the **Standard Assets**, Unity is still in transition to the new **Scriptable Render Pipeline** (**SRP**) and other advancements, while there's a treasure trove of assets available that were developed for older versions of Unity. Some of these assets will automatically be converted when you import them into Unity. Others, such as Materials, can be upgraded to the current project's render pipeline using the **Edit** | **Render Pipeline** menu. In the case of particle materials (at the time of writing) using particle shaders, these do not automatically convert to URP. So, let's do this first ourselves. Follow the steps given next:

1. Duplicate the **ParticleFirecloud** material (**Edit** | **Duplicate**) found in `Assets/Standard Assets/Particle Systems/Materials/` folder, and name it `ParticleFirecloud URP`
2. Drag the **ParticleFirecloud URP** material onto the **Fire Particles** | **Particle System** | **Renderer** | **Material** slot
3. Change its **Shader** to **Universal Render Pipeline / Particles / Unlit**
4. Drag the `ParticleFilecloud.png` texture (found in `Assets/Standard Assets/Particle Systems/Textures/` folder) onto the **Base Map** texture chip (or use the **Base Map** | doughnut-icon to find it)
5. Set its **Surface Type** to **Transparent**
6. Set its **Blending Mode** to **Additive**

Next, modify its **Shape** and **Emission** parameters, as follows:

1. Near the top of the Particle System **Inspector**, find the **Shape** panel, and check to enable it
2. Select **Shape** | **Sphere**, and set its **Radius** to `0.1`
3. Find the **Emission** panel and check to enable it
4. Then, set **Rate of Time** to `15`
5. At the top of the Particle System **Inspector** is the *main panel* with uncategorized parameters—let's set some of these, as follows:
    - **Duration**: `2.00`.
    - **Start Lifetime**: `1`.
    - **Start Speed**: `0`.
    - **Start Size**: `0.5`.

Next, we'll animate the particles, as follows:

1. In the particle system main panel, for **Start Rotation**, click the **selector icon** on the right and choose **Random Between Two Constants**. Then, fill in the values `180` and `-180`.
2. Set the **Start Color** and then select **Gradient** (right-side selector), and then, pick a range of colors such as yellow to red, as shown here:

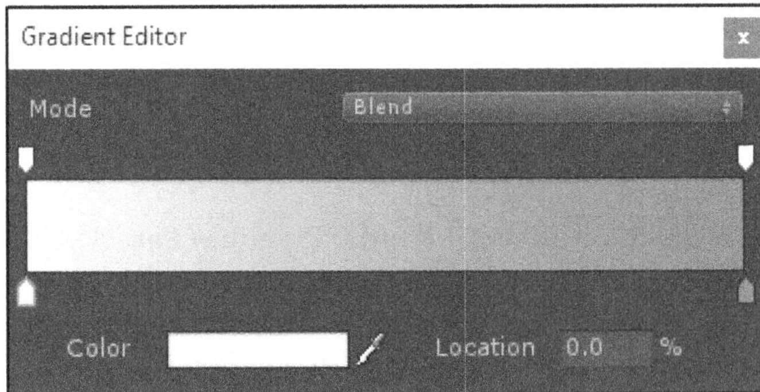

3. Find the **Color Over Lifetime** panel. Check to enable it. Click the slot to open its **Gradient Editor**. We want to adjust the **Alpha** curve so that it starts at **Alpha** `0` at **Location** `0%`, then becomes **Alpha** `255` at `10%`, and then fades out over time back to **Alpha** `0` at `100%`. The editor is shown here:

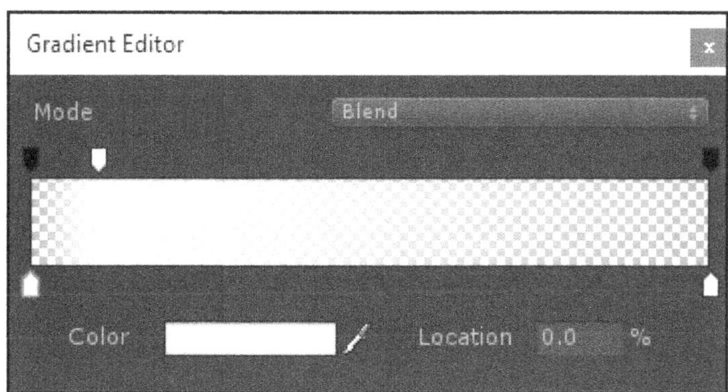

4. Next, set the **Velocity Over Lifetime**—find that panel and check to enable it, using **Random Between Two Constants**. For each **Linear X, Y, Z** value, set min and max values to `-0.05` and `0.05`, respectively.

At this point, we have a really nice-looking fireball, but it's much bigger than our red shooter ball. We should adjust the fireball so that it's about the same size. We can temporarily enable the FireBall's renderer for reference. Follow the steps given next:

1. Re-enable the FireBall's **Mesh Renderer**
2. Adjust the particle system scale—for example, by changing the **Transform** | **Scale** to (`0.2, 0.2, 0.2`)
3. Once you have it right, disable the **Mesh Renderer** again

Complete the setup by telling the **Ball Game Controller** to use this prefab, as follows:

1. **Save** your edits to prefab and return to the scene edit mode (press <)
2. With **Ball Game Controller** selected, drag the **FireBall** prefab from the **Project** window onto the **Object Pooler** | **Prefab** slot

Now, when you press **Play**, the shooters will fire FireBalls. *Oh wow!* Here is a screenshot of the gameplay window paddling an incoming fireball:

Next, we'll work on our level design, using a cool skull platform asset I found on the Asset Store.

Skull environment

To spice up our game even more, we should find a more exciting environment. Searching the Asset Store, I found the *Skull Platform* free asset (`https://assetstore.unity.com/packages/3d/props/skull-platform-105664`). You can use it too, or find something different. Assuming you've found and installed the Skull Platform asset, we'll add it to our scene. (I won't walk you through the import steps, but don't forget to convert the materials to URP using **Edit | Render Pipeline | Universal Render Pipeline | Upgrade Project Materials to UWP**.) First, let's render our target as a skull, as follows:

1. Drag **Platform_Skull_01** (found in the `Assets/Skull Platform/Prefabs/` folder) as a child of **Target** (under `TargetWall`)
2. Set its **Transform Rotation** (`0, 0, 180`) and **Scale** (`0.3, 0.3, 0.3`)
3. Select the **Target** and disable its **Mesh Renderer**

Let's illuminate the target more dramatically. Follow the steps given next:

1. Create a new **Spotlight** as a child of **Target** by right-clicking | **Light** | **Spotlight** to shine on the skull.
2. I used the following settings: **Position** (0, `-12`, `1`), **Rotation** (`-40`, `180`, `180`), **Range**: `4`, **Color**: `#FFE5D4`, and **Intensity**: `3`.
3. **Indirect Multiplier** is not supported in URP, so set it to `0`.

Next, let's add the big platform as a backdrop instead of the ground plane. The quickest way is to merge in the **Demoscene** they provide. We do this by temporarily having two scenes open, ours and theirs, so that we can move the things we want from theirs, then remove their scene. Use the following steps to move the objects we want from the Platform demo scene into our own game:

1. Create an **Empty** game object in the **Hierarchy** root, name it `SkullPlatform`, and **Reset** its **Transform**.
2. Drag a copy of the Skull Platform's demo scene named **Platform** (`Assets/Skull Platform/Demo/` folder) into the **Hierarchy.** We now have two scenes open, ours and theirs.
3. Select the Demo's **Scene**, **Lighting**, and **Particles** objects and drag them as children of **SkullPlatform**.
4. Now that we have the assets we want, we can remove their scene altogether. (Right-click the **Platform** scene in **Hierarchy** and choose **Remove Scene**. When prompted, choose **Don't Save**.)
5. Set the **SkullPlatform Position** to (`0`, `-1.5`, `0`) so that it's just below the ground plane.
6. Select the **GroundPlane** and disable its **Mesh Renderer**.

Now, we'll set up the scene environment lighting. Follow the steps given next:

1. Delete the **Directional Light** from the scene **Hierarchy**.
2. Open the **Lighting** window. If it's not already a tab in your editor, use the **Window** | **Rendering** | **Lighting** | **Environment** tab and dock it next to the **Inspector**.
3. Set its **Skybox Material** to **Sky** (provided in the Skull Platform package).
4. Set **Environmental Lighting** to **Color**, then section, set **Ambient Color** to RGB `(20, 20, 20)`.
5. Go even further and check the **Fog** checkbox (in **Other Settings**), with **Color RGB** to (`20, 20, 20`), **Mode: Exponential**, and **Density** to `0.03`.

Here is a screenshot of the scene with the skull platform environment and lighting. *Sweet!*

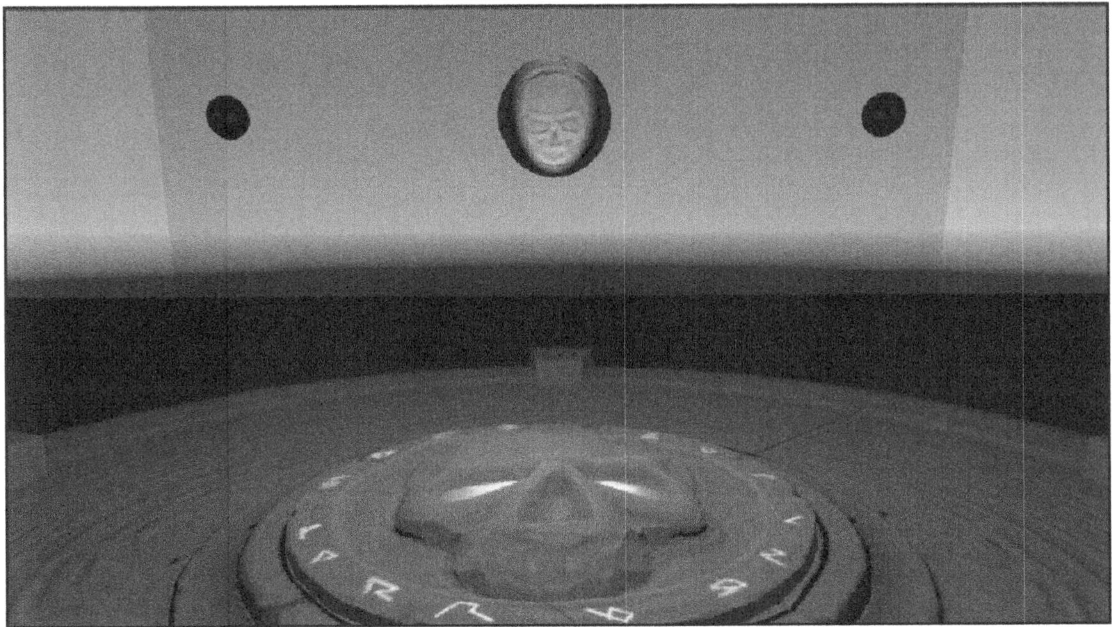

When you press **Play**, it's exactly the same game we had before but it feels a whole lot cooler, don't you think? Let's add one more feature to shoot the fireballs at you much faster and synchronize this to the beat of some heavy dance music.

Audio synchronization

Many popular VR rhythm games, such as Audio Shield and Beat Saber, synchronize the projectiles coming toward you to the beat of the music. How can we add that to our game? One method is to compose a timeline manually that maps the music timings to projectiles (and other artifacts) that you'll experience playing a specific song. Beat Saber, for example, has its own Beat Saber Level Editor that opens a music file (OGG or WAV) and lets you create a Beatmap and content within its graphical editor. Then, you save your composition to a data file. When you launch the song in Beat Saber, it uses the Beatmap file to play the game. You could also do this directly in Unity using the **Timeline** window (we work with Timelines in `Chapter 12`, *Animation and VR Storytelling*).

For this project, we'll do this procedurally, using code that "listens" to your music and detects beats in the song at runtime, triggering a new fireball on each beat. Unity provides an API for sampling audio source data, including `AudioSource.GetSpectrumData` and `GetOutputData`. Extracting actual beats in the music from this data is not trivial and requires a lot of math and some understanding of how music encoding works. Fortunately, we found an open source script that does this for us, called **Unity-Beat-Detection** (`https://github.com/allanpichardo/Unity-Beat-Detection`). It conveniently provides Unity Events for `onBeat` events, which we'll use. (It also provides `onSpectrum` events, with music frequency bands per frame, which you could use too—for example, to change the color of the fireball or other things based on frequency bands, such as a music visualizer.) Proceed as follows:

1. Download the `AudioProcessor.cs` script from GitHub (`https://raw.githubusercontent.com/allanpichardo/Unity-Beat-Detection/master/AudioProcessor.cs`) or refer to the copy we've provided with the files for this book for your convenience.
2. Drag the file into your **Project** `Assets/Scripts` folder.
3. For your music, find any MP3 or WAV file that has a nice beat, and import it into your project.

   We looked on SoundCloud NoCopyrightSounds track (`https://soundcloud.com/nocopyrightsounds/tracks`) to find one named *Third Prototype - Dancefloor* (`http://ncs.io/DancefloorNS`).

4. In the **Project** window, create a folder named `Audio`.
5. Import your music into Unity by dragging the audio file into the **Project** window `Assets/Audio/` folder (or use **Assets** | **Import New Asset**).

To implement this feature, we'll make a **MusicController** and then modify the `ShooterBallGame` script to use its beats to fireballs. In Unity, do the following:

1. In **Hierarchy**, create an **Empty** game object and name it `MusicController`.
2. Add the **AudioProcessor** script as a component.
3. Note that it automatically adds an **Audio Source** component too.
4. Drag your imported music file onto the **Audio Source** | **AudioClip** slot.

5. Drag **MusicController** itself onto the **Audio Processor | Audio Source** slot.

Note the **G Threshold** parameter on **Audio Processor** can adjust the sensitivity of the beat-recognition algorithm.

6. Now, update the `ShooterBallGame` script on `Ball Game Controller` as follows. Add the following two lines to the `Start` function, which adds a listener to the `processor.onBeat` event:

```
AudioProcessor processor = FindObjectOfType<AudioProcessor>();
processor.onBeat.AddListener(OnBeatDetected);
```

7. Then, we will replace the `Update` function with the `OnBeatDetected` function. That is, instead of using a timer to decide when to shoot a new fireball in `Update`, we shoot one based on the beat events. Also, we'll randomly decide to shoot from either the left or right shooter location. **Delete (or comment out) the entire** `Update` **function**. Then, add this code:

```
void OnBeatDetected()
{
    if (Random.value < 0.5f)
    {
       ShootBall(shooter0);
    }
    else
    {
       ShootBall(shooter1);
    }
}
```

Press **Play** and go at it! *Whoohoo,* we have our own version of Audio Shield! A screenshot of active gameplay is shown here:

In this final version of the project in this chapter, we made some major improvements by focusing beyond the basic game mechanics (launch a ball, hit the ball, aim for the target). We first replaced the simple red bouncy ball with a fireball, using the Unity Particle System. Then, we replaced the simple level environment with an interesting 3D Skull Platform asset found on the Asset Store. Lastly, we improved the game mechanics by synchronizing the fireballs to rhythmic beats of music, using an open source script that analyzes the music source as it's playing at runtime.

Summary

In our journey through this chapter, we experienced software development as an iterative process, changing, reworking, and improving our game multiple times. Some changes were big, while others were small. We built games that use the Unity Physics Engine and other features.

First, we explained in layman's terms the relationship between Rigidbody, Colliders, and Physic Materials, and explored how the physics engine uses these to determine the velocity and collision of objects in the scene. Then, we considered the life cycle of game objects and implemented an object pooler that helps avoid memory fragmentation and GC, which can lead to performance problems and VR discomfort.

Using what we learned, we implemented several variations of a ball game, first aiming for a target with your head, and then using hand paddles. We modified the game so that, instead of serving balls from above, using gravity, we shoot them from in front and apply a velocity vector. Lastly, we juiced up our game, changing the bouncy balls into fireballs, adding a cool level environment, and synchronizing the fireballs to music beats. In the end, we have a good start to making our own version of a music rhythm-beat VR game.

In the next chapter, we will see another, more practical example of a virtual interactive space. We are going to build an interactive art gallery space that you can move through and query the artwork for information and details.

10
Exploring Interactive Spaces

Successful **virtual reality** (**VR**) applications put the player into a believable place and allow them to explore and interact with objects in the environment. In this chapter, we'll explore the creation of an interactive space and introduce some new development topics, including level design, 3D modeling, and data management, to implement an interactive space you can experience in VR. The scene is a photo art gallery where you can showcase your own photos. We'll design a simple floor plan that your visitors can move around via teleportation.

You will learn how to use ProBuilder, Unity's built-in level design package, to create an architectural space, including extruding shapes to make walls, doors, and windows. You will also learn about data management using lists, data structures, and scriptable objects. In addition, you will gain more experience with lighting, materials, interaction, and teleportation components. By the end of the chapter, you'll have built a completed interactive art gallery where your visitors can explore your favorite images.

In this chapter, we are going to discuss the following topics:

- Using ProBuilder in Unity to construct a simplistic art gallery building
- Interacting with objects and metadata
- Data structures, lists, and scriptable objects
- Using teleportation

Technical requirements

To implement the projects and exercises in this chapter, you will need the following:

- A PC or Mac with Unity 2019.4 LTS or later, an XR plugin for your device, and the XR interaction toolkit package installed
- A VR headset supported by the Unity XR platform

You can access or clone the GitHub repository for this book (`https://github.com/PacktPublishing/Unity-2020-Virtual-Reality-Projects-3rd-Edition-`) to optionally use assets and completed projects for this chapter, as follows:

- Asset files for you to use in this chapter are located in `UVRP3Files/Chapter-10-Files.zip`.
- All completed projects in this book can be found in a single Unity project at `UVRP3Projects`.
- The completed assets and scenes for this chapter can be found in the `UVRP3Projects/Assets/_UVRP3Assets/Chapter10/` folder.

Using ProBuilder and ProGrids

For this project, we're going to design an interactive art gallery. We just need a simple, small art gallery exhibit room, about 24 x 36 feet. The room is so simple, in fact, that it could easily be built within Unity using 3D cube primitives, but we'll take this opportunity to introduce you to the **ProBuilder** package included with Unity. If you prefer, you can skip this section and build the floor and walls using Unity cubes. Or, you could use the `GalleryBuilding.obj` file provided in the files for this chapter.

ProBuilder is a package of tools that allow you to build, edit, and texture geometry within Unity. It's intended to be used for in-scene level design, prototyping, and playtesting. In this project, we'll use ProBuilder just enough to get you started, along with the tools of its companion, ProGrids. Keep in mind that there's a lot more to it than will be covered in this chapter. For more information on **ProBuilder**, **ProGrids**, and **Polybrush** (introduced in `Chapter 4`, *Using Gaze-Based Control*), also check out the documentation and tutorials, including the following:

- *ProBuilder package documentation*—`https://docs.unity3d.com/Packages/com.unity.probuilder@latest/manual/overview.html`
- *Unity at GDC—Rapid worldbuilding with ProBuilder* video (March 29, 2018)—`https://www.youtube.com/watch?v=7k-81UEluyg`
- *Unity Blog—ProBuilder joins Unity offering integrated in-editor Advanced Level Design* (February 15, 2018)—`https://blogs.unity3d.com/2018/02/15/probuilder-joins-unity-offering-integrated-in-editor-advanced-level-design/`

In this project, we will limit our use to a few ProBuilder features, including creating shapes, extruding and moving faces, creating and bridging edges, and snapping to a grid. The first step is to install the ProBuilder and ProGrids packages using the following steps:

1. Open the **Package Manager** window by selecting **Window | Package Manager**.
2. Ensure the filter dropdown in the upper-left corner of the window is set to **All**.
3. Locate the package by typing `Pro` in the search field.
4. Install ProBuilder by selecting **ProBuilder** from the list of packages, and then click **Install**.
5. Also, install the **Samples** package for your render pipeline. Assuming you're using **Universal Render Pipeline** (**URP**) in this project, on the **Universal Render Pipeline Support** item, click **Import into Project**.
6. Install **ProGrids** by selecting **ProGrids** from the list of packages, and then click **Install**.

Before using the tools for our project, let's take a quick tour of the editor interface for ProGrids and ProBuilder.

Using the ProGrids editor interface

Back in `Chapter 2`, *Understanding Unity, Content, and Scale*, I introduced the Unity **Scene** editor window, including the use of its built-in grid-snapping tools. ProGrids is an advanced version of this feature available in a separate package. Once installed (as per the preceding instructions), open the ProGrids window using **Tools** | **ProGrids** | **ProGrids Window**, and a new toolbar is added to the **Scene** window, on the left-hand side of the window, as shown in the following screenshot:

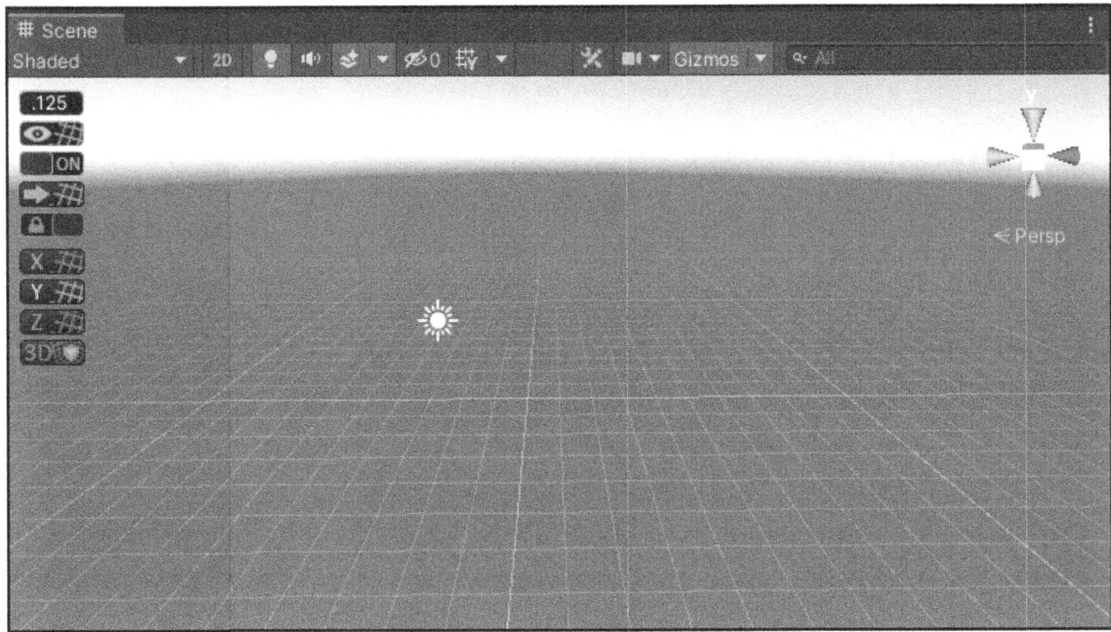

These ProGrids interface icons, from top to bottom, perform the following functions:

- **Snap Size**—sets the size of the grid's snapping increment (default: 0.125 meters)
- **Grid Visibility**—toggles show/hide gridlines in the **Scene** view
- **Snapping Enabled**—switches on/off the snap-to-grid behavior
- **Push to Grid**—snaps all selected objects to the grid
- **Lock Grid**—locks the perspective grid in place
- **Set Grid Planes**—lets you choose to display grids for a single axis (**X**, **Y**, **Z**), or all three at once (**3D**).

Grid snapping operates on the transform of the object currently being edited. You can modify snap settings, including the snap size, and enable/disable snapping while you edit. You can set the grid visibility, including showing/hiding the gridlines, locking the grid in place, and choosing on which axis plane to show the grid. We will learn to use them as we go along in this chapter. To remind you what each icon does, simply hover the mouse over it to get a tooltip. Also, each of these has a keyboard shortcut, details of which can be found here: `https://docs.unity3d.com/Packages/com.unity.progrids@latest/manual/hotkeys.html`.

Next, we'll introduce the ProBuilder editor interface.

Using the ProBuilder editor interface

As mentioned, ProBuilder is a package of tools for building, editing, and texturing 3D geometry within Unity. As with any 3D editing tool, ProBuilder can seem complex, especially for those new to 3D editing, since you're operating on 3D objects from a 2D computer screen. However, they've tried to keep things reasonably easy by providing context-sensitive menus and natural integration with the familiar Unity Scene editor tools.

To begin exploring and using ProBuilder, open the window by selecting **Tools | ProBuilder | ProBuilder Window**. This opens the ProBuilder tools window (described further shortly) and a small **Edit Mode Toolbar** inside the **Scene** window, as shown in the following screenshot:

Edit modes define what you are selecting and editing in your scene. In the leftmost position is the **Object** mode—this is the standard Unity edit mode. When you make a selection in **Object** mode, you're selecting the entire object Mesh. The other three icons, in order from left to right, are for **Vertex**, **Edge**, and **Face** edit modes. We'll learn to use these modes as we work through this project.

The basic concept of mesh editing is that an object mesh consists of vertices, edges, and faces. Actually, these are different parts of the same whole object. These are defined as follows:

- A **Vertex** is a point, such as the corner of a cube.
- An **Edge** is a straight edge made by two vertices.
- A **Face** is a flat facet made from three or more edges.
- An **Object** is all of these parts of a mesh.

The four edit modes apply to these four element types that make up an object mesh.

It's important to note that ProBuilder's geometry mesh is differs from the standard Unity mesh because the ProBuilder mesh contains additional metadata required by the ProBuilder tools. So, you cannot edit ordinary Unity objects using ProBuilder tools, such as ones imported from OBJ or **Filmbox** (**FBX**) files. However, you can convert such objects to ProBuilder meshes if required. Likewise, you can export ProBuilder meshes to standard OBJ or other format files for editing in external 3D software, but again, those models will no longer contain the ProBuilder metadata and cannot subsequently be edited using ProBuilder tools in Unity.

Also, when you open the ProBuilder window, the **ProBuilder** tools window is opened, as shown in the following screenshot:

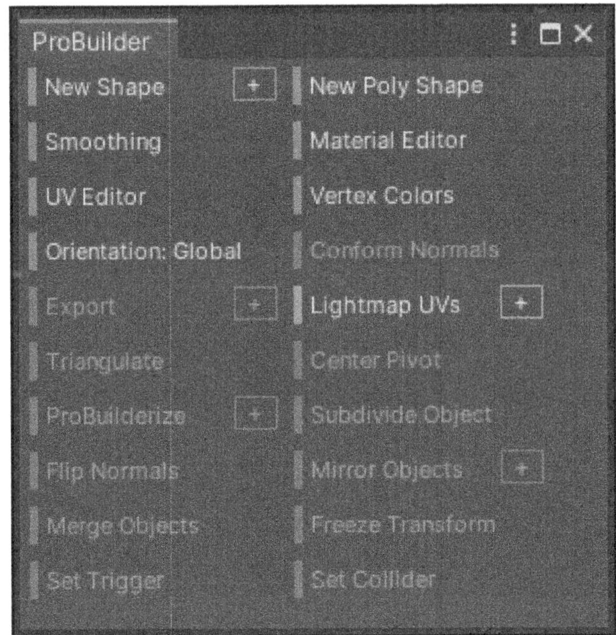

Note that this is a free-floating window that can be resized, and—optionally—docked, as with any window in the Unity Editor layout. You can choose between text and icon display modes, using the three-dot menu in the upper-right corner of the screen. The previous screenshot shows the menu in text mode, and the following screenshot shows it as icons, docked above the **Scene** edit window (throughout this chapter, we'll use Text mode menus for readability):

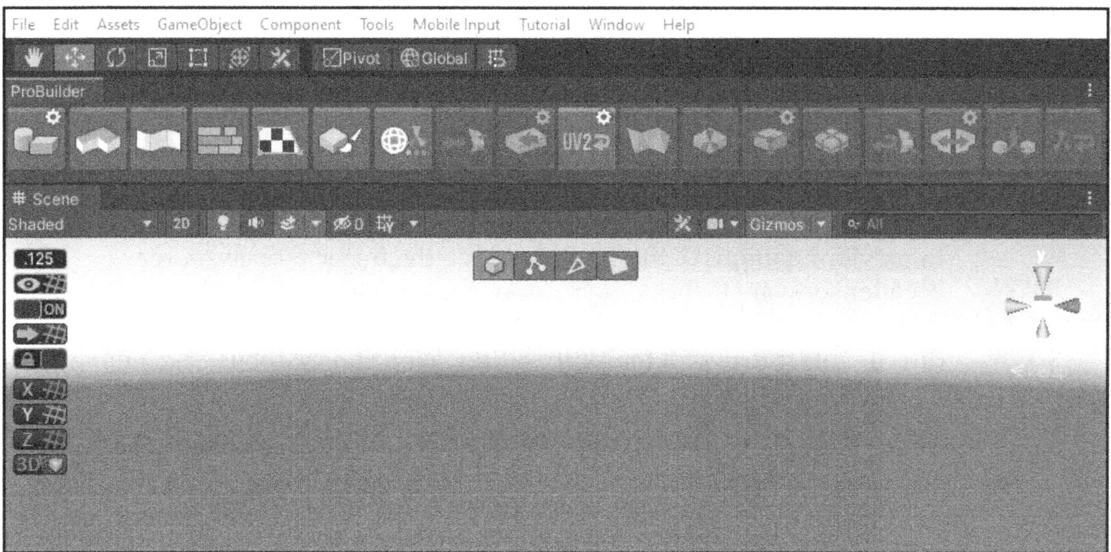

Rather than going through each of the tools now, I'll introduce the ones we need as we use them in this chapter. Each tool has a tooltip; simply hover over the item to show the tooltip after a short delay, or use *Shift* + *hover* to see the tips immediately. The tooltip also shows the keyboard shortcut for picking the tool, which can make your workflow more efficient than repeatedly mousing back to the toolbar each time you need to change tools.

Some of the tools require a ProBuilder mesh element to be selected; otherwise, the tool is grayed out. Some tools are useful only for specific mesh element types and edit modes (Face, Edge, Vertex). The ProBuilder menu will show only the current relevant menu tools and hide the others.

Many tools have tool-specific options. You may notice that the text mode view uses a **+** icon to open the options panel, while the icon view uses a *gear* icon for the same. Or, you can **alt-click** (**option-click** on a Mac) to see the options window for a given tool.

Lastly, ProBuilder has a rich offering of settings available in the project **Preferences** window, found by selecting **Edit** | **Preferences** | **ProBuilder**. We won't go into them here, but feel free to explore these settings and read more at `https://docs.unity3d.com/Packages/com.unity.probuilder@latest/index.html`.

ProBuilder, combined with ProGrids, provides a powerful extension to the Unity Editor for creating and editing geometry, especially architectural structures and scene environments. Given this brief introduction, we can now begin building our art gallery.

Constructing the art gallery building

For this project, we are first going to construct an art gallery building to display artwork and provide a space for the user to interact. If you'd like to skip this topic, you can use the prebuilt `GalleryBuilding.obj` file included with the downloadable files for this project. If you'd like to make the building from scratch using ProBuilder, continue with this section.

In previous editions of this book, we used the free and open source **Blender** software (`https://www.blender.org/`) to construct the art gallery building. Since then, Unity acquired ProBuilder, and these tools are now directly integrated with the Unity Editor. While not as robust as Blender, ProBuilder provides the tools we need for this project.

To begin, I've drawn a simple floor plan on an 11" x 8.5" piece of graph paper and scanned with a desktop scanner (`gallery-floorplan.png`). Each square of the graph paper is a one-foot scale. It's just a rectangular room with two entrances, and interior walls to display artwork, as shown in the following screenshot:

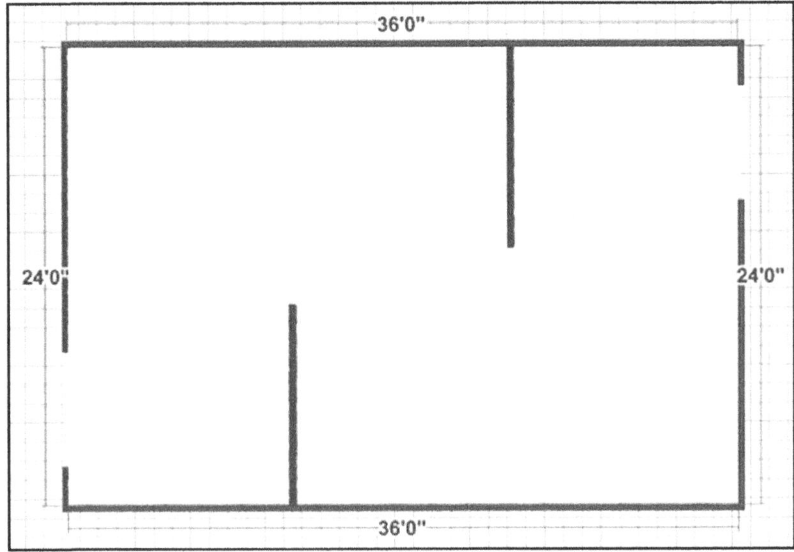

To build the gallery, we'll add this sketch to the scene as a reference image. Then, we'll draw the walls, including perimeter and interior walls, and create a ceiling with a skylight while learning and using the basic features of ProBuilder.

Using a floor plan sketch

The first step is to optionally add the floor plan sketch to the scene, temporarily, as a visual reference for our construction process. To add the sketch image to the scene, create a 3D Quad on the `Y=0` plane, and a material using the image as a texture. First, let's import the image and create a material as follows:

1. Create a new scene by selecting **File** | **New Scene**.
2. Save it to a new file by clicking **File** | **Save As**, and name it `Scene-10-1-Gallery`.
3. Import the `gallery-floorplan.png` image file by dragging it from your system explorer into the **Project Assets** `Textures/` folder (or use **Assets** | **Import New Asset...**).
4. Create a new Material with this image texture. In your **Project** `Materials/` folder, use the "+" **button** | **Material** and name it `Floorplan Material`.
5. Set the Material to use an Unlit shader by selecting **Shader** | **Universal Render Pipeline** | **Unlit**.
6. Drag the `gallery-floorplan` texture from the **Project** window onto the **Floorplan Material** | **Surface Inputs** | **Base Map** chip (left of the label).
7. Make it semi-transparent by setting **Surface Type** | **Transparent**, and set its **Base Map** color to white (`#FFFFFF`) with **Alpha** `128`.

Now, add a Quad plane with the correct scale. We'll set it up so the top-left corner of the paper is at the world space origin, and we'll scale it so one square on the paper (one foot) is scaled in meters (Unity's units). The calculation is as follows: the landscape width of the paper is 11 inches, and contains 42 squares; each square corresponds to one foot, so the paper is 42' wide or 12.8 meters. Thus, we need to scale the 11-unit Quad by 1.164 times (that is, 12.8 m / 11" = 1.164). Perform the following steps:

1. Add an empty GameObject at the origin using **GameObject** | **Create Empty**, and rename it `Floorplan`.
2. Then, reset its transform (**Transform** | **right-click** | **Reset**).
3. As a child of **Floorplan**, add a Quad using **GameObject** | **3D** | **Quad**.
4. Transform the quad to lay flat on the **Y** plane with its upper-left set **Scale** (`11, 8.5, 1`), **Rotation** (`90, 0, 0`), and **Position** (`5.5, 0, -4.25`).
5. Select its parent **Floorplan** and set its **Scale** to (`1.164, 1.164, 1.164`).
6. Drag the **Floorplan Material** from the **Project** window onto the **Floorplan** GameObject.

The resulting **Scene** and **Hierarchy** is shown in the following screenshot, viewing the scene from the top using an isometric view (to achieve this view, click the green **Y** cone on the view gizmo in the upper-right corner of the **Scene** window, and click the gizmo's **white-square** to switch to **Iso** view mode):

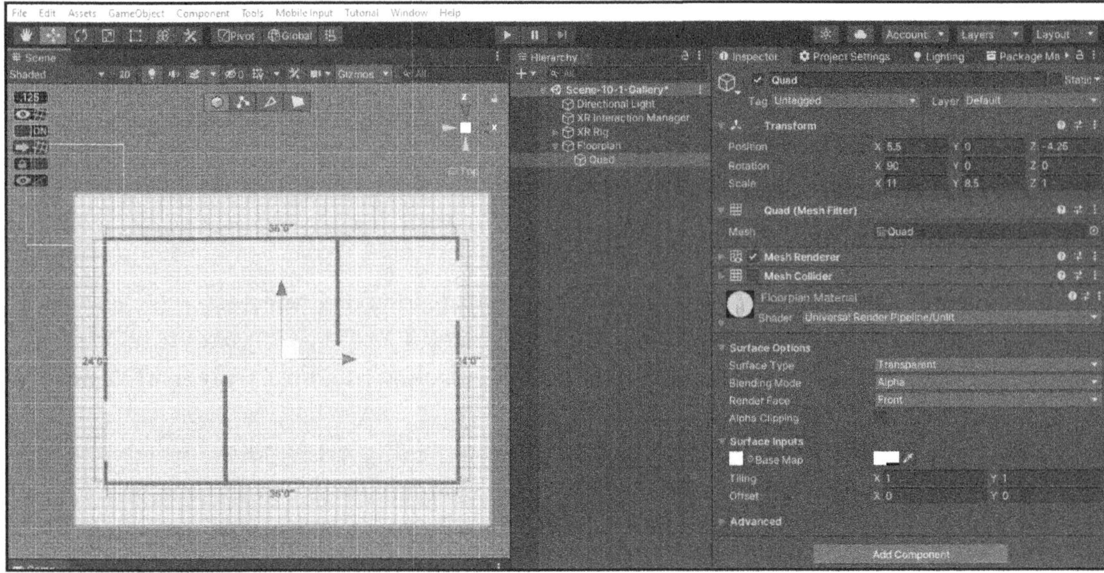

Please note that while we're trying to be precise, this sketch is just a guide. Unity is not an architectural design software and, certainly, our scanned hand-drawn paper sketch is not an engineering drawing. But it will be fine for our purposes.

Now, we can jump into ProBuilder and create a floor, before adding the walls and ceiling.

Creating the floor

We'll create a floor from a ProBuilder cube object. First, please make sure you have the **Scene** view and tools set up the same as mine, as shown in the preceding screen capture, including the following:

- Top-down scene view—if not set, click the green **Y** axis cone on the viewing gizmo in the upper-right corner of the **Scene** window.
- In the ProGrids toolbar, **Snap Increment** is set to `.125`, the **Guidelines** are visible, and **Snapping** is on.

We'll make the floor foundation larger than the perimeter walls, creating a terrace structure around the outside of the building. For now, we'll make it 15 by 12 meters. Follow the steps given next to create a floor:

1. Create an empty GameObject with **+** | **Create Empty**, naming it `Gallery Building`, and resetting its transform using right-click | **Reset**.
2. In the ProBuilder menu window, open the **Shape Tool** options window, using the **+** button on the **New Shape** item (or gear icon if you're in **Icon View** mode).
3. Ensure that the **Shape Selector** dropdown is set to **Cube**.
4. Set the **Shape Settings** | **Size** to (`15, 0.1, 12`).
5. Press **Build** to create the object in the scene.
6. Rename the new Cube object in **Hierarchy** to `Floor`, and ensure that it's a child of **Gallery Building**.
7. Position the **Floor** at the origin so its *top face* is exactly at `Y=0` level, by setting **Position** (`0, -0.05, 0`).
8. To make sure the **Floorplan** sketch is still visible, raise the `Floorplan` game object a bit to **Position** (`0, 0.1, 0`).

The **Shape Tool** window settings we used are shown in the following screenshot:

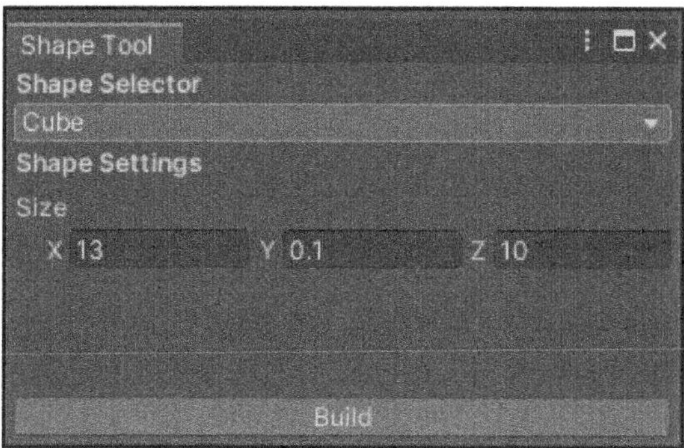

We can change the color of the floor to help distinguish it from the walls using the ProBuilder **Vertex Colors** feature. This may be temporary, as you can assign an actual material later. Follow the steps given here:

1. Select the **Floor** option in the **Hierarchy** window.
2. Choose **Vertex Colors** from the ProBuilder menu to open the **Vertex Colors** window.
3. Using one of the default colors such as orange, press **Apply**, as illustrated in the following screenshot:

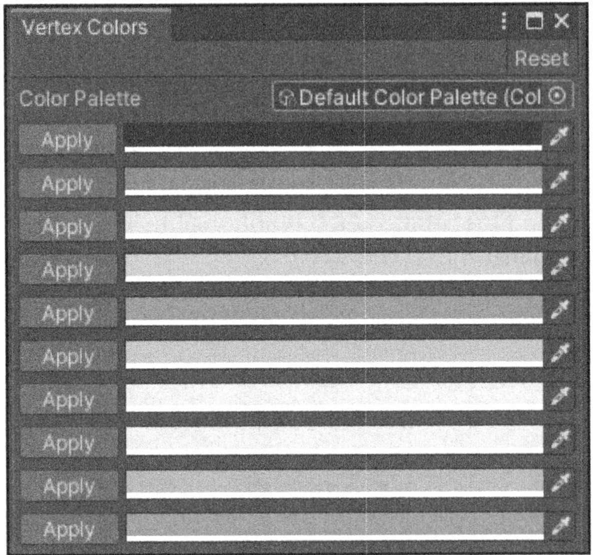

Gridbox Prototype Materials is a free asset from Ciathyza in the Asset Store that contains lightweight grid materials for prototyping scenes with ProBuilder. Refer to `https://assetstore.unity.com/packages/2d/textures-materials/gridbox-prototype-materials-129127`.

The resulting scene is shown in the following screenshot, with both the **Floor** and the **Floorplan** visible:

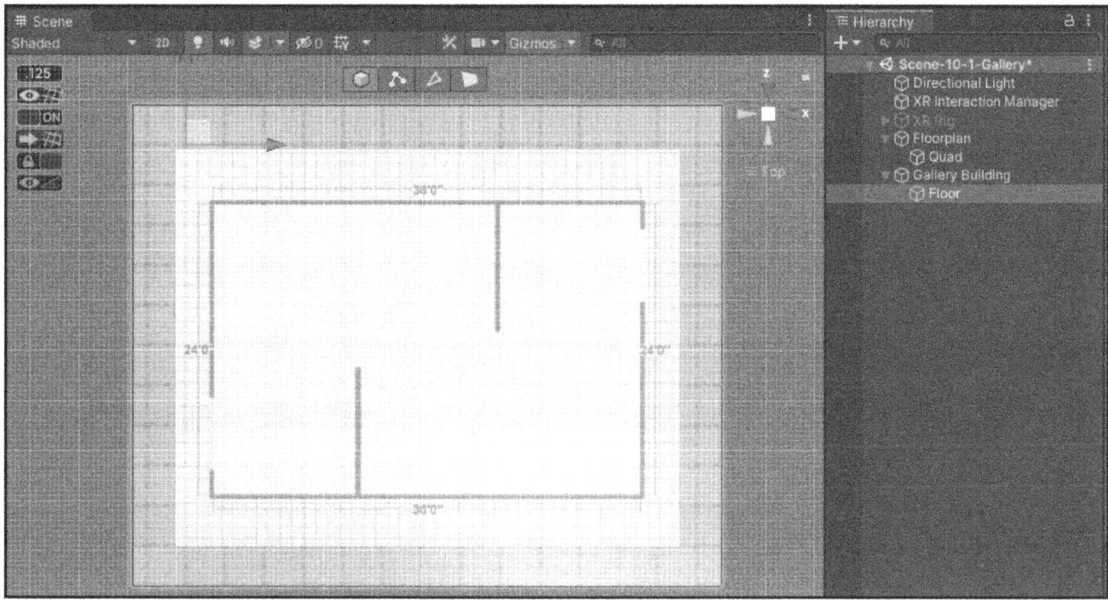

Now, we can move on to creating each of the walls by inserting a cuboid shape and extruding it along the perimeter.

Creating the walls

There are several ways to create perimeter walls with ProBuilder. We'll use a technique to create the north-side wall first. Then, we'll cut a post in the corner by inserting an edge loop and extrude it for the eastern wall, and repeat this process for the other two walls, creating the four perimeter walls. We'll use a similar process for the inner walls, and then punch holes for the doorways.

To assist our work, let's turn on the **Dimensions Overlay** cues by selecting **Tools** | **ProBuilder** | **Dimensions Overlay** | **Show**. As we work, the dimensions of the objects we're editing will be shown in the **Scene** window. Also, if our floor plan sketch is hidden, elevate it slightly—for example, changing the **Position** of **Floorplan** to (`0, 0.1, 0`).

Let's now create the north wall, sized 11 meters wide and 3 meters tall, using the **Shape Tool**. We'll set the wall thickness the same as our **Snap Size**, `0.125`, as follows:

1. Open the **Shape Tool** window, using the **+** button on the **New Shape** item.
2. Set **Shape Selector** | **Cube**.
3. Set **Shape Settings** | **Size** to (`11, 3, 0.125`).
4. Press **Build**.
5. Rename the new object `Walls`.
6. Ensure **Walls** is a child of **Gallery Building** in **Hierarchy**.
7. Set the wall's **Position** to (`0.875, 0, -1.25`).

The following screenshot shows a perspective view in the **Scene** window of this northern wall of the building:

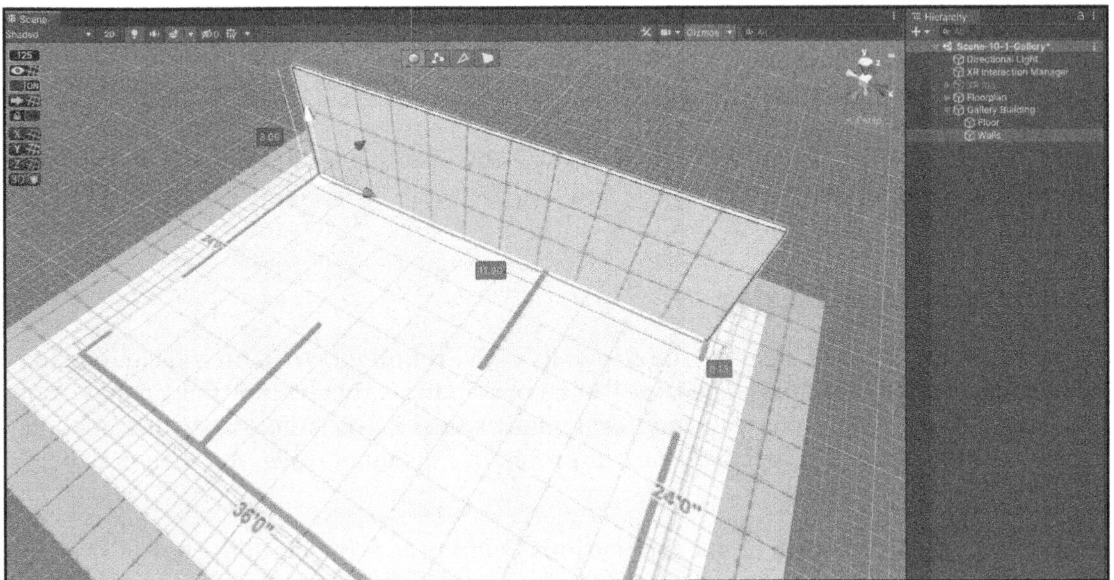

For the east wall along the right of the building, we'll make an edge loop the thickness of the walls (0.125 m) and extrude it in the **-Z** direction, using the following steps:

1. With the **Walls** object selected, in the ProBuilder edit mode toolbar, select the **Edge Selection** tool (second icon from the right).
2. Select the horizontal edge facing you at the top of the wall.

3. In the ProBuilder menu window, choose **Insert Edge Loop**. This creates an edge loop on the wall.
4. On the edge loop in the **Scene** window, grab the red **X** axis move cone and slide it toward the right side, leaving a 0.125 m band on the wall, as shown in the following screenshot:

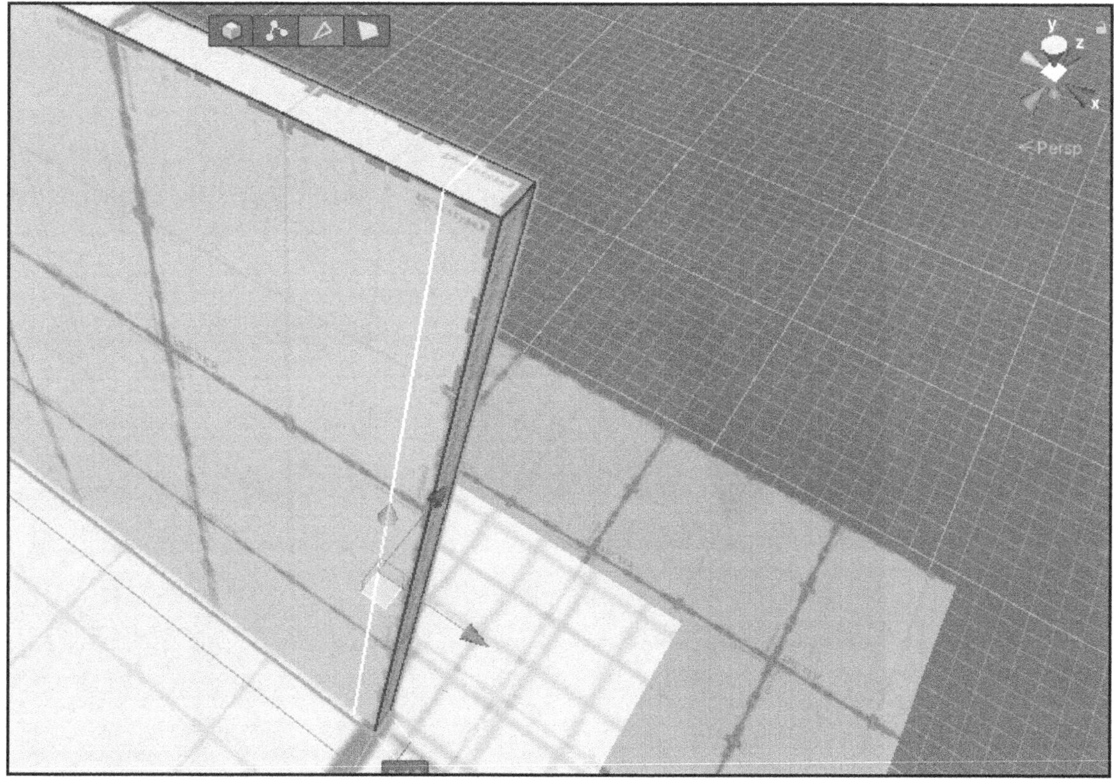

Next, we'll switch into **Face Selection** mode and select the south-facing narrow face, extruding it to the south-east corner of the building, using the following steps:

1. On the ProBuilder edit mode toolbar, choose the **Face Selection** tool (last icon on the right).
2. Select the south-facing narrow face on the wall.

3. Extrude the face by pressing *Shift* + *click* on the blue **Z** axis move cone, and drag it toward the south-east corner, as shown in the following screenshot:

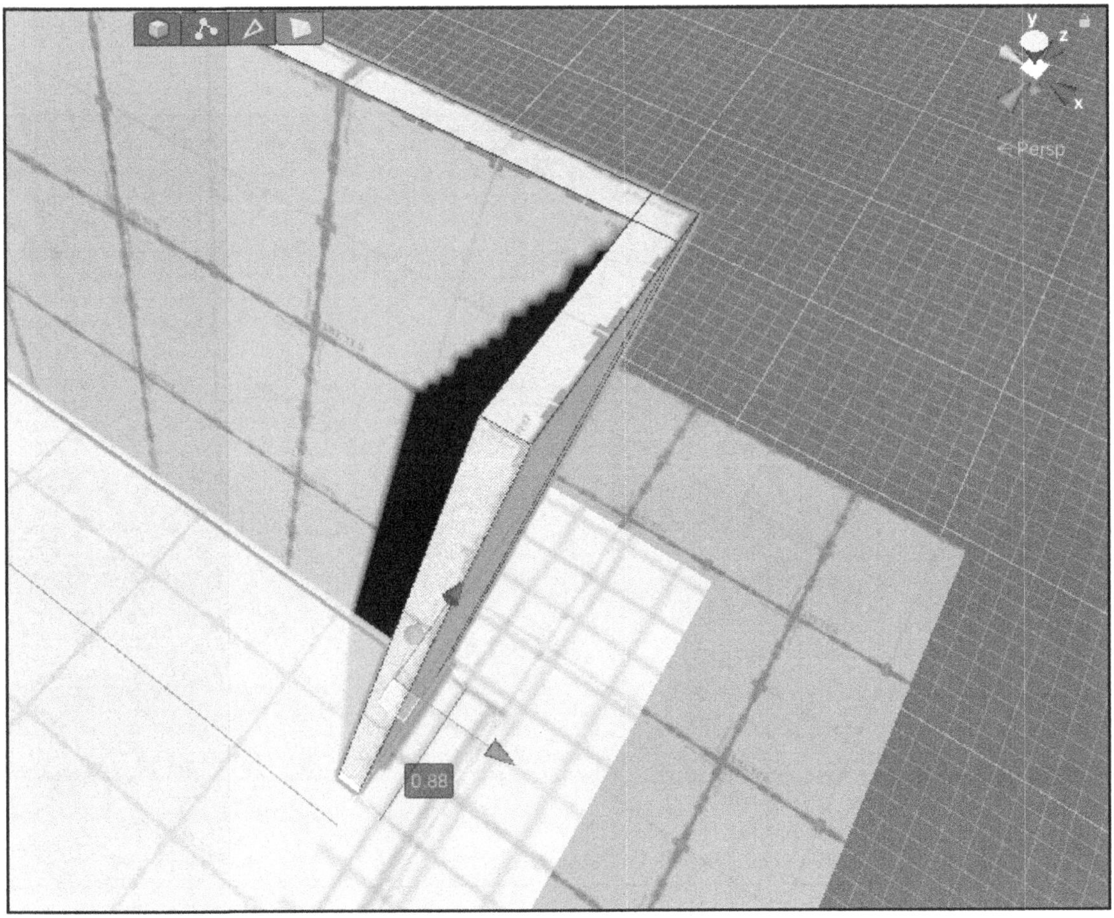

The process of **extrusion** extends the shape by adding additional parts and pieces to the geometry. In **Face Selection** mode, for example, when you *Shift* + *click* and drag to extrude a face, you are adding a new part to the mesh. Conversely, when you click and drag (not pressing *Shift*) to move a face, you are modifying the position of that element but not adding new ones to the object.

After releasing the mouse click, you can adjust the wall by continuing to click the **Z** axis and move the cone to the corner, as shown in the following screenshot:

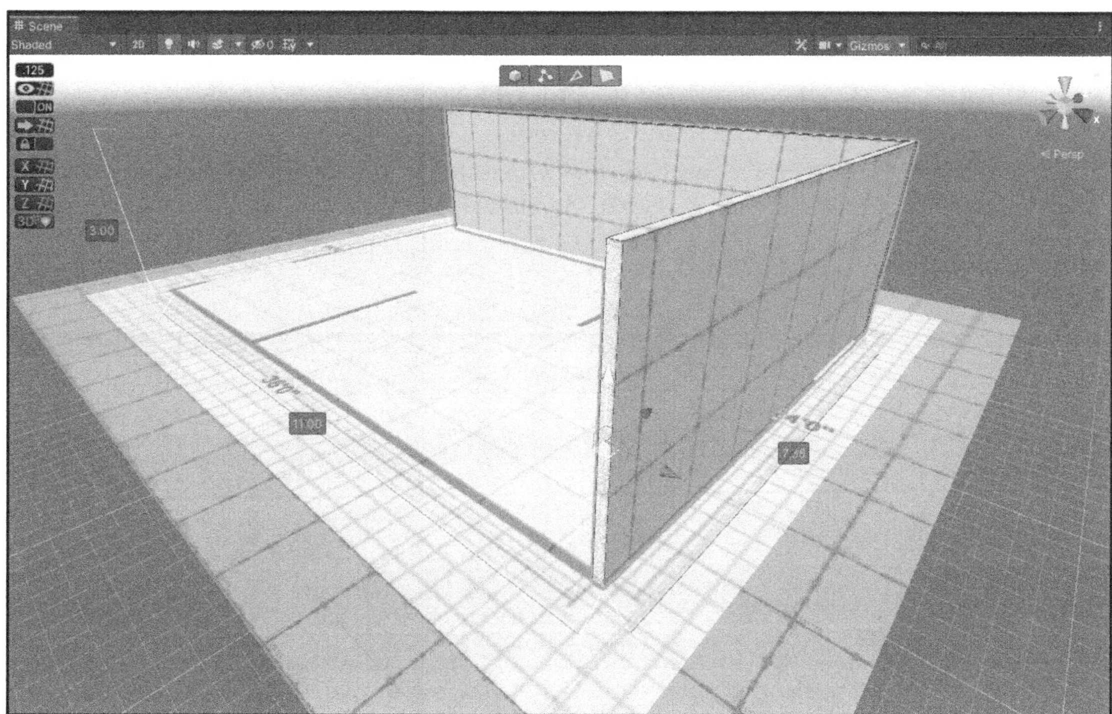

Now, repeat these steps to create the other two walls, as follows:

1. On the ProBuilder edit mode toolbar, choose the **Edge Selection** tool (second icon from the right), and then select a top edge of the east wall.
2. From the ProBuilder menu, choose **Insert Edge Loop**.
3. Then, slide the loop to the south corner, leaving a `0.125` band.
4. Choose the **Face Selection** tool (last icon on the right).
5. Select the west-facing narrow face on the wall.
6. Extrude the face by *Shift* + *clicking* on the red **X** axis move cone, and drag it toward the south-west corner.
7. Unclick, and then continue adjusting the wall by clicking the **Z** axis move cone to the corner.
8. Repeat to draw the western wall, connecting to the northern one and completing the enclosure.

Drawing the interior walls is a very similar process, as follows:

1. Choose the **Edge Selection** tool, and then select a top edge of one of the long walls.
2. Select **Insert Edge Loop** and slide the loop into position for the interior wall.
3. Select the top edge again, and then **Insert Edge Loop**, and slide the edge to make the interior wall face 0.125 units wide.
4. Choose the **Face Selection** tool, select the interior wall face, and then *Shift* + *click* the blue **Z** axis move cone to extrude the wall toward the interior of the room.
5. Repeat these steps for the opposite interior wall. The result can be seen in the following screenshot:

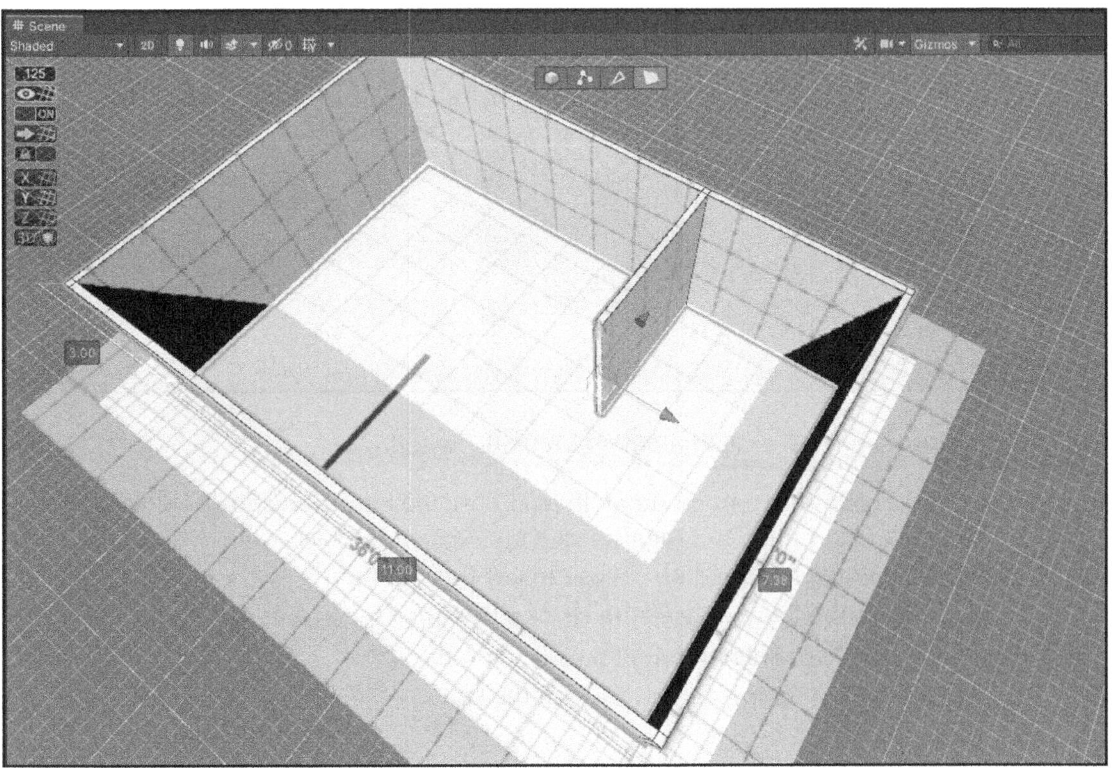

We now have a floor and walls (both perimeter and interior ones). At present, there's no way to get in or out of the room! Let's add some openings for entrances in the next section.

Making holes for entrances

The entrances on either side of the room are indicated on the sketch drawing as gaps in the walls. We'll use this as a guide to decide where to create ours. There's more than one way to accomplish this. We're going to use Edge Loops again to make new faces for the entrance area, delete them, and then connect the edges of the door frame. To do that, follow these steps:

1. Choose **Edge Selection** mode from the edit mode toolbar.
2. Choose a horizontal edge at the top of the wall.
3. Select **Insert Edge Loop**, and drag it into position for one side of the entrance.
4. Repeat *steps 1-3* for the other side of the entrance.
5. Choose **Face Selection Mode** from the **Scene** toolbar.
6. Select the outward-facing face of the entrance, and press *Backspace* to delete it.

You might think we're done because you can see through the wall into the room. But the inner-facing side of this wall is still present; it's just not rendered when you're looking from its behind. Let's remove that now, as follows:

1. Rotate your scene view so that you're looking at the inside of the wall. The wall entrance is solid again.
2. Select the inner-facing face of the entrance and press *Backspace* to delete it too.

While editing in ProBuilder selection modes, the *Backspace* keyboard key will delete the selected element. Beware: the *Delete* key will delete the entire object, as is standard in Unity. If you hit *Delete* by mistake, use *Ctrl + Z* to undo.

There's one more step to observe. If you examine the door frame, you'll notice there are no faces. We need to add them, as follows:

1. Choose **Edge Selection** mode.
2. *Shift + click* to multi-select both inner and outer edges of the left side of the entrance.
3. Select **Bridge Edges** from the ProBuilder menu to create a new face bridging these edges.

4. Repeat *steps 1-3* for the right side of the doorframe. The result can be seen in the following screenshot:

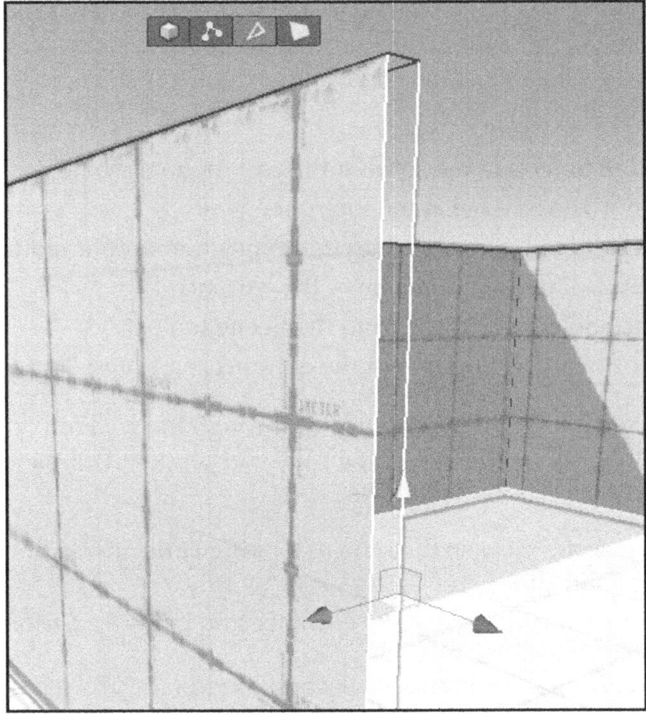

Now, repeat all the steps in this topic for the other entrance on the opposite side of the room. With that done, at this point, you can hide the **Floorplan** sketch image by disabling the **Floorplan** GameObject. The resulting room now looks like this:

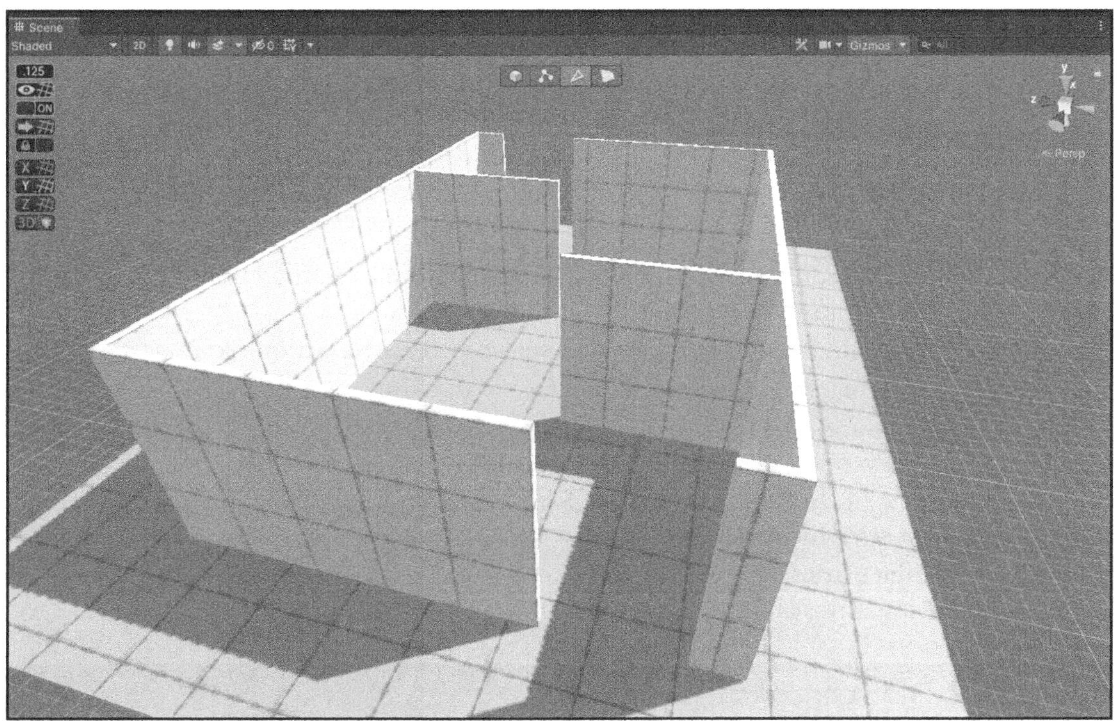

Next, we'll add a roof with a skylight.

Creating a roof and skylight

We'll make a roof from a Cube object, as we've done for the floor and walls. Perform the following steps:

1. In the ProBuilder menu window, open the **Shape Tool** options window, using the **+** button on the **New Shape** item (or gear icon if you're in **Icon View** mode).
2. Ensure the **Shape Selector** dropdown is set to **Cube**.
3. Set the **Shape Settings** | **Size** to (`11, 0.125, 7.375`).
4. Press **Build** to create the object in the scene.
5. Rename the new Cube object in **Hierarchy** to `Roof`, and make sure that it's a child of **Gallery Building**.
6. Position the roof at the origin so its top face is exactly at Y=0 level, by setting **Position** (`0.875, 3,-1.25`).

Before moving the whole object, such as our roof, to a new position, remember to switch the edit mode to **Object Selection** on the ProBuilder edit mode toolbar. **Object Selection** mode is the normal Unity edit mode that lets you operate on the object's transform rather than its mesh.

To make a skylight in the roof, we'll extrude the face using the **Scale Tool**, and then delete the faces and repair the edges as we did for the entrance, as follows:

1. In the standard **Scene** edit toolbar (above the **Scene** window), select the **Scale Tool** (fourth icon from the left).
2. In the ProBuilder edit mode toolbar, select the **Face Selection** tool.
3. In the **Scene** window, select the top face of the **Roof.**
4. Modify your **Scene** view so that you can see inside the building, and press *Shift* + *click* to also select the inside face of the roof.
5. Using the **Scale Tool** gizmo, press *Shift* + *click* on the center of the white square to extrude-scale the roof.
6. Shape the extruded planes as you like, using the scale handles, as shown in the following screenshot:

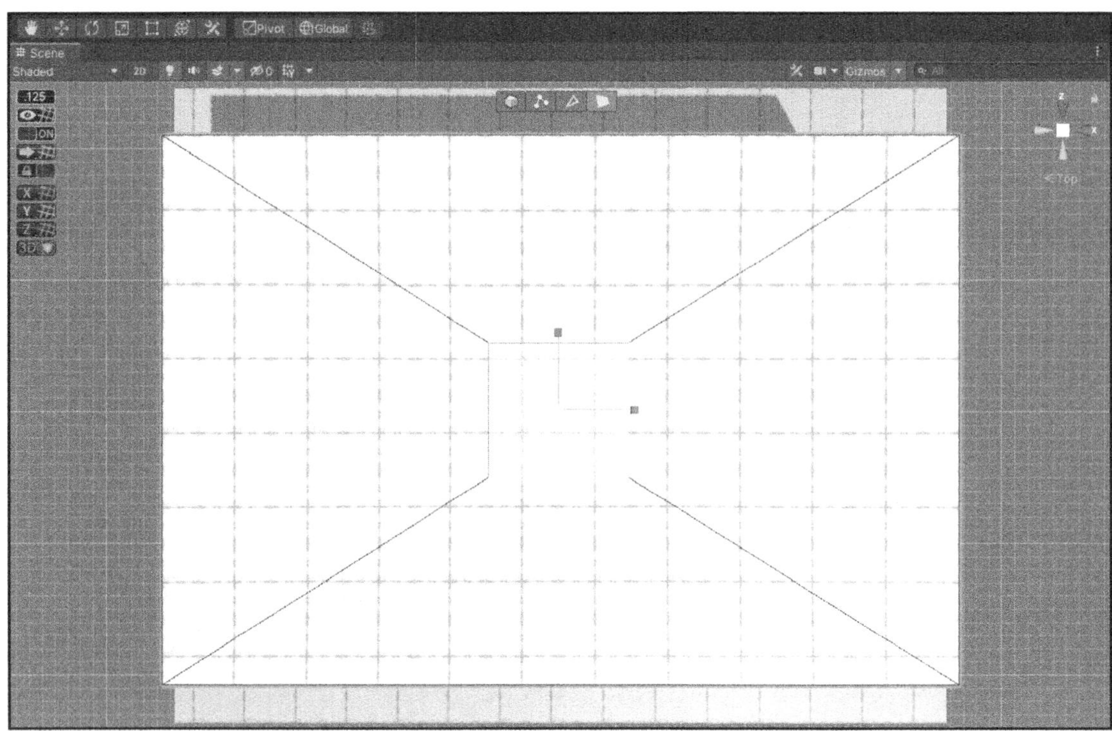

Then, position this extruded face where you want the skylight to be, as follows:

1. Change the Unity edit tool to the **Move Tool** (first icon on the left of the edit toolbar above the **Scene** window).
2. Move the faces to the position you desire.
3. Double-check from inside the building that the skylight is not on top of an interior wall!
4. Use the *Backspace* key to delete the faces for the skylight.

As we saw with the entrances, deleting the faces has left unconnected edges on the window frame. Use the **Bridge Edges** function to fix this, as follows:

1. Select the **Edge Selection** tool.
2. *Shift* + *click* the two inner and outer edges on one side of the window frame.
3. Select **Bridge Edges** from the ProBuilder menu.
4. Repeat *steps 2* and *3* for the other three sides of the window frame.

If the Scene view looks too dark, you can disable lighting in that window by toggling the lightbulb icon in the **Scene** window toolbar, and/or click **Generate Lighting** in **Window** | **Rendering** | **Lighting window**. Likewise, you can autogenerate the **Lightmaps** checkbox in the **Lighting** settings window—just beware, as this can slow down your workflow as the scene gets more complicated.

The following screenshot shows the art gallery building from the inside, with directional sunlight streaming in through the skylight:

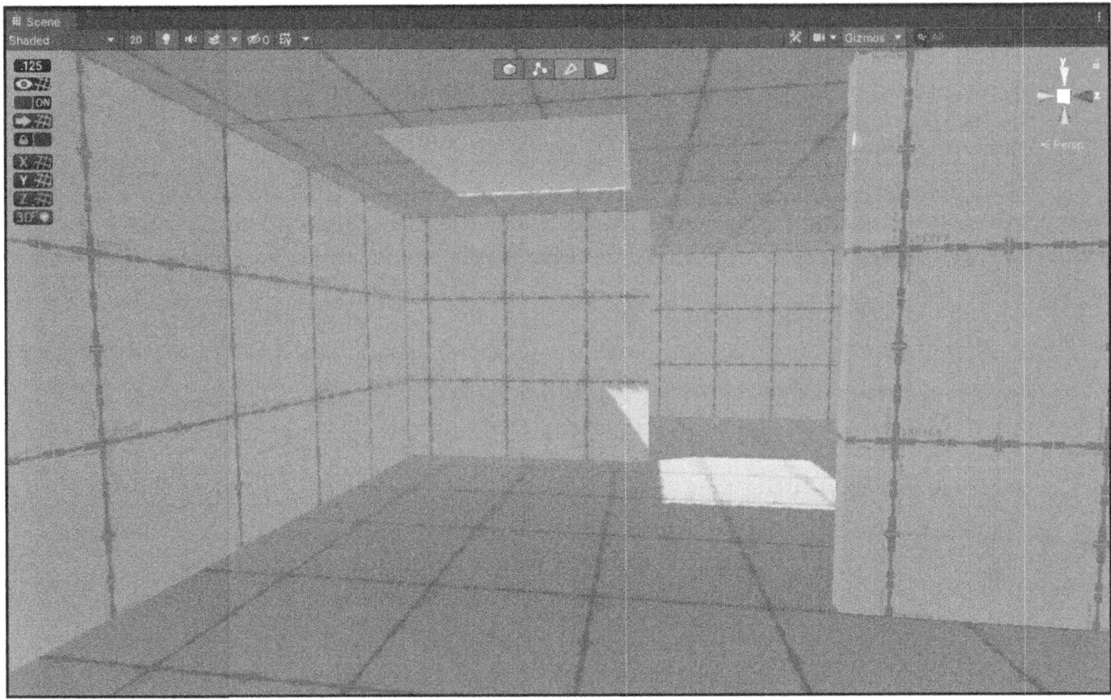

We have completed the construction of our art gallery building. You can save the model as a non-ProBuilder asset using the **Export** function in the ProBuilder menu. To export the floor, walls, and roof into a single file, multi-select the three objects when you export (export as a group, including children objects). An exported `GalleryBuilding.obj` file is included with the files for this project.

Great job! We now have the architectural structure of the room that we'll use for the art gallery, including perimeter walls, interior walls, and a ceiling with a skylight. Now, we can assemble our scene and add the artwork to the gallery.

Assembling the scene

If you've been following along, you now have a scene with the **Gallery Building** object we just created. If not, perform the following steps to create a new scene and import the building model provided with the files for this chapter:

1. Create an empty scene using **File | New Scene**.
2. Save it to a new file, **File | Save As**, and name it `Scene-10-1-Gallery`.
3. Import the `GalleryBuilding.obj` file by dragging it from your system explorer into the **Project** window `Assets` folder, or use the **Assets | Import New Asset...** menu.
4. Drag the **GalleryBuilding** from the **Project** window into the scene **Hierarchy**.
5. Reset its **Transform** by using right-click | **Reset**.

Now, we can set up the scene for VR with an XR camera rig. To do this, follow these steps:

1. Add an XR rig by selecting **GameObject | XR | Stationary XR Rig** (or **Room-Scale XR Rig**, if you prefer).
2. Position the rig at the north-east entrance, setting **Position** (`12, 0, -3`) and **Rotation** (`0, -90, 0`).
3. If your default camera height is on the floor, then, for development, elevate the **XR Rig/Camera Offset** position to (`0, 1.4, 0`).

For this project, I'll use a stationary camera rig. If you prefer to make it room-scale, please read the *Room-scale considerations* topic at the end of this chapter. We can make the gallery room look nicer by applying some **physically-based rendering** (**PBR**) textures next, and then adjust the scene lighting.

Replacing the building materials

We've been using default materials for the building. Let's now improve on that. There are many sources of material textures in the Asset Store and across the internet, both free and for a fee. The textures I am using here have a free-to-distribute license for this book and are from `https://3dtextures.me/`. The texture files are included with the files for this book, or you can download the same from the following links, and then import them into your **Project** `Assets/Textures` folder, as usual:

- Wood floor: `https://3dtextures.me/2018/02/14/wood-floor-007/`
- Plaster walls: `https://3dtextures.me/2019/02/15/plaster-rough-001/`

To begin, create separate materials for each **Floor**, **Walls**, and **Roof** (ceiling) GameObject of **Gallery Building** by following these steps:

1. In your **Project** window `Assets/Materials/` folder, create a new material, using "+" | **Material**, and name it `Gallery Floor Material`.
2. Drag the material to the **Floor** GameObject of the gallery.
3. Create another material named **Gallery Walls Material**, and drag it to the **Walls** GameObject.
4. Likewise, create a material named **Gallery Ceiling Material**, and drag it to the **Roof** GameObject.

For the ceiling, let's just keep it smooth (untextured) and white, as follows:

1. Select the **Roof** game object in **Hierarchy**.
2. Set its color to white by selecting **Gallery Ceiling Material** | **Base Map** | **[color swatch]** | `#FFFFF`.

For the walls, we'll use a plaster material. The textures I found create a pretty dramatic rough texture, so we'll smooth that down so it looks more like textured drywall that you're more likely to see in a gallery. Select the **Walls** GameObject in **Hierarchy**, and on its shader **Surface Inputs**, set the following (if you don't have these files, you can skip these steps):

1. Set the color swatch to white (`#FFFFFF`).
2. From the **Project** window, drag `Plaster_Rough_001_COLOR` onto the **Base Map** texture chip.
3. Drag `Plaster_Rough_001_ROUGH` onto the **Metallic Map** texture chip.
4. Drag `Plaster_Rough_001_NORM` onto the **Normal Map** texture chip.
5. If you see a prompt that the texture has not been imported properly for the **Normal Map** texture type, click **Fix Now**. (This will change its **Texture Type** to `Normal Map` for you.)
6. Drag `Plaster_Rough_001_OCC` onto the **Occlusion Map** texture chip.
7. Reduce the roughness by setting the **Normal Map** value to `-0.1`.

For the floor, we'll use a wood plank flooring material. The textures I found seemed to make the planks too short and narrow, so we'll scale them and darken them a little. Select the **Floor** game object in **Hierarchy**, and on its shader **Surface Inputs**, set the following:

1. From the **Project** window, drag `Wood_Floor_007_COLOR` onto the **Base Map** texture chip.
2. Set its color swatch to an off-white color (`#C5C5C5`).

3. Drag `Wood_Floor_007_ROUGH` onto the **Metallic Map** texture chip.
4. Set its **Smoothness** to `0.333` so it's not too shiny.
5. Drag `Wood_Floor_007_NORM` onto the **Normal Map** texture chip.
6. If you see a prompt that the texture has not been imported properly for the **Normal Map** texture type, click **Fix Now**.
7. Drag `Wood_Floor_007_OCC` onto the **Occlusion Map** texture chip.
8. Set **Tiling X Y** to (`0.5, 0.5`) to enlarge the textures.

The empty gallery now looks like this:

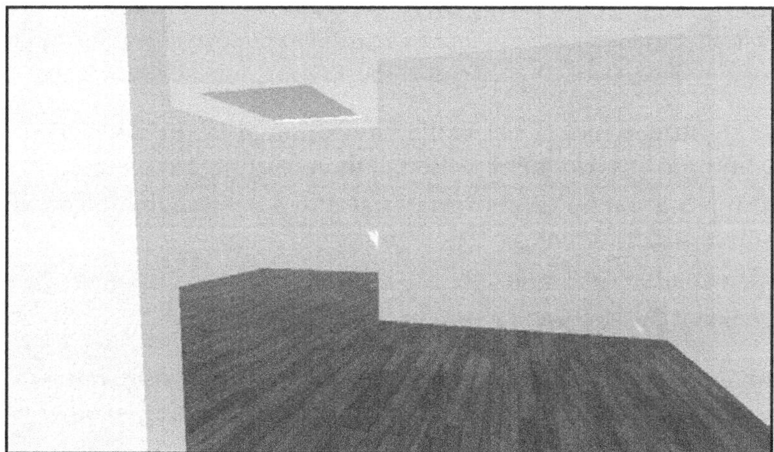

By the way of a final step in setting up the level design, let's tune the lighting and add a skybox.

Tuning the lighting

Check that your scene lighting is being generated (baked). For this project, it may be simplest to keep the **Auto Generate** functionality enabled. However, if that gets in the way of your workflow, turn **Auto Generate** off, but then don't forget to press the **Generate Lighting** button periodically to re-bake your lightmaps. Follow these steps:

1. Open the **Lighting** window (**Window** | **Rendering** | **Lighting**) (or **Lighting Settings** in Unity 2019).
2. Select the **Scene** tab.
3. Ensure **Mixed Lighting** | **Baked Global Illumination** is checked.

4. Set **Lighting Mode: Baked Indirect**.
5. Ensure **Lightmapping Settings | Progressive Updates** is checked in Unity 2020+ (for Unity 2019, choose **Lightmapper: Progressive CPU**).
6. At the bottom, use the **Auto Generate** checkbox to enable or disable autogenerated lightmaps.
7. When **Auto Generate** is disabled, press **Generate Lighting** to manually bake the current lightmaps.

In this scene, the user can see the sky from the entrances and skylight. Presently we're using just the boring default Unity skybox. Back in `Chapter 2`, *Understanding Unity, Content, and Scale*, I suggested you import the **Wispy Skybox** asset into the project. If you don't have it yet, you can get it now at `https://assetstore.unity.com/packages/2d/textures-materials/sky/wispy-skybox-21737`. To add the skybox, follow these steps:

1. In the **Lighting** window, select the **Environment** tab in Unity 2020 (for Unity 2019, find the **Environment** section at the top of the **Scene** tab).
2. At the top is a slot for **Skybox Material**. Press the doughnut icon, which opens the **Select Material** dialog.
3. Search using the `wispy` string.
4. Select one of the skyboxes to use in the scene.

The skybox's sun may not match the angle of your **Directional Light**, but let's not worry about that right now. However, we can control the interior lighting in other ways. On the same **Environment** tab or section, proceed as follows:

1. Set the **Environment Lighting | Source** to **Color**.
2. Set the **Ambient Color** to **Warm Sunlight** or an incandescent hue such as **RGB** (`190, 180, 160`).

Personally, I like the mood this creates. Feel free to experiment and discover what works for you. One more thing. The gallery building will not change in this scene, so we can help Unity optimize its processing by marking it **Static**, as follows:

1. Select the **Gallery Building** parent in **Hierarchy**.
2. In **Inspector**, in the upper-right corner, check the **Static** checkbox.
3. When prompted **Do you want to enable the static flags for all the child objects as well?** press **Yes, change children**.
4. If your baked lighting in this scene looks much darker, try making the **Roof** game object not static by unchecking its **Static** checkbox.

Unity may take a few seconds to regenerate the lighting when lightmaps are autogenerating. Alternatively, in the **Lighting** window, press the **Generate Lighting** button. We've added some physically-based materials to the walls and floor, and then set up the scene with a skybox, lighting, and baked lightmaps for static objects. Now that we have a gallery, we need to put some art on it!

Creating the artwork rig

Our next step is to create a reusable artwork rig with a picture frame, lighting, information plaque, and a teleportation pod that defines its optimal viewing position. Then, we'll hang the art on the walls of the gallery. We'll construct one rig in the scene, and then save it as a prefab. Later, we'll apply the actual images.

Defining an artwork rig

The artwork rig will consist of a picture frame (cube), a photo plane (quad), and a spotlight, all relative to the artwork's placement on the wall. Let's get started by doing the following:

1. Create a container object by navigating to **GameObject** | **Create Empty**, renaming it `ArtworkRig`.
2. Create the frame. With `ArtworkRig` selected, right-click and select **3D Object** | **Cube**, and name it `ArtFrame`.
3. Leaving the origin of the rig at floor level, let's set the default height of the art image frame at 1.4 meters high. In **Inspector**, set the ArtFrame **Position** to (`0, 1.4, 0`).
4. Give it some thickness, setting its **Scale Z** value to `0.05`.
5. Also, let's assume a `3:4` aspect ratio, so set its **Scale Y** value to `0.75` (scale `1, 0.75, 0.05`).

Place the **ArtworkRig** on the wall facing the north-east entrance (upper-right corner of the plan sketch). It may help to hide the **Roof** of the **Gallery Building** object (uncheck its **Enable** checkbox option) and change the **Scene** view to a top-down view and **Iso.** Now, place the **ArtworkRig** on the wall, as follows:

1. Select the parent **ArtworkRig** object.
2. Rotate it to face east, **Rotation** (`0, -90, 0`).
3. Use the **Move Tool** to position it on the wall. The **Position** that works for me is (`8.3, 0, -2.9`).

Next, we'll build up the artwork rig by adding an image placeholder mounted on a black matte board, as follows:

1. Make the frame black. Navigate to **Assets** | **Create** | **Material**, and name it `ArtFrame Material`.
2. Set its **Base Map** color to a charcoal black color.
3. Uncheck its **Specular Highlights** and **Environment Reflections** checkboxes so that it renders matte.
4. Then, in **Hierarchy**, select the **Frame** option, and drag the `ArtFrame Material` material to `ArtFrame`.
5. To make the image placeholder, with `ArtFrame` selected in **Hierarchy**, right-click and navigate to **3D Object** | **Quad**.
6. Name it **Image**.
7. Position **Image** just in front of the frame so that it's visible; set **Position** to (`0`, `0`, `-0.8`), and scale it so that it's slightly smaller than the frame by setting **Scale** to (`0.9`, `0.9`, `1`).
8. Create a material for the images. Navigate to **Assets** | **Create** | **Material**, and name it **ArtImage Material**.
9. Drag **ArtImage Material** to the **Image** object.
10. Set the **Base Map** color to white so that the photo's full texture fidelity will be rendered. Leave **Specular Highlight** and **Reflections** enabled if you want the photos to have a glossy finish.

Usually, any artwork has a spotlight shining on it. Let's add that now.

Adding a spotlight

Let's add a spotlight to the rig and bake it, as follows:

1. First, put the ceiling back in by checking off the **Enable** checkbox option for the **Roof** child object of **Gallery Building**.
2. With `ArtworkRig` selected in **Hierarchy**, right-click and navigate to **Light** | **Spotlight**.
3. Position it one and a half meters away from the wall (**Z**=`-1.5`) and up near the ceiling. The exact height doesn't matter much since we don't actually have a light fixture. I set **Position** to (`0`, `2.4`, `-1.5`).

4. Now, adjust the `Spotlight` value so that it appropriately illuminates the artwork. I set **Rotation X** to `30`. Adjust the light parameters to your liking, such as **Inner/Outer Spot Angle** (`38, 45`), **Range** to `3`, and **Intensity** to `3`.
5. Set the light **Color** to white (`#FFFFFF`).
6. The lights will not move so we can bake it, but the frame will be dynamically resized (see later in this chapter), so set **Light** | **Mode** to **Mixed**.

We set the light mode to **Baked** to reduce the runtime costs of shading and shadow calculations. Likewise, we can make the entire artwork rig **Static**, since it won't be moving at runtime either. Then, let's save the rig as a prefab before we duplicate it throughout the scene. This will make it easier to make changes later that propagate to all the instances in the scene. Proceed as follows:

1. Select `ArtworkRig` in **Hierarchy**.
2. Enable the **Static** checkbox in the upper-right corner of its **Inspector**. When prompted **Do you want to enable the static flags for all the child objects as well?** press **Yes, change children.**
3. Save the rig as a prefab, and drag it to your **Project** `Assets/Prefabs` folder.

The results are shown in the following screenshot:

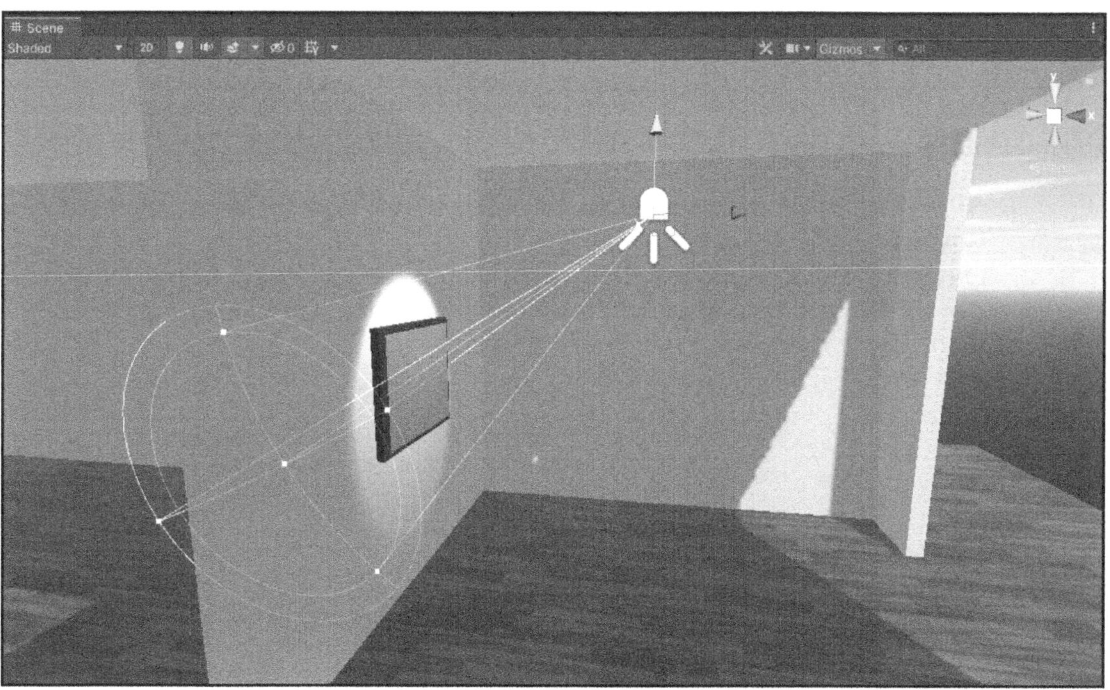

Now, we can set up the exhibition by placing artwork throughout the gallery.

The exhibition plan

The next step is to duplicate the `ArtworkRig` on each wall where we want to display the images. Position it and rotate as needed. If you follow the plan shown in the following diagram, your exhibition will display 10 images, indicated by the stars:

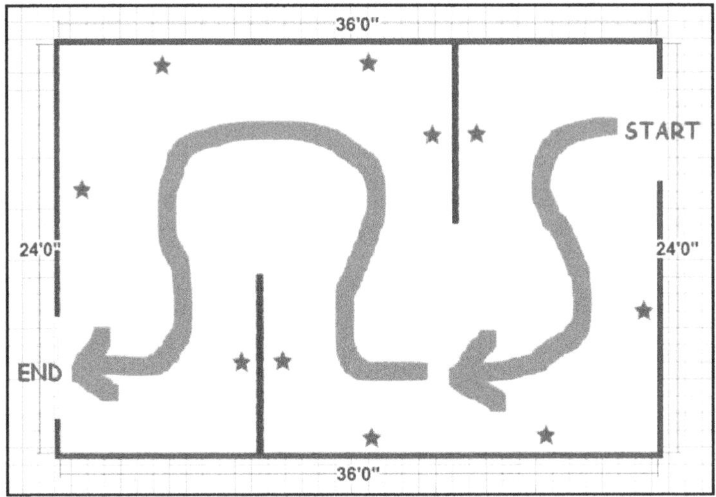

The following are the steps to take to duplicate the `ArtworkRig` on each wall:

1. As before, it may be easier to hide the ceiling and change the **Scene View** panel to **Top** and **Iso**.
2. On the top left of the **Scene View** panel, change the **Transform Gizmo** toggles so that the tool handle is placed at the **Pivot** point rather than **Center**. See the following screenshot:

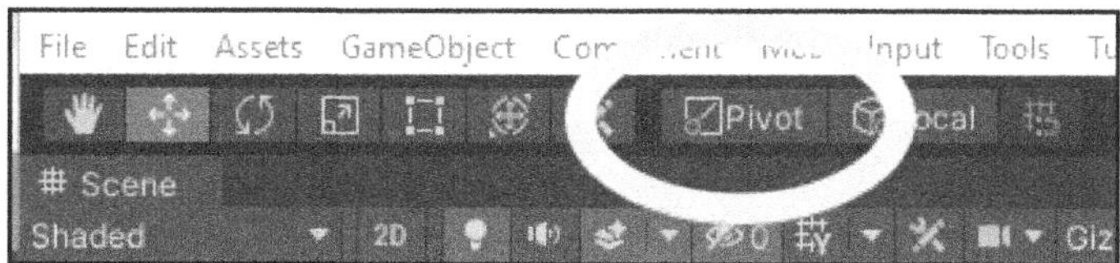

3. Create a new **Empty** game object, **Reset** its transform, and name it `Artworks`.
4. Drag the existing **ArtworkRig** so it's a child of **Artworks**.

For each location, place an artwork in the gallery. You may need to first turn off **Snap to Grid** if you presently have it enabled, and then follow these steps:

1. Select an existing **ArtworkRig** in the **Hierarchy**.
2. Duplicate **ArtworkRig** by right-clicking on **Duplicate**, or by pressing *Ctrl* + *D*.
3. Rotate the rig so that it faces the correct direction by setting **Rotation Y** to `0`, `90`, `180`, or `-90`.
4. Position the rig on the wall.

The settings that work for my gallery are provided in the following table (and assume your **Artworks** transform is reset to the origin):

Index	**Position X**	**Position Z**	**Rotation Y**
0	8.3	-2.9	-90
1	11.75	-6.2	90
2	9.3	-8.475	180
3	6.5	-8.475	180
4	4.77	-7	-90
5	8.1	-3	90
6	5.7	-1.4	0
7	2.9	-1.4	0
8	1	-4	-90
9	4.6	-7.1	90

The following screenshot shows the player's view of the scene so far:

Well, this is starting to look pretty good. So far, we've created an art gallery building, created an artwork prefab rig, and arranged the rigs on the walls to set up the exhibition. Now, we just need to put some lovely pictures into those picture frames.

Adding pictures to the gallery

Please find 10 of your favorite photos from your photo library to use and add them to a new **Project Assets** folder named `Photos`. Or, use the ones I've included in the files for this book, a collection of freely usable nature photos found on Unsplash (`https://unsplash.com/`). Add the photos as follows:

1. Create a photos folder, then navigate to **Assets** | **Create** | **Folder** and name it `Photos`.
2. Import 10 photos by dragging and dropping them from your OS file explorer into the `Photos` folder that you just created (or navigate to **Assets** | **Import New Asset...**).

We are going to write a script named `PopulateArtFrames` that, given the list of images, will add them to each **ArtworkRig** in the scene. Create the script as follows:

1. In **Hierarchy**, select `Artworks`.
2. Then, in **Inspector**, navigate to **Add Component** | **New Script** and name it `PopulateArtFrames`.

3. Open the new script for editing, as follows:

```
public class PopulateArtFrames : MonoBehaviour
{
    public Texture[] images;

    void Start()
    {
        int imageIndex = 0;
        foreach (Transform artwork in transform)
        {
            GameObject art = artwork.Find("
                ArtFrame/Image").gameObject;
            Renderer rend = art.GetComponent<Renderer>();
            Material material = rend.material;
            material.mainTexture = images[imageIndex];
            imageIndex++;
            if (imageIndex == images.Length)
                break;
        }
    }
}
```

What is going on here? First, we declare a public array of `Textures` named `images`. You will see that this will appear in the **Inspector**, so we can specify which photos to include in the scene.

This script is attached to the `Artworks` container object, which contains as children the **ArtworkRigs**. When the app starts, in `Start()`, we loop through each of the **ArtworkRigs**, finding its **Image** child object. For each image, we get its **Renderer** component's **Material**, and assign a new **Texture**, that being the next image in the list. We use an `imageIndex` variable to increment through the list, and stop when we've run out of images or run out of **ArtworkRigs** without causing an indexing error.

The astute reader may wonder why, since all the **ArtworkRig Image** objects use the same **Material**, wouldn't changing the material on any one object change them all? In fact, Unity takes care of that by cloning the material into a new unique one when you modify its texture (or other attributes) at runtime. So, each **ArtworkRigs Image** gets its own **Material** with its own **Texture**, and thus, each picture in our gallery is different.

To finish this up, let's perform the following steps:

1. Save the script and return to the Unity editor.
2. With `Artworks` selected in **Hierarchy**, unfold the **Populate Art Frames** script component in **Inspector** and unfold the **Images** parameter.
3. Set the **Images Size** value to `10`.
4. Find the images you imported in the `Photos` folder under **Project** `Assets/` and drag them, one at a time, into the **Images** slots as **Element 0** through **Element 9**, as shown in the following screenshot:

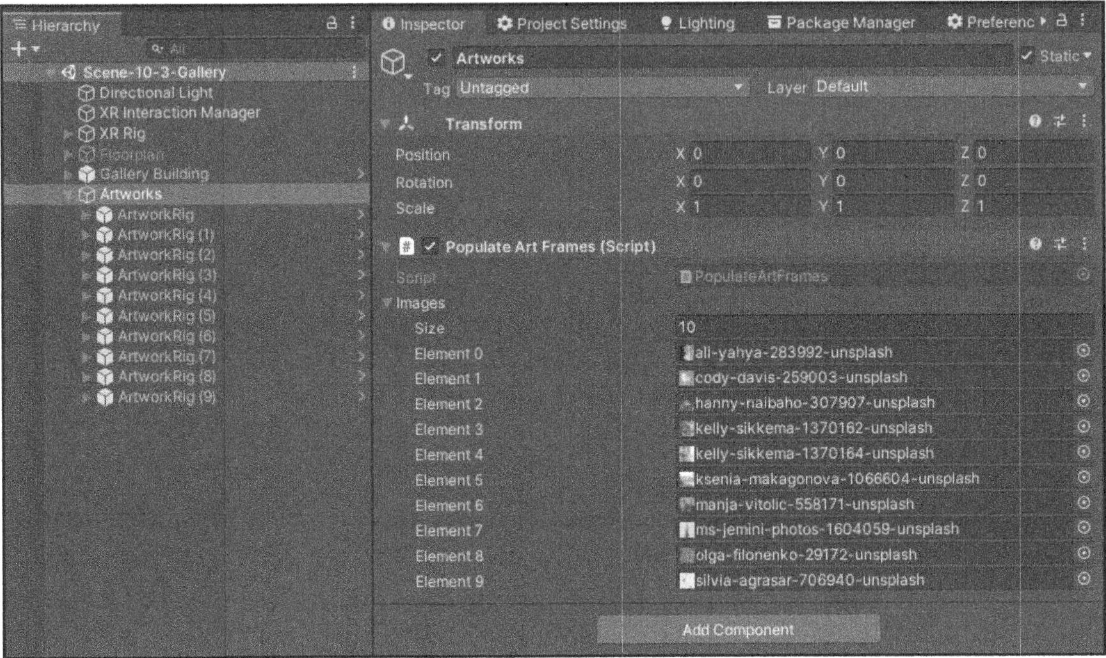

When you click on **Play mode**, the artwork in the scene will get populated with the images in the order that you specified. Here's a view from inside the gallery:

That's pretty nice! We could stop here, but let's suppose we want to track more data than just the images for each artwork, such as artist, title, and description. Let's add the ability to add metadata to our photos.

Managing art info data

We will consider several software design patterns to manage metadata associated with each photographic art piece, including in the first two sub-topics—separate lists and data structures—for your edification. Then, we'll actually use **Scriptable Objects** (explained next) as the preferred data management technique in our project.

Using lists

One approach to adding more data about each photo could be to add more lists to the `PopulateArtFrames` script, one for each of the data fields. For example, the script may contain the following code (no need to add this code yourself—this is only for teaching purposes):

```
public Texture[] images;
public string[] titles;
public string[] artists;
public string[] descriptions;
```

In such a case, the **Inspector** would show the following (I limited the list to four items for brevity):

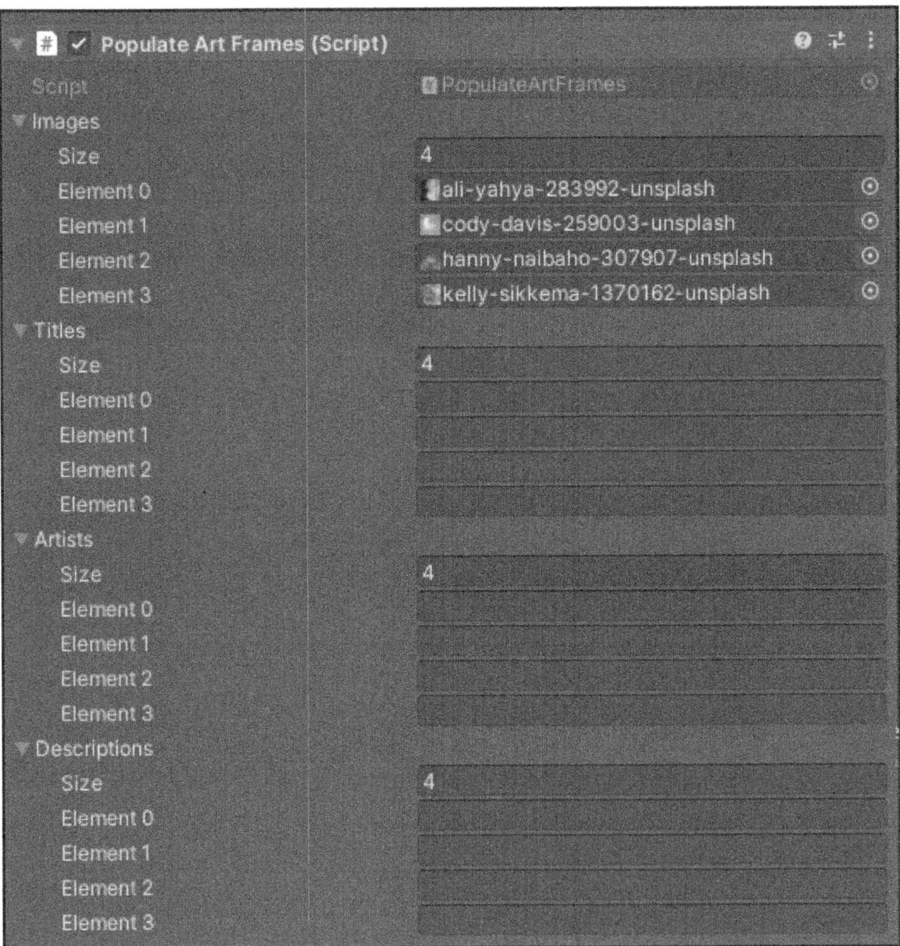

When you have lists in the Unity **Inspector**, it's not unusual to want to be able to rearrange the order of items without having to copy/paste the element values. While Unity (at this time) does not include re-orderable lists, there are plugins that do the job. For example, the free **NaughtyAttributes** package (`https://assetstore.unity.com/packages/tools/utilities/naughtyattributes-129996`) includes, among other things, a `ReorderableList` attribute you can use with your lists.

As you can imagine, this could get very unwieldy. To change the fourth image in the scene (**Element 3**), for example, you'd have to go to all the lists and change the **Element 3** item in each list separately (**Images, Titles, Artists, Descriptions**), which makes it easily prone to mistakes and hard to maintain. Things could get very out of sync.

Using data structures

A better approach could be to write a C# `struct` (or `class`) as a data structure that contains each of the fields we want, and then make the list in `PopulateArtFrames` as this type. For example, the script may read as follows (no need to add this code yourself—this is only for teaching purposes):

```
[System.Serializable]
public struct ArtInfo
{
    public Texture image;
    public string title;
    public string artist;
    public string description;
}

public class PopulateArtFrames : MonoBehaviour
{
    public List<ArtInfo> artInfos = new List<ArtInfo>();
```

In the preceding example snippet, we declare a separate data structure named `ArtInfo` defining our data fields. Then, in `PopulateArtFrames`, we declare it as a `List` (which must be initialized with the `new List<ArtInfo>()` call). In the script, we'd then reference the textures—for example, as `artInfos[i].image`. Also, we need to say that it is `System.Serializable` so that the list appears in the editor **Inspector**, as follows:

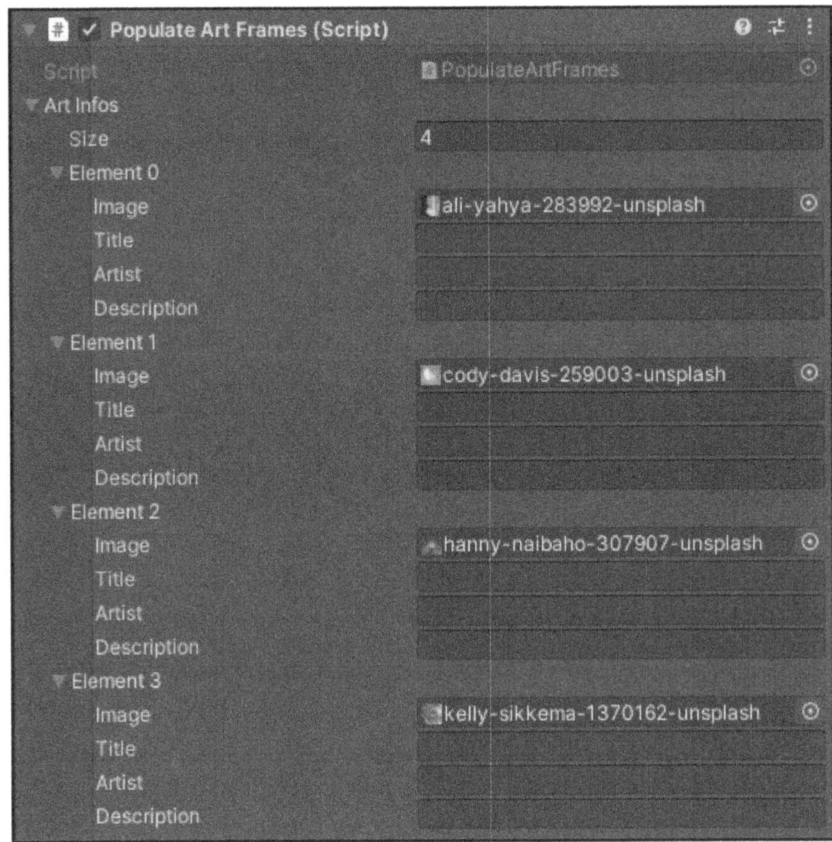

Now, we have a list of `ArtInfo` elements that we can fill in, and the data for each element is grouped together. Another benefit of this structure is it could be more easily populated from an external data source, such as a cloud-based **JavaScript Object Notation** (**JSON**) or **comma-separated values** (**CSV**) file, or a database query.

If you are interested in loading data from a database, there are a number of approaches, outside the scope of this chapter. But briefly, if you do find a source of CSV data, this handy CSV parser (`https://github.com/frozax/fgCSVReader`) is basic but gets the job done. If you are in need of a JSON parser (from a web-based **representational state transfer** (**REST**) **application programming interface** (**API**), for example), consider the **JSON .NET For Unity** package (`https://assetstore.unity.com/packages/tools/input-management/json-net-for-unity-11347`), or another similar one.

Using scriptable objects

In the previous examples, the art info data is maintained on a **GameObject** in the Scene hierarchy. As a software design, this is not really where the data belongs. Data objects are not game objects and should be managed separately. In the Scene hierarchy, we define the level design and game behaviors. **ArtworkRigs** have spatial transforms, renderers, and other components for runtime behaviors, including physics. But other data can live outside the scene hierarchy. For this, Unity offers **Scriptable Objects**. Let's see how to manage our art info data as Scriptable Objects. Begin by writing a new `ArtInfoData` script for the Scriptable Object, as follows:

1. In the **Project** window `Asset/Scripts/` folder, right-click and select **Create | C# Script**.
2. Name the script `ArtInfoData`.
3. Then, open the `ArtInfoData.cs` script for editing, as follows:

```
[CreateAssetMenu(menuName = "My Objects/Art Info")]
public class ArtInfoData : ScriptableObject
{
    public Texture image;
    public string title;
    public string artist;
    [Multiline]
    public string description;
}
```

Rather than inheriting from `MonoBehaviour`, we define this class as a `ScriptableObject`. Since scriptable objects are not added to the scene **Hierarchy**, we need a way to create them in the **Project** `Assets` folder. At the top of the script, I've added a `CreateAssetMenu` attribute, which generates a menu item in the Unity Editor for the object. Using this attribute makes it easy, as follows:

1. Save the script and return to Unity.
2. In the **Project** window, select your `Photos` folder where you imported your image textures. We'll create the **ArtInfoData** objects in the same folder.
3. In the Unity editor's main menu, navigate to **Assets** | **Create**.
4. You will see a new item, **My Objects**, with a submenu with an **Art Info** item, as directed in the `CreateAssetsMenu` property attribute in our script, as shown in the following screenshot:

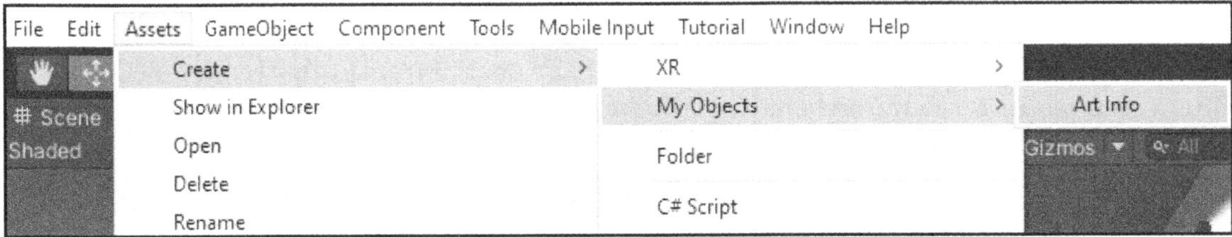

5. Choose **Art Info** to create an instance. It may be helpful to name the object similar to your images. For example, if you have **PictureA**, name it `PictureA Info`.
6. Drag the image texture onto the scriptable object's **Image** slot.
7. Add information for the **Title**, **Artist**, and **Description** too.

Here is a screenshot of an **ArtInfoData** object with some data filled in:

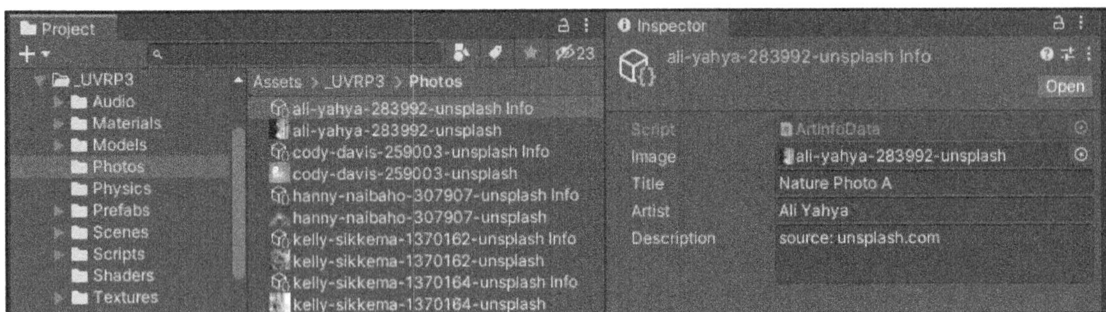

Repeat these steps for all your pictures. When you're done, your art data will be **Project** assets along with the photo images.

Now, to use these scriptable object assets in the project, we could modify the `PopulateArtFrames` script to use a list of the `ArtInfoData` asset objects we just created. But to make this more object-oriented, we'll refactor how we did it before. We're going to eliminate the `PopulateArtFrames` script and instead, let each artwork rig populate its own data. Let's write a new `ArtInfo` script for the **ArtworkRig** that takes an `ArtInfoData` object and sets up its own image based on the given data object. Create a new script named `ArtInfo` and open the script for editing, as follows:

```
public class ArtInfo : MonoBehaviour
{
    public ArtInfoData artInfo;
    public GameObject image;

    private void Start()
    {
        Renderer rend = image.GetComponent<Renderer>();
        Material material = rend.material;
        material.mainTexture = artInfo.image;
    }
}
```

Save the script. In Unity, remove the **Populate Art Frames** component from the **Artworks** object, and open the **ArtworkRig** prefab for editing, as follows:

1. In **Hierarchy**, select the **Artworks** object and, in **Inspector**, remove the **Populate Art Frames** component by right-clicking | **Remove Component** (or using the three-dot icon menu).
2. In the **Project** window `Assets/Prefabs/` folder, open the **ArtworkRig** prefab for editing by double-clicking it.
3. Drag the `ArtInfo` script we just created from the **Project** window onto the **ArtworkRig** object.
4. Drag the **Image** child onto the **Art Info** | **Image** slot.
5. Leave the **Info Data** slot empty for now.
6. Press **Save** to save the prefab, and return to the Scene **Hierarchy**.

The following screenshot shows the **ArtworkRig** prefab being edited as I described, with the **Art Info** component:

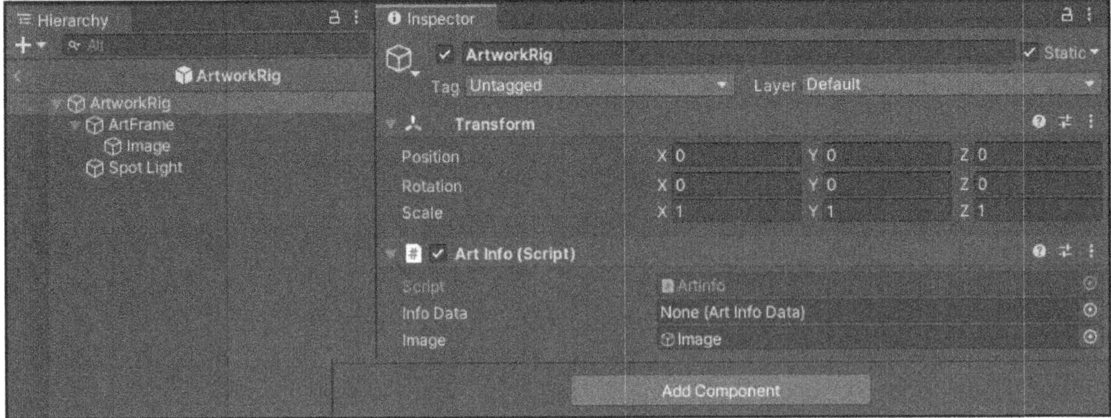

Now, in **Inspector**, we just need to assign the **Art Info** data objects to each rig object. The following screenshot shows one of the **ArtworkRigs** set up:

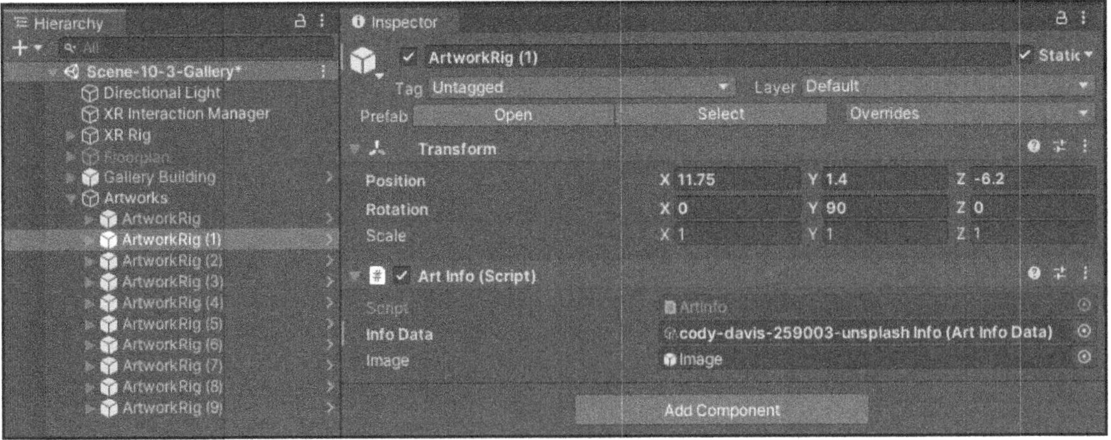

Press **Play**. The artwork images get loaded during `Start` just like before, but we've made the underlying implementation more object-oriented. By making each **ArtworkRig** responsible for its own data rather than using a top-down controller for populating the data, and using Scriptable Objects for the art info data, we have extended our app to handle more info about each art picture. Now, we can go ahead and show this info within the gallery.

Displaying the art info

We now have more information on each art piece, and can incorporate that into our scene. We will add a world space user interface (UI) canvas to the ArtworkRig. If you'd like a reminder introduction to Unity's canvas and UI elements, please look at `Chapter 6`, *Canvasing World Space UI*.

The info plaque will be a small canvas next to each picture, with a title text UI element. Let's build it into the **ArtworkRig** prefab. Open the **ArtworkRig** prefab for editing. Then, add a world space canvas, as follows:

1. Add a child canvas, **GameObject| UI | Canvas**, and name it `InfoPlaque Canvas`. (Note: if you wanted to make any of the UI on this canvas interactable, you should use **XR | UI Canvas** instead).
2. Set its **Render** mode to **World Space.**
3. Set the canvas **Width**: `640`, **Height**: `480`, **Rotation** (`0, 0, 0`).
4. If you recall, the canvas scaled in world space will be 640 meters wide! Set the **Scale XYZ** to `0.0006`.
5. Next, create a child panel, **+ | UI | Panel**.
6. Visually adjust the position of **InfoPlaque Canvas** using the move gizmo. I found this works: **Pos** (`0.8`, `1`, `-0.01`). (Leave the child panel at `0, 0, 0`).

Now, we can add text UI elements for the title, artist, and description. I'll use a **Vertical Layout Group** for this. In the following, I provide my recommended settings (you can do what works for you):

1. On the **Panel** game object, add a **Vertical Layout Group** using **Add Component | Layout | Vertical Layout Group.**
2. Set the **Child Alignment** to **Middle** and **Center**.
3. Check the checkboxes for **Control Child Size: Width** and **Height** and **Child Force Expand: Width** and **Height**.
4. Add a child text element to the panel, using **Create UI | Text - TextMeshPro**, (or simply **Text** if you don't have the `TextMeshPro` package installed), and rename it `Title`.
5. Set some default title text in **Text Input**, such as `[Title text]`.
6. Use the following settings: **Font Size | Auto Size** checked; **Vertex Color** to black; **Alignment**: **Middle, Center**; **Wrapping:** `Enabled`; **Overflow:** `Overflow`; **Extra Settings | Margins | Left:** `40`, **Right:** `40`.

7. Duplicate the **Title** element, and rename it `Artist`. Set its **Text Input** to `[Artist name]` and **Auto Size Options | Max |** `48`, and **Font Style: I** (for italics).
8. Duplicate the **Title** element again, rename it `Description`, set **Text Input** to `[Description text]`, and **Auto Size Options | Max | 48.**

One more thing. Previously, we decided that the **ArtworkRig** can be **Static** in the scene. This should also be the case for the new UI canvas.

1. With the **InfoPlaque Canvas** selected, check that the **Static** checkbox is in **Inspector**.
2. Answer **Yes Change Children**, when prompted.
3. **Save** the prefab changes.

Now, we can modify the `ArtInfo` script to add new variables for the text UI elements and set their `text` property, as follows:

```
using TMPro;
using UnityEngine;

public class ArtInfo : MonoBehaviour
{
    public ArtInfoData infoData;
    public GameObject image;
    public TMP_Text title;
    public TMP_Text artist;
    public TMP_Text description;

    private void Start()
    {
        Renderer rend = image.GetComponent<Renderer>();
        Material material = rend.material;
        material.mainTexture = infoData.image;

        title.text = infoData.title;
        artist.text = infoData.artist;
        description.text = infoData.description;
    }
}
```

That was easy. Save the script, and then, while still editing the **ArtworkRig** prefab, assign the UI elements to the variable slots, as follows:

1. Drag the **Title** element from **Hierarchy** to the **ArtInfo | Title** slot.
2. Drag the **Artist** element to the **ArtInfo | Artist** slot.

3. Drag the **Description** element to the **ArtInfo | Description** slot.
4. **Save** the prefab edits.

The following screenshot shows the **ArtworkRig** prefab being edited, and its **ArtInfo** component populated with the UI text elements:

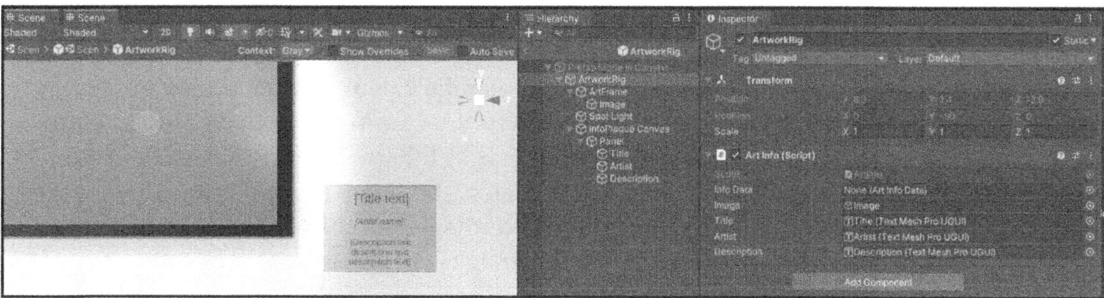

Now, when you press **Play**, the picture images and title text will get initialized on `Start` for each of the artwork rigs. Here's one of the photos with its info plaque:

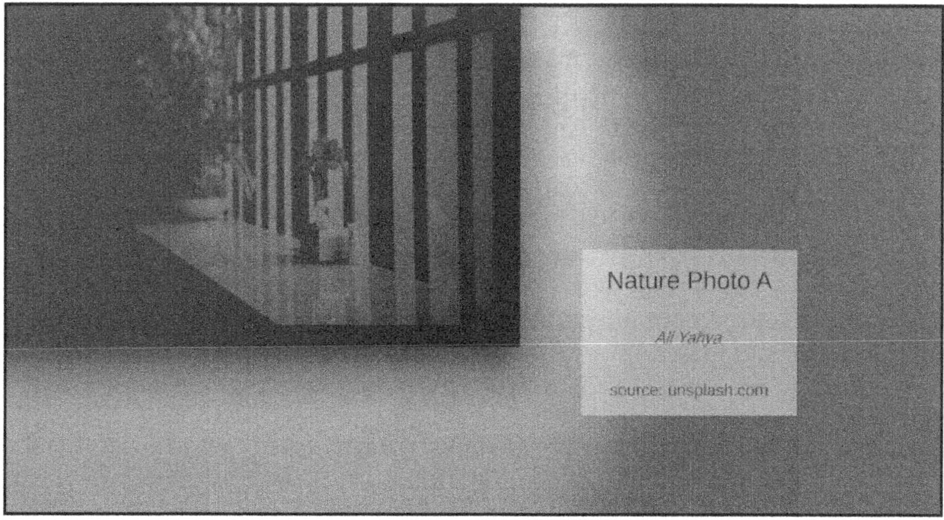

So, now, we have a good-looking art gallery room, with art rigs strategically arranged on the walls throughout the room. We manage the art data using scriptable objects that define the artwork for each station. At present, we've defined all the pictures with a 4:3 aspect ratio, but that's not the actual shape of many of our photos. Let's fix that next.

Adjusting for image aspect ratio

You probably noticed that some of your pictures appear squished, since our framed image is shown at a fixed size and aspect ratio. What we really would like is for the frame and image to adjust themselves, depending on the dimensions of the image.

When Unity imports a texture, it prepares it (by default) for **graphics processing unit** (**GPU**) rendering as an object material texture, which includes resizing it to a square power of two (for example, 1024 x 1024, 2048 x 2048). If you adapt your project to load images at runtime—for example, from the `Resources` directory, or from the device's photostream, or over the web—then you will probably have access to the image file's metadata header that includes its pixel width and height. Unfortunately, because of using imported textures, Unity only provides the size of the imported scaled image, not the originals. One solution is to change the **Advanced Import Settings** for the images we're using, as follows:

1. From your **Project** `Assets/Photos/` folder, select an image texture.
2. In **Inspector**, under **Advanced**, change **Non Power of 2** to **None**.
3. Press **Apply**.

Repeat this for each image in the project. (You can multi-select images in the **Project** window using *Ctrl* + *click* and change all their settings at once). Note that this also decompresses the image, so what might start out as a 400k `.jpg` file becomes a 3 MB file, or a 24-bit image in the project, so be cautious of the width and height of the source images you choose to use.

Not scaling textures to a power of two can be bad for performance, startup time, and memory usage of your app. If you have more than a few images, you should avoid this approach. One solution would be to add the image aspect ratio as another field of the `ArtInfoData` scriptable object, and manually set that value when you set up the data. Then, change the `ArtInfo` script to use this value instead of calculating it.

In `ArtInfo.cs`, add the following helper function, which returns a normalized scale of a texture. The larger dimension will be 1.0 and the smaller one will be a fraction. For example, an image that is 1024w x 768h will get a scale of (1.0, 0.75). It also maintains the current relative scale of the picture using the **Z** scale value, since that's not changed by our aspect ratio calculation, but will be changed by the **Scale** tool!

Modify `ArtInfo` first by adding a `TextureToScale` private function that normalizes the image scale to 1.0 for the larger of width or height, and sets the other dimension to the aspect ratio, as follows:

```
private Vector3 TextureToScale(Texture texture, Vector3 scale)
{
    if (texture.width > texture.height)
    {
        scale.x = 1f;
        scale.y = (float)texture.height / (float)texture.width;
    }
    else
    {
        scale.x = (float)texture.width / (float)texture.height;
        scale.y = 1f;
    }
    return scale;
}
```

The function takes the original scale of the frame and modifies the **X** and **Y** scale, but preserves the original frame depth (**Z**). Add a new public variable for the `frame`, as follows:

```
public Transform frame;
```

And then, add this line to set the frame's scale:

```
frame.localScale = TextureToScale(infoData.image, frame.localScale);
```

Save the updated script. Then, in Unity, add the frame reference. Also, now that we're changing the frame at runtime, it should no longer be flagged as **Static**. Proceed as follows:

1. Open the **ArtworkRig** prefab for editing.
2. Drag the **ArtFrame** to the **Frame** slot in the component.
3. With **ArtFrame** selected in **Hierarchy**, uncheck its **Static** checkbox in **Inspector**, and answer **Yes, Change Children** when prompted.
4. **Save** the prefab.

Now, when you play, the framed images are scaled with the correct aspect ratio, like the one shown here:

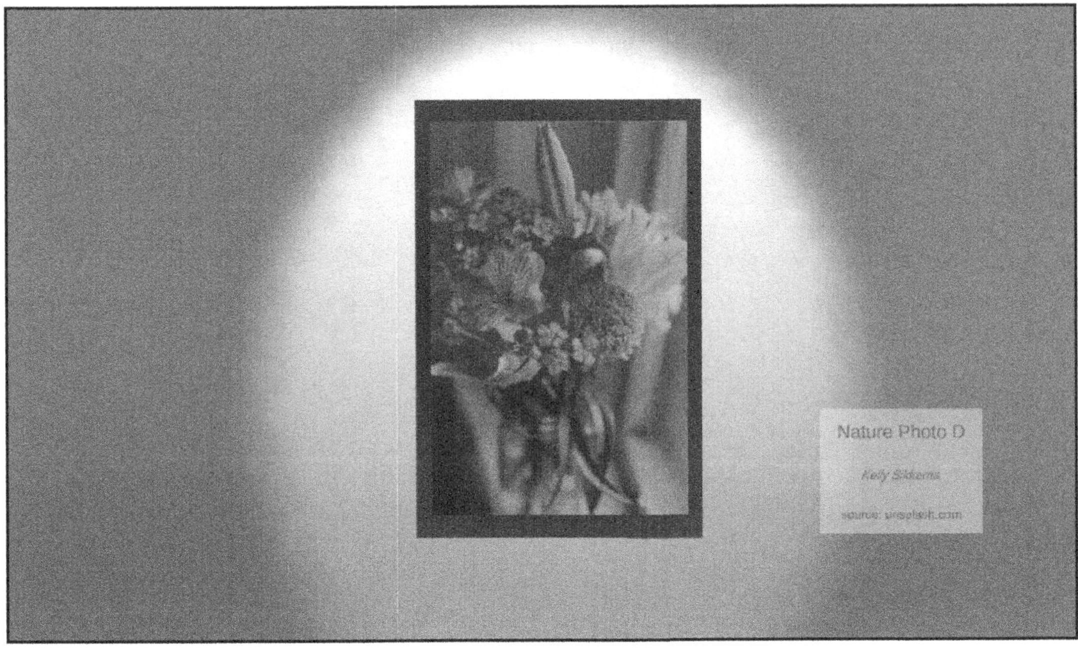

Wow, this is pretty exciting! Viewing the scene in VR, I really wish I could move around the gallery and look at each photo up close. Let's add teleportation to that.

Teleporting around the gallery

We've done so much, and yet have not discussed moving throughout the gallery level. In `Chapter 7`, *Teleporting, Locomotion, and Comfort,* we examined various ways of implementing locomotion and teleportation. Let's now set up specific teleportation spawn points that provide an optimal viewing pose for each artwork picture in the gallery.

We'll begin by adding the XR Interaction Toolkit's Locomotion System to our scene, including teleportation and snap turning. You can set it all up component by component (**Teleportation Provider**, **Snap Turn Provider**, **XR Ray Interactor** line types and renderer, and so on). For brevity, let's just borrow the demo rig provided with the **Unity XR Interaction Toolkit examples** we already installed in `Chapter 7`, *Teleporting, Locomotion, and Comfort* (and which can be found at the following GitHub repository: `https://github.com/Unity-Technologies/XR-Interaction-Toolkit-Examples`). Add the **XRRig Demo** object to the scene with the following steps:

1. In the **Project** window, search for `XRRig_Demo` (for example, `Assets/Prefabs folder`) and drag the prefab into your **Hierarchy**.
2. Copy the **XR Rig** | **Transform** you had (**right-click** | **Copy Component**), and paste it onto the new **XRRig_Demo** | **Transform** (**right-click** | **Paste Component Values**).
3. Delete the **XR Rig** you had.

Or, if you prefer to set it up manually yourself, start with the following steps:

1. Select the **XR Rig** in **Hierarchy**.
2. Add a **Locomotion System** by selecting **Add Component** | **search locomotion** | **Locomotion System.**
3. Add a **Teleportation Provider** to the **XR Rig** by selecting **Add Component** | **search teleport** | **Teleportation Provider.**
4. Add **Snap Turn Provider** by selecting **Add Component** | **search snap** | **Snap Turn Provider.**
5. Wire up the thumbsticks on both controllers. Set **Snap Turn Provider** | **Size** to `2`, and then drag **LeftHand Controller** and **RightHand Controller** to the **Element 0** and **Element 1** slots.
6. Set up the ray line visualizers on the controllers—for example, change its **XR Ray Interactor** | **Line Type** to **Projectile Curve** and modify the **XR Ray Interactor, Line Renderer, XR Interactor Line Visual** as needed, as well as create a new **Material** for **Line Renderer**.

Now, we can update **ArtworkRig** to offer a teleport pod, taking the player to an ideal viewing position in front of each picture. I suppose a good viewing position is about one and a half meters back from the picture. We can add a **TeleportAnchor** object at that location, within **ArtworkRig**, on the floor. Let's add that now, as follows:

1. Open the **ArtworkRig** prefab for editing.
2. From the **Project** window, locate the **TeleportAnchor** prefab (use the search field) (for example, in `Assets/Prefabs/`).

3. Drag it to the scene and set its **Position** to (`0, 0, -1.5`).
4. Create a material for the anchors. Navigate to **Assets** | **Create** | **Material**, and name it `TeleportAnchor Material`.
5. Set the material's **Shader** to **Universal Render Pipeline/Unlit**, **Surface Type** to **Transparent**, and **Base Map** color to black with **Alpha** `40`.
6. Drag **TeleportAnchor Material** to the **Teleport Anchor** | **Mesh Renderer** | **Materials** | **Element 0** slot.
7. **Save** the prefab.

Conveniently, in the **ArtworkRig**, the anchor is always facing the photo, so when the entire rig is positioned in the room, and the player teleports, the player will always end up facing that particular rig's image.

That should do it! Press **Play**. You can now press down on the thumbstick button and point the hand controllers at a teleport anchor, and it'll highlight. Click the trigger (or whichever button you've configured) to teleport to that location and be turned facing the picture at that station. Here is a screenshot of me teleporting to a new spot in the gallery:

If you're sitting comfortably in a chair enjoying the gallery, this works well. But there could be trouble if you get up and walk around in VR. Let's discuss this problem next.

Room-scale considerations

The gallery-level layout we have designed works best in seated or standing tracking mode. Our use of the zig-zag partitions, for example, is not a good idea in room-scale VR unless you take care to not allow the player's play space (chaperone boundaries) to cross these walls. This can be done, but you would need to make the overall space larger, perhaps adaptive to the actual play-space size, and add conditions to the teleportation feature that we implement later in the chapter, complicating our examples.

The following screenshot is a depiction of an initial position for XR Rig, showing that the play-area boundaries (green lines) fit neatly within the gallery viewing space for the first **ArtworkRig**. It may not fit so easily at the other viewing situations, so you'd need to make adjustments to discourage the player from walking through walls. Also, while this is the default length and width, the player's actual space will vary to their configuration. To fully accommodate these possibilities, it may be necessary to go to a procedurally generated level layout, where the position and scale of the walls are determined at runtime based on the player settings. Have a look at the XR Rig position here:

As you can see, the level design for VR has many considerations, such as whether the player is stationary or using room-scale tracking; whether this is expected to be a passive experience or one with a lot of interactivity; whether the game objects (and lighting) are stationary and can be marked static, or will be changing at runtime.

Summary

In this chapter, we built an art gallery scene from scratch, starting with a 2D plan, drawing and using the ProBuilder tools to construct a 3D architectural structure. We built a scene around the model, adding PBR materials and environmental lighting. Then, we built an artwork rig consisting of an image, a picture frame, and a spotlight, and placed instances of the rig on various walls throughout the gallery. Next, we imported a bunch of personal photos and wrote a script that populates the art frames at runtime. Adding more detailed data about each piece of artwork, we explored several ways of managing lists of non-graphical data and settled on an object-oriented approach, where each rig is responsible for handling its own data, stored in Scriptable Objects. Finally, we added the ability to teleport around within the art gallery level, using the XR Interaction Toolkit locomotion system.

You have learned some of the basics of mesh editing and 3D modeling, while further exploring issues of lighting, rendering, and materials. You learned different design patterns for managing data apart from GameObjects and MonoBehaviours, including Scriptable Objects that are kept as project assets but not in the scene hierarchy. These are important skills for any 3D Unity project, but especially VR ones.

In the next chapter, we will take a look at a different kind of VR experience, using pre-recorded 360-degree media. You will build and learn about photospheres, equirectangular projections, and infographics.

11
Using All 360 Degrees

360-degree photos and videos are a different way of using **Virtual Reality** (**VR**) that is widely accessible to consumers today, both in terms of experiencing them as well as producing and publishing them. Viewing prerecorded images requires much less compute power than rendering full 3D scenes, and this works very well even on low-end mobile VR devices (such as Oculus Go) and mobile phone-based headsets such as Google Cardboard.

In this chapter, we will learn about using 360-degree media is Unity for VR projects. To begin, I will explain the difference between regular photos and spherical projections (equirectangular) and then demonstrate this in several cases, including crystal balls, globes, and inside-out *magic orbs*! Then, we'll create a new scene so that we can view 360-degree photos within VR and add a user interface to let the user switch between pictures. Likewise, we'll also learn how to use 360-degree videos in the scene. Skyboxes are a more traditional use of 360-degree media in computer graphics and Unity scenes, so we'll see how to apply 360-degree assets as a skybox. Lastly, we'll consider methods of capturing the 360-degree images of your Unity projects, in the Editor and possibly at runtime, so that your users can share them.

In this chapter, we will cover the following topics:

- Understanding 360-degree media and formats
- Using textures to view globes, photo spheres, and skyboxes
- Adding a 360-degree video to your Unity projects
- Capturing 360-degree images and video from within your Unity app

Let's get started!

Technical requirements

To implement the projects and exercises in this chapter, you will need the following:

- A PC or Mac with Unity 2019.4 LTS or later, the XR plugin for your device, and the XR Interaction Toolkit installed
- A VR headset supported by Unity XR Platform

You can access or clone the GitHub repository for this book (`https://github.com/PacktPublishing/Unity-2020-Virtual-Reality-Projects-3rd-Edition-`) to use the following assets and completed projects for this chapter:

- The asset files for you to use in this chapter are located in the `UVRP3Files/Chapter-11-Files.zip` folder.
- All the completed projects for this book can be found in a single Unity project at `UVRP3Projects`.
- The completed assets and scenes for this chapter are located in the `UVRP3Projects/Assets/_UVRP3Assets/Chapter11/` folder.

Exploring 360-degree media

The terms **360-degree media** and **virtual reality** are being tossed around a lot lately, often in the same sentence. Consumers may be led to believe that it's all the same thing, it's all figured out, and it's all very easy to produce, when, in fact, it is not that simple. Generally, the term **360-degree media** refers to viewing prerecorded photos or videos in a manner that allows you to rotate your view's direction to reveal content that was just outside your field of view.

Non-VR 360-degree media has become relatively common. For example, many real-estate listing sites provide panoramic previews with a web-based player that lets you interactively pan around to view the space. Similarly, Facebook and YouTube support uploading and playback of 360-degree videos and a player with interactive controls so that you can look around during the playback. Google Maps lets you upload 360-degree panoramic photos, much like their Street View, which you can create with an Android or iOS device or a consumer camera (for more information, visit `https://www.google.com/maps/about/contribute/photosphere/`). The internet is teeming with 360-degree media!

With a VR headset, viewing 360-degree media is surprisingly immersive, even still photos. You're standing at the center of a sphere with an image projected onto the inside surface, but you feel like you're really there in the captured scene. Simply turn your head to look around. It's one of those things that gets people interested in VR the first time they see it. Let's learn more about this media and its file formats before we use them in a Unity project. This will include understanding equirectangular (spherical) projections, seeing how VR works to make 360-degree media feel immersive, and issues concerning stereo 360-degree media.

Understanding equirectangular projections

Ever since it was discovered that the Earth is round, mapmakers and mariners have struggled with how to project the spherical globe onto a two-dimensional chart. The variations are plentiful and the history is fascinating (if you're fascinated by that sort of thing)! The result is an inevitable distortion of some areas of the globe. As a computer graphics designer, it's perhaps a little less mysterious than it was to ancient cartographers because we know about *UV Texture mapping*.

To learn more about map projections and spherical distortions, visit `http://en.wikipedia.org/wiki/Map_projection`.

Three-dimensional object models in Unity are defined by *meshes* – a set of `Vector3` points connected with edges to form triangular-shaped facets. You can unwrap a mesh (in ProBuilder or Blender, for instance) into a flattened 2D configuration to define the mapping of texture pixels to the corresponding areas on the mesh surface (UV coordinates). A globe of the Earth, when unwrapped, will be distorted, as defined by the unwrapped mesh. In computer graphics, the resulting image is called a **UV texture image**.

This UV mapping of the texture to the geometry mesh can be arbitrary and depends on the artistic requirements at hand. However, for 360-degree media, this is typically done using an **equirectangular** (or a Meridian) projection (for more information, visit `https://mathworld.wolfram.com/EquirectangularProjection.html`), where the sphere is unraveled into a cylindrical projection, stretching the texture as you progress toward the north and south poles while keeping the meridians as equidistant vertical straight lines.

The following image (see *Tissot's indicatrix* for more information) shows a globe with strategically arranged identical circles (illustration by Stefan Kühn):

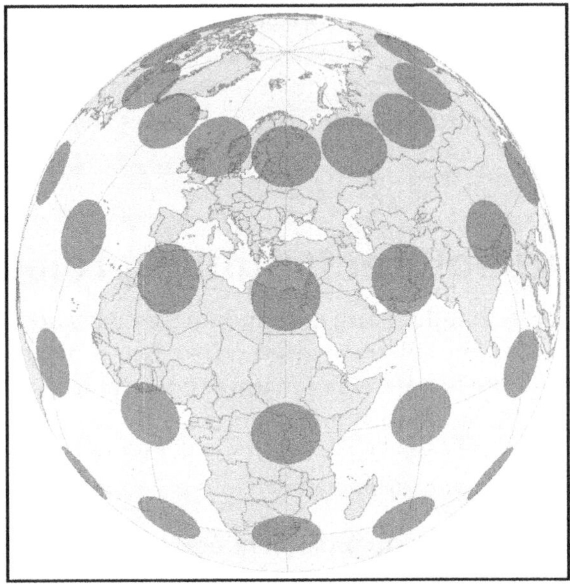

The following image shows the globe unwrapped with an equirectangular projection:

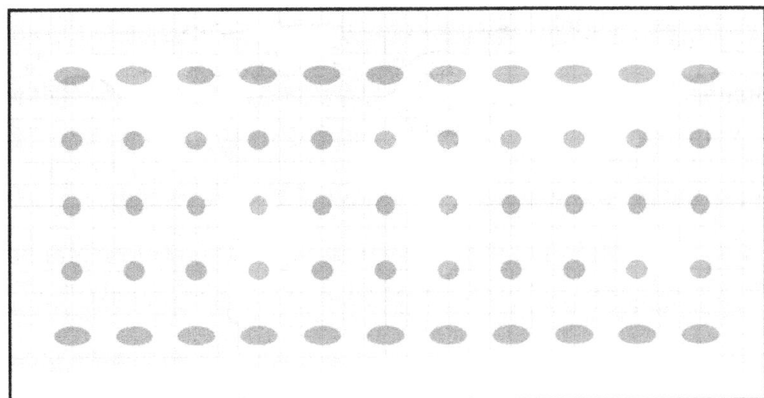

Illustration by Eric Gaba – Wikimedia Commons user: Sting

We will use an equirectangular mesh for our photospheres and an appropriately projected (warped) image for its texture map. Now, let's understand how these image projects are used in VR.

VR is hacking your field of view

OK, but why is 360-degree media in VR so compelling? There's a huge difference in how we experience viewing a 360-degree video on a flatscreen versus inside a VR headset. First of all, consider the field of view and peripheral vision. For example, an IMAX cinema theater with larger screens than those in conventional cinema theaters encompasses more of your peripheral vision and has a wider **Field Of View** (**FOV**). A mobile phone or computer monitor, at a natural viewing distance, is about a 26-degree FOV. A movie theater is 54 degrees, while IMAX is 70 degrees. Oculus Rift and HTC VIVE are about 120 degrees. In terms of human vision, one eye can see about 160 degrees, and both eyes combined provide about a 200-degree horizontal field of view.

For more information about FOV adjustments in conventional video games, read the excellent article *All about FOV* (July 18, 2014) at `http://steamcommunity.com/sharedfiles/filedetails/?id=287241027`.

But in VR, there's more! In VR, you're not so obviously limited by the FOV and physical dimensions of the screen because you can easily move your head to change your view direction at any time. This provides a fully immersive view, that is, horizontal 360 degrees as you look side to side and 180 degrees when you look up and down. With your head still in VR, the field of view is only significant with regard to the outer reaches of your peripheral vision and eyeball movement. But move your head (at the neck or full body) and the software detects the change in head pose (viewing direction) and updates the display. The result is that you believe to have an uninterrupted view of the 360-degree image. In addition, you probably have two eyes. We'll consider stereo views next.

Stereo 360-degree media

To capture monoscopic 360-degree media, you can use a consumer 360-degree camera. These cameras typically have a couple of back-to-back super-wide-angle lenses and corresponding image sensors. The resulting images are stitched together, using clever algorithms to avoid seams, and the result is processed in an equirectangular projection. When viewing it in VR, each eye sees the same 360-degree photo. For landscapes, such as mountain views or other large areas, where the subject is more than 20 meters from your viewing position, it is fine because there is no parallax; that is, each eye sees pretty much the same thing from the same viewing angle. But if the photo includes objects closer to you, it will look incorrect, or at least artificially flattened, because you expect parallax where each eye has a slightly different view.

What about a true 360-degree stereo? Shouldn't each eye have its own photosphere offset from the other eye's position? To capture *stereo* 360-degree media, it cannot simply be photographed by two 360 cameras from two viewpoints; instead, it has to be constructed by stitching together images from a rotating stereo pair. The distance between camera images simulates a human's separation between their eyes (**interpupillary distance**, that is, **IPD**). There is a new generation of consumer cameras (such as *Fuze Camera*, `https://vuze.camera/`, with eight cameras), and high-end professional camera rigs that arrange as many as 16 separate cameras in a cylindrical array and can cost as much as $15,000. Advanced image processing software then constructs stereographic views.

Google introduced an advanced file format for stereo 360-degree video called **omni-directional stereo**, or **ODS**. It is a variant of conventional equirectangular projections with the advantages of avoiding bad seams or dead zones, it is pre-rendered for faster playback, and video uses conventional encoding so that you can edit using conventional tools.

For a more detailed explanation of the challenges and geometry of stereo 360-degree media captures, see the Google whitepaper *Rendering Omni-directional Stereo Content* (`https://developers.google.com/vr/jump/rendering-ods-content.pdf`). Also, check out the article *Stereographic 3D Panoramic Images* by Paul Bourke (May 2002) at `http://paulbourke.net/stereographics/stereopanoramic/`.

Another technology that results in stereo 360-degree viewing is called **Light Fields**. Unlike conventional photographs that capture a single pixel of light reaching the plane of the camera's light sensor (or a set of pixels, in the case of multiple cameras for stereographic media), a light field camera (also known as a **plenoptic** camera) captures not only the *intensity* of light but also the *direction* that the light rays are traveling in space. Light field cameras are fascinating, even for still photography, as the photos possess a unique ability to modify the depth-of-field focus (for example, iOS *portrait mode*) after a picture has been taken, allowing the user to blur the background more or less in an existing photo. Light field technology is rumored to making its way into consumer devices, including Apple and Android mobile phones. Light field's applications for VR are just as impressive, potentially allowing you to view a captured scene from any viewpoint and direction. However, this isn't happening in today's world. Please stay tuned – at the time of writing, I don't know of any tools that support light field images in Unity.

So far, we have learned that spherical images become distorted when flattened into a two-dimensional image and that there are different ways to accomplish this, typically using 360-degree media and an equirectangular projection. You can view such images on a flatscreen such as on Facebook, YouTube, and web browsers. In VR, the 360-degree media become much more immersive because the field of view changes with view direction, tracking the user's head movement. Stereographic 360-degree media is more advanced, providing separate views of the captured scene for each of the user's eyes. Now that we have a better understanding of the nature of 360 images and videos, let's begin using them in a Unity project. We'll start with spherical photo globes.

Having fun with photo globes

To begin exploring these concepts, let's have a little fun and apply ordinary (rectangular) images to 3D spheres. First, let's take a regular photo and apply it as a texture to a sphere, just to see what it does and how bad it looks. Then, we'll use a properly distorted equirectangular photosphere texture. You'll see why that's required to make a globe look correct, but you'll also need a compatible mesh geometry for the project to look right. Lastly, we'll invert the shader we're using to view the globes so that the image projects onto the inside of the sphere instead of the outside. Then, we'll play with it as a *magic orb* in VR.

Seeing crystal balls

"Auntie Em! Auntie Em!" cried Dorothy in the *Wizard of Oz* 1939 movie as she gazed into a crystal ball, seeking help from the Wicked Witch. Let's consider making a crystal ball using Unity, *my little pretty!* In `Chapter 8`, *Lighting, Rendering, Realism,* we considered techniques we can use for custom materials, including simulating metal and glass surfaces. We'll apply similar settings in our semi-transparent crystal ball material. And to give an impression of thickness to the glass, we'll project the image onto a smaller sphere with a ball.

First, set up a new scene for this chapter by performing the following steps. We can use a stationary XR camera rig for this:

1. Create a new scene by navigating to **File** | **New Scene**. Then, navigate to **File** | **Save As...** and name it `PhotoGlobes`.
2. Add a stationary XR Camera Rig to the scene using **GameObject** | **XR** | **Stationary XR Rig**.

3. Set the XR Rig's **Position** to (`0, 0, -1`).
4. For the **Game** window view, while in the Unity Editor, elevate **Camera Offset** above the ground and set its **Position Y** to `1.4`.
5. For VR, I always like to set **Main Camera | Clipping Planes | Near** to zero (`0.01`).

Let's set up the scene environment with a ground plane and a skybox. If you've installed the Wispy Sky package, as suggested in previous chapters (`https://assetstore.unity.com/packages/2d/textures-materials/sky/wispy-skybox-21737`), add a skybox to the scene as follows:

1. Open the scene's **Lighting** window via **Window | Rendering | Lighting settings**.
2. Select the **Environment** tab at the top of the window (Unity 2020+).
3. At the top is a slot for **Skybox Material**. Press the **doughnut-icon**, which opens the **Select Material** dialog.
4. Search using the `wispy` string.
5. Select one of the skyboxes to use in the scene, such as `WispySkyboxMat2`.

While we're in the **Lighting** window, let's auto-generate the lighting for when we work on the crystal ball materials:

1. In the **Lighting** window, select the **Scene** tab at the top.
2. Uncheck the **Mixed Lighting | Baked Global Illumination** checkbox.
3. Check the **Auto Generate** checkbox at the bottom of the window.

For a default environment, let's just create a simple ground plane, as follows:

1. Create a new plane by navigating to **GameObject | 3D Object | Plane** and reset its transformation using the **Transform** component's three-dot icon | **Reset**. Rename it `Ground Plane`.
2. Create a new material named `Ground Material` using **Assets | Create | Material** with a **Base Map** color such as `#543C30`.

I'm using the `EthanSkull.png` image that was provided with this book (drag and drop it into your **Project** `Assets/Textures` folder). Then, perform the following steps:

1. Create a new sphere by navigating to **GameObject | 3D Object | Sphere** and name it `CrystalBall`.
2. Set its **Position** to (`-0.5, 1.25, 0.2`).

3. Create a new material named `CrystalBall Material` using **Assets** | **Create** | **Material** and drag it onto the **CrystalBall** sphere.
4. In the **CrystalBall** inspector window, unfold its **CrystalBall Material** settings.
5. Set its **Surface Type** to **Transparent**.
6. Set its **Base Map** color to white (`#FFFFFF`) with **Alpha** `123`.
7. Set the **Metalic Map** factor to `0.9`.
8. Set the **Smoothness** factor to `0.9`.

Now, for the inner image projection, we'll add another sphere, as follows:

1. With **CrystalBall** selected in **Hierarchy**, right-click and select **3D Object** | **Sphere** and name it **CrystalBall Image**.
2. Reset its **Position** to (`0, 0, 0`) and **Scale** it to (`0.95, 0.95, 0.95`).
3. Create a new material named `CrystalBall Image Material` using **Assets** | **Create** | **Material** and drag it onto the **CrystalBall Image** sphere.
4. Set its **Surface Type** to **Transparent**.
5. Drag the texture named `EthanSkull` (you can use any photo you want) onto the **Base Map** texture slot (on its left, and set its **Base Map** color to white (`#FFFFFF`).
6. Set the **Base Map** color's **Alpha** to `123` like the outer sphere.
7. To make it brighter, we'll add an Emission. Check the **Emission** checkbox.
8. Drag the same **EthanSkull** image onto its **Emission Map** texture slot and set its **Emission** color to white.
9. Uncheck its **Specular Highlights** and **Environment Reflections** boxes; we'll let the outer sphere render those.

Not bad! For even better fidelity, we can add a **Reflection Probe** to the scene, as follows:

1. Select **GameObject** | **Light** | **Reflection Probe.**
2. Set its **Position** to the same as that of **CrystalBall** (`-0.5, 1.25, 0.2`).
3. For this example, set its **Type** to **Realtime** and **Refresh Mode** to **Every Frame** (in real projects, you'll probably want to keep it **Baked**).

Now, press **Play**. The resulting scene will look like this:

Is that scary or what? No worries. The projected image may be distorted, but it looks wicked cool. For some applications, a little distortion is an artistic intent, and you don't need to worry about it. Just for fun, let's add a little rotation script while we're at it. Create a new script on the **CrystalBall** game object by navigating to **Add Component** | **New Script** and name it `Rotator`. Open the script and write the following inside it:

```
public class Rotator : MonoBehaviour
{
  [Tooltip("Rotation rate in degrees per second")]
  public Vector3 rate;

  void Update()
  {
    transform.Rotate(rate * Time.deltaTime);
  }
}
```

Note that I added a `Tooltip` attribute for the Unity Editor that gives the developer (your coworkers or you, in the future) more details regarding how to use the `rate` values. Then, set the rotation rate so that it spins around the y-axis 20 degrees per second by going to the **Rotator Script** component and setting **Rate** for **X**, **Y**, **Z** as (`0`, `20`, `0`). Save the scene and try it in VR.

If you're interested in more realistic glass simulation shaders for your crystal balls, look on the Asset Store at `https://assetstore.unity.com/?q=glassorderBy=1`. Just be sure to select one that is compatible with the render pipeline being used in your project.

Note that transparency should be used sparingly in VR applications as it requires additional rendering passes per pixel, potentially slowing your frame generation and causing unwanted latency.

This spherical rendering of a regular rectangular image has clearly made it distorted. What if we want an image that's neatly mapped to the surface curvature of the sphere? That's what we'll do next to render a globe.

Rendering globes

To make the texture surface of the globe appear correct, we should use an equirectangular (photosphere) image projection. Let's make another sphere and add a texture, as we just did, but this time using a texture made for this purpose. Import the `Tissot_euirectangular.png` image, which is included with this book (and available on Wikipedia at `https://en.wikipedia.org/wiki/Tissot%27s_indicatrix#/media/File:Tissot_behrmann.png`), into your `Texture` folder and perform the following steps:

1. Create another new sphere and name it `Globe`.
2. **Position** it at (`0.75, 1.25, 0.2`).
3. Create a new material named `Globe Material` and drag it onto the **Globe** sphere.
4. Drag the texture named `Tissot_equirectangular` onto the **Base Map** texture slot (on its left) and set its **Base Map** color to white (`#FFFFFF`).
5. Add the `Rotator` script if you want.

Try it in VR. Take a close look at the globe, as shown in the following screenshot:

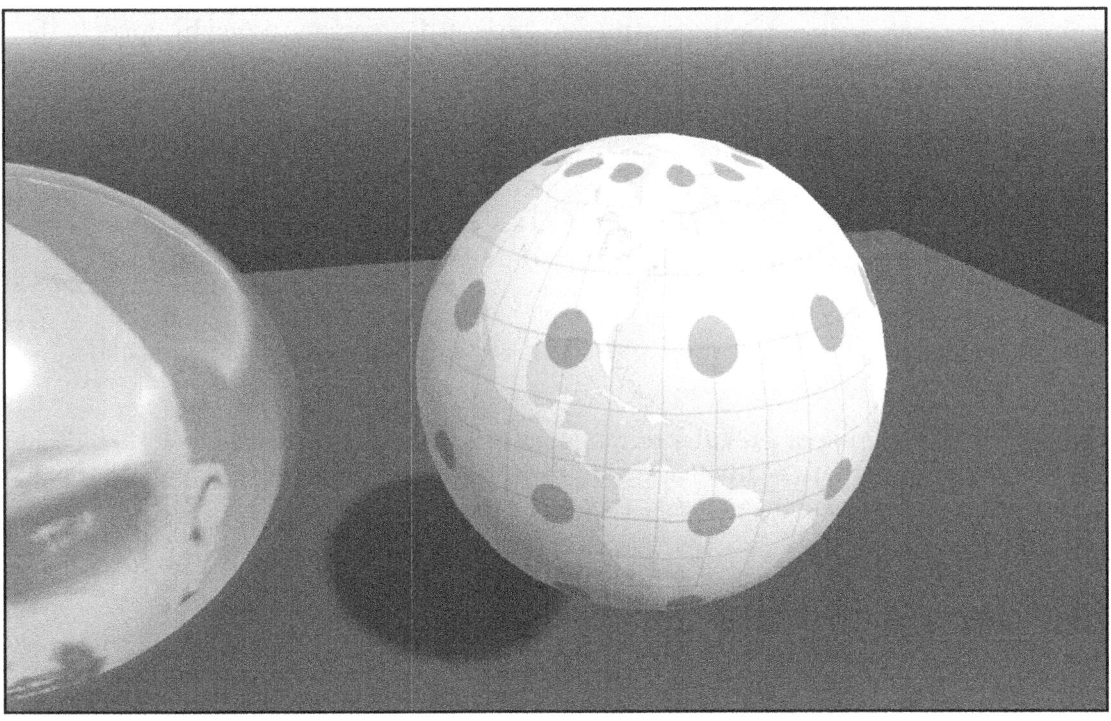

Hmm, it's still not right. Note that, unfortunately, the Tissot circles are oval, not circular, except along the equator. It turns out that the default sphere provided in Unity does not mesh well for equirectangular texture maps. Instead, I have provided one designed specifically for this purpose, `PhotoSphere.fbx` (which happens to be the default sphere model in 3D Studio Max). Let's try it out:

1. Import the `PhotoSphere.fbx` file by dragging it into your **Project** `Assets/Models` folder (or through the **Assets** | **Import New Asset...** menu).
2. Create a new equirectangular sphere by dragging the `PhotoSphere` model from **Project Assets** into **Scene**.
3. Set its position and name it `Globe2`.
4. Drag the same **Globe Material** we just created onto **Globe2**.
5. Add the `Rotator` script if you want.

Now, try this in VR. *Much better*. You can see that the texture is correctly mapped now; the circles are round (and the underlying mesh grid is more regular):

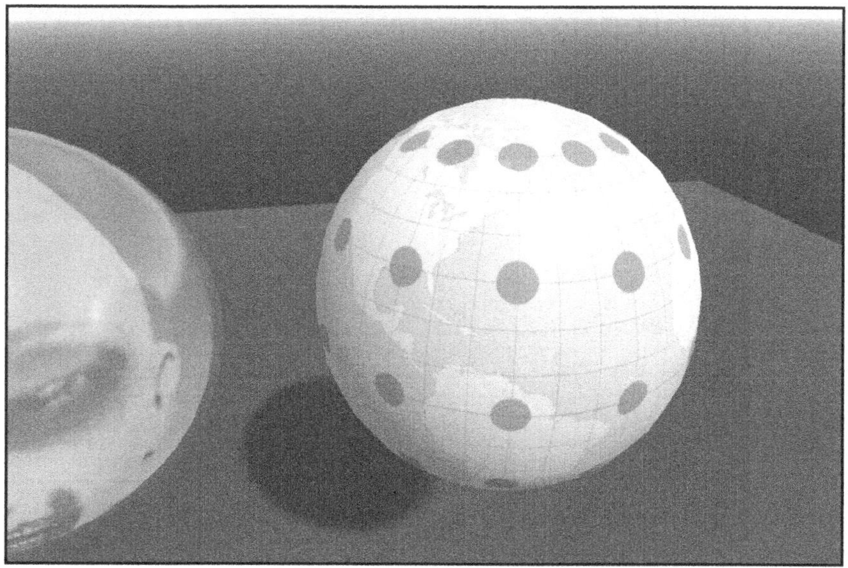

Now, you can apply any 360-degree photo to the globe, thus creating your own *photo-globes* or virtual Christmas tree ornaments!

To expand on this topic, you could build a nice model of the Solar System, for example. Equirectangular texture maps of each of the planets and moons can be downloaded for free from Solar System Scope (`https://www.solarsystemscope.com/`). Data regarding the rate of rotation (day/night) and orbit (around the sun) can be found on the NASA site (`https://nssdc.gsfc.nasa.gov/planetary/factsheet/index.html`). A complete Unity tutorial project can be found in the book *Augmented Reality for Developers* (`https://www.amazon.com/Augmented-Reality-Developers-Jonathan-Linowes/dp/1787286436`).

Next, let's turn the globe inside-out and make a mini-world from what I like to call *magic orbs*.

Handling magic orbs

The inverse of a globe is a photosphere. Where a globe maps an equirectangular texture onto the outside surface of a sphere, a photosphere would map the texture onto the inside surface, and you view it from the inside so that it surrounds you.

For our examples, I'm using the `Farmhouse.png` image, which is provided with this book and looks as follows. Feel free to use your own 360-degree photo, whether you have a 360-degree camera such as the Ricoh Theta or another brand, a photo stitching app for Android or iOS, or you just download one from any number of photo sources on the web:

As we've seen, Unity ordinarily renders only the outward-facing surfaces of objects. This is determined, mathematically, as the *normal* direction vector of each facet of its surface mesh. A plane is the simplest example. Back in `Chapter 2`, *Understanding Unity, Content, and Scale,* we created a big-screen plane with an image of the Grand Canyon on it. When you are facing the plane, you see the image. I don't know if you realized this, but if you were to move around behind the plane, it is not rendered, as if it were not in the scene at all. Similarly, suppose there is a cube or sphere in front of you; you will see it rendered, lit, and shaded. But if you put your head inside the object, it seems to disappear, because you're now looking at the inside faces of the object's mesh. This is all handled by the **shader**. And since we want to change it, we need to modify our material to render the inside (back) faces.

Before we do full 360-photo viewing, for fun, let's first consider a special case: *magic orbs*. For this example, we'll look at the sphere from the inside, mapping a 360-degree image onto its inside surface. We'll put a solid colored *shell* around the outside. You have to stick your head into the sphere to see what's there, or grab the sphere and "put it on your eyes!"

To build it, follow these steps. First, we will create a translucent red outer shell:

1. Create a sphere in the scene named `MagicOrb` using **GameObject** | **3D** | **Sphere**.
2. Set its **Position** somewhere within reach, such as (`-1, 1.25, -1`).
3. Create a new material by navigating to **Assets** | **Create** | **Material** and name it `MagicOrb Shell Material`.
4. Drag **MagicOrb Shell Material** onto the **MagicOrb** game object.
5. Set the material's **Surface Type** to **Transparent** and the **Base Map** color to a red (for example, `#FF4242`) with **Alpha** `200`.

The inward-facing photosphere will be concentric with the shell, so we'll make it a child and add the equirectangular texture image, as follows:

1. Create a child photosphere by dragging a copy of the `PhotoSphere` model from the **Project** `Assets/Models/` folder into **Hierarchy** as a child of **MagicOrb**. Rename it `Farmhouse PhotoSphere`.
2. Create a new material by navigating to **Assets** | **Create** | **Material** and name it `Farmhouse Inward Material`.
3. Drag **Farmhouse Inward Material** onto **Farmhouse PhotoSphere**.
4. On **Farmhouse Inward Material**, change **Shader** to **Universal Render Pipeline/Unlit**.

Now, here's the clincher. We will change the shader so that it renders the "back" (inside) faces instead of the front ones, as follows:

1. Change its **Render Face** to **Back** so that it renders the inside of the sphere instead of the outside.
2. Drag the `Farmhouse` texture from your **Project** `Assets/Textures/` folder onto the **Base Map** texture slot (left of **Base Map**).
3. Set the **Base Map** color to white (`#FFFFFF`).
4. To ensure the texture appears as a mirror image on the inside of the sphere, set its **Tiling X** to `-1`.

The following screenshot shows the scene we built:

While the Scriptable Render Pipeline shaders such as the UWP/Unlit one we're using offers the **Render Face | Back** option in the **Inspector** window, not all shaders do. If your project is using the older standard (built-In) pipeline, for example, you may need to write a custom shader to cull the front faces and render the back ones. It's easy! In that case, simply select **Assets | Create | Shader | Unlit Shader** and edit the shader script by adding the line `Cull Front` (immediately after the `Tags` line). Then, use this new custom shader in your material's **Shader** setting.

At this point, if you **Play** the scene and move your head so it's inside the orb, you'll see the farmhouse scene! (Or simply in the Editor, temporarily drag the **MagicOrb** game object in the **Scene** view directly onto the **Main Camera** position). Let's make this interactive using the XRI **Grab Interactable** component, as follows:

1. On **MagicOrb**, make it interactable by selecting **Component | XR | Grab Interactable.**
2. We don't want it to fall to the ground, so disable gravity by unchecking the **Rigidbody | Use Gravity** checkbox.
3. Also, we don't want it to move from physics interactions, so disable **Physics** by checking the **Rigidbody | IsKinematic** checkbox.
4. Because our intent is to place the orb on your face, change the camera's near clipping plane to almost zero using **Main Camera | Clipping Planes | Near** | `0.01`.

Now, when you play the scene in VR, use the hand controller to grab the orb and pull it to your face, as depicted in the following screenshot. It's like peering into an eggshell!

In VR games and experiences, photo globes and magic orbs have been used as a teleportation mechanism. As a player, you grab a globe depicting another scene, put it on your face, and you are teleported into that world. See the *Capturing 360-degree media* section for how to capture a 360-degree photo of your Unity scenes.

Well, that was fun. We made a 3D crystal ball with a projected image, a photo globe, and even magic orbs. For the crystal ball, we used a normal rectangular image as the texture and rendered it using a transparent shader for a glass-like effect. For globes, we learned how to use an equirectangular 360-degree photo wrapped on a photosphere mesh to make it look non-distorted, as expected. Then, for magic orbs, we rendered the image on the inside of a sphere and made it intractable, so that the player can pick up the ball and "put it on" their eyes to get an immersive 360-degree photo effect. Now, let's really put ourselves inside the 360 images, starting with writing a 360-degree photo viewing app.

Viewing 360-degree photos

Yes sir, it's all the rage these days. It's better than panoramas. It's better than selfies. It may even be better than Snapchat! We're finally getting to the moment that you've been waiting for! It's 360-degree photos! We covered a lot of topics in this chapter, which will now make it fairly easy for us to talk about a 360-degree photo viewer. To build one, we'll just make a very big sphere with shader back faces rendered as they were previously. Start with a new empty scene:

1. Create a new scene by navigating to **File** | **New Scene**. Then, navigate to **File** | **Save As...** and name it `PhotoSphere`.
2. Add a stationary XR Camera Rig to the scene using **GameObject** | **XR** | **Stationary XR Rig**.
3. Set the XR Rig's **Position** to (`0`, `0`, `0`).

Now, to view a 360-degree photo, we simply make a giant sphere with the image on its inside, as follows:

1. Create an equirectangular sphere by dragging the `PhotoSphere` model from the **Project** `Assets/Models/` folder into the scene (as imported from `PhotoSphere.fbx` in the previous example).
2. Reset its **Transform Position** (`0`, `0`, `0`) and set its **Scale** to (`10`, `10`, `10`).
3. Create a material using **Assets** | **Create** | **Material** and name it `PhotoSphere Material`.
4. Drag **PhotoSphere Material** onto the **PhotoSphere** game object.
5. Set the material's **Shader** to **Universal Render Pipeline / Unlit**.
6. Set **Render Face** to **Back**.
7. Set the **Base Map** color to white (`#FFFFFF`).
8. To ensure the texture appears as a mirror-image on the inside of the sphere, set its **Tiling X** to `-1`.
9. Drag a 360-degree photo, such as the `Farmhouse` image we've been using, onto the **Base Map** texture slot (left of **Base Map**).
10. On the **Photosphere** game object, disable its renderer lighting properties by setting **Mesh Renderer** | **Lighting** | **Cast Shadows** | **Off**, then **Probes** | **Light Probes** | **Off**, then **Reflection Probes** | **Off**, and then uncheck the **Dynamic Occlusion** checkbox.

Press **Play**. You should now see the photosphere surrounding you in the scene. The following screenshot shows a Scene view zoomed out of the photosphere so that you can see the Main Camera's location and its viewport FOV depicted with gray lines:

You may find that the default texture resolution and/or compression are not of a high enough quality for your taste. To modify the resolution, follow these steps:

1. Select the texture image in the **Project** window (`Farmhouse.png`).
2. In **Inspector**, change **Max Size** to a larger number, such as `8192`.
3. Set **Compression** to **High Quality**.
4. Press **Apply** to reimport the texture.

Note that the actual file size (at the bottom of **Inspector**) can grow exponentially, thus affecting the final size of your app, load times, and runtime performance. You can configure these settings on a per-platform basis. Now, suppose you want to build a 360-degree photo viewer using images from the web. We'll consider that next.

Viewing 360 images from the web

We can now view 360 images, so let's develop the project into a 360-degree photo viewer that grabs images from the internet. Currently, if you build the Unity project with the current scene, the Farmhouse equirectangular image will be compiled into the assets of the built project. Instead, now, we'll provide URLs of images on the web and load them into the app on demand.

Let's start by making an **ImageController** object and write a script that loads images using the following steps:

1. Select **GameObject | Create Empty**, name it `ImageController`, and reset its **Transform**.
2. Create a new attached script by going to **Add Component | New Script** and name it `WebImages`.
3. Open the script for editing.

   Write the script as follows:

```
using UnityEngine;
using UnityEngine.Networking;

public class WebImages : MonoBehaviour
{
 public string imageURL;
 public Renderer imageRenderer;

 private void Start()
 {
     StartCoroutine(GetWebImage(imageURL));
 }

 IEnumerator GetWebImage(string url)
 {
     using (UnityWebRequest webRequest =
          UnityWebRequestTexture.GetTexture(url))
     {
         // request and wait for the result
         yield return webRequest.SendWebRequest();

         if (webRequest.isNetworkError || webRequest.isHttpError)
         {
             Debug.Log(webRequest.error);
         }
         else
         {
             Debug.Log("Got data " + webRequest.responseCode);
             var texture = DownloadHandlerTexture.GetContent
                                                 (webRequest);
             // use the following with Universal Render
                   Pipeline/Unlit shader
             imageRenderer.material.SetTexture("_BaseMap",
                                                 texture);
             // use the following with built-in shader
             //imageRenderer.material.mainTexture = texture;
```

```
                }
            }
        }
```

Here, we declare two variables: the `imageURL` string is the web address of the image file, while the `imageRenderer` string is the photosphere GameObject's renderer. When the app starts, we call `GetWebImage` in a coroutine, which uses the `UnityWebRequest` networking API, which is configured to get texture files from a web server (see `https://docs.unity3d.com/ScriptReference/Networking.UnityWebRequestTexture.GetTexture.html`). It initiates a web request to the given URL and waits for a result to be returned from the web server. If the request fails, we report the error. If it's successful, we assign the received `GetContent` to the `imageRenderer` material texture. (Of course, you could add improved in-app error reporting if the web request fails).

Note that `UnityWebRequestTexture.GetTexture` only supports JPG and PNG formats.

Save the script. Now, find an equirectangular image on the web somewhere. Then, in Unity, paste its URL in the **Image URL** slot. For example, in `photopin.com`, search for the word `equirectangular`, select **Get Photo** for one of them, and then copy the download link for one of the image sizes, as shown in the following screenshot:

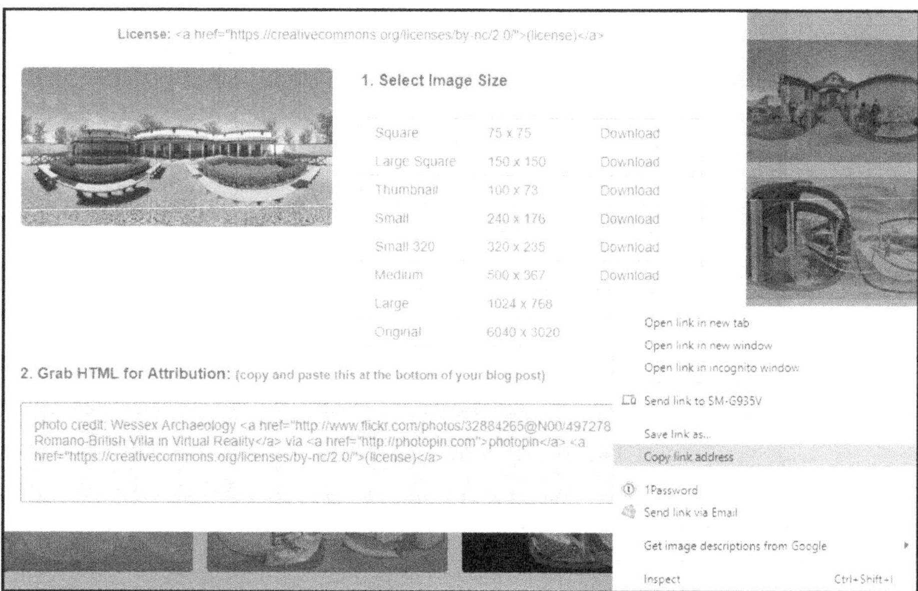

The following screenshot shows the URL pasted into the **Web Images** | **Image URL** slot:

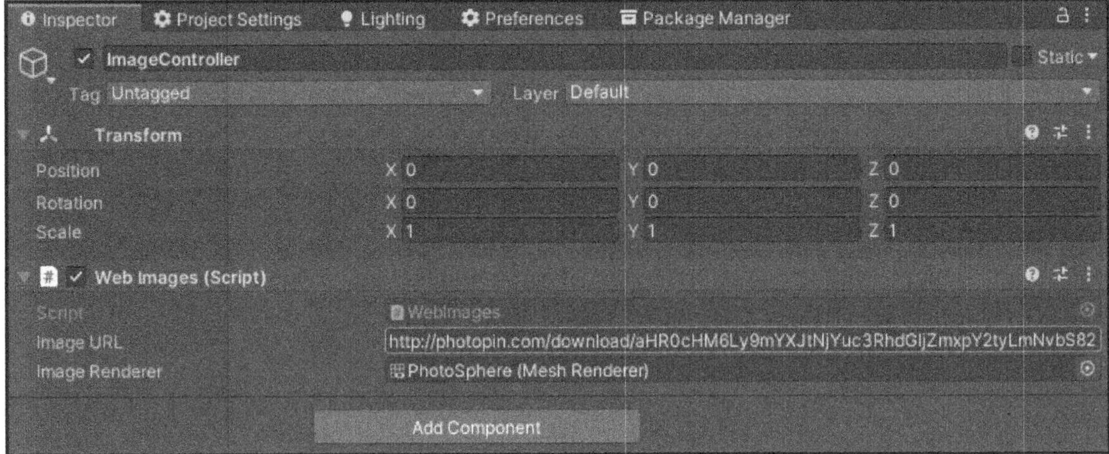

When you **Play** the scene, your script will make a web request to the given URL, download the image, and assign it to the photosphere's material. Let's expand this feature so that it uses a list of images and provides a UI menu for switching between 360 images at runtime.

Adding an image viewer UI

For completeness, let's add a simple user interface so that we can select different images. In `Chapter 6`, *Canvasing the World Space UI*, we learned about using a world space XR canvas for UI. In this case, we'll add a button dashboard UI that follows the player. The buttons on the panel will be thumbnails of the images to load, and since we're loading these images from the web, we'll use a **Raw Image** component instead of the Unity UI sprite **Image** (this avoids having to convert the image texture into Unity's internal Sprite data).

In the previous chapter, `Chapter 10`, *Exploring Interactive Spaces*, we considered various ways of managing image data. In this case, we'll make an array of `struct` that includes links for a thumbnail image, a full 360-degree image, and an attribution string (which may be required by the image source website). First, let's modify `ImageController` in order to define an array of `struct ImageData`, as follows:

```
using UnityEngine.UI;

[System.Serializable]
public struct ImageData
{
    public RawImage buttonImage;
```

```
        public string thumbnailURL;
        public string imageURL;
        public string attribution;
    }

     public class WebImages : MonoBehaviour
    {
        public ImageData[] imageData;
        public Renderer imageRenderer;
```

We declare `struct ImageData` with a `[System.Serializable]` attribute so that it will appear in the Unity Inspector as the `ImageData` array.

When we make buttons in the scene, they'll call a `LoadImage` function with the image's `index`. Add that function now. It calls `GetWebImage`, which we wrote earlier, with `imageURL` for the given index:

```
        public void LoadImage(int index)
        {
            StartCoroutine(GetWebImage(imageData[index].imageURL));
        }
```

Also, let's load up the button's thumbnail images on `Start`, as follows. This calls a similar `GetWebButton` function that loads the thumbnail version of the image into the button's **Raw Image** texture:

```
        private void Start()
        {
            foreach (ImageData data in imageData)
            {
                StartCoroutine(GetWebButton(data.buttonImage,
                    data.thumbnailURL));
            }
        }

        IEnumerator GetWebButton(RawImage rawImage, string url)
        {
            using (UnityWebRequest webRequest =
                 UnityWebRequestTexture.GetTexture(url))
            {
                // request and wait for the result
                yield return webRequest.SendWebRequest();

                if (webRequest.isNetworkError || webRequest.isHttpError)
                {
                    Debug.Log(webRequest.error);
                }
```

```
            else
            {
                Debug.Log("Got data " + webRequest.responseCode);
                rawImage.texture = DownloadHandlerTexture.GetContent
                                                        (webRequest);
            }
        }
    }
```

Save the script. Now, back in Unity, create a canvas with four buttons, as follows:

1. Create an XR Canvas by selecting **GameOjbect** | **XR** | **UI Canvas** and rename it `Button Canvas`.
2. In **Hierarchy**, unfold **XR Rig / Camera Offset** and drag **Button Canvas** to a child of **Camera Offset**.
3. Set its **Scale** to (`0.001, 0.001, 0.001`). As we know, this is the scale of one canvas pixel in world coordinates.
4. Set its **Position** to a comfortable distance, such as (`0, -0.65, 1.6`).
5. Set its **Width, Height** to (`1260, 200`).
6. Create a child **Panel** by right-clicking on **Button Canvas** and selecting **UI** | **Panel**.
7. On the **Panel**, select **Add Component** | search for `layout` | **Horizontal Layout Group**.
8. Uncheck the **Child Force Expand** checkboxes for **Width** and **Height**.
9. Set its **Spacing** to `20`.

Next, we can create four buttons on the panel by using **Raw Image** instead of **Image**, as follows:

1. Create a child **Button** by right-clicking on **Panel** and selecting **UI** | **Button**.
2. Set its **Width, Height** to `300, 200`.
3. Disable (or delete) its child **Text** object.
4. Remove its **Image** component using the component's three-dot menu | **Remove Component**.
5. Use **Add Component** | search for `image` | **Raw Image**.
6. From **Hierarchy**, drag the same **Button** game object onto its own **Button** | **Target Graphic** slot.
7. On its **Button** | **On Click**, press the **+** button to add a new event action.

8. Drag the **ImageController** game object from **Hierarchy** onto the event's **Object** slot.
9. In the **Function** selection list, choose **WebImages | LoadImage**.

The button will look as follows in the **Inspector** window:

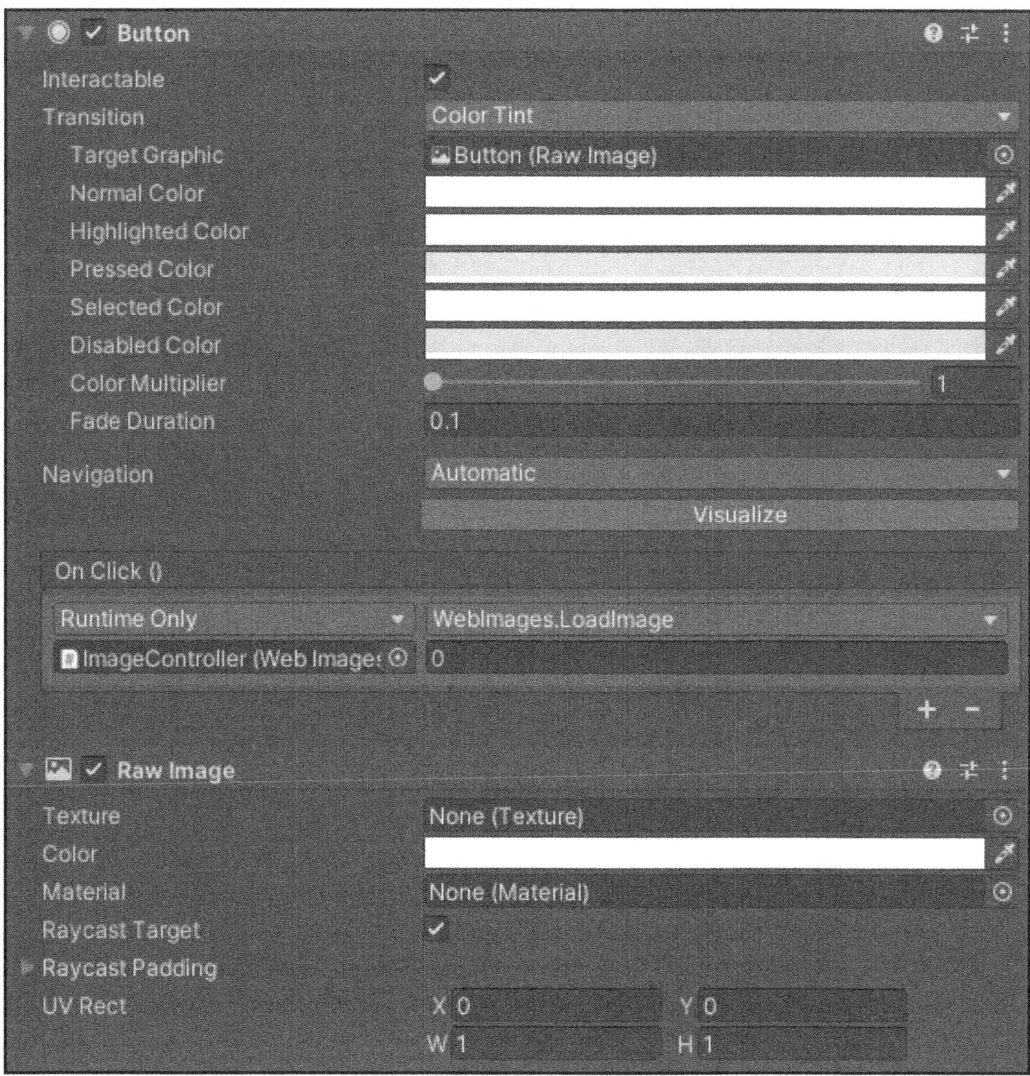

We want four of these buttons. Follow these steps to do this easily:

1. Select **Button** in **Hierarchy**.
2. Make three duplicates using *Ctrl* + *D*.

The **Scene** and **Hierarchy** windows will now look as follows:

Now, we can wire up the buttons to load the corresponding images for each image index, 0 through 3:

1. Select the first **Button** game object under **Panel**.
2. Ensure the **On Click | WebImages.LoadImage** parameter is set to `0`.
3. Select the second **Button (1)** object and set its **LoadImage** parameter to `1`.
4. Select the second **Button (2)** object and set its **LoadImage** parameter to `2`.
5. Select the second **Button (3)** object and set its **LoadImage** parameter to `3`.

Begin to populate **Image Data** in **ImageController** in order to reference the **Button** images. There will be four of them, one for each button, as follows:

1. Select **ImageController** in **Hierarchy**.
2. Set its **Web Images | Image Data | Size** value to `4`.
3. For **Element 0**, drag the **Button** game object from **Hierarchy** onto the **Button Image** slot.
4. Repeat these steps for the other three buttons.

Finally, populate the **Image Data Thumbnail URL**, **Image URL**, and **Attribution** slots with real data from the web. Remember that you need to use the actual download URL for our web requests, not simply a web page (HTML) that contains the target image. I picked four interesting images at random from Photopin (`http://photopin.com/free-photos/equirectangular`). For example, the data for my first one, which can be found at `https://www.flickr.com/photos/32884265@N00/49727861697`, can be found at the following links:

- Thumbnail: `http://photopin.com/download/aHR0cHM6Ly9mYXJtNjYuc3RhdGljZmxpY2tyLmNvbS82NTUzNS80OTcyNzg2%0AMTY5N182NzVlZWUzZjMxX3QuanBn%0A?photo_id=49727861697`
- Large Image: `http://photopin.com/download/aHR0cHM6Ly9mYXJtNjYuc3RhdGljZmxpY2tyLmNvbS82NTUzNS80OTcyNzg2%0AMTY5N182NzVlZWUzZjMxX2IuanBn%0A?photo_id=49727861697`
- Photo credit: Wessex Archaeology

As shown in the following screenshot, the filled out **Image Data** array contains four elements, where each element references a **Button Image** component, links to the thumbnail and image files, and provides a text string with attribution details:

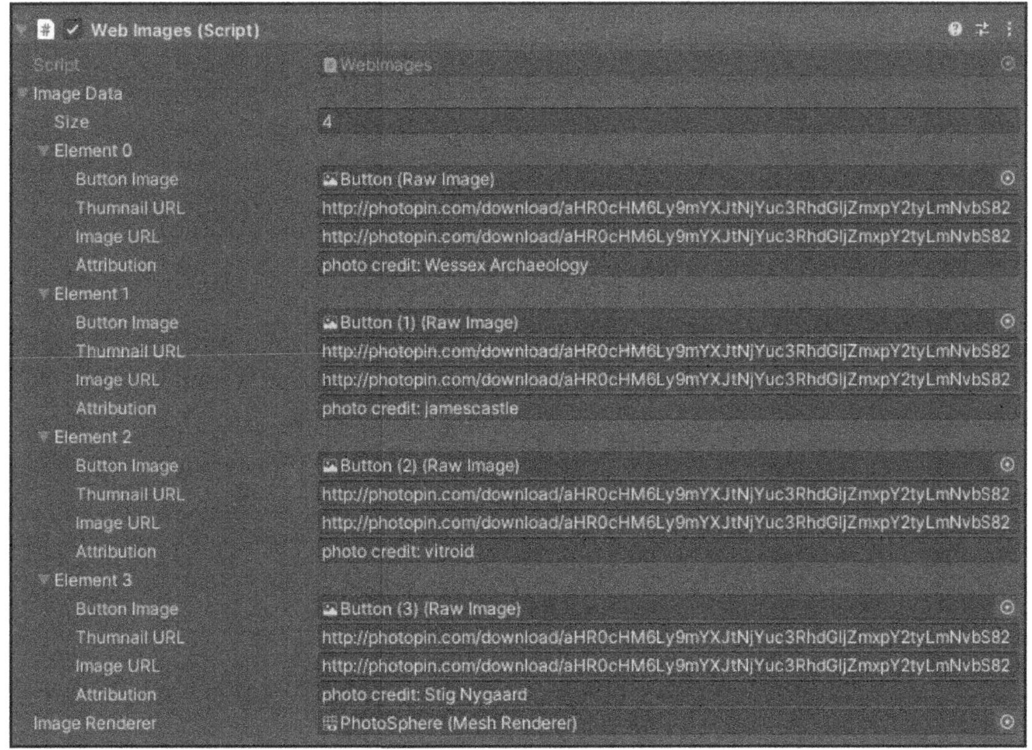

When you press **Play**, the menu buttons get filled with the thumbnail images. Clicking on one of the buttons by aiming the hand controller and pressing the select button will load the corresponding equirectangular image into the scene. The following is a screen capture of me viewing some 360-degree photos in the app, pointing to and selecting one of the images from the menu:

If you develop this into a full application, be sure to add a canvas panel to display the image attribution text and other metadata as needed. You will also probably want to add a "Loading" message/spinner to give the user feedback after a thumbnail button is clicked. Many image repository websites provide developer API and web services so that you can search, get, and even put (upload) photos from your application; for example:

- Flickr (`https://www.flickr.com/services/api/`)
- Unsplash (`https://unsplash.com/developers`)
- Google 360 Media (`https://developers.google.com/vr/discover/360-degree-media`)

In this project, we created a 360-degree photo viewer using a photosphere with a back face render. We added thumbnail-sized button images that the user can click, which then calls the `LoadImage` function we wrote to load the image from the corresponding URL from the web and show it in the scene. This works perfectly for still images. However, 360 videos are at least as popular as photos, so we'll learn how to view those next.

Playing 360-degree videos

The steps for playing a 360-degree video are pretty much the same as adding regular rectangular videos to a Unity project, that is, using a `Video Player` to render the video onto a `Render Texture`. In the case of 360 videos, we can render that Render Texture inside a photosphere, as we did in the previous section. Let's build that now.

If you do not have a 360-degree video handy, search for web-free downloads and pick one that's not too long and of a limited file size. (Try googling `360 videos download` – `https://www.google.com/search?q=360+videos+download`). The example used here (licensed under Creative Commons) can be found at `https://en.wikipedia.org/wiki/File:Hundra_knektars_marsch_p%C3%A5_Forum_Vulgaris.webm` (the file download link is `https://upload.wikimedia.org/wikipedia/commons/f/fb/Hundra_knektars_marsch_p%C3%A5_Forum_Vulgaris.webm`). It's very low resolution (1,920 x 860) and is just being used for this demo. Usually, you'll want at least 4K (4,096 x 2,160) or greater.

To download 360 videos from YouTube, you can use tools such as **4kvideodownload** (`https://www.4kdownload.com/products/product-videodownloader`).

Import a 360-degree video into your project by dragging the file into your **Project** `Assets` folder. You have the option of using Unity's built-in transcoder to ensure compatibility with your target platform. Follow these steps:

1. Drag your video file from the Windows Explorer (or OSX Finder) into the Unity **Project** `Assets/` folder.
2. In its **Inspector**, you may want to use the built-in transcoder by checking the **Transcode** checkbox.
3. In lieu of flipping the video mirror-image in **Material** | **Tiling** | **X**, you can check the **Flip Horizontally** checkbox.
4. If you receive errors when running the conversion, you might want to try changing **Codec** from **Auto**. I have found success using **Codec** | **VP8**.
5. Press **Apply**. It can take a while to run the conversion.

Depending on the format of your video, you may need to install QuickTime on your system first before you can import it into Unity, for the conversion of codec.

Note its pixel dimensions. If you're not sure, you can view it in **Inspector**. At the bottom, choose **Source Info** from the preview select list, as shown in the following screenshot:

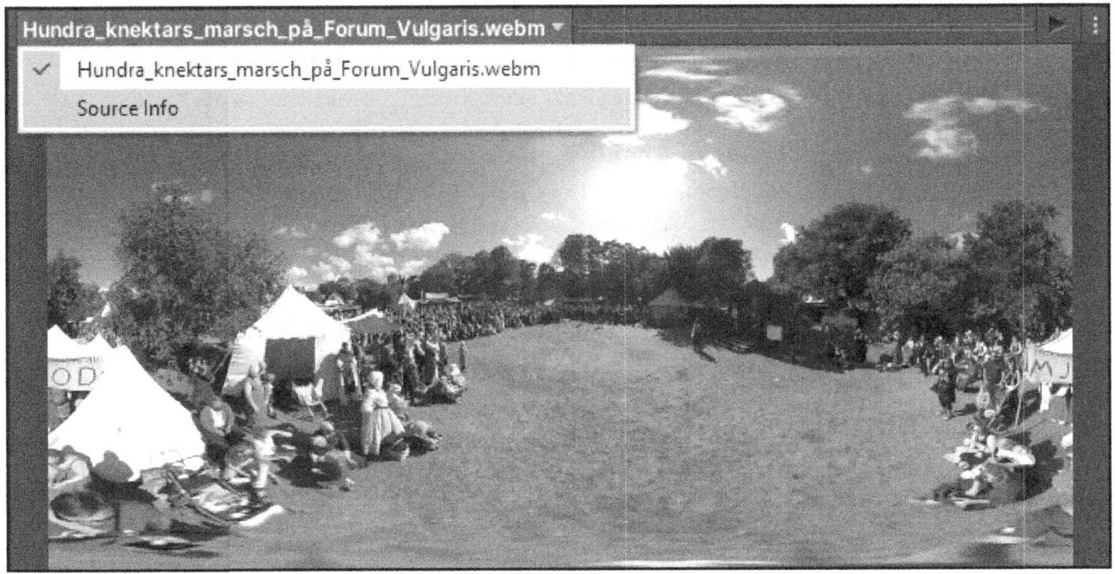

Start a new scene and include an XR Rig located at the origin, as follows:

1. Create a new scene by navigating to **File** | **New Scene**. Then, navigate to **File** | **Save As...** and name it `VideoSphere`.
2. Add a stationary XR Camera Rig to the scene using **GameObject** | **XR** | **Stationary XR Rig**.
3. Set the XR Rig **Position** to (`0`, `0`, `0`).

The first step is to add a `VideoPlayer` component to your project, as follows:

1. Create an empty object **(GameObject** | **Create Empty)** named `VideoPlayer`.
2. Click **Add Component** | **Video Player**.
3. Drag your video file onto the **Video Player** | **Video Clip** slot.
4. Check the **Play On Awake** checkbox and the **Loop** checkbox.
5. Ensure **Render Mode** is set to **Render Texture**.
6. You may need to set **Video Player** | **Aspect Ratio** to **Stretch**.

Note that if your video contains an audio track, it will play automatically since **Video Player** | **Audio Output Mode** is set to **Direct**. If you prefer, you can add an **Audio Source** component to the player and then change **Audio Output Mode** to **Audio Player**. You will also notice other options in **Video Player**, including **Source** being set to **Video Clip**, which can be changed to **URL** if you want to play videos from the web.

Now, we will create a Render Texture, a special Unity texture that will be rendered at runtime by the video player:

1. In your **Project** `Assets` folder, go to **Create** | **Render Texture** and name it `Video Render Texture`.
2. Set **Size** to exactly the size of your video (my demo is `1920, 800`).
3. Setting **Anti aliasing** to **2 samples** is recommended.
4. You can set **Depth Buffer** to **No Depth Buffer**.
5. In some cases, the video does not render correctly using the default **Clamp Wrap Mode**, so try setting **Wrap Mode** | **Repeat**.
6. Select **VideoPlayer** in **Hierarchy** and drag this **Video Render Texture** onto its **Video Player** | **Target Texture** slot.

The resulting **VideoPlayer** in the **Inspector** window can be seen in the following screenshot:

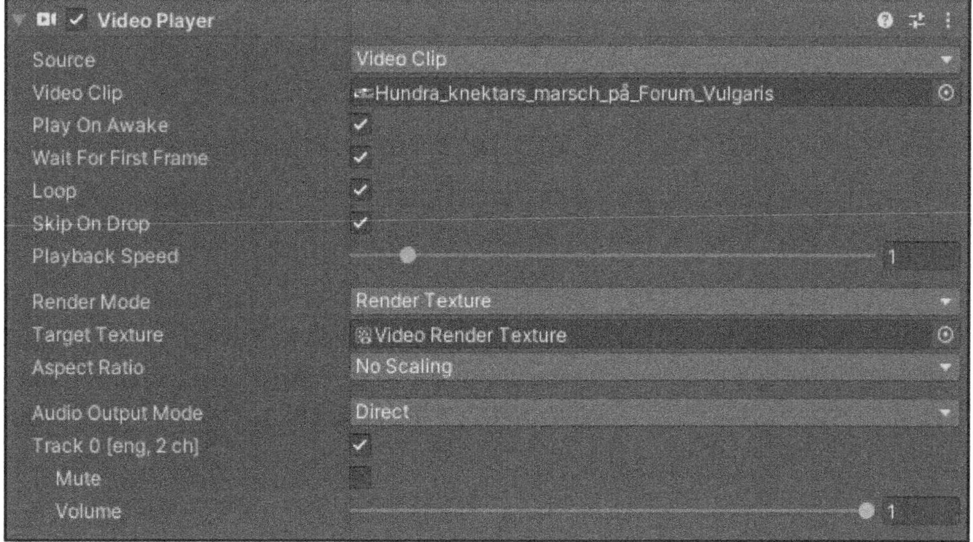

Now, create your photosphere, as we did previously in this chapter:

1. Create an equirectangular sphere by dragging the `PhotoSphere` model from the **Project** `Assets/Models/` folder into the scene (as imported from `PhotoSphere.fbx` in the previous example). Rename it `VideoSphere`.
2. Reset its **Transform Position** (`0, 0, 0`) and set its **Scale** to (`10, 10, 10`).
3. Create a material using **Assets** | **Create** | **Material** and name it `VideoSphere Material`.
4. Drag the **VideoSphere** material onto the **VideoSphere** game object.
5. Set the material's **Shader** to **Universal Render Pipeline / Unlit**.
6. Set **Render Face** to **Back**.
7. Set the **Base Map** color to white (`#FFFFFF`).
8. Drag **Video Render Texture** from the **Project** window onto the **Base Map** texture slot (left of **Base Map**).
9. To ensure the texture appears as a mirror image on the inside of the sphere, set its **Tiling X** to `-1`.
10. On the **VideoSphere** game object, disable its renderer lighting properties by setting **Mesh Renderer** | **Lighting** | **Cast Shadows** | **Off**, then **Probes** | **Light Probes** | **Off**, then **Reflection Probes** | **Off**, and then uncheck the **Dynamic Occlusion** checkbox.

Press **Play**. You now have a basic 360-degree video player built with Unity.

When building for Android and iOS, you must put your video file (such as MP4) into a folder named `StreamingAssets` in your **Project** `Assets`. For more information on this and other considerations for video players and codecs, see the Unity documentation at `https://docs.unity3d.com/ScriptReference/Video.VideoPlayer.html`.

As with all Unity components, the video player has an API and can be controlled via scripting. For example, to pause the video with a button click, you could add a script to `VideoPlayer`. The following script, when attached to the **Video Player** game object, will pause and resume the video when the user presses the right trigger button on the hand controller:

```
using UnityEngine;
using UnityEngine.Video;

public class PlayPauseVideo : MonoBehaviour
{
    private VideoPlayer video;
```

```
    private void Start()
    {
        video = GetComponent<VideoPlayer>();
    }

    private void Update()
    {
        if (Input.GetButtonDown("XRI_Right_TriggerButton"))
        {
            if (video.isPlaying)
            {
                video.Pause();
            }
            else
            {
                video.Play();
            }
        }
    }
}
```

For additional tips, check out the tutorial from Unity called *Getting started in interactive 360-degree video: Download our sample project* at `https://blogs.unity3d.com/2018/01/19/getting-started-in-interactive-360-video-download-our-sample-project/`.

In this project, we built a 360-degree video player scene. Using the standard Video Player component and a Render Texture asset, as needed for playing any video in a Unity scene, we rendered an equirectangular 360-degree video inside a photosphere to experience it in VR.

Next, we'll consider how to view 360-degree photos and videos using Unity Scene skyboxes instead of photosphere game objects.

Using Unity skyboxes

Back in the old days, or at least before 360-degree photos, we simply referred to 360 images as ***skyboxes*** as the way to create background imagery in computer graphic landscapes. **Skyboxes** depict what's far on the horizon, may contribute to the ambient lighting of the scene, can be used for rendering reflections on object surfaces, and are not interactable. Unity supports skyboxes as part of the **Lighting Environment** for each scene. We used skyboxes already in a few of the previous chapters' projects (including Wispy Sky and Skull Platform). Common sources of skyboxes include cylindrical panoramas, spherical panoramas (360 images), and a six-sided cube. We won't consider the cylindrical one since it's less useful for VR. We'll look at cubemaps first.

Six-sided or cubemap skyboxes

A skybox can be represented by six sides of a cube, where each side is akin to a camera capturing its view pointing in each of the six directions, as illustrated here:

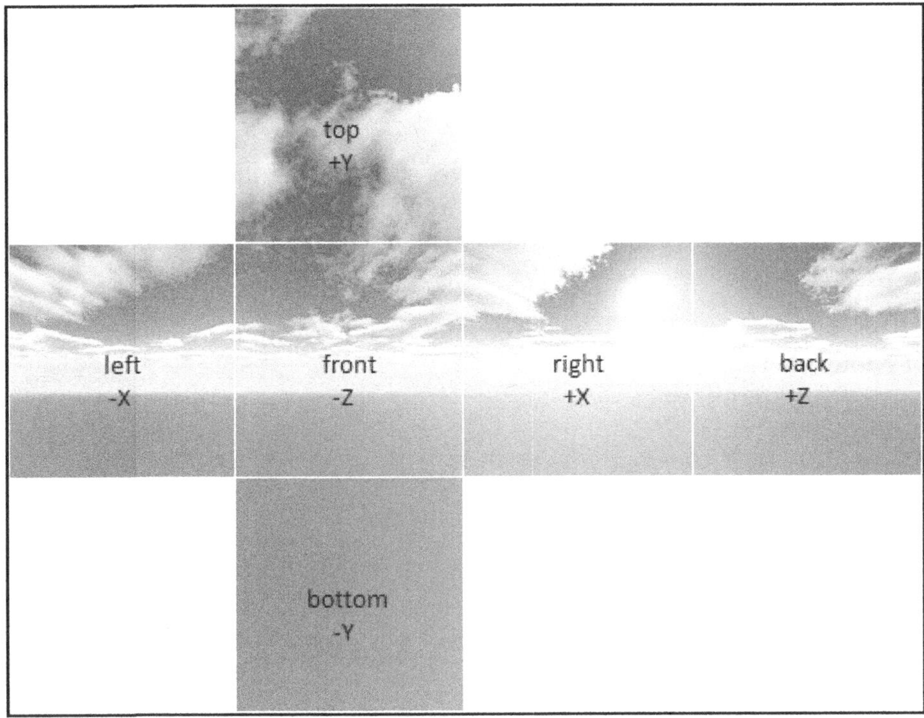

Given these six images as textures, you'd create a *six-sided* skybox material like the one shown in the following screenshot for the WispySky cubemap. Then, you would set it in the **Lighting** window as the Skybox Material for the scene. Alternatively, you could combine the six images into a single *cubemap* image, laid out in a similar fashion:

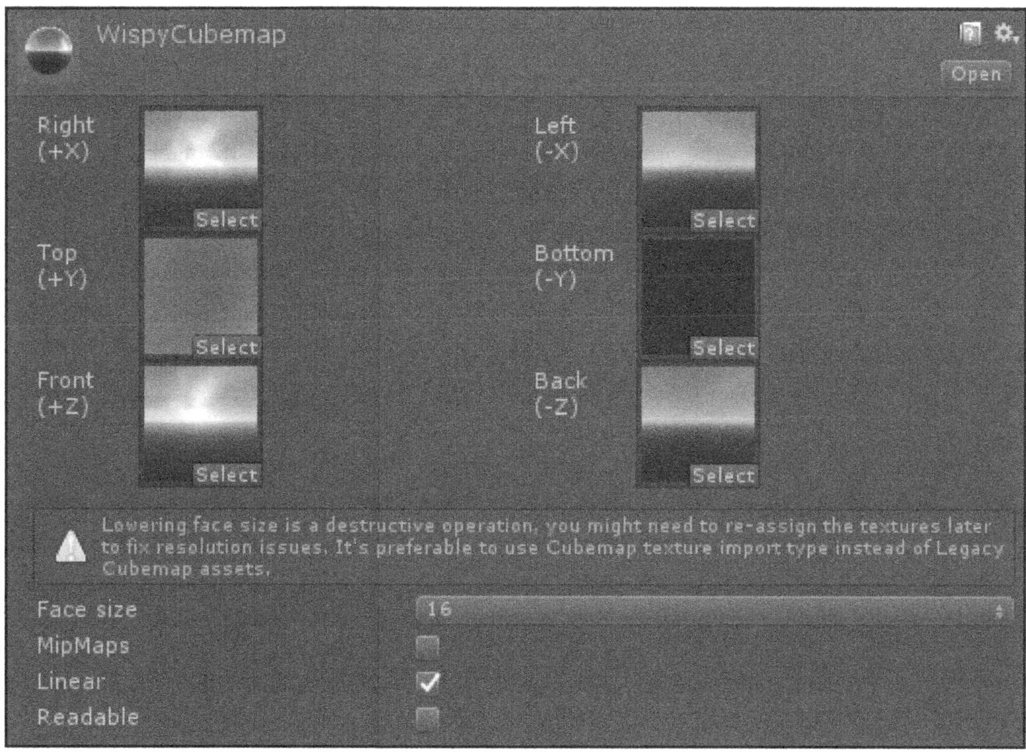

Cubemaps have an advantage because equirectangular textures waste pixels since the image is stretched at the top and bottom poles of the spherical projection. On the other hand, care must be taken to properly design images so that they'll smoothly stitch together and not cause seams or other visual artifacts.

A variant over traditional cubemaps is the **Equi-Angular Cubemap** (**EAC**). EAC strives to have even more uniform pixel sizes and "equal angle pixel distribution in 3D." (See `https://blog.google/products/google-vr/bringing-pixels-front-and-center-vr-video/` for more details.)

However, most 360-degree media today, especially coming from consumer cameras, use equirectangular projections, also known as spherical panoramas. We'll examine this next.

Spherical panoramic skyboxes

Using a 360-degree photo for a skybox is referred to as a *spherical panoramic*. Earlier in this chapter, we used a spherical game object to render an equirectangular texture and placed the player camera centered inside it. Now, we'll use the same image in a skybox. (Note that this will also work for 180-degree content). Start with a new empty scene:

1. Create a new scene by navigating to **File** | **New Scene**. Then, navigate to **File** | **Save As...** and name it `Skybox`.
2. Add a stationary XR Camera Rig to the scene using **GameObject** | **XR** | **Stationary XR Rig**.
3. Set the XR Rig's **Position** to (`0`, `0`, `0`).

Let's try using the `Farmhouse.jpg` file again that we used earlier, this time as a skybox:

1. Create a new material via **Assets** | **Create** | **Material** and name it `Farmhouse Skybox Material`.
2. For the material's **Shader**, choose **Skybox** | **Panoramic**.
3. Drag your 360 image (`Farmhouse.jpg`) onto the **Spherical** texture area.
4. Set **Mapping** to **Latitude Longitude Layout**.
5. Set **Image Type** to **360 Degrees**.

The **Material** settings are shown here:

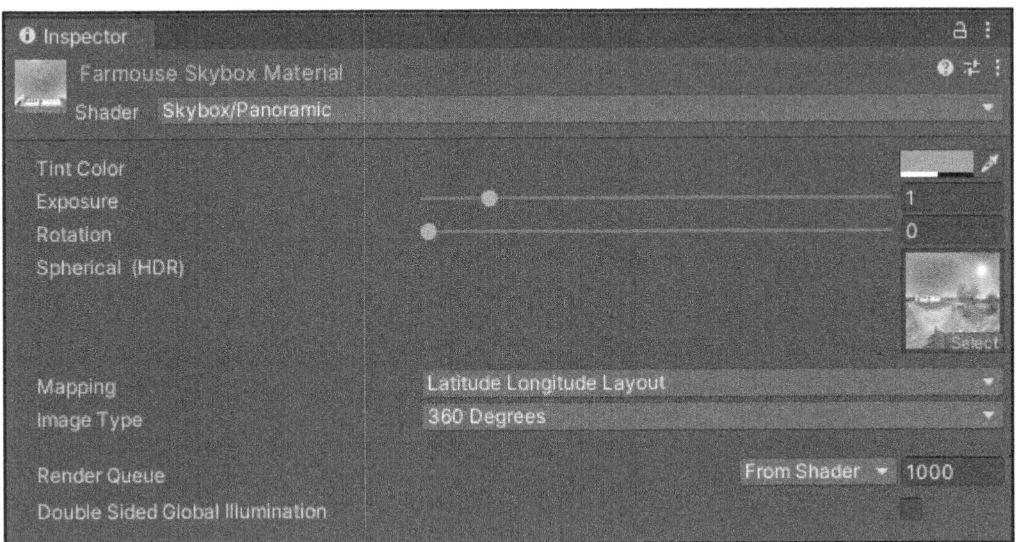

Now, to use it in your scene, follow these steps:

1. Open the **Lighting** window tab (if you're not in your Editor, navigate to **Window** | **Rendering** | **Lighting**).
2. Choose the **Environment** tab.
3. Drag your `Farmhouse Skybox Material` onto the **Skybox Material** slot.

The **Lighting Environment** settings are shown here:

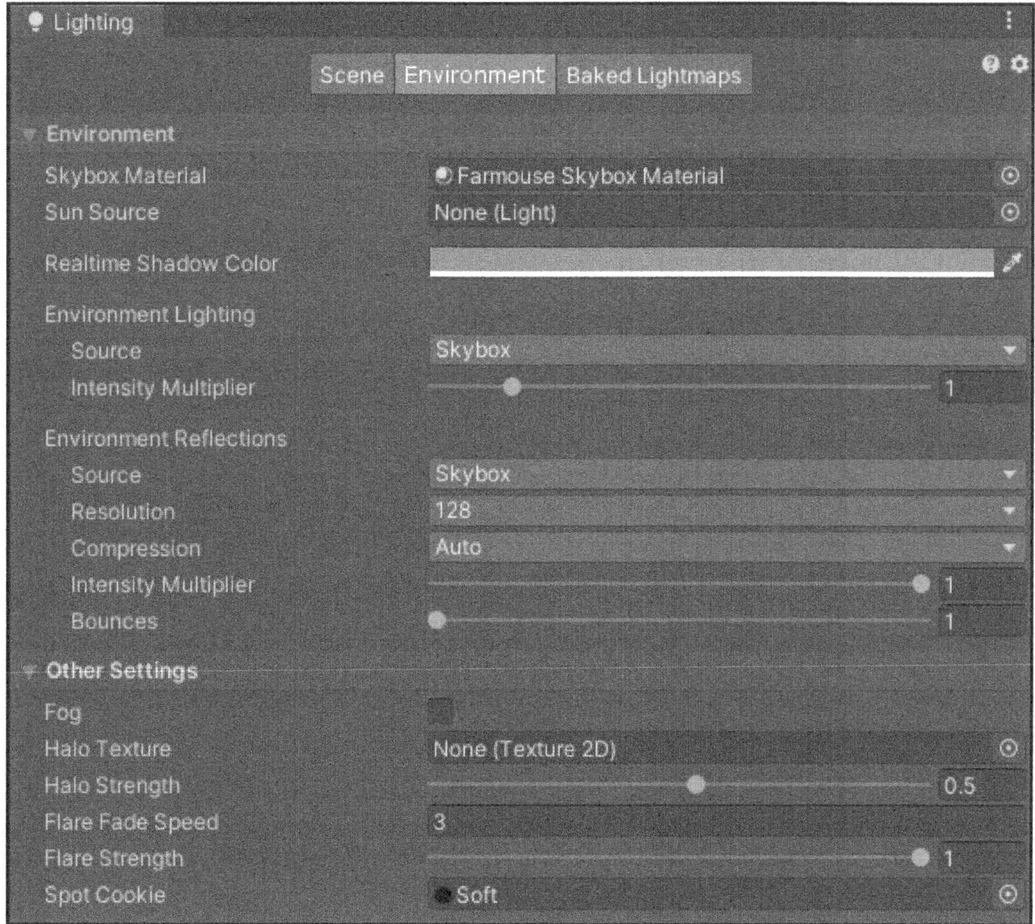

Press **Play**. *Voila!* You should now see the photosphere surrounding you in the scene. That was almost too easy. Thank goodness!

One thing that's interesting is that since skyboxes are always rendered as if at a very far distance away, the camera will always be at the center of the photosphere. Thus, we don't need to set the camera rig at the origin, and we don't need to use a stationary XR Rig. Wherever you move, the skybox will surround you just the same. If your 360 image contains content (people or objects) that are relatively near, this may feel very unnatural, as if the objects have been projected or flattened against the spherical projection (which they are!). This is why skyboxes are generally used for landscapes and large open spaces.

At this point, you can add more content to your scene. After all, we're in Unity and not just making a generic 360-degree photo viewer. Enhance your lovely outdoor scene by adding falling snow or leaves (for example, see the *Falling Leaves* particle package at `https://assetstore.unity.com/packages/3d/falling-leaves-54725`). You can also use videos with skyboxes. We'll look at this in detail in the next section.

360-degree video skyboxes

Turning your skybox into a 360-degree video player is nearly identical to the steps outlined previously for the spherical game object version. We won't repeat everything again, but briefly, it goes as follows:

1. Set up a **Video Player** to playback the video source to a **Render Texture**.
2. Set up a **Skybox Material** that will receive a **Render Texture**.
3. Set the scene to use **Skybox Material**.

Note that, according to Unity, equirectangular videos should have an aspect ratio of exactly 2:1 (or for 180-degree content, 1:1) for the skybox shader. Also, many desktop hardware video decoders are limited to 4K resolutions, while mobile hardware video decoders are often limited to 2K or less, limiting the resolution that can be played back in real-time on those platforms.

In this section, we considered how to use equirectangular, panoramic, and six-sided cubemap images in the Scene's skybox for viewing 360-degree media. Next, we'll address the question of how to capture a 360 image within your game, for sharing on the internet or for even using at an asset itself (such as teleporting via magic orbs).

Capturing 360-degrees in Unity

We've talked about using 360-degree media captured using 360 cameras. But what if you wanted to capture a 360 image or video from within your Unity app and share it on the internet? This could be useful for marketing and promoting your VR apps, or just simply using Unity as a content generation tool but using 360-degree video as the final distribution medium. First, I'll explain how to capture 360 images, including cubemaps and reflection probes, within Unity with a simple script. Then, I'll suggest some third-party tools you should consider that have more features.

Capturing cubemaps and reflection probes

Unity includes support for capturing scene views as part of its lighting engine. A call to `camera.RenderToCubemap()` will bake a static cubemap of your scene using the camera's current position and other settings.

The example script given in the Unity documentation, `https://docs.unity3d.com/Documentation/ScriptReference/Camera.RenderToCubemap.html`, implements an editor wizard for capturing a cubemap of your scene directly in the Editor, and is included here:

```
using UnityEngine;
using UnityEditor;
using System.Collections;

public class RenderCubemapWizard : ScriptableWizard
{
    public Transform renderFromPosition;
    public Cubemap cubemap;

    void OnWizardUpdate()
    {
        string helpString = "Select transform to render from
            and cubemap to render into";
        bool isValid = (renderFromPosition != null) &&
            (cubemap != null);
    }

    void OnWizardCreate()
    {
        // create temporary camera for rendering
        GameObject go = new GameObject("CubemapCamera");
        go.AddComponent<Camera>();
        // place it on the object
        go.transform.position = renderFromPosition.position;
```

```
            go.transform.rotation = Quaternion.identity;
            // render into cubemap
            go.GetComponent<Camera>().RenderToCubemap(cubemap);

            // destroy temporary camera
            DestroyImmediate(go);
        }

        [MenuItem("GameObject/Render into Cubemap")]
        static void RenderCubemap()
        {
            ScriptableWizard.DisplayWizard<RenderCubemapWizard>(
                "Render cubemap", "Render!");
        }
    }
```

To run the wizard, follow these steps:

1. Create an **Empty** game object for the camera position to capture from named `Capture Position`.
2. Create a cubemap asset where we will render the captured image by selecting **Assets | Create | Legacy | Cubemap**.
3. Set **Face Size** to a high resolution, such as `2048`.
4. Check the **Readable** checkbox.
5. Now, run the wizard from the script we just wrote by selecting **GameObject | Render into Cubemap**.
6. Drag the **Capture Position** object into the **Render From Position** slot.
7. Drag **Cubemap** from the **Project** window into the **Cubemap** slot.
8. Press **Render!**

This `.cubemap` file can now be used in a Skybox Cubemap material.

A similar but different approach is to use **Reflection Probes**. They're normally used by objects with reflective materials to render realistic surface reflections (see `https://docs.unity3d.com/Manual/class-ReflectionProbe.html`). A Reflection Probe captures a spherical view of its surroundings and is then stored as a cubemap. Scene designers will strategically place multiple reflection probes in a scene to provide more realistic rendering. You can repurpose a Reflection Probe as a 360 image capture of your scene! Since they're intended for reflection lighting, they're usually low-resolution.

Unity chooses where to store the Reflection Probe lightmap file (`.exr`), depending on your lighting settings. To save it under your `Assets` folder (rather than the GI cache), go to the **Lighting** tab, enable **Baked Global Illumination**, and disable **Auto Generate**. This will generate the refection probe `.exr` file in a folder with the same name as your scene.

Try adding one to your scene by navigating to **GameObject** | **Light** | **Reflection Probe**. Set **Resolution** to a high value, such as `2048`. Then, press **Bake**. You can then assign this `.exr` file to a Skybox Cubemap material, making a quick and easy 360 scene-shot.

While interesting to consider, both these techniques may not be practical since the resulting image resolution is very low, especially for viewing in VR. In that case, you may need to consider a third-party tool from the Asset Store.

Using third-party capture tools

There are a number of packages that allow us to capture 360 images and video in Unity. These packages may support mono - and stereoscopic capture, sequenced captures for video encoding, and possibly other features for color conversion, anti-aliasing, camera image effects, and 3D spatialized audio.

A Unity Blogs post from January 2018 (`https://blogs.unity3d.com/2018/01/26/stereo-360-image-and-video-capture/`) explains how to capture ODS stereo cubemaps and convert them into stereo equirectangular textures. This feature is based on Google's **omnidirectional stereo** (**ODS**), which was described at the beginning of this chapter. To capture a scene in the Editor or a standalone player, call `camera.RenderToCubemap()` once per eye. Unfortunately, the post references and recommends the now deprecated and unsupported Unity **GenericFrameRecorder** tool (`https://github.com/Unity-Technologies/GenericFrameRecorder`).

The basic workflow of these packages is to capture an equirectangular image (or skybox) from a specific location in the scene, as we did in the previous section. To capture a stereo 3D view, you capture two images – one for each eye – separated by a given virtual **interpupillary distance** (**IPD**). To assemble a video, you repeat the captures once per update as the scene and/or camera animates, and then convert the hundreds of still frame photos into a single video. This creates a challenge for the software to capture and save the frame fast enough (for example, 30 fps).

Try and search for `360 capture` (`https://assetstore.unity.com/tools/camera?q=360%20capture`) or something similar. I won't review these packages here. Some are free, while others are at a modest cost. Some packages only run in the Unity Editor. Others can also be built into your game, allowing your users to capture and share 360-degree media of their runtime gameplay.

Summary

360-degree media is compelling because VR tricks your FOV by updating the viewable area in real-time as you move your head around, making the screen of your HMD seem to have no edges. We started this chapter by describing what 360-degree images are, as well as how the surface of a sphere can be flattened (projected) into a 2D image by using equirectangular projections in particular. Stereo 3D media includes separate equirectangular views for the left and right eyes.

We began exploring this in Unity by simply mapping a regular image on the outside of a sphere, and were perhaps frightened by the distortions. Then, we saw how an equirectangular texture covers the sphere evenly for rendering a globe. Next, we inverted the sphere with an inverted shader, mapped the image inside the sphere, and made it a 360-degree photosphere viewer that can load photos from the web. After that, we added video.

Then, we looked at using skyboxes instead of a game object for rendering 360-degree media. We saw how Unity supports cubemaps, spherical panoramas, video skyboxes. Lastly, we explored capturing 360-degree media from within Unity scenes using Unity's built-in API and third-party packages.

As 360-degree media becomes more and more prevalent, you may find yourself increasingly needing to include it in your VR projects. In fact, it's becoming a medium in itself for storytelling, documentaries, and education. In the next chapter, we'll consider more ways to implement stories in VR using 3D animation and timelines by building a short VR cinematic experience in Unity.

12
Animation and VR Storytelling

The stories we tell, and how we tell them, say a lot about who we are and what we will become. Storytelling between humans is as primal as any human activity and the basis of interpersonal communications, mythology, religion, historical record, education, entertainment, and all of the arts. VR is emerging as one of the newest, and potentially most profound, storytelling media formats.

In the previous chapter, we looked at 360-degree media, which itself is becoming its own medium for VR storytelling, especially for non-fictional documentaries, which are capable of transmitting human experience and creating immersive empathy for humanitarian crises. Many of the tools and lessons we will cover in this chapter can also be used with 360-degree media, but we're going to focus on 3D computer graphics and animation here.

For this project, we are going to create a little VR experience – a simplistic story about a bird who gains its wings and learns to fly. We will start with an audio track to define the sequence and timeline for the animation. You will learn how to use Unity Timeline tracks to compose the animated story sequence. Then, you'll learn how to animate 3D assets by recording Animation Clips and using the third-party **DOTween** package. You'll also learn how to use the Animator for animated character sequences and transitions – in this case, a flying bird – and how to control it via C# script.

In this chapter, we are going to learn about the following topics:

- Importing and using external models and animations
- Using Unity Timelines to activate and animate objects
- Using the Animation editor window to edit property keyframes
- Controlling an Animator controller from C#
- Making a story interactive for VR

By the end of this chapter, you'll be able to create your own VR stories using the gamut of animation tools in Unity.

Technical requirements

To implement the projects and exercises in this chapter, you will need the following:

- A PC or Mac with Unity 2019.4 LTS or later, the XR plugin for your device, and the XR Interaction Toolkit installed
- A VR headset supported by the Unity XR platform

You can access or clone the GitHub repository for this book (`https://github.com/PacktPublishing/Unity-2020-Virtual-Reality-Projects-3rd-Edition-`) to optionally use the following assets and completed projects for this chapter:

- The asset files for you to use in this chapter are located in the `UVRP3Files/Chapter-12-Files.zip` folder.
- All the completed projects for this book can be found in a single Unity project at `UVRP3Projects`.
- The completed assets and scenes for this chapter can be found in the `UVRP3Projects/Assets/_UVRP3Assets/Chapter12/` folder.

Additional assets are required to run this project, as described in this chapter. Note that opening the completed project of `Chapter12` from GitHub may generate errors until all the required assets have been imported.

Composing our story

OUR STORY: Music begins. You start in a dark scene and notice a small tree sapling in the ground in front of you. It starts to grow into a full-sized tree. As dawn breaks, a bird's nest appears, and we notice it has an egg in it. The egg begins to shake and then hatches. A baby bird emerges, hops around, grows, and tests its wings. Finally, in daylight, it flies away to freedom.

Our story is about birth, growth, spreading your wings (literally and figuratively), and moving on. We will start with a music soundtrack and animate our graphics based on its parts.

We will be using free, off-the-shelf assets. Of course, you can use your own music and graphics, but we'll assume you're following along using the ones we have selected, which are all available online for free (links will be provided where necessary). As an instructive project, it's minimalist and not embellished with effects that you might expect of a polished product, but if your 9-year old cousin or nephew made it, you'd be very proud of them!

The soundtrack we will use is a rendition of The Beatles and Paul McCartney song, "Blackbird." (A download link for this can be found in the next section, and a copy is included with the files for this chapter for convenience). Based on our `mp3` recording of the song, we've sketched out a rough timeline plan of our VR experience on a chart, as shown here:

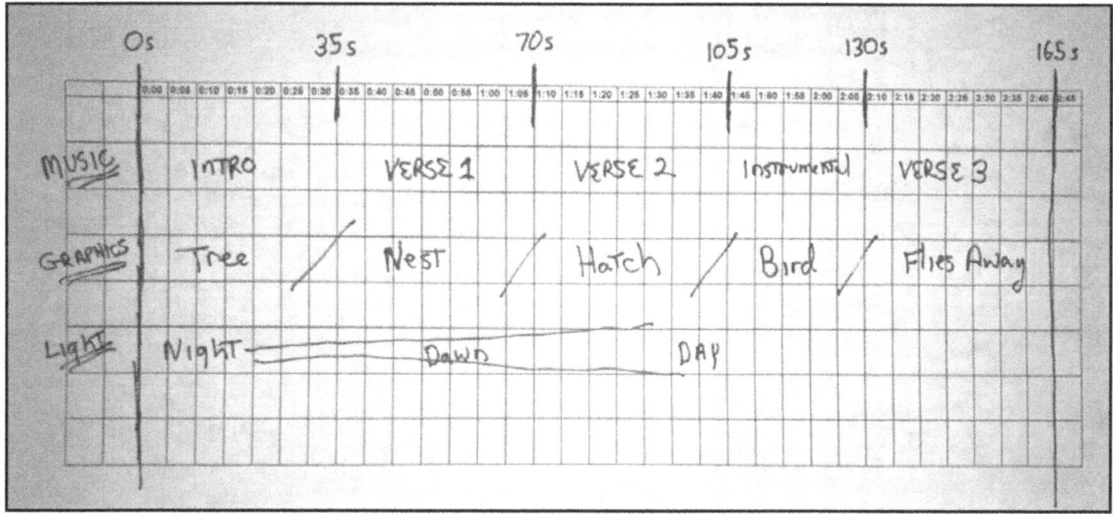

As indicated, the entire song is 165 seconds (2:45). It starts with a 35-second instrumental intro, then verses one and two (also 35 seconds each), a 25-second instrumental, and then verse three, which is 35 seconds long. We'll use this to divide our story into five segments.

Plenty of other features ought to be planned out as well. The scene lighting, for example, will start in the dark of night and gradually lighten the sky into dawn and then daytime. Now, we will collect the primary assets we plan to use in the project and create an initial starting scene.

Gathering the assets

As mentioned previously, we're going to build our story from a variety of sources, all of which contain free and simplistic assets. Some of these assets are included in the GitHub files for this book. Others, while free, require you to download them yourself from the Asset Store as we cannot redistribute the files.

The following assets are included in this book's GitHub repository, with permission from the authors:

- Music: The Beatles and Paul McCartney song, "Blackbird," performed by guitarist Salvatore Manalo:
    - File: `Audio/The Beatles (Paul McCartney) Blackbird cover.mp3`
    - Source: `https://youtu.be/chSrubUUdwc`
- Tree and Rocks:
    - File: The `NatureStarterKit/Models/` folder
    - Source: Nature Starter Kit 1, `https://assetstore.unity.com/packages/3d/environments/nature-starter-kit-1-49962`
- Nest And Egg:
    - Use the `NestAndEgg` prefab file provided with this book:
    - File: The `NestAndEgg/` folder, which contains prefab files and materials.
    - Original source: Tutorial for using Cinema 4D: `https://www.youtube.com/watch?v=jzoNZslTQfI`. Our version has been modified and converted into FBX format.

The following assets are free from the Asset Store. Please download and install them now:

- Living Birds: `https://assetstore.unity.com/packages/3d/characters/animals/living-birds-15649`
- Wispy Skybox: `https://assetstore.unity.com/packages/2d/textures-materials/sky/wispy-skybox-21737`
- DOTween: `https://assetstore.unity.com/packages/tools/animation/dotween-hotween-v2-27676`

If and when you import DOTween, you'll also be prompted to go through an extra setup procedure. Press **Setup DOTween...** when prompted and then press **Apply**.

As we did when importing other assets in previous chapters, you may need to convert the imported materials into the current render pipeline, as follows:

1. Select **Edit** | **Render Pipeline** | **Universal Render Pipeline** | **Upgrade Project Materials to URP Materials**.
2. When prompted, click **Proceed**.
3. You may see messages in the **Console** window, but they should disappear when you press **Clear**.

This project uses a tree model that was created using Unity's built-in **Tree Creator** tools (`https://docs.unity3d.com/Manual/class-Tree.html`). At the time of writing, the new Scriptable Render Pipelines (URP, HDRP) do not come with compatible versions of the **Nature/Tree Creator** shaders. (Tree Creator is rumored to become deprecated but is currently a normal Unity feature. Instead, Unity recommends developers use **SpeedTree**, `https://docs.unity3d.com/Manual/SpeedTree.html`, a superior third-party tool but with a significant monthly price tag). I have configured the tree with the URP versions of the `SpeedTree8` shaders. Unfortunately, these generate errors in **Console** and do not support Wind Zones, but otherwise, the project still runs OK. Alternatively, you may find URP compatible shaders in the Asset Store, such as **Lux URP/LWRP Essentials** (needs to be purchased), which includes URP versions of the **Nature/Tree Creator Bark Optimized** and **Nature/Tree Creator Leaf Optimized** shaders (`https://assetstore.unity.com/packages/vfx/shaders/lux-urp-lwrp-essentials-150355`). This shader was used in the screenshots for this chapter.

The Universal Render Pipeline does not (currently) support Unity Tree Creator. The files for this chapter, which can be found on GitHub, use the `SpeedTree8` shader, which renders without "pink" materials but may generate errors in the console and does not support Wind Zones. Despite the errors, the project still runs OK. For your own projects, when using Tree Creator, consider purchasing a compatible shader such as **Lux URP/LWRP Essentials** (`https://assetstore.unity.com/packages/vfx/shaders/lux-urp-lwrp-essentials-150355`).

Now, we can start to build the story scene.

Creating the initial scene

We're going to make a simple, cartoonish, minimalist scene using a plane for the ground and some rocks, a bird's nest with an egg, and a bird. Follow these steps to get started:

1. Create a new scene by navigating to **File** | **New Scene**. Then, navigate to **File** | **Save As...** and name it `Blackbird`.
2. Add a stationary XR Camera Rig to the scene using **GameObject** | **XR** | **Stationary XR Rig**.
3. Set the XR Rig's **Position** to (`0`, `0`, `-3`).
4. If not present, add an Audio Listener to the child **Main Camera** by selecting the camera. Then, go to **Add Component** | **Audio Listener**.
5. Create a 3D **Plane** named `GroundPlane`, reset its **Transform** properties, and then **Scale** it to (`10, 10, 10`).

6. Create a new **Material** named `GroundMaterial`, set its **Base Map** color to a dark earthy brown (such as `#251906`), and drag the material onto the plane.
7. Uncheck the material's **Specular Highlights** and **Environmental Reflections** checkboxes.

We are using a simple ground plane as it gives the cartoon aesthetic we want. But this could be an opportunity for you to explore the Unity Terrain system. This is another rich and very powerful topic, where you can "paint" complex landscapes with mountains, valleys, trees, and grasses. See the manual at `https://docs.unity3d.com/Manual/script-Terrain.html`.

Initialize the lighting settings and skybox as follows:

1. Open the **Lighting** window with **Window | Rendering | Lighting** (**Lighting Settings** in Unity 2019).
2. Select the **Scene** tab.
3. In Unity 2020+, click **New Lighting Settings** to create the initial lighting parameters.
4. For now, check the **Auto Generate** lightmaps checkbox (if updates get slow while working on the scene, uncheck this box but remember to periodically press **Generate Lighting** to update your lightmaps).
5. Select the **Environment** tab.
6. Set the skybox by pressing **doughnut-icon** to the right of **Skybox Material**, search for `wispy`, and select **WispySkyboxMat2**.

Now, add a tree and some rocks by following these steps:

1. From the `Assets/NatureStarterKit/Models/` folder in the **Project** window, drag **Tree** into **Scene**. Reset its **Transform** properties so that it's at the origin.
2. If you've installed alternative Tree Creator shaders for URP, such as the Lux URP Essentials package, substitute them now. In **Inspector**, on **Optimized Bark Material**, set its **Shader** to **Lux URP/Nature/Tree Creator Bark Optimized**. Likewise, for **Optimized Leaf Material**, set its **Shader** to **Lux URP/Nature/Tree Creator Leaf Optimized**.
3. Add a few rocks near the tree and move them so that they're partially buried below the ground. You might put these under an **Empty** game object named `Environment`. Assuming you've reset the **Environment** object's **Transform**, use the following table to arrange the rock positions.

4. Then, add a **WindZone** using **GameObject** | **3D Object** | **WindZone** so that the **Tree** object responds to wind and its leaves rustle. (Note that **WindZone** requires a compatible tree shader).

The rocks in my scene have been placed as follows (all at **Scale** `100`):

Prefab	**Position**
`rock03`	`(2.9, -0.6, -0.26)`
`rock03`	`(2.6, -0.7, -3.6)`
`rock04`	`(2.1, -0.65, -3.1)`
`rock01`	`(-6, -3.4, -0.6)`
`rock04`	`(-5, -0.35, 3.8)`

Caution: Duplicating objects in the **Hierarchy** window may increment the postfix number in its name, so a duplicate of `rock03` will be named in `rock04` in the **Hierarchy** window, which is not the same as the prefab `rock04`. This can get confusing, so rename it something such as `rock03-1` instead.

My scene layout, including the tree and arrangement of rocks, is shown in the following screenshot:

Press **Play** to see how the scene looks so far in VR. The leaves of the tree will rustle because we added a **Wind Zone** to the scene. Next, we'll add the nest:

1. Drag a copy of the **NestAndEgg** prefab into the scene from the **Project** window's `Assets/NestAndEgg/` folder.

2. **Scale** and **Position** it on the ground so it's easily in sight, near the tree, and not too small. We chose **Position** (`0.5, 0.36, -1.2`).
3. Set its **Scale** (`0.2, 0.2, 0.2`).

Now, add a bird. The **Living Birds** package doesn't contain a blackbird, but it does have a **Bluejay**, which is close enough!

1. From the **Project** window's `Assets/living birds/resources/` folder, drag the `lb_blueJayHQ` prefab into the **Hierarchy** window.
2. For convenience, rename it `Bluejay`.
3. **Scale** and **Position** it so that it appears full-grown and perched on the edge of the nest. We chose **Scale** (`8, 8, 8`), **Position** (`0.75, 0.4, -1.25`), and **Rotation** (`0, 135, 0`).

The model we are using comes with animation clips that we'll control later in this project. Like most character animations, it runs an `Idle` animation initially when you press **Play**. Check how it looks in VR to validate it's what you expect. It's always much different within VR than the view you see on a flat-screen. Our scene and hierarchy can be seen in the following screenshot:

So far, we've started with a project plan. This included gathering a layout of the time sequence, collecting the assets we plan to use, and building an initial scene with the environment and main game objects that will be part of the story. Now, we can begin defining the Timeline sequence, first with the audio track.

Timelines and Audio tracks

Earlier, we planned out the movie using a graph paper timeline. Unity provides a **Timeline** tool for implementing this almost directly. Timelines consist of one or more tracks that play over time. Timelines can control many different objects and different types of tracks. As we'll see and explain as we build this project, Timelines can have **Audio Tracks**, **Activation Tracks**, **Animation Tracks**, **Signal Tracks**, and more. Timelines are a type of Unity *Playable*. Playables are runtime objects that "play" over time, updating each frame based on their prescribed behavior. Animations are playables too. For more details, see `https://docs.unity3d.com/ScriptReference/Playables.Playable.html`.

Confirm that the **Timeline** package has been installed with your project (ordinarily, it is installed by default) and add or upgrade it if necessary using the following steps:

1. Open **Package Manager** using **Window** | **Package Manager**.
2. Select **Packages In Project** from the filters list in the top-left of the window.
3. If **Timeline** is present and it needs to be updated, select its **Update** button.
4. If **Timeline** is not present, choose **All** from the filter list, type `timeline` into the search area to locate it, and **Install** the package.

For now, we'll add a **Timeline** to the project and add an **Audio Track**. To create the **Timeline** object and open it in the **Timeline Editor** window, follow these steps:

1. In **Hierarchy**, create an **Empty** game object, reset its **Transform** properties, and name it `Blackbird Director`.
2. Open **Timeline Editor** by selecting **Window** | **Sequencing** | **Timeline**.
3. In the window that opens, you will see a message stating, **To begin a new timeline with Blackbird Director, create a Director component and a Timeline asset** with a **Create** button.
4. Press the **Create** button.
5. You will be prompted to save a new **Playable** asset in your **Project** `Assets/` folder (I like to use a `Playables/` subfolder). Name it `Blackbird Timeline`. Then, press **Save**.

At this point, you may have noticed a few important things just happened:

- The **Blackbird Timeline** asset was created in the `Assets` folder you specified.
- A **Playable Director** component was added to the **Blackbird Director** game object, associating it with that **Blackbird Timeline**.
- The **Timeline Editor** window is open for **Blackbird Timeline**.

The following screenshot shows the **Blackbird Director** inspector with its **Playable Director** component. A **Playable Director** controls when and how a **Timeline** instance plays, including whether to **Play On Awake**, and **Wrap Mode** (what to do when the Timeline is done playing; that is, **Hold**, **Loop**, or **None**):

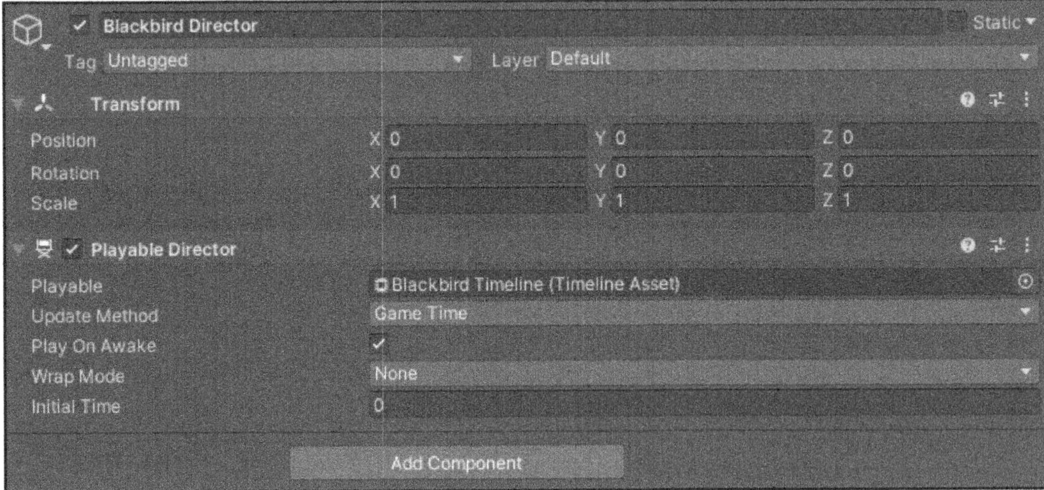

Now, let's add an **Audio Track** containing our Paul McCartney song to the timeline by following these steps:

1. Locate the `mp3` file (named `The Beatles (Paul McCartney) Blackbird cover.mp3`) in your **Project** `Assets/Audio/` folder, and drag it directly onto the **Timeline Editor**.
2. Press **Play** to play your scene as normal. The music should start playing.

Here is the **Timeline Editor**, which now contains the Paul McCartney **Audio Track**:

The white vertical cursor, or *playhead*, indicates the current time frame. The time scale is in **Seconds** (if yours is **Frames**, change it using the gear icon in the upper-right). The track's **Audio Source** remains empty (**None**) since we added the clip directly.

You can scale the view using the scroll wheel on your mouse. View all by pressing *A* on your keyboard. When the Timeline contains multiple tracks, you can focus on a specific clip by pressing *F* on the keyboard.

You may notice that, in the upper-left of **Timeline Editor**, there are preview control buttons, similar to a video player would. These let you play a preview of the **Timeline** itself, rather than the whole scene using the usual Editor **Play** button.

In this scene, we decided to make the music ambient audio. The audio will play in 2D mode when no audio source GameObject is selected. If you want to play it as spatial audio, emanating from a specific location in the scene, you should create an object with an **Audio Source** component and put that object in the Timeline track instead.

We just added an **Audio Track** to the Timeline. Another type of Timeline track is known as an **Activation Track**. Associated with a specific game object, an **Activation Track** will enable or disable that game object at the specified times. We'll look at this in more detail next.

Using a Timeline to activate objects

According to our plan, when the timeline starts, the bird's nest will be hidden (the **NestAndEgg** object). At the 35-second mark, it becomes enabled. Also, when the nest is first enabled, it should contain **WholeEgg**. Then, at the 80-second mark, it is hidden the **HatchedEgg** is enabled instead. The **NestAndEgg** game object hierarchy, as shown here, contains the **Nest** itself, a **WholeEgg** object, and a **HatchedEgg** object (which contains the two eggshell halves):

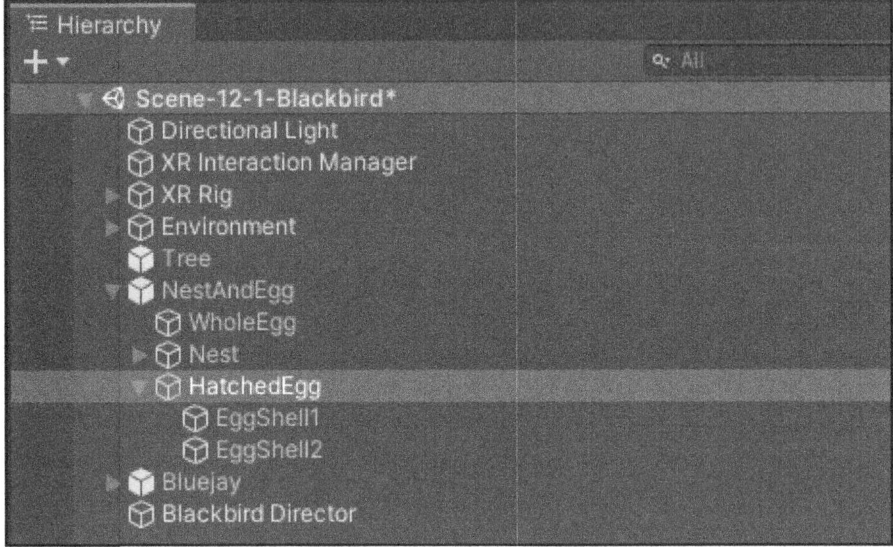

Now, let's add the activation sequence to the Timeline. You can view the results of these and the following steps in the screenshot further down:

1. With **Blackbird Director** selected in **Hierarchy**, drag the **NestAndEgg** object from **Hierarchy** into the **Timeline Editor** window.
2. A menu will pop up, asking you what type of track to add; choose **Activation Track**.
3. Ensure the Timeline units are **Seconds**, not **Frames**. Use the gear icon in the upper-right of the **Timeline** window to select it.
4. A small rectangular track marker will be added to the track. Click and drag it into place.
5. Position and size the track so that it starts at about `35:00` and ends at the end of the track, that is, `165:00`.

Now, for the eggs. Although the egg models are children of **NestAndEgg**, they can be activated separately from the parent (of course, only when the parent itself is already enabled) by following these steps:

1. Drag the **WholeEgg** object from **Hierarchy** onto **Timeline** as an **Activation Track.**
2. Position it so that it starts at the same start time as **NestAndEgg** (about `35:00`) and ends at about `60:00`.
3. Drag the **HatchedEgg** object from **Hierarchy** onto **Timeline** as an **Activation Track**.
4. Position it so that it starts at `60:00` and ends at `165:00`.

Similarly, activate the bird when the egg hatches, at the 60-second mark:

1. Drag the **Bluejay** object from **Hierarchy** onto **Timeline** as an **Activation Track**.
2. Position it so that it starts at `60:00` and ends at `165:00`.

The Timeline with **Activate Tracks** should now look as follows. On the left, you can see that each track has an object slot containing the game object being controlled by the track:

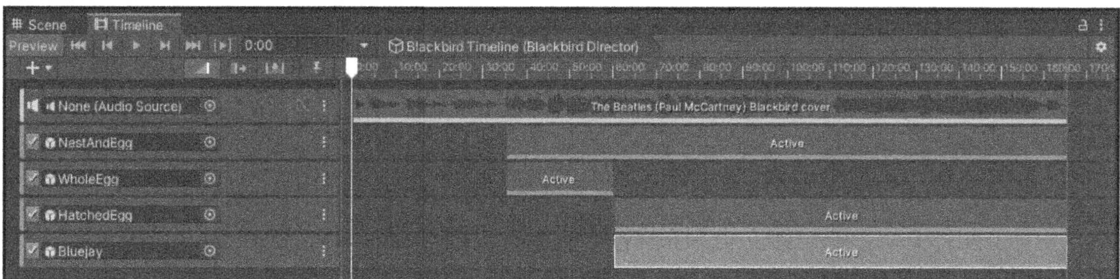

By using **Preview Play** (the control icons in the upper-left of the **Timeline Editor**), you can play and review these tracks. You can scrub through the time frames by dragging the white *Playhead* cursor. You will see the nest, eggs, and bird activate and deactivate as specified.

We now have a Timeline in the scene and laid down four Activation Tracks that specify when specific game objects in the scene become visible (Active) or not, including **Bluejay**, **NestAndEgg**, and its child objects **WholeEgg** and **HatchedEgg**. The timings have been synchronized with the audio music track we're using as the basis. Now, we can start to animate them. In particular, we're going to change the Transforms of several objects, including increasing the scale of the **Tree** and **Bluejay** objects over time to make them grow. Let's add that now.

Recording an Animation Track

As you would expect, in addition to audio and activation tracks, Timelines can include animation tracks. Unity's animation features have evolved over the years and **Timeline** greatly simplifies basic animation capabilities within Unity. You can create and edit animations directly within **Timeline** without having to create separate **Animation Clips** and **Animator Controllers**. We will look at these in more detail later in this chapter. For now, we will start simple by animating just a few **Transform** parameters on the tree and the bird, thus adding a growing tree and a growing bird to the scene.

A growing tree

We want to animate the tree so that it grows from being small (scale `0.1`) to full size during the first `30` seconds of the Timeline. We'll do this by adding an **Animation Track** for the **Tree** object, and then recording the parameter values at each keyframe time:

1. Ensure **Blackbird Director** is selected in **Hierarchy** and that the **Timeline Editor** window is open.
2. Drag the **Tree** object from **Hierarchy** into the **Timeline** window.
3. Select **Animation Track** as the type of track we are adding.

Now, we can begin recording the keyframes, as follows:

1. Ensure the playhead cursor is set to `0:00`.
2. Press the red **Record** button on the **Tree** track in **Timeline** to begin recording.
3. Select the **Tree** object in **Hierarchy**.
4. Set its **Scale** to (`0.1, 0.1, 0.1`).
5. Slide the playhead to the 30-second mark.
6. With **Tree** still selected in **Hierarchy**, set its **Scale** to (`1, 1, 1`).
7. Press the blinking red **Record** button again to stop recording.
8. Click the small graph icon to reveal the animation curve, as shown here (using the lighter Unity Editor theme so that the curve will be more visible in the image):

As you can see, our **Timeline** now has an **Animation Track** that references the **Tree** game object. It has two keyframes, one starting at `0` and one ending at `30` seconds. Unity fits a gentle curve to ease in and ease out the transition between the polemic key values. When you grab and slide the playhead cursor across the timeline curve, you will see that the tree change size in your **Scene** window. If you press the **Preview Play** icon, you can play the animation. The following sequence of frames depicts this animation:

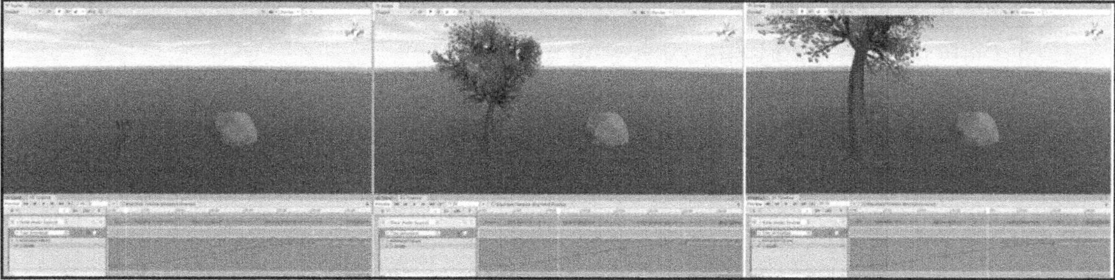

Throughout this book, we've looked at various ways to implement simple animations like this growing tree. Here, we recorded an animation clip that interpolates **Scale** between two `Vector3` values and applies an easing curve. This makes sense because it's just one track of a larger **Timeline**. In prior projects, we animated a single object with the `Update` function, or in a `Coroutine`, along with a `timer` variable to interpolate changes from one frame to the next using `Time.deltaTime`. Another way to do this, as we'll see later in this chapter, is by using a great (and free) third-party tool called **DOTween** (`https://assetstore.unity.com/packages/tools/animation/dotween-hotween-v2-27676`).

We've recorded an animation of the tree growing from a small scale to full size. Let's do a similar growth sequence for the bird.

A growing bird

Once the egg in the nest hatches, we want a tiny bird to pop out, and then let it grow (quickly) to full size. To do this, we can repeat the previous exercise, this time increasing the size of the **Bluejay** object. Scale it from a baby bird (**Scale** = `1`) to full size (**Scale** = `8`) for 10 seconds between the 60- and 70-second marks. Use the following steps to do so:

1. Ensure **Blackbird Director** is selected in **Hierarchy** and that the **Timeline Editor** window is open.
2. Drag the **Bluejay** object from **Hierarchy** into the **Timeline** window.
3. Select **Animation Track** as the type of track we are adding.
4. Ensure the **Playhead** cursor is set to `60:00` or exactly when **HatchedEgg** becomes visible.
5. Press the red **Record** button on the Bluejay track in **Timeline** to begin recording.
6. Select the **Bluejay** object in **Hierarchy**.
7. Set its **Scale** to (`1, 1, 1`).
8. Slide the playhead to the 70-second mark.
9. With `Bluejay`still selected in **Hierarchy**, set its **Scale** to (`8, 8, 8`).
10. Press the blinking red **Record** button again to stop recording.

Now, if you scrub the Timeline between the 60- and 70-second marks, the bird will grow from small to full-sized.

In this section, we've learned how to use the Timeline recorder to create animation tracks that modify the **Transform** Scale of both the **Tree** and **Bluejay** objects with a simple curve between a start and end value. Naturally, animations can be more complex with many keyframes in-between, manipulating many object parameters over time. Next, we'll make a more involved animation depicting the nest falling gently from up in the tree.

Using the Animation editor

Next, we'll create another animation track in order to animate the nest so that it starts positioned in the grown tree and then drifts slowly to the ground, wafting like a falling leaf. We want it to exhibit a gentle rocking motion. This is a little more complicated than the simple two-keyframe animation we just did, so we'll do our work in a separate **Animation Window** instead of the narrow track band on **Timeline Editor**. It will animate from `0:35` to `0:45` seconds.

Animations are based on **keyframes**. To animate a property, you need to create a keyframe and define the property values for that frame in time. In the previous example, we had just two **Keyframes**, for the start and end **Scale** values. Unity fills in-between values with a nice curve. You can insert additional **Keyframes** and edit the curve's shape. We will use these for the wafting nest.

A wafting nest

We are going to make the nest fall gently from the tree. We already have a **Timeline Activation** track for the **NestAndEgg** object, which activates it (makes it visible) in the scene. We will now add another track to animate the **NestAndEgg** object's **Transform**. Let's assume your scene already has the nest positioned on the ground, which is where we want it to end up. Create the track with the following steps:

1. Drag the **NestAndEgg** object from **Hierarchy** into the **Timeline** window.
2. Select **Animation Track** as the type of track.
3. Set the playhead cursor to `35:00`, which is where the **NestAndEgg** game object becomes activated. (Note that the **Record** icon will be disabled when the object is inactive. The playhead must be within the object's **Activation** track's **Active** range.)
4. Press the **Record** icon for the **NestAndEgg** animation track to begin recording.
5. Select the **NestAndEgg** object in **Hierarchy.**
6. Copy the current **Transform** values to the clipboard (in **Inspector**, select the three-dot icon on the **Transform** component and select **Copy Component**).
7. In the **Scene** window, ensure **Move gizmo** is currently selected.
8. Reposition the nest up in the **Tree**. object. **Position Y** = `5` worked for me.
9. Slide **Playhead** to `45:00`.
10. In **NestAndEgg Inspector**, click the Transform's three-dot icon and select **Paste Component Values**.
11. Press the blinking red **Record** button again to stop recording.

Having defined an initial **Animation** recording, we can now work on it in an **Animation** editor window:

1. On the track, click the little menu's three-dot icon to its right.
2. Select **Edit in Animation Window**, as shown here:

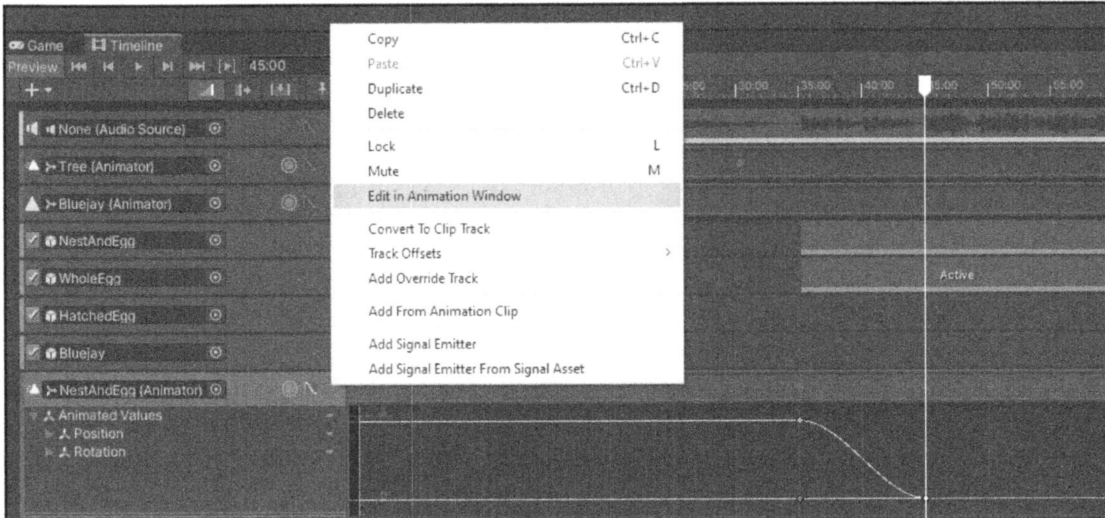

The goal is to animate a subtle floating action where the **Nest** object gently rocks from side to side (*X* and *Z* axes) and rotates lightly on each of the axes. To do this, first, we'll "anchor" the **Nest** object at the beginning, middle, and end of the fall. (We already have the begin and end positions.) Then, we'll add a couple more keyframes with arbitrary values to implement the gentle motion.

Animation Window has two view modes: **Dopesheet** and **Curves**. The **Dopesheet** view lets you focus on the keyframes for each property. The **Curves** view lets you focus on the transitions between **Keyframes**. These are shown in the screenshot further down. Using the **Dopesheet** view, we're first going to ensure we have keyframes at the start and end times, and one in-between. Add keyframes at 35, 40, and 45 seconds, as follows:

1. If not present, add **Rotation** properties too (**Add Property | Transform | Rotation** | "+").
2. Position the **Playhead** at the start of our animation (`35:00`).
3. Click **Add Keyframe icon** in the control bar, on top of the properties list (highlighted in the following screenshot).

4. Move **Playhead** about halfway, to `40:00`.
5. Click **Add Keyframe icon**.
6. Again, make sure there's **Keyframe** markers at the end (`45:00`).

You can use hotkeys to move between **Keyframes**. Press *Alt* + . (*Alt* + *period*) for the next **Keyframe**, *Alt* + , (*Alt* + *comma*) for the previous **Keyframe**, and *Shift* + , (*Shift* + *comma*) for the first **Keyframe**.

Now, we'll add a **Keyframe** at `37:30`:

1. Move **Playhead** to **37:30**.
2. Click **Add Keyframe icon**.
3. Click the red **Record** icon in the upper left to capture new values.
4. Select the **NestAndEgg** object in **Hierarchy**.
5. In the **Scene** view, using the **Move Tool** gizmo, move the **Nest** object a little bit along the X and Z axes (about 0.4 units).
6. Using **Rotate Tool**, rotate the **Nest** object gently on any combination of axes (up to 10 degrees).
7. Move **Playhead** to `42:30` and repeat *steps 2-6*.
8. Press the red **Record** button again to stop recording.

The resulting **Animation Window** in the **Dopesheet** view, with its **Position** and **Rotation** property values, is shown here at **Keyframe** `42:30`. The **Add Keyframe icon** is highlighted for you:

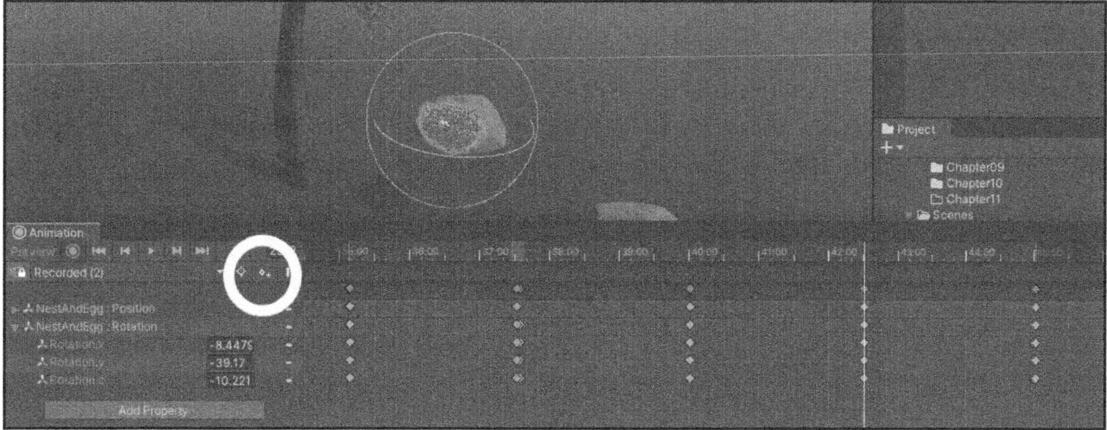

The **Curves** view lets you focus on the transitions between **Keyframes** and allows you to adjust the values and shape the curve splines. My current **Curves** view is shown here:

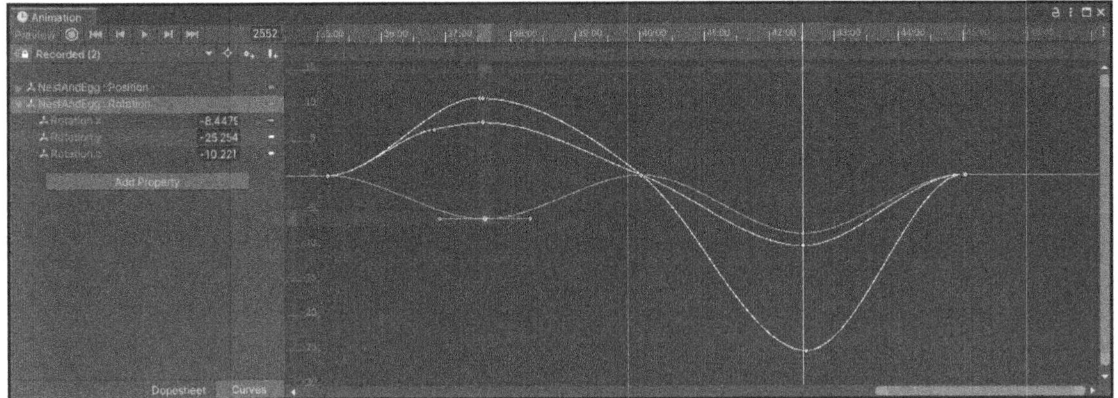

The length of the scrollbars in **Animation Window** indicates the current zoom view. The oval ends of each scrollbar are grabbable controls that let you directly adjust the zoom, as well as the position of the view.

Go back to the **Timeline Editor** window. You can slide the **Playhead** cursor to see animations in your **Scene** window or press the **Preview Play** icon to play them.

Here, we have seen that the Timeline Animation tracks are a fast way to record and adjust your animation clips. But if you want more control and detail, open that clip in an Animation window, where you can add new keyframes, add additional properties, and modify the curves. It's the same Animation Clip as in the Timeline track, but with just a more detailed editor window.

So far, we've been animating just the Transform properties of game objects. However, you can animate just about any object property that is visible in the **Inspector** window. We'll look at this in more detail next.

Animating other properties

Lighting is an important consideration in 3D animation and no less so for virtual reality storytelling. In our story, we want the lighting to start at night and progress through dawn to daylight. We'll do this by manipulating the **Directional Light** game object, a **Point Light**, and **Skybox Material**. The **Directional Light** game object has **Intensity** parameters we can animate directly. The skybox is defined with a material, so we are going to have to write a script to control its contribution to the lighting in the scene.

Animating lights

For dramatic effect, let's make the scene slowly fade from night to daytime. We will turn off **Directional Light** at the start and slowly increase its **Intensity**:

1. Select **Blackbird Director** in **Hierarchy** and open the **Timeline Editor** window.
2. Drag the **Directional Light** object from **Hierarchy** onto the **Timeline** and select **Animation Track**.
3. Press its **Record** button.
4. Ensure **Playhead** is at `0:00`.
5. Select **Directional Light** in **Hierarchy** and change its **Intensity** parameter to `0`.
6. Move the **Playhead** to `40:00`.
7. Set **Intensity** to `1`.
8. Press the blinking **Record** button to end the recording.

The Directional Light's animation track with the **Intensity** parameter curve is shown here:

The other parameters of the light can also be animated, including its **Color** and the **Transform Rotation** angles if we wanted to change the angle of the "sun" shadows and tint over time. Just imagine the possibilities!

Now, let's add a **Point Light**. For dramatic effect, position it near the **Nest** object's resting position. This will illuminate the baby tree at first, and focus the user's attention on the egg in the nest once the nest settles onto the ground:

1. Select **GameObject** | **Light** | **Point Light**.
2. In the **Scene** view, use the **Move Tool** gizmo to position it near the **Nest** object at **Position** (`0.65, 0.75, -2.25`).
3. Select **Blackbird Director** and open **Timeline Editor**.
4. Drag **Point Light** onto **Timeline Editor**.
5. Choose **Activation Track**
6. Enable the light from `0` to about `95` seconds, sometime after the egg hatches.

Things are looking pretty good!

In conventional games and videos, the director can focus the audience's attention with techniques such as close-ups, changing the depth-of-view focus, and using cutscenes. But in VR, these techniques are not available and the user can be looking anywhere at any given time. Techniques for grabbing the player's attention in VR include point or spot lighting, visual effects and sound effects at the location of interest, and possibly waiting for the player to turn to look in that direction before proceeding with the sequence.

Our **Timeline** is starting to get a little crowded. Let's move the lights into a **Track Group**:

1. In **Timeline**, choose "+" | **Track Group**.
2. Click its label and name it `Lights`.
3. Drag each of the light tracks into the group.

Use **Group Tracks** to organize your **Timeline** in a nested tree structure.

Fading in the **Directional Light** game object helps set the mood. But it's the skybox that is really going to make the difference between night, dawn, and daylight. We'll consider how to animate the skybox's light intensity next.

Animating a scripted component property

As you can see, you can animate just about any **GameObject** property that you can modify in the **Inspector** window. This includes your own C# script component's serialized properties. We want to fade the environmental lighting from night to day. There are several ways to achieve this. We've decided to do this by modifying the skybox material's **Exposure** value (`0` is off, while `1` is all the way on). But **Timeline** can only animate **GameObject** properties, and this is a **Scene** property, not a **GameObject**. So, what we'll do is create an empty **GameObject**, named **Lighting Controller**, and write a script that controls the skybox material. At the beginning of this project, we added a skybox material to the scene (that is, `WispySkyboxMat2`).

Since we're going to dynamically modify the skybox, we do not want to bake the global illumination (that would defeat our objective). Uncheck the **Mixed Lighting Baked Global Illumination** checkbox. Note that in a larger scene, this can have a serious impact on performance and should be avoided in lieu of finding another way of accomplishing the same visual effects, but it will be OK in this project.

To understand how this will work, select the `WispySkyboxMat2` material and, in its **Inspector**, see what happens when you slide the **Exposure** value between `1` and `0`. This fades the brightness of the skybox. We will animate this value to modify the ambient light in our scene. But Animations can only modify **GameObject** parameters, so we'll write a script:

1. Create a new C# script and name it `SkyboxExposure`.
2. Open the script and write the following:

```
public class SkyboxExposure : MonoBehaviour
{
    public Material skyboxMaterial;
    public float exp = 1.0f;

    private float previousExp = 0f;

    private void Update()
    {
        if (exp != previousExp)
        {
            skyboxMaterial.SetFloat("_Exposure", exp);
            previousExp = exp;
        }
    }
}
```

In `Update`, we check if the public `exp` value has been changed (for example, by the **Timeline** director) and send it to `skyboxMaterial` using `SetFloat`. (Material/Shader properties can be modified using the string reference to the property name). Save the file. In Unity, we'll make a **Lighting Controller** object that uses the script as follows:

1. Create an **Empty** object in **Hierarchy** named `Lighting Controller`.
2. Add the `SkyboxExposure` script to this object.
3. Drag the **WispySkyboxMat2** asset from the **Project** window onto its **Skybox Material** slot (or whichever material you currently have assigned in **Lighting** | **Skybox Material**).

Now, let's animate this parameter:

1. Select **Blackbird Director** in **Hierarchy** and open the **Timeline Editor** window.
2. Drag the **Lighting Controller** object from **Hierarchy** onto **Timeline** and select **Animation Track**.
3. Press its **Record** button.
4. Ensure **Playhead** is at `0:00`.
5. Select **Lighting Controller** in **Hierarchy** and change its **Exp** parameter to `0`.
6. Move **Playhead** to the `100:00`.
7. Set **Exp** to `1`.
8. Press the blinking **Record** button to end the recording.

The **Timeline Editor** window with a **SkyboxExposure** track is shown here:

Press **Play**. The scene lighting will fade from night to day as the skybox material's **Exposure** animates from `0.0` to `1.0`. (Note that it's not available in the **Timeline** preview **Play**, just the Editor **Play**). Here is a sequence of screenshots showing the skybox's intensity as it animates:

With that, we've controlled the mood and lighting of the scene using **Timeline** tracks. **Directional Light Intensity** is faded in over time. A small **Spot Light** is activated and deactivated to draw the user's attention. Finally, the exposure of **Skybox** (lightness) is also animated by **Timeline** using a helper `SkyboxExposure` script attached to a **GameObject** that the **Timeline** track can reference.

You can also use separate animation clips as another Playable asset you can add and sequence in Timeline tracks. We'll look at that next.

Using Animation clips

For the next animation example, we'll get the egg to wobble and shake before it hatches. We will create a simple animation and make it loop for its duration. To illustrate, we'll make an **Animation Clip** of the **WholeEgg** object rattling and then add it to **Timeline** on an **Animation Clip Track**.

Shaking an egg

To create a new **Animation Clip** on the **WholeEgg** object, follow these steps:

1. In **Hierarchy**, select the **WholeEgg** object (child of **NestAndEgg**).
2. Open the **Animation** window (**Window** | **Animation** | **Animation**).
3. You should see a message stating, **To begin animating WholeEgg, create an Animation Clip**, and a **Create** button.
4. Press **Create**.
5. When prompted for a filename, save it as `EggShaker Animation`.

We saw the **Animation** window earlier in this chapter. We're going to make a very short, 2-second animation that rotates the egg on the X and Z axes by manipulating the animation curves:

1. Show the **Curves** view using the **Curves** button at the bottom of the window.
2. Press **Add Property** and **WholeEgg** | **Transform** | **Rotation** | **+** to add the **Rotation** properties.
3. Select the **WholeEgg: Rotation** property group on the left.
4. Press *A* on the keyboard to zoom all; you should see three flat lines, one for each of the X, Y, and Z rotation axes.
5. Click the **Add Keyframe** icon in the control bar.
6. Move **Playhead** to `1:00` (60 seconds) and click **Add Keyframe**.
7. Scroll out (using the middle scroll wheel on the mouse or using the horizontal scrollbar oval-end handles) so that you can see the 2:00-minute (120 seconds) marker.
8. Move **Playhead** to 2 seconds and click **Add Keyframe**.
9. Move **Playhead** back to the 1-second mark.

Now, we'll edit the animation spline curves. If you're familiar with spline editing, you'll know there is a line at each node representing the tangent of the curve at that point and handles at the ends of the line for editing the curve. (You also modify the operation of this gizmo by right-clicking the node). Follow these steps:

1. Click the 1:00-second node for the **Rotation.X** property and grab one of the handles to make a smooth S-curve. Don't make it too steep; set it to something between 30 and 45 degrees.
2. Repeat this for the Y and Z axes, but with some variation, as shown here:

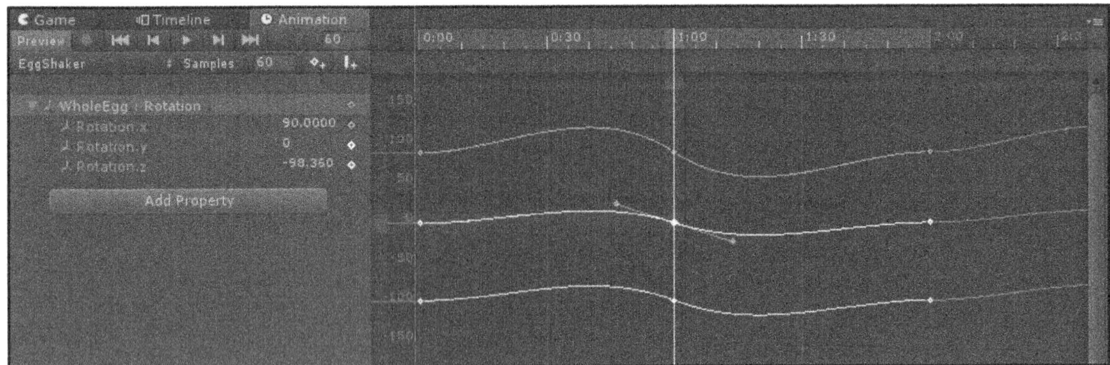

For one or two of the axes, add an extra **Keyframe** to make the curves wobble the egg a little more randomly. My final curves are shown here:

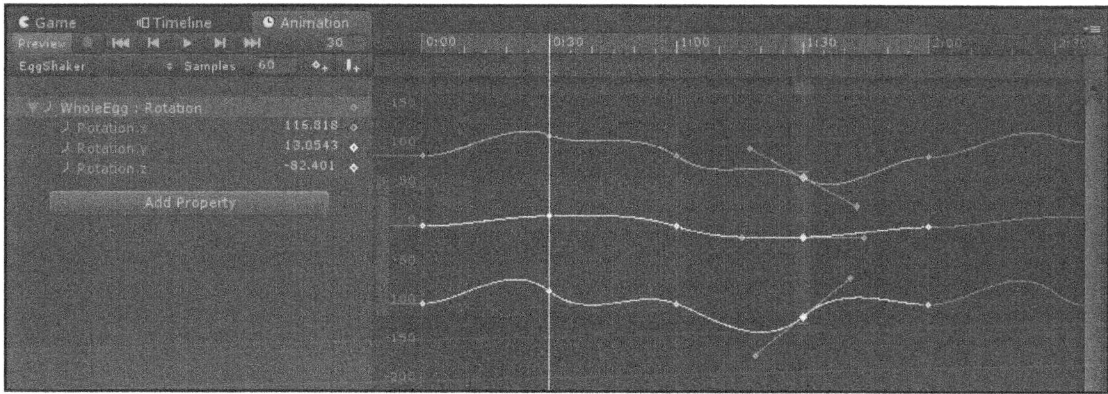

With that done (the curves can be edited and refined later), select **Blackbird Director**, open the **Timeline** window, and perform the following steps:

1. Select the **+** add button (at the top-left) and choose **Animation Track.**
2. Drag the **WholeEgg** object from **Hierarchy** onto the **Timeline** track's **Animator** slot.
3. If prompted to **Create Animator** on the GameObject, say yes to add an **Animator** component.

This time, instead of recording the track, we'll use the one we just created and make it animate back and forth, as follows:

1. Using the menu icon on the track we just created, choose **Add From Animation Clip**.
2. When prompted, choose the **EggShaker** animation from the **Select Animation Clip** window.
3. A small rectangle will be added to the track. Slide it to about `50` seconds, which is when the nest is on the ground but the chick has not hatched yet.
4. In **Inspector**, we now have more clip options. Under **Animation Extrapolation**, choose **Post-Extrapolate: Ping Pong**, as shown in the following screenshot.

5. Then, drag the right edge of the animation track to the 60-second mark, so that the animation plays for about 10 seconds:

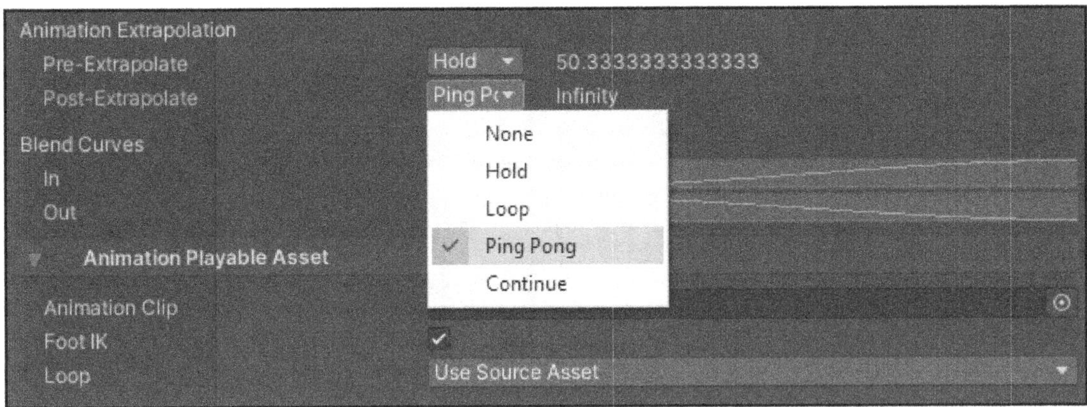

This exercise was a lot like the other animations we created earlier, but this time, we created the animation clip first in **Animation Window** and then added it to a **Timeline** track afterward. Often, animation clips can be imported into your Unity project from asset packages from the Asset Store, for example, or created in other 3D packages such as Blender, Maya, and 3D Max.

Animation Clips with **Timeline** can be quite flexible. You can even add multiple **Animation Clips** to the same **Animation Track**, and blend between them. If you need even more control, you can use an **Animator Controller** instead, as we'll see in the next section.

Using Animator Controllers

While recording animations as **Timeline** tracks is very convenient, it does have its limitations. These animations "live" in **Timeline**. But sometimes, you want to treat animations as assets in their own right. For example, you would use **Animation Clips** if you want an animation to loop repeatedly or transition between movements, blend their actions, and then apply the same set of animation curves to many different objects.

Animators were the standard way of managing *Animation Clips* in Unity before **Timeline**. It uses an **Animator Component**, an **Animator Controller**, and an **Animation Clip**. Fortunately, if you create a new **Animation Clip** on an object, Unity creates each of these items for you. But it's important to understand how they fit together.

Briefly, from the Unity Manual (`https://docs.unity3d.com/Manual/animeditor-CreatingANewAnimationClip.html`):

> *"To animate GameObjects in Unity, the object or objects need an **Animator Component** attached. This Animator Component must reference an **Animator Controller**, which, in turn, contains references to one or more **Animation Clips**."*

These objects originate from the **Mecanim** animation system that was folded into Unity a few years ago (you may still see references to Mecanim in the Unity Manual and web searches). This animation system is specially tailored for humanoid character animations (see `https://docs.unity3d.com/Manual/AnimationOverview.html`). The terminology may seem redundant and confusing. The following definitions may help (or not!). Pay especially close attention to the use of "animator" versus "animation":

- **Animation Clips**: Describes how an object's properties change over time.
- **Animator Controller**: Organizes clips in a state machine flowchart, keeps track of which clip should currently be playing, and when animations should change or blend together. It references the clips it uses.
- **Animator component**: Brings together Animation Clips, the Animation Controller, and the Avatar if used.
- **Do not use legacy Animation components**: The Animation component is legacy but the Animation window is not!
- **Animation window**: Used to create/edit individual Animation Clips and can animate any property you can edit in the inspector. Shows a **timeline**, but this is not the same as the **Timeline** window. Offers a Dopesheet versus Curves view.
- **Animator window**: Organizes existing animation clip assets into a flowchart-like state machine graph.

Timeline animation recordings also use Animation Clips; you just don't need to explicitly create them. Each recorded Animation Track in a Timeline has a corresponding animation playable file (named "Recorded (n)") in your **Assets** folder.

We will take a look at a couple of existing examples of Animators and then use the existing birds one to make our **Bluejay** fly. First, we'll review **ThirdPersonController**, which will be similar to the Ethan character we used in previous chapters. Next, we'll look at the Animator that's included in the Living Birds package we're using for our **Bluejay** object. We'll use it in our project to make the bird fly between locations in the scene.

ThirdPersonController Animator

The **ThirdPersonController** character prefab we used for Ethan in previous chapters uses an **Animator Controller** to manage humanoid animation clips on the rigged model. For curiosity, let's examine it now (although we will not use it in this scene):

1. Temporarily drag a copy of the **ThirdPersonController** prefab from your **Project** `Assets/Standard Assets/Characters/ThirdPersonCharacter/Prefabs/` folder into the scene.
2. Notice that, in **Inspector**, it has an **Animator** component and that the **Controller** slot references **ThirdPersonAnimatorController**.
3. Open the **Animator** window using **Window** | **Animation** | **Animator.**
4. You can pan or zoom into the graph using the mouse by clicking and dragging or by using the scroll-wheel, respectively.

The **Animator** graph for Ethan is shown in the following screenshot. You can see that when the character is activated (`Entry`), it initializes to the `Grounded` state. The rounded boxes are **States**; the lines between them are **Transitions**. On the left is the list of state **Properties** that the Animator can use. When `Crouch` is true (checked), for example, the animation transitions to `Crouching`, plays that animation clip, and then transitions back (and clears the `Crouch` state's boolean value):

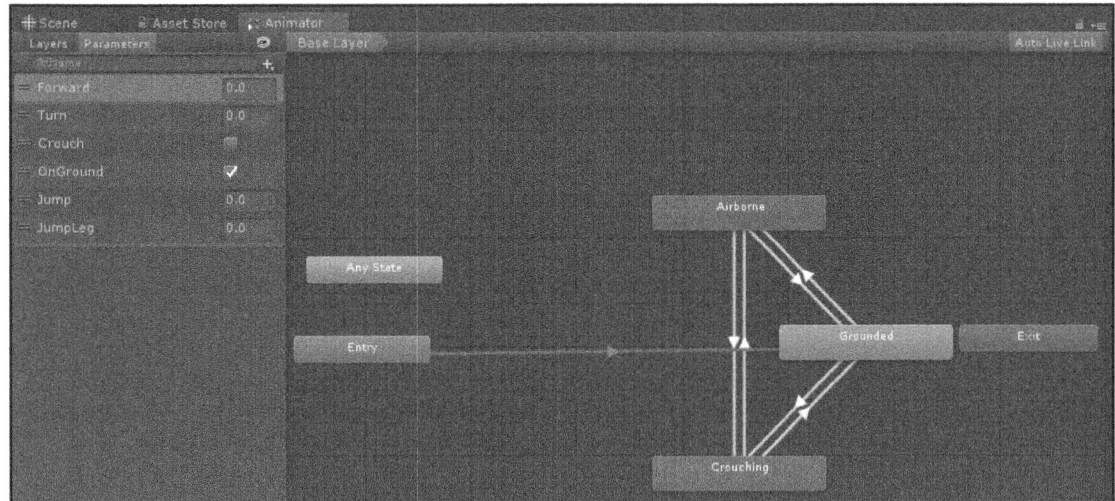

If you open the `Grounded` state (double-click it), you will see a **Blend Tree** with an impressive collection of **Animation Clips** for standing idle, walking, turning, and so on. These can be activated and combined (blended) based on user input.

That was just for show and explanation. You can now delete the **ThirdPersonController** object from the scene. Next, we'll look at another Animator, **BirdAnimatorController**, which is used by our **Bluejay** object.

Living Birds Animator

The Living Birds package comes with a lot of animation clips. You can actually open the FBX models in Blender or another animation application and examine how the models and animations are defined. These have been combined into a **BirdAnimationController**. Examine the Animator using the following steps:

1. Select the **Bluejay** object in **Hierarchy**.
2. If the **Animator** window is open, you'll see the graph. If not, open it with **Window** | **Animation** | **Animator**.

The **Animator** graph is shown here:

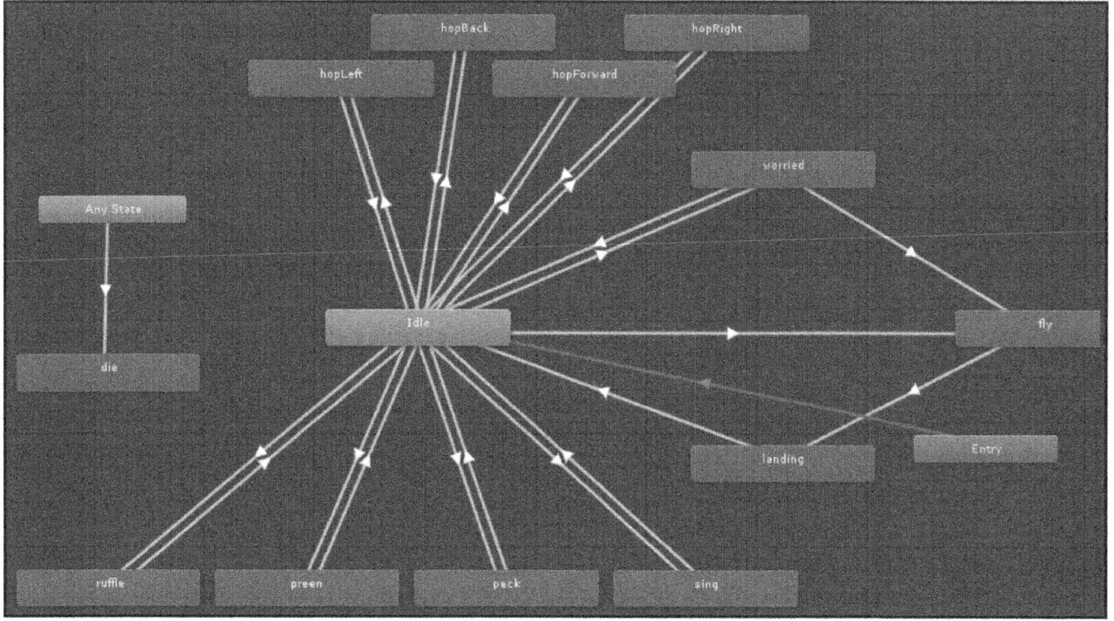

You can see that almost all the animations readily transition to and from the `Idle` one, whether `Preen`, `Peck`, `Sing`, or `HopLeft`, `HopRight`, `HopForward`, and so on. Also, notice the `Idle -> Fly -> Landing -> Idle` loop, as we're going to use that. On the left of the graph is a properties box. The following screenshot shows its **Parameters** tab. We'll be using two of these – **flying** and **landing**. These are `boolean` values that can be set to `true` or `false` from a script to affect which animation clip to play at a given time:

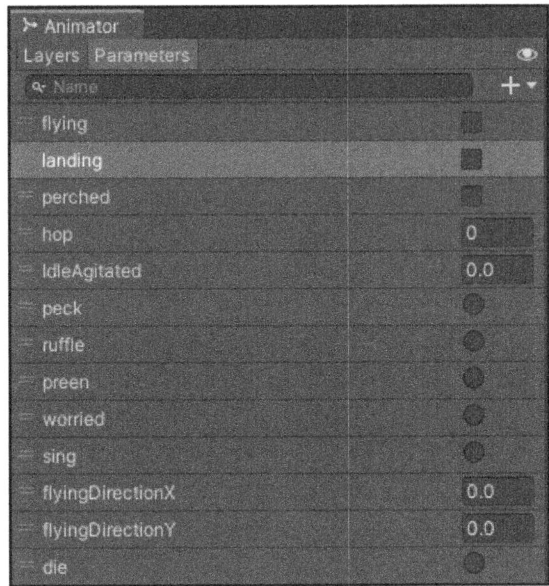

The **Bluejay** game object also has a C# script, `lb_Bird`, which invokes these Animator states and transitions. Unfortunately, like a lot of code you'll find on the internet, the Living Birds `lb_Bird` code works for its own purposes but not necessarily ours. It's designed for generating a flock of many birds that fly and land randomly, avoid collisions, and can even be killed. In our project, we have just one bird and want control over the landing locations, so we'll use the nice models and animations from the package but write our own controller script and keep it simple.

Earlier, we animated the falling nest by defining **Keyframe** positions in the animation curves. We'll do things differently for the **Bluejay** object. We'll place empty GameObjects as markers in **Scene Hierarchy** that define the key positions for the bird to fly and land. (This is a lot like using a **Navmesh** agent target to direct Ethan's movement, as we did in `Chapter 4`, *Using Gaze-Based Control,* and when using teleportation pods in our other projects*)*. Then we'll use **Timeline** to progress from one target position to the next, over time, using, as you'll see, a **Signal Track**. First, we'll create a list of locations where the bird should fly between.

Defining the fly-to targets

We are going to place a series of target locations in the scene that define where the bird will fly. To define these, we'll create a **Location Marker** prefab that also helps us visualize the position and rotation direction. Follow these steps:

1. In **Hierarchy**, create an **Empty** game object named `Bird Controller` and reset its **Transform** properties.
2. Create a child empty object child of **Bird Controller** (right-click | **Create Empty**), name it `Location Marker`, and reset its **Transform** properties.
3. Use any graphic to visualize the marker's position and direction. I'll use **directionArrow**, which is included with the default Universal Project Template in the `Assets/Models/` folder. Drag **directionArrow** into **Hierarchy** as a child of **Location Marker**.
4. Set its **Scale** (`0.25, 0.25, 0.25`) and **Rotation** (`0, 90, 0`). (For some reason, this model is not pointing forward by default).
5. Make it a prefab by dragging **Location Marker** from **Hierarchy** into the **Project** `Assets/Prefabs/` folder.
6. Set **Location Marker** | **Transform** | **Position** and **Rotation** to the same values as the **Bluejay** object.
7. Duplicate **Location Marker** (*Ctrl* + *D*) six times, setting the bird's target landing sites. Use the values in the following table as a guide:

Name	**Position**	**Rotation**	**Description**
`Location Marker`	`(0.75, 0.4, -1.25)`	`(0, 135, 0)`	The starting position of the **Bluejay** object
`Location Marker (1)`	`(3, 0.65, 0)`	`(0, 40, 0)`	Atop nearest rock
`Location Marker (2)`	`(1.9, 0, -1.7)`	`(0, -165, 0)`	Ground near **Nest** but not in it
`Location Marker (3)`	`(2.5, 0.6, -3.4)`	`(0, -200, 0)`	Atop next nearest rock
`Location Marker (4)`	`(-5.85, 0.5, -0.3)`	`(0, -70, 0)`	Next rock
`Location Marker (5)`	`(-5, 0.53, 3.7)`	`(0, 0, 0)`	Last rock
`Location Marker (6)`	`(45, 11, 45)`	`(0, 36, 0)`	In the distance

The last location should be far away. The bird will head there at the end of the video. The following screenshot shows a top-down isometric view of the scene, along with the markers:

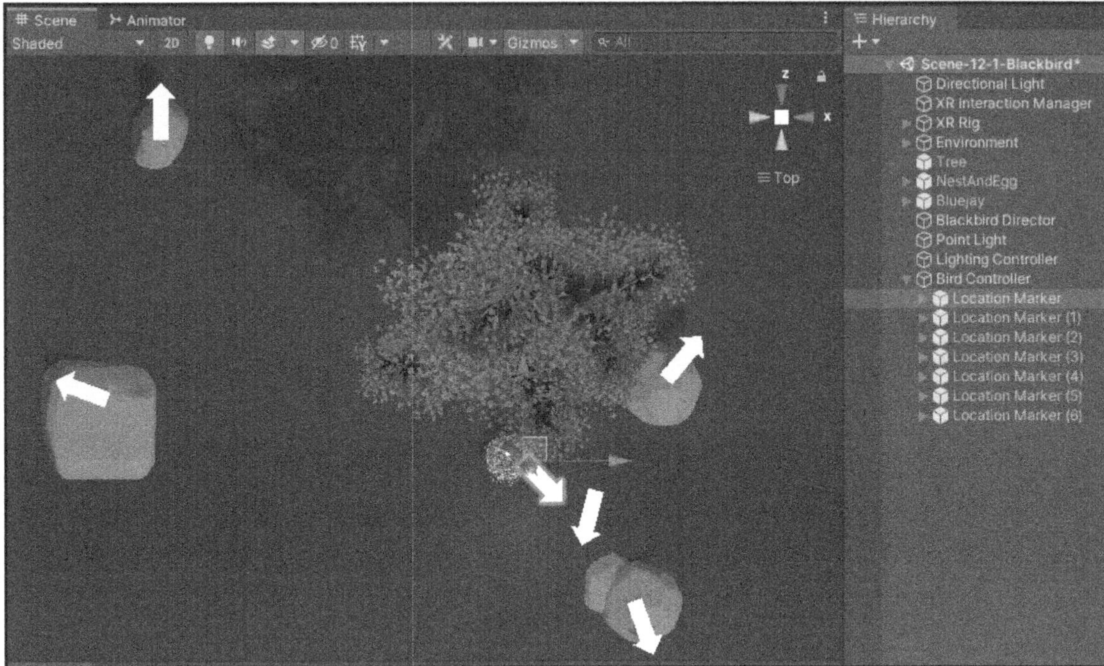

We've now defined seven location markers, beginning with the bird's initial starting location in the nest, then specifying how the bird will fly or hop from one rock to another across the scene, before it eventually flies away into the distance. Given these markers, we can now code the animations.

Using Animator hashes and DOTween to animate

To make the bird actually animate and move, we'll write a `BirdController` script containing the list of marker locations. These will move the bird from one landing site to another at the control of the Timeline. Create a new C# script on **Bird Controller**, (**Add Component** | **New Script**) named `BirdController`. To begin, declare some `public` and `private` variables at the top of the class and a `Start` function to initialize them, as follows:

```
using System.Collections.Generic;
using DG.Tweening;
using UnityEngine;
```

```
public class BirdController : MonoBehaviour
{
    public Transform bird;
    public float flightTime = 5f;
    public float turningTime = 2.5f;
    public float flyAwayTime = 20f;
    public List<Transform> targets = new List<Transform>();

    private Animator birdAnim;
    private int index;

    void Start()
    {
        // initialize references
        birdAnim = bird.GetComponent<Animator>();

        // start at first target marker
        bird.transform.position = targets[0].position;
        bird.transform.rotation = targets[0].rotation;
        index = 0;
    }
```

The `bird` variable, obviously, will reference the **Bluejay** GameObject in the scene. The `flightTime`, `turningTime`, and `flyAwayTime` variables are, respectively, the total duration in seconds for each hop from one target to the next, the time it takes to turn toward the target direction, and a separate total flight time for the last fly-away target. Then, we declare a list of `targets` transforms that we'll reference in the scene.

The `Start` function grabs a reference to the Bluejay's **Animator** component. Then, in `Start`, we initialize the bird's position and rotation to the first target transform.

Next, we write a public `FlyToNextLocation` function that will be called by **Timeline** when it's time for the bird to go to the next target location. It finds the next target transform in the list and animates the bird to that target by calling the `FlyToTarget` function, which we will write next. In the case of the final target, we'll call a different `FlyAway` function (where the bird does not hop nor land):

```
    public void FlyToNextLocation()
    {
        index++;

        if (index == targets.Count - 1)
        {
            FlyAway(targets[index].transform);
        }
        else
```

```
            {
                FlyToTarget(targets[index].transform);
            }
        }
```

Of the two fly functions, let's write the `FlyAway` one first, as follows:

```
        private void FlyAway(Transform target)
        {
            birdAnim.SetBool("flying", true);
            birdAnim.SetBool("landing", false);
            bird.transform.DORotate(target.eulerAngles, turningTime);
            bird.transform.DOMove(target.position, flyAwayTime);
        }
```

Here, we set the bird's **Animator** to begin the flying animation (calling `birdAnim.SetBool("flying", true)`). If the bird is playing its landing animation, we'll turn that off (`birdAnim.SetBool("landing", false)`). Now, the bird is flapping its wings like it's flying.

But we also need to move it within the scene from the current location to the target one. For this, we are going to use a handy third-party tool (that we installed at the start of this chapter) called **DOTween**. (See the DOTween documentation at `http://dotween.demigiant.com/documentation.php`). I love this asset. It's a very useful shortcut for many common animations you might otherwise have to write by hand using `Update` or a `Coroutine`. Here, we will rotate the bird for `turningTime` seconds to point in the given target direction (calling `transform.DORotate`). We will concurrently move its position to the target location (calling `transform.DOMove`) for the `flyAwayTime` duration.

The animation to fly from one place to another is a little more complicated as we want the bird to hop up in the air, turn toward the target, travel to the target, land at the target location, and then return to the `Idle` animations. The `FlyToTarget` function is written as follows:

```
        private void FlyToTarget(Transform target)
        {
            birdAnim.SetBool("flying", true);
            birdAnim.SetBool("landing", false);

            bird.transform
                .DORotate(target.eulerAngles, turningTime)
                .OnComplete(() =>
                {
                    birdAnim.SetBool("flying", false);
                    birdAnim.SetBool("landing", true);
                });
```

```
        bird.transform
            .DOJump(target.position, 1f, 1, flightTime)
            .OnComplete(() =>
            {
                birdAnim.SetBool("landing", false);
            });
    }
```

It starts the same as `FlyAway`, by running the `flying` animation clip (and stopping the `landing` one). Then, we also run the `DORotate` animation to turn the bird in the target direction. But when that sequence is complete, we switch the animation from `flying` to `landing` (where the bird flaps its wings in a rapid landing motion). For moving the bird to the new location, instead of a linear interpolation of the two positions, we use a handy `DOJump` function, which causes the object to appear to hop up (change in Y value) as it moves (changes in X and Z values). When the jump sequence is complete, we turn off the landing animation. Due to this, the bird will go back into its `Idle` animations.

This C# script uses an advanced lambda coding syntax that creates an unnamed function on the fly where it's needed. The `OnComplete` function requires a callback action function that is called (as the name implies) when the tween animation is complete. Rather than defining a separate function in our script, we use lambda syntax `() => { }`.

Save the script. Back in Unity, let's populate its public parameters, as follows:

1. If it's not already attached, drag the `BirdController` script onto the **Bird Controller** game object.
2. Drag the **Bluejay** game object from **Hierarchy** onto the **Bird Controller** | **Bird** slot.
3. We have seven location markers, so unfold the **Targets** parameter and set its **Size** to `7`.
4. One at a time, drag the Location Markers from **Hierarchy** into their corresponding slots in the **Targets** list.
5. Now, or at any time, you can hide the **directionArrow** objects in the **Location Marker** prefab by opening the prefab for editing and disabling that child object.

The resulting component **Inspector** window looks as follows:

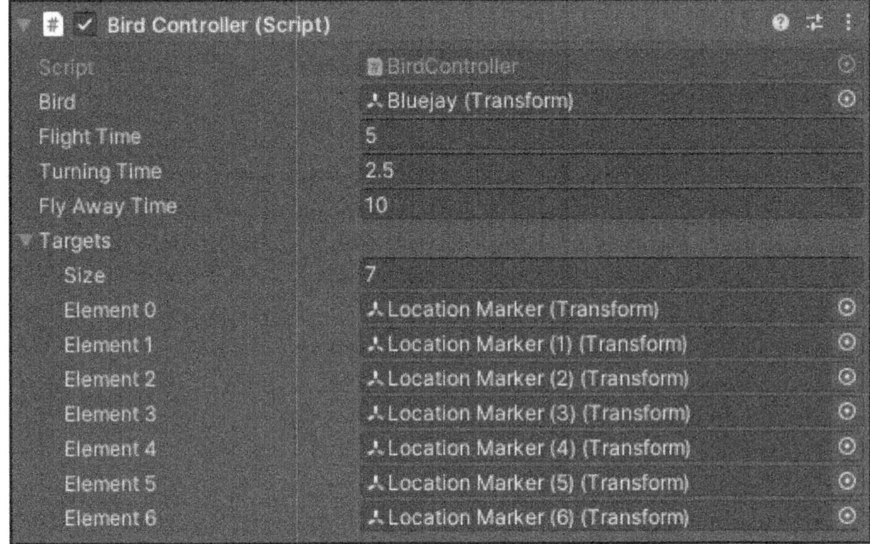

Awesome! Now, we just need to trigger the hops between targets from **Timeline**.

Using a Signal Track in Timeline

So far, we've already used several types of **Timeline** tracks, including **Audio**, **Activation**, and **Animation** tracks. Now, we'll introduce a **Signal Track**. As the name suggests, a signal is an event that triggers some action in your scene. Here, the signal will trigger a call to `FlyToNextLocation` in `BirdController`. We'll add the signal to the timeline starting at the 80-second mark and trigger it at 10-second intervals. Follow these steps:

1. Open the **Timeline Editor** window for `Blackbird Director`.
2. Drag the `Bird Controller` object from **Hierarchy** onto **Timeline** and add a new **Signal Track**.
3. Move **Playhead** to `80`.
4. Right-click the track (or use its three-dot menu) and select **Add Signal Emitter**.
5. In its **Inspector**, select **Emit Signal**. Because we haven't created one yet, press the **Create Signal...** button and name the file `Fly Next Signal`.
6. In its **Signal Receiver** component, add a new **Reaction** (if necessary, press the + button), drag **Bird Controller** onto the **Object** slot, and in the **Function** list, select **Bird Controller | FlyToNextLocation**.

Signal Emitter looks as follows:

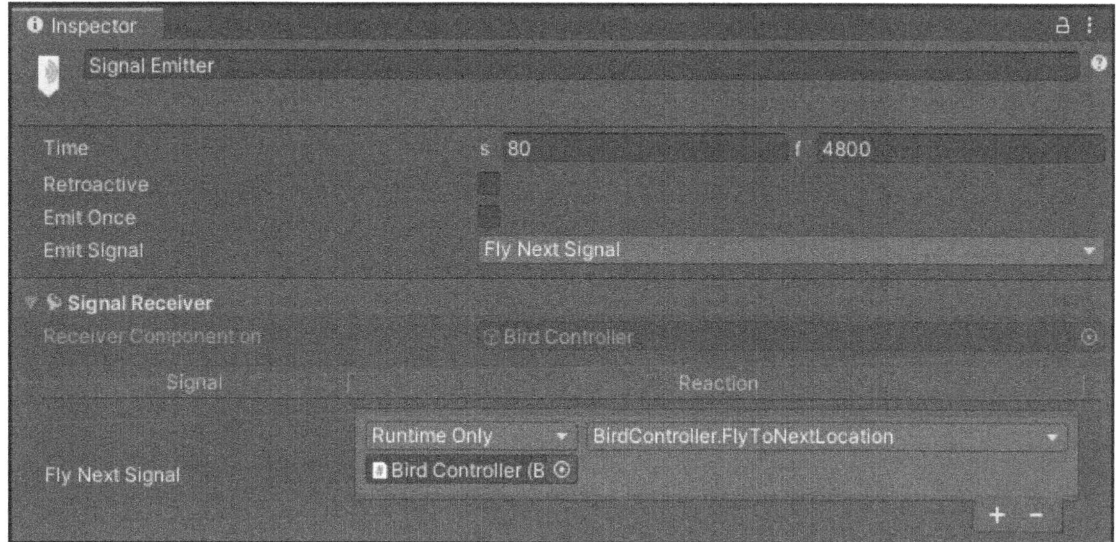

Now, add the remaining signals to **Timeline** with the following steps:

1. Slide **Playhead** to `90` seconds.
2. On the track, select the three-dot icon | **Add Signal Emitter**.
3. In **Inspector**, set **Emit Signal** to **Fly Next Signal**.
4. You can actually duplicate the signal marker. Right-click and select **Duplicate** and slide it to the 100-second mark (or type `100` into its **Time** parameter).
5. Repeat s*tep 4* for the remaining three signals (at `110`, `120`, and `130` seconds, respectively).

Timeline, along with the six signals we've defined, is shown in the following screenshot:

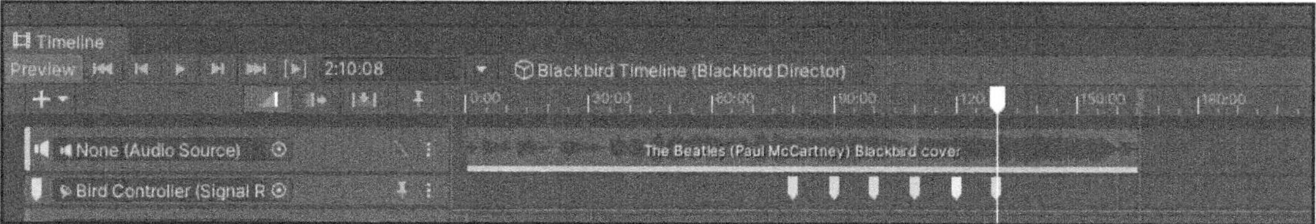

You just need to press **Play** now and you'll experience a wonderful short animated story. The following are a few frames of the **Bluejay** object flying from the initial target (**Location Marker**) and landing on the next one (**Location Marker (1)**):

Note that if you receive a `NullExceptionError` message in the `lb_Bird.cs` file, it's because our implementation is not using the original package's `lb_BirdController` but our own. You can fix this problem by modifying (near line `457`) it so that it checks the `controller` variable is not `null` before trying to reference it, as follows:

```
void FlyAway(){
   if(!dead){
     StopCoroutine("FlyToTarget");
     anim.SetBool(landingBoolHash, false);
     if (controller)
         controller.SendMessage ("BirdFindTarget",gameObject);
   }
 }
```

The following is one more dramatic view of our happy bird flying off toward the horizon to the song lyrics, *"Blackbird singing in the dead of night; Take these broken winds and learn to fly... All your life; You were only waiting for this moment to be free"*:

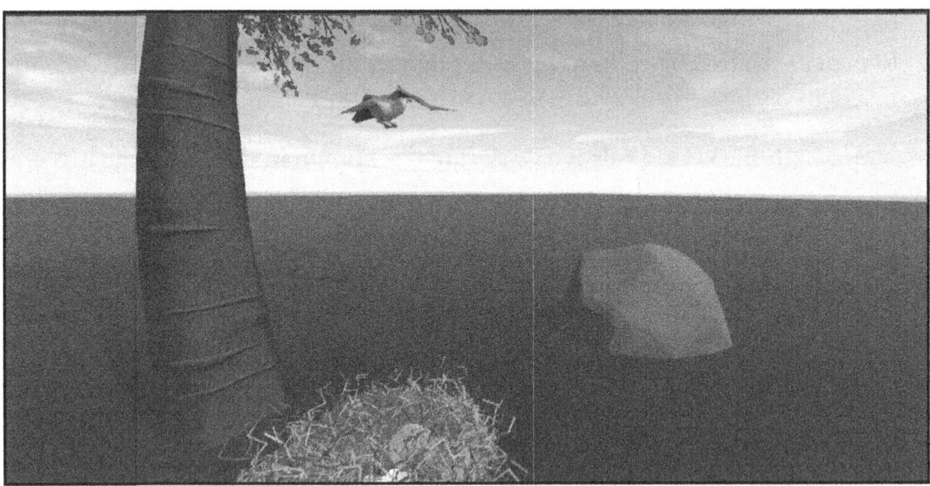

There we have it! We started with a timeline storyboard, collected the assets we needed for the project, and assembled them into a **Timeline** sequence with multiple tracks. In this last part, the story really comes alive as we used an Animator Controller that's called from our own control script to make the bird flap its wings to fly and land. We also used **DOTween** animations to rotate, move, and jump the bird from one target location to the next. It may be nice to watch as a video, but play it in virtual reality for a real experience!

Currently, the user's participation in the story is entirely passive. It plays and the user watches. Let's add a little bit of interactivity to the scene.

Making the story interactive

So far, we've used **Timeline** to drive our entire VR story experience from start to finish. But in fact, **Timelines** are a playable asset like others in Unity. For example, if you select the **Blackbird Director** object and look in **Inspector** at its **Playable Director** component, you'll see it has a **Play On Awake** checkbox and that it's currently checked. What we're going to do now is not play on awake, but rather start playing on a user event, namely looking directly at the small tree for a few seconds. When the story ends, we'll make it reset itself.

Look to play

An interesting design pattern for VR application is to wait for the player to look at something before it starts animating or otherwise becomes active in the scene. After all, it'd be a shame for the user to not notice things and miss all the action! We'll demonstrate this idea in our project by waiting for the user to look at the small tree before beginning to play the Timeline. First, we'll add a **LookAt Target** that encases the small tree and then use that to trigger playing the timeline. We'll also display a countdown text. (In `Chapter 6`, *Canvasing World Space UI*, we used a World Space Canvas, but now, we'll simply use a 3D text object, assuming you already have TextMeshPro installed via **Package Manager**). Follow these steps:

1. Select `Blackbird Director` and uncheck the **Play On Awake** checkbox.
2. For reference, set the **Tree** game object's **Scale** to its starting keyframe **Scale** (`0.1, 0.1, 0.1`).
3. In **Hierarchy**, create a cube (**GameObject | 3D Object | Cube**) and name it `LookAt Target.`

4. Scale and place it to encase the small tree. Use **Scale** (`0.4, 0.5, 0.4`) and **Position** (`0, 0.3, 0`).
5. Disable its **Mesh Renderer** but keep its **Box Collider**.
6. Add a 3D text object as a child by right-clicking | **3D Object** | **Text - TextMeshPro**. Rename it `Countdown Text`.
7. Set **Text Mesh** | **Font Size** to `72`, **Alignment** | **Center**, and **Transform** | **Scale** to (`0.2, 0.2, 0.2`). Set its **Position Z** to `-0.5`.
8. Create a new C# script on the cube (**Add Component** | **New Script**) named `LookAtToStart` and write it as follows:

```
using UnityEngine;
using UnityEngine.Playables;
using TMPro;

public class LookAtToStart : MonoBehaviour
{
    public PlayableDirector timeline;
    public float timeToSelect = 4f;

    private Transform camera;
    private TMP_Text countdownText;
    private float timer;

    void Start()
    {
        camera = Camera.main.transform;
        countdownText = GetComponentInChildren<TMP_Text>();
        timer = timeToSelect;
    }

    void Update()
    {
        // Do nothing if already playing
        if (timeline.state == PlayState.Playing)
            return;

        // Is user looking here?
        Ray ray = new Ray(camera.position,
             camera.rotation * Vector3.forward);
        RaycastHit hit;
        if (Physics.Raycast(ray, out hit) &&
             (hit.collider.gameObject == gameObject))
        {
            if (timer > 0f)
            {
```

```
                    timer -= Time.deltaTime;
                    countdownText.text = timer.ToString("F0");
                    countdownText.gameObject.SetActive(true);
                }
                else
                {
                    // go!
                    timeline.Play();
                    countdownText.gameObject.SetActive(false);
                }
            }
            else
            {
                // reset timer
                timer = timeToSelect;
                countdownText.gameObject.SetActive(false);
            }
        }
    }
```

This script is similar to the ones we wrote in `Chapter 4`, *Using Gaze-Based Control*. We use the Main Camera and determine the direction the user is looking in. Using the physics engine, we call `Physics.Raycast` to cast a ray in the view direction and determine if it hit this object, that is, **LookAt Target**. If so, we start or continue a countdown timer and show the countdown text. When the counter reaches zero, we play the Timeline. Meanwhile, if we look away, we reset the timer.

Save the script. In Unity, drag the **Blackbird Director** game object onto the **Look At to Start | Timeline** slot. Try it out by pressing **Play**. **Timeline** will not start playing, instead waiting for you to look at the tree sapling for a few seconds and then calling `timeline.Play` to start the animations. The countdown text gives you feedback on this, as shown in the following screen capture:

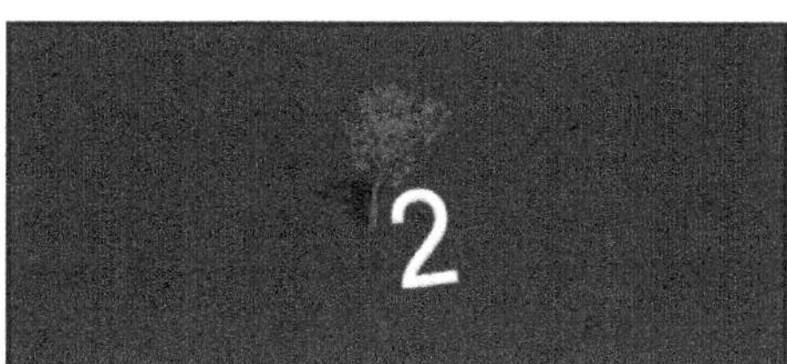

We used the player's head pose (viewing direction) to make the scene more interactive. The story does not start until the player is paying attention.

Now, we have a new problem. When **Timeline** was set to **Play On Awake**, the user would immediately see the Timeline from the beginning. But now, the scene starts in the state that the developer (you) last saved. That is, the sky is not dark, the tree and bird are active and full-sized, and so on. Instead, the experience should start basically at the first frame of the Timeline while waiting for the user to start playing the story. Let's fix this.

Resetting the initial scene's setup

You could manually go through each and every game object in the scene and ensure it has been saved with the same initial state as the start of the Timeline. Not only is this tedious but it's error-prone since you or another developer could save the scene with an object in some unexpected state. Instead, we'll add a little hack that plays the timeline for a brief `0.1` seconds to reset the objects to their starting state. We will implement this using a coroutine. Follow these steps:

1. Modify the `LookAtToStart` script as follows. Add a new variable, `resetSetup`, and initialize it to `true`, as follows:

```
private bool resetSetup = true;
```

2. Add a `PlayToSetup` function, which will be run as a coroutine. As we know, coroutines are a way to run a function, let Unity do other stuff momentarily, and then resume where you left off (via the `yield` statement). Here, we start playing the Timeline, go away for `0.1` seconds, and then tell the Timeline to stop playing:

```
IEnumerator PlayToSetup()
{
    timeline.Play();
    yield return new WaitForSeconds(0.1f);
    timeline.Stop();
}
```

3. Call the coroutine from `Update` when we want to reset the setup:

```
void Update()
  {
    if (timeline.state == PlayState.Playing)
       return;

    if (resetSetup)
    {
```

```
            StartCoroutine(PlayToSetup());
            resetSetup = false;
        }
```

We also want the scene to reset after the Timeline plays all the way through, so we set `resetSetup` as soon as the timeline starts playing. It'll be recognized once `timeline.state` is no longer playing:

```
...
        // go!
        timeline.Play();
        resetSetup = true;
    }
```

4. Press **Play**.

Look at the tree. Enjoy the experience. When it ends, you're reset to the beginning and can look at the tree again to replay the story.

We're going to stop developing now. Some suggestions regarding how to improve the interactivity and user experience include doing the following:

- Add a particle effect around the tree to indicate that it's a trigger.
- Highlight the tree as visual feedback when you're looking at it.

Here are other suggestions for interactable objects you could add to the story:

- Looking at the egg in the nest causes it to hatch sooner than its default timing.
- When you look at the bird while it's idle, it will turn to look back at you.
- If you poke the bird with your hand controller, it jumps out of the way.
- You can pick up a rock and throw it to kill the bird (*nooo, just kidding!*).

Now, let's recap this chapter.

Summary

In this chapter, we built an animated VR story. We began by deciding what we wanted to do by planning all the necessary details, including the timeline, music track, graphic assets, animation sequences, and lighting. We imported our assets and placed them in the scene. Then, we created a Timeline and roughly estimated when specific objects will be enabled and disabled using an Activation Track. Next, you learned how to animate several objects, including growing the tree and bird, floating the nest, and making the egg wobble. You also animated the lighting and learned how to animate game object parameters other than Transforms.

You also used Animation Clips and an Animator Controller in order to use animations imported from a third-party package, Living Birds. You wrote a control script that calls the Animator to tell the bird when to flap its wings for flying or landing. We then defined location markers to define where the bird will hop, fly, and land from one rock to another and then fly away into the distance. The control script animated this movement using the DOTween tools package. Lastly, you learned how to add interactions to the story and how to use gaze-based control to start and replay the experience.

In the next final chapter, we will dive into the technical details of optimizing your VR projects so that they run smoothly and comfortably in VR. We will consider the different areas that affect performance and latency, from model polygon count, to Unity scripting, to bottlenecks on the CPU and GPU.

13
Optimizing for Performance and Comfort

As we've mentioned throughout these chapters and projects, the success of your VR app will be negatively impacted by any discomfort your users feel. It is a fact that VR can cause motion sickness. The symptoms of motion sickness include nausea, sweating, headaches, and even vomiting. It can take hours – perhaps an overnight sleep – to recover. In real life, humans are susceptible to motion sickness: riding a roller coaster, a bumpy airplane, a rocking boat. It's caused when one part of your balance-sensing system thinks your body is moving but other parts don't.

In VR, this could occur when the eyes see motion but your body doesn't sense it. We've considered ways you can design your VR apps to avoid this. With locomotion, always give the user control over their first-person movement. Try to avoid riding-the-rails experiences and especially avoid free-falling. Display a horizon line or dashboard in the foreground so that the player at least feels like they're grounded in a cockpit if not on solid ground.

The opposite is also true: when your body feels motion but your eyes don't see it, this can also cause motion sickness. Even a very subtle discord can have a bad effect. In VR, a major culprit of this is motion-to-pixel latency. For example, if you move your head but the view you see doesn't keep up with the movement, that can cause nausea. Causes of latency in VR are often because your application has too much to compute during each frame, so rendering a frame takes longer than it should, slowing down the frame rate the user experiences. This chapter addresses ways to optimize your application to improve performance, reduce the computation per frame, reduce latency, and give your users a more comfortable experience.

Although this chapter is at the end of this book, we do not mean to suggest that performance issues be left for the end of your project's implementation. The old software development adage "first get it to work, then get it to work faster" doesn't necessarily apply to VR development. You need to pay attention to performance and comfort throughout your development process, which we will address as the main topics in this chapter, including using the Unity Profiler window, optimizing your 3D models, using Static objects in the scene, and using best practices for optimizing your C# code. This chapter will cover the following topics:

- Using the Unity Profiler tools
- Optimizing your artwork and 3D models
- Optimizing your scene and rendering options
- Optimizing your code
- Runtime performance analysis

By the end of this chapter, you will be able to use Unity's **Profiler** tools to analyze and diagnose performance issues, flag static objects, and provide other performance optimizations. We will start with a quick introduction to the **Profiler** and **Stats** windows.

Technical requirements

To implement the projects and exercises in this chapter, you will need the following:

- A PC or Mac with Unity 2019.4 LTS or later, the XR plugin for your device, and the XR Interaction Toolkit installed
- A VR headset supported by the Unity XR platform

You can access or clone the GitHub repository for this book (`https://github.com/PacktPublishing/Unity-2020-Virtual-Reality-Projects-3rd-Edition-`) to optionally use the following assets and completed projects for this chapter:

- The asset files for you to use in this chapter are located in `UVRP3Files/Chapter-13-Files.zip`.
- All the completed projects for this book can be found in a single Unity project at `UVRP3Projects`.
- The completed assets and scenes for this chapter can be found in the `UVRP3Projects/Assets/_UVRP3Assets/Chapter13/` folder.

Using the Unity Profiler and Stats windows

Optimizing can be a lot of work, and there is a learning curve to get the hang of it. The good news is that it can be accomplished incrementally. Tackle the more obvious, bigger bang-for-their-buck things first. You can accomplish a lot with little or no visual degradation after a bit of experimentation. The Unity Editor includes two built-in tools that can be used to assess performance: the **Stats** window and the **Profiler** window, both of which I will introduce in this section.

The Stats window

The **Stats** window shows real-time rendering statistics when you press **Play** in the Unity Editor. Reviewing and understanding these statistics is your first line of call when it comes to evaluating and improving the performance of your app, and it can help you decide which optimization strategies, including those covered in this chapter, to tackle first. In the **Game** window, enable **Stats** by pressing the **Stats** button. The output of doing this can be seen in the following screenshot:

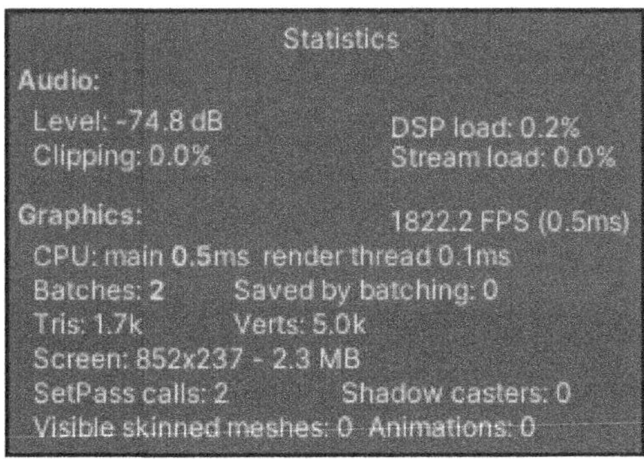

The actual statistics displayed will vary, depending on your current build target (see `http://docs.unity3d.com/Manual/RenderingStatistics.html`), including the following:

- Graphics **frames per second** (**FPS**) and time per frame
- **CPU** time per frame
- **Tris** (**triangles**) and **Verts** (**vertices**) geometry to be rendered in the frame
- **Batches** of graphic data efficiently grouped together for the GPU

In VR, you want to pay close attention to the frames per second. The minimum acceptable rate varies, depending on your target device, but generally, for desktop devices, you should aim as high as 120 FPS, while 60 FPS (or 75 FPS) is considered an absolute minimum. The Sony PlayStation VR accepts 60 FPS but uses hardware to automatically double the rate to 120 FPS to compensate. Windows Mixed Reality HMD will throttle the frame rate between 90 and 60, depending on the graphics processor hardware on your computer, allowing laptops with slower mobile GPU to run VR. The Oculus Quest mobile VR device's target is 72 FPS.

When in the Unity Editor's **Play** mode, the FPS is not necessarily the same as you'd experience when running a built executable in your device, so it should be used as an indicator, not necessarily as an actual value. But, thankfully, it does not include any editor-only processing such as drawing the **Scene** view.

Examining the **CPU** time per frame and comparing that with the overall graphics time per frame will tell you whether your app is CPU-bound or GPU-bound; that is, which process is the bottleneck slowing you down the most. The CPU is used for physics calculations, geometry culling, and other operations that prepare the data for rendering in the GPU. On the other hand, the GPU runs the shaders and actually generates the pixel values for display. Knowing if you're CPU- or GPU-bound can help direct your focus for what optimization efforts are required to improve your game's performance.

The **Tris** and **Verts** values show the size of your geometric models' meshes that are drawn. Only the visible faces of your meshes are counted, so your scene could include much more. The values in **Stats** are the geometry the camera is looking at, not including any vertices outside the view, and after any occluded surfaces and back faces have been removed. This culling is performed by the CPU. As you move the camera or as objects in the scene animate, the numbers will change. As we'll see in the next section, reducing the poly count of your models can lead to significant gains in performance.

The **Batches** value is an indicator of how hard your GPU is working. The more batches, the more rendering the GPU must perform each frame. The number of batches, not the size of a batch, is the bottleneck. You can reduce batches by reducing and/or combining the geometry in your scene. Since it's faster to have fewer (albeit larger) batches than lots of small ones, you can tell Unity to optimize the graphics by combining more geometry into larger batches and pump that through the GPU pipeline.

When profiling and optimizing, write down (or take screenshots of) the stats and label them, perhaps in a spreadsheet, to log your progress and measure the effectiveness of each technique that you try.

Next, we'll take a look at the **Profiler** window.

Overview of the Profiler window

The Unity **Profiler** window is a performance instrumentation tool that reports how much processing time is spent in various areas of your game, including rendering and scripts. It records the statistics during gameplay and shows them in a timeline graph. Clicking various parts lets you drill down into the details. The Profiler can be seen in the following screenshot (see `http://docs.unity3d.com/Manual/Profiler.html`):

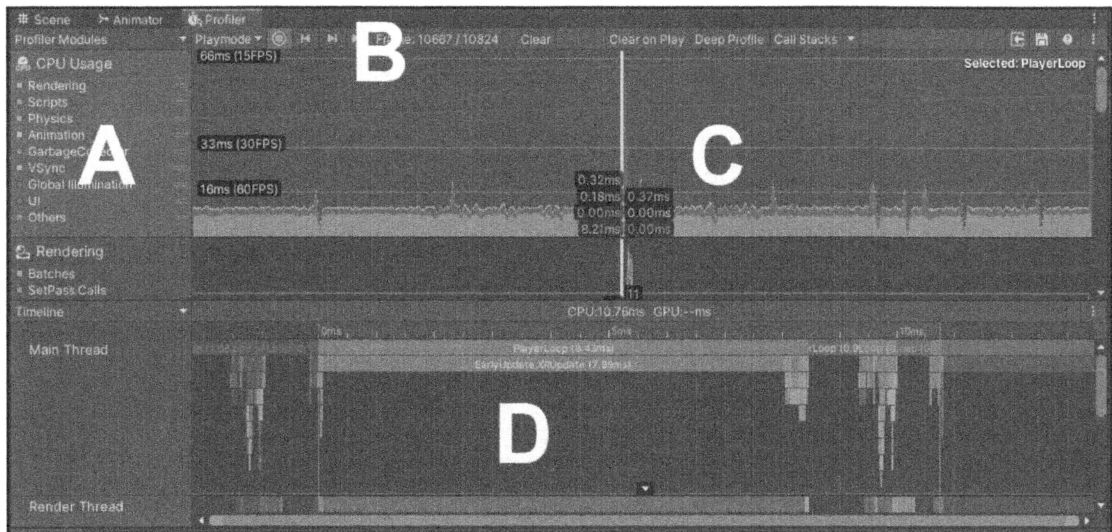

The Profiler compacts a lot of information into a small space, so you should recognize its various parts to understand what you're seeing. On the left (**A**) are the Profiler modules, that is, the list of areas that you can monitor through the Profiler. Along the top of the window is the Profiler controls toolbar (**B**), which enables you to record profiling data as your application runs and navigate through profiled frames. The white vertical line in the profile tracks is the playhead, indicating the current frame being examined. Underneath the toolbar are the profile tracks (**C**). Scroll down the **Tracks** pane to reveal more. You can add and remove tracks using the **Add Profiler** select list.

Each track includes stats for many parameters pertaining to that category of processing. For example, **CPU Usage** includes **Scripts** and **Physics**, while **Rendering** includes **Batches** and **Triangles**. The visual graph helps you easily detect anomalies. When troubleshooting, look for stretches and spikes where the data exceeds your expected thresholds. The bottom panel (**D**) shows details for the current frame and selected module that can really help you drill down into your scene to determine what processes are working and when.

You can profile your application running in the Unity Editor or remote profile builds running in a separate player, such as a mobile device.

When you discover a situation that requires deeper analysis, you can enable the **Deep Profile** button at top of the window. **Deep Profile** lets you drill down into more detail, recording all the function calls in your scripts. This can be useful if you wish to see exactly where time is spent in your code or other systems. Note that deep profiling only works in the Editor rather than remote profiling the build running on your target device, and it incurs a lot of overheads that may cause your game to run very slowly. So, in general, you'd run the Profiler without Deep Profile, and only when you find a trouble spot would you enable Deep Profile to try and discover the root cause.

As a complement to the Profiler, there is also a new **Profile Analyzer** tool (presently in preview mode) that helps you conduct a multi-frame analysis of your profile data by aggregating and visualizing frame data from the Profiler. Use **Package Manager** to install the Profile Analyzer tool (see `https://docs.unity3d.com/Manual/com.unity.performance.profile-analyzer.html`).

Now that you have the stats and profiler tools at your disposal, you can begin analyzing and diagnosing performance issues in your project.

Analyzing and diagnosing performance problems

The first line of attack in evaluating performance problems is to determine whether the bottleneck is on the CPU or the GPU. When your app is CPU-bound, the CPU (general central processor) is taking too long to execute its tasks. When your app is GPU-bound, the GPU (graphics processor) is taking too long to execute its tasks. Therefore, you need to be familiar with not just how your application is implemented but also how Unity carries out its work.

The Unity engine play loop (for example, calls to `Update` and `FixedUpdate`) is performed by the CPU. Likewise, any C# code that you write is run on the CPU. If your app is CPU-bound, you should first determine whether the cause is in components you have written versus how you're using Unity's built-in ones. Physics calculations and animations are performed by the CPU. The CPU is also used in the rendering pipeline to select which objects are candidates to be rendered in the current frame, and then prepares the geometry and texture data and feeds them to the GPU as vertices, triangles, normals, and other attributes, including the shader parameters. The more complex and detailed your geometry, the more work that happens on the CPU.

The GPU renders the geometry into pixels for display on the screen, re-rendering the screen every frame update. GPUs are very good at parallel processing so that they can calculate the value of multiple pixels concurrently from the same input data that was fed from the CPU. The code that runs on the GPU is called a **shader**. We've been selecting and using various shaders throughout this book in our materials and setting some of their properties (and ignoring other properties). Unity compiles your shaders into multiple efficient shader variants based on the properties being utilized.

But in practice, the line is not always so clearly drawn between CPU and GPU responsibilities. For example, Unity will normally organize meshes on the CPU, but you could be using a geometry shader on the GPU. Unity will build batches on the CPU or use instancing on the GPU. You can perform calculations on the CPU or in a compute shader on the GPU. Once you've identified whether the performance bottleneck in your project is within the CPU or GPU, you can use the Profiler to try and see what specific processes are consuming the most time. The basic workflow is as follows:

1. Use the Profiler on your project, looking for general areas of poor performance and/or latency spikes.
2. Enable Deep Profile and examine sample frames to determine, or at least form a hypothesis for what's causing the issue.
3. Make a change to your project.
4. Repeat the preceding steps, profiling the effect of that change.

When it comes to diagnosing problems, sometimes the third step, *Make a change to your project*, is not necessarily an attempt to fix the problem – it could be there to give more insight into what is going on. For example, if you guess that a particular `Update` call in one of your components is the root cause of the problem, you might temporarily disable that component or comment out a few lines of code to see whether that produces an improvement. If so, then you can figure out an alternative, more efficient way to implement that same feature.

Now that you are familiar with the Stats and Profile tools, you can begin to analyze and diagnose performance issues in your project. Causes of performance problems can be attributed to the geometry of your game object's artwork, scene illumination, C# code, and GPU rendering. We'll consider each of these in turn in the following sections.

Optimizing your art

The one thing that you have the most control over in your project is the content of your scenes. And sometimes, it's these very same intentionally creative decisions that have the greatest negative impacts on performance. Maybe you want hyper-realistic graphics with high-fidelity sound because *its gotta be so awesome!* Realizing you must dial that down may constitute a difficult design compromise. However, it's also likely that, with a little creative thinking and experimentation, you can achieve (nearly) identical visual results with much better performance.

"Quality" is not only how it looks, but also how it feels. Optimizing for user experience, including high frame rates and low latency, is as fundamental a design decision as visual quality.

In general, try to minimize the number of vertices and faces in your model's meshes. Avoid complex meshes. Remove faces that will never be seen, such as the ones inside of solid objects. Clean up duplicate vertices and remove doubles. This will most likely be done in the same 3D modeling application you used to create them in the first place. For example, **Blender** has built-in tools for this. Also, there are third-party tools that you can purchase to simplify model meshes.

Be sure to check out Unity's **Import** settings for your FBX and OBJ models, including options to compress and optimize your meshes. See `https://docs.unity3d.com/Manual/FBXImporter-Model.html` for more details.

In order to demonstrate these ideas, let's set up a scene with a high polygon count model, replicate that model 1,000 times, examine it in the Profiler, and try some optimization techniques. To begin with, we'll need a high-poly model. It's not unusual for 3D artists to produce models with a ridiculously high number of polygons that are virtually unusable in a game engine such as Unity. I recently found a model on **Sketchfab** that will do fine for our demonstration – a 3D version of the *NPC meme man* (see `https://knowyourmeme.com/memes/npc-wojak`) created by TANMATE. You can download a copy of this OBJ file from Sketchfab (`https://sketchfab.com/3d-models/meme-manmr-succspecial-meme-fresh-head-3d1f49bc7e6e446fb0d97e98cd40e749`) under the Creative Commons license, and a copy is included on the GitHub repository for this book, along with the modified versions of the model that will be used in this tutorial.

My local file is named `mememan-original.obj`. The original model has over 500,000 triangles and is over 37 MB in size. Let's suppose you didn't notice or mind this size and used the file as-is in your Unity project. In Unity, create a new scene with the `mememan-orginal` model, as follows:

1. Create a new scene (**File** | **New Scene**) and then save it (**File** | **Save As**) with the name `Optimization`.
2. Select **GameObject** | **XR** | **Stationary XR Rig**.
3. Create a ground plane using **GameObject** | **3D Object** | **Plane** called `Ground Plane`, reset its **Transform**, and create a material with a neutral **Base** color such as `#908070`.
4. Open the **Lighting** window using **Window** | **Rendering** | **Lighting**, select its **Scene** tab, click **New Lighting Settings** (Unity 2020+), and check the **Auto Generate** checkbox for lightmaps.

Now, add a copy of the Mememan, normalize its size, and save it as a prefab:

1. Create an empty game object using **GameObject** | **Create Empty**, name it `Mememan`, and **Position** it at (`0, 1, 1`).
2. Drag a copy of `mememan-original` into the scene as a child of the `Mememan` object we just created.
3. Set its **Scale** (`0.35, 0.35, 0.35`) and **Rotation** (`0, -135, 0`) so that it fits inside a single one-unit cube and is facing the camera.
4. Make it a prefab by dragging the root **Mememan** object into your **Project** `Assets/Prefabs/` folder.

Let's look at its **Stats** and **Profile** information and make a note of some values:

1. In the **Game** window, press **Stats** to open the **Stats** window.
2. Also, open the **Profiler** window using **Window | Analysis | Profiler.**
3. Press **Play.**

The **Game** window has the following scene and **Stats** window that shows, on my hardware, the graphics hovering around 160 FPS, CPU main 6 ms, with 11 batches:

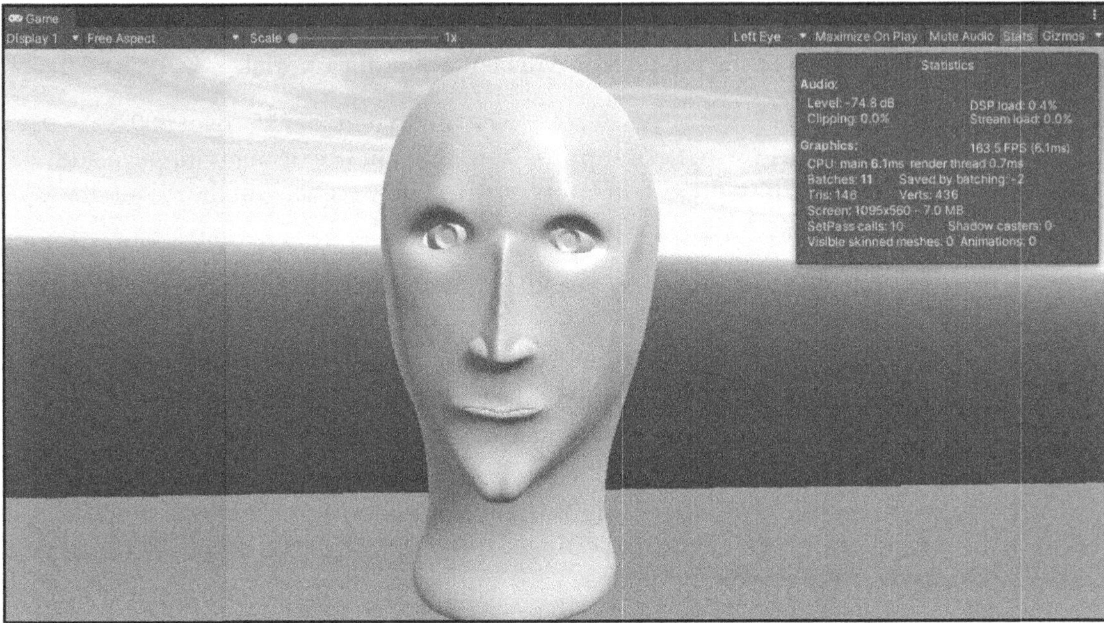

The corresponding **Profiler** window is shown in the following screenshot:

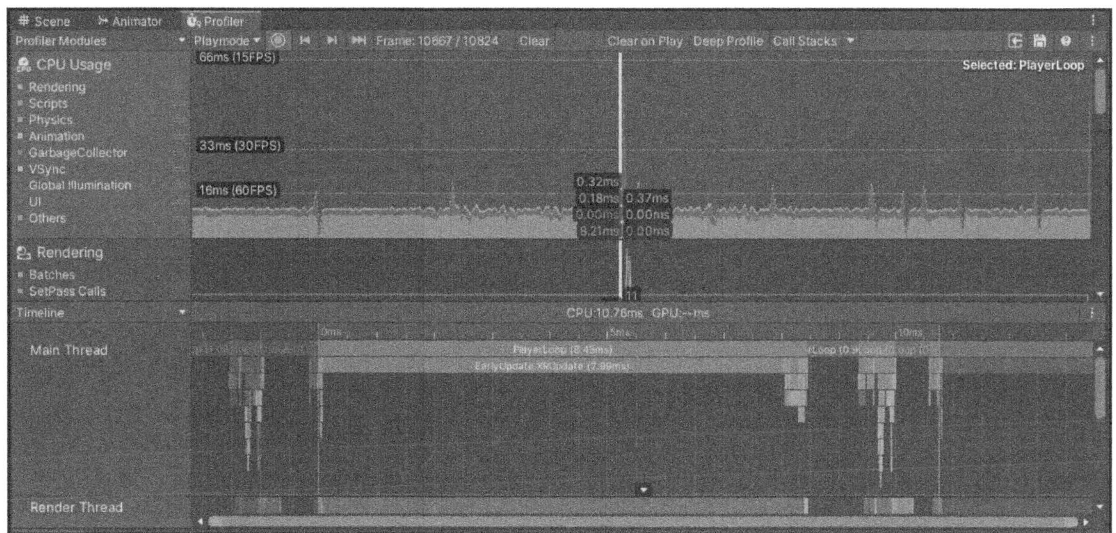

This scene is too simple for us to gather much in the way of meaningful statistics. Let's create 1,000 copies of the Mememan in the scene by following these steps:

1. Create an **Empty** game object and name it `Object Replicator`.
2. Create a new C# script on it called `ObjectReplicator` and write it as follows:

```
public class ObjectReplicator : MonoBehaviour
{
    public GameObject prefab;
    public Vector3Int dup = new Vector3Int(10, 10, 10);
    public Vector3 delta = new Vector3(1.2f, 1.2f, 1.2f);

    void Start()
    {
        Vector3 position = transform.position;
        for (int ix = 0; ix < dup.x; ix++)
        {
            for (int iy = 0; iy < dup.y; iy++)
            {
                for (int iz = 0; iz < dup.z; iz++)
                {
                    position.x = transform.position.x + ix
                         * delta.x;
                    position.y = transform.position.y + iy
                         * delta.y;
                    position.z = transform.position.z + iz
                         * delta.z;
                    GameObject go = Instantiate(prefab, transform);
```

```
                    go.transform.position = position;
                }
            }
        }
    }
}
```

This script takes a `prefab` object and instantiates it `dup` number of times (`10`) in each of the X, Y, and Z axes, offsetting each by `delta` units (set to `1.2`), thereby generating a total of 1,000 instances of the prefab. Save the script. Then, back in Unity, set up and assign the replicator parameters, as follows:

1. Select `Object Replicator` in **Hierarchy** again and drag the **Mememan** prefab from the **Project** `Assets/Prefabs` folder to its **Prefab** slot.
2. Set the `Object Replicator` **Position** to (`-5, 0, 1`) as the origin of our stack of objects.
3. Save the scene and the project (**File | Save**, and **File | Save Project**) as this may crash your system!

Press **Play**. The generated scene in the **Game** window is shown in the following screenshot (with the camera rig pulled back so that the whole thing is within view). You can see that our frame rate has dropped to a dramatically slow 2 or 3 FPS and that **Graphics** went to 1,011 **Batches**:

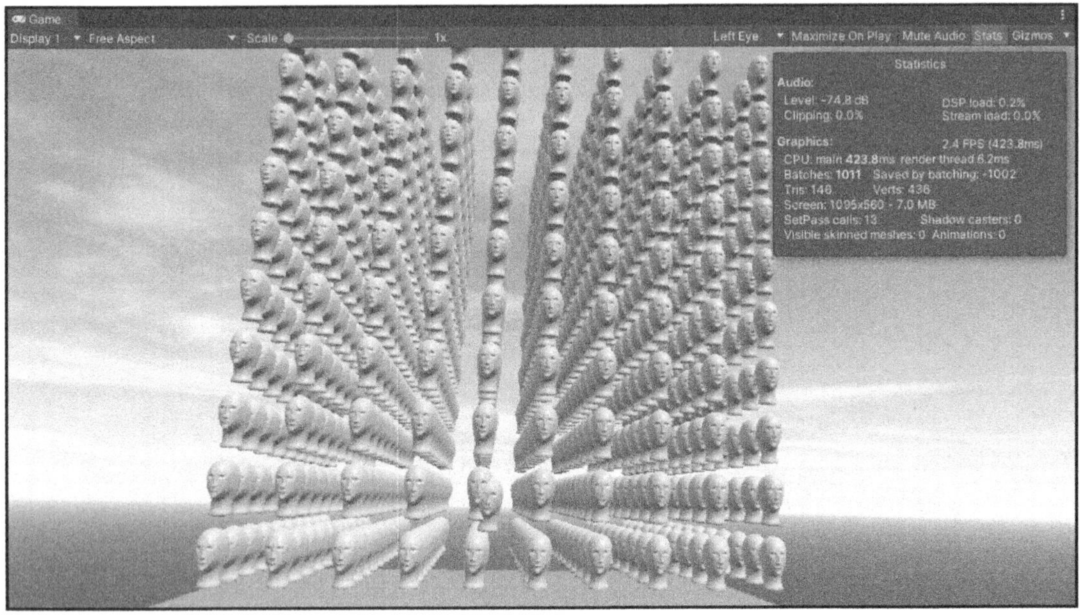

Now that we have a poorly performing scene, let's see what we can do about it. First, we will try to reduce the polys by decimating the model and then further reduce the polys by dynamically choosing the level of detail based on their distance from the camera.

Decimating models

One thing we can do is try to simplify the 3D models before we import them into Unity. If you select the `mememan-original` object in your **Project** window's `Assets/` folder, you will see that it consists of a mesh named **default** with **515365** triangles, as shown in the following screenshot:

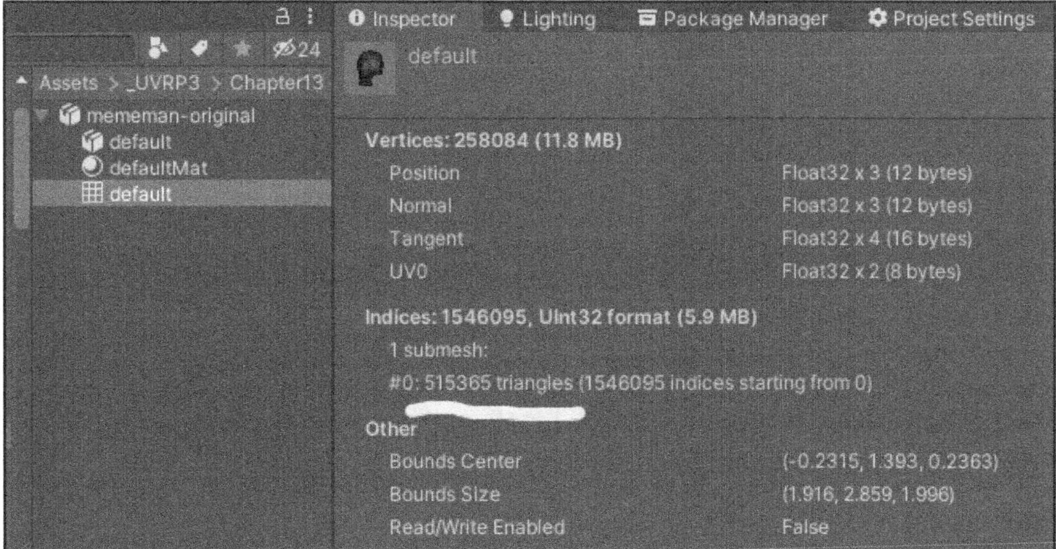

We should reduce the number of faces on the mesh, or *decimate* the model. I have used the separate (free and open source) Blender application (`https://www.blender.org/`) to produce a set of modified models. The following screenshot of the Blender editor shows where to find the **Decimate** modifier tool (`https://docs.blender.org/manual/en/latest/modeling/modifiers/generate/decimate.html`). It is set to `0.1` **Ratio**, thus reducing the number of triangles (tris) from 500,000 to 50,000. This is only for your reference, should you want to try it yourself:

I decimated the model from 500,000 triangles to 50,000, 5,000, 2,500, 1,000, and 500 triangles, and saved them into separate FBX files in this project. The results are shown in the following composite image. Reading the image clockwise from the top right, you can see that the density of the mesh reduced with the number of triangles (and corresponding file size):

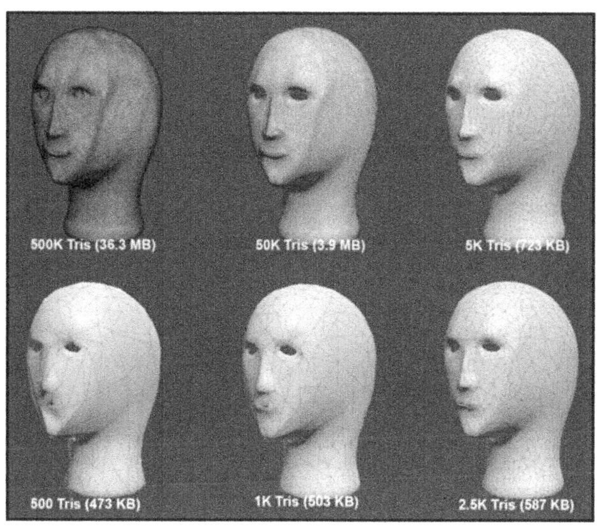

Depending on your requirements, preferences, and the size of the object in the camera view, you might find an acceptable version in the smaller models. (Of course, automated tools can only take you so far – manual editing and refinement may still be required; for example, the rim of the face and shape of the lips in this example have lost a lot of definition and may need work). Personally, I like the 2,500 version – it's relatively small and still works. Let's use that in our scene. Its filename is `mememan-2.5k.fbx`. Let's create and use a new prefab for this version of the model by copying the **Mememan** prefab and replacing its model using the following steps:

1. In the **Project** window's `Assets/Prefabs/` folder, select the **Mememan** prefab and select **Edit | Duplicate** from the main menu.
2. Rename the copy `Mememan-decimated`.
3. Double-click `Mememan-decimated` to open it for editing.
4. Drag the `mememan-2.5k` model from the **Project** `Assets/Models/` window into **Hierarchy.**
5. Copy/paste or set the transform we used to normalize the model earlier (**Rotation Y**: `-135`, **Scale**: `0.35`).
6. Delete the `mememan-original` object in the prefab **Hierarchy**.
7. Save the prefab and exit to the scene **Hierarchy**.
8. Select the **Object Replicator** object in the scene **Hierarchy**.
9. Drag the **Mememan-decimated** prefab from the **Project** `Assets/Prefabs/` window to the **Object Replicator | Prefab** slot.
10. Save the scene using **File | Save.**

Press **Play**. Much better! As shown here, it's now running faster at about 50 FPS. There's still room for improvement, but this is much better:

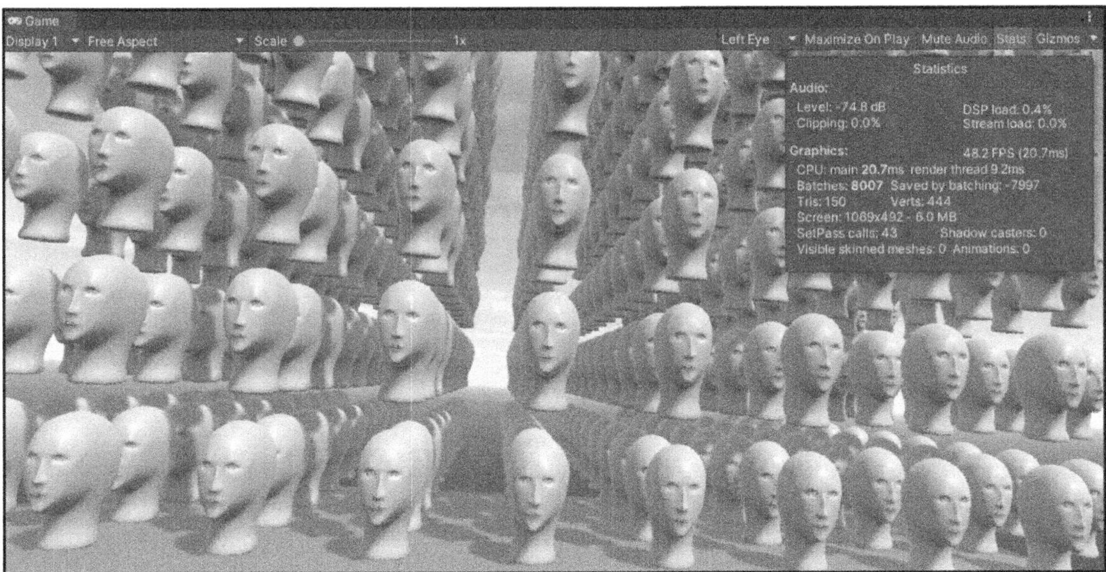

This example does not consider another important characteristic of 3D modeling and art – the texture maps and materials used with the objects, as we've seen in other project chapters of this book, including `Chapter 8`, *Lighting, Rendering, Realism*. Material properties and shaders work as a fantastic substitute for geometric mesh details. With careful application of **Physically-Based Rendering** (**PBR**) materials composed of textures maps for base texture, surface normal, occlusion, metallic, and other surface properties, you can get fantastic results in terms of performance, file size, and rendering flexibility – better than you can hope to achieve with overly dense model meshes.

There are a number of LOD tools available in the Unity Asset Store to help manage levels of detail and even generate decimated meshes from your models. Unity itself is toying with such a tool, AutoLOD, which is available free on GitHub (`https://blogs.unity3d.com/2018/01/12/unity-labs-autolod-experimenting-with-automatic-performance-improvements/`).

It may occur to you that we could get away with a lower detail model when the object is further away from the camera and vice versa with the higher detail version when closing up. Let's take a look at this now.

Levels of detail

Reviewing the scene, you may realize that a higher poly object may only be needed when you're near it. As the object recedes further into the distance, a lower poly version does just fine. Unity understands this and provides a component to automatically manage levels of detail, called **LOD Group** (see `https://docs.unity3d.com/Manual/LevelOfDetail.html`). Let's use this now. We'll create a group of Mememans with each of the detail level versions. Follow these steps:

1. In **Hierarchy**, create an **Empty** game object, name it `MememanLOD`, and reset its **Transform.**
2. Drag a copy of the **mememan-2.5k** model as a child of `MememanLOD`.
3. Drag a copy of the **mememan-1k** model as another child.
4. Finally, drag a copy of the **mememan-500** model as yet another child.
5. Set the **Transform** details we used to normalize the model earlier (**Rotation Y**: `-135`, **Scale**: `0.35`) for all three models.
6. Select the parent **MememanLOD** object and select **Add Component** | **LOD Group.**

Look at the **LOD Group** component in **Inspector**. Notice that it has several ranges for when to use one model or another based on camera distance, labeled **LOD0**, **LOD1**, and **LOD2**. The range is a percentage of the object's bounding box height relative to the screen height. When closest, the **LOD0** objects are active. Further away, those will be deactivated and the **LOD1** ones will be active, and so on. Let's assign the LOD groups now:

1. Select **LOD0**.
2. Drag the **mememan-2.5k** game object from **Hierarchy** onto the **Add** button.
3. Select **LOD1**.
4. Drag the **mememan-1k** game object onto the **Add** button.
5. Select **LOD2**.
6. Drag the **mememan-500** object onto **Add** as well.

In practice, I modified the preceding steps so that they use a prefab version of the imported model objects to ensure consistent use of materials and other properties.

The following is a screenshot of **LOD Group** in the **Inspector** window:

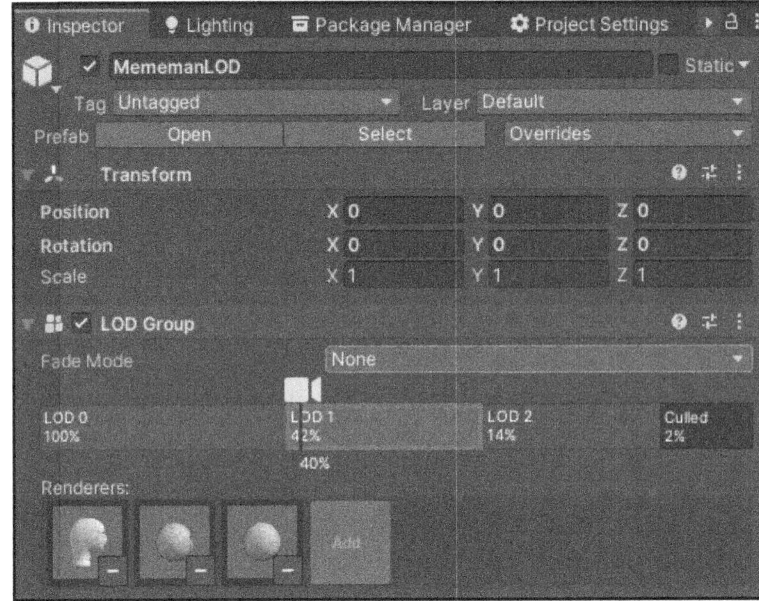

Notice that there is a little camera icon on the top edge of the LOD group graphic. You can select and slide it across to preview the LOD activations based on camera distance. You can also configure the active range of each LOD (percentage) by sliding the edge of each area box. The **Scene** view and **Hierarchy** we created can be seen in the following screenshot, with the camera at a distance that activates the **LOD 1** graphics:

Now, let's try it in our scene:

1. Save it as a prefab by dragging the `MememanLOD` object to your `Project Prefabs` folder.
2. Select the **Object Replicator** game object in **Hierarchy** and drag the `MememanLOD` prefab to its **Prefab** slot.

Press **Play**. The scene looks essentially the same in VR but we have now achieved our target, rendering at 120 FPS or higher. The ones closest to us are the 2.5K tri heads, the middle contains the 1K ones, and the models furthest away contains the low poly 500-tri version of the model, as shown in the following screenshot:

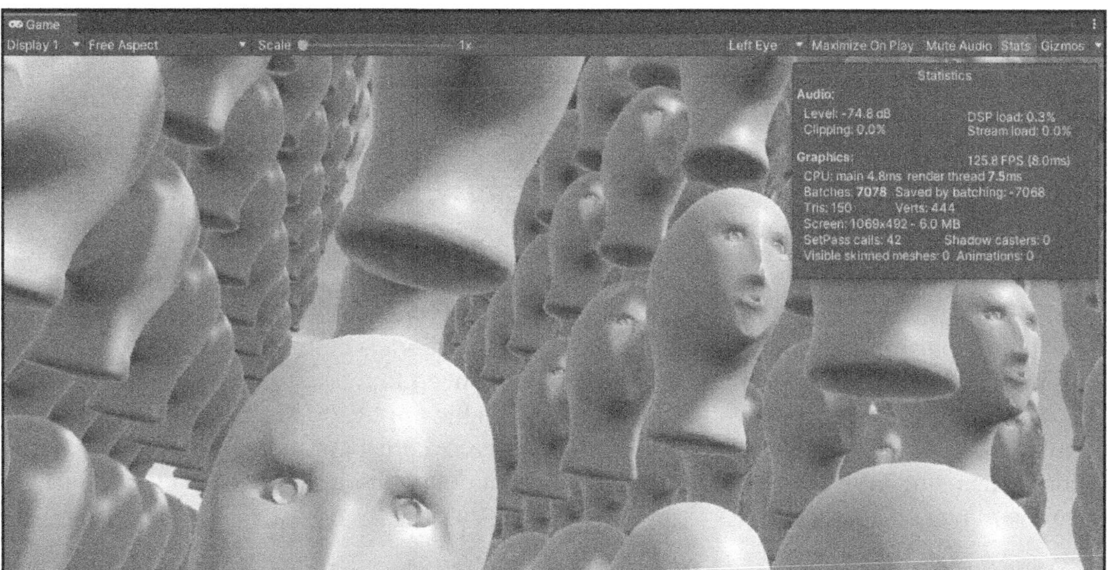

The **Profiler** timeline, as shown in the following screenshot, is busy but maintains an acceptable frame rate:

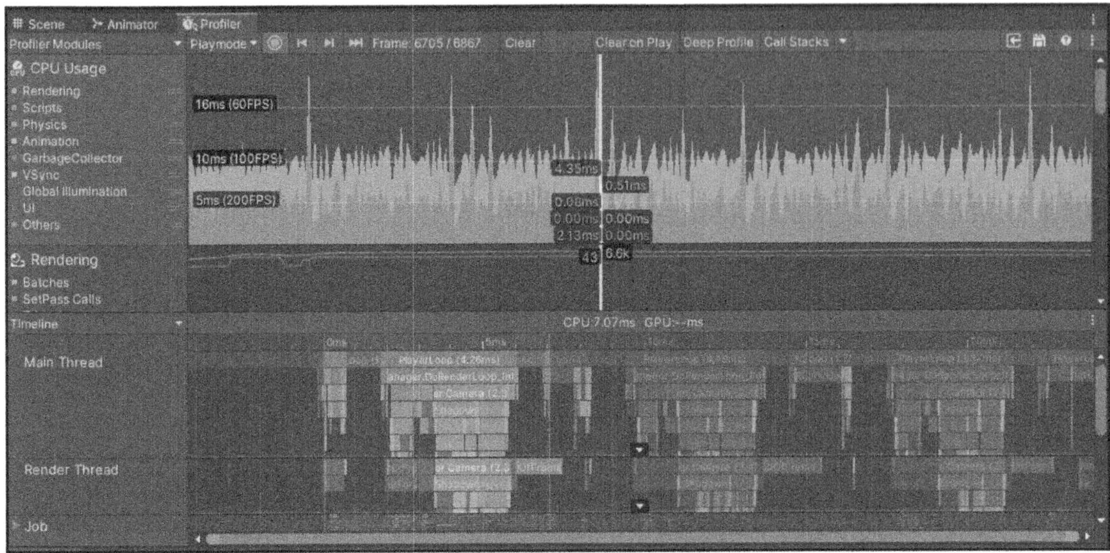

In this section, we have seen how high-poly models can have a significant detrimental effect on the performance of our app. Simplifying your models before they're even imported into Unity is a good first step, but you may need to work with your 3D artist to keep the integrity and quality you require, as well as the application of the material's texture and shader properties. Then, you can get greater control of the models instantiated in the scene using LOD groups to choose the level of detail based on the object's distance from the player and camera.

In addition to your art objects, the next step in terms of optimization might be how your scene itself is organized, including tagging game objects as **Static**.

Optimizing your scene with static objects

Another way of optimizing your scene is to let Unity pre-compute a lot of the processing work in advance rather than at runtime. You can do this by informing Unity that specific objects will not change or move in the scene. This is accomplished by defining these game objects as *static* and then *baking* them into specific Unity system contexts, including lighting, occlusion, batching, navigation, and reflection probes. In the top-right of the **Inspector** window for each game object is a **Static** checkbox that can be used to set the object to **Static** for all Unity systems that can use it. Alternatively, you can choose the down arrow to select the static setting for individual systems, as shown in the following screenshot:

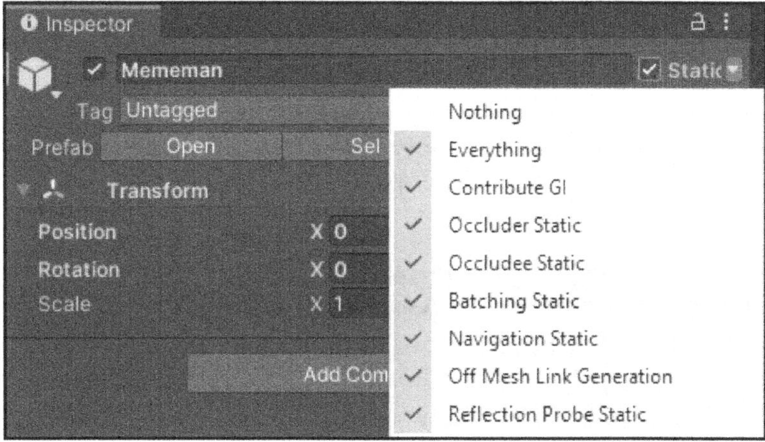

Ordinarily, if you're going to make an object **Static**, go ahead and check **Everything**, unless you know you need to refine it. The specific **Static** flags are as follows:

- **Contribute GI**: Use this object when precomputing lighting data, general illumination, lightmaps, and shadows (see the **Window** | **Lighting** | **Lighting** window). We used this in the art gallery scene in `Chapter 10`, *Exploring Interactive Spaces*.
- **Occluder / Occludee**: Use this object when precomputing occlusion culling, which divides the scene into static volumes that can be quickly removed when out of view, saving processing by possibly eliminating many objects from consideration at once. We'll try using this next.
- **Batching**: Include this object when batching draw calls to the GPU (see `https://docs.unity3d.com/Manual/DrawCallBatching.html`).

- **Navigation** and **Off Mesh Link**: Use these objects when generating a **Navmesh** for AI characters. (We used this in `Chapter 4`, *Using Gazed-Based Control*, when we baked a **Navmesh** for Ethan's walkable areas in the scene.)
- **Reflection Probe**: Use this object when precomputing Reflection Probes whose **Type** is set to **Baked** (See `Chapter 8`, *Lighting, Rendering, and Realism*).

Let's try out some examples by setting up the scene, baking the lighting, and then adding occlusion culling.

Setting up the scene

To demonstrate the use of static game objects, we cannot use the dynamically instantiated **Mememan** GameObjects generated by the `ObjectReplicator` script at runtime because, by definition, a **Static** GameObject must be present and unchanging in the Unity Editor and built into the app, not instantiated at runtime. But given we have this script, we'll use it to our advantage by playing the scene to generate the 1,000 objects, then copy/paste them into the **Hierarchy** window that we save with the scene. Follow these steps:

1. In **Hierarchy**, select **Object Replicator** and drag the **Mememan-decimated** prefab from **Project Assets** onto its **Prefab** slot.
2. Press **Play**. Note that **Object Replicator** now has 1,000 children game objects named **Mememan-decimated(Clone)**.
3. While playing, in the **Hierarchy** window, right-click the **Mememan-decimated** object and select **Copy.**
4. Stop **Play** mode.
5. From the main menu, select **Edit | Paste**, which inserts a copy of **Object Replicator** and all 1,000 of its children into the **Hierarchy** window.
6. Rename it `Mememan Borg`.
7. In **Inspector**, remove the **Object Replicator** component of **Mememan Borg** by **right-clicking | Remove Component.**
8. In **Hierarchy**, select the **Object Replicator** GameObject and deactivate it by unchecking its checkbox at the top-left of **Inspector**, as we no longer want to use it.

Now, we have all the instantiated models in the **Hierarchy** window, as shown in the following screenshot:

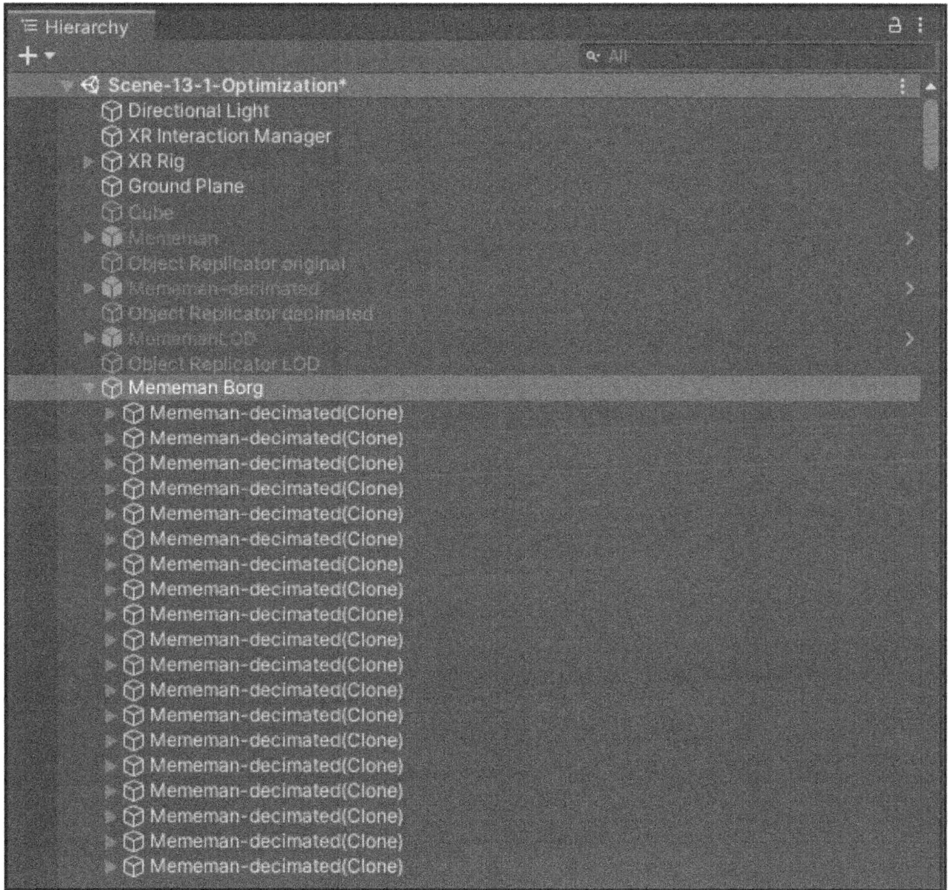

A problem with this technique is that all the Mememan children are now unpacked; that is, they've lost their association with the original prefab asset. To avoid this, you could write the version of the replicator script as an *Editor Script* to achieve a similar result and preserve the prefab link. Editor scripts extend the features of the Unity Editor and are not compiled into your final built application. For example, it could add a **BorgMaker** menu item to the Editor menu that may prompt you with a dialog box asking for the prefab object, duplication counts, and offset parameters, much like our `Object Replicator`. Writing scripts that customize and extend the Unity Editor is common practice. If you're interested, see *Manual: Extending the Editor* (`https://docs.unity3d.com/Manual/ExtendingTheEditor.html`) and the *Editor Scripting Intro* tutorial (`https://unity3d.com/learn/tutorials/topics/scripting/editor-scripting-intro`).

Next, we'll bake the scene lighting by making these objects **Static**.

Lighting and baking

The use of lights in your scene affects the frame rate. You have a great deal of control over the number of lights, types of lights, their placement, and their settings. Use baked lightmaps whenever possible, which precalculates the lighting effects into separate images rather than at runtime. Use real-time shadows sparingly. When an object casts shadows, a shadow map is generated, which will be used to render the other objects that might receive shadows. Shadows have a high rendering overhead and generally require high-end GPU hardware. Let's see the impact of using baked lightmaps on our scene:

1. Select `Mememan Borg` and click its **Static** checkbox in the upper-right corner of **Inspector**.
2. When prompted, answer **Yes, change children**.

If you get an error stating **Mesh doesn't have UVs suitable for lightmapping**, select the imported FBX model in your **Project** window, choose **Generate Lightmap UVs**, and select **Apply**.

Depending on your **Lighting** settings, the lightmaps may begin generating right away. Review and modify the lightmap settings, as follows:

1. Open the **Lighting** window by selecting **Window | Rendering | Lighting.**
2. With **Auto Generate** checked, it will start generating lightmaps any time your scene changes.
3. Alternatively, uncheck it and click **Generate Lighting** to build them manually.

It can take several minutes or more to generate the lightmaps in a complex scene. The following screenshot shows one of the baked lightmaps in the **Lighting** window's **Baked Lightmaps** tab, along with a **Preview** of the lightmap texture for its **Baked Directionality**:

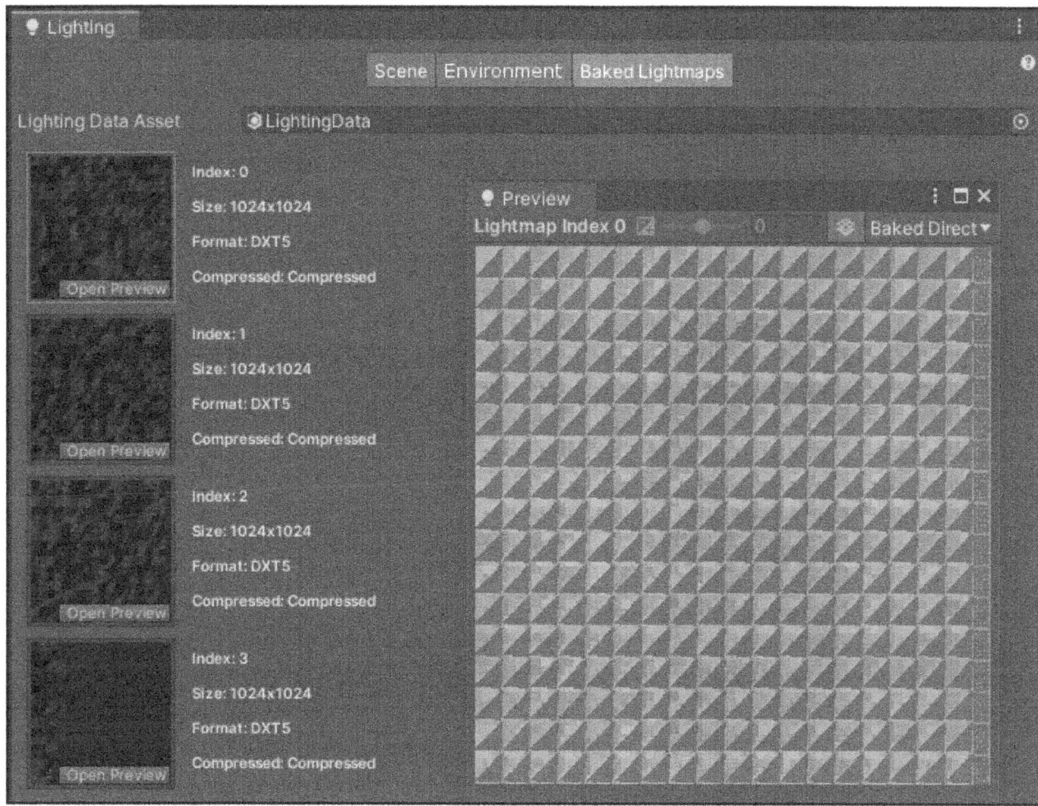

Here are some more tips when dealing with lighting and performance:

- Avoid dynamic shadows altogether, especially on mobile devices. You can substitute by using a "blurry blob" underneath moving things.
- Check your project's **Quality Settings** (**Edit** | **Project Settings** | **Quality**). Use fewer **Pixel Lights** (on a mobile, limit them to 1 or 2). Use **High Resolution** on **Hard and Soft Shadows**.
- You can have as many baked lights as you want. Baked lighting produces high-quality results, whereas real-time shadows can appear blocky.
- When baking, you can improve lightmap quality by increasing the baked resolution (a 40-100 pixel resolution is reasonable).
- Use light probes with baked lighting to illuminate dynamic objects.
- Use reflection probes for reflective surfaces. These can be static (baked) or dynamic (real-time).

To render a shadow blob under moving objects, in the past, it was recommended to use a Projector shader (see `https://docs.unity3d.com/Manual/class-Projector.html`) instead of dynamic shadows. Unfortunately (at the time I'm writing this), Unity does not provide a Projector shader that is compatible with URP. Alternative solutions include the Kink3D kDecals system (`https://github.com/Kink3d/kDecals`) or simply adding a Quad object at the base of your character with a blob texture on it.

Light probes (either real-time or baked) and the shaders you use (and the shader options) can make your scene look really amazing. However, they can also have a significant effect on performance. Balancing aesthetics and graphics performance is an art and a science.

Next, we'll take a look at flagging game objects as static for occlusion culling.

Occlusion culling

As we've seen, the less geometry that's rendered each frame, the better. Whether or not you are using high- or low-poly models, Unity still needs to figure out which faces are in view. This process is split into **viewport clipping** and **occlusion culling**. Clipping occurs on objects completely outside of the camera view. Unity includes built-in occlusion culling on the CPU when determining what data to send on to the GPU for rendering. When there are a lot of overlapping objects, perhaps we could help Unity out by giving it some clues.

Occlusion culling disables the rendering of objects altogether when they are not seen by the camera because they are obscured (occluded) by other objects (see `http://docs.unity3d.com/Manual/OcclusionCulling.html` for more details). It examines your scene and, using the bounding boxes (extents) of each object, divides the world space into a hierarchy of cubes. When Unity needs to determine if an object is within view, it will throw away any objects whose culling box is obviously outside of the view and continue through the hierarchy.

To demonstrate this, we'll bake **Occlusion Culling** of our 1,000 object called **Mememan Borg**. Assuming all the GameObjects are marked as **Static** (including the **Occluder** and **Occludee** flags), you can generate it with the following steps:

1. Open the **Occlusion Culling** window using **Window** | **Rendering** | **Occlusion Culling.**
2. Click **Bake** (at the bottom right of the window).

This may take a while. The following screenshot shows a visualization image in the **Scene** window showing **Camera Volumes** (white) and **Visibility Lines** (green). Only a portion of the 1,000 objects remains in the scene after the ones outside the camera's view have been culled. Due to this, less data needs to be processed in the frame:

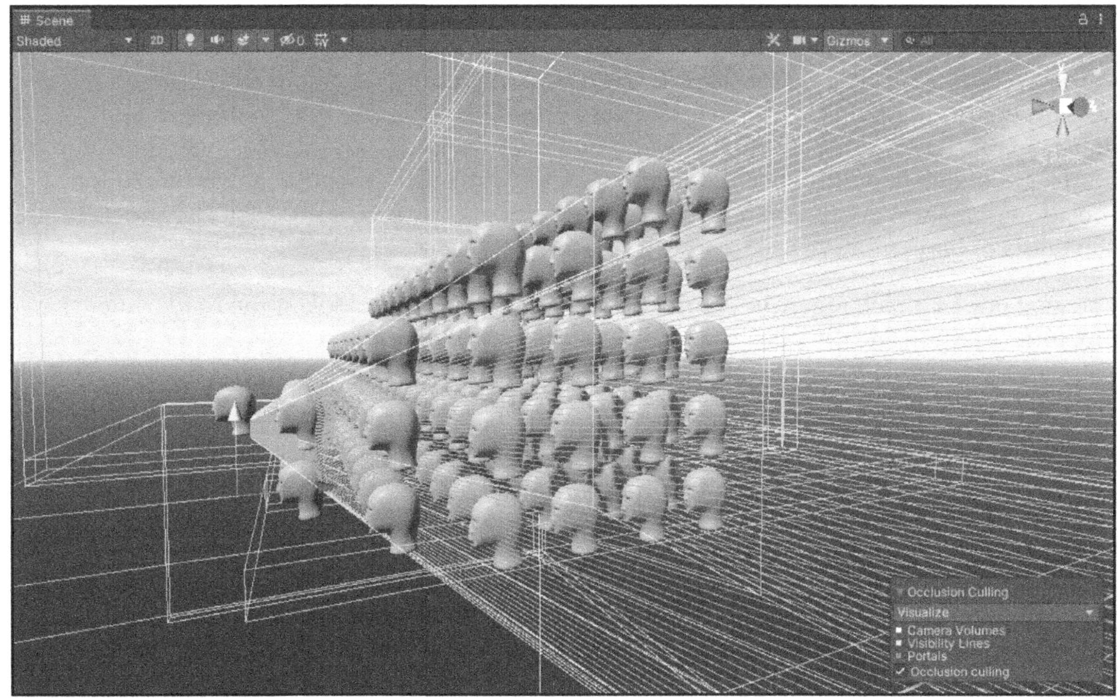

Unity's built-in occlusion culling is automatically performed at runtime and calculated on the CPU. Precomputed **baked** occlusion culling is most beneficial when your app is GPU-bound due to overdraw where the same pixels are rendered more than once in a frame. According to the Unity manual, "Occlusion culling works best in scenes where small, well-defined areas are clearly separated from one another by solid GameObjects. A common example is rooms connected by corridors."

Note that we could have, but didn't, distinguish Occludees versus Occluders in our scene. Occludees are objects that get occluded. Occluders are ones that may be in front, occluding the others. Translucent objects that do not occlude should be marked as Occludees, but not Occluders.

Occlusion can be further controlled with the use of **Occlusion Area** components and **Occlusion Portal** components. An **Occlusion Area** defines a view volume or area of the scene where the camera is likely to be at runtime. When the occlusion data is baked, Unity generates the data at a higher precision within View Volumes. An **Occlusion Portal** lets you control occlusion at runtime, which is useful for objects that can be open or closed, such as a door.

In this section, we have learned how to improve performance and help Unity by reducing the number of runtime calculations with precomputed, or baked, information, including lightmaps and occlusions. This is achieved by flagging specific GameObjects in the scene as **Static** and then baking the specific system that we want. This is a strategic optimization consideration and very much depends on our particular project, scene, objects, and behaviors in play.

The next line of attack regarding performance is taking a closer look at the rendering pipeline.

Optimizing the rendering pipeline

There are a number of important performance considerations that are specific to how Unity does its rendering. Some of these may be common for any graphics engine. Recommendations will vary, depending on your target platform (for example, desktop VR versus mobile VR), your render pipeline (for example, Universal Render Pipeline versus High-Definition Render Pipeline), and Project Quality settings. There are many articles on the internet offering recommendations on which settings to use to optimize your VR apps, and it's not unusual for someone's advice to contradict that of someone else. Here are some good ones:

- In **Graphics Project Settings**, select the **render pipeline** (**RP**) settings object for the project. This may have been set up by default when you chose a **Project Template** from **Unity Hub** when the project was first created.
- In your chosen RP settings object (for example, **UniversalRP-HighQuality** versus **UniversalRP-LowQuality**), set **Anti Aliasing (MSAA)** to **2x** or **4x** (multi-sampling anti-aliasing). This is a low-cost, anti-aliasing technique that helps remove jagged edges and shimmering effects.
- In the RP settings object's **Renderer**, use**ForwardRenderer**. This is the default for the **Universal Render Pipeline** (**URP**).

- In **Quality Project Settings**, disable the use of **Realtime Reflection Probes.**
- In **XR Plugin Project Settings**, use **Single Pass Stereo Rendering**. It performs efficient rendering of a parallax perspective for each eye in a single pass.
- In **Player Settings**, enable **Static Batching** and **Multithreaded Rendering**.

This is a sample of the settings from across various settings windows in the Unity Editor, including **Graphics** settings (**Edit** | **Project Settings** | **Graphics**), **Quality** settings (**Edit** | **Project Settings** | **Quality**), **XR Plugin** settings (**Edit** | **Project Settings** | **XR Plugin Management** | **Oculus**, for example), and **Player** settings (**Edit** | **Project Settings** | **Player** | **Other Settings**). The render pipeline settings are stored in an asset file in your **Project** window and can be edited in that object's **Inspector**.

Perhaps the biggest bang-for-the-buck is a feature in Unity that groups different meshes into a single batch, which is then shoveled into the graphics hardware all at once. This is much faster than sending the meshes separately. Meshes are actually first compiled into an OpenGL **vertex buffer object** or **VBO**, but that's a low-level detail of the rendering pipeline. Each batch takes one draw call. Reducing the number of draw calls in a scene is more significant than the actual number of vertices or triangles in the batch. For mobile VR, for example, stay around 50 (up to 100) draw calls. There are two types of batching: **static batching** and **dynamic batching.**

For static batching, simply mark the objects as **Static** by checking off the **Static** checkbox in the Unity **Inspector** for each object in the scene. Marking an object as **Static** tells Unity that it will never move, animate, or scale. Unity will automatically batch together the meshes that share the same material into a large. single mesh. The caveat here is that meshes must share the same **Material** settings: the same texture, shader, shader parameters, and the material pointer object. How can this be, since they're different objects? This can be done by combining multiple textures into a single macro-texture file or **TextureAtlas** and then UV mapping as many models as will fit. It's a lot like a sprite image used for 2D and web graphics. There are third-party tools that help you build these.

A useful analytics tool for checking the resources in your scene, including active textures, materials, and meshes, is the Unity Resource Checker, which can be found here: `https://github.com/handcircus/Unity-Resource-Checker`.

Dynamic batching is similar to static batching. For objects that are not marked as **Static**, when **Dynamic Batching** is enabled, Unity will still try to batch them, albeit it will be a slower process since it needs to think about it frame by frame (the CPU cost). The shared **Material** requirement still holds, as well as other restrictions such as vertex count (less than 300 vertices) and uniform **Transform Scale** rules. For more details and other caveats governing batching draw calls, please refer to the Unity documentation at `http://docs.unity3d.com/Manual/DrawCallBatching.html`. By default, **Dynamic Batching** is ***disabled*** in the URP settings.

When managing textures in C# scripts, use `Renderer.sharedMaterial` rather than `Renderer.material` to avoid creating duplicate materials. Objects that receive a duplicate material will opt out of the batch.

Another concern in the rendering pipeline is sometimes referred to as the pixel fill rate. If you think about it, the ultimate goal of rendering is to set each pixel on the display device with a correct color value. If Unity has to paint any pixels more than once, that's more costly. For example, watch out for transparent particle effects, such as smoke, that touch many pixels with mostly transparent quads.

For VR, Unity paints into a frame buffer memory that is larger than the physical display dimensions, which is then post-processed for ocular distortion correction (barrel effect) and chromatic aberration correction (color separation), before getting tossed onto the HMD display. In fact, there may be multiple overlay buffers that get composited before post-processing.

This multipass pixel filling is how some advanced renderers work, including lighting and material effects such as multiple lights, dynamic shadows, and transparency. VBO batches with materials that require multipass pixel filling get submitted multiple times, thus increasing the net number of draw calls. Depending on your project, you may choose to either optimize the heck out of it and avoid multipass pixel filling altogether, or carefully curate the scenes with an understanding of what should have high performance and what should have high fidelity.

You can use **Light Probes** to inexpensively simulate the dynamic lighting of your dynamic objects. Light probes are baked cubemaps that store information about direct, indirect, and even emissive light at various points in your scene. As a dynamic object moves, it interpolates samples of the nearby light probes to approximate the lighting at that specific position. This is a cheap way of simulating realistic lighting on dynamic objects without using expensive real-time lights. We discussed light probes in `Chapter 8`, *Lighting, Rendering, Realism*.

In this section, we learned more about opportunities to tune the graphics and render pipeline in your project, if needed, to squeeze out extra performance. It's important to become familiar with the many parameters available to you in the **Graphics**, **Quality**, **Render Pipeline**, **Player Settings**, and **XR Plugin** settings. Visit the default settings in your project and, from time to time, experiment with the effects of changing one or two values at a time. In practice, Unity is getting better every day at automatically optimizing the render pipeline for you and provides well-balanced default sets of parameter values for high-, medium-, and low-quality graphics. But there's comfort in knowing that if (or when) you need to fine-tune it, the settings are available to you.

There's one other major area of concern that affects performance, especially when your project is CPU-bound: the C# code you have written.

Optimizing your code

Another area prone to performance problems and ripe for optimization is your C# script code. Throughout this book, we have used various coding best practices, without always explaining why. (On the other hand, some examples in this book are not necessarily efficient, in favor of simplicity and explanation). In `Chapter 9`, *Playing with Physics and Fire*, for example, we implemented an object pool memory manager to avoid repeatedly instantiating and destroying game objects that cause memory **garbage collection** (**GC**) issues, which, in turn, slows down your app.

In general, try to avoid code that repeats a lot of computation over and over. Try to pre-compute as much work as you can and store the partial results in variables. At some point, you may have to use a profiling tool to see how your code is performing under the hood. If the Profiler indicates that a large amount of time is spent in the scripts that you've written, you should consider another way to refactor the code so that it's more efficient. Often, this is related to memory management, but it could be math or physics. For tips from Unity, see `http://docs.unity3d.com/Manual/MobileOptimizationPracticalScriptingOptimizations.html`.

Please follow coding best practices, but otherwise, avoid going out of your way with *premature optimization*. One mistake people make is putting too much effort into optimizing areas of their code that don't need it, thus sacrificing readability and maintainability in the process. Use the Profiler to analyze where the performance bottlenecks are and focus your optimization efforts there first.

Let's take a closer look at the Unity play loop and life cycle of GameObjects and then consider some suggestions for writing efficient code.

Understanding the Unity life cycle

Like all video game engines, when your game runs, Unity is executing a giant loop, repeating each frame update over and over. Unity provides many *hooks* to tap into events at just about every step in the game loop. The following is the life cycle flowchart, annotated from the Unity Manual page's Execution Order of Event Functions (`https://docs.unity3d.com/Manual/ExecutionOrder.html`). The two event functions you are most familiar with, `Start` and `Update`, are highlighted with large arrows. The dots highlight a number of other events we'll reference in this section:

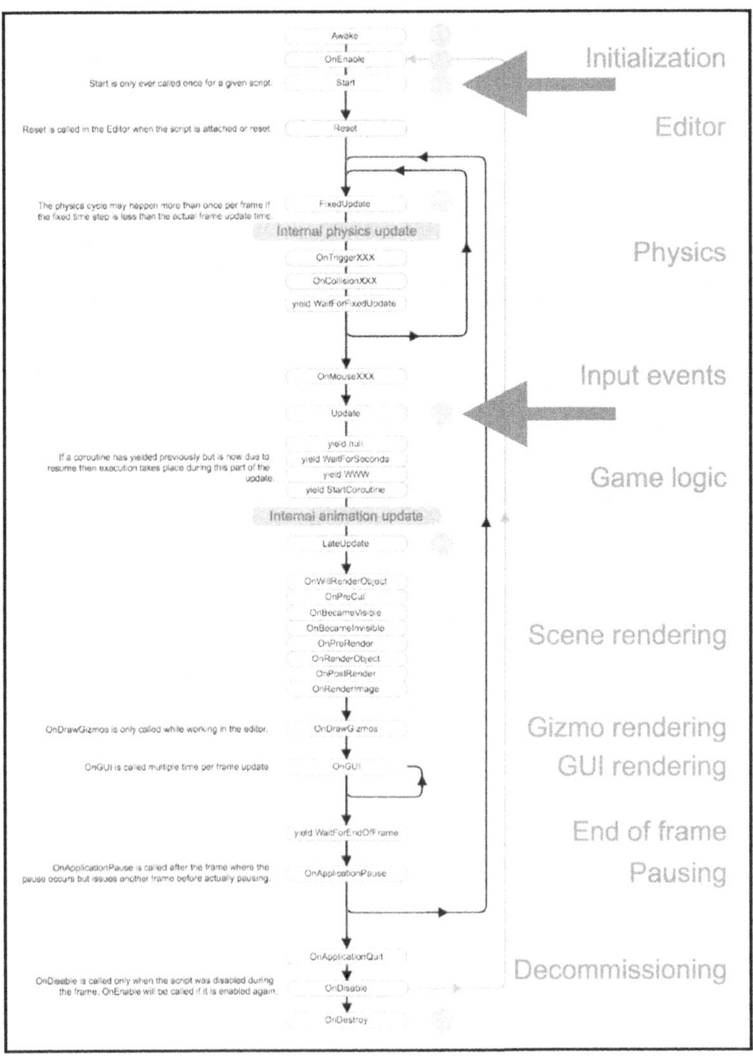

Reading from the top of this chart, when your game starts, each GameObject's component (which is derived from the `MonoBehaviour` class) will be initialized with a call to `Awake`. Then, `OnEnable` and then `Start` is called. `Awake` and `Start` are only called once in the life cycle of an object. `OnEnable` is called each time the GameObject is enabled, at the start, and also if deactivated and reactivated. Unless you need to use `Awake` or `OnEnable`, we typically initialize objects in `Start`.

Skipping down to the **Game logic** section, `Update` is called on each frame iteration. Note the loop line/arrows in the chart. (The physics engine has its own loop timing for dealing with `RigidBody`, which may be more frequent than the frame updates. You hook into that with `FixedUpdate`.)

The `OnDestroy` event is called to decommission the object.

For the current discussion, the important thing to notice is which events are within the game loop and which are outside. Now, let's look at ways to write efficient scripts.

Writing efficient code

We want to keep all of the code within the game loop (such as `FixedUpdate`, `Update`, and `LateUpdate`) as lean as possible. Move any initialization into `Awake`, `OnEnable`, or `Start`. We also want to precompute and cache any computationally expensive work in the initialization functions.

For example, a call to `GetComponent` (and its variants) is expensive. As we've seen in many of the scripts in this book, it is a best practice to get references to any components that `Update` will need beforehand, outside the game logic loop, in `Start`. Likewise, finding the `Camera.main` reference can be slow. Consider the following example script, which detects a gaze-based hit by ray casting from the camera and displays the hit count in a text element on the screen:

```
public class HitScore : MonoBehaviour
{
    private int score = 0;

    void Update()
    {
        RaycastHit hit;
        Ray ray = new Ray(Camera.main.transform.position,
                          Camera.main.transform.rotation *
                            Vector3.forward);
        if (Physics.Raycast(ray, out hit))
        {
```

```
                score++;
                GetComponentInChildren<Text>().text =
                    "Score: " + score;
            }
        }
    }
```

For each Update, perhaps 120 times per second,
I'm calling GetComponentInChildren and calling Camera.main (twice!). In the following code, we have refactored the script to precompute any initialization into Start using private variables and making the Update function more efficient:

```
public class HitScore : MonoBehaviour
{
    private int score;
    private Transform camera;
    private Text scoreText;
    RaycastHit hit;

    void Start()
    {
        score = 0;
        camera = Camera.main.transform;
        scoreText = GetComponentInChildren<Text>();
    }

    void Update()
    {
        Ray ray = new Ray(camera.position,
             camera.rotation * Vector3.forward);
        if (Physics.Raycast(ray, out hit))
        {
            score++;
            scoreText.text = "Score: " + score;
        }
    }
}
```

Likewise, if you have code in Update that does not need to be called every frame, turn off the calculations using a state variable (and an if statement) when they are not needed, as follows:

```
public bool isWalking;

void Update()
{
    if (isWalking)
```

```
        {
            character.SimpleMove(camera.transform.forward * 0.4f);
        }
    }
```

You can go even further than this. If you need to make regular updates but not as often as every frame, you can do this in a coroutine instead of `Update`. In the following code, for example, a `DoSomething` function is performed twice a second rather than at the game's normal frame rate. Note that I'm also precomputing the `WaitForSeconds` delay so that a new one is not reallocated every iteration:

```
    private WaitForSeconds delay;
    private Coroutine co;

    private void Start()
    {
        delay = new WaitForSeconds(0.5f);
    }

    private void OnEnable()
    {
        if (co == null)
            co = StartCoroutine(SlowUpdate());
    }

    IEnumerator SlowUpdate()
    {
        while (true)
        {
            DoSomething();
            yield return delay;
        }
        co = null;
    }
```

The coroutine is restarted in `OnEnable` rather than `Start` because if you deactivate a GameObject, any coroutines running in any of its components are automatically stopped. If you expect the `SlowUpdate` function to be running any time the object is active, you must restart the coroutine yourself. Also, for safety, I'm keeping a reference of the running coroutine (`co`) to make sure we don't accidentally have two instances of the `SlowUpdate` coroutine running at the same time for this specific object.

Other than moving expensive API calls out of `Update` into an initialization function or a coroutine, there are some APIs that should be avoided altogether if possible. Here are a few:

- Avoid `Object.Find("ObjectName")`. To obtain a reference to a game object in your scene, do not call `Find`. Not only is `Find` (by name) expensive, as it must search the **Hierarchy** tree, it is brittle (might break) if you rename the object it is looking for. If you can, define a `public` variable to reference the object and associate it in the **Editor Inspector**. If you have to find the object at runtime, use **Tags** or perhaps **Layers** to limit the search to a known fixed set of candidates.
- Avoid `SendMessage()`. The legacy use of `SendMessage` is computationally expensive (because it makes use of runtime *reflection*). To trigger functions in another object, use Unity **Events** instead.
- Avoid fragmenting memory and garbage collection. Temporary allocations of data and objects may cause memory to fragment. Unity will periodically go through the memory heap to consolidate free blocks, but this is expensive and can cause frames to skip in your app.

Another area of optimization is Unity Physics. In previous chapters, we mentioned using layers for ray casting in order to limit the objects Unity needs to search, for example, for gaze-based selection in VR. Likewise, physics collision detection can be limited to objects on specific layers by defining a **Layer Collision Matrix**. Refer to the manual page on *Optimizing Physics Performance* (`https://docs.unity3d.com/Manual/iphone-Optimizing-Physics.html`) and the *Physics Best Practices* tutorial (`https://unity3d.com/learn/tutorials/topics/physics/physics-best-practices`).

For more coding best practices and optimization suggestions, see the Unity best practices guide, *Understanding Optimization in Unity* (`https://docs.unity3d.com/Manual/BestPracticeUnderstandingPerformanceInUnity.html`). In this section, we learned about the Unity play loop and hooks in each GameObject life cycle. We then saw several techniques for optimizing our own code by reducing the amount of CPU processing in each frame `Update`.

As we mentioned earlier, the Profiler is very useful for determining where and what in our code may be causing our project to slow down. However, running the Profiler in the Unity Editor's **Play** mode has limitations, especially, for example, if you're targeting an Android device but obviously, Unity is running on your desktop. For that, you'll want a better picture of the runtime performance of the actual device.

Runtime performance and debugging

Graphics hardware architectures continue to evolve toward a performance that benefits rendering pipelines for virtual reality and 3D graphics. VR introduced requirements that weren't very important for traditional video gaming just a few years ago. Latency and dropped frames (where rendering a frame takes longer than the refresh rate) took a back seat to high-fidelity AAA rendering capabilities. VR needs to render each frame in time and do it twice: once for each eye. Driven by the requirements of this emerging industry, semiconductor and hardware manufacturers are building new and improved devices, which will inevitably impact how content developers think about optimization.

That said, you should develop and optimize for the lower specs that you want to target. If such optimizations necessitate undesirable compromises, consider separate versions of the game for high- versus low-end platforms. VR device manufacturers have started publishing minimum/recommended hardware specifications, which take much of the guesswork out of this. Start with the recommended Unity settings of your target device and adjust them as needed.

For instance, for mobile VR, it is recommended that you tune for CPU-bound rather than GPU-bound usage. Some games will make the CPU work harder, while others will impact the GPU. Normally, you should favor CPU over GPU. Running in the Editor is not the same as running on a mobile device. However, you can still use the Profiler while running in the device.

It can be useful to have a developer mode in your app that shows a **heads up display (HUD)** with the current **frames per second (FPS)** and other vital statistics at runtime. To make your own FPS HUD display, add a UI **Canvas** to your scene with a child `Text` object. The following script updates the text string with the FPS value:

```
public class FramesPerSecondText : MonoBehaviour
{
    private float updateInterval = 0.5f;
    private int framesCount;
    private float framesTime;
    private Text text;

    void Start()
    {
        text = GetComponent<Text>();
    }
    void Update()
    {
        framesCount++;
        framesTime += Time.unscaledDeltaTime;
```

```
            if (framesTime > updateInterval)
            {
                float fps = framesCount / framesTime;
                text.text = string.Format("{0:F2} FPS", fps);
                framesCount = 0;
                framesTime = 0;
            }
        }
    }
```

Some VR hardware producers also provide their own tools. Oculus, for example, offers a suite of performance analysis and optimization tools (`https://developer.oculus.com/documentation/pcsdk/latest/concepts/dg-performance/`), which includes extensive documentation and a workflow guide for developers. Good stuff! It also includes a **Performance Profiler** and a **Performance Head-Up Display**, both of which you can add to your Unity projects.

Summary

Latency and low frames-per-second rates are not acceptable and can cause motion sickness in VR. We are bound by the capabilities and limitations of the hardware devices we run on and their SDKs. In this chapter, we dove into some of the more technical aspects of making great VR by considering four separate areas that affect performance: the artwork, the scene, the rendering pipeline, and the code. This was a survey of the profiling and analysis techniques you can use and suggestions on how to address performance problems. This is no way a prescription for your own specific project, nor is this a complete treatment of this deep topic. This also gets into system architecture and engineering problems that may not be everyone's forte.

We started this chapter by introducing the built-in Unity **Profiler** and **Stats** windows, our primary weapons in this battle. To illustrate the impacts of designing models and materials, we built a scene with 1,000 high-poly Mememan objects, examined the performance stats, and learned a couple of ways to improve the frame rate: decimating the models (making them lower poly) and managing the **level of detail** (**LOD**) in the scene. Then, you learned about the things you can do at the scene level using static objects, baked lightmaps, and occlusion culling.

Next, we looked at the rendering pipeline and gained some insight into how it works. Then, you learned how to use the recommended **Quality**, **Graphics**, and **Player** settings, VR optimized shaders, and runtime tools to analyze and improve performance. After that, you learned about the basic practices for optimizing your C# scripts. A key to this is understanding the Unity life cycle, game loop, and expensive API functions, thus encouraging you to make frame `Update` processing as lean as possible.

It should be abundantly clear by now that developing for VR has many facets (pun intended). You work hard to create an awesome project with beautiful models, textures, and lighting. You try to provide a thrilling interactive and immersive experience for your visitors. At the same time, you should also be thinking about the requirements of your target platform, rendering performance, frames per second, latency, and motion sickness. It's never too early to focus on performance. It's a mistake to start too late. Follow the recommended best practices that are easy to implement while keeping your code and object hierarchy readable, clean, and maintainable. However, take a thoughtful, scientific approach to troubleshooting and performance tuning by using the Profiler and other tools to analyze your project so that you can zero in on the root causes rather than spending time on areas that may yield little net effect.

> *We developers rapidly become immune to all but the most obvious rendering errors, and as a result, we are the worst people at testing our own code. It introduces a new and exciting variation of the coder's defense that "it works on my machine" – in this case, "it works for my brain."*
>
> *– Tom Forsyth, Oculus*

Developing for VR is a moving target. The platform hardware, software SDKs, and the Unity 3D engine itself are all changing and improving rapidly. Books, blog posts, and YouTube videos can be readily superseded as products improve and new developer insights emerge. On the other hand, great strides have already been made to establish best practices, preferred Unity settings, and optimized device SDKs that address the needs of VR developers.

With VR becoming mainstream, it is coming into its own as a new medium for expression, communication, education, problem-solving, and storytelling. Your grandparents needed to learn to type and read. Your parents needed to learn PowerPoint and browse the web. Your children will build castles and teleport between virtual spaces. VR will not replace the real world and our humanity; it will enhance it.

Other Books You May Enjoy

If you enjoyed this book, you may be interested in these other books by Packt:

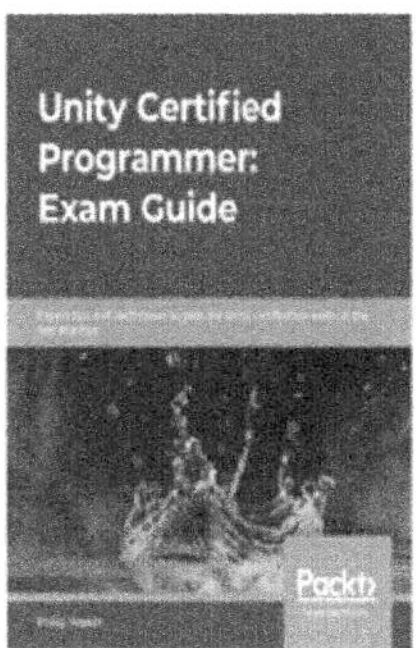

Unity Certified Programmer: Exam Guide
Philip Walker

ISBN: 978-1-83882-842-4

- Discover techniques for writing modular, readable, and reusable scripts in Unity
- Implement and configure objects, physics, controls, and movements for your game projects
- Understand 2D and 3D animation and write scripts that interact with Unity's Rendering API
- Explore Unity APIs for adding lighting, materials, and texture to your apps
- Write Unity scripts for building interfaces for menu systems, UI navigation, application settings, and much more
- Delve into SOLID principles for writing clean and maintainable Unity applications

Unity Game Optimization - Third Edition
Dr. Davide Aversa, Chris Dickinson

ISBN: 978-1-83855-651-8

- Apply the Unity Profiler to find bottlenecks in your app, and discover how to resolve them
- Discover performance problems that are critical for VR projects and learn how to tackle them
- Enhance shaders in an accessible way, optimizing them with subtle yet effective performance tweaks
- Use the physics engine to keep scenes as dynamic as possible
- Organize, filter, and compress art assets to maximize performance while maintaining high quality
- Use the Mono framework and C# to implement low-level enhancements that maximize memory usage and prevent garbage collection

Leave a review - let other readers know what you think

Please share your thoughts on this book with others by leaving a review on the site that you bought it from. If you purchased the book from Amazon, please leave us an honest review on this book's Amazon page. This is vital so that other potential readers can see and use your unbiased opinion to make purchasing decisions, we can understand what our customers think about our products, and our authors can see your feedback on the title that they have worked with Packt to create. It will only take a few minutes of your time, but is valuable to other potential customers, our authors, and Packt. Thank you!

Index

B

C

H

I

J

S

T

U

V

W

X

Y

Z

Made in the USA
Coppell, TX
11 August 2020